The Medieval Islamic Republic of Letters

the MEDIEVAL ISLAMIC REPUBLIC *of* LETTERS

Arabic Knowledge Construction

MUHSIN J. AL-MUSAWI

University of Notre Dame Press

Notre Dame, Indiana

Notre Dame, Indiana 46556
www.undpress.nd.edu

Manufactured in the United States of America

Library of Congress Cataloging-in-Publication Data

Musawi, Muhsin Jasim, author.
The medieval Islamic republic of letters : Arabic knowledge construction / Muhsin J. al-Musawi.
pages cm
Includes bibliographical references and index.
ISBN 978-0-268-02044-6 (paperback)—ISBN 0-268-02044-2 (paper)
1. Arabic literature—1258–1800—History and criticism. 2. Islamic literature—History and criticism. I. Title.
PJ7535.M87 2015
892.7'09004—dc23

2014047954

∞ *The paper in this book meets the guidelines for permanence and durability of the Committee on Production Guidelines for Book Longevity of the Council on Library Resources.*

CONTENTS

ACKNOWLEDGMENTS

My interest in the Arabic thrust of medieval and premodern Islamic culture has a long history, and it is certainly bound up with my engagement with the *Thousand and One Nights* (The Arabian Nights). The material that I collected and worked on regarding medieval Islamic culture took many directions later, and from the present project another one has branched off with a focus on the complexity of the *nahḍah* (the modern Arab awakening or renaissance, as it is often called). But, practically speaking, the current book started with two invitations early in 2001, the first from the editors for *Arabic Literature in the Post-Classical Period*, Roger Allen and D. S. Richards, who invited me to write a survey essay, published under the title "Pre-modern Belletrist Prose," covering the prose section in that volume. I hereby express my gratitude to both of these editors and to the publisher, Cambridge University Press, and in particular to my dear friend Roger Allen, who cherished the book and provided generous suggestions and support throughout the years of preparation. I also extend thanks to Bruce Craig and to Th. Emil Homerin for the invitation to participate in the *Mamluk Studies Review* issue on Mamluk literature, with my essay "Vindicating a Profession or a Personal Career? Al-Qalqashandī's Maqamah in Context." Without their devotion to Mamluk studies, many scholars would not risk treading in this thinly nurtured field. Although these two essays are not included in the present book, they are nevertheless part of the background that substantiates its argument. Many thanks are due to Marlis Salih, editor for *Mamluk Studies Review*, for reproducing part of chapter 3 as "The Medieval

Islamic Literary World-System: The Lexicographic Turn" (*Mamluk Studies Review* 17, 2013), and for the invitation to give a talk on the medieval Islamic republic of letters at the University of Chicago, April 27, 2012. The two anonymous readers for the University of Notre Dame Press were no less helpful in providing extensive notes and queries. I also need to thank my colleagues and friends Suzanne P. Stetkevych at Georgetown University and Li Guo at the University of Notre Dame for their invaluable comments and notes. Thanks are due as well to my former students and present colleagues Anne-Marie McManus at Washington University in St. Louis and Nizar Hermes at the University of Oklahoma for going through an early version of the manuscript and making some insightful suggestions. I also thank my colleagues Moneera al-Ghadeer, Visiting Professor at Harvard University, and Bilal al-Orfali from the American University of Beirut for helping in the acquisition of some relevant material. To my assistant Joscelyn Shawn Ganjhara Jurich go sincere thanks for helping out in locating images; and similar thanks go to the Turkish scholar Osman Yilmaz.

For their help with a generous subvention, I express gratitude to the Warner Fund of the University Seminars at Columbia University. Ideas in this book were presented early on at the University Seminar on Arabic Studies, and I express gratitude to the discussants, George Saliba, Richard Bulliet, and Pierre Cachia. For the reproduction of images and illustrations, thanks and acknowledgments are due to the Beinecke Rare Book & Manuscript Library, Yale University, and to Moira Fitzgerald in particular for her help; to Houghton Library at Harvard University, and to Mary Haegert and Robert Zinck for making the acquisition of images a smooth process; to Dār al-ʿIlm lil-Malāyīn for reproduction of images from their publication *Muṭālaʿāt fi al-shiʿr al-Mamlūkī wa-al-ʿUthmānī*; and to Süleymaniye Library, Esad Efendi 3638, Istanbul, for the reproduction of the image from Ikhwān al-Ṣafāʾ. My warm gratitude goes to my friend the Iraqi painter Dhia Azzawi for providing the art for the cover of this book; and to Wendy McMillen from the Press for her attention to artistic production.

Warm thanks go to Stephen Little, the acquisition editor at the University of Notre Dame Press, for his early interest in the project and his keen attention to every step in the acquisitions process. I am also particularly impressed by the painstaking and thorough attention showed by Rebecca DeBoer, the copy editor at the Press. Her focus on every detail, keen eye, and pertinent suggestions are unique and deserve the highest appreciation. It would be churlish not to end with thanks to my family (Bahira, my daughters Wafa and Zainab, and my son Adnan), who have to suffer through my long hours of preoccupation with other people of premodern times.

ILLUSTRATIONS

The following are reproduced in the gallery after p. 146.

Figure 1. Ikhwān al-Ṣafāʾ (The Pure Brethren; 908–980), *Rasāʾil ikhwān al-ṣafāʾ wa khullān al-wafāʾ* (Epistles of the Pure Brethren and the Sincere Friends), Baghdad, MS dated 686/1287. Istanbul, Süleymaniye Library, Esad Efendi 3638, fol. 4v. Courtesy of Süleymaniye Library.

Figure 2. *Al-ʿAwāmil al-Miʾah* (The One Hundred Regents), by ʿAbd al-Qāhir ibn ʿAbd al-Raḥmān al-Jurjānī (d. 1078?), translated into Persian verse. A grammatical work on Arabic syntax. Beinecke Rare Book & Manuscript Library, Yale University.

Figure 3. *Talkhīṣ Miftāḥ al-ʿUlūm* (Resumé of the Key to the Sciences), by Muḥammad ibn ʿAbd al-Raḥmān Jalāl al-Dīn al-Qazwīnī, Khaṭīb Dimashq (d. 739/1338). Beinecke Rare Book & Manuscript Library, Yale University.

Figure 4. *Dalāʾil al-Khayrāt wa-Shawāriq al-Anwār fī Dhikr al-Ṣalāh ʿalā al-Nabī al-Mukhtār* (Guide to Blessings and Shining Lights Regarding Prayers on the Chosen Prophet), by Abū ʿAbd Allāh Muḥammad ibn Sulaymān al-Jazūlī (d. 1465). One of the most famous books of prayer in Islamic literature. Undated, but most likely copied in the eighteenth century. Beinecke Rare Book & Manuscript Library, Yale University.

Figures 5a, b, and c. *Kitāb al-Ḥujjah fī sariqāt ibn Ḥijjah* (The Damning Evidence of ibn-Ḥijjah's Plagiarisms), by Shams al-Dīn Muḥammad ibn Ḥasan al-Nawājī (d. 1455), undated, MS Arab 285, Houghton Library, Harvard University.

Figure 6. The Tree-like Poetic Form. Bakrī Shaykh Amīn, *Muṭālaʿāt fī al-shiʿr al-Mamlūkī wa-al-ʿUthmānī*, 182. Beirut: Dār al-ʿIlm lil-Malāyīn, 2007.

Figure 7. The Geometrical Form in the Poetry of the Middle Period. Bakrī Shaykh Amīn, *Muṭālaʿāt fī al-shiʿr al-Mamlūkī wa-al-ʿUthmānī*, 213. Beirut: Dār al-ʿIlm lil-Malāyīn, 2007.

An Inventory of al-Ḥillī's Reading List and Library in Rhetoric. Al-Ḥillī, *Sharḥ al-kāfiyah al-badīʿiyyah fi ʿulūm al-balāghah wa- maḥāsin al-badīʿ* (The Explication of the Sufficient *Badīʿiyyah* Ode in Rhetorical Sciences and Adornments in Innovativeness). Ed. Nasīb Nashāwī. Beirut: Dār Ṣādir, 1982.

PRELIMINARY DISCOURSE

Khuṭbat al-kitāb

This book argues that the large-scale and diverse cultural production in Arabic in the postclassical era (approximately the twelfth through the eighteenth centuries) was the outcome of an active sphere of discussion and disputation spanning the entire medieval Muslim world.[1] I explore this production over a long temporal stretch and across a vast swathe of Islamic territories. My focus is on the thematic and genealogical constructions that were of greatest significance to the accumulation of cultural capital, which, I argue, constitutes a medieval Islamic "republic of letters."[2] My emphasis is also on human agency and on the sites and methods of conversation, discussion, compilation, and writing that are of most relevance to the development of this communicative sphere. Although the fact that Arabic is the language of the Qurʾān necessarily entails its dominance in the battle to ensure a place for vernacular literatures, I redirect attention away from that battle and toward individual writers, grammarians, and lexicographers as active players in a larger Islamic cultural pursuit.

The pervasive Islamic consciousness that takes the Arabic language as its pivotal point, given its bearing on Qurʾānic studies and the emerging strategies of study and discourse, seems more important here than a metropolitan-peripheral demarcation, despite the marked presence of local, regional, and national production. Under precarious and ever-shifting politics, centers at any given time may be replaced by other centers, and scholars are compelled to develop their own counterstrategies in a vast Islamic domain where theological studies hold sway. Thus, the issue of centers and peripheries is secondary in relation to cultural activity. Arabic grammar, for instance, which is basic to training in the religious sciences, *kalām* (scholastic theological discourse), and disputation, cannot be described as an ethnic-bound pursuit. It is the foundation for every other pursuit in Islamic knowledge.[3] The prioritization of Arabic is evident in the study of rhetoric, where heavy emphasis was placed not only on figures and tropes but also on methods and strategies of application and analysis, and which enlisted the efforts of numerous scholars east of the Arab region proper. Such innovations contributed to the development of a cultural sphere that was greater than any single territorial center.

Lending credence to this premise of a medieval Islamic republic of letters is the fact that literary production spilled over into a variety of sites, such as mosques, hospices, educational institutions, markets, and other public spaces. It involved a rigorous conversation among authors, coteries, particular texts, poems, theories, and insights, which took the form of glosses, marginal explications, correspondence, epistles, and disputes and debates over a centuries-long period. Nearly every postclassical cultural production communicates some involvement and participation in this republic. Philological inquiry, for example, as manifested in lexicons, disputes, speculative theological treatises, and their marginalia, often either consciously integrates with or else rebels against one or another system of thought and politics, and thus contributes to an accumulating rhetorica over the long period under consideration. Rhetors and texts are the marked traces in this genealogical succession.

The focus on rhetoric in this book implies a recognition of its significance to the littérateurs, grammarians, poets, lexicographers, and copyists of this republic of letters. As I argue throughout, rhetoric is a combative verbal domain, where battles are fought and achievements inscribed. Its dense figures and tropes distance it from the strictly official discourse that is usually upheld in traditionalist circles, with their marked distrust of logic and hermeneutics.[4] The recourse in rhetoric to indirection, or *laḥn al-qawl* (i.e., implicitness), and to *taʿrīḍ* (dissimulation, connotation, concealment) signifies the other side of written and verbal transactions in this *jumhūr* (majority) of littérateurs, which is the basis for Arab and Muslim modernists' application of the term *jumhūriyyah* (i.e., republic). In this verbal domain, the root and conjugation of the verb *jamhara* also connote dissimulation. Hence, both verb and noun are loaded in Arabic in a binary structure, negation, or *taḍādd* (based on opposites or contrasts — *aḍdād*), implying both revelation and concealment.[5] Unless we perceive this philological undertaking in relation to the rise of *badīʿ* (inventiveness and innovation) and the subsequent multiplication of a *badīʿiyyah* ode (i.e., encomium to the Prophet in poetry and poetics, with specific application of figures and examples in each verse) for more than six centuries,[6] we are bound to overlook this development as a countermovement to an official discourse that was bent on attenuating the presence of the Prophet's family in popular memory. Until the eighteenth century, littérateurs' shows of veneration are downplayed as mere Sufi or Shīʿī aberrations.

The present project also concentrates on genealogical constructions in lexicography, dynastic growths in chancery institutions, apprenticeship, mentorship, and the exchange between public and private spheres in poetry and art. On the material level, the outcome is manifested in impressive biographical dictionaries, encyclopedias, and *khizānāt* (treasure troves), that is, multivolume productions that encapsulate authors' comments on and engagements with widely circulated and celebrated forms of knowledge. The overall cultural production that documents contemporary literary life and the culture industry (authorship, street performance, copying, book marketing, and so forth) presents a strong case for the appellation of "the medieval Islamic republic of letters." Rather than being bound to a specific cultural form or formative episode, this designation refers to a general condition that makes it possible for scholars, modes, genres, and ideas to consort with each other over time and to thereby create new cultural trends and projects, along with an ethos of reciprocity, exchange, and obligation. Cultural genealogies are established, not necessarily as uniform structures but rather primarily as distinctive systems of thought and inquiry. There is no better evidence for this hypothesis than the cumulative effect in cultural production in every field of knowledge in the long period under consideration. The thoughtful discourse and the gravity of issues that are raised often provoke parody and biting satire from less canonized authors. Along with the growing body of reading publics in the medieval Islamic world—as attested to by the lucrative business of copyists[7]—public sites turned into recognizable centers for innovative and alternative cultural production, which often held traditionalists at bay and even forced chancery officials to admit the writings and anecdotes of professionals and craftsmen into their compendiums and encyclopedias.

The culture industry produced an enormous corpus of treatises, compendiums, lexicons, commentaries, glosses, and supplements in history, geography, philosophy, speculative theology, philology, rhetoric, topography, and other domains in the humanities, along with scientific inquiry and research. Updated modes of communication, writing, and *mukhtara'ah* (invented) terminology confront us with the need to re-address rigorously the cultural complexity of the postclassical period. Through the consolidated efforts of littérateurs, philologists, lexicographers, speculative theologians, and epistolographers in Islamic domains, prototypes and forms of literary value systems and conceptualized republics of letters emerged, where cultural capital and consumers seem to be entangled in an ongoing transaction. In one marked case, a grammatical tradition that takes shape in ibn Wahb al-Kātib's (d. after AH 334/AD 946)[8] groundbreaking *Burhān* in the tenth century connects genealogically with Abū Ya'qūb al-Sakkākī's (d. 626/1229) *Miftāḥ*,[9] opening up the field of grammar and rhetoric to a succession of abridgements, commentaries, and explications for over seven centuries, setting grammar free from earlier limits, and situating it within larger inquiries in knowledge and life.

Classical Arabic, although experiencing many ups and downs, was already established in Islamic dominions by the twelfth century as the language of religion, rhetoric, epistolography, and, at times, philosophy and science. Its very strength as the language of the Qur'ān and hence its dominant status, however, also curtailed its availability for a much-needed conflation of popular and classic literary forms, which was given sporadic impetus by certain middle-period poets and rhetors. Problematic as this is for my reading of a republic of letters—a point that will be discussed in due course—the fact of this republic needs to be argued in terms of an enormous cultural capital that could not have retained value and availability had it not been meeting, in its times, the needs of Islamic literate communities. The Arab and Muslim modernist view that the literary output of the medieval Arab and Islamic nation-states is ineffectual has to do with the role of these modernist native elites — such as the prominent Egyptian writers Salāmah Mūsā (1887–1958), Ṭāhā Ḥusayn (1889–1973), and Aḥmad Ḥasan al-Zayyāt (1885–1968) — who have long internalized a European Enlightenment discourse and looked with suspicion and distrust at the past and its massive accumulation in cultural capital.[10]

The book argues its case, therefore, against the widespread disparagement of the postclassical Islamic era (medieval and premodern) as one of literary decadence, degeneration, and darkness. The modernists' disillusion with that cultural production was primarily informed by a European discourse but was also driven by a misreading of the compendious and commentarial effort of the period, a misreading that could not discern the significant redirection of cultural capital to escape imitation, while simultaneously assimilating ancient and classical knowledge. In fact, by appropriating and classifying these sources rather than duplicating them, postclassical scholars and littérateurs embarked on what Pascale Casanova terms a "diversion of assets."[11]

A number of recent works have raised similar concerns and contributed significant insights that could correct the modernist misreadings of particular authors or texts. However, little has been done to account for the large-scale literary production that continued for centuries across the Islamic world under circumstances of social and political upheavals, wars, invasions, and drastic shifts in ideology and methods of reasoning. Indeed, there is even less concern with social networks, sites of production, and the significance of biographical, lexical, topographical, and encyclopedic constellations as representative landmarks in a republic of letters.

Because such a discussion demands a focus on specific centers for the transmission, acquisition, and construction of knowledge, this work emphasizes the importance of Cairo, not only as the site for a substantial part of this cultural production but also as a medieval-premodern epicenter where travelers, scholars, exiles, poets, and others settled, argued, and met fellow scholars. Founded in the tenth century as the capital of the Fatimid Caliphate (909–1167), Cairo largely escaped the destruction that befell many other metropolitan centers as a result of the Mongol invasions. It turned into a repository of libraries, archives, and centers for learning that no other city outshone during the period under consideration. As a center for writers from all over the world, Cairo occupied a special place of honor from the tenth through the fifteenth centuries, according to two prominent contemporaries of the Mamluk period, ibn Khaldūn (d. 808/1406) and al-Qalqashandī (d. 1418). The erudite Russian Arabist Ignatii Lulianovich Krachkovskii argues that Egypt possessed a literature unequalled anywhere else in the East.[12] Intellectuals from both east and west, whether fleeing political upheavals or settling in Cairo temporarily while on their way to Mecca, viewed it as "the garden of the Universe, the orchard of the World," as ibn Khaldūn reports in his *Taʿrīf*.[13] Al-Qalqashandī notes that Cairo "benefited from the most honorable of writers as no other kingdom did," and that "it had the kind of notables and men of letters that no other country had."[14]

Cairo of the middle and premodern period was an epicenter of both material production and symbolic capital. The nature of its growth and its shifting body politic place us squarely within a cosmopolitan nexus that witnesses a dialogue among schools of thought, scholastic controversies, scientific achievements, poetic innovations and shifts in expression, the massive use of prose for statecraft, and soaring heights of Sufi poetry that simultaneously derive and refract worldliness from common tropes. Its cosmopolitan culture was partly its own, but also to a large extent was forced on it by virtue of place. Situated at the crossroads to Mecca, to Africa, to the Mediterranean, to Syria, and to eastern Asia all the way to the borders with China—which ibn Baṭṭūṭah (d. 1369) would reach and describe—Cairo was a place but not an identity. What was its own and what was brought to the place and its people involve and define its makeup at that particular historical intersection, one in which another, non-Arab element (i.e., the Mamluk and Ottoman dynasties) enforced its presence while acclimatizing itself to the accommodating Islamic space. Fighting its way between its own populations and its Arab and Afro-Asian communities, especially the Maghribi component and the superimposed Mamluks and Ottomans, this City-Victorious, as its name al-Qāhirah signifies, emerges cosmopolitan but also as an Arab-Islamic metropolitan epicenter. The influx of scholars, poets, travelers, and entrepreneurs continued markedly into the nineteenth century and played a significant role in giving the city its cosmopolitan features.

Pascale Casanova in her *World Republic of Letters* argues that "the exceptional concentration of literary sources that occurred in Paris over the course of several centuries gradually led to its recognition as the center of the literary world."[15] Such a description is no less applicable to Cairo; it stood to the postclassical Islamic world as Paris stood to Europe. It was the space where the learned functioned as transmitters and providers of knowledge on multiple levels. Their encyclopedic bent and their appropriation of antecedent tradition did not detract from their other literary pursuits. As an example, consider Shams al-Dīn al-Nawājī (d. 859/1455). His books comprise not only anthologized material on erotica and wine but also rigorous readings and criticism. A copyist famed for his copying skills, an anthologist, and a sharp critic, especially in his criticism of contemporaries, al-Nawājī is typical of many scholars whose role, production, and diversified interests placed them in dialogue with each other as well as with a wide body of readers, who obviously were keen to peruse their books and manuals.

The concentration of scholars, authors, and copyists in Cairo and, to a lesser degree, in Damascus, Aleppo, and other Islamic centers west of the Arab region valorized Arabic; but it also prompted the "revolutionary vernacularizing thrust" that was noticeable throughout the Islamic world.[16] This vernacularizing effort made heavy use of lexical transmission, appropriation, and transference of Arabic grammar, rhetoric, and poetics. National languages also brought into Arabic their own distinctive traits, a point that will receive further attention in the following chapters. Although the process of linguistic and cultural differentiation is particularly noticeable in the new states to the west of the Arab region, it should be seen in terms of the valorization of a wide political and cultural field. Every new political formation ended up with an increasing dependence on and appropriation of Arabic for religious, scholastic and symbolic reasons. Arabic itself underwent some of its most serious transformations, in the form of nonclassical modes and practices that were theorized by several prominent scholars, and in the upsurge of the so-called *ʿāmmī* (colloquial) poetry. Hence, in spite of linguistic divergence, a common Islamic literary, theological, and symbolic field emerged that warrants the present discussion of an Islamic republic of letters. The massive production that has unsettled Arab modernists attests to this cultural space.

In this book I examine an extensive corpus through various lenses. Underlying patterns of social networking are always present to account for the ultimate material presence of cultural production. Travel, pilgrimage (*ḥajj*), migration, the search for libraries and centers of learning, assemblies (*majālis*), diverse modes of writing and compilation, and treasuries of knowledge (*khizānāt*) all function as the means and mediums, as well as self-sufficient pursuits, in the makeup of a broad republic of letters.

I attempt to demonstrate that a layered structure held together the seemingly disparate modes of writing, rewriting, compilation, revision, commentary, and disputation in nearly every field of knowledge and gave them validity and meaning over a long period of power struggles and knowledge construction. Only through examining such a layered structure of multiple, challenging, cultural spectrums can we escape the temptations of an ethnically-based identitarian politics outside the canvas of an Islamic culture with its many ideologies and forms of self-constitution. Indeed, the stupendous encyclopedic growth and the dynamic channels of disputation, emendation, gloss, rewriting, invention of new modes in poetry, recitation, and so on confront us with questions that become more acute whenever we understand these activities as simultaneously peripatetic and stationary—depending on the appropriate location or settlement across the Islamic world, from central Asia to Timbuktu, a world that was traversed by ibn Baṭṭūṭah between 1325 and 1354.[17] This Moroccan traveler, whom Jawaharlal Nehru rightly ranks "amongst the great travelers of all time,"[18] could not narrate his travels without a "cultural script" that constituted his frame of reference.[19]

Travel accounts are not the only traces of a republic of letters in this Islamic map. In more than one sense, a compendium, gloss, or praise poem to the Prophet, for example, often traversed lands, challenging other texts and literary practices and putting down new roots in more than one place. The "street," as opposed to scholars and other elites, has always been part of this vibrant encounter and unfolding, and on many occasions it displays its own opposite poetics or discourse, while in other instances its case may be played out against innovations in theological discussion. Ultimately, the present book seeks to contribute to an understanding of this formative process in the transmission and acquisition of knowledge in its entirety, as larger than any one of its many component parts and hence more complex than has been recognized. This republic of letters, whose topography is mapped out in the course of this study, resists compartmentalization. By presenting it thus, the book attempts to provide a solid base to engage with Islamic societies in a crucial period of their shared cultural history.

But before we address further the resistance of Arab and Muslim modernists to their past, it is appropriate to take a closer look at the textual community of the Mamluk period in Arab-Islamic history (1250–1811),[20] especially in terms of the transmission and reconstruction of knowledge. Although the term "republic" is used here as a conceptual framework, an edifice, to account for a literary world-system in which Arabic functions as the dominating language, its appropriation in this book entails no equation between Latin and Arabic in relation to national vernacular languages. Even with the disintegration of the caliphate that started early in the tenth century, Arabic was the proper medium and resource for a community of scholars and readers across the Islamic lands, scholars who happened to interact, correspond with each other, hold meetings and debates, and thenceforth establish a repertoire of texts in encyclopedic or commentary form. The medieval Arab-Islamic "republic of letters," although very different from this term and its applications in Western scholarship, presents a rich construction of knowledge made possible through Arabic. As the language known to every Muslim scholar, Arabic facilitates transmission through a number of channels and networks. Wanderlust and the search for knowledge are also among the dynamics that this book explores in order to map out the means and outcomes in this transmission and acquisition of knowledge. Books, modes of writing and recitation, assemblies, correspondence, and conversation complement each other in the structure of this republic over such a long period. For example, a prototype for a collaborative encyclopedic work, a tenth-century joint project that will be discussed later in this volume, was perhaps in the minds of many when they embarked on supplementing each other's work with book-length studies and commentaries. The case for a republic of letters made possible through Arabic is even stronger for Sufis, who were in need then, as they are now, of connecting to a nuanced Qur'ānic hermeneutic.

Indeed, there is no shortage of prominent names and movements that demonstrate significant social networking. Patterns for this networking had already been set, not only by geographers, intelligence informants in military conquests, and postmasters (*Aṣḥāb al-barīd*; sing. *Ṣāḥib al-barīd*) and their network, but also, more significantly, by Sufis, scholars and polymaths, and travelers. Across these networks is always a gravitating fulcrum, exemplified by the compelling commitment to undertake the *ḥajj* (pilgrimage to Mecca) as duty, ritual, and as part of a craving to meet fellow scholars and Sufis and to make use of the libraries in Mecca and Medina that were endowed by prominent emirs, kings, and sultans from the Arab world, Anatolia, Persia, and Africa.[21] For example, the itineraries of the Sufi grand shaykh, the Andalusian Muḥyī al-Dīn ibn al-ʿArabī (d. 638/1240);[22] of the saint Abū al-ʿAbbās al-Mursī (d. 1287), whose shrine is in Alexandria; and of the latter's father-in-law, the Sufi master Abū al-Ḥasan al-Shādhilī (d. 1258), range from Muslim Spain through North Africa, from Alexandria or Cairo to Mecca and other places, and show how travel, pilgrimage, accumulation of knowledge, and Sufi mentoring together built up significant genealogies in Islamic thought and life. *Hajj* can turn into a transformative experience, as the case was with the Andalusian Sufi master ibn al-ʿArabī. His meeting with al-Niẓām, the highly gifted and inspiring daughter of Shaykh Abū Shujāʿ from Iṣfahān, and his sojourn in Mecca (1201–1204) were behind his highly acclaimed and controversial collection of poetry *Tarjumān al-ashwāq* (The Interpreter of Desires) and the voluminous *Meccan Revelations* (*Al-Futūḥāt al-Makkiyyah*). Celebrated travelers such as the Andalusian ibn Jubayr (d. 1217) and the Moroccan ibn Baṭṭūṭah, along with historians and theologians such as ibn Khaldūn[23] and the erudite scholar and speculative theologian Saʿd al-Dīn al-Taftazānī (d. 791/1389) of Taftazān (Khorasān),[24] traversed lands and established themselves as recognizable and influential presences in this republic of letters.

Both Mecca and Cairo functioned like stars, pulling writers and literary production into their orbits. Writer, text, and genre all become dynamic links in the process. It is not surprising that post-ʿAbbasid Cairo became a center where competition, professional rivalry, and theological discussion and difference throve. Here, and indeed with cultural centers across the Islamic east, authors and scholars were not the only players. The region or city-state became a vigorous participant as well, affecting the lives and fortunes of other players. Their life accounts testify to the validity of the argument of this book that ideas, people, coteries, and networks are complementary components in the constitution of this republic.

The configurations and constellations of postclassical Islamic knowledge, extending well into the eighteenth century—a much larger and more productive "republic of letters" than the French encyclopedia project that originally invoked the term[25]—complemented, built upon, and far exceeded in diversity, scope, geographical range, and target the foundation that had been laid in the late Umayyad (661–750) and ʿAbbasid (750–847) eras.[26] At the same time, it must also be acknowledged that there was an equally large production of works of lesser merit over these centuries, which were intended to nourish a broad populace in quest of knowledge. Muslim elite treatment of the recent past tends to discount the masses and hence to denigrate medieval and premodern writing addressing these publics.

The reader of this book will emerge with an understanding of the medieval and premodern period in Arab-Islamic culture that is totally at variance with Arab and Muslim modernists' denigration and rejection of the past as a period of decadence and stagnation. By associating the political loss of an Arab center for an Islamic empire after the Mongol invasion of Baghdad in 1258 with cultural decadence, they fail to dissociate political disintegration from the ongoing cultural dissemination and exchange across the Islamic world. This twentieth-century outlook is a notable sign of failure on the part of the architects of modernity to connect effectively with a rich culture of their past, and it is also largely responsible for their failures to establish emotive and cultural links with the Muslim populace. The cultural and historical gap that results can easily induce architects of regression to involve regions and peoples in schisms and disorder. Hence, the study of past culture is a study of societies and their political economies. What is lost on modernists is a simple premise expressed by Casanova in her *World Republic of Letters*: "It is necessary to be old to have any chance of being modern or of decreeing what is modern."[27] In a review of her book, Joe Cleary puts this point as follows: "Only countries that can claim a venerable and distinguished historical stock of literary capital get to decree what is and is not 'fashionable' in literary terms."[28]

Leading elites in Asia and Africa, long before the advent of postcolonial theorists, were often enmeshed in cultural dependency, largely exemplified by an internalization of Enlightenment discourse. Thus, the relationship with a cultural past assumes great importance in our search for a better understanding of movements, attitudes, and concepts in the postclassical era, since culture provided shared codes that were not lost on either the *khawāṣṣ* (or *khāṣṣah*: elite) or the *ʿawāmm* (*ʿāmmah*: the common public).[29] This was especially the case in a volatile political climate run not only by dynasties with different interests in and engagements with culture, but also by less conspicuous powers on both material and intellectual levels. Let us remember that the Islamic narrative tradition of the same period leaves us a massive record of tyrants and rulers who would turn into helpless beings in the presence of a revered shaykh or a prominent scholar.[30] The *Thousand and One Nights* is, after all, a testimony to the power of knowledge. No wonder, then, that this work made such a successful entry into Europe through its French translation of 1704–1712. *Contes Arabes*, or the *Arabian Nights' Entertainments*, drew attention across Europe, including that of the enlightened leaders of thought in France, England, and Germany. Yet it is only one example of the highly diverse literary productions of the Islamic republic of letters.[31]

My use of this term, given its current association with Casanova's *World Republic of Letters*, merits further attention, not only to decenter the latter's conceptualization of a Europeanized world-system but also, and primarily, to direct attention to traditions that antedate the European model and perhaps problematize a global application of the term. Casanova's world republic cannot accommodate non-European cultures of the recent past. Paris, as the center around which Casanova's republic turns, is the site that accrues, recapitulates on, and also delivers recognition, a case that, in her argument, is seemingly proved not only by its cultural exports to the rest of the world but also by its cultural imports—its assimilation of other works from ex-colonies and cultural peripheries.[32] The idea of a metropolis exerting both centripetal and centrifugal cultural forces obviously depends on material and cultural circumstances, as was the case for an earlier Baghdad, where the symbolic power of the city as the central pivot of Islam lasted even as its contribution went into decline, before its eventual downfall as a result of the Mongol invasion in 1258. In this case, the notion of a symbolic capital derives from the caliphal order, which leads a reputable jurist and judge like the Egyptian ibn Duqmāq to bewail the city's fall as a universal catastrophe.[33]

Although ibn Duqmāq's view of Baghdad is commensurate with Casanova's assessment of Paris, it obviously exposes at the same time the pitfalls involved in any generalized equation that would link the interdependency of the print industry and the rise of a "world republic of letters." The medieval and premodern period in Islamic history may illustrate failures in economy and politics, but it does not illustrate backwardness and stagnation, a point with which Peter Gran strongly engages.[34] The actual achievements in cultural production in terms of written culture are sufficiently problematic to raise numerous questions about Eurocentric totalizing constructs in the form of structuralist polarizations. During the period under consideration, monographs, massive lexicons, and encyclopedic dictionaries were composed across Islamic lands, along with an active quest for knowledge and the rise of individual library collections and archival repositories. While medieval and premodern Islamic culture attests to Casanova's stipulation concerning the unsustainability of an equation between political/economic growth and cultural prominence, it also disputes her definition of the world republic of letters in terms of a post-Renaissance Europe. Even if we accept the term as involving "winner-nations and winner-cities,"[35] the period and culture under consideration offer us the opportunity for questioning such umbrella terms.

It stands to reason that a return to the study of an earlier cultural period, albeit with a different understanding and new methodology, is unwarranted unless there is a pressing need for it, a need that pertains to structures of knowledge in relation to colonial and postcolonial imperatives, including identitarian politics.[36] The present project therefore questions now and then contemporary sources that propagate a wholesale rejection of the cultural values of the postclassical period. It also seeks to reveal the oscillation that is characteristic of another segment of Arab and Muslim literati, between an edgy and shy approval and occasional expressions of denial of any worthwhile literary production of the period under consideration. Morover, it attempts to uncover the omissions in the rhetorical disclaimers of modernity and instead to construct a countermapping of a textual terrain involving conflict and struggle.[37] My interdisciplinary critique conforms to a contemporaneous definition of the term *adab*, one through which aesthetics, the sciences, and crafts or professions transform the cultural landscape at the same time as they undergo ruptures and shifts. The first half of this book focuses on cultural dynamics, formations, and production; the second half concentrates on human agency and sites of scriptoria, and especially on rhetoric and epistles concerning disputation or argumentation, as dynamic forces in the fabric of discussion- and reading-communities, of forums of governance and authority, and of common or street life. Within such a framework, specific subgenres are discussed in support of my basic premises.

In mapping out and analyzing the Islamic cultural scene, the book argues its case through four underlying concerns, which necessarily overlap and hence resist easy categorization. The first is that of networks of travelers, scholars and poets, coteries and ensembles, and also books and discussions that generate ideas, positions, and a multifaceted production of rejoinders, commentaries, marginalia, contrafactions (understood as deliberately differentiated reproductions, or the use of previously existing material in conjunction with new or different texts), abridgements, compendiums, and lexicons. The second is the valorization of the role and presence of professionals, scholars, and poets whenever they effect a communal and confederational site of discussion, such as Sharaf al-Dīn Abū ʿAbd Allāh Muḥammad ibn Saʿīd al-Būṣīrī al-Shādhilī (d. ca. 694–696/1294–1297), Saʿd al-Dīn Masʿūd al-Taftazānī (d. 791/1389), Ṣafī al-Dīn al-Ḥillī (d. 750/1349), Jamāl al-Dīn ibn Nubātah (d. 768/1366), Ṣalāḥ al-Ṣafadī (d. 764/1363), Abū Bakr. b. ʿAlī ibn ʿAbdullāh ibn Ḥijjah al-

Ḥamawī (d. 837/1434), and many others.[38] The third concern is an attempt to account for the rise of specific modes of writing, discourse, and enunciation, as in the proliferation of al-Būṣīrī's Mantle Ode and its apparatus in innovative rhetoric, the soaring esotericism of the Sufi language, and many other significant manifestations of change. The last underlying concern is with methodologies that perpetuate and outline such categories as the rationalist, the theologian, and the traditionalist, or, as summed up by Jalāl al-Dīn al-Suyūṭī (d. 1505), the ways of the Arabs (i.e., traditional reading) and the ways of non-Arabs.

The first chapter, "Seismic *Islamica*: Politics and Scope of a Medieval Republic of Letters," attempts to lead the reader into the thickness of the term "Islamic" as it functions across different territories, places, and periods of time, exploring the complexities and common features of its use. It navigates through a number of prominent names, texts, and modes of discourse that are the shared property of Muslim societies. Its purpose is to ground the general reader as well as the specialist at the intersection of past and present so that each may recognize the relevance of medieval Islamic literate culture and knowledge to the present, especially given the rise of contemporary conservative Islamic movements. Throughout, I interrogate Arab and Muslim modernists' internalization of the European Enlightenment disparagement of the Middle Ages. This chapter acquaints the reader with networks, circles, travelers, books and modes that create a conversation site among Islamic communities. Within this site, cities, city-states, and dynamic subgenres and modes of cultural production are all active players, indeed no less so than individual intellectuals and travelers.

Chapter 2, "A Massive Conversation Site: The Word Empire," begins mapping out cultural trajectories and sites that native advocates of modernity inevitably overlooked in their zealous duplication of a seductive Europe. It addresses, first, the tenth-century prototype for an Islamic republic of letters as exemplified by the scholarly and highly sophisticated encyclopedic work of the Brethren of Purity in Basra. With its rigorous analysis of all fields of knowledge and its significant insights into the most problematic issues in philosophy, theology, sciences, and language, this anonymous work raised as much opposition as did Diderot's *Encyclopedia* project. The chapter then turns to the emphasis during the middle period, although with different methods, on lexicography. The enormous lexicographic activity can be justified as manifestations of ethnic awareness in non-Arab Islamic lands, or as a bulwark against invasions and wars of destruction. This chapter, however, probes into the lexical activity itself—its social range and politics, its engagement with dialects and idiolects—to account for the lexicon as a kind of compiled nation, retained and guarded in a world that cannot sustain independence.

Chapter 3, "The Lexicographic Turn in Cultural Capital," continues the discussion. Along with a distinctive lexical interest, it looks at compendiums, which usually grow into *Khizānāt* (treasure troves, or treasuries) even though they may begin as explications of a poem or epistle. In this period, book properties are no longer the same, since large-scale production, competition, and diversity bring into full play an active conversation that displays itself in commentaries, abridgements, rewriting, and an ever accumulating corpus of gloss and marginalia. The search for new titles for such books makes an interesting case in the study of paratexts and thresholds, that is, textually permeating prologues and textual openings, as indices of mutation and change in cultural production and the accumulation of cultural capital. In more than one sense, this compilation fervor and the book industry signify a solid base for a literary world-system.

Chapter 4, "The Context of an Islamic Literate Society: Epistemological Shifts," addresses thorny and problematic issues in this cultural production. According to the custom in this medieval period, an explanation of a verse or image can lead to a discussion of grammatical or lexical issues of relevance, which in turn can lead the explicator into discussions of social life, religion, philosophy, science, education, conflicts, and historical accounts, before returning to the starting point. Other treasuries developed differently under other types of division and subdivision. None is a mere accumulation of information and documentary record; all are conversations with others, who happen to be writers, theologians, poets, and grammarians. The loosening of the conventions of authorized report, and of written and oral transmission (audition), made this conversation enriching, providing the reader with firsthand knowledge of social and cultural life, the very kind of knowledge that modern anthropology obtains from informants. More than any historical account, these compendiums and treasuries take us into private and public spaces, including assemblies, and put us in touch with people going about their daily pursuits. Autobiographical and biographical elements take over. Even works that purport to be concerned with specific genres, such as *mujūn* (licentious verse), lead us into the life of specific quarters within urban centers.[39] In those locations, common pursuits establish different speech registers, which invade elite discourse and force compilers to copy and circulate them among readers. These suburban speech registers, which find a place in the poetry of the Baghdadi ibn Ḥajjāj (941–1001) and others, for example, and which claim the attention of the eminent Egyptian poet and writer ibn Nubātah (d. 1366), also explode the myth of territorial and geographical demarcations. Ibn Nubātah was able to speak to the Moroccans and the Baghdadi in their specific dialects, whereas a poet such as Rashīd al-Dīn al-Waṭwāṭ (d. 573/1182) mastered Arabic as well as Persian, composing poetry in both languages. On the other hand, one finds eminent poets across the Islamic lands, such as the Indian Ghulām ʿAlī Āzād Bilgrāmī (1704–1786), who were so well versed in Arabic and its poetics as to have a significant share in Arabic poetry and rhetoric.[40]

This chapter, then, sets the tone for chapter 5, "Superfluous Proliferation or Generative Innovation?" With a particular focus on compendiums and the implications of the birth or maturation of certain modes and movements, this chapter argues that a discussion sphere derived its vitality and invigoration from the written and oral transmission, inscription, copying, correspondence, and personal contact that made up an Islamic republic of letters across the Islamic world and beyond. Against heavy odds, the wide-ranging endeavor evident especially in Arabic works consolidated the acquisition of knowledge not only through books, translation, commentary, gloss, compendiums, and modes of recitation and praise to the Prophet, but also through street performance, assemblies, and public spaces such as markets, mosques, hospices, and colleges. Texts, along with modes of expression and circulation, militate against boundaries and converse with each other across distant locations and centers in a surprising argumentative way. Methods and achievements should raise questions about certain inherent failures in this Islamic construction of knowledge, but such questions cannot be argued independently of the power relations existing both before and after the advent of European colonialism.

Chapter 6, entitled "Disputation in Rhetoric," consists of a sustained reading of the growth of rhetoric as the defining discursive dynamic. It explains this growth as a cultural phenomenon with an underlying religio-political base that lays a greater emphasis on the Prophet and thence the community. It reads the rise of rhetoric in the study and analysis of critical philology as significantly tied both to the increasing awareness of the street, as shown specifically in compendiums that accommodate popular forms of knowledge and poetry, and also to the shift in philological inquiry to the underlying social, economic, and political layers that interact with linguistic and grammatical (and hence logical) formations. These also connect to a conspicuous engagement with issues of clarity, critical inquiry, eloquence, and forms of effective discourse simply because the rise of the chancery as the center of power, as well as the urgent need for disputations in an increasingly polarized cultural sphere, requires a great amount of skill and sophistication. The reported instance of Tīmūr's debate with ibn Khaldūn and Damascene theologians, for example, directs our attention to disputation and argumentation as highly developed strategies, especially in times of war.[41] The rhetoric of empires and the rise of philological inquiry are tied to each other. Theological and literary discourse often blends with a studied engagement with grammar and logic, as various commentaries on and supplements to primary texts indicate. This preoccupation cannot be understood apart from a dynamic cultural argumentation that passed through many "instabilities," not only across the primary contending camps, such as the traditionalists, speculative theologians, and the rationalist remnant, but also from both the rising Shīʿī *kalām* that retained its early tenth-century acumen and the Sufi poetics of esotericism and devotional service.[42] Moreover, classical poetics was challenged not only by praise poetry to the Prophet but also by the growing investment in street and marketplace poetry. Craftsmen and professionals used poetry as one way of expressing themselves, their roles, identities, and presences as social groups. These are the people who, after all, challenged invasions and in a number of cases (such as the defense of the Damascus fortress) were behind the heavy losses inflicted on Tīmūr's army in 1401.[43] They were also among the groups whose services were pivotal in building up new empires at the expense of their demolished homelands. Thus, Aḥmad ibn ʿArabshāh (1389–1450) writes of Tīmūr's exploits in Damascus and his draining of Syria of its artisans as follows: "Meanwhile he gave himself to seeking excellent men and masters of arts and crafts and men that had skill," and he "ordered slaves of Zinj [Zanzibar] to be collected, of whom he sought to possess more and preferred them to others."[44]

Chapter 7, "Translation, Theology, and the Institutionalization of Libraries," continues the emphasis on logic and rhetoric through a discussion of issues of translation. As the most contentious site of all, translation bore the brunt of traditionalist attacks for introducing speculative theology and dialectic reasoning. But the debate is not as clear-cut as it seems, for grammarians, most of whom were logicians, also disputed translators on other grounds with respect to the latters' canonization of Greek philosophy and logic. The chapter therefore explores *grammatica* as a comprehensive framework for a "tabulated knowledge grid," or a "tabulated space of knowledge," to borrow from Michel Foucault.[45] Rhetors, grammarians, and poets were among the dynamic participants in the makeup of this grid across the Islamic world. This construction or reconstruction of knowledge, moreover, in no way obstructed the rise of popular forms of knowledge. Despite the resistance of certain members of the elite, many others found themselves highly intrigued by the unrestrained flow of street anecdotes, joviality, poetry, and poetics.

Hence, chapter 8, "Professions in Writing: Street Poetry and the Politics of Difference," focuses on poetics and politics at the social fringes and their mediations and modulations. Artisans enforced their place in compendiums, such as ibn Ḥijjah's (d. 1434) *Treasure Trove*, where erotics and homoerotics also had some share. Sufi symptomatology and cryptology crept into other compendiums to unsettle traditionally oriented minds, while finding more currency among mass audiences through Sufi gatherings, recitation sessions, and other means of transmission. The Sufi presence cannot be an ordinary one, for, as multiple accounts make clear, it was so conspicuous that some writers and grand Sufis decided to write back against phony Sufis. On the other hand, despite their light impact and their dissociation from centers of power, Sufis secured the loyalty of certain governors and rulers, especially during the Ottoman and Safavid rule.[46] This intersection leads us smoothly to questions about centers of power and their chanceries, where power articulates its relations and intentions through prose and the deliberate manipulation by prominent scribes, the eminent practitioners of the belletristic tradition.

The book concludes on this note, because these centers of power happened to function as an institutionalized belletristic space, a think tank for city-states, kingdoms, and empires. Many of the most brilliant epistolographers, lexicographers, grammarians, and even poets were once members of the chancery, where prose functions as the "canon of politics," as al-Qalqashandī neatly put it in the culminating volume to his massive compendium of chancery and epistolary art. Yet this site of power comprises only one aspect of the construction of knowledge, for, as discussed in chapter 8, the street and its peripheral continuums in Sufi *khānaqās* and *zāwiyas* had their own input, foreshadowing Johann Gottfried Herder's popular concept of the underlying spirit of a nation.[47] Hence, both spaces, with their highly diverse sites of production and conversation, provide a contentious tabulated space, a knowledge grid involving both harmony and dispute. Indeed, a seismic *Islamica* finds itself there, in these knowledge constellations where Islamic thinkers, writers, and poets from different origins, lands, and forums find their way to pronounce views, carry on discussions, and engage in occasional polemics. Many paid with their own lives for their thoughts, while others suffered imprisonment. Others, meanwhile, failed the challenge of decentralized rule and its coterminous free cultural space and hence stood against innovation and difference. It is to the credit of this rich *Islamica*, as the cauldron for knowledge acquisition and contention, that it explored and mapped out various regions of thought, leaving Islamic societies an enormous corpus with which to wrestle in approval, compromise, or rejection. The legacy is weighty and the burden is heavy. Such is the nature of a seismic challenge.

chapter one

SEISMIC *ISLAMICA*

Politics and Scope of a Medieval Republic of Letters

> This is a record of travel [ibn Baṭṭūṭah's] which is rare enough today with our many conveniences.
>
> —Jawaharlal Nehru, *Glimpses of World History*, 752

> When he [Tīmūr] had filled the bag of his cupidity with precious things and had gradually milked every drop clear or foul . . . he let his soldiers plunder at will, seize any they wished as prisoners, destroy suddenly and slaughter, burn and drag into bondage without restraint. . . . Wisdom became fickle, sagacity was stunned and thick clouds of affliction gathered, and I call Allah to witness that those days were a sign among the signs of the last day; and that that hour showed the conditions of the last day.
>
> —Ibn Arabshah, *Tamerlane, or Timur the Great Amir*, 157

There is perhaps no better instance of the complexity of the politics of medieval and premodern Islamic cultural life, and hence of the formation of an Islamic republic of letters, than the historic meeting between the eminent scholar and historian ibn Khaldūn (d. 808/1406) and the Mongol emperor Tīmūr (Tamerlane; 1336–1405) outside the gates of

Damascus in 803/1401.[1] Its significance for this first chapter derives not only from its problematic narrative in relation to other accounts of prominent fourteenth- and fifteenth-century travelers and scholars and their networks, but also from its pertinence to the constitution of the republic of letters during and in the aftermath of invasions and wars. The Arab-Islamic world was about to witness the collapse of another center and the ultimately supreme military domination of the Mongol empire, along with its increasingly consolidated cultural capital of language, rhetoric, and historiography.

The meeting of the two men combined the primary elements in social networking. Conquest and invasion, in the form of military deployment against the Levant, comprised gathering intelligence not only on military matters but also on prominent scholars in Damascus. Such information partly led to Tīmūr's meetings with ibn Khaldūn and the latter's ultimate commitment to documenting these meetings as evidence of his social theory, which was based on the principle of group solidarity. The occasion can also be read as the intersectional space for a mixed agenda and a means of testing the ways in which modernist and postcolonial lenses choose to engage with the past. Cutting as it does across conceptualizations of nation and categories of ethnicity and ethos, this meeting confronts readers with an immediate need to recover an Islamic understanding of "Dār al-Islām" (the abode of Islam as an inclusive domain), a concept that may rise above ethnic demarcations but may still succumb to more restrictive dynastic applications, which bring with them significant consequences. This historic meeting is also problematic because it directs attention to the manipulation of religion and its concomitant cultural capital in a conquest that has an ethnic core, a core that Tīmūr makes clear in his discussion of historiography and pre-Islamic or Mesopotamian lineage, addressed below. Philological and political explorations, however, cannot be understood apart from economic needs and grand confrontations with other rising powers across the Mediterranean. By wrecking the Levant and planning to conquer the western Arab flank, Tīmūr was facing a possible confrontation with his ancestors' allies, the Franks. In ibn Khaldūn's short autobiographical sketch of that meeting, we are led into Tīmūr's exceptional mind and will to imperial power. Tīmūr was only one emperor among many competing powers and dynasties that also witnessed, cherished, or undermined cultural growth across a long period rich in knowledge production. The meeting subsumes not only the politics of power but also the geography of the Islamic world, its east and west, and the implications of knowledge construction beyond the context of dynastic rule on the large scale.

To the credit of the Mongol conqueror, the thirty-five meeting sessions, spread over forty-eight days, confirm his pursuit of disputation, a trait that was matched only by his voracious desire for conquest and the destruction of every other urban center that competed with his cherished Samarqand. The imperial pursuit was as ruthless and destructive of human and cultural property as any postcapitalist invasion. In preparation for storming Damascus, and also shortly thereafter, the emperor made use of the sessions with the historian and thinker ibn Khaldūn to gather information about lands, resources, theological and philosophical controversies, craftsmen, scholars, and other notables of the Arab-Islamic world and Muslim Spain. The meetings of the two men were held both at Tīmūr's instigation and ibn Khaldūn's own choice, the result of discreet suggestions from Damascene notables in order to avert the calamity of the city's capture.[2] Ibn Khaldūn, an accomplished intellectual, historian, and scholar, the chief Maliki judge in Mamluk Egypt, a native of Tunisia and noted administrator in Granada and Morocco, and an expert in social and economic politics, brought with him a vast knowledge of Andalusia (Muslim Spain), the entire western flank of the Arab-Islamic world (*al-Maghrib*), Africa, and certainly Egypt, the kind of knowledge that an ambitious conqueror like Tīmūr needed in order to ensure expansion and rule that would sustain a Tīmūrid empire (1370–1506).[3] The whole Islamic world was about to fall into the Mongol emperor's hands, with the help of this noted scholar, who found in Tīmūr the proof of his theory of the paradigmatic rise and fall of empires and the function of group solidarity in substantiating, inciting, and consolidating the drive for conquest.[4] Over these forty-eight days, Tīmūr acquired from ibn Khaldūn an extensive knowledge about the region, including its geography, demography, natural and human resources, and present and future prospects.

The last part of ibn Khaldūn's multivolume history includes his autobiography, although without the account of the historic meeting and of the last eleven years of his life, which are found in other autobiographical pieces.[5] Scholars have tended to focus on his introductory volume, or Prolegomena (*al-Muqaddimah*), where he pursues a highly sophisticated theoretical discussion of history, state, society, and the formation of culture.[6]

The father of sociology and history as a science was no minor figure, and it is to ibn Khaldūn's credit that he had and still has a substantial impact on historical theorists, sociologists, linguists, literary scholars, and Islamic jurists. His acquiescence to Tīmūr's desire for expansion may present him as complicit in a devastating expansion; yet ibn Khaldūn shows no qualms with respect to the politics of the meeting. On the contrary, his smooth narrative presents the occasion as an act of recognition and reciprocal arrangement, a gift exchange that Tīmūr and his entourage fully appreciated. The historian is also not bothered by the ethnicity of the conquest; throughout North Africa and until very recently, Islam and Arabism overlap, and no such contradiction or separation is implied, unlike the case in the Arab east. Ibn Khaldūn's counter-endeavor, aimed at contacting Moroccan rulers and acquainting them with the situation, might be a saving grace or a genuine warning, which does not contradict his appreciation of the conqueror.[7] Ibn Khaldūn's social theory could have turned him away from nationalist imperatives, despite the impending calamity that was about to change the political map drastically and relegate Damascus, Cairo, and the rest of the Arab world to a secondary, peripheral status. Medieval scholars' positions with respect to these grave issues seem to be quite problematic and are more complicated than those of contemporary Arab modernists, with their sweeping rejection of the recent past and of its intimidating cultural capital.[8]

This historic meeting cuts across many divides. In ibn Khaldūn we have both the humanist and also an effective participant in Islamic "scholastic" knowledge in its most excessive exegetical domain; the shrewd negotiator trying to save people from impending destruction; and the theorist who is carried away by a theory that demands cogent proof of the group solidarity dynamic needed to generate conquest and control empires. In that meeting, the Islamic world is encapsulated in a nutshell. The struggle for power takes Islam as an ideological pretext for the establishment of a rule based on tribal, ethnic, and other broadly defined confederations. On the positive side, ibn Khaldūn can serve as the iconic and also charismatic embodiment of the Maghrib, not only because he "clung stubbornly to his special Maghrib, or Moorish, garb," but also because his identitarian politics connects us symbolically with the Maghribi community of scholars, Sufis, and entrepreneurs who happened to form a substantial portion of the Cairene and urban elite between the tenth and eighteenth centuries.[9] It is not surprising, therefore, that Maghribi culture and ibn Khaldūn's writings in particular received great attention in the eighteenth century.[10] In other words, in him as a scholar and signifier we also have the Muslim west both in conversation and at war with the Muslim east. This state of affairs does not preclude ups and downs in the lives and careers of individuals and communities. Scholars, artists, artisans, poets, and scientists are caught in the middle, as accomplices, captives, and, on some rare occasions, independent minds and talents.

Indeed, Tīmūr's unflinching purpose of establishing Samarqand as a unique metropolis, one that could outshine the former ʿAbbasid Baghdad, generated an insatiable desire for culture that took the form of enforced migrations of artisans, scholars, and scientists to Samarqand. From the twelfth and even into the nineteenth century, choices were never easy. The Arab center could not hold for long, despite the invigorating presence of Cairo amid other centers subject to rise and fall, such as Granada, Fez, Damascus, Herāt, Tabrīz, Balkh, Bukhārā, Hamadhān, Ṭūs, Samarqand, Iṣfahān, Khwārizm, Khurāsān, Marv, and others. As if mapping out a geographical scope for Islamic knowledge, the discerning master of eloquence Badīʿ al-Zamān al-Hamadhānī (known as the "wonder of the age"; d. 398/1008) takes these and other cities as the sites for his short, eloquent, and witty narratives of ruse, the *Maqāmāt* (Assemblies), which present their locales as culturally active and thriving cities under the control of shaky and unstable regimes.[11]

Knowledge under Duress

Postclassical Islamic cultural life since the mid-tenth century has resisted attempts at categorization on the bases of ethos, ethnos, and logos. Instead it demands a reading (or indeed a rereading) of the period that takes the free, enforced, or deliberate conversations among artisans, poets, and scholars across Islamic lands as an ongoing struggle, a contestation among priorities that cannot be grasped outside the context of power relations. Culture, although upheld and kept alive in poetry, art, and social relations, cannot be argued independently of the ever-shifting grounds that at times compromise the sober-mindedness and agility of scholars. As an example, certain scholars are fully prepared, for instance, to criticize ibn ʿArabshāh's (d. 1450) biography of Tīmūr, *ʿAjāʾib al-maqdūr fī nawāʾib Tīmūr* (The Wonders of Destiny Concerning the Calamities Wrought by Tamerlane), for its "Persianate" style and lack of sympathy for his subject,[12] without giving due consideration to the personal intervention in a narrative of an author who was taken captive in Damascus by Tīmūr at the age of twelve.[13] Unlike compromised historians who write for power motives, but also like many who unflinchingly subscribe to one theological stand, ibn ʿArabshāh is obviously bent on setting the record straight against somebody who destroyed his birthplace, Damascus, and who claimed the intention to interrogate and dismantle the Arab official discourse of power since the Umayyads (r. 661–750).[14] This subjectivity notwithstanding, he offers firsthand accounts of Samarqand as a thriving place for scholars and also highlights the positive aspects of Tīmūr, which were used by the Renaissance poet and playwright Christopher Marlowe (1564–1593) in his play of two parts, *Tamburlaine the Great*. Indeed, ibn ʿArabshāh's description of Tīmūr's physical features, his proclivity for disputation, and his interest in learning are juxtaposed with descriptions of his cruelty and destructiveness. Albeit with styles that succumb to the contentious qualities of the languages that ibn ʿArabshāh mastered, his hybrid grammaticality and diction represent but one aspect of the period under consideration here, namely, the struggles between Arabic as the language of religion, rhetoric, and poetry, on the one hand, and, on the other, the growing prevalence of Persian and Turkish as the languages of the new Islamic political order in its enormous shift eastward. His account lays bare the problematic in cultural formations, between conquest and the commensurate constitution of cultural centers and coteries. The Islamic world was turned into a large theatre of disputation, embodied in multiplying commentaries and other forms of writing. There is a noticeable shift in the transmission of knowledge eastward, as Hamid Dabashi argues, but the same transmission places ibn Baṭṭūṭah and ibn ʿArabshāh, for example, in conversation with a broad Islamic order that was always either in conflict or else rapprochement with the west.[15] The west itself was already there in the east, not only through an unabating influx of Greek logic, via translations, into Islamic speculative reasoning, but also through contacts in Andalusia and Sicily and during the Crusades. The east/west paradigm could not hold for long, and a struggle for power beyond borders took place, as Tīmūr's conquests demonstrate. Transmuted into an epicenter of learning and elegance, Samarqand could not outlast its Tīmūrid-enforced cultural feeding: lettered cities also require their own self-generated dynamics.

While invasions and conquests led to the growth of some city-states and the destruction of others, there is nevertheless a resilient human will that escapes the rigid constraints of ascending political powers and disturbs their seemingly homogeneous façade. Ibn ʿArabshāh's life-itinerary is merely one among many similar examples that demonstrate the other dynamic in the "republic of letters," namely, its networking, which confronts us with an interactive Islamic web, a cluster of *Islamica*, a pattern of vast possibilities that traverse geographies in pursuit of a book, a scholar, a poet, a manuscript, or a noted *majlis* (assembly). Born to a Turkish father and an Arab mother in Damascus, ibn ʿArabshāh was captured in 1401 and carried away to Samarqand by Tīmūr's invading army, where he acquainted himself with Persian, Turkish, and Mongolian languages in the process of later becoming private secretary for the Turkish Sultan, Muhammad II, son of Bāyazīd. He returned to Damascus in 824/1421 and finally settled in Cairo. There he suffered imprisonment once again under Sultan al-Ẓāhir Juqmaq, bequeathing to us before his death in 1450 a large number of prominent disciples, numerous books, and a high level of scholarship. The life of ibn ʿArabshāh can thus be cited as an index of Tīmūrid times and their cultural achievements, all at the expense of human life and urban growth. Such were, in fact, the vagaries and outcomes of those troubled times.

Transmitters of Knowledge

If ibn ʿArabshāh's enforced migration at the age of twelve during the Tīmūrid heyday of Samarqand led him paradoxically to greater knowledge and achievement, there were others who were simply driven by wanderlust. Although free from the dangers of political captivity, this urge was no less binding on others, such as the Moroccan ibn Baṭṭūṭah (d. 1377), whose journeys took him in the opposite direction from that of the Mongol army. Traveling deep into central Asia and ending up in China, he also acted as a judge in Delhi and the Maldives. There and in other places of residence, he became acquainted with notables, converted people to Islam, married, and came across old friends and relatives. In him, the abode of Islam was deterritorialized, and issues of dogmatic stratification and regimentation lost ground. Turned into a lyrical subject like any distinguished poet, this traveler sang the *riḥlah* theme as an ultimate human odyssey shorn of limits. In an amazing travelogue (1325–1354) that eludes questions of identity and language, ibn Baṭṭūṭah, as the unique Islamic subject, takes us to Islamic lands as confederational sites of possibilities where rigid scholasticism is put aside and other ways of communication, understanding, and also difference are found.[16] In more than one sense, his travels provide an index of social networking patterns, through his contacts, his self-presentation as a jurist, his sociability, partial affiliations with coteries and brotherhoods, attendance at ceremonies and Friday congressional prayers, subscription to officialdom, and many other activities.

The adventures of the human agent in this struggle for knowledge open up wide cracks in the shell of consensus that had defined and marked a portion of scholastic thought among jurists and theologians. In this type of thought, there was a sustained emphasis on religious paraphernalia as a means for turning religions into playgrounds for political manipulation. Tīmūr was no exception to this practice. In justifying his conquest and the invasion of Aleppo and Damascus, Tīmūr played out a theological grievance against those who had humiliated the family of the Prophet.[17] But the politics of conquest can also give way to a cultural dynamic of need that ends up putting knowledge at the service of power. No wonder, then, that the Tīmūrid court hosted every kind of worthy scholar. Knowledge in the service of power is more than a handmaiden.

Otherwise, how can we explain the presence in the papal court of the Moroccan Ḥasan al-Wazzān, who was baptized at St. Peter's in Rome on January 6, 1520, as Johannes Leo de Medicis? (He also kept an Arabic version of his name, as Yuḥanna al-Asʿad al-Gharnāṭī.) He was presented to Pope Leo X Medici (r. 1513–1521) at a time when the latter was making preparations for a crusade to northern Africa. Leo Africanus, as a willing collaborator, seemed to the pope to be no less than a heavenly token, a gift presented for the pursuit of his mission. The records mention al-Wazzān as falling first into the hands of Spanish corsairs near Crete in June 1518, while on his return journey to Tunisia from Arabia and Egypt, where he had witnessed in Rosetta the Ottoman conquest of Egypt in 1517. With his knowledge of Timbuktu, Sudanic Africa, and the northern African coast, Leo compiled his *Geography of Africa* in 1520, a work that was translated into several languages and had a lasting influence on colonial thought until the early twentieth century.

Although he is believed to have died as a Muslim in either Tunisia or Fez in 1550, Ḥasan al-Wazzān's role as broker and collaborator is even more problematic than that of ibn Khaldūn. His conversion paved the way for a colonial pursuit under the guise of a crusade. Caught between interest and fear, the Moroccan scholar, born in Granada in 1488, a few years before its fall in 1492, could have lost all hope of a possible Andalusian dawn. But both the recurrence of instabilities in the region as occasions for further dissension among scholars and also their surrender of status and respect to the interests of local authorities raise questions; these questions concern not only consensual theologies but also Islamic politics in an age of conquest involving the Mongols (1256–1353, followed by the Tīmūrid empire, 1370–1506), the Safavids in Persia (1501–1722), and the Ottomans (1300–1914). In one case, we have a crisis and two different resolutions. The Muslim subject, the young ibn ʿArabshāh, met Tīmūr and witnessed the combination of ambition, aspiration, cruelty, and magnanimity that dimmed in his mind any prospects of an ideal rule. On the other hand, ibn Khaldūn met the emperor over a prolonged period of time and ended up with a completely different worldview, one that consolidated his own historiographical theory. From ibn Khaldūn's autobiographical notes we know that Tīmūr was curious about Muslim Spain and possibly thought of regaining it after conquering Morocco. Moving in the opposite direction from Hulagu's alliances with Frankish powers, Tīmūr contemplated a world order, supreme and triumphant, with Samarqand as its center. Leo Africanus's complicity with the papacy obliquely confirms ibn Khaldūn's paradigm of rise and fall, in that it seems to convey a sense of opportunism, a resignation to a politics of reversal whereby the Franks would continue their colonial onslaught under papal guidance.[18] Ibn Baṭṭūṭah may seem at first to be only a wayfarer, a traverser of lands, a cartographer, and devout Muslim subject whose faith is beyond borders and ethnicities and whose wealth lies in an imagination and fecundity of tales, reports, and descriptions. And yet, when put together, those accounts could have made up the material needed by Leo Africanus for his *Description of Africa*, a work that G. J. Toomer rightly describes as "a principal source for European knowledge of the Islamic world."[19] Caught historically at the intersection of an ascending European imperialism, as signified by the symbolic loss of Granada in 1492 (and subsequently underlined by the Spanish invasion of the African coast and the proposed papal crusade), eastern empires were engulfed by the notion of a single-handed triumphalism among three contenders whose playground was the Islamic East: Tīmūrids, Ottomans, and Safavids. Just as imperial motivation requires an idea in order to give the pursuit of conquest both form and flame (or "solidarity," according to ibn Khaldūn's theories), similarly, religion was played out in full just as it was in Europe, but also within the ethos and ethnos of conquest.

The Mongol Court as Site for Debate: Al-Taftazānī and al-Jurjānī

Tīmūr's court in fact mimicked the ʿAbbasid court, not so much in procedural matters and statecraft—which Mongol traditions ran differently—but rather in courting and calling on scholars and poets from every part of the world to settle in Samarqand and to participate in disputations, discussions, and philosophical or theological debates. These were ways of reflecting the kudos befitting an empire. Tīmūr's court was no less than a central Asian prototype of a dynamic republic of letters. The case of Tīmūr himself—a split subject, an emperor of multiple leanings, affiliations, and interests—is quite problematic. Although emperors share the qualities of a fractured mind in the shadow of their absolute desire for conquest, Tīmūr's mixed Sufi, Sunni, and ʿAlid faith is unique. The Mongol appropriation of Sharīʿa (*yāsā*) as a device for conforming to their rituals, practices, and needs is well known; it helped them to forge an open space for cultural florescence. It was common for famous scholars to be invited or brought from Islamic lands to adorn the court and participate in discussions that touched on this triple affiliation. Possibly it was Hārūn al-Rashīd (r. 786–809) or his son al-Maʾmūn (r. 813–833) who was in Tīmūr's mind as he pursued these invigorating discussions and debates.

A further example tells us more about this practice. Soon after conquering Khwārizm (781/1379), Tīmūr's attention was drawn to the highly reputed scholar, rhetor, and theologian Saʿd al-Dīn al-Taftazānī (d. 791/1389), who at the time was enjoying the support and protection of a number of patrons, princes, and rulers in Gurganj, Herāt, Kalistan, Ghujuwan, and then Khwārizm, all of which fell to Tīmūr's conquest in 780/1379. Although al-Taftazānī was given the leading religious office in Sarakhs, Tīmūr would soon bring him to his court, along with his friend and protégé al-Sayyid al-Sharīf al-Jurjānī (d. 816/1413), who was captured during the conquest of Fars and Shiraz.[20] These eminent Muslim scholars of Persian origin—with their lasting devotion to Arabic rhetoric and philology—were two of the many illustrious names adorning Tīmūr's court. In one public theological debate between the two, moderated by the Muʿtazilī scholar Nuʿmān al-Dīn al-Khwārazmī (as assigned by Tīmūr), al-Sharīf al-Jurjānī emerged the victor, an outcome that was condoned by Tīmūr, who credited the latter with "an edge over his rival as a descendant of the Prophet's family."[21] The verdict displeased al-Taftazānī, who had an impressive record as a scholar, theologian, and philosopher and whose influence would continue throughout the sixteenth and seventeenth centuries in the Arab region and in the rest of Asia. Ibn Khaldūn is just one authority of many who testify to the popularity of his writings.[22] The books of both contenders were part of the curricula in Islamic theology as taught or discussed in assemblies, schools, and intellectual circles.[23] The debate was obviously conducted in Persian, as the official language of the empire; but those scholars and their precursors, such as the renowned al-Ghazālī (d. 1111), ʿAbd al-Qāhir al-Jurjānī (d. 471/1078), Fakhr al-Dīn al-Rāzī (d. 606/1209 in Herāt), and Naṣīr al-Dīn al-Ṭūsī (d. 672/1274), circulated their writings in Arabic.

The meetings between Tīmūr and ibn Khaldūn in 803/1401 may have been conducted in Persian or, although only partly, in Chaghtai

Turkish. Their conversations were mediated through a translator assigned by Tīmūr himself.[24] It is worth keeping these facts in mind whenever a comparison is drawn between an Islamic republic of letters and the republic of letters in France on the eve of its imperial expansion. French was the language both of an empire and of the encyclopedia project—and regardless of the scholarly concerns of the architects of the latter, such as Voltaire (d. 1778) and Jean le Rond d'Alembert (d. 1783), its use was symptomatic of the desire for a confederated Europe led by France. The issue of language is therefore central not only to a republic of letters but also, and markedly so, to a burgeoning empire. In other words, emperors made a point of using their official language, while scholars and diplomats felt more assured of their argument and also of their respectability in using their own languages, and especially Arabic, as an acceptable medium among Muslims. Language, outside its binding Qurʾānic use, remains a contested space.

Dynamic Production and Producers

As both a nexus and a medium for possibilities and instabilities, the Muslim subject is not the only problematic agent in the formation of a broad Islamic republic of letters. A notable example of how compilations, texts, and modes of communication and proclamation generated a large knowledge grid is the work of Yāqūt al-Ḥamawī (al-Rūmī; d. 1229), a slave to a trader, who grew into a formidable scholar, biographer, and bibliophile. Yāqūt was able to access the rich libraries of the Caspian Sea, especially Marv in present-day Turkmenistan, before the devastation wreaked by Mongol invasions. In Marv he conducted research for his unparalleled compendiums: "I used to pasture there [in the library], make use of its bounties; and my attachment to the library made me forget every other country, and distracted me from family and sibling, and most of the advantages of this book [i.e., *Muʿjam al-buldān*, The Dictionary of Nations and Countries] were gathered there."[25] This compendium and his voluminous Dictionary of Littérateurs (*Muʿjam al-ʾudabāʾ* or *Irshād al-arīb ilā maʿrifat al-adīb*) are no mere gleanings of material culled from secondary sources.[26] They include character sketches, original documents, and observations along with material conveyed in personal correspondence with the compiler. Both dictionaries would generate others, as supplements, improvements, and also as evidential and authoritative bases in lexicography and historical and literary accounts. A dictionary as source material functions as an encyclopedic base and a discussion site for contemporaries and successors. Significantly, apart from Yāqūt's compendiums and their many supplements over the next six centuries, the practice of dictionary writing brought with it a chain of commentaries, erudite explications that make use of contemporary cultural life, and literary treasure troves. Prominent names participated in this knowledge grid, as I will demonstrate in this volume, and the outcome testifies to an invigorating culture industry whereby the littérateur, poet, or thinker, through a network of associates and readers, assumes the role of a public intellectual. Yāqūt's words, "my attachment to the library made me forget every other country," attest to the formation of a deterritorized republic of letters. The dictionary that grows out of a mind and skill in conversation with a library of rich holdings turns into a new country, a verbal but empowering one, that becomes soon after a source for others, including lexicographers.

Another example is a text by a scholar and Sufi master that opened up loci of interpretations, interrogations, and tests of faith: ibn ʿArabī's (d. 638/1240) *Fuṣūṣ al-Ḥikam* (translated as *Bezels of Wisdom*). Over no less than three centuries, in a process that involved scholastic practitioners, humanists, poets, historians, and rulers—from ibn Taymiyyah, al-Taftazānī, and ʿAbd al-Raḥmān Jāmī (d. 1492) to ʿAbd al-Ghanī al-Nābulusī (d. 1143/1731)—ibn al-ʿArabī's text proved to be a test for the Muslim community in matters of interpretation, one that begins and ends in language. The divide between traditionalists and grammarians, rhetoricians, and theologians often rested on both surface and deep (esoteric and metaphorical) levels of meaning. However, seeming accessibility and impregnable ease (*al-sahl al-mumtaniʿ*) may pose a challenge in that they paradoxically invite both surface interpretations and more discerning ones. Such was the case with the *Bezels of Wisdom*, which engendered raging controversies in support of or against the Sufi master.[27]

The Traveling *Qaṣīdah* in a World-System

Apart from texts as dynamic players in their own right, various modes, conventions, and genres of literature were vigorously pursued and spread across Islamic lands and adjacent cultures, as was the case in southern Europe. Hence it is almost impossible to discuss triumphalist poetics, for example, without reference to the vagaries of the *qaṣīdah* (formulaic ode) in Asia and Africa.[28] Especially in triumphalist court poetry, which was once the epitomic display of allegiance and praise, the *qaṣīdah* structure takes leave of its Arabic origins in the process of its travels, in order to strike a deal with the emperor, the sultan, or the shah, and to configure a new transaction of gift exchange between the panegyrist and the ruler, one that is well suited to its time in thriving cities, city-states, and empires. Always accompanied by some historical record, the *qaṣīdah* also turns into a register of power and glory. Although the increased celebration of Iranian cultural life in the tenth century coincided with the weakened presence of the ʿAbbasid metropolis of Baghdad, the direct encouragement of the Ghaznavid court led to the canonization of the panegyric, especially during the reign of Maḥmūd of Ghazna (d. 421/1030), Sultan Masʿūd I (d. 433/1041), and Sultan Muḥammad (r. 421/1030 and 432/1041).[29] But no matter how Persianized the ode became, it was indebted in form to its Arabic original. As Franklin Lewis argues: "The poets who canonized the Ghaznavid qasida, including among others, ʿAsjadi, Farroxi, Ğayżâyeri, Manučehri, and ʿOnṣori, derived the forms and motifs of their Persian qasidas (either directly or indirectly) mostly from the model of the Arabic *qaṣīda* (especially the two-part form as practiced by al-Mutanabbī [a prominent Arab poet of the tenth century]), and only somewhat from the 10th century Persian panegyrics."[30] Indeed, for many poets, such as Manūchihrī Dāmghānī (d. 1040/41), their "famous 'Arabic' *qaṣīdahs*" were cited or chosen by specialists like E. G. Browne as "typical" odes.[31] Although "heavily influenced" by the Arabic panegyric model,[32] every other branching out within the vernacularizing tradition brought about some divergence. Even the Arabic *qaṣīdah* witnessed a number of turns and changes, thereby providing an elastic rather than a restrictive model, one that allowed differences, including the nonclassical arts discussed by al-Ḥillī. On the other hand, the increased use of

Arabic words and expressions in the *sabk-i ʿIrāqī* (the style of Iraq) tradition is noticeable in Iranian poetry of the mid-twelfth to sixteenth centuries, accompanied by a density of images and a resort to the esoteric expressions characteristic of Sufi poetry.[33]

As usual in cultural transactions, there is a struggle to import elements from adjacent cultures, depending on the need and the desire to innovate. The Arabs drew heavily on Hellenistic thought when they felt the need for a form of disputational logic that has its roots in political upheaval and sectarian or ethnic divides. And while logos may have always held the upper hand in literary and theological conventions and also innovative movements, these are also tied to facts on the ground. Al-Jāḥiẓ, for instance, makes enormous use of Greek, Persian, and Indian sources in nearly all of his books, especially *al-Maḥāsin wa-l-Aḍdād* (Embellishments and Opposites), in order to consolidate his humanistic urge to disseminate culture as a form of cultivated sobriety. In his epistles, on the other hand, he prefers to show the positive and powerful characteristics of races, ethnicities, gender, and nations. It is always advisable to read al-Jāḥiẓ's works in full rather than to treat them piecemeal. His sober-mindedness and rationalist application laid a solid foundation for humanistic discourse, one from which no one, even those least appreciative of his works, can ever be free. Abū Ḥayyān al-Tawḥīdī (d. 1023) was to serve as his successor in the eleventh century. Their humanist endeavors have no limits, and both demonstrate great acumen in the way in which they benefit from other cultures—not only from Hellenistic philosophy and logic, Persian administration and statist ethics, and Indian intellect and expertise in mathematics, but also, and to a large extent, from the street and ordinary life.

For a time al-Tawḥīdī enjoyed the patronage of the Buyid vizier, ibn Saʿdān (d. 375/985), a patronage that was rare in the life of the logician and philosopher.[34] He may have known a number of languages, including Persian, since he was an active participant in philosophical assemblies and circles, especially that of Abū Sulaymān al-Manṭiqī Sijistānī (932–1000).[35] By the end of the tenth century, a good number of writers and poets were familiar with Persian, as appears clearly in Abū Manṣūr al-Thaʿālibī's (d. 429/1039) *Yatīmat al-dahr* (Solitaire of the Ages on the Excellences of the People of the Era) and also in ʿAlī b. al-Ḥasan al-Bākharzī's (d. 467/1075) *Dumyat al-qaṣr fī ʿuṣrat ahl al-ʿaṣr* (The Palace's Crimson Statue and the Nectar of the People of the Epoch). Furthermore, the same era gave an impetus to Persian letters, which made enormous strides under the tutelage of the Ghaznavids, Seljuqids, and Mongols, thus confirming what Dabashi has described as "a manifest imperial imagination staging otherwise its latent defeats—a paradox that made Persian poets and literati creatively passive-aggressive in overcoming and outstaging their Arab counterparts."[36] During the Mamluk period, between the thirteenth and sixteenth centuries, the frequent recurrence of quotations from and allusions to Persian poetry also point to the rise of Persian letters as well as the increased recognition accorded to literary production. A paradigm of center versus periphery, although in tandem with the shift in political power, might not hold up here, not only because of the already established presence of an ancient Persian culture that was assimilated into the rising ʿAbbasid political order, in particular, but also because of the ongoing shared literary codes between Arabic and Persian. Even if there were many instances of differentiation from Arabic, the latter was not as indomitable as Latin was for the French, for example, a point that will receive further problematization below.[37] Anthologies and compendiums abound with Persian poetry rendered from Persian into Arabic. Such familiarity with Persian literature can also be traced in poetic practices that make use of broken or modified metrics in Persian in order to conform to singing and hence lyrical pursuits. As noted by the versatile Indian poet Ghulām ʿAlī Āzād Bilgrāmī (1704–1786), the prominent Egyptian poet al-Bahāʾ Zuhayr (d. 1258) used one of those metrics; this observation, however, overlooks the presence of the same modified meter in Abū al-Faraj al-ʾIṣfahānī's *Kitāb al-Aghānī*.[38]

Literary exchange on either equal or less than equal bases may lead to extreme disruptions that relate to a poet's attempts at destabilizing a convention or a code. Such is the case with Ḥāfiẓ's (d. 1390) use of a verse by Yazīd ibn Muʿāwiyah (d. 64/683), who was known for his love of worldly poetry. In a wine poem (*khamriyyah*), the earliest on record, Yazīd says: "I am poisoned [by love], and have no antidote, nor any charm [to protect me]; / pass round the wine-cup and proffer it then, O cup-bearer." According to Sūdī Busnavī (a ninth-century/sixteenth-century commentator), as referenced by Julie Scott Meisami, the line is reworked via *taḍmīn* (embedding) by Ḥāfiẓ to read as follows:

> O *sāqī*, pass the wine-cup round and proffer it;
> for love at first looked easy, but difficulties have come to pass.

No wonder, argues Sūdī, that the embedded quote raised the objections of Safavid poets like Ahlī Shīrāzī and Kātibī Nīshāpūrī. Ahlī responds in verse:

> One night I saw lord Ḥāfiẓ in a dream,
> and asked him, "O peerless one in virtue and in learning:
> Why did you bind Yazīd's verse to yourself,
> despite all your virtue and perfection?"
> He answered, "You don't understand the point:
> The unbeliever's property is licit to the believer."[39]

Although this is not a case of theft (*sariqah*),[40] and is parenthetically set apart from the rest of the *ghazal*, it is critiqued on other grounds. To cite, include, and even contrafact (imitate as a poetic convention) implies an affinity with the source subject, which the Safavids ideologically decried. On another level, the daring inclusion of a verse that was notoriously available among the poet's audiences conveys the notion of a strong literary community, sufficiently familiar with even the most obscure counterviews. Such an inclusion of a verse by an Umayyad who was known as a reveler at best and as an opponent of the family of the Prophet invites us to reconsider our assumptions concerning extreme sectarian or ethnic divides and to look instead for the makeup of an actual humanist tradition that goes beyond Arab/Persian and Turkish or Indian paradigms. A correspondence is to be found between the refined *ghazal* of Ḥāfiẓ, for example, and the love poetry of the Arab poet Jamīl, as noticed by Meisami, but variations emerge on other levels, including concepts, themes, and style. In this domain of interaction and dialogue, of accumulation and dissemination, we confront significant manifestations of exchange, constellations of poetry and poetics, and a consortium of ideas. In other words, we find another multifaceted republic of letters that stretched across different lands, regions, languages, and communities.

Ghazal Conversations

Poetry clearly forges deep emotive links; this is especially the case in the *ghazal* tradition, with its significantly pervasive tropes of madness. What starts as story and is given form in poetry would develop to become a mode in *ghazal* poetics and a trope for the sobriquet *majnūn*, or mad as the one possessed by love. The *majnūn* trope in poetry relates to real names, such as that of Qays ibn al-Mulawwaḥ (first/seventh century), also called the madman of the ʿĀmir tribe, whose love for his cousin Laylā and the enforced separation from her was the reason behind his madness. However, madness here does not imply wayward behavior; rather, it is the projection of the beloved into the seen and perceived. The lover passes into a Sufi-like state, becoming subsumed into the image and soul of the beloved in order to become her in *ḥulūl* (incarnation) fashion, the one who sees, talks, and perceives. Abū al-Faraj al-ʾIṣfahānī warns, however, that there were so many poets under the same name and so much written in the tradition of love and madness that due caution is needed in sifting the poetry of love and madness originating in seventh-century Arabia. That same tradition later found impetus in the lyrical fecundity of Persian poets, narrators, and painters; it grew on its own and reached into illustrated manuscripts as a phenomenal expression of human love, beyond caste or class.[41] The third of Nizami Ganjavi's five narrative poems, *Khamsa*, focuses on a malady that transforms the lover into another person who is lost in a world filled by the image of the beloved; hence everything makes sense only through her image. In 1299, Amir Khusrow Dehlavi presents us with *Majnun o Leyli*, treating the same theme but showing more interest in the literariness of the narrative. Jāmī completed his *Layla and Majnun* in couplets in 1484. No less significant is the work of Jāmī's nephew, Abd-Allah Hatefi (d. 1521), whose *Layli o Majnun*, the first in his *Khamsa* (pentalogue), is so impressively wrought that it stands on its own as an independent work of art. Expanding into India and Turkish domains, the story of love and madness is in need of no origin, in that it generates its own versions, imitations, and appropriations to fit into new communities and cultures. In the world of collaborative *Islamica*, this narrative, whether in poetry, prose, or painting, forges another link, emotive to the extreme and tightly binding as if in resistance to the forces of destruction and war and their ultimate condition of severance and disintegration. The human longing for rapprochement cultivates and is cultivated within a tradition of writing and speech, or communication, whereby discourse and poetics are humanized and made people's property, although it is not that of jurists and scholars of law, with their regimentation of impossibilities and forebodings. Poets are the voices of humanity; they repeat, along with a tenth-century littérateur, "Poets alone, not tutors [i.e., grammarians], may pass judgment on poetry!"[42]

Even religion, much to the chagrin of many a jurist, is played out as poetry in the middle and premodern period. This was due to the phenomenal presence and dissemination all over Asia and Africa of encomiums to the Prophet, which continue to occupy the place of honor in *dhikr* (remembrance of God) festivities and ceremonies.[43] The typical *qaṣīdah* or ode structure, canonized as the ancient model worthy of emulation throughout Arab and Islamic lands, undergoes reinvention in terms of form and sociopolitical function. Building on Rajāʾ al-Sayyid al-Jawharī's reading of Abū Jaʿfar al-Andalusī's commentary on ibn Jābir's *badīʿiyyah*, Suzanne P. Stetkevych succinctly explains that the *badīʿiyyah* "is a curious subgenre of *madīḥ nabawī*." She adds: "Though commonly defined as merely a praise poem to the Prophet in which each verse exemplifies a particular rhetorical device . . . , it is precisely a *muʿāraḍah* (a contrafaction, or counter-poem, that follows the rhyme and meter of the base poem)."[44] While investing in the literary devices, images, and structures of the pre-Islamic ode, the *badīʿiyyah* creates its own functionality not only through emotive links with the populace, but also through its transactional terms with the Prophet and his memory rather than with any other patron. Instead of conceding to a theologically imposed poetics through the paradigm of Quʾrānic "inimitability" that continued to inform critical discourse for a long time, the *badīʿiyyah*, with its accompanying compendiums in rhetoric, shifts attention to the Prophet. Hence a humanizing poetic propensity has gained in impetus, as will be made clear later in this volume. The *Burdah* (Mantle Ode) and its *badīʿiyyah* (innovative ode with deliberate abundance of figures of speech) outgrowths were soon to become a unifying factor across Islamic lands among both the educated and the illiterate.[45] As a significant practice, it was also used by Arab Christian poets, such as the Syrian al-Khūrī Nīqūlāws al-Ṣāʾigh (d. AH 1169), and the Lebanese Arsā b.Yūsuf al-Fākhūrī (d. AH 1301), in praise of Jesus.[46] While avowedly an encomium, this poetry shifts attention from ordinary panegyrics to another level, one that dims worldly pursuits in a quest for Prophetic intercession. Here, Arabic seems to be playing a unifying role without political support. To borrow and redirect Hamid Dabashi's phrase with respect to "Persian literary humanism," Arabic was used and practiced since the mid-tenth century in the shadow of "world conquerors" and non-Arab empires and dynasties.[47]

A Mantle for Islamic Nationhood: Genealogy of a Subgenre

The term "republic of letters" begs for a more nuanced interpretation when applied to the sweeping popularity of a *qaṣīdah* such as Muḥammad ibn Saʿīd al-Būṣīrī's (1211–1294) Mantle Ode (*al-Burdah* or *al-Burʾah*).[48] Of Amazigh descent from a Ṣanhāja tribe, al-Būṣīrī received sufficient education in Cairo to become recognized as an established poet, entitled to mentor his juniors, such as the poets ʾAthīr al-Dīn Muḥammad ibn Yūsuf Abū Ḥayyān al-Andalusī (d. 725/1325), Abū al-Fatḥ b. Sayyid al-Nās al-Yaʿmarī (d. 734/1334), and ʿIzz al-Dīn b. Jamāʿah (d. 735/1335). Both the poet and his poem were soon to be the center of widespread attention. The recitation of his Mantle Ode in *dhikr* ceremonies and lamentations for the dead, its use for amulets, and its status as an object of emulation and study, present us with a case that requires a further broadening of the idea of a republic of letters. The Mantle Ode turned into a semiotic space for identification with an Islamic world-system of Sufi adoration and rapture across Asia and Africa. The poet, whose tomb became a revered shrine in Alexandria, and who followed the Shādhilī (named after the Andalusian Sufi master Abū al-Ḥasan al-Shādhilī) order in Sufism, claimed that the Mantle Ode was his gift to the Prophet in exchange for the Prophet's intercession on his behalf in a dream that cured him of paralysis. Regarded as a sacred recitation, this ode, ever since its appearance, has brought into being a rich concordance of other odes, recitations, and discussions. It has evolved as a unifying Islamic recitation, a group, communal, and congressional exercise, and a nucleus for communication and theological and literary study. An ode that is beyond borders and is an incentive for collaborative networking and sociability cannot be less than an ideal example of the republic of letters. It functions as medium, effect, and generator of duplicates and festivities. It was also a political tool, a sanctified gift worthy of Tīmūr, which ibn Khaldūn presented to him as second only to the Qur'ān, and which the emperor treated with great reverence: "Then I presented the Burda to him; and he asked me about it and about its author, and I told him all I knew about it."[49]

Al-Būṣīrī's Mantle Ode invokes other variants, such as Muḥammad ibn Faḍl Allāh al-Hindī al-Burhānpūrī's (d. 1620) *al-Tuḥfah al-mursalah 'ilā al-Nabbī* (The Gift to the Prophet), which turned its latent Sufism into an encapsulation of ibn ʿArabī's thought. It is certainly among many, including Āzād Bilgrāmī's ode, that set the scene for the late eighteenth-century infatuation with the Mantle Ode, an infatuation that gathered even more momentum as a result of French Orientalists' familiarity with the poem. Indeed, this infatuation turns into seduction at certain historical moments, such as that of the Napoleonic expedition of 1798. In an ambivalent stance between resistance and temptation, the speaker in Shaykh Ḥasan al-ʿAṭṭār's (1766–1835) *Maqāmah* sounds intrigued, tempted, and eventually "seduced" by the French Orientalist's command of the native's literary heritage.[50] The Orientalist is made to discuss verses from the thirteenth-century poet al-Būṣīrī's Mantle Ode, but, based on the protagonist's recapitulation with verses of his own on being infatuated, as "arrows fill [his] heart," we may infer that the verses they discussed pertain to the *ghazal* tradition.[51] With admiration and the same infatuation, the chronicler of late eighteenth-century Egypt, ʿAbd al-Raḥmān al-Jabartī (1756–1825), dwells on the French Orientalist's memorization of the Mantle Ode with gusto.[52] The Orientalist's pursuit of popular Islamic tradition was not a personal whim; it falls within the needs of an empire to reach into Muslim minds and "structures of feeling," to borrow Raymond Williams's apt phrase,[53] in order to ensure a hegemonic presence.

Pascale Casanova's argument with respect to Paris and its centripetal and centrifugal roles could have been expanded and problematized, beyond what is a celebratory narrative, in order to account for the imperial use of native traditions to seduce and lead native elites. The case is even stronger, in our present example, when Mantle odes and other intercessionist poems and poems of praise become so popular and numerous as to invite scholars such as the Bombay scholar and poet Faiz Allāh Bhār to compile, in 1893, his *Tuḥfat al-muslimīn: A Moslem Present; An Anthology of Arabic Poems about the Prophet and the Faith of Islam.*[54] Compilations in Arabic were already in demand, as the enormous Nabhāniyyah collection of 1902 tells us.[55]

The Ode as Medium of Sociability

Rather than an aberration, the subsequent emulation of al-Būṣīrī's Mantle Ode and the extensive use of rhetoric to supplement or mutate this tradition in the so-called *badī'iyyah* form of inventiveness complements a poetic pursuit that also finds expression in compendiums of poetry, which indicate on the part of their compilers (both scholars and critics) a commitment to propagate poetry as a field of knowledge operating on structures of feeling, connecting to a political unconscious, and forging links with or against the state apparatus. Apart from the popularity of poems, which ensures a place in compendiums, poems are often conducive to sociability; hence their centrality to the republic of letters. In assemblies, poetry recitation often calls for comments and invokes discussions that, on many occasions, draw the attention of a biographer, critic, or bibliophile. In other words, it generates its own public sphere in the ongoing formation of a republic of letters. Complementing al-Tha'ālibī's *Yatīmat al-dahr* (Solitaire of the Age), with its listing of hundreds of examples of poetry from across the Islamic dominions along with short biographical notes and selections, the renowned scion of Nishapur, Abū al-Ḥasan 'Alī ibn al-Ḥasan al-Bākharzī (d. 467/1075), compiled his *Dumyat al-qaṣr* (The Palace's Crimson Statue), in which five hundred and thirty contemporary poets are cited in a voluminous work dedicated to the Seljuq vizier, Niẓām al-Mulk (Nezam al-Molk al-Tusi; d. 1092). In both compilations, it is taken for granted that poets are familiar with the languages and cultures of the age, but that they all write in Arabic, as the language with which to disseminate knowledge under an Islamic umbrella. In this sense, Islam is not a religious entity that confines, nor is it a product of rigidity and dogma, but rather a way of life, a culture of accommodation that assumes and adopts the color and taste of each milieu. With the mushrooming of a variety of dynasties and sultanates within the larger framework of Islamic dominions, the need to bring together poetry and poets across the different regions was a priority that was pursued with diligence. What was lost in centralization was compensated for in compendiums: a textual empire is given both form and shape through these voluminous combinations, which serve as the poetically synergized cartography for a once central empire that no longer exists, a textual simulacrum for a nonexistent original.

Poetic compilations were able to restore sufficient knowledge to their readers, who may have felt a need for them in order to connect back to an earlier poetic tradition. Although al-Bākharzī's compendium reveals an awareness of this tradition, it also brings into the picture fresh innovations, the poetics of the street and the common people, a tendency that was also to develop in Mamluk Cairo in particular, where in the twelfth and thirteenth centuries artisans fully participated in a poetic tradition. Such a poetic propensity on the part of artisans could hardly be something new, as is duly explained by Ṣafī al-Dīn al-Ḥillī (d. 750/1349).[56] The substantial presence of such poetic expression as an urban phenomenon in Mamluk Cairo (just as it had been in Baghdad and Basra at an earlier date, and in Iran and central Asia since the fifteenth century) signifies recognition on the part of scholars and critics of the multifaceted literary domains that existed beyond the privileged space of the learned and the early hierarchy of literary genres.[57] This democratization of space as a central characteristic of the republic of letters finds its textual representation in compendiums that collapse the separate categories of theological, philosophical, and literary thought, along with whatever relates to professions, crafts, painting, poetry, and song, in order to speak to society in its entirety, and also in terms of its ethos and abandon.

Although the language of pre-Islamic odes could be considered an echo from the past, its rebirth in the *badīʿiyyah* tradition that was popular all over Asia and Africa should lead us to reconsider any such hasty judgments. Apart for this rejuvenating presence, it should be recalled that prototypical *qaṣīdas* cut across every genre of Islamic *adab* and poetry. They are present in *nasīb* (amatory mood) or the love and *ghazal* tradition, in wine poetry, and in song, as shown in al-ʾIṣfahānī's voluminous *Kitāb al-Aghānī* (The Books of Songs). Al-ʾIṣfahānī, of Umayyad extraction but born in Iṣfahān in 897, was educated in Baghdad and settled in Aleppo, Rayy, and other cities. He was an exemplary seeker of knowledge, who was able to bring together in his vast collection the lives of artists, singers, and poets, of men and women, in conversation across time and space. Poised between rupture and ease, death and love, sacrifice and hedonism, recklessness and restraint, a valorized deterritorialized space emerges in his works that lays down a combination of the explosive and the collaborative in a republic of letters, which was bound to assume other forms and images in years to come.

As the language of the Qurʾān, Arabic linked nations and narration across the Islamic lands. Books, modes, genres, and practices were continually in motion, even during the most disruptive times. One might be surprised to read, for instance, books authored by Ghulām ʿAlī Āzād Bilgrāmī in Persian, Urdu, and Arabic, along with his native Braj. Nicknamed Ḥassān al-Hind after the pre-Islamic and ultimate poet of the Prophet, Ḥassān ibn Thābit (d. 674), because of his versatile grasp of Arabic and his poetry and studies in the language, Bilgrāmī is another littérateur whose career and achievements exemplify this republic of letters.[58] He was not only conversant with Arabic metrics and their variations in Persian verse but also familiar with poets from pre-Islamic times onward. *Subḥat al-marjān*, his compendium that interacts with writers in the *badīʿiyyah* tradition, is impressive. By his time, *badīʿiyyah* variations had multiplied, and *Burdah* (Mantle odes) and panegyrics addressed to the Prophet had become popular across Asia and Africa, from Delhi and Herāt to Timbuktu and West Africa. Throughout this era of Islamic politics, especially controversial issues relating to the caliphate and *Wilāyah* or *Imāmate*,[59] Arabic was a cauldron for rhetoric, a language to be stretched, explored, and set in compendiums and ever-growing lexicons across the Islamic world, each one claiming perfection while containing verbatim sections or smaller segments culled from antecedents. Authorship and circulation are the markers of a volatile space.

A Language for a Republic?

Cultural phenomena such as compendiums and lexicons were not a redundant exercise or superfluous activity, but rather the result of a dogged commitment on the part of the best lexicographers across Islamic dominions, who regarded Arabic as their world, both now and hereafter. Their lifelong preoccupation with and veneration of Arabic cannot be adequately comprehended by secularized modernists, who thus fail to recognize the driving force behind such encyclopedic efforts over the centuries. The modernist depreciation of premodern Arabic cultural production amounts to a substantial disengagement from a tradition that was much needed for the promotion of education and culture in the newly emerging Islamic nation-states.

It is significant that the majority of compendiums and lexicons were produced in Cairo. Although most were single-authored, they usually involved the collaboration of many other scholars as consultants, along with a wide variety of source material, correspondence, and reports. For itinerant scholars and traveling texts, Mamluk Cairo played an important role as a meeting place. As both a centrifugal and a centripetal body, Cairo served as habitat and the site of exile, as was the case with ibn Ḥijjah al-Ḥamawī (d. 837/1434), Jamāl al-Dīn ibn Nubātah (d. 768/1366), and many others. The city was also relatively free from constraints, due to a decentralized intelligentsia, as discussed in the last chapter. It was both a host and a discussion space. This space was negatively affected for some time during and after the Ottoman conquest (1517) and the subsequent imposition of Turkish as the official language. However, the city would recover some of its cultural luster thanks to the presence of other cultural centers, both immediately adjacent and also relatively distant. Scholars from Aleppo, Damascus, and Fez, all the way to Timbuktu in present-day Mali, Iṣfahān, and Bukhārā settled in Cairo or at least stopped there for a while. Others were satisfied with an imaginary stopover, which was sustained and given shape through Sufi networks and an innovative reliance on the antecedent tradition of poetry and writing. Such was the case with al-Taftazānī, Saʿdī al-Shīrāzī,[60] ibn Baṭṭūṭah, Ḥasan al-Wazzān (Leo Africanus), ibn al-ʿArabī, ibn Khaldūn, ibn ʿArabshāh, and numerous other scholars and poets. Arabic had to engage in a struggle against the Ottoman imposition of Turkish, one lamented by lexicographers. The result was a weakened or even hybrid Arabic historiography, as found in the language of ʿAbd al-Raḥmān al-Jabartī's (d. 1825) documentation of the state of Cairo and Egypt.[61] For some writers, such as the seventeenth-century satirist Yūsuf al-Shirbīnī, author of *Kitāb hazz al-quḥūf* (Brains Confounded), scholars have ventured so far in hermeneutic superfluity that they deserve a satiric gloss.[62]

Although Arabic remained the language of arts and theology, it could not be the language of political power, as it had once been in the Umayyad and ʿAbbasid periods. At that time of imperial growth, the caliphate and its elite opened up to cultural influx but granted Arabic a privileged status in their assemblies, correspondence, and rewards. Only this particular aspect of Umayyad official discourse, and especially its traditionalist discourse, can hegemonically claim Arabic as a kind of privileged territory of wealth and power. Hence, Arabic as the Umayyad official discourse only partially justifies Dabashi's otherwise significant critique of "Arab literary imperialism as the *modus operandi* of the dominant ideology of conquest."[63] Indeed, a number of historical details militate against Dabashi's premise with respect to Persian and Arabic. The premise seems to subscribe to Casanova's argument with respect to the burgeoning of the French in 1549 as a "vernacular national literature [that] has been founded by differentiating itself from the literature of another neighboring people and by refusing the domination of another language, the apparently indomitable Latin."[64] While admittedly language is a battle space, as I argue below, we should keep in mind that Persian was a dominating language in the Arab east, with the exception of Arabia and Yemen, before sometime during the Umayyad reign. Its reappearance as an official language by the end of the tenth century cannot be put forward as an example of a newly valorized vernacular language. Moreover, the Umayyads inherited from the Sassanid a Persian-oriented administration, statecraft, and financial system in Iraq and a Greek-oriented system in Syria. Persian and Greek were used in those domains until sometime during the reign of the fifth caliph ʿAbd al-Malik ibn Marwān (685–705). In other words, during the heyday of so-called Arab "literary imperialism," the empire was run differently, and literary and philological pursuits were a primarily courtly or independent enterprise. As such, Arabic continued to enlist the participation of scholars and littérateurs across the Islamic world.

Under the governor of Iraq al-Ḥajjāj ibn Yūsuf (d. 713), Arabic replaced Persian through the diligent effort of the bilingual Persian Ṣāliḥ ibn ʿAbd al-Raḥmān al-Sijistānī when he worked with the secretary in charge, the Persian Zādānfarrūkh b. Būrī. Thus Mardānshān, the son of Zādānfarrūkh b. Būrī, reportedly cursed Ṣāliḥ: "May God exterminate you as you have exterminated the Persian language!" According to Franz Rosenthal's reading, "The Persians offered 100,000 dirhams to Ṣāliḥ should he declare himself incapable of introducing Arabic as the language of financial administration."[65] Under the Umayyad caliph ʿAbd al-Malik, Arabic gradually replaced Greek for financial administration in Syria.[66] In other words, power can be decisive in changing language, but it also manipulates all philological resources in order to consolidate a state or an empire. Identitarian politics, including Arabism, becomes secondary in this consolidation process. The Umayyad caliph exerted an effort to impose Arabic as the language of the empire throughout, a strategy that meant enlisting the support not only of the Arab tribes that provided the military corps and personnel, but also that of Berbers and all other Muslims under the banner of the Qurʾān. The move consolidated the Islamization of the empire and hence its legitimacy among other Islamic nations. Yet the legitimation process through Arabic was not necessarily opposed to an enormous importation of Persian, Indian, and Greek sources. A translation movement had thrived since the days of the Umayyad (Marwānid) caliph Khālid b. Yazīd b. Muʿāwiyah, who called on a group of Greek philosophers to undertake a translation project in alchemy and other sciences.[67] Translation is no mere transfer of books and treatises from one language to another; rather, it is a dynamic space of negotiation that tends to unseat any linguistic monopoly. The "literary imperialism" premise also cannot hold for the ʿAbbasids, not only because the Sassanid statecraft from Khurāsān was already implemented and exercised by the new dynasty, but also because of the deliberate political shift away from Umayyad ideological thought that is succinctly expressed in al-Jāḥiẓ's epistle on the Umayyads. In that epistle, al-Jāḥiẓ chose as his target the lingering Umayyad presence among the elite who tried to make a return through the back door of the rift between the ʿAbbasids and their presumed cousins, the ʿAlīds.[68]

Mobilizing Mourning Rituals

The mounting regression to a pre-Islamic aristocratic discourse, though significantly reduced during the initial period of the ʿAbbasid caliphate (roughly 750–930), provoked the rise of a counter-discourse as part of a political pro-ʿAlid or Shīʿī Buyid (r. 934–1055) takeover of the weakened ʿAbbasid caliphate. The Persian dynasty institutionalized mourning rituals to commemorate the death of the Prophet's grandson. The latter's name occurs only cursorily in official historical discourse, such as the fourteenth-century historian ibn Kathīr's report on the year (AH 352) when the Buyid ruler, Muʿizz al-Dawlah ibn Buwayh, issues an order whereby "markets be closed, and women should wear coarse woolen hair cloth; they should go into the markets with their faces uncovered/unveiled and their hair disheveled, beating their faces and wailing over Husayn Ibn Abi Talib [*sic*]."[69] In the era of the Safavid dynasty (1502–1736), these mourning rituals would receive further institutionalization and undergo significant transformation, especially in matters of narrative, as reciters or narrators began recounting events in assemblies and memorial gatherings. In the sixteenth century the practice of *rowzeh khani* (hence the Iraqi colloquial *rowzakhūn*, or remembrance reciter) was instituted as a narrative ritual to commemorate the tragedy at the Battle of Karbalāʾ in 680, now a defining paradigm in Shīʿism.[70]

This process of remembrance, involving these practices and their transformation, is of some significance in the context of discursive controversies, since scholars tend to regard literate culture as separate from these practices, which possessed sufficient resilience to resist elite censorship or repression. Mobilization of a sense of tragedy among communities takes place through an internalization of the narrated and performed event, the betrayal of the Prophet's grandson, and its provocation of a collective sense of guilt. The narrative and performance of the event creates a community in mourning that is larger than any individual or collaborative project. The classical Muslim historian al-Ṭabarī (d. 923) and other authorities make use of Abū Mikhnaf's record to document that harrowing rupture in Islamic history.[71] This material, in turn, received further attention and institutionalization that led to the composition in 1502 of Hoseyn Vaʿez Kashefi's *Rowzat al-Shuhadāʾ* (The Garden of Martyrs), a work that draws on Saʿīd al-Dīn's *Rowzat al-Islām* (The Garden of Islam) and al-Khwārazmī's *Maqtal Nūr al-aʾimmah* (The Murder Site of the Light of the Imams). Other changes in the ritual occurred during the Qajar (r. 1796–1925) era, when the mourning narrative (*rowzeh khāni*) developed to become *Shabīh khāni*, a ritual drama or theatrical performance in the streets, along with processions (*mawkib*) for mourners. This ritual led a number of European travelers to write about the tragic aspect of "The Persian Passion Play," as Matthew Arnold called it in an article under that title.[72]

These developments in discourse that treated of the strong divide between Islam as the faith effectively practiced by the Prophet and avowedly followed by his family and ardent companions, on the one hand, and, on the other hand, as that of the Meccan aristocracy as represented by the Umayyads, can serve as the defining point in discussions of humanistic and scholastic developments in Islamic *adab* and thought. As mentioned earlier, the greatest humanist in the Arab tradition, al-Jāḥiẓ, focuses succinctly on this defining point. He was writing in order to expose the new Umayyad advocates (i.e., those among his contemporaries), whom he called *nābitat ʿaṣrinā* (the reemerging clan of our age).[73] Yet his pointed critique against them should not be seen as siding with the ʿAlīds, for he directs his criticism at the concept of the Imamate as well.[74] Al-Jāḥiẓ, the sober-minded Muʿtazilī, could not hide his reluctance to believe in *ilhām* (inspired knowledge) or prophetic succession, but he does grant the Prophet's family the power of faith, uprightness, and righteousness.

No less significant to this approach to the politics of the postclassical *Islamica* are the declarations, rituals, and practices that attended the emergence of protest among the Shīʿites. Mourning rituals were not initiated by the command of the Buyid ruler; however, it was that ruler's order that allowed repressed emotions and feelings to find expression in ways that are as diversified as human behavior can be. Official sanction gives communal feelings ways of venting themselves, which are necessarily opposed by those who view matters differently. No wonder, then, that ibn Kathīr and many other followers to date of the school of ibn Ḥanbal (241/855) have been unable to condone practices that they understand as signs of unbelief. Yet rituals have their poetic tradition, as found not only in *marāthī* (elegies) but also in Mantle odes, *nasīb* (amatory) preludes, and lyricism. They also connect to the *qaṣīdah* as epic reconstructions, a tradition of poetry, the examples of which may serve as axial constructions throughout the Islamic literary heritage across Asia and Africa. Such poetic expressions thereby grant us, as their readers, itineraries of connection that are more subtle than the easily harped-on divides of ethnic possibilities. Their relevance to the study of street performance, carnival, and other popular manifestations of collective performance emanates from the increasing self-awareness of the street in urban space. They can be read in tandem with the rise of popular epics and the tendency to write down what was once only part of a collective memory,[75] a kind of political unconscious that runs deep below the surface, as Frederic Jameson argues.[76] Studied or placed in the context of a conflated national-popular literature, usually associated with Herder's conceptualization of a German nationhood,[77] these popular rituals, festivities, and epics are no less foundational for cultural capital than the belletristic cultural tradition. The city of Cairo alone witnessed the composition of several famous popular epics, such as *Sayf ibn Dhī Yazan*, *al-Amīra Dhāt al-Himmah*, *al-Sīra al-Hilāliyyah*, and *al-Ẓāhir Baybars*.[78]

Reinvented Lexical Communities

Arabic is the centerpoint of an interactive *Islamica*, with its intricate webs and byways, not because Persian, Turkish, Urdu, Swahili, and a number of other languages were less productive or synergic, but because Arabic happened to be the language of Muslim communities. Similarly, the centrality of Cairo in no way minimizes the important role, say, of

Tabrīz as the capital of the Il-Khanids (1256–1353), and those of other city-states that happened to pass through phases of rise and fall throughout the postclassical Islamic period. Cairo, however, as mentioned in the Preliminary Discourse, escaped destruction and remained beyond the immediate vagaries of devastating onslaughts from Asian invasions.[79] As a safe enclave, it functioned in a way similar to its multiplying compendiums and lexicons. If the city was able to reinvent itself in a prolonged struggle for survival, so do the compendiums and lexicons, which reached a peak in Murtaḍā al-Zabīdī's (d. 1205/1790) voluminous *Tāj al-ʿArūs* (The Bride's Crown), a lexicon that brings alive an Arab culture in all of its massive comparatist frameworks.[80] Using his many contacts, his travels across Arab and Islamic lands, and his sustaining connections with the North African region, al-Zabīdī was able to make use of a wealth of written material, antecedent lexicographic authority, and human sources. He brought an Arab and Islamic world into a multivolume lexicon with entries that turn into series of glosses and commentaries. In André Lefevere's reading in his *Translation, Rewriting, and the Manipulation of Literary Fame*, seemingly secondary activities—such as rewriting, translation, editing, compilation, and, by extension, lexicography—reinvent their originals in such a way as to popularize, propagate, reinterpret, edit, and abridge them in order to meet new expectations and demands, and thereby reach larger audiences.[81]

No less of a reinvention is the illustrated book, which received great encouragement and impetus in cities other than Cairo. The Persian and Mongol art of illustration was the most sophisticated medium in the reinvention of narrative and poetry. Sequences of illustrations reached and impressed audiences even beyond the specific linguistic domain of each work. Often bilingually adorned with a calligraphic narrative, these illustrated and embellished books remain one of the greatest wonders of a cultural florescence, a celebration of the human beyond limits, as Dabashi convincingly argues.[82] Whether under the same influence after the Mongol invasion (1258) or in response to earlier Seljuq rule (1038–1194), Baghdad was witness to the curious process of illustration or use of frontispieces for books usually associated with philosophy and logic, such as the collective encyclopedic work *Rasāʾil Ikhwān al-Ṣafāʾ wa Khullān al-Wafāʾ* (The Epistles of the Pure Brethren and the Sincere

Friends) that was prepared in Baghdad in 686/1287.[83] The double frontispiece has "scholars in conversation, reading, writing, arguing, surrounded by pupils," as Anna Contadini rightly notes. Closely corresponding to the preface, which the "Pure Brethren" meant as a contract with their readers, the frontispiece underscores their explorations in the humanities, metaphysics, mathematics, science, and music, and the proposed transmission of knowledge that they intimate in their mission statement to the reader.[84] Both this illustration and its originating text serve as a prototype for a republic of letters, one that encompasses and mutates the components of this republic and its functional social networks. No less important are the illustrated books with numerous plates produced in Wāsiṭ, to the south of Baghdad, such as al-Qazwīnī's *ʿAjāʾib al-makhlūqāt* (The Wonders of Creation and the Oddities of Existence), available as an illustrated manuscript in 678/1280.[85] Also of importance to this Islamic network was the illustrated reproduction of al-Ḥarīrī's *Maqāmāt* carried out by the copier and illustrator, Yaḥyā ibn Maḥmūd al-Wāsiṭī, in Baghdad (634/1237).[86] Another is *Kitāb al-Aghānī* (the Book of Songs; illustrated vol. 17, 1217–1219).[87] In specifically underscoring these illustrated books, I am drawing attention to their presence among audiences and communities that clearly cherished them and boosted their popularity.

The other development in painting occurs in response to urban space. If we assume that Cairo and Iṣfahān, for example, witnessed both urban growth and the rise of a class of artisans that was sufficiently strong to call for treatises by market inspectors, written to record and regulate in detail these professions and their measures and performance, then the very care and attention devoted in painting, for instance, to lower walks of life, rather than to the court and the privileged classes, can be explained as a natural outcome. Hence, the shift in Reza Abbasi's (1565–1635) production toward common life is an index of this change in urban space, one that would also be similarly represented in writing, poetry, and other modes of expression.[88] However, the shift itself should not be regarded as region-specific. The renowned traveler ibn Baṭṭūtah (from Tangier) tells us that a picture of a foreigner traveling in China was circulated by the Chinese authorities everywhere in case a wrong or a misdeed were committed by or against that person. On the other hand, early on in the days of the ʿAbbasid caliph al-Muʿtaṣim, colored painting was already in practice; and Andalusian art shows not only colored paintings of rulers, along with wall paintings, but also many other paintings where Christians and Muslims share in activities such as chess or music.[89] This noticeable shift toward the representation of common life thus occurs in a confederacy of arts. There are hundreds of such artifacts, poems, book illustrations, performed recitations, and other means of communication that confront us with another trajectory of communication and education across Islamic lands.

Vagrant Intellectuals

Given that this book focuses on Arabic as the language of communication and expression that gave way to other languages soon after the actual loss of a center, Baghdad, to the Buyids (934–1055), it is worthwhile to assess the ways in which Arabic was able to establish its presence and efficacy beyond the enormous cultural inception generated by the Qurʾān and its sciences. Perhaps there is no better guide to the intricate vagaries and achievements in languages than the one offered by Badīʿ al-Zamān al-Hamadhānī (d. 398/1008), mentioned above, in his *Maqāmāt*. Prominent in his own times and "remarkable for his choice and correct Arabic, the elegance of his epistles and the beauty of his poetry," as the polymath and philologist Abū Manṣūr al-Thaʿālibī (d. 429/1039) notes,[90] he was also a great traveler to cities and states, from Kkurāsān, Sijistān (Sistan), Herāt, the kingdom of Ghazna, and Nishāpur to Kufa, Mosul, and Baghdad. Badīʿ al-Zamān al-Hamadhānī offers us a model of the scholar as a humanist of his time. Limiting his protagonist's journeying to West Asian states and cities, Badīʿ al-Zamān maps out the vagaries of cultural life and the increasing gap between the learned and the court. Vagrant intellectuals turn into dissenters and destabilizers of absolutism. Furthermore, their presence as the elusive protagonists in widely circulated prose foretells the subsequent role of the intellectual as an entrepreneur, whose expertise must prove itself in a lucrative market. Not bound by identitarian politics, and self-presented as a businessman with cultural commodities for sale to whoever pays the most, an intellectual such as Abū Ḥayyān al-Gharnāṭī (full name, Athīr al-Dīn Muḥammad of Granada; d. 745/1344) can equally serve the interests of the Arabic language or provide a basic grammar for the Turkish language. In these cases, the expert and eloquent protagonist or vagrant intellectual redraws the cultural map, not only geographically within a broad Islamic domain but also as knowledge that is accessible outside of princely courts, for example, in mosques, markets, and the streets. Badīʿ al-Zamān's "republic of letters" is discernible in many biographical sketches of a solid scholarly career and contacts, but his *Maqāmāt* (Assemblies) present gatherings where discussion is pursued as an independent inquiry. In other words, he plays havoc with common terms of patronage. The humanist tradition releases knowledge from shackles and lets it make its way into every kind of public space. The analogues of Badīʿ al-Zamān's *Maqāmāt* appear soon afterward, converting modes, tropes, and genres and merging styles into hybrid systems and compendiums that set Arabic in motion as a great humanist endeavor: hence my reservations with respect to defining Arab humanism as necessarily tied to conquest and gain.[91] Badīʿ al-Zamān's protagonist is the shadowy figure of Abū al-Fatḥ al-Iskandarānī, but he is also an eloquent scholar and a trickster whenever wit and agility are required to beat a community on its own terms. Always the intruder on companies that take themselves seriously as distinguished scholars, Abū al-Fatḥ breaks through the crust or veneer of knowledge in order to penetrate its core, and thence to demonstrate from within its life and warmth; "every age has its Jāḥiẓ," as he informs one company. That destabilizing dictum is equivalent to saying, "Every age has its Shakespeare." In other words, canonization is downplayed to accommodate change and mobility among scholars, social groups, cultural norms, and literary genres. Throughout the *Maqāmāt*, as short narratives with a particular focus on social, economic, and cultural issues, Badīʿ al-Zamān uncovers ruptures, uncertainties, cracks, and pitfalls, and guides knowledge back to its humanist resourcefulness. In other words, during the zenith of knowledge construction in the tenth century, the *Maqāmāt* author leads us to the fringes of society and its forms and methods of knowledge, while at the same time interrogating the mainstream discourse in the *Māristān* (Asylum) *Maqāmah* (no. xxiv) and in that of Ḥulwān (no. xxxiii; a town beyond Baghdad). In both, he is engaged with issues of abstract knowledge that can become confusing to the layman. In breaking down and indeed subverting totalities, including argumentation over minute issues in speculative or rationalist thought and grand proclamations in literary canonizations, Badīʿ al-Zamān al-Hamadhānī paves the way toward further achievements in knowledge, beyond any privileged domain.

The eloquent wanderer serves as a model. He is able to roam widely across different lands, always with Arabic and other languages as his weapons and tools in an age of struggle for power. The famous Buyid vizier, al-Ṣāḥib ibn ʿAbbād (d. 385/995), gave al-Hamadhānī a Persian verse to render into metrical Arabic, a test that proved too easy for him.[92] The rise of Persian was already evident by then, but Arabic remained the yardstick among the literati regardless of their race. Such an accomplished poet, writer, scholar, and epistolographer as Badīʿ al-Zamān al-Hamadhānī received great acclaim as the "wonder of the age" in an era that already owned such illustrious names as the author and compiler of the voluminous *Book of Songs*, Abū al-Faraj al-ʾIṣfahānī (d. 967); the highly controversial rationalist and skeptic poet and prose writer Abū al-ʿAlāʾ al-Maʿarrī (d. 1058); the celebrated Abū al-Ṭayyib al-Mutanabbī (d. 965); the exceptional poet Abū Firās al-Ḥamadānī (d. 968); the great philologist ibn Fāris (d. 1004); and the Ikhwān al-Ṣafāʾ (Pure Brethren), whose prototypical republic of letters takes the form of a systematic classification and analysis of all knowledge in a unified corpus.[93] The prominent names in the Arabic tradition also happened to be well versed in other languages, Persian included, and had made it a standard practice to switch among metrical practices as a show of dexterity and competence.

What I would like to dispute here, in particular, is the mistaken notion that Arabic was exercised primarily as a scholastic tool, a mechanism in the hands of the powerful, a one-sided enterprise that was nomocentric—scholastically centered on law and regulations—rather than homocentric.[94] Every language has its play of power with others and within itself, among different classes, groups, and societies. At the time when no Arab dynasty was actually a ruling authority (with the exception of a territorialized one in Morocco, for example), the traveler ibn Baṭṭūṭah narrates conversions to Islam and the use of Arabic everywhere. He also narrates meeting familiar faces from his own hometown Tangier far away in Anatolia, Delhi, and the Maldives.[95] The accommodating Islamic dominions were meeting sites for wayfarers and fortune seekers far removed from their homelands. It was also not uncommon to come across calamities befalling individual writers and scholars, ranging from conspiracies against some thinkers, the execution of others, and personal decisions on the part of yet others to burn their own books in sheer frustration and disappointment, as was the case with Abū Ḥayyān al-Tawḥīdī. But with all these vagaries and achievements in mind, Arabic remains a desirable privilege, not only as a means of acquiring knowledge but also as the ultimate accomplishment in Qurʾānic sciences. Littérateurs such as Āzād Bilgrāmī in eighteenth-century India used Arabic for a substantial portion of their poetry and criticism, as if to make a case for the "republic of letters" even at a time when Arabic was in eclipse.

A Dialogic Space for the Republic

Across the many cultural ruptures, uncertainties, and discontinuities we can pick up elusive connections, in spite of apparent labyrinths and incongruous individual undertakings. Otherwise, how can we rationalize Āzād Bilgrāmī's engagement with most of the salient markers of the republic of letters, with its intricate webs, discussions, salons, and echoes across vast lands and periods? The republic as the dialogic space for poetics and politics claims its freedom from power as the condition for its humanist conversations. Hence, the use of Arabic and the spread of a culturally oriented Islamic identification in no way negate the racial manipulation of genealogical divides to ensure privilege in times of conquest. Across Islamic lands in times of conquest (including that of Andalusia), for example, rulers were keen to gain the support of their tribes or the races they counted on for one reason or another. Arabs acquired the better agricultural lands in Andalusia, for instance, and to a degree in Khurāsān as well. But a changing politics would soon displace this racial prioritization after the Turks were singled out as the people most suitable for warfare. Following al-Jāḥiẓ and early writers and historians, for instance, Abū al-Ḥasan ʿAlī al-Bayhaqī (ibn Funduq; d. 565/1169) would divide up regions and nations according to their exceptional traits: the Persians were known for ethics; the Turks for horsemanship and warfare; the Chinese for the arts; Greeks for wisdom, medicine, and logic; Indians for astronomy and mathematics; Byzantines for medicine; and Arabs for the science of genealogy and proverb.[96] These divides were taken for granted in the body politic. It was a given that reliance on essentialized racial traits would speed up and secure a better state apparatus. Although whimsical rulers might ignore such criteria, as ibn Baṭṭūṭah observed during his stay in Delhi, it is difficult to ignore the dynamics of these basic identifications. Genealogy, as a science highly acclaimed by al-Bayhaqī, resonates with his boast of an Arab descent at a time when Arab lineage was not in demand. A knowledgeable author and a prolific writer of books, including one on genealogy, al-Bayhaqī succumbed to a tradition whereby the Arab race derives nobility from its association with the Prophet. In other words, we have another line of legitimation that derives moral power from faith—not from dynastic rule, as was the case with the Umayyads and ʿAbbasids, but from the family of the Prophet. No wonder al-Bayhaqī was also the author of a commentary on Imam ʿAlī ibn Abī Ṭālib's sermons, sayings, and proverbs in his *Nahj al-Balāghah* (English translation: *The Peak of Eloquence*), which has been a central text for Shīʿites and other Muslims.[97]

Legitimation, then, demands dual lines of approach: one is to claim nobility in association with aristocracy; another settles on ethos, involving a number of utopian promises and also protests. The first line may well draw us into an Arab problematic that survived in the so-called *ʿAṣabiyyah* (solidarity) principle as developed by the historian ibn Khaldūn, which is patrimonial and tribal to the extreme, despite Islam's counterproposal of confederacy among Muslim peoples. It was certainly given impetus during the era of the caliph ʿUthmān (d. 656). Although political and administrative imperatives would soon displace these priorities, the genealogical principle obliquely gained ground from the parallel application of chains of transmission to ascertain the Prophet's hadiths and Arab historiography. Both lines left an abiding mark on claims of legitimacy that have endured, and drove many prominent writers to cite a genealogical tree to claim an Arab descent, even when Arab ascendancy was no longer tenable.

Such was the case, for instance, with Badīʿ al-Zamān al-Hamadhānī, Abū al-Faraj al-ʾIṣfahānī, and al-Bayhaqī (i.e., ibn Funduq). These itineraries and divided aims only serve to complicate the politics of the medieval Islamic republic of letters as an encompassing term for the period that extends from the twelfth to the late eighteenth centuries. They place us directly at a number of intersections that can be neither easily categorized nor summed up by hasty conclusions of the kind often encountered in the writings of many Arab and Afro-Asian modernists. The following chapters will aspire to explain and defend these arguments.

chapter two

A MASSIVE CONVERSATION SITE

The Word Empire

There are many reasons that warrant a sketch of the parallels between two collaborative efforts, one in the Islamic world and the other in Europe. The former took place in the southern Iraqi city of Basra in the tenth century, and the latter in late seventeenth-century France. A number of factors curtailed the Islamic project, while the European one had the advantage of congenial conditions, including the rising intellectual ferment and collaborative spirit that were integrating and dynamic forces in the Enlightenment. In its four sections and parts, Jean Le Rond d'Alembert's (d. 1783) *Preliminary Discourse*, which accompanied the first volume of Diderot's *Encyclopedia* (1751), is often read as the fruition of the late seventeenth-century European republic of letters.[1] The confederation of scholars and writers involved in the *Encyclopedia* set the stage for other philosophers and thinkers to implement new methods of inquiry and discourse. In Richard Schwab's words, "by the end of the seventeenth century, the members of the European international republic of letters were developing an awareness that cumulatively they were a force in the world, and this birth of a self-conscious sense of power among the literati proved to be one of the revolutionary events of modern times."[2] He adds: "For the first time large numbers of people were coming to the bracing conclusion that the progress of humanity could be carried forward indefinitely in this world, and men of letters felt they were the prime movers of that progress." With the publication of the first volume of the *Encyclopedia*, the collaborators and contributors to the project brought that spirit of inquiry into effect. D'Alembert's *Preliminary Discourse* is often cited as the concise introduction to the Enlightenment. Although it was the work of d'Alembert, the *Discourse* was also written in response to and in conversation with his associates in a circle consisting of Diderot, Jean-Jacques Rousseau, Étienne Bonnot de Condillac, and a large number of other correspondents and thinkers, including Voltaire. The amount of scrutiny in method and the range of ideas that wrecked the orthodox foundations of an old regime of thought are taken as the crystallization of that republic of letters and hence of the Enlightenment.

We have the right, then, to look for other prototypes that antedate this European project. In fact, in the Islamic world order there already existed a basic Islamic collaborative compendium composed by a number of scholars and thinkers in Basra, namely, the first encyclopedic work in Islamic philosophy, compiled by Ikhwān al-Ṣafāʾ (The Pure Brethren; 908–980), with the title *Rasāʾil Ikhwān al-Ṣafāʾ wa Khullān al-Wafāʾ*[3] (Epistles of the Pure Brethren and the Sincere Friends).[4] The fifty-two epistles circulated anonymously by a group of four authors[5] culminated in *al-Risālah al-jāmiʿah* (The Comprehensive Epistle), or *Jāmiʿat al-jāmiʿah* (Super Comprehensive Epistle).[6] Although we have no information on other team-authored encyclopedias in the medieval Islamic world, the groundwork for collaborative efforts in knowledge construction was thereby laid, although these efforts developed in different directions.

A Prototype for a Republic of Letters

The encyclopedia of the Pure Brethren comprises four sections with an opening "*mathesis*" treatise (*al-riyāḍiyyah*) of many chapters, covering in sub-epistles the topics of algebra, mathematics, logic, analogy, calculus, geometry, music, categorization, and many others, with the aim of bringing each disciple to a level of knowledge that is humanized and grounded in the ancient (Greek) and Arab and Indo-Persian sciences. It is a systematically organized project that digests and interrogates accumulated and translated knowledge and that is always bracketed by an invocation of God. Worth noting here is that *mathesis*, defined as "the science of calculable order" in Foucault's account of sixteenth-century Europe,[7] had already reached a very advanced stage when the Brethren recorded and circulated their corpus of information. The first part of the Brethren's collection lays the groundwork for other explorations and draws the reader into the thick of the Islamic rationalist/speculative episteme, thus demanding a certain caution lest the epistles encounter the wrong audience and fail to attain their purpose. It is followed by others on the natural, psycho-rational, and metaphysical-theological sciences. Conversant with Greek philosophy and Indo-Persian sciences, the Brethren come across terms with no equivalent in Arabic and leave them in their transliterated form. Although the presence of transliterated words attests to the increasing *dakhīl* (that which is foreign; intruding) in the Arabic language, it should not be confused with the speculative theologians' expansion in conjugational forms, which will be discussed in chapter 6. It falls rather into the category of Greek loan words, a register already endorsed and practiced by translators.

Like the eighteenth-century French encyclopedia, the Brethren's epistles were to provoke a counter-discourse from certain traditionalists. The caliph al-Mustanjid (1124–1170) lent his support to conservative jurists who shunned the work as heretical and, as a result, ordered the collection to be burnt. The epistles provoked other prominent conservatives as well. The renowned scholar Taqī al-Dīn Aḥmad ibn Taymiyyah (d. 1328) rejected them as heretical, esoteric, and ultimately damned, as being contrary to Islam. This is no ordinary confrontation, since it also explains how this contentious terrain foreshadows a rather intense theological controversy, one that manages to fragment and halt the growth of Islamic philosophical inquiry thereafter. Even so, another line of support for philosophical pursuits made itself felt throughout Islamic lands, as we will see in due course. In the genealogy of ideas, a lead was probably taken from the earlier Ismāʿīlī blend of Greek/Islamic thought,[8] as found in the contributions of Abū Yūsuf Yaʿqūb ibn ʾIsḥāq al-Ṣabbāḥ al-Kindī (Latin: Alkindus; 185–256/805–873) and of Abū al-Naṣr al-Fārābī (Alpharabius; 870–950). Ikhwān al-Ṣafā'’s constructed knowledge order was the basis on which Abū ʿAlī al-Ḥusayn b. ʿAbd Allāh ibn Sīnā (Avicenna; d. 428/1037) and later Naṣīr al-Dīn al-Ṭūsī (d. 672/1274) were able to build a philosophical discourse with a solid foundation in science, which would continue to inform the pursuit of knowledge. The renowned historiographer ibn Khaldūn (d. 808/1406), for one, wrote his *Lubāb al-Muḥaṣṣil* (The Essence of *al-Muḥaṣṣil*; i.e., al-Ṭūsī's critique) as a synthesis of the latter's contribution to philosophy, a work that was nearly lost due to the heavy attacks it suffered at the hands of traditionalists in unstable political situations. The raging controversies that took place involving traditionalists, rationalists, theologians, and also Sufi Shaykhs (another subject of controversy) provide us with a large corpus of works that resonated heavily in certain regions, as can be inferred from popular or "street" responses and debate sessions.[9]

Other examples can also lead us to appreciate the pursuit of knowledge in the medieval period, but it is worth noting that the controversial epistles of the Brethren were not meant for either the layman or the untrustworthy. Instead, they aim at the salvation of the soul through the purification of the heart and the acquisition of knowledge. They beg their reader to cherish their contents, to peruse them by following the same structure and organization in the different sections and chapters, and to avoid letting them fall into the hands of the unworthy.[10] Their aim is not to provide a mere preliminary introduction or synopsis, like a *khuṭbah* to explain the design of a book, but rather to provide a rigorous systematization of all of Islamic thought. Philosophy (*ḥikmah*) and theology can thereby receive sustained attention in connection with human life and a guiding reason, but also in terms of the grand context of the cosmos. Throughout the epistles, the sciences of language, social and natural science, statecraft, logic, philosophy, and ancient knowledge (that of the Greeks) are invoked in a lucid display of explication and argumentation. Abū ʿAlī ibn Sīnā (Avicenna) would follow this direction and take it further; Abū Ḥāmid al-Ghazālī (d. 505/1111) is stuck in-between philosophical reasoning, logic, and Sufism, although with a large dose of Ashʿarite speculation; al-Ṭūsī retains the human soul at the center of thought; whereas Ashʿarite logic resonates more with al-Kindī's thesis that revelation is superior to reason as a source of knowledge. Although the compatibility between philosophical reasoning and natural and speculative theology is always a point of argument, an emphasis on the intellect (*ʿaql*) remains a constant. All these scholars and their ideas are pitted against the traditionalists who fear reasoning and speculative tendencies.

To draw further comparisons between the two projects—the French *Encyclopedia* and the Brethren's Epistles—one can argue that both stem from a network of associates, assemblies, conversations, and correspondence. They necessarily rely on some recent or ancient authority in order to interrogate outworn or prognostic and visionary concepts in favor of empirically proved or upheld views. Not all of the contributors to the French model are known; but the Basra Brethren chose anonymity as necessary to strategic dissimulation. Political authority, as represented by Frederick the Great, was appreciative of d'Alembert's *Preliminary Discourse*,[11] but such could not be the case for the Basra Brethren, who were afraid of a culturally unreliable consumer. Nevertheless, there is still an outcome from them, a delivery, consisting of a multivolume encyclopedia. Whenever there is an encyclopedia, there stands behind it a belief in a community of consumers in need of a comprehensive repository of updated knowledge. The providers as a group also cherish their common commitment, not as ordinary scholars or researchers, but as leading intellectuals.

Apart from its basic constructions in acquired knowledge, the collaborative encyclopedia of the Brethren has Arabic as its language, Basra as its site of production, and anonymity as its authors' absence or metaphorical death. In other words, it has already negated an author-centered category for the sake of the free transmission and facilitation of knowledge, which does not deny the authors' deliberate choice of precautionary dissimulation (concealment) to escape persecution. Furthermore, the encyclopedia was collaborative in the sense that it was the outcome of discussions and joint reasoning. It has no place as such for single authorship. Produced in a city famous for its innovation in philological inquiry, analogical reasoning, and intellectual leadership, this collaborative project must have been more challenging in its own times than many of Casanova's models. No less interesting is the fact that the nineteenth-century publication of the Brethrens' project was prefaced by none other than the Syrian-Lebanese "master" Buṭrus al-Bustānī (1819–1883), a renowned *nahḍah* (revival) pioneer, whose scholarly efforts in lexicography, journalism, social justice, and the education of women were invaluable. His preface aligns him with other advocates of modernity, but it also sets him apart as highly selective in addressing the massive production of an earlier period. The significance of the preface also stems from directing our interrogation toward the basics that sustain specific projects such as the French one and its integration into the Enlightenment.

When we look back upon the Basra pioneering teamwork, however, we confront a different turn in cultural production following its publication. Even when we rely on reports from and correspondence with contemporaries, or on antecedent authorities, we still possess no other such group-authored work. One explanation for this lacuna relates to the availability of other means of configuration, the collection of material and discussion sessions, and a process that necessarily precludes team-authorship while achieving practically the same end. The other explanation is state intervention and, on many occasions, persecution of thinkers, as was the case during the reign of a number of ʿAbbasid caliphs and later authorities. Team authorship is often accompanied by secrecy, especially when a group of thinkers and writers collaborate in a written forum that often serves as a declaration of seminal and groundbreaking interventions, which in turn can lead to sharp opposition and discord, as was the case with the Brethren of Purity in Basra. In such cases, private and selective circulation works better than open publication. Such projects, as well as the preparation of compendiums, assemblies, discussion sessions, and commentaries, have their own formation processes over time. Hence, a conceptualized republic of letters turns into an ongoing project that draws its sustenance from an ever-accumulating cultural capital. Its demise or failure occurs whenever there are counter-circumstances, including a power politics that intervenes negatively against its three foundational and constituent components, namely, networking, where communication is contingent on the "rattle"—the clatter and commotion—of different languages in a dialectic of alignment and conflict between Arabic and struggling vernacular literatures; human agency, as exemplified in an integrated body of intellectuals with a clear-sighted notion of their role in transformation and change; and an accumulated cultural capital that feeds and defines a cultural script.

Structural Components of a Republic of Letters

Rather than simply offering a history of ideas, the present project partly adopts a Foucauldian exploration of the conditions that enable these movements and of the conflicts and fluctuations that led certain ideas to either thrive or falter. Reflecting on the neoclassical period in Europe, Foucault argues: "If one wishes to undertake an archaeological analysis of knowledge itself, it is not these celebrated controversies that ought to be used as the guidelines and articulation of such a project. One must reconstitute the general system of thought whose network, in its positivity, renders interplay of simultaneous and apparently contradictory opinions possible." After "dispersing the undefined circle of signs and resemblances, and before organizing the series of causality and history, the *episteme* of Western culture had opened up an area to form a table over which it wandered endlessly, from the calculable forms of order to the analysis of the most complex representations" in a "tabulated space" of knowledge classified under "theories of language, classification, and money."[12] The reader may perhaps see no particular rationale for this partial comparison with Foucault's analysis, unless he or she is acquainted with the massive (if random) migration of a large number of Arab/Islamic manuscripts to Europe throughout the Middle Ages and well into the eighteenth century.[13] The fact that they take root in Europe, in controversy or otherwise, certainly raises questions regarding their original milieu, but such an investigation would take us away from the project at hand. In other words, my aim here is not to provide answers to the failure of knowledge to establish an orderly state in many Arab and Muslim regions; rather, it is to deal with the constitution of a grid of relationships and connections in Islamic culture that may help to explain for us what Foucault defines, with respect to what he calls the "Classical Age" in Europe, as "the general configuration of knowledge."[14]

The turn in Islamic culture toward the pursuit of knowledge in general cannot be summed up by any single event or phenomenon. Certainly, the turn to written texts was consolidated and given impetus by the manufacture of paper.[15] The shift to the written on a massive scale, upon the advent of a political state in Islam (Muʿāwiyah's seizing of power in 661), signifies a move away from a view of the universe as a microcosm of what Foucault calls the "privileged creation" of the macrocosm.[16] But some comparisons and contrasts need to be established here. Foucault ascribes to sixteenth-century Europe an episteme "in which signs and similitudes were wrapped around one another in an endless spiral,"[17] leading in the end to a perception of the microcosm as the sign of the macrocosm, "the visible marks that God has stamped upon the surface of the earth."[18] The Brethren of Purity invoke Neoplatonic premises in an otherwise sustained scientific analysis; occasionally they indulge in a number of detours, such as one subsection with the heading "The Resemblance of the Human Body to the Circles beyond the Orbit of the Moon": "If you ponder the buildup of the human and meditate upon it, you find all *mawjūdāt* (manifestations of existence), with all representations in there, this is why the philosophers call it a microcosm, for there is a resemblance to whatever is in the macrocosm."[19] As argued by G. P. Conger, the Brethren used analogy as "a more generalized cognitive and conceptualizing mode," thus preparing the way for further explorations in the construction of knowledge.[20] According to Conger, "the theory that man is a microcosm first becomes imposing [in their work]. It is no longer fragmentary, but fundamental; and it is no longer isolated, but linked up with a comprehensive and correlated world-system."[21] The universe conveys *āyāt*[22] (signs), contained in language, pointing to the omnipresence of God, but there is also an emphasis on *jadal* (argumentation; the art of pleading) in the Qurʾān, which celebrates human reason.[23] Resemblance, at least before the advent of Islam and its confrontation with both old and contemporary habits of thought and practices, was once a sign, a meaning, and a conjuncture of marker (idol) and belief.[24] The Brethren of Purity take such ideas further by bringing into their discussion whatever can be classified and included within the basic structure of their epistles, keeping in mind all the while the need of their readers to be addressed persuasively in the face of a rising class of jurists and also traditionalists. Indeed, in *Al-Burhān fi wujūh al-bayān* (Demonstrating the Modes of Eloquent Expression), Abū al-Ḥusayn Isḥāq b. Ibrāhīm b. Sulaymān b. Wahb al-Kātib (d. after 334/946) claims to be able to glean the signification of a thing by way of four manifestations: resemblance; binary opposition; the indivisible essence, which may carry internal contradictions without damage to itself; and the occasional or effect (*ʿaraḍ*) that pertains to whatever can be described or conjoins with epithet and attribute.[25] The gradual urban change, cultural diversity, and the ultimate separation between faith and the state in the Islamic world served to amplify the separation between things and words,[26] emptying language of its spontaneous flair, its transparency, and hence its lamented purity. No wonder there would appear lexicons, books in grammar and philology, collections of poetry, compendiums of anecdotes, and secretarial manuals to support the lucrative vocation of *kuttāb* (epistolographers, writers, and secretaries) in a rising and expanding empire beginning during the early years of the eighth century. This is even more the case in the medieval and premodern period, despite the opposing but limited proliferation of Sufi loci that reconstitute language as corresponding to the language of God, a point that will receive more attention in the concluding chapter.

Arabic happened to be the space where thought, conflict, affiliation, and struggle were pronounced and regained their actual or symbolic value. It therefore makes sense to start from there, in and within the sphere of language. As I have argued earlier, conversation, debate, and rebuttal all occur within the domain of Arabic as the language of the Qurʾān. All conflict is played out in a language grid of philological explanation, lexical derivation or conjugation, and systematic argumentation or wholesale refutation. Especially for jurists, language and rhetoric in particular has to be mastered. Thābit ibn Qurrah (d. 288/901) goes so far as to think of rhetoric as an inclusive rubric, in which *fiqh* (jurisprudence) is only a subdivision.[27] In other words, controversies and differences continued to rage, coming into being through engagement with political and theological issues from the earlier period of Islam that caused rifts among thinkers, theologians, and jurists, and that ultimately led to a buildup of a massive repertoire of hermeneutics.[28]

The "Rattle" of Languages

Networking occurs within languages, but it is consolidated by a common sphere of discussion, competition, and interaction, where some differentiated spaces hold sway over others. The literal battles and wars waged throughout the long period under consideration can blind us to the raging "rattle" of competitive languages, the commotion in philology and linguistic studies, and the excessive explorations in Arabic lexicography. The Tunisian lexicographer and prominent compiler of the indispensable lexicon *Lisān al-ʿArab* (The Arab Language), Muḥammad b. al-Mukarram ibn Manẓūr (d. 1311), bemoaned the decreasing interest in Arabic among the learned and the counter-vogue for translation.[29] Ibn Manẓūr looked on Arabic as the upholder of Qurʾānic culture and hence of a triumphant Islam spreading across the globe. In contrast, the Mamluk, especially Circassian, body politic in Egypt saw itself as split between an Islamic centrism with Arabic as its proclaimed official language—"*lisānun ʿArabiyyun mubīn*" (a clear Arabic language)—on the one hand, and, on the other, the Kipchak or Oghuz tribal confederacies with which they were affiliated.

Ibn Manẓūr's worry was certainly prompted by the tendency among the professional classes to have works translated from Arabic and Persian into these Turkish dialects. Finding that translation for the ascending Turks was a lucrative business, scholars and other professionals must have shifted their attention to translation. Translation in this case becomes the nexus for shifting power relations. Along with the translations done at the behest of the court of one center or another under the emerging dynasties, professional translators grew up as a class of their own, with solid grounding in competing languages. To make use of writings in Arabic in order to consolidate a rising dynasty or to substantiate its Islamic legitimacy, translations from Arabic into Persian and Turkish multiplied over time. On the other hand, the ascending Turks made use of Persian and Arabic poetry, along with history and science, to build up libraries of their own, as befitting an empire. Although there were many translations from Arabic into Persian, as I will discuss later, the medieval period, specifically the Mamluk era, witnessed a rough competition with Arabic among the Mamluk elite. Robert Irwin correctly concludes that it "is difficult to consider the Turkish literature of Mamluk Egypt in isolation from that of the Golden Horde, Khwārizm, Anatolia and Azerbaijan."[30] But, with the rise of Ottoman triumphalism, Anatolian Oghuz was to become the dominant medium for translation. Along with the translation movement itself, there was also an effort to place Turkish at the nexus of imperial consolidation, one that was forced to take grammar and lexical accumulation seriously. It should not be surprising, then, that some Arab scholars were also involved in translation from Arabic to Turkish and in providing teaching manuals in grammar and good writing. *Al-Idrāk li-lisān al-Atrāk* (The Acquirement of the Turkish Language), which served as the basic grammatical tool throughout the Ottoman domains, was written by none other than the Andalusian scholar Abū Ḥayyān al-Gharnātī (d. 745/1344),[31] who had settled in Cairo and received the patronage of the Mamluk state through its viceroy, Sayf al-Dīn al-Arghūn. Adept in Turkish and Persian, he was also a noted poet and littérateur.

If Pascale Casanova thinks of Joachim du Bellay's *La défense et illustration de la langue française* (1549) and the establishment of the French Pléiade as a basic restructuring and hence expansion of a world-system that was the sphere for a world republic of letters,[32] then we can argue similarly for the place of Turkish in the rising Ottoman Empire. On the other hand, Abū Ḥayyān al-Gharnātī's career as a philologist (basically a grammarian), translator, theologian, and poet of Andalusian origin, with his multiple residencies and identities, confronts us with the need to regard such a migrational itinerary as one of the distinctive landmarks in an Islamic republic of letters. He made use of his literary talent in versification to make Arabic grammar accessible, just as in the popular *Alfīyyah* by ibn Mālik (d. 672/1274), himself an Andalusian who settled in Aleppo and then Damascus.

The Rise of Polyglotism

Apart from the market for manuals to train people to speak Turkish as spoken in Cairo, the city began to court and attract a number of notable Turkish scholars, such as Sayf-i Sarāyī, who was also the translator of Saʿdī's classic Persian text, *The Gulistan* (Rose Garden), into Kipchak Turkish.[33] On the other hand, Sultan Qānṣūh al-Ghūrī commissioned Sharīf Ḥusayn ibn Ḥasan to translate Firdawsī's *Shāhnāmah* into Ottoman Turkish. Although al-Ghūrī was well versed in Persian and wrote poetry in both Turkish and Arabic, as the translator explains in his introduction, he wanted the work to be familiar to the rest of his emirs. Among the Mamluk elite, patronage took different directions: Yashbak, for example, was known for his support of Persian scholars. Both Yaʿqūb Shāh and Pīr Ḥajji enjoyed his patronage. The Mamluk court offered strong patronage to Turkish scholars from the Golden Horde and other regions, and some emirs were notably enthusiastic about endowing schools and centers of learning where Turkish jurists and scholars could pursue their instruction. The Ḥanafī school of law was a particular beneficiary and was promoted through the patronage of such sultans as al-Ẓāhir Tātār (r. 824/1421) and the emir Sayf al-Dīn Sarghitmish al-Nāṣirī.

On the other hand, although the emir Yashbak b. Mahdī al-Ẓahirī al-Dawādār (d. 1480) wrote in Turkish, he was no less fond of Arabic and Persian. His career is of particular significance to the formation of literary world-systems that have some Islamic presence. He commissioned Shams al-Dīn Muḥammad ibn Ajā al-Ḥalabī (d. 881/1476), for example, to translate al-Wāqidī's *Futūḥ al-Shām* (*The Syrian Conquests*) into Turkish.[34] A lover of books, he was also behind the ornamented production of al-Būṣīrī's *al-Kawākib al-Durrīyah* (The Pearly Stars [Mantle Ode]). According to Muḥammad ibn ʿAbd al-Raḥmān al-Sakhāwī (d. 902/1497), Yashbak asked him to write *Al-Tibr al-masbūk fī dhayl al-sulūk* (The Cast Gold as Supplement to al-Maqrīzī's chronicle *al-Sulūk*).[35] Both sultans Muʾayyad al-Shaykh and al-Ẓāhir Tātār combined a humanist interest in poetry and the arts with a keen familiarity with sciences. The other sultan known for having similar interests was al-Ashraf Qāytbāy (r. 872–901/1468–1496); and his son Muḥammad was no less so. Of special interest was their preoccupation with religious and especially Sufi poetry and *ghazal*. It was said that Qāytbāy himself wrote love lyrics and Sufi poems. The continuing dominant interest in treatises on war, manliness, and swordsmanship was nothing new; ever since early ʿAbbasid times this interest had been regularly regarded as the trademark of Turks.[36] Writing poetry and pursuing other arts in Turkish was a lucrative business, as we may understand from the patronage available and the complaints of lexicographers such as ibn Manẓūr.

There are a number of factors however, that condition and also impact the choice of language, all in terms of power relations. Along with the taste for Sufi poetry and ritual, and in line with the vogue of the Mantle Ode, for example, there was a revival of the classical Arabic poem among the Ottomans.[37] Fitting into a taste for splendor and pomp, the panegyric mode was popular among the Ottoman elite and ruling class, a point that draws the attention even of nonspecialists such as André Lefevere.[38] The *qaṣīdah* mode in particular derives its acumen from its association with power. Even when the poet is a brigand, the form itself and its celebration of self, tribe, and group bring into the poetics a strong functional drive that happens to carve and thence mold a dominant politics. Its codified presence attests to this dominance, which the Ottomans were pleased to transfer and duplicate in their court. In Lefevere's view, the "Ottoman Empire . . . produced a coterie literature centered on the court of Istanbul and closely modeled on classical Arabic examples, whereas the literature produced in the country at large, modeled on Turkish traditions, was never taken seriously by the coterie group and always rejected as 'popular' if referred to at all."[39] This cultural activity was not confined to patronage, translation, disputation, duplication, copying, and teaching; for, as we will notice later, professional groups, including some Sufis, also had an interest in poetry and writing, along with their respective crafts. Indeed, the dynamic popular sites, including markets, mosques, assemblies (*majālis*), *zāwiyas* (Sufi circles and sites), and many more, that are enumerated in the *maqāmāt* tradition lead us into the more invigorating public domains of cultural production. Medieval and premodern Cairo provides a great topographical space of markets, alleys, mosques, libraries, and street corners, as we gather from Taqī al-Dīn al-Maqrīzī's (d. 1442) *Khiṭaṭ*.

Hence, Cairo itself as a specific cosmopolitan space is no less important than other factors for the makeup of the Islamic republic of letters. Cairo was a meeting point for massive movements of people from the Arab west, Muslim Spain, Sicily, Africa, and central Asia and Anatolia. To give the reader a sense of Cairo as epicenter, I quote from ibn Baṭṭūṭah's account of the city of Akrīdūr (Egerdir, northeast of Isparta in present-day Turkey, i.e., Sabartā), where he was lodged "in a college opposite the main congressional mosque and occupied by the learned professor, the worthy pilgrim and sojourner [at the Holy Cities] Muṣliḥ al-Dīn."[40] Ibn Baṭṭūṭah adds: "He had studied in Egypt and Syria, and lived for a time in al-ʿIrāq."[41] In other words, even in accounts of diversified learning experience, Cairo stands out as a desirable destination. The place was also receptive to cultural intrusions that usually and in due time became enmeshed in the host culture. The presence of the Mamluks in the circles of leadership tells us much about the Cairene culture, as well as the historicity of non-Arab leadership. Ever since the reign of the eighth ʿAbbasid caliph, al-Muʿtaṣim (d. 842), who was born to a Turkic slave mother, there had been a sustained dependence on Turks, Persians, and Mamluks from across east Europe and central Asia as a much-needed component for the administration of the state. Establishing ethnic identities within an Arab core involved the Islamic state in a process of de-ethnicization, for the hybrid social fabric would soon involve culture in a diaglossic condition, whereby a thickly layered practice of dialects and formal languages was in effect, resulting in a competitive struggle for ascendancy.

The Human Agent as Structural Component

The Brethren of Purity ask their readers to guard their epistles: "So those who get hold of these epistles should not let them go into the hands of those who do not deserve them or who are not well-disposed to them, but should not repress their circulation nor withhold them from reaching those who deserve them."[42] Caught between their avowed intention to disseminate knowledge and their fear of an antagonistic response, the Brethren underscore a basic problem in Islamic thought that would soon turn into a pattern of libel against scholars and writers, under the rubric of blasphemy, apostasy, and unbelief. The rising number of traditionalists and a professional class of jurists found in the rigid codification of Islamic law a lucrative trade that they could easily sell to the state and other empowered groups. In line with the instinct of self-preservation, this codification and systematization of Islamic law, best manifested in market-inspectors' manuals, was used to manipulate the common people and to compel authorities to persecute and execute thinkers and Sufis.[43] Although historical accounts provide us with many instances in which rulers and centers of authority rely on scholars and may have them as their companions, we need to keep in mind that even in these cases, scholars were very careful, lest their discourse convey a blatant difference from or disagreement with those holding power. As mentioned in chapter 7, ibn Wahb al-Kātib warns scholars not to correct kings and caliphs when they make noticeable solecisms. In another instance, it is reported that al-Ṭūsī was able to intervene on behalf of prominent prisoners only indirectly, through astrological readings to Hulagu Khan (d. 1265). On other occasions, rulers succumbed to pressure from empowered groups and ordered eminent scholars, scientists, and Sufis to be executed. Although other cultures have similar deplorable records, the situation in Islamic culture became so acute at times that it might have generated a reluctance among all scholars to bring theology, philosophy, and science into direct conversation with statecraft and the political uses of religion.

Apart from issues of professional competition and the struggle to preserve or achieve a distinguished professional status, such as that attained by scribes or jurists as a class or tribe, another stratum with a unique hybrid status was conspicuously present in the Mamluk and premodern periods: the *awlād al-nās* (sons of Mamluks born to mothers of the Arab elite). As Ulrich Haarmann demonstrates in his essay "Arabic in Speech, Turkish in Lineage,"[44] this group contained many illustrious names, including al-Ṣafadī, ibn Iyās, ibn Taghrībirdī, ibn al-Dawādārī, ibn al-Turkumānī, ibn al-Manglī, ibn Sūdūn, and Nāṣir al-Dīn Muḥammad ibn Jankalī al-Bābā. These writers, with their diverse interests, genres, styles, and modes, whose works include history, narrative, biography, fabula, humor, and poetry, valorize cultural production and free it from territorization. Their focused affection for and celebration of Arabic as part of their identity and as the venue for their writing and speech entitle them to be viewed as the spearhead in creating a universalized space whereby Arabic reigns as the language of the learned. More than their counterparts in lexicography, they can be thought of as foremost in the medieval Islamic republic of letters. These names were among the most prevalent, not only in the quality and quantity of their production but also in their networking activities, as evidenced by their historiographical, biographic, and compendium production. Less keen on ornate prose and more suited to a communicative style, they found a successful niche with a wide readership. Their navigational style is ideal for a republic of letters, because they preferred to negotiate rather than to turn such a space into a fixation. As noted earlier, in chapter 1, Aḥmad ibn Muḥammad ibn ʿArabshāh's (d. 854/1450) scholarly itinerary shows the degree of recognition he received; he could offer a license (*ijāzah*) to notables such as ibn Taghrībirdī to teach his own writings. In Cairo, he sketched Sultan al-Ẓāhir Jaqmaq favorably in his *al-Taʾlīf al-Ṭāhir* (The Disinterested Composition; i.e., unsolicited biography), which takes the sultan as the model to be matched. In this work, as in his *Fākihat al-khulafāʾ wa-mufākahat al-ẓurafāʾ* (Fruit of Caliphs and Humor of the Refined),[45] he subscribes to the mirror-for-princes genre as a reformist gesture, in that it seeks to both edify and entertain. The combination of instruction and amusement in these fables recalls the appropriation by ibn al-Muqaffaʿ of the middle-Persian *Panjatantra* as the Arabic *Kalīlah wa-Dimnah*. Ibn ʿArabshāh's corpus is enormous, including his biographical account of Tīmūr (Tamerlane), discussed earlier. Contemporary scholars regard the relatively minor impact that ibn ʿArabshāh had on his contemporaries as being principally caused by an ornate, "torturous and metaphor-laden rhymed," Persianate style, which lacks the ease with which his disciples and also his contemporaries write.[46]

The case of ibn ʿArabshāh is one among hundreds where the author is both an outcome and cause of a number of circumstances and elements. While scholars often display a penchant for speaking truth to those in power and perhaps suffering the consequences, more than one style is adopted toward this end: indirection, in the manner of fables, is one of these. By putting three traditions and languages into a single nutshell and working closely with the common people, the literati, and the elite, ibn ʿArabshāh's career and life manage to encapsulate the intricate crossroads in this republic of letters. His achievements direct our attention to many other intellectuals within the medieval and premodern period whose mastery of languages was phenomenal. Ahead of him in time, for example, was the poet and rhetor Rashīd al-Dīn al-Waṭwāṭ, the chief secretary in Khurāsān. Adept in both Persian and Arabic, he could write the same poem in the same metric form and rhyme in both languages, a feat celebrated by Yāqūt al-Rūmī al-Ḥamawī al-Kātib (d. 626/1229), as will be observed in due course.

In Cairo of the middle and premodern periods, as the accommodating space for everyone, multilingual scholarly achievements take multiple directions and turns. Another worthy example is that of Kemalpaşazâde, the renowned Ottoman historian and Shaykh al-Islam (the head of the religious institution during the reign of Süleyman [r. 1520–1566]). When he accompanied Selim I (r. 1512–1520) on the massive military invasion of Mamluk Egypt, he embarked on the translation from Arabic of the works of the noted Mamluk historian Abū al-Maḥāsin ibn Taghrībirdī. Kemalpaşazâde, who was a scholar in jurisprudence and Qurʾānic studies as well as a historian, wrote a book on Arabic philology, entitled *Daqāʾiq al-ḥaqāʾiq* (The Subtleties of Verities). In Persian, he produced a poetry collection, *Nigaristan* (The Picture Gallery), which was modeled on the Persian poet Saʿdī's *Golestān*. In other words, we have an Ottoman scholar, historian, and poet who was also well-placed in the Ottoman imperial administration, thus providing us with an exemplary case for an "Islamic" trajectory that cuts across the three dominant language traditions, with their ever-shifting centers, but for which Cairo functioned as a sort of cultural lighthouse.

Hundreds of examples corroborate the rise of polyglotism among the learned and the significant practice of multilingualism in meetings, conversations, and writing. Specific instances also bring us closer than usual to the correspondence and exchange that went on between rulers and writers outside of court rituals. On the positive and pleasing side, one can cite the poetry of "the Sultan of Shīrāz and Persian Irak," Shāh Shāh (d. 1384), written during the ordeals of Tīmūr's ascendancy. Although strained and perhaps distressed by the raging conflicts and wars, he still had time to combine serious scholarship with a love for poetry in Arabic and Persian, which ibn ʿArabshāh found worth quoting in his biography of Tīmūr. Shāh Shāh, an accomplished scholar in Qurʾānic exegesis, writes in Arabic such *ghazal* as the following:

> If my life were spent in love
> And the cause of my long suffering ceased not to delay,
> Would I not keep her love, whenever the rising sun scatters
>   its beams anew,
> Though wasting destroy me?
> He who has not tasted the pure sweetness of love in youth,
> Truly I know he is utterly a fool.

No less exquisite is his love poetry in Persian:

> O thou who art peerless beauty to the taste of lovers,
> If ever I choose in thy stead
> Or neglect thy memory, may my life be accursed? And if by thy cruelty
>   I die and my life-blood flows,
> Let all see to my affairs,
> We will commit to the Best Protector.[47]

Lexical Authentication for Imperial Rule

More problematic is the ever-expanding territory that was the object of imperial ambitions and the communication demands of such a grand but arduous undertaking. For someone like Tīmūr, to claim to be the ruler of the world requires knowledge of other tongues, especially Arabic. Ibn Khaldūn refers to him speaking through an interpreter in "*al-lisān al-mughlī*," which according to Walter Fischel's note on this phrase is probably "Eastern Turkish or Jaghaṭāi Turki, a dialect spoken throughout Central Asia and generally used by Mongols in their Uighur writing."[48] On the same page, ibn ʿArabshāh denies that Tīmūr knows Arabic; though he "understood enough, but no more" of Persian, Turkish, and the "Monghul" language. On the other hand, ibn Khaldūn's commissioned account of the Maghrib was translated for Tīmūr into Persian, although the use of Mongolian as an official language of communication with other states is indicated by the existence in the Mamluk chancellery of a specific division dealing with correspondence in Mughlī.[49] This may sound of little consequence for the argument of this chapter; but its thrust leads us well into the implication of language in issues of lineage, leadership, and historical validation of a worldwide supremacy. With this primacy given to lexical excavation, even historiography is held suspect, as ruling powers make up and endorse their own narratives. Thus, when ibn Khaldūn cited the authority of the major Arab and Muslim historian Muḥammad ibn Jaʿfar al-Ṭabarī (d. 923), Tīmūr retorted: "We do not depend on at-Tabari."

Before exploring the reasons for this denial, we should recall that al-Ṭabarī's *Tārīkh al-Rusul wa-l-mulūk* (The History of the Prophets and Kings) was already translated into Persian by Muḥammad ibn ʿAbdullāh al-Balʿamī (d. 996) for the Samanid ruler Manṣūr ibn Nūḥ (d. 976), a knowledgeable monarch who commissioned other translations from Arabic to consolidate his Islamic rule, ensure legitimacy, and build up a powerful state grounded in Persian identitarian politics and foundational Islamic tenets. Although ibn Khaldūn was eager to make use of al-Ṭabarī's highly regarded historical authority, Tīmūr preferred to dispense with it, especially since that historical record was called on to corroborate ibn Khaldūn's view of Nebuchadnezzar as "one of the last kings of Babylon." To Tīmūr, there were more reasons to draw a filiation with the latter, as both Persian and Mongol from the mother's side. Thus Tīmūr argues: "This means that he was a descendent of Manūjihr; it is the name of the first Persians; it means 'silver face,' and this was because of his beauty, for 'mainū' in Persian means 'silver,' and they shorten it by eliminating the letter 'yāʾ,' and say 'manū'; and 'jihr' or 'shihr' means 'face'; hence Manūshihr." He adds: "And we are related to Manūshihr on our mother's side." He was reminding the scholar that Nebuchadnezzar "was only [one] of the Persian generals, just as I myself am only the representative of the sovereign of the throne [not of a royal blood]."[50] While Tīmūr tries to build up a legitimating genealogy of power and rule, ibn Khaldūn attempts to consolidate a theory of group solidarity led by a powerful dynasty. No wonder the historian addressed the interpreter as follows: "This is another reason which prompted my desire to meet him [Tīmūr]."[51]

Tīmūr's manipulation of lexical excavation to prove his right to rule over the Islamic territory centered previously in Baghdad should not be taken lightly. The battle in Islam itself, its political divides and sects, rests on exegetical analysis of the Qur'ān and authentication of the Prophet's sayings in support of one point or another. Tīmūr would like to locate the legitimate roots for his rule in pre-Islamic times, in order to undermine once and for all any converse applications of official Islamic legitimacy logic. The historian was almost ready to give up his authenticating authority, al-Ṭabarī, to appease Tīmūr, who was keen to establish a genealogy that was already claimed by his court historians. The use of lexical authentication to corroborate his lineage supports the argument of this chapter that lexicography strongly invents, reinvents, and cements identitarian politics. The justification and legitimation process pursued in these meetings between the historian and the emperor conveys a remarkable mixture of personal experience, genealogy, historiography, lexicography, and even, perhaps, factors of physiognomy—ibn Khaldūn had an impressive appearance that was well-received by rulers.

Cairo beyond Tīmūr

No less important than the theoretical framework that informs the Islamic republic of letters is the fact that Tīmūr gave up his earlier plan to invade Cairo and the Maghrib. This historical fact saved the city from the fate of such major cultural centers as Seistān, the capital of Khurāsān, Herāt, Jurjān, the capital of Khwārizm, and Iṣfahān. Thus ibn ʿArabshāh writes: "The era dating from the spoiling of Khwārizm is called *ʿAẓāb* [suffering and torture], as that from the spoiling of Damascus is called *kharāb* [ruins]."[52]

The movement toward Cairo and later Damascus, following the devastation caused by Tīmūr's invasion of other cities and kingdoms, directs our attention to the vagaries of politics and cultures.[53] A significant migration toward these two cities and other cities in northern and western Africa took place, especially among Sufis. If there was ever a challenge posed to dominant ways of thought and their unfolding in language, this occurred through the agency of Sufism, not so much because Sufis had such an intention, but rather because Sufism involved a liberated sensibility in a loving God's universe. The apparently self-denying empowerment of Sufism necessarily brings with it other means of ascendancy; binaries of ethnos and logos lose their cogency in an undefined context, an unworldly space of a kind that cannot be claimed by any triumphal minority. Sufi works were read, cherished, and admired even by those in the centers of power, and especially by ascendant Ottomans from the late fourteenth century onward, yet Sufism is able to occupy an abstract or apolitical space because it does not present a material challenge to authority.

Even so, Sufism is a challenge to official schools of thought since it disturbs and unsettles their paradigms of self-righteousness and dogma. In one of ibn Baṭṭūṭah's anecdotes, a certain Sufi shaykh could exert so much miraculous power over those whose rationalist thought he wanted to confound that he was able to render them paralyzed until they relented. And this anecdote is merely one among others that illustrate the narrator's antagonism toward rationalist philosophy.[54]

Scholars from far and wide visited or settled in Damascus and Cairo to discuss their work or the work of others, and lexicographers and erudite polymaths eagerly explored new possibilities of investigation and disputation. Still others turned to producing compendiums and used their spare time for writing verse. Poets could be found in a chancery or a literary salon, but locations in the street and square were even more inviting for genuine poetic production. Poetry of the street was scattered, but so abundant as to draw the attention of compilers and authors of compendiums and treasure troves, who found this poetry sufficiently different and invigorating to adorn their work.

Cultural Production as a Structural Component

The physical side of cultural production, which will receive further attention in the next chapter, deserves some mention here as part of mapping out the formation of an Islamic republic of letters. It is worth keeping in mind that the Brethren of Purity built up their encyclopedic work through conversation, discussion, and their reading of antecedent and contemporary authorities. They carried out a sharp dissection of extant knowledge in order to move beyond traditional narrative and its venues of transmission and instead to apply philosophical and speculative reasoning in a systematic interrogation of ideas and phenomena. The Brethren were even more concerned, however, with making a systematized grid of knowledge available to a cultivated segment of society, which in turn might lead Islamic societies forward. Interest in their work, as manifested particularly in a thirteenth-century illustrated manuscript of their epistles, would continue ever afterward as part of a rising interest in theological reasoning.

What with massive dictionaries, biographical compendiums, and authored books in every discipline, the library of works in the Islamic world grew over centuries as part of a process of ongoing communication, emulation, explanation, gloss, refutation, debate, and counter-discourse.[55] Furthermore, voluminous biographical dictionaries, with their habitual insertion of texts from notables and authors, continued to increase in number from the eleventh century onward before eventually giving way to more limited dictionaries, covering only a century or so of authors, including some from the margins of social or religious life.[56] Such works include Yāqūt al-Ḥamawī's (d. 626/1229) *Muʿjam al-ʾudabāʾ* (Biographies of the Littérateurs) and *Muʿjam al-buldān* (The Dictionary of Nations and Countries), which served as a basis for other types of compendiums. To this list can be added lexicons like ibn Manẓūr's *Lisān al-ʿArab*, ibn Khallikān's (1211–1282) biographical work *Wafayāt al-aʿyān* (Obituaries of the Notables), ibn Shākir al-Kutubī's (d. 764/1363) and Ṣalāḥ al-Dīn al-Ṣafadī's (d.? 764/1363) supplements,[57] and other single-century biographical dictionaries. Such compilations involved a systematic textual configuration and codification, whereby the informed compiler presides over his creations as empowered spaces to lead readers into a shared knowledge. Compilers and writers of commentaries are not to be regarded as mere knowledge intermediaries; they wielded authority through their selection and choice of material, not to mention their proclaimed goal of resurrecting the dead through their own words and those of others. As knowledge-provider for the Muslim community, the littérateur, historian, administrator, and compiler Shihāb al-Dīn Aḥmad al-Nuwayrī (d. 733/1333) went so far as to insert full books and chapters by other authors in his massive *Nihāyat al-arab fī funūn al-adab* (The Ultimate Goal of the

Learned).[58] Such voluminous works map out a society and its individual scenes and lives across time, space, and cultures, and in so doing, they redefine a library as more than any particular books or private collections. Indeed, the noticeable appearance and popularity of supplements, or *dhayl* (literally, "tail"), attests not only to a scholarly endeavor to contribute to a general knowledge repository, a library, but also to the presence of human agency, the devoted scholar and professional, who is in conversation with others across time in the pursuit of knowledge.

Such "macrogenres,"[59] the poetic innovations in content and form, and a massive cultural archive of "institutionalized" and "reading" communities mark an epistemological shift in cultural production. Compendiums, encyclopedias, rejoinders in book form, and book- or treatise-length reflections and correctives imbue this cultural milieu with conversational and communicative dimensions that tempt one to invoke the idea of a common public sphere. This cultural movement is initiated as a redefinition of the moral and hence the political order, making use of a broad-scale remapping of knowledge genealogies and antecedent authorities, rhetorical innovations, and verbal discoveries or inventiveness. These factors all vie both to establish and to consolidate a textual homeland of calligraphic and conversational dimensions.[60] Although political upheaval was bound to curtail dissemination, these cultural manifestations also reveal an interior dynamic contestation; they stimulate and enhance the foregrounding of linguistic, textual, and aural practices that often serve as preconditions for the emergence of peoples, ideas, and both "public" and elite texts.[61] In textual terms, the shift is away from a text that is patron- or ruler-bound and hence subservient, and toward a self-sufficient enterprise, one that is patron-free and thenceforth situated among both the learned and the ordinary reading publics. While making extensive use of the achievements of the ʿAbbasid cultural heyday, this shift is particularly noticeable for its scholarly or public concerns. To be sure, we still come across works specifically addressed to rulers or patrons, and certainly there is a substantial record of thinkers and authors who lost their lives because of their differences in opinion and method from their rulers.[62] The dominant trend, however, is to move far beyond court-based productions, a trend that is traceable in numerous poems, compilations of anecdotes, and authored treatises and manuals. There is less focus on the education of prospective leaders and rulers, as found earlier in works such as al-Jāḥiẓ's *Risālah fī ṣināʿat al-quwwād* (Epistle on the Constitution of Leaders), written for the heirs of either the Caliph al-Muʿtaṣim (833–842) or al-Mutawakkil (847–861). Notwithstanding this work's announced purpose to persuade the privileged and powerful that knowledge is a comprehensive endeavor that precludes nothing and requires a familiarity with the rest of the society, al-Jāḥiẓ's *Risālah* is nevertheless intended as an instructive manual for the royal youth.[63]

This kind of knowledge needs to be situated within an order of one sort or another, one in which discursive battling and the prioritization of genres can be analyzed and pursued. An overall archaeology is needed to explore these developments in terms of epistemological shifts from a basic ternary mode, which collapses signs and the signified into one of resemblance, to a binary mode that assigns representation to signs.[64] Throughout the disputes among speculative theologians (especially Ashʿarites) and rationalists, for example, there was a tendency to assign to imaginings a perception from which they emanate.[65] Along with other common and distinctive features, I venture to argue that a substantial epistemological turn also explains the inability of what Theodor Adorno calls the "antipodes" or "patriarchs of modernity" to come to grips with unsettling explorations that absorb antecedent knowledge, its *ʿulūm* and *rusūm*, while creating new paths and legitimizing others that had survived from the past and but were never previously accommodated as central to knowledge.[66]

Authors and Preachers in Conversation

Both the rhetorical and epistemological shifts that are conspicuously noticeable can be summed up as follows. First, there is a turn toward a more conversational style in narrative writing and poetry, a blend of street language with a standard written one, as seen in the histories of Muḥammad ibn Iyās's (d. 930/1524) *Badāʾiʿ al-zuhūr fī waqāʾiʿ al-duhūr* (The Choicest Blooms Concerning the Incidence of Dooms) and Abū al-Maḥāsin Jamāl al-Dīn Yūsuf b. Taghrībirdī's (d. 874/1470) *Al-Nujūm al-zāhirah fī mulūk miṣr wa-l-Qāhirah* (The Glorious Stars of the Kings of

Egypt and Cairo). This feature can be seen clearly when these works are compared with narratives such as those of Jalāl al-Dīn al-Suyūṭī (d. 911/1505), ibn Ḥajar al-ʿAsqalānī (d. 852/1448), and more conservative jurists. Second, along with this conversational poetics, which seeps into popular poetic subgenres, there is a rhetorical shift toward an extensive use of the double entendre, which was the topic of book-length studies (along with contestations and rejoinders). This dominating trend should be seen as a movement beyond representation and toward dissimulation and dissemblance. Its political significance goes beyond its immediate poetic implication. It is presented as a case of obliqueness, *muʿāraḍah*,[67] which ibn Wahb al-Kātib defines as deriving from "contrasting a commodity with another in price and sale" and used in order to signify "juxtaposition between two different speech articulations." He adds that "it is used in *taqiyyah* (the prudent withholding of opinion/precautionary dissimulation) and when addressing a person feared for his malice."[68] Third, concealment and evasion as stylistic practices gradually give way to a more open, exposed, and naked discourse, which culminates in Yūsuf al-Shirbīnī's (d. 1094/1685) masterly work, *Kitāb hazz al-quḥūf bi-sharḥ qaṣīd Abī Shādūf* (Brains Confounded by the Ode of Abū Shādūf), a literary detour into peasantry as a subject previously closed to littérateurs.[69] This work plays havoc with a solid canon that staunchly adhered to verisimilitude and truth, while at the same time enrolling in its ranks jurists of disputable and unreliable knowledge.[70] Unless we are to regard this undermining of the canon as the zenith of a steadily growing, scathing criticism of pseudo-jurists, ultraconservative traditionalists, and sham Sufis, then we are bound to miss its significance in the way that it foreshadows and anticipates the enormous present-day manipulation of religion as a lucrative business, through social media and satellite broadcasting. Furthermore, the movement among the medieval and premodern literati toward the social fringes in both matter and manner, and the increasing presence of a conversational mode in writing, both serve to unseat canonical priorities and their hold on literary criticism, exegetical exploration, and hadith scholarship. With the multiplication of cultural centers in cities and regions such as Cairo, Aleppo, Khurāsān, and Khwārizm, for instance, the widespread correspondence of scholars and travelers, exchanges of visits, and traveling theories and ideas initiated a cultural dynamism that was perpetuated by the fight against heavy odds and also by a tendency to consolidate localized knowledge formations.

Let us take three examples. One is a report by the traveler ibn Baṭṭūṭah on his visit to Shīrāz. Speaking of women there, he writes: "These wear boots, and when out of doors are swathed in mantles and head-veils, so that no part of them is to be seen, and they are [noted for] their charitable alms and their liberality. One of their strange customs is that they meet in the principal mosque every Monday, Thursday, and Friday to listen to the preacher, sometimes one or two thousands of them, carrying fans in their hands with which they fan themselves on account of the great heat. I have never seen in any land an assembly of women in such numbers."[71] In another report of preaching at a mosque in the city of Tustar (in Arabic: Tushtar), on the east bank of the Kārūn river, the traveler stayed at the college of the versatile and pious imam Sharaf al-Dīn Mūsā, whom he had met a number of times in Ḥijāz, Syria, and Egypt: "He delivered discourse with solemnity and dignity, making extempore use of all kinds of learning, interpretations of the Book of God, citation of the traditions of the Apostle of God, and dissertation upon their meanings." Ibn Baṭṭūṭah adds: "When he finished, bits of paper were thrown to him from all sides, for it is a custom of the Persians to jot down questions on scraps of paper and throw them to the preacher, who answers them."[72] Preaching here functions as a learning experience, where worshippers act as active participants. The city as a center for learning, with private colleges run by the imams themselves, assumes its grandeur and significance not only from business and commerce but also from these colleges.

The third example is even more telling. Sa'd al-Dīn al-Taftazānī (d. 791/1389) introduces his *Muṭawwal* (The Elaborate or Expanded) with an encomium addressed to the province of Khwārizm. He had settled there, after all, in order to be able to converse with rhetors in the tradition of the famed scholars of Jurjān like 'Abd al-Qāhir al-Jurjānī. He found no better epithet to celebrate Khwārizm than its association with that illustrious name and the center Jurjān: "Jurjāniyyat Khwārizm." He collected and prepared his material before putting it together in Herāt (in the western part of Afghanistan bordering Iran) after the devastating wars in Khurāsān and Khwārizm.[73] In short, although the work of scholars was often disrupted by disturbances and wars, they were nevertheless determined to maintain a conversation with each other in an invigorating Islamic culture.

Archaeological Inventories

Lexicographical research and a multiplicity of lexicons signify a shift in the practice and use of languages from orality to writing. The contemporary reception and understanding of such research, however, varies across time and space. Upon the first appearance of lexicons as specialized pursuits setting standards for correct usage and pure articulation, beyond the intrusion of foreign words or dialects and idiolects, they were regarded as belonging to a poetics that tends to establish its legitimation as part and parcel of a political system, a system with its roots in a privileged Arab core (i.e., Quraysh). But after developing in the tenth century into lexicons of words, meanings, and roots, they were viewed as limited in value to their immediate practice and use—a position that would undergo serious revision in the thirteenth and fourteenth centuries, when lexicons turned into custodians of an Islamic narrative. The encyclopedic Abū ʿAbdullāh Muḥammad ibn Aḥmad ibn Yūsuf al-Kātib al-Khwārazmī (d. 387/987), for example, was not enthusiastic about lexicography, which is "but an instrument for the attainment of moral excellence."[74] During the tenth century, when the waning empire was still host to a vast culture, lexicons were no more than vessels for words and grammatical correctives. Due to the relatively new urban phenomena and the continued communication with the Bedouin Arab, as testified to in Badīʿ al-Zamān al-Hamadhānī's (d. 1007) *Maqāmāt*, there was no great urgency yet to uphold lexicons as the referential centers for both the learned and students, as spectrums for their debates and conversations, and as tests of their mastery of other sciences.

The Battle for Lexical Hegemony

Al-Khwārazmī's fellow grammarians and lexicographers focused on solecism as a stigma among the learned, and some caliphs treated it as a punishable offense. In *Shams al-ʿūlum wa-dawāʾ kalām al-ʿArab min al-kulūm* (The Sunlight of the Sciences and the Treatment of Ancient Arabic Speech for Inflicted Wounds), the Yemeni magistrate Ṣafī al-Dīn Nashwān b. Saʿīd al-Ḥimyarī (d. 575/1180) makes a plea for the preservation of language from incorrect usage and solecism in speech.[75]

The problem here goes back to the early expansion of the empire and the migration of different peoples into Islamic centers, as well as the increasing distance in time and space from the pure use of language, namely, among the Aʿrāb or the Bedouins.[76] Early on, al-Jāḥiẓ (d. 255/869) accepts solecism in pleasantries, witty and humorous sayings, and jokes, a point that Shihāb al-Dīn Aḥmad al-Qalqashandī gladly and approvingly reports in his *Ṣubḥ al-aʿshā* (The Dawn of the Benighted) as follows: "Beware that solecism is rampant, and forms of speech [tongues] are so altered that to speak grammatically and eloquently is looked upon with disdain. Expediency necessitates copying people, confining the use of the standard classical Arabic to reading the Qurʾān, hadiths, and poetry, along with rhymed speech, scripts, and correspondence."[77]

The issue was not unique to the early medieval period, for it is reported that the caliph Hārūn al-Rashīd once asked the philologist and grammarian Yaḥyā b. Ziyād al-Farrāʾ (d. 207/822) if he ever spoke ungrammatically. The philologist's response comes as follows: "The natural disposition of the Arab is to speak with correct syntax; whereas the natural disposition of urbanized Arabs is to speak ungrammatically."[78] There is also an epistemological side to this response that conveys a loose link with canonized knowledge (the Qurʾān and the hadith). Pragmatic and factual turns in urban life perhaps entailed such negligence and consequent laxity in the acquisition and application of rhetorical knowledge.

At a later period, and following the appearance of Abū al-Naṣr Ismāʿīl ibn Ḥammād al-Jawharī's (d. 398/1008?) *Muʿjam al-Ṣiḥāḥ fī al-lughah* (The Lexicon of Correct Arabic),[79] there was a greater focus on the right path toward lexicographic training as central to the knowledge of religion, and also as a means of counteracting the sense of loss of a "golden" past, which reverberates strongly in popular culture. Lexicography and rhetoric received further impetus and attention due to mounting political confrontation, wars, urban mobility, and the attendant processes of social and cultural transformation. If solecism was the most serious challenge to lexicographers and grammarians until the eleventh century, at a later period it was merely one concern among many others. The rise of a codified theological discourse also provoked a counteraction prompted by popular preachers, poets, and rhetors. The tendency among littérateurs to make their products more marketable was no less conspicuous, as emerges clearly from the titles of works on wine and *mujūn* (ribaldry, bawdiness, licentiousness). But insofar as the "empire of words" is concerned, cultural production manifests an enormous lexicographic shift, which in turn is closely connected to the competitiveness among different languages and vernaculars, a competitiveness that is reflected positively in the vogue for lexicographic compilations, inquiries in rhetoric and grammar, and the remarkable rise in commentaries about widely circulated texts.[80] Given the significant modes of networking in the Islamic world by the eleventh century, the widespread intellectual participation, a massive accumulation in cultural production, and a prominent prototype for a republic of letters (the tenth-century Epistles of the Pure Brethren), still, the issues of sustainability, durability, and anticipated breakthroughs in scientific and intellectual achievement remained problematic, inviting us to look more deeply at particular aspects of Islamic culture.

chapter three

THE LEXICOGRAPHIC TURN IN CULTURAL CAPITAL

In the argument of Pascale Casanova's *World Republic of Letters*, the major restructuring and hence proliferation of the literary world-system are neither totally ordained by academic institutionalization processes, nor confined to the systematization of language through a difference from and struggle against a hegemonic Latin. In her view, these events are no less motivated and driven by the corporate effort of grammarians and writers, an effort that, in the case of English, drew impetus from a sustained privileging of literature in a self-assertive nationalism.[1] In applying her European model to the medieval and premodern Islamic cultural world, one can argue that grammar, lexicography, and literary production assume even greater significance, as evidenced in the massive production and demand.

As an exemplary man of letters, the Andalusian poet, philologist, and grammarian Abū Ḥayyān al-Gharnāṭī (d. 745/1344), for example, who settled in Cairo and the Levant, made popular the teaching of Turkish grammar. His Turkish grammar manual was a landmark in the rise of Turkish as the language of empire. That rise coincided with the upsurge in lexicographic activity in Turkish, Persian, and Arabic. In Persian, poets such as Asadī Ṭūsī and Qaṭrān Tabrīzī prepared the way for Moḥammad

Nak̲javānī's (728/1328) *Ṣeḥāḥ al-fors*, which was based on Asadī's dictionary but took as its model Abū al-Naṣr Ismāʿīl ibn Ḥammād al-Jawharī's (d. 398/1008?) Arabic lexicon *Muʿjam al-Ṣiḥāḥ fī al-lughah* (The Lexicon of Correct Arabic).[2] As in the use of Latin by the rising European vernaculars, both Turkish and Persian made enormous use of Arabic antecedent authority, spelled out in a lexical activity whereby rhetoric was the discursive domain for scholars. Al-Jawharī's lexicon was invaluable to the expanding Ottoman Empire. Mehmet bin Mustafa Vankulu (d. 1592) rendered it in a bilingual Arabic–Turkish dictionary, which was among the first seventeen texts that Ibrahim Muteferrika published in Istanbul in 1729, as *Vankulu Lügati*. The copious front matter in *Vankulu Lügati*, its inserted imperial edict and religious fatwās, is no less than a summons of authority on the part of the publisher to exercise and disseminate this imperial venture.[3] (This renowned publisher was the first Muslim to be credited with establishing a printing press.)[4]

On the other hand, the edition of al-Jawharī's *Ṣiḥāḥ* that was begun by E. Scheidius with a Latin translation appeared only in part at Harderwijk in the Netherlands in 1776. This lexicon, with its forty thousand entries arranged alphabetically according to the last letter of the word root, served as the base and model for the enormous lexical effort during the Mamluk period. Its centrality to the effort is not confined to the fact that it was a model, however, or to its material, which was incorporated by the Tunisian Muḥammad b. al-Mukarram ibn Manẓūr (d. 711/1311) in his massive compilation, *Lisān al-ʿArab* (The Arab Language). The career of its author is equally exemplary for a republic of letters. Al-Jawharī was born in Farab (southern Kazakhstan), received his early education in Baghdad and Hejaz, and worked on his dictionary in Nishapur, where he died. Indeed, lexicographers had unique careers that presented them as seekers of knowledge. Al-Zabīdī, with whom this lexicographical tradition came full circle, was born in the Indian town of Bilgram and remained there until he was fifteen, then resided in the Yemenite city of Zabīd, before settling for good in Cairo.[5] Another example is ʿAlī ibn Aḥmad ibn Maʿṣūm, with his many books in Arabic on the Arabic language and literature. Born and raised in Medina until the age of fifteen, he spent the rest of his life in India. Even his journey by sea from his birthplace in Medina to India is described in terms of a literary tradition that informs his language and comments. Its title is *Salwat al-gharīb wa-aswat al-arīb* (Comfort for the Stranger/Consolation for the Resourceful). But, as Joseph Lowry rightly notes, ibn Maʿṣūm "is an example of the continuing vitality of Arabic as an international language of literature and culture, apart from the religious writings, in the late seventeenth and early eighteenth centuries."[6] In other words, these scholars represent the model Islamic scholar, whose search for knowledge inevitably leads to centers of learning, and whose devotion to Arabic knows no bounds. Ethnic or residential roots faded, and a commitment to Arabic as the language of a Muslim community became paramount, even when its grammar and lexical models were deployed to promote competing languages and vernaculars, such as Turkish and Persian.

Turkish and Persian came into their medieval standardized forms as the languages of empires as a result of the rule of the Buyids and Seljuks and the Mongol institutionalization of Persian as the official language. Arabic was on the defensive throughout. Yet the devotion and skill of its writers, lexicographers, and other professionals in the book industry consolidated its already well-established lexical base, turning it in the field of rhetoric into a world-system. Arabic was the medium for an Islamic culture with far-reaching explorations not only in theology, logic, and philosophy but also in poetry, prose, and the performing arts. The great lexicographic achievements during the medieval and premodern period are numerous,[7] but at an early stage they culminated in the epochal lexicographical achievement of ibn Manẓūr's *Lisān al-ʿArab* (The Arab Language), mentioned above and in the previous chapter, a work known for its systematic and comprehensive arrangement that takes into consideration the needs of actual use and reference. Under each root or variation and conjugation are examples of use and misuse that make each entry a lively encounter, especially since these examples are taken verbatim or in a condensed form from antecedent authorities, which receive due citations. To date, this work is practically unsurpassed. It was followed by Aḥmad ibn Muḥammad al-Maqrī Abū al-ʿAbbās al-Fayyūmī's (d. 770/1368) *al-Miṣbāḥ al-munīr* (The Enlightening Lamp), which holds a prominent place among lexicons in the long period under discussion. Al-Fīrūzābādī (d. 817/1415) produced his *al-Qāmūs al-muḥīṭ* (The Encompassing Ocean or Lexicon) soon after, to be followed by Abū al-Fayḍ

Muḥammad Murtaḍā al-Zabīdī's (d. 1205?/1791) voluminous *Tāj al-ʿarūs min jawāhir al-Qāmūs* (The Bride's Crown from the Pearls of the Lexicon), which provides some balance to al-Fīrūzābādī's *al-Qāmūs* (Lexicon), including further information and the incorporation, nearly in full, of ibn Manẓūr's indispensable *Lisān al-ʿArab*.[8]

In the context of the present discussion of the republic of letters in the Mamluk and Ottoman periods, it is essential to recognize that these lexicons are no mere listings of words and meanings: ibn Manẓūr's *Lisān*, for instance, is a thoughtful reclamation of the lexical space that includes an extensive treasury of proverbs, maxims, poetry, and prose, along with Qurʾānic verse and reference, and hadith. Words place the reader into a network of negotiation and correspondence that manages to revive and hold both the ancient and the more recent past in dialogue. Thus, this work is of immediate relevance to the Mamluk era and its dynamics of innovative encyclopedic creativity as a part of knowledge acquisition. On the other hand, this lexicographic fervor sets the stage for its unconditional espousal by the *nahḍah* or *yaqaẓah* (Arab awakening) advocates. Although they had their own point of departure on other matters, they could not resist the compelling lexicographic achievement of the Mamluk period.

The ways in which proponents of the *nahḍah* engaged with past lexicons are worth seeing through Aḥmad Fāris al-Shidyāq's (1805–1887) analysis of lexicographic activity in his meticulously researched *Al-Jāsūs ʿalā al-Qāmūs* (Spying on al-Fīrūzabādī's Lexicon).[9] He describes ibn Manẓūr's *Lisān al-ʿArab* as follows: "It is reported that it lists eighty thousand items; and it is wonderful in its transmissions, refinement, amendments, and organization: but it is limited in circulation compared to other lexicons. It came after the first age [of the Mamluk period] and was contemporaneous to the time of the author [al-Suyūṭī] of *Al-Muzhir* [*sic*; al-Suyūṭī came later]. May God have them all in His mercy."[10] Al-Shidyāq seems puzzled by the following neglect on the part of al-Suyūṭī: "It is strange that Imam al-Suyūṭī does not mention the author of *Lisān* among those who have authored in the field of language." On the other hand, al-Suyūṭī mentions ibn Manẓūr in his *Bughyat al-Wuʿāt*.[11] However, it is the lexicon that provokes al-Shidyāq's interest: "It is a book in language, philology, grammar, conjugation, hadith explication, and Qurʾānic exegesis." He justifies repetition as being a meticulous transference of information from each primary lexicon. He concludes that "it is the best book ever authored in language, but its enormous size led to its limited circulation; it discourages students from buying it."[12] Al-Shidyāq makes use of the occasion to criticize al-Suyūṭī for other omissions and also to underline the significance of al-Jawharī's (d. 398/1008?) *Muʿjam al-Ṣiḥāḥ fī al-lughah* (The Lexicon of Correct Arabic). To him, al-Jawharī sets the standard of correctness as applied by the Bedouin Arabs, with whom he was in conversation during his stay in Iraq and Hejaz.[13] Al-Jawharī's lexicon received high acclaim and was to undergo reviews, updates, and amendments; it was followed only a year later by Aḥmad ibn Zakariyyā al-Qazwīnī ibn Fāris's (d. 395/1004) *Muʿjam maqāyīs al-lughah* (Language Standards Compendium).[14]

In methodological terms, al-Shidyāq brought into the discussion another element that underscores the conversational milieu in the middle period. Biographers, explicators, and littérateurs, in their entries and obituaries on authors and compilers, write about these individuals' works. There is also the element of comparison; al-Shidyāq has a comparatist bent and sets out to evaluate each author or compiler against the other, especially if another commentator, such as al-Suyūṭī, has omitted something of significance. Hence, in order to correct the ancestor (al-Suyūṭī) who applauds al-Fīrūzabādī's *al-Qāmūs* while overlooking the role of *al-Ṣiḥāḥ*, he explains: "*Al-Ṣiḥāḥ* has the advantage over *al-Qāmūs* in that it is distinguished by clarity of expression, the consolidated support of the Qurʾān, hadith, Arab proverbs and maxims, and grammatical, linguistic, and conjugational rules. The author often applies a speech construct and structure along with an explanation of lexical items."[15] Al-Shidyāq is meticulous, but selectively so. Ibn Manẓūr admits that he has emptied the contents of early lexicons into his enormous dictionary, letting each entry include and appropriate their successive items. The primary sources that he cites are many.[16] Indeed, ibn Manẓūr's preface to his work is more or less a reclamation of Arabic and its placement at the center of culture, along with an apology for omissions and a disclaimer of faults, in that he chooses to describe himself merely as the provider of an accessible concordance. The reclamative tone is more assertive, corresponding as it does to what al-Shidyāq wants the lexicographic enterprise to become.

His reclamation of ibn Manẓūr brings to mind the latter's lament, described in the last chapter, that in his time, "to speak in Arabic was often seen as a drawback," and his statement, "I have compiled the contents of this work in an age whose people are not proud of their own native language."[17] The lament should not be taken lightly, for power relations and the loss of Arab political primacy and hence the diminishing role of Arabic in centers of power drove many to search for benefit and profit elsewhere. Al-Fīrūzabādī is no less aware of the problem, but he recognizes the survivalist potential in the Arabic language, despite what is "befalling its people." He laments that schools are the only space where Arabic is studied and promoted. But the diligent lexicographer nevertheless overlooks ibn Manẓūr's *Lisān* and instead offers deserved plaudits to al-Saghānī's lexicon *al-ʿUbāb* (The Vast Ocean), ibn Sīdah's *al-Muḥkam* (The Concise), and al-Jawharī's *al-Ṣiḥāḥ*. He admits that in his time *al-Ṣiḥāḥ* was the most popular, a verdict that leads him to adopt its contents in full but adding in red what is disputed, updated, and corrected. In anticipation of further lexicographic efforts, he explains the reasons behind this abridged version of his voluminous *al-Lāmiʿ* (The Superb Lexicon), which amount to no more than the need to make it more accessible. He nevertheless sets a modernist (*muḥdath*) criterion, in that he negates antecedent recurrence as being a value in its own right. He quotes the poet Abū Tammām's remark that "there is so much that is untouched by ancients for their descendants to pick up." Moreover, al-Fīrūzabādī proclaims the lexicographic effort and "the science of language" as "sufficient enough to cover the basic needs of every science," and Islamic law in particular.[18] Such negation of antecedent authority is no ordinary matter, and had it been followed up in a wider range of knowledge, it could have left an abiding impact on the construction of knowledge.

Models for *Nahḍah*

Both the need to consolidate correct usage and the broader circulation of Arabic, along with its centrality to every other pursuit, entitles al-Fīrūzābādī's well-organized, neat, and affordable lexicon to its place as an important antecedent treasury, important not only to the *nahḍah* and its valorization of lexical inquiry and research but also, and very much so, to eighteenth-century scholarship. Murtaḍā al-Zabīdī's massive *Tāj al-ʿArūs* (The Bride's Crown), which followed it, might be his best achievement, crowning his other solid contributions to hadith scholarship, philology, and literature. But we need first to notice his choice of the title. In line with his elegies of longing and pining addressed to his dead wife, al-Zabīdī chose a feminine subject as the title for his lexicon.[19] Unlike most works by his predecessors, the "Bride's Crown," perhaps along with a few others, opens up the field of writing for the public inclusion of women. In the late eighteenth century, "women did appear in the chronicles."[20] After studying with the lexicographer and hadith scholar Muḥammad b. al-Ṭīb al-Fāsī (d. 1170/1756), with his commitment to clarity of usage and his extensive use of hadith in explication, al-Zabīdī combined empirical research with the medievalist's interest in root formation and conjugation. Like a free and independent anthropologist, unhampered by any binary other than that of correct versus actual usage, he undertook travels, research, meetings, and contacts to corroborate his lexicon. His celebrated salon in Cairo was a meeting place for discussions and a workshop for significant compilations. He made use of every available source, especially his antecedent authority, al-Fīrūzabādī. His students were expected to carry out further projects and to enrich the cultural scene with studies in philology, hadith, poetry, and history. Noticeably, early lexicographers' inclusion of the description of regions and peoples received further impetus in al-Zabīdī's dictionary, which treats demography, geography, and medicine as among the areas of interest for the rising reading public. The interest in lexicography in the eighteenth century is reminiscent of the thirteenth and fourteenth centuries, when lexicographic research reached an unparalleled level. Peter Gran noted that "six out of the ten copies of a standard dictionary in al-Azhar's library were made in the eighteenth century."[21]

Concomitant with this lexicographic interest was the revived interest in Abū al-Qāsim al-Ḥarīrī's (d. 516/1122) *Maqāmāt* and *Durrat al-ghawwāṣ* (The Diver's Pearl). The renewed celebration of the *Maqāmāt* is unique to the times. Studies on and copies of the *Maqāmāt* had multiplied, perhaps starting with Shihāb al-Dīn al-Khafājī's (d. 1069/1653) study and his emulation of the genre.[22] To memorize the *Maqāmāt* was part of learning good Arabic, as was the tradition in al-Ḥarīrī's days. In the eighteenth century the practice was followed by nearly everyone trying to master eloquence in speech and clarity in writing. Along with this noticeable revival was the rise of commentaries on al-Qazwīnī's (d. 739/1338) *Talkhīṣ al-Miftāḥ* (The Resumé of the Key), the latter being an abridgement or resumé of *Miftāḥ al-ʿulūm* (Key to the Sciences) by Yūsuf ibn Abī Bakr al-Sakkākī (d. 626/1229).[23]

Two other prominent trends that are uniquely typical of eighteenth-century Egypt have puzzled scholars. The first was the interest in the battle of Badr (17 Ramadan/13 March 624), an interest for which Peter Gran could not find a reason other than asking a question: "Is it possible that the eighteenth-century writers of the Battle of Badr felt a renewed sense of identification with the forces of Muhammad [against the nonbelieving aristocracy of his tribe]? Did they feel that they, too, were struggling in a rather hostile environment against powerful odds?"[24] While it sounds rhetorical, the question still begs for answers, especially if we read it alongside the second trend: the increasing concern for the populace, which was already spelled out in al-Shirbīnī's *Hazz al-quḥūf*, with its dashing satire on elitism, pedantry in scholarship, and the compendious and commentarial surplus, and its biting irony directed toward certain religious circles and sham Sufism.[25] Committed Sufis were already involved in reaching out to the masses. To reach peasants and lower classes, Sufis resorted to the *mawwāls* (*mawāwīl*) and other popular forms of colloquial poetry,[26] a means that was deprecated by the "doyen of literature" Ṭāhā Ḥusayn (1889–1973) and others when it continued to hold sway in the twentieth century.[27] The combined interests in a colloquial *mawwāl*, in the *faṣīḥ* ("pure") of al-Ḥarīrī, and in lexicography and philology are not unrelated to the attention bestowed on the Battle of Badr as the victory of a message that rests on Qurʾānic inimitability (*iʿjāz*). All these were part of the makeup of a political unconscious that could have taken a more nuanced and overt form of resistance—not only against Ottoman occupation but also against another discursive force that continued to hold sway in centers of power. The official Islamic discourse and its core, which were substantially formed by *nābitat ʿaṣrinā*, as al-Jāḥiẓ called the Umayyad clientele during the ʿAbbasid period, and consolidated through the privileged class, posed no ordinary challenge to a rising learned class in eighteenth-century Egypt. In their Sufi struggle and revisionist reading of tradition, they were increasingly aware of how the second Umayyad caliph Yazīd used to sing of the war achievements of the Meccan aristocracy in the following Battle of ʾUḥud (23 March 625) against the Prophet and his companions, a battle that retained for the Meccan aristocracy a sense of victory and power and proved an Islamic vulnerability in war tactics and a weakness in mobilization. "Had my masters at the Battle of Badr seen . . ." was the Umayyad slogan and trope for the recovery of rule and their supremacy.[28] The middle period witnessed a strident Umayyad discourse, concealed under the garb of consensual *sunna* and partly resisted by prominent scholars and jurists such as al-Suyūṭī. A countermovement, expressed in the praise to the Prophet poem, the *badīʿiyyah*, made a comeback in the eighteenth century.

Given that philology was the stage and means for this discussion, it was bound to receive the attention it did throughout the middle and premodern period. Its rise to prominence, as manifested in the study of tribal and lexical roots, attributes, applications, usage, and methods of authentication and argumentation in poetic and prose domains, is a sign of contestation in a struggle for ascendancy. The philologist is a much-needed player in the staging of power relations. On the other hand, the nineteenth century also underwent similar challenges, and hence its intellectuals found a considerable resonance in the prolegomena of ibn Manẓūr and al-Fīrūzabādī.[29] The battleground was primarily lexicographic.

The Fight for Culture: Compendiums and Commentaries

The standard critique of Arab and Islamic modernity is primarily centered on a rejection of a politics of loss and failure, leading many modernists—and Ṭāhā Ḥusayn was no exception—to categorize the middle period as one of petty accomplishments, albeit with cultural centers in Cairo and Damascus, Morocco, Khwārizm, and Khurāsān.[30] In their negative reading of the past, such modernists rarely acknowledge its accomplishments in terms of writing. Indeed, they regard the compendium, a conspicuous landmark of medieval and premodern production, as a sign of intellectual exhaustion and lack of creativity. Portrayed in the dominant modernist discourse as a merely passive container, the compendium becomes a trope for hagiography, superstition, visitations, rampant esoteric practices, excursions in craftsmanship, and whatever else connotes a lack of rationality. In such a depiction of premodern Arabic tradition, it is not difficult to recognize the borrowing from Enlightenment critiques.[31] Those among Arabs and non-Arabs who fit into Adorno's critique of the "patriarchs of modernity" and who denigrated the cultural products of such a lengthy period have been unable to grasp the totality of the Islamic cultural endeavor both before and after the fall of Baghdad in 1258. Shocked by the sheer quantity of writing, many scholars have confused it with pedantry and mere imitation. Even granting that such features are present, they comprise only a small byproduct within an immense repository. Unfortunately too often defined by political upheaval and the loss of an imaginary or real Arab-centered polity, the lengthy premodern era remains relatively understudied, especially in terms of what Brinkley Messick associates with a "calligraphic state," namely, the shared discursive features taking the form of "authoritative expression" that find their way into "the practices of a number of important institutions."[32]

At this juncture it may be useful to recall once more Foucault's discussion of a similar compendious pursuit in sixteenth-century European commentaries and to consider how far his explanation can be applied to the medieval Islamic gloss and commentary. He quotes Montaigne: "There is more work in interpreting interpretations than in interpreting things; and more books about books than on any other subject; we do nothing but write glosses on one another."[33] Foucault comments that "these words are not a statement of the bankruptcy of a culture buried beneath its own monuments; they are a definition of the inevitable relation that a language maintained with itself in the sixteenth century."[34] The last qualification, the emphasis on historicity, resonates with his argument that the relation of languages to the world is one of analogy, where resemblance stands unchallenged as the base for a written knowledge. Taking the scriptures as a point of departure, Foucault's analysis is an attempt to define commentary and gloss as the infinite proliferation of interpretation that justifies the "sovereignty of an original text."[35] He adds: "And it is this text, by providing foundation for the commentary, that offers its ultimate revelation as the promised reward of the commentary." Thus, it is the "interstice occurring between the primal Text and the infinity of Interpretation" that accounts for the proliferation in interpretation, commentary, and gloss, which take writing to be a substantial part of the "fabric of the world."[36]

I draw attention here to this analysis for a number of reasons, not the least being the way in which commentary and compendia in the premodern period of Arab-Islamic thought have tended to be denigrated among modernists. Islamic medievalists usually focused on the compendium as a treasury of knowledge; the compiler is thus a producer who aims to provide readers with a reservoir of information that would otherwise be inaccessible in its original form, since it can only be found in scattered books. The compendium emerges as a lexical index of knowledge, a place where words are listed not only for their etymology or resemblance, or for their "infinity of adjacent and similar fidelities of interpretation"[37] within a ternary "system of signs,"[38] but rather primarily for their encyclopedic range across different fields of knowledge and communication. Ibn Manẓūr's lexicon was a conspicuous model, with its reliance on books of geography, demography, history, and literature. The commentary, by contrast, can function differently when it is addressed to the learned and highly sophisticated class of literati, people already well-versed in philosophy, geography, history, philology, and pure science. Thus, the books that emerged over a number of centuries as commentaries on Abū Yaʿqūb al-Sakkākī's (d. 626/1229) *Miftāḥ al-ʿulūm* (Key to the Sciences) are not mere dabblings in philological inquiry, nor are they casual explanations and interpretations; instead they regularly unearth the uses of rhetoric and its intricate workings in Arabic, as exemplified in written and oral knowledge. They bring the spheres of philosophy, philology, speech acts, semantics, and semiology into conversation, as if to construct intertwined and highly integrated exchanges of information and opinion, as was the case in the responses to al-Khaṭīb al-Qazwīnī's (d. 739/1338) *Īḍāḥ al-Miftāḥ* (The Explicator of the Key) and *Talkhīṣ al-Miftāḥ* (The Resumé of the Key), or ibn Sīnā's *Al-Ishārāt wa al-Tanbīhāt* (translated as *Remarks and Admonitions*).[39]

To relocate the discussion in terms of cultural dialectics, whereby conflict and struggle sustain a dynamic process that is larger than the outcome of wars and invasions and is related to the conceptualization of a republic of letters, we need to consider first whether literary overproduction can be a problem. What if we regard the economics of surplus, especially in matters of contrafaction, parody, and parallel scholarly or explicatory maturations, as both an accumulation and a dispersion that make use of an open space in a relatively decentralized state? What if we question the practice of authorized transmission, or reading and reporting, as a dynamic of a nonbinding gift transaction? What if we read carefully, not T. S. Eliot's "Tradition and the Individual Talent," with his statements on the ephebe's or neophyte's dependency on ancestors, but rather the renowned Egyptian poet ibn Nubātah al-Miṣrī's (686–768/1287–1366) sophisticated summation of the ongoing dispute among scholars on the scope of plagiarism (i.e., broadly-based intertextuality) as specific to a world-system? He stipulates: "I have seen how the by-products of people's thoughts [*natā'ij afkār al-nās*] are no more than progeny passed on from one to another and from nations whose poetries originate side by side on this earth."[40] This conceptualization of a universal world order whereby ideas, signs, and images freely emerge and configure applies as well to the functions of the Mamluk state. Although identified as Mamluk, its openness to the world at large signifies the same notion.

Although the Mamluk state was able to claim an Islamic hegemonic order and rule in many regions in the Arab world, it was much less centralized than the earlier ʿAbbasid or Umayyad empires. It was also only one part of a larger Islamic world with a widespread production in philosophy, theology, science, and philology. For lengthy periods, individual sultanates and emirates exercised autonomous rule. Indeed, beyond Mamluk domains, there were sovereign sultanates, such as Khwārizm, that witnessed a very active and thriving cultural life. Yāqūt, for one, describes the spread of public and private libraries and book markets in Khwārizm from the twelfth century onward.[41] On the other hand, traditionalist Islamic discourse in the Arab east continued to set the tone for a nostalgic yearning for a past Golden Age of an Islamic order, a tone that would necessarily denigrate the present. Thus, as mentioned briefly in the Preliminary Discourse, the fall of Baghdad to the Mongols in 1258 was bewailed by no less than the Egyptian jurist and scholar ibn Duqmāq as the loss of a center, since the universe "was now left without a caliph."[42] It is no wonder that the Mamluks were desperate to bring a caliph in person from Baghdad as a symbolic Islamic presence, although with no more than a ceremonial role.[43] Al-Maqrīzī provides us with an example of a symbolic gesture on the part of the token-caliph, the ʿAbbasid Aḥmad ibn al-Ẓāhir (al-Mustanṣir), who drew up a letter of allegiance to the Mamluk Sultan Baybars that in fact assigns the latter the authority of the caliph: "For the Commander of the Faithful thanks you for these feats, and admits that, had it not been for your care, the ruptures could have been too vast to be patched. Hence we are hereby endowing you with the rule of the lands of Egypt, the Shām (Syria), Diyār Bakr, the Ḥejaz, Yemen and the Euphrates, and the lands that come under new conquests all over, and assigning to you administering their military and populations."[44] Scholars are not far off the mark when they view the shadow play (*Bābah*) of the Cairene oculist ibn Dāniyāl (d. 1310) as a burlesque of that period, one in which the caliph, his descendants, and the Mamluk sultan were all muddled in their intentions and aspirations.[45] Furthermore, during the same period the city of Cairo in particular became an attractive location for learned scholars and littérateurs, in that there was sufficient mobility, opportunity, resources, and renowned scholarly circles and institutions to stimulate intellectual activity.[46] Other cities, such as Damascus, Aleppo, Fes, Qairawān, Bukhārā, Samarqand, and Khajand, also had their own literate culture, assemblies, reading sessions in private or public spaces, book markets, and learned or learning circles; but Cairo had inherited the cultural traditions of the Fatimids (969–1171) and their successors, the Ayyubids (1171–1250), and offered a cultural climate that was particularly conducive to the growth of knowledge. The attraction was primarily cultural, given that the pursuit of knowledge did not guarantee financial reward. The learned and their disciples were not necessarily affluent. Al-Maqrīzī lists ordinary jurists and instructors as fifth in the scale of income.[47] In comparison, their income may have been somewhat better in Damascus.

There were multiple sessions in jurisprudence, *adab*, and grammar, which took place at times in different sections of city mosques.[48] We have on record the names of highly recognized scholars who started their careers as merchants, booksellers, slaves and copyists, or sons of porters,[49] and whose studies on grammar and lexicography served as the bases for their eventual scholarly repute and recognition.[50] Compendiums and anthologies appeared to be one format in a culture industry for meeting the demand for partial reading and discussion of public texts in large or private reading sessions, as documented by scholars who have done research on the processes of teaching and learning during this period. In other words, the compendium is not a servile reproduction, an unoriginal collation of material, and hence a superfluous piece of work, but rather is one of the learning tools, like manuals and formularies, needed to accommodate educational demands. They served as means in the production of knowledge.[51] Throughout these manuals and the centers and means of learning, such as libraries, mosques, and other sites of education, Arabic and its sciences held sway. In other words, the lexical base as broadly defined in ibn Manẓūr's entries sets the stage for, in Foucault's terminology, the tabulation of knowledge.

A careful navigation between the twin poles of textual systems and deviations from the norm can also help in the process of restoring this enormous bulk of cultural production to the center of an Arab-Islamic conceptualization of knowledge. It also necessitates a more serious engagement with the substantial work done so far in textual and philological inquiry, including contributions to the reconstruction of the concept of knowledge in classical Islam.[52] But to argue the case in more positive terms, especially in the context of late nineteenth- and early twentieth-century interlocutors, it is perhaps worthwhile to speculate on issues that may serve to reclaim the relevance of that knowledge to the so-called push toward modernity, or "awakening," at the turn of the nineteenth to the twentieth century, in spite of its negative perspective. The *nahḍah* or awakening was itself another perpetuation of the republic of letters, one that happened to take place within a mixed discursive space where the European Enlightenment held sway.[53] Its revivalist stance was intended to balance the paradoxically "charming" incursion of European historical models.[54] Even so, this ambivalent space had room for conjecture and positivist thought. The battle over the medieval body of knowledge, with its lexicographical fervor, surplus of production, and density of titles, and the eventual sense of loss among its reluctant heirs (i.e., modernists) tend to blur the picture and prevent us from looking in depth at the mechanics of production, the significations and markers that must have connected this production economically and culturally to its milieu, and the systematic institutionalization of a book industry. The book in its many formats and targets had reached its zenith within the available means of production in the medieval and premodern period. Its front material and divisions received systematic lexical differentiation and naming, to guide or respond to readers' expectations. Hence, paratexts and peritexts provide us with a register of priorities and an index of tastes. They function as an established lexical code among producers, mediators, and consumers.[55]

Markers of a Complex Phenomenon

Other noticeable markers are worth mentioning as part of identifying the complex process of acquisition and dissemination of knowledge in the period under consideration. One relates to the kind of prefatory note that was common among scholars of that period. It was not only a *khuṭbah*, explaining the purpose and structure of the book, but also and primarily an autobiographical itinerary that traced the history of composition or compilation. An example is the prefatory note to Saʿd al-Dīn al-Taftazānī's (d. 791/1389) *Muṭawwal*, which concludes with an expression of some anxiety lest the book suffer at the hands of the stubborn or the dogmatic. In expressing such concerns, Saʿd al-Dīn al-Taftazānī echoes Ṣafī al-Dīn al-Ḥillī (667–750/1278–1349), "for obduracy and obstinacy are rampant, and jealousy and disputation are widespread."[56] But no matter how authors and writers approach the latter issue, it still signifies an active climate of ideas. Among writers and scholars there were significant differences on scholarly, theoretical, ethnic, and sectarian levels, but these appear in their writings as part of an ongoing conversation. Difference and blunt antagonism are signs of their authors' liveliness and activism. Had they been passive and pacifists, they would not have taken the trouble of disputation and research. As a dynamic arena where difference is played out in full, the premodern scene is a highly complex one, with its praise poetry to the Prophet, the rise of compendiums in every field of knowledge, the exhilarating pace of textual and philological exploration, and the tendency of writers to engage with each other across time and space and develop a combative linguistic, theological, and informational arsenal, perhaps partly to counteract the vicissitudes of wars and occupations. As these activities gain momentum and generate rejoinders through more words and lexical multiplication, we need to interpret them in relation to the seemingly peripheral matter: the title page, the invocations of the divine for blessing and consecration (*basmalah*), the expressed gratitude to God (*ḥamdalah*), the praise to the Prophet and his companions and family, prayers, divisions of contents, sectional subtitles, epigraphs, postfaces or addenda at the back, and cover. Along with these are marginal notes, thresholds or openings for chapters, prologues, epilogues, colophons, illustrations, prefaces, and copyists' stamps. The *basmalah* and *ḥamdalah* may take a short or a long form to include the writer's invocation of God's help and also to establish the writer's identity as a Muslim subject, a point that may be further consolidated by a reference to the writer's *madhhab*, or official Islamic school of law, such as Mālikī or Ḥanafī. Chosen or inherited eponyms proliferate. As designated forms of affiliation that conclude a surname, these eponyms empower the writer among a specific constituency. They underscore the pertinence of the text, define its logic and content, and address an identifiable Islamic community. Thus ibn al-Ḥājib, discussed below, identifies himself as a Mālikī theologian. The name, title, dedication, and invocation are important thresholds and identifications. The text derives its cohesion and plausibility from their visibility. Illustrations complement the narrative or the poem, populate its empty spaces and holes, and lend concreteness to abstract and allusive or elusive passages, as is the case with the illustrations for the Epistles of the Brethren of Purity.[57] Other good examples are Iranian manuscripts of *Majnūn Laylā*. In the Baghdadi school of Yaḥyā ibn Maḥmūd al-Wāsiṭī (d. 1237), as it has survived in his illustrations of the *Maqāmāt* of Abū al-Qāsim al-Ḥarīrī (1054–1122), the illustrator cares for the community and the group rather than the single protagonist, a point that matches and augments the increasing awareness among writers and painters of the artisanal, mercantile, and laboring classes. No less present in a book, along with the author, is the copyist. The copyist for ibn Abī al-Iṣbaʿ's book, Ḍiyāʾ al-Dīn Mūsā b. Mulḥam, could not take himself out of the transaction between the author and the reader, and hence he concludes the book with a poem in praise of this relatively small book in comparison to the customary voluminous output, in which he also identifies himself as the copyist. By means of this short poem, the copyist elevates his calligraphic skill as an artisan to the level of the author and places himself among critics with some say about the matter at hand.[58]

Thresholds that consist of titles, prologues, and the customary bracketing of the author's name between a religious invocation of the names of God, the Prophet, and his family and companions, usually lead us into *khuṭbat al-kitāb*. But as usual, it is here that the author will refer to himself as the shaykh, or *ʿālim*, whose honorific title is ameliorated by being "God's worshipper," His "slave." The author's expressions of humility should be read, however, as a declaration of independence and self-respect and the denial of any servitude or subservience to humans. The case is different when there is patronage, for here the author may distinguish his economic dependency from an ideological subservience that would imply the loss of independent thinking. In most cases, however, an undifferentiated kind of patronage is involved, which combines the three components of economics, ideology, and status into a single package: to be supported finanically and also to be endowed with a dignified status, the poet or author must renounce or tone down any ideological difference that cannot fit into a codified system pleasing to the patron.[59] This type of undifferentiated patronage is manifested in the form of a plain encomium.

But there is more to guide us into the intricacies, not only of levels of patronage or of independence in relation to material identifiers, but also of the text itself. The highly developed rhetoric and its sophisticated poetics resituate us in a critical space where every term summons up concrete images. As these common, shared poetics and peripheral matter generate more poetics in the ongoing cultural production, they contribute to the constitution of an Islamic literary world-system. The pre-Islamic poetics of the erotic prelude, the *nasīb*, which recalls the departing beloved and her tribe through an engagement with the remains and ruins of a campsite, reemerges under a different guise and name. What rhetoricians call *barāʿat al-maṭlaʿ* and *barāʿat al-istihlāl* (felicitous and suggestive openings), such as loaded preludes, bring about the impact of the place. Through its associations with the pre-Islamic amatory poetic opening and evocations of desire and longing, the recollected or invoked site collapses the spatial and the philological. While the site invokes memory, the antecedent tradition of the relevant poetics serves as a base for the newly constituted verbal threshold of recollection and personal itinerary. Thus al-Mutanabbī says: "Greeting to a site where once a slender one captivated you!"[60] Indeed, Ṣafī al-Dīn al-Ḥillī's elaborate rhetorical canvas led many to expound on this territory with more derivations or referents, and with professional or artisanal documentation that most often consolidated a concrete base for a poetics that at this juncture derived its wording and imagery from the human body, from crafts such as embroidery, from material such as silk or metal, and from physical abodes.[61]

Within this active attention to rhetoric, style, and book writing, texts and their layout invited experimentation and innovation in inscription, copying, and embellishment. Even within the text itself, the roles of the author or copyist and the artist are obvious. Both the *taqdīm* (preface), *khuṭbah* (plan and intention), and subdivisions or headings (*ru'ūs*) express, for example, the author's choices and convey a specific plan that appears more conspicuously in adapted or appropriated translations, such as Abū Isḥāq al-Kindī's (d. 870) adaptation of ibn Nāʿimah al-Ḥimṣī's translation of the *Enneads* by the third-century philosopher Plotinus, wrongly attributed by a later scribe to Aristotle.[62] Indeed, a later translator makes it clear that he *naqala* (transferred) what al-Kindī *aṣlaḥa* (corrected and appropriated).[63] The adaptor probably wrote the prologue not to explicate the emergence of the copied and circulated text, and the labor involved in making it available, but primarily to connect the book to a large corpus of philosophical discourse in which al-Kindī was a major player.[64]

Paratexts are not supplementary material (*dhayl*), for dedications and divine invocations function as the text in action. They are not to be confused with what is added later by publishers and editors, and they need to be considered only as they appear in their manuscript form. They may emerge as divisions within the text, such as those Aḥmad ibn ʿArabshāh (1389–1450) provides in his biography of Tīmūr, for example. He makes a point of separating an anecdotal narrative of some relevance from the main thrust of his coverage of Tīmūr's conquests. Thus, we come across portions that are placed under the category of *maqṭaʿ* (section) and "story."[65]

On other occasions, and these are abundant in the manuscript tradition of the period under consideration, there are marginal notes that could have been an afterthought, an addition by a copyist, disciple, or transmitter. The marginal note is no less functional than a commentary or a gloss, but the latter may well grow into another book. Whenever margins and colored lines, passages, or words multiply, we understand that the author is struggling to cope with exceptions, current notions, and usage that require attention. But matters can become more complicated whenever a number of scholars across the many Islamic lands and the long period under consideration derive stimulation and impetus or a clue from another author's gloss, or from a marginal and border note (*ḥāshiyah*). The gloss may well grow into another expanded *ḥāshiyah* or *sharḥ* (commentary, gloss, and explication), *takmilah* (complement, addendum, or supplement), or *dhayl* (supplement). Indeed, these *shurūḥ* (sing. *sharḥ*) were taken so seriously by scholars and their reading public that it is rare not to find extant copies of them. I take the *ḥāshiyah* (marginalia, commentary, scholium) to be a significant turn in the formation of a scholarly network, not only as a dynamic interaction between an antecedent authority, usually in the form of a groundbreaking book, and a successor, but also as a component in a growing chain of analysis and discussion. In other words, its recurrence in the fields of logic, philosophy, grammar, theology, and lexicography over a long temporal span confronts us with a solid, scholarly, genealogical succession, which could not have accumulated as cultural capital without a demanding market. An example is the commentary written by ʿAbdullāh ibn Shiḥab al-Dīn al-Ḥusayn al-Yazdī of Iṣfahān (d. 981/1573) on Saʿd al-Dīn Masʿūd al-Taftazānī's (d. 791/1389) *Tahdhīb al-Manṭiq* (The Refinement of Logic). Nearly two centuries separate the author from the later commentator. Both books often formed part of the theological curriculum outside the ultraconservative domains. Apart from authentication and elucidation, the commentary divides its concerns into philological inquiry and hermeneutics in a very concise Arabic that includes the commentator's corrections, objections, and disagreements. Logic, theology, and grammar work together and allow the commentator to touch on schools of thought and their methods of inquiry, including Ashʿarites, Muʿtazilah, and Imamates (Shīʿīs).[66]

Among the most prominent cases, next to the commentaries in rhetoric on praise odes to the Prophet, are those that deal specifically with al-Sakkākī's *Miftāḥ al-ʿulūm* (Key to the Sciences). The number of books and commentaries on this work is astounding. This scholarly production takes place in a highly specialized domain, the greatest merit of which, for educated readers, derives from its bearing on the study of religious texts and its systematic and highly nuanced and persuasive instruction in the art of logic and grammar. The rationale behind these efforts receives due promotional impetus through the abridgement by the noted scholar and rhetorician Muḥammad ibn ʿAbd al-Raḥmān Jālāl al-Dīn al-Qazwīnī (d. 739/1338), also known as Khaṭīb Dimashq, who hits a sensitive nerve in his resumé of al-Sakkākī's *Miftāḥ*. He praises the Key as "the best in rhetoric" for its organization, editing, and gathering of principles and roots. But he justifies his abridgement because the primary text or source "is not devoid of padding, digression, and complexity, lacking clarification and abstraction and hence inviting abridgement."[67] In other words, the explicator or editor is here playing the role of the discerning reader, someone who is aware of the needs of others among the reading community. He justifies the effort behind his resumé (*talkhīṣ*) as an inevitable response to the demands of a literate society to make al-Sakkākī's work "accessible" and "easy for its readers to understand."[68] This rationale opens the door for further endeavors in the same direction. Each critic or editor has to justify a scholarly effort, and Saʿd al-Dīn al-Taftazānī (d. 791/1389) gives further explanations for his expanded reading and explication of al-Qazwīnī's abridgement, which was obviously so popular among scholars that it invited scholars to expand, explicate, and comment in order to meet the needs of a growing readership. Al-Taftazānī embarked on a double venture. He issued both an abridgement (*Mukhtaṣar*) and an extended version (*Muṭawwal*). He begins by explaining the reason behind his effort as an obligation to release rhetoric from the many misunderstandings and dogmatic explications that beset it. He decided to settle in Khwārizm because "Jurjāniyyat Khwārizm is the abode of noble men and the haven of the upholders of virtue." There he obtained "the treasuries of knowledge" while consulting knowledgeable rhetors.[69] Working diligently on al-Qazwīnī's abridgement, he celebrates his "*muṭawwal*" as being both comprehensive and meticulous, a feat that can be substantiated by the number of commentaries that followed it.[70] Al-Sharīf al-Jurjānī's (d. 1413) commentary demonstrates the impossibility of such a claim and the inevitable limitations of any project in rhetoric.[71]

Within the lexical domain, in other words, terminology and systematic classification of rhetoric place Arabic into a territorial space occupied by rhetors, grammarians, and logicians. Book production relies on this contribution to legitimize its presence. The astounding multiplication of commentaries attests to this turn, which could be seen as an ultimate appropriation of specialized knowledge to the needs of the Islamic street. *Sharḥ* in this case can take many forms, as commentary, explication, marginal notes, and annotations. It can add, emend, explicate, and expand on the original. Its origins, development, and stupendous growth should not be treated as some kind of secondhand or duplicated project. Like manuals, these works flourish and expand whenever there is a thriving reading climate and a community of scholars to participate in discussion. The trend is a testament to a burgeoning book industry and a dynamic cultural climate, which forced scholars to settle in congenial spaces that would make it possible for them to pursue their research, analysis, and consultation. Hence *sharḥ* as a scholarly pursuit belongs among the primary concerns and interests of participants in a republic of letters, which is larger than any body politic. The *sharḥ* often turns into another encyclopedic enterprise with a plan and strategies of explication, along with erudite annotations that touch on other works, as the significant endeavors that we have been discussing make clear. But each explicator directs his *sharḥ* in the domains with which he is most familiar. Al-Taftazānī leads it into speculative theology; while his nineteenth-century publisher decided on his own to have Imam Jalāl al-Dīn al-Suyūṭī's *Itmām al-dirāyah* (Completion of Knowledge) on grammar and rhetoric bracket al-Sakkākī's text. The publisher speaks of this bracketing as "embroidering and embellishing" its "forelocks."

Al-Sakkākī's *Miftāḥ* (Key) provokes just as many commentaries as al-Ḥillī's *Kāfiyah* ode and its explanation, and yet each signifies a specific trend in reading, analysis, and annotation. The *Miftāḥ* places grammar into rhetoric in order to reorient speculative theological reasoning neatly within the domains of the Arabic language and its sciences. The studies of Qur'ānic "inimitability" are brought back into a combined study of logic, grammar, rhetoric, and poetry. Thus, for instance, we have *Al-Kāfiyah fī al-naḥw* (The Sufficient Guide in Syntax) by the prominent grammarian and speculative theologian ibn al-Ḥājib (d. 1249), and soon after, *Sharḥ Kāfiyat ibn al-Ḥajib* by Raḍī al-Dīn Muḥammad Astarabādhī (d. after 1284); another *Sharḥ* by ʿAbd al-ʿAzīz ibn Jumʿah ibn Zayd (d. 1297); yet another by no less than Muḥammad ibn Ibrāhīm ibn Jamāʿah (d. 1333); and even another by Ṣalāḥ ibn ʿAlī ibn Mahdī al-Zaydī (d. 1446) with a different title from the preceding ones. It bears the title *Al-Najm al-thāqib: Sharḥ Kāfiyat ibn al-Ḥājib* (The Piercing Star: Elucidating the Sufficient Guide by ibn al-Ḥājib). More grammarians and philologists would expound on *al-Kāfiyah* throughout the next six centuries, especially in the eighteenth century. But we should look at this concordance in terms of the objective circumstances that compelled scholars to carry on such a project in grammar throughout the thirteenth century in particular. Itineraries in the pursuit of grammar cannot be random engagements across a crowded paratextual map. They build on and reflect on each other so densely that we end up with a scarcity of titles and the apparent resignation of some scholars to this fact: they merely add their names to their subgeneric commentary, for example, in the case of the explicator al-Raḍī, *Sharḥ al-Raḍī*. In the latter case, however, al-Raḍī's resignation also implies a new contract with the source, an exchange that may elicit further responses and commentaries, as was the case in al-Raḍī's commentary. Put together, these works form the curriculum for training in syntax. Hence Muḥammad al-Shawkānī (d. 1834), for example, cites these books among required readings.

On other occasions, the text at hand raises serious issues in theological thought, logic, and grammar, and therefore calls for the intervention of solid scholars across Islamic lands. Such was the case with ibn al-Ḥājib's *Mukhtaṣar al-muntahā al-ùṣūlī* (The Resumé of the Ultimate Theological Basics). ʿAḍud al-Dīn Ijī (d. 1355) wrote his *sharḥ* (commentary) on ibn al-Ḥājib's Resumé. His commentary was followed by the marginal gloss of Saʿd al-Dīn al-Taftazānī (d. 1389) and another by al-Sharīf ʿAlī ibn Muḥammad al-Jurjānī. These three are among the most prominent scholars and speculative theologians of their time. Thus, when the gloss, as *ḥāshiyah* (pl. *ḥawāshī*: marginal explications and annotations), was reproduced later in print, the text itself is either showcased in a bordered layout with each explanation and commentary on the left, right, top, and bottom, or it disappears altogether whenever al-Ijī's commentary replaces it. The reciprocity between the host's text and that of the guest undergoes serious transformation when the original author is sufficiently knowledgeable to raise more questions and commentaries or simply invites further explanations. In fact, the analogy of host and guest becomes problematic in these intersectional spaces, where theologians and critics scrutinize every textual and conceptualized unit in detail, depending on which copy is at hand. These include the Moroccan linguist and scholar Muḥammad ibn al-Ṭayyib (d. 1756), the author of *Riḥlah ilā al-Hijāz*, who was also known in his time for a significant series of *shurūḥ*. The *shurūḥ* attest to the popularity of the text under review, a case that applies to almost every book of significance, not only in hadith and theology but also specifically in grammar and philology. Ibn Hishām al-Anṣārī's (d. 1360) *al-Mughnī al-labīb ʿan kutub al-aʿārīb* (The Adroit Substitute for Grammar Books) is a case in point. It has its own *sharḥ* (commentary) by Muḥammad ibn Abī Bakr al-Damāmīnī (d. 1424?), a solid scholar, poet, and littérateur. Ibn Hishām's other books, such as *Shudhūr al-dhahāb* (Snippets of Gold), also received a number of *shurūḥ*.

The *shurūḥ* phenomenon, which puzzled modernists such as Jurjī Zaydān and brought about much of their biting criticism of the past period, signifies a number of things that are lost on most modernists.[72] The first is the high demand for these *shurūḥ* in their time; otherwise, writers and scholars would not have wasted their time and effort on such painstaking projects. Among the well-known and wealthy Cairo booksellers, with a network of copyists, was Muḥammad ibn Ibrāhīm ibn Yaḥyā al-Waṭwāṭ (1235–1318), an encyclopedist and author in natural sciences. His wealth indicates a lucrative business. Second, there is the genealogical accumulation of a specific undertaking in theology, logic, or grammar, for example, that requires further elucidation and commentary to meet a horizon of expectations under different circumstances and times. In this sense, the commentary is not different from a translation. And third, there is the inevitable change in taste and milieu that requires a different "cultural script" to fit into acceptable cultural norms.

The semiotics of titles is no less significant. Titles are meant to lead the reader into the text and trap him in its intricacies. Thus, ibn al-Ḥājib's *Kāfiyah* (The Sufficient Guide) in the area of syntax generates other *Kāfiyas* in different domains, such as Ṣafī al-Dīn al-Ḥillī's (d. 750/1349) *Kāfiyah* in poetry and rhetoric. On the other hand, the use of *saj'* (rhymed wording) in these titles cannot be either a random choice or a mere show of dexterity and craft. In response to a horizon of expectation and need, the writer may have wanted his production to be compatible with current needs and demands. In these titles we encounter resonance, assonance, intonation, paronomasia, antithesis, contrafaction, and also referents that send us to the body of the text and its intertexts and subtexts. Thus, we come across 'Abd al-Rahīm ibn 'Abd al-Raḥmān al-'Abbāsī's (d. 1556) *Kitāb Sharḥ shawāhid al-Talkhīṣ al-musammā Ma'āhid al-tanṣīṣ* (Designating Familiar Texts: A Commentary of the Evidentiary Verses in *al-Talkhīṣ*),[73] for example, which implicates us in the study of a series of samples, referents, and intertextual documentation while meeting the disposition for resonance in titles.[74] The terms *ma'āhid* and *tanṣīṣ* are loaded, not only with the immediate contractual denotative of the first and the textuality of the second, but also because both work in unison to connote the thresholds as textual and semiotic openings of the text. On the other hand, although the word *tanṣīṣ* refers to a textual documentation of references, it derives from the verb *naṣṣa* (noun *naṣṣ*: text) that comes with the preposition *'alā* to mean "stipulate in writing." The moment the author or philologist undertakes the pursuit of documentation, textual analysis, and annotation, he or she is deeply involved in scriptoria. Peritexts and paratexts signify, then, a dense writing tradition, where lexicography holds sway.

The noticeable semiotics found in titles of the middle period is a practice that involves something more akin to marketplace language than the rhetorically rich titles of the classical Islamic period. There is less emphasis on the originating rhetorical preoccupation with *i'jāz* (inimitability) and eloquence. The plain attributes in secretarial or other manuals, which constitute a regular phenomenon until the twelfth century, give way to a process based more on a craft, profession, or a marketplace transaction. Ibn Sanāʾ al-Mulk (d. 608/1211) follows this road in his *Dār al-ṭirāz* (House of Brocade), which is a unique study of *muwashshaḥ* as intricately woven cloth or an embroidered gown in a textile house.[75] On the other hand, this same shift toward professional and marketplace semiotics entails kinesis, a dramatic normative predication on a rhetorical figure. The subgenre *muwashshaḥ*, which the author and poet ibn Sanāʾ al-Mulk explores in *Dār al-ṭirāz*, combines in the title its stimulating attributes as a street-staged performance and an abode of art. Two significant examples that respond and play on each other through processes of parody and subversion are those of al-Ṣafadī and ibn Ḥijjah. The latter's *Kashf al-lithām* (exposing, unveiling) is a counter-discourse to the former's *Faḍḍ al-khitām* (meaning: unsealing, deflowering, and resolving). This battle within titles that reflect on each other in order to undermine content is fought in masculinist terms over a feminized body of tropes and figures of speech, such as *tawriyah* (puns). At times, the reliance on a Qurʾānic verse from the "Sura of Light," for example, can generate other titles. Muḥammad ibn Saʿīd al-Būṣīrī (1211–1294) uses *Al-Kawākib al-Durriyyah* (Pearly Stars) as a title for his praise (Mantle) ode to the Prophet, borrowing from the verse on the light of God.[76] The use became so popular that it lent itself easily to other variations, not only in poetry but also in a *maqāmah* addressed to a patron rather than to the Prophet, unlike the source ode. Such is the *maqāmah* by the eminent chancery scribe Shihāb al-Dīn Abū al-ʿAbbās Aḥmad b. ʿAlī b. Aḥmad ʿAbd Allāh al-Qalqashandī (d. 1418).[77] The itinerary taken by this term, from a specific reference to God's light to the Prophet and then to a patron, cannot be an ordinary one, and must be seen in terms of a comprehensive drive to humanize knowledge. In this context, titles that make use of concrete terms such as pearls and gems abound, and the whole book industry dances in lively and kinetic imagery.

Private Libraries and Scholarly Networks

With all of the above in mind, I continue to engage with the contentious modern critique of medieval and premodern cultural production as a point of departure. My focus is on issues that have incurred serious disparagement, especially issues that pertain to lexical proliferation and its systematization in a culture industry. These relate to authorship, legitimation and validation, rhetoric and its possible superfluity, genealogical construction, transactional codes among peers, fellows, and mentors, public communication and reading, and the impact of an entire milieu. Very often all of these issues, or at least a substantial subset of them, show up in one type of production, such as the so-named *badīʿiyyah* (encomium to the Prophet exemplifying figures of speech and rhetorical apparatus), with its wide circulation and vogue among the learned and common publics. Through a remapping of cultural production, along with its previous archival validation or an alternative rapport with reading publics, new concerns and classifications emerge, each with its concomitant definitions of identity, space, authority, and, most importantly, language and rhetoric.

The surge in rhetorical experimentation and the shift away from official discourse, coupled with a sustained undercurrent that dismantles generic or representative divides between high and low—all characteristics of the premodern era—require a different kind of analysis of the production of knowledge. The enhanced devotion to rhetoric that has engendered so much negative criticism against a so-called age of superfluity is an accurate reflection of a full-scale grammatical and linguistic movement aimed at reorienting literate culture, which in turn was a feature of a strongly established, multidisciplinary effort characteristic of ninth- to eleventh-century knowledge. Elaborated effectively among rhetors, the growth in the rhetorical corpus was often played out among aspiring scholars, such as the students and fellows of Jār Allāh al-Zamakhsharī (d. 538/1144), a scholar who gave credence and legitimacy to a remarkable network of disciples actively involved in presentations, rejoinders, and disputations. The case of the poet and rhetor Rashīd al-Dīn al-Waṭwāṭ (Vatvat), the chief secretary in Khurāsān (d. 573/1182), with his guide to rhetorical figures in *Ḥadāʾiq al-siḥr fī daqāʾiq al-shiʿr* (The Groves of Enchantment in the Secrets of Poetry), is a case in point.[78] Al-Waṭwāṭ's network, as shown in his published letters, demonstrates the significance of this activity in reconciling views, raising questions, strengthening disputations, and ultimately contributing to profound philological knowledge. Al-Waṭwāṭ made it possible for scholars to be hosted at his own location, where they could work on certain books and matters in which they would receive authorization to transmit and teach.[79] Although his book relied on its author's knowledge of the *Tarjomān al-balāghah* (Guide to Eloquence; written 507/1114), by the Persian scholar Muḥammad ibn ʿUmar al-Rādūyānī, its systematic approach was widely recognized by prominent poets and critics across the Islamic lands. His bilingual expertise and competence as a poet and rhetorician were admired by Yāqūt al-Rūmī al-Ḥamawī al-Kātib in his massive biographical dictionary (d. 626/1229); he was "the most knowledgeable of people in Arabic language," in which he excelled, just as he did in his native Persian. He wrote poetry in both languages, in the same rhyme, rhythm, and equivalent wording. In the "Groves of Enchantment," he lists and supplies examples of fifty-five figures and tropes.[80] Similarly, the brilliant Egyptian rhetor and poet Abū Muḥammad Zakī al-Dīn ʿAbd al-ʿAẓīm ibn Abī al-Iṣbaʿ (d. 654/1256) set a model for the Iraqi merchant, eminent poet, critic, and scholar Ṣafī al-Dīn al-Ḥillī (d. 750/1349). Like his predecessor, al-Ḥillī also argues the case for his contribution to rhetoric in terms of a detailed recognition of antecedent authority, which took the form of a cultural production that was perused, digested, or critiqued by the successor scholar. In these cases, a chain of tutors and a genealogy of readings can be retrieved.[81] From this process books emerge as the most conspicuous presence in the makeup of a newly authored text that, in the case of al-Ḥillī, for example, was to become pivotal not only for theorizations regarding rhetoric but also for the perpetuation of a new dynamic—namely, the encomium to the Prophet, not to the court, as a means of retention and reclamation of Islamic legitimacy ever since the era of the "rightly guided" caliphs.[82] Placed at the center of literate culture, this dynamic also leads the discussion of the inimitability of the Qurʾan (*iʿjāz*) on to another sacral but rarely trodden territory. A new sphere for discussion was to grow alongside these other discussions, one that was to enlist the participation of readers, policy makers, historians, biographers, speculative theologians, grammarians, lexicographers, and every writer of note. Despite the devastation that affected their lands and their libraries as a result of the Mongol invasions, networks among the learned still proved sufficiently vigorous to inject fresh energy into the scene.

We need to keep in mind here Jār Allāh al-Zamakhsharī's place in defining lines of demarcation in scholarship between Arabs (which in this context means writers devoted to the Arabic language, not a particular racial group) and non-Arabs. In the thirteenth century, certain books specifically address the criteria for the assessment of non-Arab poetry, referring in this case to the poetry written in Persian as the official language under the Mongols. Along with al-Rādūyānī's Guide to Eloquence noted earlier, these included Muḥammad ibn Qays al-Rāzī's (d. 1232) *Al-Muʿjam fī maʿāyīr ashʿār al-ʿAjam* (The Compendium on the Principles of Non-Arab, "Persian" Poetry). The amount of Sufi poetry composed in Persian between the eleventh and fourteenth centuries may well explain the need for bilingual works of criticism or others written only in Persian. However, this trend should not be confused with the development of multiple modes of analysis among scholars. Initially, some used the method of the speculative theologians and others followed habitual and traditional ways of reading and analysis. The latter was followed particularly by Jalāl al-Dīn al-Suyūṭī and a chain of other critics until al-Zabīdī's proclaimed preference for the "Arab" way, as being the uncontaminated traditional reading.[83]

But both criticism and rhetoric also show the influence of two discourses of specifically analogical reasoning: the Muʿtazilite and the Ashʿarite. These discourses were politicized further following the Ottoman conquest of Egypt in 1517 and the emergence of the Safavid Iran (1502–1736) under Shah ʿAbbās (r. 1588–1629), when both Azerbaijan and Shirwan were annexed to Iran. Among later arrivals from Iran to Damascus was Mullah Maḥmūd al-Kurdī (d. 1663), who settled and taught there using the method that his biographers and historians, such as Muḥammad Amīn al-Muḥibbī (d. 1699), specify as the method of verification (commentary and annotation), *taḥqīq*, as practiced in *kutub al-aʿājim* (the books of non-Arabs).[84] Although this phrase replaces that of *al-qudamāʾ* (the ancients, i.e., the Greeks), from the twelfth century on it assumed a broader application, in line with the resurgence of national languages across Islamic lands. With Hulagu Khan's (d. 1265) sweeping and devastating conquests of lands all across Asia and the Near East, the Persian language received legitimation as the official language of the Mongol empire, giving it, in Hamid Dabashi's phrase, world dimensions. At a later date, the Kurdish scholar Ibrāhīm al-Kūrānī (d. 1690) was notably mentioned as a scholar with whom such prominent Arab scholars as ʿAbd al-Ghanī al-Nābulusī (d. 1731) and Abū al-Mawāhib al-Ḥanbalī (d. 1714) studied rhetoric, grammar, and philology.[85]

While setting the scene for future generations of scholars, al-Zamakhsharī's circle was particularly bent on making its point by applying Muʿtazilite reasoning in rhetoric and claiming Arabic as its deliberately acknowledged language of choice. The influence of the circle on other scholars thus was variable. No less vigorous was the group of scholars that took al-Sakkākī's "Key to the Sciences" as the subject of analysis and discourse, including al-Qazwīnī and al-Taftazānī. Entrenched between Muʿtazilites and Ashʿarites, analysis and logical reasoning in the study of language and its enunciation in poetry and prose consolidate a discursive constellation of its own, with many different voices and applications. To a certain extent, traditional philology found itself marginalized and as a result began to reach into domains that were once closed to literati, including the street and its speakers.

Shifting discursive and conversational positions manifest an acute sense of crisis, especially around the mid-thirteenth century. As if to ward off the haunting memory of the sack of Baghdad by the Mongol army in 1258 and the consequent imperial campaign to impose Persian or their own language, a countermovement took place. This amounted to a vast accumulation of compendiums, lexicons, dictionaries, rejoinders, encyclopedic topographies, geographies, and histories, along with works composed on every other field of knowledge, which closely rivals the output of the heyday of productivity in ʿAbbasid Baghdad. Benefitting greatly from this invigorating cultural activity and encyclopedic productivity, the Mamluk state in particular derived moral and administrative power from the institution of the chancery as an administrative and cultural center maintained by its elite. The latter, in turn, engendered a vigorous atmosphere of competition, one that involved not only members of departments such as finance, the military, and the chancery, but also an ever-increasing number of other kinds of authors who chose to operate outside statist domains in order to exercise their independence and sense of ownership. As a consequence of this increase in productivity, a new textual regime was established in nearly every branch of knowledge, although the dominant ones were those involving issues of statecraft, social order, moral and religious thought, worldly pursuits, and sensory or visionary experience.

As a natural consequence of this cultural milieu, we find a number of epistles, or *maqāmāt*, that focus specifically on disputation, debate, or dialogue among the three leading administrative departments: finance, military, and chancery—the last being the primary domain for writers, or *arbāb al-aqlām* (lords of the pen).[86] While such assiduous activity was clearly important to the process of state building, at the same time it should arouse suspicions on our part, not with respect to the rules of supply and demand, or of competition and advancement among writers, but rather with respect to its unsettling magnitude. The questions that arise are thus: Are we in the presence of Jorge Luis Borges's idea of a minutely drawn map that negates its original?[87] Is this an institutionalization in rhetorical form of a paper empire, of words on words, and *kalām ʿalā kalām* (metadiscourse)? Yet even when this rhetoric is negated by modernists as superfluity, this negation only testifies to its presence in a rich culture, which necessarily takes language as its field. "The disclaiming of rhetoric," says Christine Brooke-Rose, "is itself a figure of rhetoric."[88] Was this enterprise essentially constructed on antecedent authorities or on a contemporary inventory of poets, prose writers, Sufis, speculative theologians, and rationalists, each category having its effect on extraction, conjugation, patching, inversion, derivation, abstruse reasoning, and logical postulations, not to mention hundreds of other ways for coming up with new meanings from the same root or name?[89] However, the simulacrum is no paper tiger. Instead, it raises questions, invites conceptualization, and also leads to action. Perhaps in anticipation of a disintegrating Mamluk order as a result of the Ottoman invasion of Egypt (1517), it lays the groundwork in words for formulating a displacement of both notions and nations.

chapter four

THE CONTEXT OF AN ISLAMIC LITERATE SOCIETY

Epistemological Shifts

> Knowledge is my capital; reason the foundation of my religion;
> love is my base; and yearning is my boat; the mention of God
> is my confidante, trust is my treasure, and sadness my mate;
> learning is my weapon and patience my garb; satisfaction my gain,
> poverty my pride; austerity my profession; certainty my strength;
> sincerity my savior; obedience my lineage; jihad my comportment;
> and the ultimate joy is in prayers.
>
> —Muḥammad ibn ʿAbdullāh (the Prophet; d. 8 June 632)[1]

A question that confronts us as readers and scholars may relate to other properties in the makeup of a republic of letters in the medieval period. Popular-national modes that were taken to be formative in Johann Gottfried von Herder's view of a valorized cultural sphere apply with even greater force to the Islamic scene as we read it in its literary manifestations. These were to receive further impetus through the poetry and writing of popular poets and Sufis, as will be discussed in chapter 8. In matters relating to the increasing power of the Arab-Islamic street, we are tempted as never before to interrogate the comparable presence of the social multitude in the medieval Islamic world, as seen in its practices, rituals, recitations, slogans, odes, songs, banners, and colors—elements that in our era receive wide circulation through social media and satellite broadcasting. In such a context we need to recall that, in their own time, the stunning vogue of both the Mantle odes (praise poems to the Prophet) and the *badīʿiyyāt* subgenre as additionally and primarily exemplifying figures of speech involved more than ordinary public recitations.[2] They also entailed Sufi *dhikr* rituals (invocations of God's attributes and those of the Prophet, and recitation) that, through the attainment of an ecstatic state, practically annihilate the material burden of the body in the hope of fusion in the divine. In the narrative base of the dream behind the mystical ode, a metaphysical stage is already set, which recapitulates a common belief in the veracity of a hadith whereby the Prophet says: "Whoever sees me in a dream, then surely he has seen me for Satan cannot impersonate me."[3] The ode comes as a muse's gift in exchange for a graceful blessing from the Prophet in the form of healing. To recite the ode or to comment on it becomes a participatory act in this process of transfiguration.

The spectacular growth of replications, superseding contrafactions, and commentaries on the *Burdah* (Mantle) poem involves many skillful excursions in rhetoric and thus acquaints us with graphic, firsthand accounts of communities and writers or poets. One such example is ibn Ḥijjah's *Sharḥ* for his ode *Taqdīm Abī Bakr* (Giving Precedence to Abū Bakr),[4] with its mixed genres and street songs, the metrics of which bring the period closer to the post-*nahḍah* era of social change.[5] Both al-Būṣīrī (d. 696/1296) and al-Ḥillī, the first as the recognized *Burdah* (Mantle Ode) poet and the second as the forerunner in directing it into the art, craft, and rhetoric of inventiveness, highlight the dream as the generating power for poetry and rhetoric. This was not the case for ibn Ḥijjah, who simply pursued his project, a poem and a compendium, as a superseding contrafaction and as a show of mastery in poetry and rhetoric. He may have preferred to omit the dream motif simply because it had already been exhausted as a deus ex machina or a pseudo emplotment practiced by tricksters, as in al-Hamadhānī's *Maqāmah* of Iṣfahān. The trickster Abū al-Fatḥ claimed in a congressional mosque prayer that he saw the Prophet in a dream: "Then he taught me a prayer and admonished me to teach it to his people. So I wrote it down on these slips of prayer with the perfumes of khalūq, musk, saffron and socc, and whoever asks for a copy as a gift, I will present it to him, but whosoever hands me back the cost of the paper I will accept it."[6] With or without the intercessional dream, the ode in praise to the Prophet is among the significant markers of a massive accumulation of cultural capital for over five centuries after al-Ḥillī. Each treasury, compendium, commentary, or dictionary has, we should assume, a readership.

There must be reasons for this considerable, long-running cultural output. Other than the logical surmise that in times of crisis, people tend to adhere strongly to certain practices and pursuits and especially to education, one might suggest that the literati were keen to sustain a vigorous presence for themselves. Given that a relatively decentralized state structure in Mamluk and other precarious sultanates could no longer offer them wide and sustained patronage, there inevitably emerged another plausible space, in which the literati could exchange views among themselves and their constituencies of readers.

Terms of Exchange: Problems of Authorized Transmission

Rather than writing being a process whereby legitimacy could be bolstered through author/patron transactions, the most dynamic part of writers' production moves beyond the subject of authorship and the subsequent *samāʿ* (the certified and authorized audition whereby a specific disciple was given a license to have a book read, copied, circulated, sold, discussed, and passed through contrafaction, parody, and commentary).[7] Authors often belonged to the same social and economic groups as their readers, and contemporaneous or posthumous circulation was rampant. On some occasions, the authorized fellow and companion (*ṣāḥib*) of the writer or his reader might be accused of plagiarism, or raids on the original source, based perhaps on sheer proximity and hence a particular affinity with the reported material. A case in point is ibn Nubātah al-Miṣrī's (686–768/1287–1366) scathing critique directed at his authorized disciple, the polymath Ṣalāḥ al-Dīn ibn Aybak al-Ṣafadī (696–764/

1296–1363). In ibn Nubātah's confrontational work, entitled *Khubz al-shaʿīr* (Barley Bread; i.e., the proverb goes, "barley is eaten and despised"), the terms of transmission and reporting are questioned.[8] The licensing process (*ijāzah*, a license to transmit) in his day underwent some drastic shifts in application.[9] It became not the result of a choice between, on the one hand, authoritative *riwāyah* or transmission based on *samāʿ* (certified audition) from the immediate author and, on the other hand, *dirāyah* (cognizance) as basically grounded in understanding and reasoning,[10] but rather a confrontational posture, as was the case between ibn Nubātah and al-Ṣafadī and also between Ḥasan Shams al-Dīn al-Nawājī (799–859/1386–1455) and his mentor and fellow-scholar, Abū Bakr ibn Ḥijjah al-Ḥamawī (767–837/1366–1434).

The license to transmit was no ordinary matter: it was given to a disciple on the basis of a strong belief in his capacity, commitment, faith in the subject of transmission, and intimate familiarity with both the work and the author. Nowhere are these features and claims more closely documented and transcribed than in ibn Ḥijjah's text of ibn Nubātah's authorization of al-Ṣafadī, in response to a request from the latter. The two documents are unique,[11] not only because ibn Nubātah admired and celebrated his junior, the prolific littérateur, encyclopedic scholar, and daring literary controversialist ibn Ḥijjah, but also because there is a textual, moral, and intellectual reciprocity between the two sides of the transaction. Ibn Nubātah and al-Ṣafadī appear as rounded characters, alive, knowledgeable, and on familiar terms with each other. In the end, their words and syntax interact and converse, as befits a republic of letters. The request and the warm response open up a genealogical space for readings, authors, mentors, companions, and reminiscences that in the end become a microcosmic republic of letters.

Writing a Contemporary Cultural Scene

The record of ibn Nubātah's and al-Ṣafadī's confrontation, which is both confessional and documentary, offers a striking background against which to assess subsequent cases of disparagement between authors. But neither those disparagements nor the early laudations detract from a broader context of discussion, within which accusations by authors of raids on each other's work demand a careful reading on our part of the other side of plagiarism, namely, the side of absorption and identification. The matter is so convoluted that at times it is easy to confuse texts and authors. Ibn Ḥijjah could not liberate himself from his formative apprenticeship to the poetry of al-Ḥillī and ibn Nubātah; al-Ṣafadī received the authorization to transmit and report on behalf of ibn Nubātah, and yet he was unable to dissociate his frame of reference from these prominent figures or their community of littérateurs, theologians, historians, and polymaths. Al-Ḥillī and ibn Nubātah saw themselves as being independent from, but also in conversation with, their forebears. Al-Nawājī was on such intimate terms with his mentor, ibn Ḥijjah, that he copied in his own hand the latter's *Qahwat al-inshāʾ* (The Intoxication of Chancery), and yet he wrote the most scathing criticism of ibn Ḥijjah's "plagiarisms."[12] A no less interesting case relates to the sardonic epistle penned by the Andalusian poet and prominent Cordoban ibn Zaydūn (d. 1071) against his rival in politics and love for the princess Wallādah (d. 1091). This epistle was converted into an occasion for two significant but opposite excursions in intellectual history, composed later by ibn Nubātah and al-Ṣafadī.[13] In the end, one concludes that there existed an intricate web of readings, transmissions, suggestions, premises, insights, and also controversies, which is linked to (and builds upon) other webs, spilling over into compendiums and lexicons where proper names are merely signifiers that may have lost their signified in the plethora of scholarly contributions.

This engagement with particular texts takes the place of any kind of radical shift in the mechanics of cultural genealogies and issues of cultural affiliation. We are dealing here with a phenomenon that is both contemporary and ancient in its ancestry, and that functions in the medieval Islamic world as a catalyst for a growing circle of poets, writers, jurists, and philologists who happened to correspond, meet, transmit, and comment on each other's work. Over the thirteenth to the eighteenth centuries, a significant body of material supports the idea of a republic of letters that built upon many assemblies, confederations, alliances, meeting sites, personal libraries which were open to scholars, and dynastic and other ruling courts. This kind of textual web does not amass a faceless but substantial ancestry of ancients or moderns, like the littérateurs of the ʿAbbasid era. Nor does it have recourse to an unidentified principle that is designated only by "shifters," such as we find in Abū Muḥammad ʿAbd Allāh ibn Muslim ibn Qutaybah's (d. 276/889?) *Al-Shiʿr wa-l-shuʿarāʾ*.[14] Nor does it aim to target somebody to expose or defend, as had been the tradition at an earlier stage. On the contrary, identification of the names of antecedent writers in such cases is painstakingly carried out by the learned descendant, who takes pride in having his own work as the center of attention. However, this same trajectory is still problematic. Although the personal element is significantly underscored in the rare biographical sketches within compilations or manuals by poets, critics, epistolographers, or theologians, the general tendency is to present only the autobiographical or biographical details that are of literary or communal significance.

There are two dimensions to the rise of an autobiographical/biographical poetic: one is specifically centered on crafts, occupations, and professions, where poets in particular create a pun or make a point in a humorous celebration of their calling and craft, using for that purpose the professional epithet or agnomen (as we shall see with poets of popular verse studied in subsequent chapters). The circulation, transmission, and compilation of a poetic production signify not only its artistic or aesthetic efficacy but also its reception in a literate culture, where it invites distribution and achieves visibility within the available framework for larger audiences. The other dimension relates to processes of systematic authorization, whereby prominent writers and mentors acquire disciples and fans from among aspiring scholars, who will document their life and works. It is not only one's personal life that counts, despite its significance for authorized biographical compilations,[15] but also the presence of the person in the formation of an innovative stance, a movement, or a milieu. Here, the subjective "I" is hidden and camouflages its presence in a genealogy or network of people and books, as if (although actually not) in accord with an old theological objection to the grammarians' use of the term "regent" (*ʿāmil*), since the latter, according to Ashʿarite theology, is the exclusive property of the Omniscient.[16] Autobiography creeps into an abundance of biographical dictionaries, authorial testimonials, and authorized audition, at times covering a substantial portion of a "treasury" or compendium. However, this tendency is part of a broader framework, one that can be termed "calligraphic,"[17] in the sense that each production either responds to another or prepares itself for the subsequent appearance of dialogues and refutations. In these latter contributions, an authorial self emerges as the author tries to vindicate a profession or position or to draw attention to an achievement. While the public representational site may be minimized, an authorial presence takes over, but not as a dominant factor. Authors speak of their readings, dialogues, interventions, travels, and correspondence, and on occasion they harp on the playful, the humorous, and the ribald. Although there is always the possibility of a history for textual genealogies of affiliation, mentorship, and apprenticeship, the middle period is distinguished by monographic or compendious responses and recapitulations. At times, the main purpose of the production or composition seems to involve the decomposition of another work, not only through a systematic emptying of significations but also as the result of a systematic process of undermining.[18]

This process of displacement through a differentiated engagement with an original work could not have assumed the significance it did, had it not been for an active climate of ideas in which writing was a lucrative and profitable business on both the material and the moral levels. The case of ibn Ḥijjah is an example. A prolific writer, insightful critic, poet, and scholar, he can easily become a center for controversy and debate. He is described by al-Sakhāwī as "the knowledgeable imam and littérateur, the first among his peers, and the most advanced in the knowledge of literary arts. He has great achievements in poetry and prose, possesses valor and good manners, but is prone to vain glory [boastful vanity/excessive elation over one's achievements]."[19] Many of his compositions tend to be confrontational and contrafactional. Two of the most well known are *Burūq al-ghayth al-ladhī insajam* (The Lightening of the Concordant Rain), in which he deliberately undermines Ṣalāh al-Dīn al-Ṣafadī's commentary on the poet al-Tughrāʾī's *Al-Ghayth al-ladhī insajam ʿalā sharḥ lāmiyyat al-ʿajam lil-Tughrāʾī* (The Concordant Rain in Explicating al-Tughrāʾī's Poem *Lāmiyyat al-ʿAjam*), and a work on rhetoric, *Kashf al-lithām ʿan wajh al-tawriyah wa-al-istikhdām* (Unveiling Double Entendre and Pivoting),[20] which is a verbatim reproduction of the chapter in his *Khizānat al-adab* (The Ultimate Treasure Trove of Literature) and deliberately imitates the title of one of al-Ṣafadī's (d. 1363) works, *Faḍḍ al-khitām an al-tawriyah wa-al-istikhdām* (punning on opening up and sealing the discussion of the two figures, the double entendre and pivoting). His famous ode in book form, *Taqdīm Abī Bakr*, and its accompanying explication are intended to surpass and supersede al-Ḥillī's *Al-Kāfiyah* (Sufficient Ode) and its own rhetorical apparatus.[21] In contrast, his other important contribution to the study of the arts of popular poetry and especially *zajal*, namely, *Bulūgh al-amal fī fann al-zajal* (The Ultimate Achievement in the Art of Zajal), complements and at times duplicates Muḥammad ibn Muḥammad ibn al-Habbāriyya's (1023–1115) *Dīwān al-ṣādiḥ wa-al-bāghim* and Ṣafī al-Dīn al-Ḥillī's study of these arts.[22] If he was well known, as the documentary record has it, for his displays of vanity and arrogance in the treatment of contemporaries, it was only to be expected that he would have been subject to various kinds of scathing attack and vituperative criticism. Al-Nawājī's book *Al-Ḥujjah* [or *al-muḥajjah*] *fī sariqāt ibn Ḥijjah* (The Damning Evidence of ibn Ḥijjah's Plagiarisms) is only one among many that critiqued him.

Cultural Trafficking in a Communicative Sphere

Notwithstanding the disputed moral grounds for controversies such as these, they are nonetheless of great significance. They demonstrate a vibrant cultural environment, one that is sufficiently competitive to raise questions, initiate disputes, and establish terms for discussion. Moreover, the relevance of these discussions to an effervescent cultural scene cannot be overestimated. To stretch further the marketplace analogy already proposed several times in the course of my analysis, such discussions of plagiarism involve a much larger theoretical issue than Harold Bloom's anxieties of influence or the anthropological terms of gift exchange can explain. What we have in these discussions is an effort to impose rules on an incontrollable and free activity.[23] Language and its lexical landscape are an open arena for controversial players who find in decentralization, travel, pilgrimage, schools and education, mosques and their sessions, markets and assemblies, and books and the accumulation of books an inviting space. This space is already opened up to accommodate all sorts of activity where only the most eloquent and prolific can make an achievement and carve out a distinction for themselves. An open culture market economy is set loose, with only a few critics fighting to contain and control it. Even the efforts of these critics is no more than an oblique systematization of such activity—not to shun it but rather to canonize it as central to this economy.

Given that the discussions of plagiarism are not addressed to any particular authority or center, their freedom from restrictions and constraints is conducive to an open forum, a communicative sphere in which both readers and writers are audience and arbiters. In contrast to early centralized activities, the ruler's court has no function here. The ruler perhaps only rarely cares for or even understands what is going on. On the other hand, ibn Ḥijjah's *Khizānat al-adab* (Treasure Trove of Literature) manages to function as such an open forum, although the voice of the narrator has the ultimate say not only in selection, argumentation, and commendation or refutation, but also in plagiarizing or raiding the ideas and images of others. Given that in such matters there is no juridical opinion to set up checks and balances, as under postindustrial bourgeois rules, nor is there a political or statist center to expose and condemn, this space is open to trafficking in plagiarism; it is a competitive sphere run wild. The caliphal court or any other center of authority could have been the arena for deciding such disputations, as it had been during the ʿAbbasid era, for example, but it did not play this role during that of the Mamluks. A decentralized political sphere is reflected in this trafficking phenomenon, one in which only personal moral grounds can function as a contract, one that remains nonbinding. All this is carried out under the "terms" of a loose agreement on the need to make cultural production available and known to everyone in the period following the sack of Baghdad and the losses incurred by its libraries, including private and special or rare collections. The shift in the very definition of plagiarism is indicative of such a loose agreement, one that may be resorting to a counterfeit justification which expands without due consideration of the early theoretical grounds for plagiarism based on verbal rather than thematic practices.[24]

Abū ʿAlī Muḥammad ibn al-Ḥasan al-Ḥātimī (d. 998) in his *Ḥilyat al-muḥaḍārah* (The Ornament of Ensembles) offers a wide scope for plagiarism and its gradations between what is acceptable and what is to be censored. The new horizons that virtually open the floodgates for this kind of trafficking, however, are worth recognizing. While building on antecedent knowledge, such as al-Qāḍī ʿAlī ibn ʿAbd al-ʿAzīz al-Jurjānī's (d. 392 /1001) *Al-Wasāṭah* (Work of Mediation),[25] middle-period critics and grammarians eschew any such restrictions. Al-Jurjānī's classifications of plagiarism fall into three categories, occasioned by the always controversial poetic persona and contribution of al-Mutanabbī: thematic, verbal, and semiotic or rhetorical. Under the first category are notions and meanings that are common to people all over the world. But even newly invented notions can circulate easily and in due time merge into the common and shared. Poets in particular can emulate and exchange such themes, a case that differs from a deliberate raid on a specific use and choice of words and images that belong to a specific author; and, according to Ḍiyāʾ al-Dīn ibn al-Athīr (d. 1239) in his training manual for scribes, *Al-Mathal al-sāʾir fī adab al-kātib wa-al-shāʿir* (The Popular Model for the Literary Discipline of the Secretary and the Poet), there can be gradations in such things. There is a difference between copying, transforming, and raiding, which takes the form of what he terms "peeling" (i.e., detaching the image from its context). These criteria are categorized further in a discriminating critique penned by the Mamluk critic ibn Abī al-Iṣbaʿ, which looks at textual trafficking in the following terms: a sharing of meaning or wording; and a kind of telepathic transfer or mind reading that allows contemporaries to encounter each other's words or notions. More conducive to the possibility of widening the borders of such trafficking are his notions of *ḥusn al-itbāʾ* and *tawlīd* (subtle emulation and inference or extrapolation), ideas that involve a close acquaintance with the works of a predecessor in order to improve on words, images, or inventiveness in verbal dexterity, brevity, and completion. Ibn Abī al-Iṣbaʿ can be seen as showing a more liberal touch when he accepts as a "contractual" bond a poet's raid on meaning and wording in prose. He even allows for a process of defamiliarization, *ighrāb*, whenever the poet is able to add an element of strangeness to the original. However, not all critics of the period have the same attitude. The noted theologian and critic Ḥāzim al-Qarṭājannī (d. 1285),[26] for example, suggests in his *Minhāj al-bulagāʾ* (The Path of the Eloquent and the Lamp for the Literati) that there can be no justification for raids on meanings unless something new is added, which cannot include the so-called "barren" meanings that are uniquely linked to specific names and usage, as in the association between "lion" and majesty, or between "tiger" and ferocity.

The middle period's critical corpus on plagiarism achieves a more systematic level in Abū ʿAbd Allāh Jalāl al-Dīn al-Qazwīnī's (d. 739/1338) *al-Īḍāḥ fī sharḥ al-miftāḥ* (Elucidation of al-Sakkākī's Key). As loathsome plagiarism, he stipulates only what is "apparent," whatever duplicates the meaning and wording of the original, a position that al-Ṣafadī also accepts in his reading of al-Tughrāʾī.[27] Plagiarism is regarded as being less problematic (while still constituting a case of plagiarism) if there is a change in syntax, structure, or part of the wording to the extent of falling into the category of *ighārah* (a raid) or replication. It involves four subdivisions, of which the third and the fourth are considered unworthy as long as they literally duplicate the original or are lower in quality, but are reckoned good whenever the resulting text is considered more effective in brevity, explication, or density, and even when it is regarded as merely equal in quality to the original, but with a degree of alteration. This process of "peeling" in meaning has three grades: preferable to the original, better than the original, or neutral. Inconspicuous, discreet, or concealed plagiarism is more subtle, since poets and writers are able to redirect the purpose but hijack the meaning from another semantic field, transfer it anew, transform it into an opposite, make it more inclusive, or improve on it. Surprisingly, ibn Ḥijjah reserves the accusation of plagiarism for specific cases that he discusses in terms of what he calls "rarities," which display the talents of the successor. His other classifications are in agreement with the other writers on the topic. But for him, as for al-Nawājī, whenever there is a correspondence between two poets in meaning and wording, then preference is to be given to the one who is already established and known, with a firm and recognizable register.

Cultural Production as Commodity

Given a sustained grammar of plagiarism as a practice—one that has accumulated its own critical corpus over the centuries—readers can justifiably raise questions with respect to veracity, or the elements and principles that inform this corpus. In other words, awareness of this grammar of plagiarism can potentially either negate the need for accusatory exchange or raise the matter to another level of arbitration. As the situation unfolds, there is an exchange of accusations in a dynamic, seemingly open space of ideas and rhetoric, a marketplace where literary production is a commodity. This space expands beyond Cairo to Aleppo, Damascus, Morocco, and Baghdad. Only Yemen remains relatively isolated from these semi-regular exchanges, a point that is rightly noticed by Qalqīlah in his core analysis of the issue of plagiarism, which he also assigns to rhetorical concerns with inventiveness and novelty, or *badīʿ*.[28]

No wonder, then, that ʿUmar ibn al-Wardī (d. 1348) can proclaim in his *Dīwān*:

> I steal of meanings whatever I can
>   and if I can surpass the ancients, I praise my feat
> But if I am on equal footing with the ancients
>   it is still to my credit to be so.

He concludes with a simple interest-bound transaction:

> A dirham issued under my name is more to my taste
>   than somebody else's dinar.[29]

In this literary transaction, privatization runs rampant; the immediate concern of all producers is to fare well in a lucrative market. But there also exists a differential schema whereby "originality" is exempted from this process of transference, through which literature and poetry are treated partly as a commodity in a supply and demand transaction. Ibn Nubātah, for one, exempts ibn al-Ḥajjāj from his surmise that poets and littérateurs fall on each other's words, images, or notions, for "the byproducts of people's thoughts" are bound to "emerge from one level on this earth."[30]

Diversity and Stratification

Beyond the binary structuring of knowledge between philosophical or speculative theology, on the one hand, and traditionalist regimentation, on the other, the middle period is especially characterized by its diversity. Although there are occasional times in which a substantial body of codified Islamic scholarship is consolidated within a legitimating juridical structure, there are also instances of contending but subtle initiatives that manage to unsettle the official or hegemonic order. These include a sustained effort to invoke and compile such different and previously unrecorded genres and types as street songs and poetry, prison narratives, and nonscholarly anthologies, and to take account of the increased involvement of female audiences, craftsmen, artisans, and traders, all alongside the reclamation of rhetoric made accessible via professional practices and common life. Such a combination of concentrated activity indeed deserves the appellation of a republic of letters. A seemingly neutral production such as a fourteenth-century *badīʿiyyah* ode can cause problems in the context of the established binary structure of discourse (i.e., traditionalist vs. speculative or rationalist theology) by initiating a process of displacement, one whereby a separate genealogy develops that strikes substantial roots not only in the ceremonies of Sufi *dhikr*, with its invocations of the divine attributes and those of the Prophet, but also, and basically, through a lengthy textual progeny—which, at a much later date (1974), results in four thick volumes of emulations, imitations, and contrafactions.[31] Even the massive lexicons, compendiums, commentaries, and encyclopedias of the middle period reveal to us vigorous personal and individual tendencies of their authors that are circulated through information, communication, discussion, and conversation, in that their authors may have once been slaves, book dealers, artisans, craftsmen, copyists, participants in public readings, or merely affiliates of other authors with their distinct trends and dispositions.[32] The kind of cultural production that we have been describing here establishes a new set of identities, affiliations, and priorities in a textual community.

Institutionalized Knowledge Undermined

It is usual to subdivide discussions of the composition of knowledge and information with the aid of categories and paradigms, such as traditionalist, speculative/theological, and rationalist—to be split yet further into linguistic, grammatical, and administrative genealogies. The sheer number of such conflated elements within each subdivision and category, however, suggests that such stratifications serve as mere covers, or distorting lenses.[33] The strikingly widespread recourse to compendiums, the rise of the polymath, and the vogue of *shurūḥ*, or explications of an original text, all suggest a process in which designated classifications and centers of institutionalized knowledge were being undermined. For a considerable length of time, lines of demarcation and classification had relied on a paradigmatic loss of a centripetal political order symbolized by the city of Baghdad. The emergence of an alternative center in Cairo was accepted, but not as wholeheartedly as had been the case with Baghdad. Political disintegration, however, did nothing to halt the ongoing growth of a republic of letters, nor was it able to arrest the expansion of reading communities and sites of public learning. On the other hand, the beliefs promulgated by the ʿAbbasid caliph al-Qādir (r. 381–422/991–1031) set the tone for a strict traditionalist prohibition of deviating movements, creeds, and practices, including those of the Ashāʿirah (Ashʿarites) and the Muʿtazilah (Muʿtazilites). The Qādirite creed was upheld not only by contemporary or later market inspectors and jurists in al-Shām (Syria) and Egypt, but also by such an eminent historian and jurist as Shams al-Dīn Muḥammad ibn Aḥmad al-Dhahabī (d. 748/1347), who was followed by others as late as the fifteenth century.[34] Although Shīʿism had been under attack for some time, since the eleventh century (this is a noticeable feature of market inspectors' manuals, such as that of al-Shayzarī, for example, and also of ibn Taymiyyah's statements of doctrine), there is also a marked dilution of such categorization. The Shīʿites were described in these documents under such designations as Shīʿism per se; rejectionist Shīʿism (*muʿaṭilah*); and also under the heading *ḥubb āl-bayt* (love for the Prophet's family). Al-Ḥillī is listed under the second label, while the lexicographer ibn Manẓūr appears under the first.

Jurists make their living through their participation in activities involving name-calling, accusation, hasty proclamations, and also the kind of polarization that helps in the establishment of a particular constituency, and hence yields a source of income. Some law experts of this period complain of the rise in the number of jurists. Centuries later, ibn al-ʾUkhuwwah, whose full name is Ḍiyāʾ al-Dīn Muḥammad ibn Muḥammad al-Qurashī al-Shāfiʿī (d. 1329), complains that his city, namely, Cairo, "is full of legists occupied with issuing *fatwās* [legal opinions] and responding to legal inquiries on points which arise."[35] In despair, he asks: "Can there be any justification for the faith in allowing for a state of affairs in which large numbers of people occupy themselves with one particular duty while another [medicine] is neglected? The only excuse is that medicine does not afford access to judgeships and governorships, which makes it possible for people to claim superiority over rivals and to acquire authority over enemies."[36]

Within the context of official (i.e., Sunni) discourse, there is also a certain shift toward another kind of middle ground, one that, while not duplicating the view of the Ashʿarites, nevertheless envisages a functional purpose for Islamic law as a means of perpetuating people's welfare and restraining confusion and chaos through transmission and reasoning. Although ʿAbd al-Malik al-Juwaynī (d. 478/1085) and his disciple, Abū Ḥāmid al-Ghazālī (d. 505/1111), had already set out the path for both ʿIzz ibn ʿAbd al-Salām (d. 660/1261) and the Andalusian Isḥāq Ibrāhīm Mūsā al-Lakhmī al-Shāṭibī (d. 790/1388) in the application of the "*ʿilm al-maqāṣid* [aims/principles]," especially in the fourteenth century, there was an urgent need for an understanding of Islamic law, as espoused by al-Shāṭibī, as being primarily concerned with "gentleness as its distinctive feature and forgiveness as its concern."[37] I draw attention to al-Shāṭibī here because it seems that his was already a household name among audiences, as shown in a tale from the collection *A Thousand and One Nights*, where a mendicant claims to have been trained in al-Shāṭibī's use of logic as a means of reorienting foundational or originary principles.[38] On the other hand, and alongside this creed (but perhaps at the same time exposing the pitfalls of coercion), there is also an enormous body of literature that exposes, repudiates, and shuns hypocritical religious practices, pretentious Sufis, and popular storytellers and preachers. Despite the recognized impact that these street preachers and storytellers exerted on the masses, ibn al-Jawzī's (d. 1201) writings are particularly focused on the role of these groups,[39] an opinion that ibn al-ʿArabī certainly shares with respect to pretentious Sufis and mediocre jurists.

At an earlier date we encounter the licentious verse of the Iraqi poet Abū ʿAbd Allāh al-Ḥusayn ibn al-Ḥajjāj (d. 391/1001).[40] With its slang and colloquial words culled from the common way of life of Baghdad, his poetry made its way throughout the middle period, leading jurists and scholars in institutionalized teaching centers to ban it, but at the same time provoking a countermovement of admiration, including the support of eminent figures such as ibn Nubātah, who collected the verses in question, al-Ṣafadī, who wrote admiringly about them, and ibn Ḥijjah al-Ḥamawī (d. 837/1434), who never tired of drawing on ibn al-Ḥajjāj's collection. Ibn al-Ḥajjāj's contribution to an underground poetics of extravagant looseness, licentiousness, and obscenity was to prove a thrilling experience, perhaps as paradoxically shocking and tantalizing as Richard Burton's edition of *A Thousand and One Nights* (*Arabian Nights*). The sensational narrative in ibn al-Ḥajjāj's poetry should not blind us to another point that I want to make: by collecting the verses involved, the Cairene ibn Nubātah is displaying familiarity with a Baghdadi dialect used by the commoners and ruffians in the Baghdadi quarter of al-Zaṭṭ (gypsies). If we accept the biographical accounts of ibn al-Ḥajjāj, there seems to be a disparity between the person of the author and the product: his poetry consists of an engagement with the fringes of society, adopting their own languages and registers, which are themselves invigorated by a high dose of exuberant poetic style with realistic overtones. This divide makes it easy for highbrow or middlebrow poets and critics of the medieval and premodern period to read, quote, collect, and discuss his poetry with great abandon. In other words, a republic of letters transcends the boundaries of learned scholars, with their circles of discussion and correspondence, and reaches into the very fringes of society. Nonclassical poetic subgenres, especially the ones with street registers, cover the lands of Islam from Andalusia and North Africa to Mosul in the north of Iraq and bring into circulation words, images, and rhythms that also raise serious questions regarding the efforts of current scholarship to assign specific geographical and territorial locations and identities to popular literature.

On the other hand, we also possess voluminous topographies and world geographies, along with biographies of notables, obituaries, chancery correspondence, and manuals of the epistolary art spanning centuries. In addition, there are extensive studies that take a poem as the pretext for the construction of an archive of notes, glosses, commentaries, other verses both known and obscure, and anecdotes. Above all, there are, as noted earlier, massive contributions to lexicography that take street-talk into account, along with its origins and deviations. Taking as an example *Masālik al-abṣār fi mamālik al-amṣār* (Tracks of Vision concerning the Domains of Cities) by the chancery secretary and eminent scholar and poet Shihāb al-Dīn Aḥmad ibn Faḍl Allāh al-ʿUmarī (d. 749/1349), it is difficult to overlook the fact that a sense of comprehensive knowledge exists, controllable and in tandem with an all-encompassing Islamic order. In other words, we have not only multiple systems of thought but also multiple methodologies, which continue to challenge scholars and, in particular, bewilder those Arab and Muslim modernists who find themselves caught between a desire to control knowledge and the lure of a positivist philosophy—a position that leads them to look with suspicion at such a massive process of cultural productivity, seemingly at odds with what has been deemed a political failure.

The Hard Politics of Rhetoric: Decentering the Sacral

This colossal reservoir of cultural productivity can be channeled back into both textual and aural genealogies, which are never absolute. For instance, we can argue for the rising power and role of epistolary art, which accompanied the expanding state apparatus from as early as the Umayyad caliphal era. An orally based context (including poetic transmission and recitation) gradually gives way to the writing environment of the chancery and the development of other forms of prose. This shift is so commonplace that it hardly needs proof; nevertheless, the increasing presence of manuals on grammar and lexicons tell us much about this literate culture and its denizens. We are dealing here, for example, with the hundreds of volumes that by the end of the tenth century are included in the listings of Abū al-Faraj Muḥammad ibn Isḥāq al-Nadīm's (d. 995 or 998) massive bibliography, *al-Fihrist*. Poetry continues to exist alongside prose, but prose begins to occupy a larger proportion of the total output, as evidenced in Shihāb al-Dīn Abū al-ʿAbbās Aḥmad ibn.

ʿAlī b. Aḥmad ʿAbd Allah al-Qalqashandī's (d. 1418) fourteen volumes of chancery correspondence, *Ṣubḥ al-aʿshā fī ṣināʿat al-inshā* (The Dawn of the Benighted in the Craft of Fine Writing).

The ongoing competition between the two subdivisions of the literary spectrum—poetry and prose—can be detected in many meta-critical accounts and epistles. The competitive scope is more problematic and cannot be characterized simply as a passing displacement process among genres. The particular sphere of discussion demands both a wide and a highly specific knowledge.[41] To be a respectable jurist, for example, one must also be a grammarian, not only because discourse and speech require a firm grounding in grammar, but also because of the close theoretical relationship between the principles of jurisdiction and those of grammar. What can be seen in modern times, among those who term themselves "*Salafis*," as an advocacy of the need to return to principles of the righteous predecessors, albeit in a selective manner that vaults over serious historical problems, is in fact merely an attempt to duplicate a long-established traditionalist perspective. Accordingly, that same perspective continues to adopt in a thoroughly cursory fashion the principles of origin and branch to be found in studies on grammar, but without the kind of acumen and depth that is found in the work of Saʿd al-Dīn al-Taftazānī (d. 791/1389), who notes that "it is the origin that is built on."[42] In the book in which he discusses the application of jurisprudence on the basis of grammatical rules, Jamāl al-Dīn al-Isnāwī (d. 772/1370) establishes the connection in terms of the originary rule, *aṣl*.[43] Grammarians go further and suggest that the originary (i.e., the Qurʾān) is the one that accommodates no other, unique and by itself, according to a monotheistic belief.[44]

The Verbal Subtext of Hegemonic Discourse

Within the area of prose composition, we thus find ourselves faced directly with a conflation of the natural and the metaphysical. Even more significant is the fact that prose evolves as the battleground for ascendancy. The broad forum of theological debate had exploited the discussion of Qurʾānic inimitability (*iʿjāz*) to such an extent that for some time it had managed to override other areas; it might even have swallowed up rhetoric in its speculative reasoning and metaphysical theology, had it not been for the emergence of another genealogical linkage that took the form of the *badīʿiyyah* ode and its appended corpus of rhetorical devices.[45] This particular development evolved from within a poetic stronghold that diverted attention away from the sacred and toward the broadly textual. It decentered the former while underscoring the significance of figures, devices of expressiveness, and tropes, which gradually call for further investigation and exemplification. In the process, it displaces the core of the theological argument through a double transposition: from inimitability and Qurʾānic exegesis to a poetic terrain that adopts as its pretext none other than the Prophet of Islam himself, in order to consolidate a realm of art through its figural and rhetorical network. And yet even this new network undergoes its own further dispersion through separate alliances between the poetics of the double entendre and that of paronomasia.[46] Each of the two has its own lineage. The former, for example, traces its roots back to the magisterial prose of al-Qāḍī al-Fāḍil (The Erudite Magistrate) ʿAbd al-Raḥīm al-Baysānī (d. 596/1200), the chief minister and secretary of Ṣalāh al-Dīn (Saladin); through the prose of Muḥyī al-Dīn ibn ʿAbd al-Ẓāhir (d. 692/1293) and his powerful chancery coterie, for whom ibn Nubātah himself (d. 1366) was proud to be the person authorized to transmit and report their accounts and writings;[47] to that of ibn Ḥijjah and dozens of the most illustrious names in the middle period. The other line finds its representation primarily in the writings of Ṣalāh al-Ṣafadī, and also partly in those of Ṣafī al-Dīn al-Ḥillī,[48] whose roots go back to the rigorous line of robust prose characterized by density in presentation, dexterity in communication, and skill in the manipulation of rhetorical figures. Although there is a great deal of overlap in usage, both these lines are noticeably powerful only insofar as each is distinguished by its own specific rhetorical abundance. Both have effective qualities of political and social mediation. What has been mistakenly treated in earlier studies as a mere exercise in rhetoric or literary virtuosity is in fact tightly linked to a discursive struggle aimed at scoring a victory in a sociopolitical or theological domain. Al-Qāḍī al-Fāḍil, for example, was singled out by Ṣalāh al-Dīn as the one responsible for the liberation of Jerusalem in 1187, a point to which I return toward the end of this chapter. However, the dispute over the validity of every term is not merely some passing controversy. In rhetoric, it is connected to the issue of representation—its duplications, simulations, uses of similes, or resemblances. The double entendre as dissimulation breaks down the representational privilege of the high arts that are popular in the classical period, and brings poetics into a public domain where wit, humor, playfulness, erotic insinuations, and intrigue are now able to run rampant. Thus, when we come to understand this genealogical structuration that is spread over a number of centuries, we can perhaps conclude that the middle period has more to offer in terms of knowledge than has been commonly assumed. The literary mapping of this period can also easily find room for further classifications and divides, in the form of categories that continue to resist limits.[49]

The Breakdown of Representation

Perhaps some examples are in order at this juncture. Let us explore first how *tawriyah* (double entendre) can break down verisimilitude through shifting meaning, leaving the door open for a variety of interpretations and distortions. The process of breaking down the notion of resemblance should not be lightly dismissed, not only because it had already been in currency as a discursive and oral practice throughout Islamic history, but also, and primarily, because, thanks to that history, it had become an evasive style on its own merits, involving a subtle and oblique reference to abuses of power. It is likewise central to intellectual analysis whenever wit falls short of accommodating argumentation. Although primarily a binary structure—a drastic departure from a resemblance ternary—its basic motion is directed toward ideas and systematic thought.

I begin by considering its basic definition, its position in the context of its kinship grid, and also the way that it constructs the relational sites that are classified in compendiums of rhetoric by a number of Muslim scholars between the thirteenth and eighteenth centuries, culminating in ʿAbd al-Ghanī al-Nābulusī's *Nafaḥāt al-Azhār ʿalā Nasamāt al-Asḥār badīʿiyyah* (The Exhalations of Flowers on the Daybreak Breezes, in

Praise of the Chosen Prophet), with its extensive rhetorical figures and devices.[50] The double entendre, in Pierre Cachia's summary, is "the use of the word in two meanings—either both inherent or one inherent and the other metaphorical—in such a way that one of the two meanings is evident and the other concealed, yet it is the latter that is intended."[51] Although the following examples of double entendre—which Cachia selects from al-Nābulusī's—are taken from poetry, Cachia's definition applies equally to prose and indeed to a whole grid of speech and discourse, including twenty-nine items in Cachia's *Arch Rhetorician* that bring together stylistic, syntactic, and semantic fields along with methods of argumentation, logical reasoning, and adage (*sententia*). Even when applied to situations where the speaker is in harmony with authority, the use of double entendre still unsettles conformity and gestures toward divides based on class and other forms of power. Al-Qāḍī Muḥyī al-Dīn ibn ʿAbd Ẓāhir, for instance, is the last person to contemplate inciting a rebellion, and yet his avowedly eulogistic verse displays a basic master-slave, male-female (*mamlūk*, *jāriyah*) divide. His use of double entendre endows the "slave" referent with another meaning, a far-fetched signified that is conveyed through the combined use of the male epithet *mamlūk* (meaning: possessed or owned) and the female *jāriyah* (thus punning on its double meaning of female slave and also running). The verses read:

Master, though my tears and blood flow out,
  Shed by the eye and spilled by the heart,
Yet need you fear no retaliation,
  For my eye is *jāriyah* and my heart is *mamlūk*.[52]

The seemingly smooth figuration works within a large sign system that pervades the Arabic dynamic in Islamic culture. Without a shared understanding, response, and practice, there is no possibility of such a proliferation of figures, signs, and recapitulations.

In this context, it is helpful to compare Michel Foucault's use of a sign system to account for epistemological shifts in the Western order of knowledge. Foucault never claims to offer a universal systematization of this idea, and his archaeological analysis strictly applies to the sixteenth-century ternary sign system in the West, with its base in resemblance. A subsequent seventeenth- to eighteenth-century binary system, he suggests, dismantles an old order, and a following ideological age takes it still further. Insofar as a system of Islamic knowledge is concerned, we need to keep in mind at least a few demarcating moments that define knowledge and set the textual terrain for further analysis. In pre-Islamic times, within a belief system that adopted idolatry, correspondence operates between sign and meaning, idol and signification. During the subsequent Islamic era, this is replaced by a divine order whereby marks or signs are God's *āyāt*. Foucault discusses knowledge in the West as having been "handed down to us by Antiquity" until well into the sixteenth century, and has this to say on the subject: "The value of language lay in the fact that it was the sign of things. There is no difference between the visible marks that God has stamped upon the surface of the earth, so that we may know its inner secrets, and the legible words that the Scriptures, or the sages of Antiquity, have set down in the books preserved for us by tradition."[53] Assuming an all-encompassing, divinely imposed order, he concludes: "The truth of all these marks—whether they are woven into nature itself or whether they exist in lines on parchments and in libraries—is everywhere the same: coeval with the institution of God."[54] If Western rationalist discourse with its scientific underpinnings was able to disorient that legacy and dismantle similitude and analogy in seventeenth-century Europe, then I would suggest that Islamic discourse between the eighth and fifteenth centuries had already amassed a significant body of rationalist reasoning and philosophical discourse by which to account for new urban and cultural realities, involving important confrontations in metaphysics with traditionalists on issues of essence and occasion, eternity and creation, and methods of reasoning. At this intersection, the Arab-Islamic double entendre settles as a sign in an ambivalent space, an unresolved order of things. On the other hand, Foucault's analysis reveals that the seventeenth and eighteenth centuries in the West involved a rupture in the relation of signs to things: "The relation of the sign to the signified now resides in a space in which there is no longer any intermediary figure to connect them: what connects them is a bond established, inside knowledge, between the *idea of one thing* and the *idea of another*."[55] This pattern that Foucault perceives in the structural transformation of a seventeenth- and eighteenth-century episteme is significant for our current investigation of the place of the double entendre in a knowledge grid. The well-known seventeenth-century logic textbook *Logique de Port-Royal* reads as follows: "The sign encloses two ideas, one of the things representing, the other of the thing represented; and its nature consists in exciting the first by means of the second."[56]

Rhetoric, as perceived and studied across Islamic regions, dwelt extensively and thoroughly on signification, especially with respect to the study of the Qur'ān beyond the casual traditionalist *tafsīr* as exegesis. The effort to prove its inimitability (*iʿjāz*) in the context of the Muʿtazilite *ṣarfah* (diversion) of Arabs from its imitation accounts for the continuing sophistication in the study of signs and relations. That effort was carried out in particular by ʿAbd al-Qāhir al-Jurjānī (d. 471/1078) in his *Asrār al-balāghah* (The Mysteries of Eloquence) and *Dalā'il al-iʿjāz* (The Evidence of Inimitability). The double entendre, being an element central to tropics of discourse for a number of poets and essayists thereafter, may include etiological relations in a "witty invention of a fictitious cause" for a natural phenomenon. The latter is usually covered under the trope *ḥusn al-taʿlīl*, discussed by Julie Meisami as poetic discovery, not invention, whereby "latent correspondences" emerge as "imaginative evocation" of a seeming causation.[57] Scholars attest to the fictitious nature of causation on the basis of relationships between nature and man, but the limit of the trope puts it squarely in a Foucauldian schema for resemblance in the preclassical (sixteenth-century) Western episteme. What ʿAbd al-Qāhir al-Jurjānī reads as phantastic or etiological analogy is interpreted by al-Zamakhsharī (d. 538/1144) as the visual marks of God's omnipresence.[58] It can break away from its limits through the use of "wit," as alluded to by G.J. van Gelder, a point that is addressed by Rashīd al-Dīn al-Waṭwāṭ (d. 573/1182).[59]

Rhetoric for the State

Rhetoric reached its highest degree of sophistication across Islamic regions, enlisting the efforts of the most prominent names in theology and philosophy.[60] Along with ʿAbd al-Qāhir al-Jurjānī and al-Sakkākī, al-Ḥillī established an enormous rhetorical grid, one that cannot be read on its own or separated from an epistemological schema of lexical density and philosophical grounds, as the contributions of ʿAḍud al-Dīn ʿAbd al-Raḥmān ibn Aḥmad Ijī (d. 1355) clearly demonstrate.[61] When these works are considered in their entirety and independently of the political contexts of upheaval and decentralization, we notice that the features that Foucault assigns to the Age of Reason in Europe, a "single network of necessities" where new forms and methods apply, enlisting "probability, analysis, combination, and universal language system,"[62] also resonate clearly with each individual effort in central and East Asia, Andalusia, and the Arab west.

But, with all that in mind, the question that should concern us at this juncture is whether in fact there exists such an Islamic order, comparable to Foucault's "single network," or even whether it held particular sway in specific regions or subregions. Apart from political upheavals and the paradigm of rise and fall in dynastic structures, as noticed and predicated on an Arab/Muslim past by ibn Khaldūn (d. 808/1406), Islam as a religious institution with valence across many regions was never able to recover from its Ottoman political system or from European colonialism. But this same verdict can also be regarded in a different light: as a failure to look the realities of this past straight in the eye, and to realize that religion and piety remained separate from the state as inaugurated by the first Umayyad Caliph Muʿāwiyah (r. 41–60/661–680), who openly opposed the claims of the fourth "rightly chosen" caliph, the Prophet's cousin ʿAlī.[63] Islamic states, or the ones allegedly Islamic, resist any recognition of the historical problematic or admission of its basic structural problems. On the other hand, the Qurʾān—as the sacred text that signifies the pivot in guidance—leads, as is the case with Hebrew or Christian scriptures, to different schools of thought and interpretation, creating competitive discourses among traditionalists, speculative theologians, rationalists, and Sufis. If the traditionalist is bent on literal or semiliteral readings and interpretations, where resemblance and similitude stand foremost as guiding principles, the Sufis in contrast turn the ternary paradigm upside down, not to replace it with a binary one but to read signifiers as mediums for something else, beyond immediate natural (or even far-fetched) relevance. Sufi semiology strips language of its denotative role and sets it free. Words and nature leave their signified behind and assume new life in the soaring ecstasy of the liberated Sufi experience, which may be seen as a partial anticipation of postmodern musings on madness and poetry, as laid out, for example, in Foucault's reflections. He states: "The poet brings similitude to the signs that speak it [i.e., the other language], whereas the madman loads all signs with a resemblance that ultimately erases them. They share, then, on the outer edge of our culture and at the point nearest to its essential divisions, that 'frontier' situation—a marginal position and a profoundly archaic silhouette—where their words unceasingly renew the power of their strangeness and the strength of their contestation."[64] He concludes: "Between them there has opened up a field of knowledge in which, because of an essential rupture in the Western world, what has become important is no longer resemblances but identities and differences."[65]

The controversy that erupted around ibn al-ʿArabī during his life and posthumously may well situate us at this significant intersection, with its indirect pull toward a paradoxical engagement with piety as practice and its resistance to traditionalism, through not only its imposed limits on the sacred text but also (and beneath the surface) its espousal of *mulk* or state ideology as the justification of absolute rule.[66] Ibn al-ʿArabī's concept of *Waḥdat al-wujūd* (unity of being; existence) was one way of breaking up correspondence and resemblance (i.e., between human and nature) and replacing them with an order that establishes both as mere mediums in an otherwise luminous existence. His Sufism, which will be considered later in this study, cannot be seen outside the context of a parallel rise of philosophical discourse and the hold of poetics on ecstatic utterances and enunciations. Whether working in unison or as manifestations of rupture, both illustrate the propensity for the ongoing consolidation of a knowledge base. In Sufi thought, as in earlier philosophical thought, a register emerges that confounds traditionalists, the fideists in particular.[67] Moreover, the degree of sophistication that was reached in rhetoric, which tends to baffle modernists and incur the charge of superfluity, should be considered the natural outcome of an enormous amount of knowledge acquisition and a widespread cultural sphere of discussion. Its seeming incompatibility with a political order marked by imperial wars and massive destruction provides us with clues to an understanding of the Islamic order as another name for disparate entities, where different identities, native traditions, customs, and newly rising aspirations for control and expansion militate against both a master narrative of one Islamic ideology and a conceptualization of a centralized empire. It is worthwhile to recall Casanova's conclusion that "literary capital is not simply a bonus or 'added extra' that automatically attends the accumulation of economic or political capital."[68] Only on rare occasions do we find rulers and monarchs striving to bring the two together, usually at the expense of other nations and cultures. Tīmūr's itinerary of bloody conquests, for example, is matched by his mastery of historical records and disputation. Thus ibn ʿArabshāh admits: "He was well-versed in books and histories, whence he sought aid in his speeches and replies."[69] In another reported incident in which the conqueror held a meeting with Damascene religious leaders and theologians, the scene conveys a mind prone to argumentation and discussion to a degree that baffled and shocked those who could not digest more than one unitary discourse, including the narrator ibn ʿArabshāh, who could not control his anti-Muʿtazilī and anti-Shīʿī sentiments.[70] The centrality of this combined knowledge to political conquest finds no better evidence than in the example of Tīmūr, but it does not necessarily detract from Casanova's premise, nor does it challenge the argument of this book that political disintegration is not concomitant with cultural failure. On the other hand, rhetoric holds sway as much as history and military strategy in times of war and expansion.

Another, albeit different, corroboration of the power of rhetoric and its relatively unique influence is the example of Ṣalāḥ al-Dīn al-Ayyūbī (i.e., Saladin; d. 1193) and his chief secretary and advisor, the Erudite Magistrate (al-Qāḍī al-Fāḍil). After the liberation of Jerusalem (October 2, 1187) and the Treaty of Ramla in 1192, Saladin made it clear how decisive was the role of such an epistolographer as the Erudite Magistrate. Saladin's praise may well remind us of another example from eighteenth-century Europe, where Frederick the Great ranked d'Alembert's *Preliminary Discourse* above the best of his own military achievements: "Many men have won battles and conquered provinces," he wrote to d'Alembert, "but few have written a work as perfect as the preface to the *Encyclopedia*."[71] It was al-Qāḍī al-Fāḍil who brought into rhetoric a definite preference for specific stylistic tropes and figures. In its comprehensive engagement with philological and semantic inquiry, rhetoric includes *ʿilm al-maʿānī* (stylistics of syntax), *ʿilm al-bayān* (science of tropes and figures), and *ʿilm al-badīʿ* (stylistic novelty and adornment). Developed and promoted over time by grammarians, logicians and poets, it courts morphology, syntax, prosody, and logic. No wonder that commentaries on purely theological questions often dwell on these features as basic to an understanding and thus interpretation of a text and its applications. The double entendre emerges as a primary structural device used by poets and epistolographers who happened to assume leading state responsibilities, particularly al-Qāḍī al-Fāḍil, Ṣalāḥ al-Dīn's minister and companion. The successor of al-Qāḍī al-Fāḍil, ibn Nubātah, boasts of his place in the established school of double entendre as rooted in the writing and poetry of al-Qāḍī al-Fāḍil, and of how he carries on the tradition, as is duly recorded in the writings of ibn Ḥijjah, who offers examples whereby *jinās* and *tawriyah* (double entendre) easily conflate. A word with a number of meanings and rhymes can also point to a distant meaning:

What charm there is in a cupbearer [*sāqī*] who says:
    if your wine is finished, then my glances will offer enough satiety
He uncovers his leg [*sāq*; i.e., embarks with enthusiasm] to quench
        our thirst [*saqā*]:
    wars of passion broke out to ensure his [*sāqī*'s] love.[72]

The different meanings of *sāq* and *sāqī* are here collapsed so as to provide a theme commonly encountered in wine and *ghazal* poetry, a blend of homoerotic and love poetry. Although a common theme, it is inserted into a dense lexical and rhetorical space that relates to a speaker who courts individualization and thereby anticipates the elimination of any presumed barriers or divides between high and low genres.[73]

There are also examples where the current terms of an "aesthetic logic of a mode of visibility" better apply, since these terms are played out in the open, free from constraint. Not circumscribed by strict adherence to rules, they accommodate the urge to have a say in poetry or social criticism.[74] Ibn Ḥijjah was obsessed by the ghost of his predecessor, Ṣafī al-Dīn al-Ḥillī, who was highly acclaimed for his inventiveness and innovation. Hence, he picks out a verse by al-Ḥillī that he paradoxically duplicates. In this verse, which uses the common or stock image of *asyāf laḥẓ* (fatal glances like swords),[75] al-Ḥillī inserts the sword of the Prophet's cousin ʿAlī into the eyes of Abū Bakr (the first, "rightly guided" caliph, implying thereby ʿAlī's renowned might and swordsmanship). The verse itself reads as follows: "Had your eyes ever seen the face of my tormentor: when visiting me after long estrangement and separation / you would have traced a welcome in my heart: and the sword of ʿAlī in the eyes of Abī Bakr." Ibn Ḥijjah duly cites this as an example of not only *tawriyah*, double entendre, but also of al-Ḥillī's *rafḍ* (rejection) of the succession process following the Prophet's death: "God will surely confront him on this for his guile and bad manners."[76] When inserting itself into the realm of street poetry, the double entendre blends even further with *jinās* (paronomasia) both to evoke amorous pleasure and to incite communal jubilation or counter-preaching. The application of metric and rhyming systems fluctuates and at times is confounded with parody, contrafaction, sarcasm, and straightforward diatribe, especially in the seventeenth century. The overall presence of rhetoric as a massive and dense practice obviously provides communities and the state with further power, which can be decisive at times in resolving issues, disputes, and wars. The negative effects of this accumulation of rhetoric cannot be underestimated. They do not stem from its sophistication but rather from its superfluity and unwarranted proliferation among rhetoricians and poets, a proliferation that invoked sarcasm and biting satire, as al-Shirbīnī's *Hazz al-quḥūf* shows.

Figure 1. Ikhwān al-Ṣafāʾ (The Pure Brethren; 908 – 980), *Rasāʾil ikhwān al-ṣafāʾ wa khullān al-wafāʾ* (Epistles of the Pure Brethren and the Sincere Friends), Baghdad, MS dated 686/1287. Istanbul, Süleymaniye Library, Esad Efendi 3638, fol. 4v. Courtesy of Süleymaniye Library.

نصرت فتح و ظفر اقبال جاه سلطنت

باد باقی بهر دوران تا هست امکان بقا

عامل اندر نحو صد باشد چنین فرموده است

شیخ عبد القاهر جرجانی پیر هدا

معنوی از وی دو باشد جمله را لفظی شناس

باز لفظی شد سماعی و قیاسی ای فتا

زان نود و یک دان سماعی هفت دیگر را قیاس

وان سماعی سیزده نوعست بی ریب و ریا

قسم اول را سماعی دان نوعش سیزده

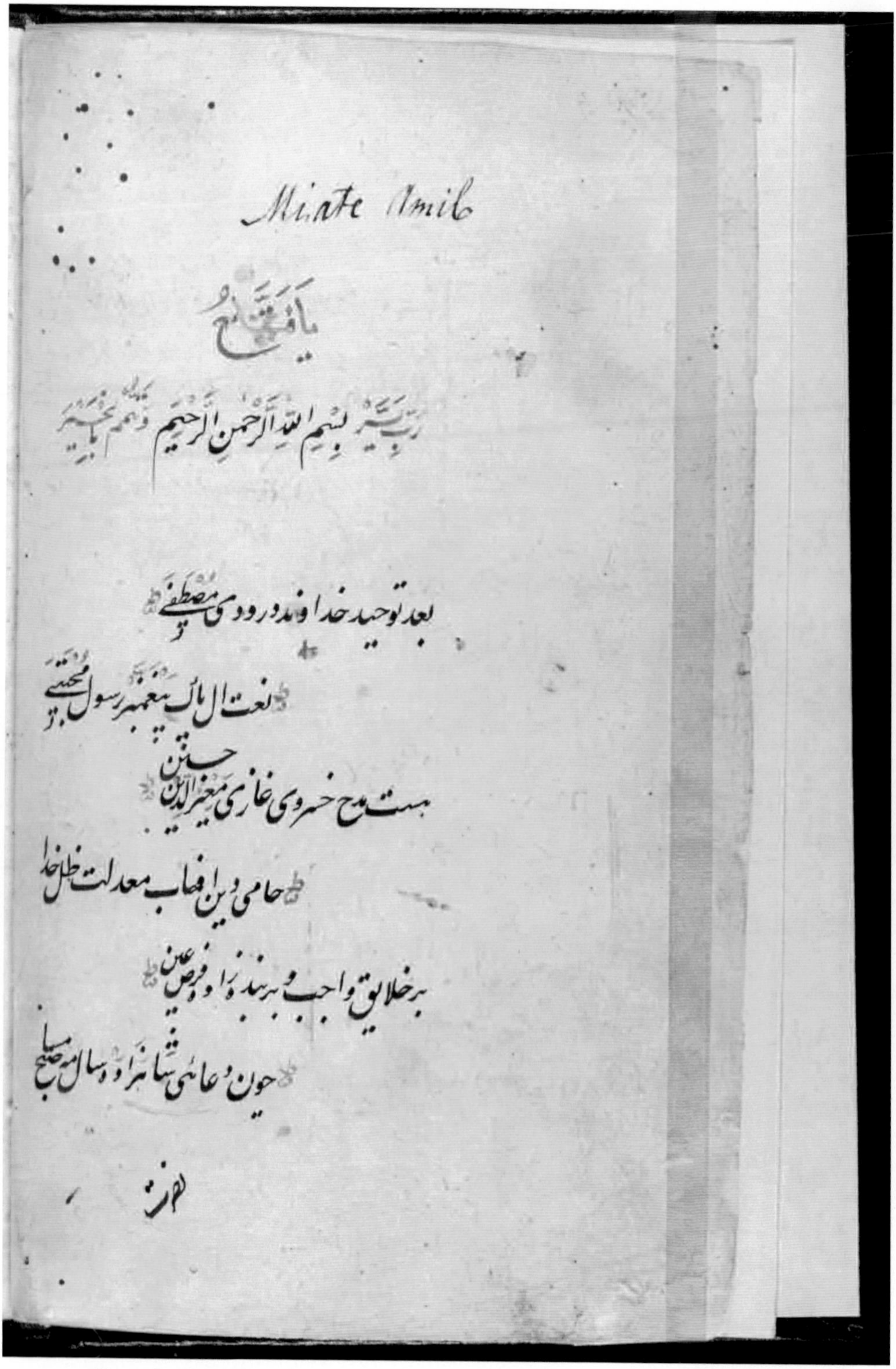

Figure 2. Al-ʿAwāmil al-Miʾah (The One Hundred Regents), by ʿAbd al-Qāhir ibn ʿAbd al-Raḥmān al-Jurjānī (d. 1078?), translated into Persian verse. A grammatical work on Arabic syntax. Beinecke Rare Book & Manuscript Library, Yale University.

الفصاحة ولما كان هذا الانواع واحوال الكتابة واشكال ذلك اشار الى
ان ان ذلك الخفا بقوله يظهر ذلك في التي مر التذكر لما تقدم من الاصول
والقواعد المذكورة في الفنون الثلاثة يمكن الاطلاع على تفاريقها
وتفاصيلها الا لعلام الغيوب فانه يظهر بتذكرها ان كلا بمن ذلك وقع
موقعه في النظر في مقتضيات الاحوال وان كلا من التسوير في التنبيه في
الكمح الذي تضمنه شملا على لطف الفالح حسطوية على حسن الخاتمة ختم الله
لنا بالحسنى ويسر لنا الفوز في الآخرة الاسنى بحق نبي وآله الامجاد
قد فرغ من تسويد فرغت من تسويد هذا المختصر المختصر بعون الله الملك
الاكبر وقت الظهر يوم الخميس من الثاني والعشرين
شهر رمضان المبارك ورزقنا في صومه وصلوته
الخشوع والاذعان والصلوة على نبيه الذي
خلق لاجله الكون والمكان وعلى آله
الذين بلغوا في الايمان واصحابه
الذين اتبعوهم باحسان
الكاتب الحقير الفقير
المذنب العاصي
المفتقر الى الله
زين العابدين
ابن حسين التزوري
اللهم اغفر له سنة ١٢٣٣

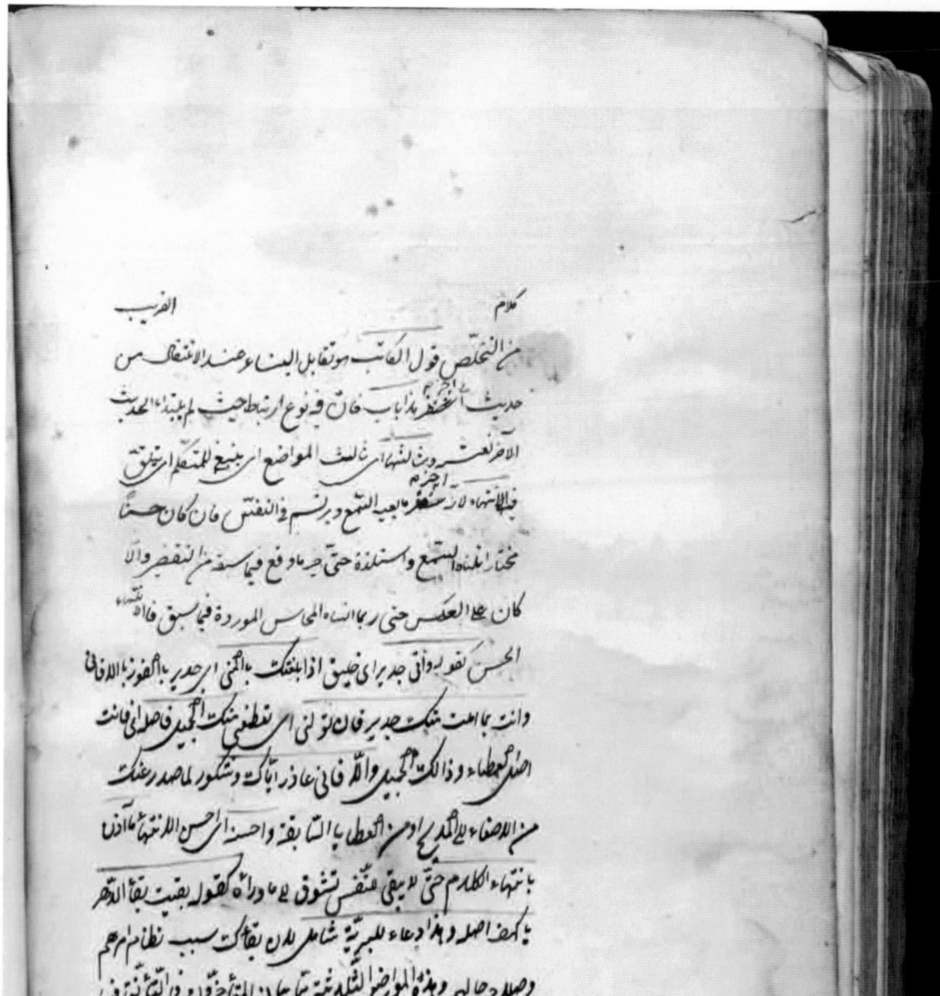

Figure 3. Talkhīṣ Miftāḥ al-ʿUlūm (Resumé of the Key to the Sciences), by Muḥammad ibn ʿAbd al-Raḥmān Jalāl al-Dīn al-Qazwīnī, Khaṭīb Dimashq (d. 739/1338). Beinecke Rare Book & Manuscript Library, Yale University.

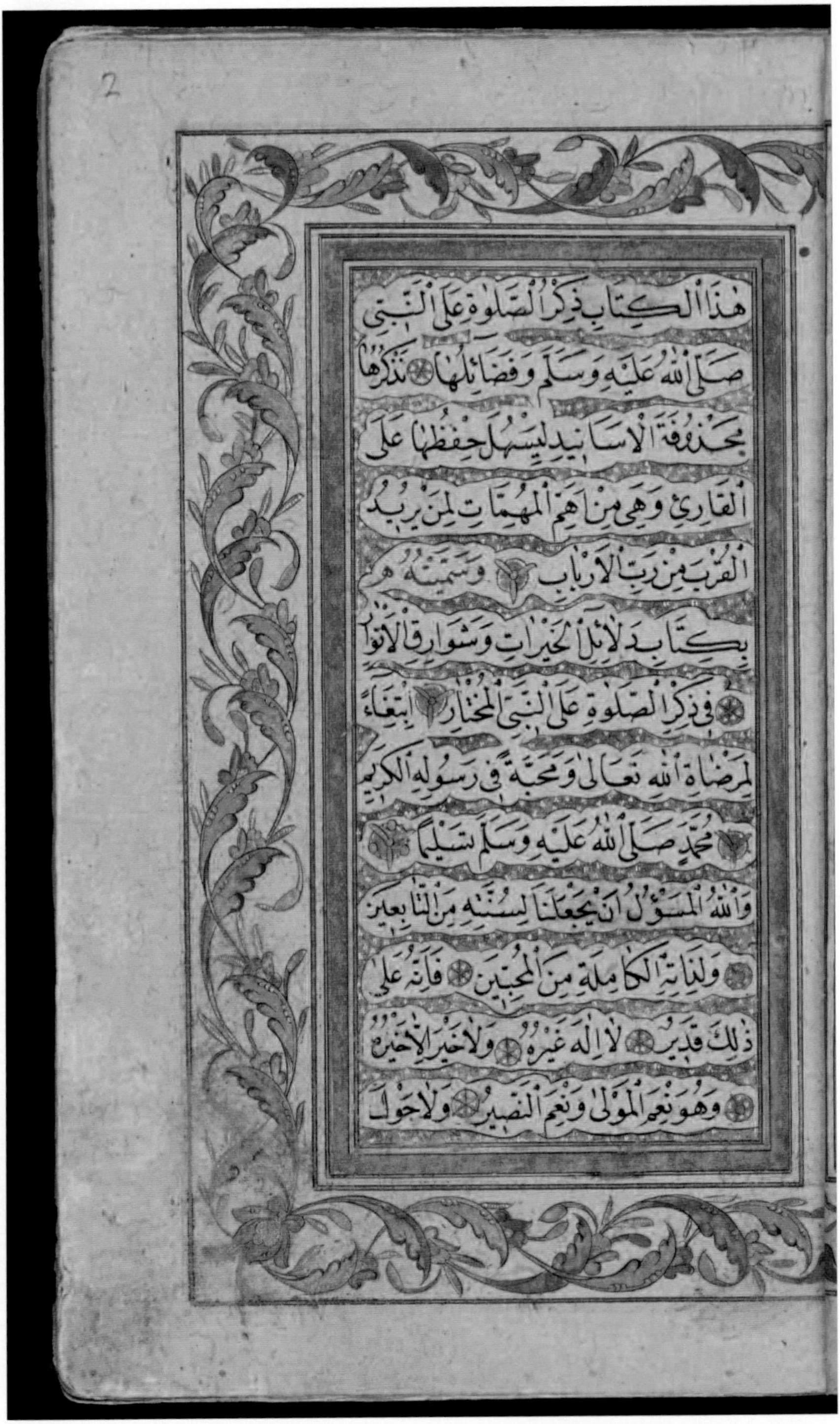

Figure 4. Dalāʾil al-Khayrāt wa-Shawāriq al-Anwār fī Dhikr al-Ṣalāh ʿalā al-Nabī al-Mukhtār (Guide to Blessings and Shining Lights Regarding Prayers on the Chosen Prophet), by Abū ʿAbd Allāh Muḥammad ibn Sulaymān al-Jazūlī (d. 1465).

One of the most famous books of prayer in Islamic literature. Undated, but most likely copied in the eighteenth century. Beinecke Rare Book & Manuscript Library, Yale University.

ولم يبرع لصاحبه ذمام وقال يجو الى كعبه هذا
البيت الحرام وكم شن الغارة على ذباء عمر
فأخلا ابياتها العامرة بالمحاسن من السكان وقال
انا قاضي الادب وامام الحقيقة نقلنا لا شك هذا
القاضي خان نعم هو ذو الفقه شاعر الباري
وهو في الشعر احد الفقهاء لا الى هؤلاء لا لمبني
وجروا ولا الى هوى لاء ثم طفى وتكبر وبغي
وبخر واجلب على الناس بخيله ورجله وحاصل
ابناء الاصالة لما يبني عن اصل حتى الله قال المرء
دمرارا وملاء من اصحابه ان مملكة مصر لم يصير لها
جمال لا به وقال مرت لو شئت كل ولصفة لبيت
ولكني ولله لو اعلين الخلا فمن مارضيت
دناكي بباب الجامع الازهر على رؤس الانامل
والاماتل كل من قرا المشرق والمغرب تحت خفي ونازل
واذا كانت النفوس كبارا تعبت في مرادها الاجسام
ولست للشعر احتاج رحي واعتمدى في جميع
نظمه ونثره على ارتجله عن مادته الاحوال

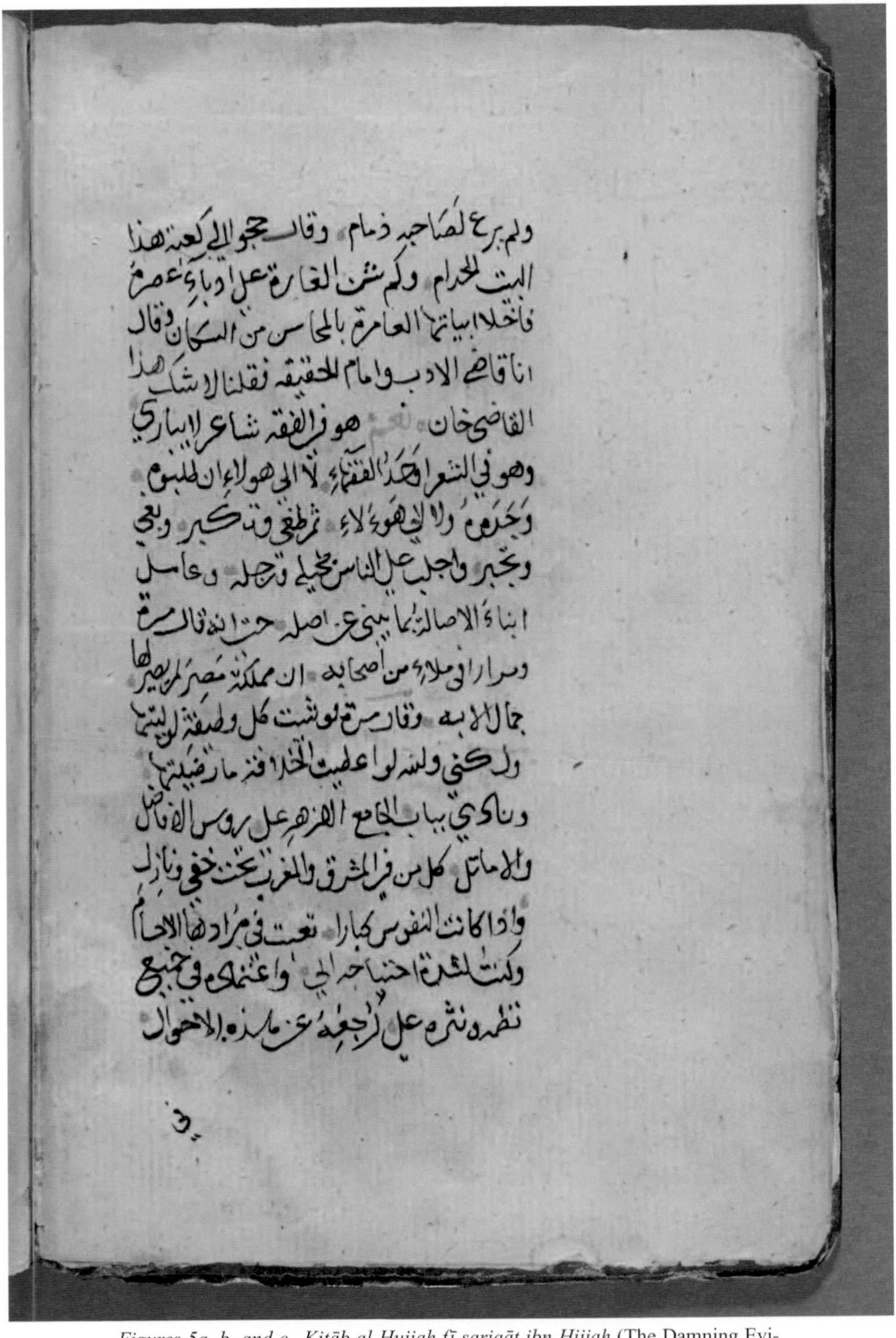

Figures 5a, b, and c. Kitāb al-Ḥujjah fī sariqāt ibn Ḥijjah (The Damning Evidence of ibn-Ḥijjah's Plagiarisms), by Shams al-Dīn Muḥammad ibn Ḥasan al-Nawājī (d. 1455), undated, MS Arab 285, Houghton Library, Harvard University.

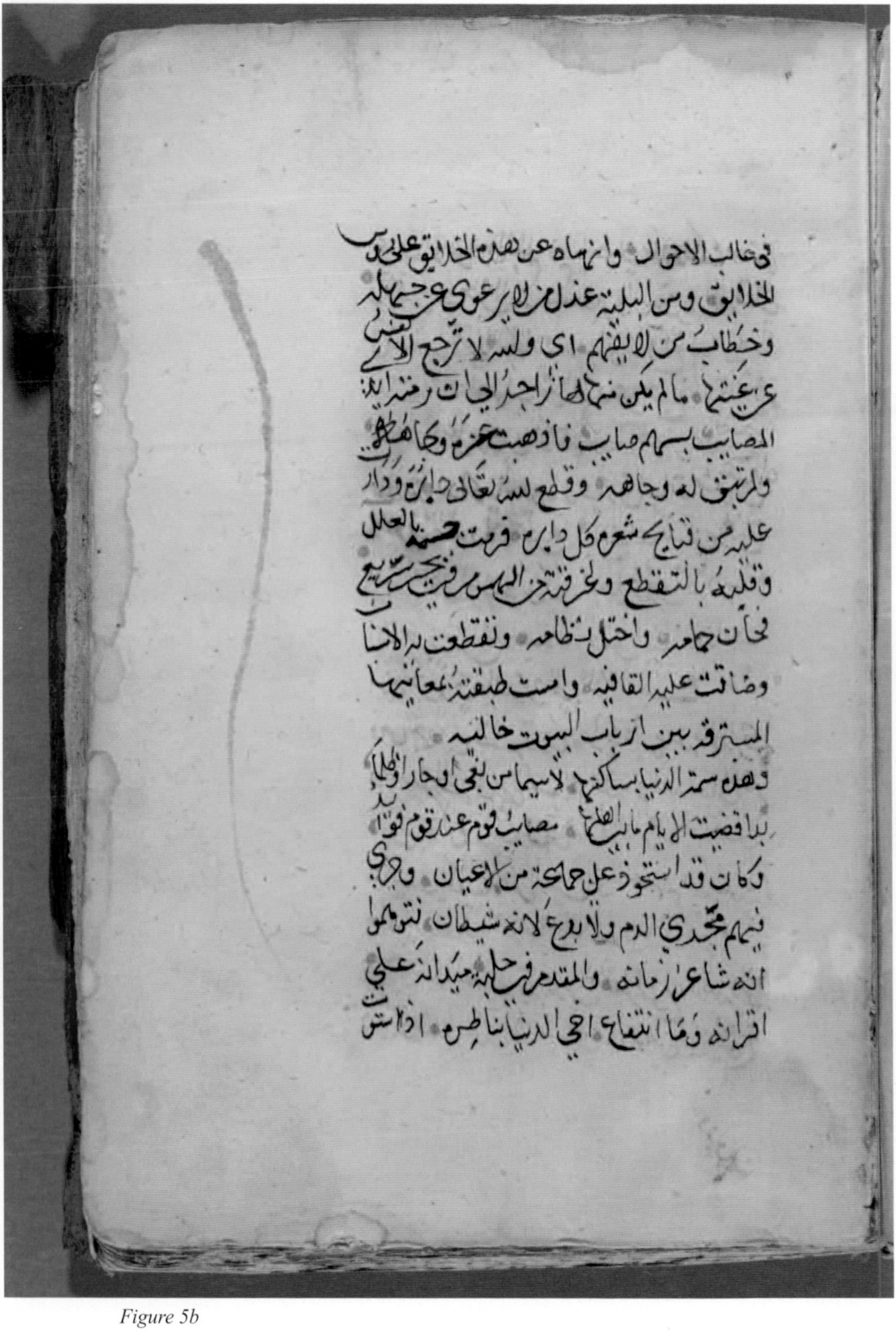

في غالب الاحوال وانهاه عن هذه الخلايق على درس
الخلايق ومن البلية عذل من لا يرعوي عن جهله
وخطاب من لا يفهم اي والله لا ترجع الا نفس
عن غيها مالم يكن منها لها زاجر اليات رمته ايدي
المصايب بسهام صايب فاذهبت عزمه وكاهله
ولم تبق له وجاهه وقطع الله تعالى جابره ودار
عليه من نتايج شعره كل داير قرمت حسنه بالعلل
وقلبه بالتقطع ولحرفته الناس في بحر سريع
فخان جامه واختل نظامه وانقطعت به الاسباب
وضاقت عليه القافيه واست لطبقته معانيها
المسترقه بين ارباب البيوت خاليه
وهذه سمة الدنيا بساكنها لاسيما من بغى او جار او ظلما
بذا قضت الايام مابين اهلها مصايب قوم عند قوم فوايد
وكان قد استحوذ على جماعة من الاعيان ومن
بينهم مجدي الدم ولا بدع لانه شيطان نشو مموا
انه شاعر زمانه والمتقدم في حلبة ميدانه على
اقرانه وما انتفاع اخي الدنيا بناظره اذا استوت

Figure 5b

عين الانوار والظلم فلم يأخذني عند ذلك مستقر
واعتبرت حركات مضطرب واستخرت الله تعالى
في تصنيف هذا الكتاب وبيان ما وقع له من الخطا
معتقدا انه الصواب [illegible] على جميع سرقاته
مجد ساله على رؤس الاشهاد بما اظهره من فضيح
عملاته مناديا عليه وسارق ابيات شعر غيره
لا يعرف النظم ولا يحسن اياك ان تسرق يا فتى
بيتا فلص البيت لا يوسن ليعلم ذووا الآداب
انه عري عن الادب ويتحقق ابنا الكتاب
انه حري بان يرد الى الكتاب
ومن جهلت نفسه قدره راى غيره منه ما لا يرى
وسميته الحجة في سرقات ابن حجة والله تعالى يعمر
[illegible] بذكره ويبدلنا من هذه الدار الفانية قصورا
عالية ويكفينا شر الذين ظلموا انفسهم فتلك بيوتهم
خاوية ولنبدأ الآن بالكلام على خطبته [illegible]
الوجوه قال لحمد لله الذي ابحر مجموع فضله ديوان
ذلك قصد بيت المناسبة في اللفظتين كلمة مجموع
ديوان

Figure 5c

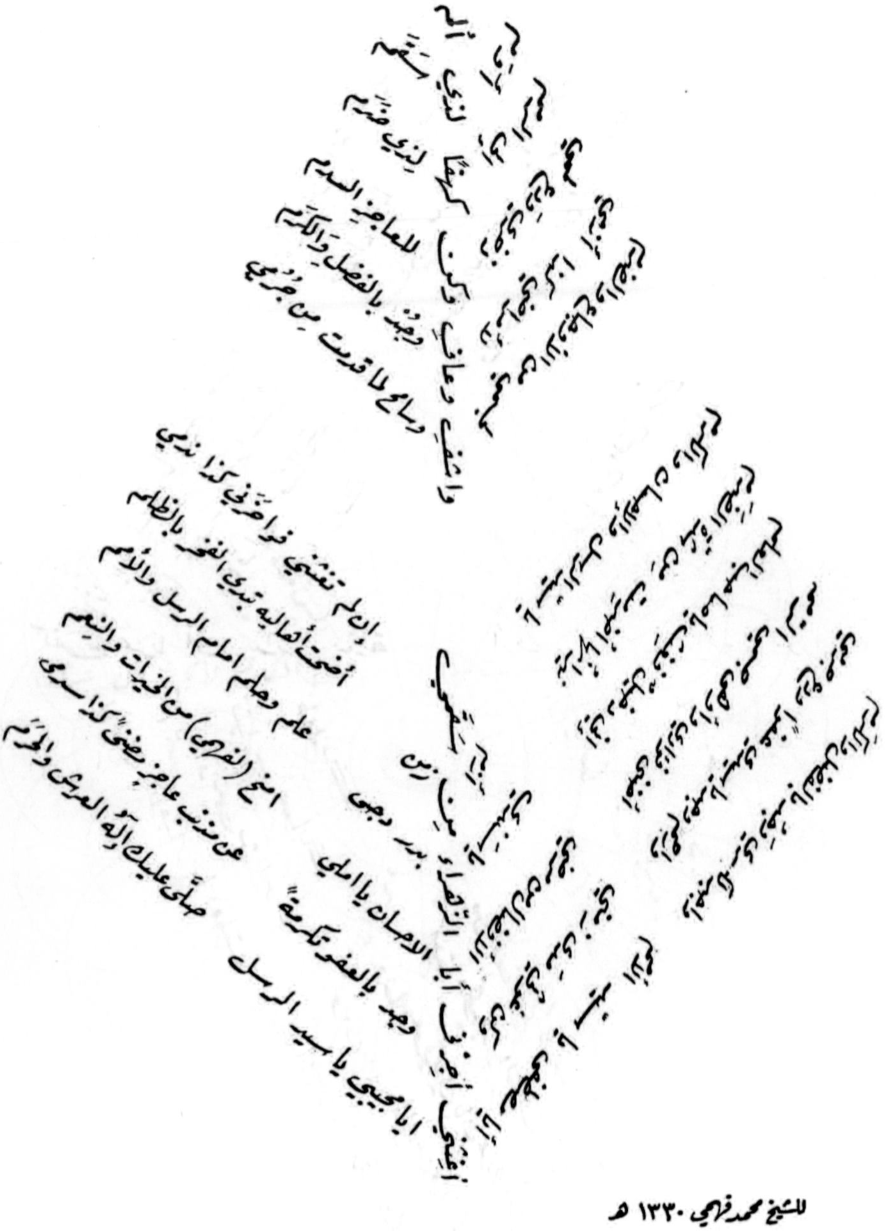

Figure 6. The Tree-like Poetic Form. Bakrī Shaykh Amīn, *Muṭālaʿāt fī al-shiʿr al-Mamlūkī wa-al-ʿUthmānī*, 182. Beirut: Dār al-ʿIlm lil-Malāyīn, 2007.

قفوت بمدح لا يضاهي ثنا فــتى ‏ على فضله تثني القوافي وتنطـــــق

قلمتُ بنظم فضلُه شاع ، رأسَ من ‏ يعاديه في العليا وعينه تـــرمـــــق

قطنت اليه في أجلّ مكانـــــــة ‏ وبين الورى في مدحه لي تَعَشَّـــق

قمرت بنظمي في الورى كلّ شاعر ‏ وبالأصل لي والله فيه تعـــــرُّق

قشعت تمامَ الجهل والله يــا فتى ‏ بمدحه قد ضَجّ العدى منه ترهـــق

قرعت .....

....

٢١٣

Figure 7. The Geometrical Form in the Poetry of the Middle Period. Bakrī Shaykh Amīn, *Muṭālaʿāt fī al-shiʿr al-Mamlūkī wa-al-ʿUthmānī*, 213. Beirut: Dār al-ʿIlm lil-Malāyīn, 2007.

An Inventory of al-Ḥillī's Reading List and Library in Rhetoric. Al-Ḥillī, *Sharḥ al-kāfiyah al-badīʿiyyah fi ʿulūm al-balāghah wa- maḥāsin al-badīʿ* (The Explication of the Sufficient *Badīʿiyyah* Ode in Rhetorical Sciences and Adornments in Innovativeness). Ed. Nasīb Nashāwī. Beirut: Dār Ṣādir, 1982.

عدة الكتب السبعين

[التي وعد في الخطبة بتفصيلها]

وهذه عدّةُ الكتبِ السّبعينَ التي وعدتُ في الخطبة بتفصيلها.

قالَ الشّيخ زكي الدين عبد العظيم بن أبي الإصبَع رحمه الله في صدر كتابه : "التحرير":

ولقد وقفتُ من هذا العلم على أربعين كتاباً، منها ما هو مُنْفردٌ به، وما هذا العلم أو بعضه داخلٌ فيه وهي:

[١و٢] نقدا قدامة

[٣] وبديع ابن المعتز

[٤] وحلية المحاضرة في صناعة الشعر لابن المظفر الحاتمي

[٥] والصناعتين للعسكري

[٦] والعمدة لابن رشيق

[٧] وتزييف نقد قدامة لإبن رشيق

[٨] ورسالة ابن بشر الآمدي التي ردّ بها على قدامة

[٩] وكشف الظلامة للموفق عبد اللطيف البغدادي

[١٠] وإعجاز القرآن لإبن الباقلاني

[١١] والكشّاف للزمخشري

[١٢] والنكت في الإعجاز للرّماني

[١٣] والجامع الكبير في التفسير له

[١٤] والتعرف والإعلام للسهيلي

[١٥] ودرّة التنزيل وغرّة التأويل للخطيب

[١٦] ودلائل الإعجاز للجرجاني

[١٧] وأسرار البلاغة له

[١٨] ونظم القرآن للجاحظ

[١٩] والبيان والتبيين للجاحظ

[٢٠] وإعجاز إبن الخطيب

[٢١] ورسالة الصولي التي قدّمها على شعر أبي نواس

[٢٢] ورسالته في أخبار أبي تمّام

[٢٣] ورسالة ابن أفلح

[٢٤] وشروح أبي العلاء الثلاثة وهي: ذكرى حبيب

[٢٥] وعبث الوليد

[٢٦] ومعجز أحمد

[٢٧] والمنصف لابن وكيع

[٢٨] والموازنة للآمدي

[٢٩] والوساطة للجرجاني

[٣٠] والغرر والدرر للمرتضى

[٣١] وكتاب الصرفة له

[٣٢] والمجاز لأخيه الرضي

وما لخصه في آخره من بديع الحديث{ وشرح حديث أم زرع للقاضي عياض}

[٣٣]

[٣٤] والحديقة للحجاري -براءة مهملة - صاحب المسهب في أخبار أهل المغرب

[٣٥] وبديع التبريزي

[٣٦] وسر الفصاحة لابن سنان الخفاجي

[٣٧]والمثل السائر لابن أثير الجزيرة

[٣٨] والإقناع للصاحب بن عباد

[٣٩] وبديع أبي اسحاق الأجدابي

[٤٠] وبديع شرف الدين التيفاشي. وهو آخر من نقل عنه في كتابه المذكور

فوقفتُ بعد أنْ أنهيتُ كتابَه المذكور مطالعةً وتحقيقاً على ثلاثين كتاباً في هذا العِلم لم يقف عليها، منها ما هو قبله، ومنها ما أُلِّفَ بعدَهُ وهي:

[١] كتابُ المفتاح لسراج الدين أبي يعقوب السكاكي رحمه الله
[٢] وكتاب الخراج لقُدامة
[٣] ونقد الشعر لابن جنّي
[٤] والكنايات للقاضي الجرجاني
[٥] والبديع لأبي أحمد العسكري
[٦] والبديع للمطرِّزي
[٧] ونقد الشعر لابن الخشّاب
[٨] والبيان لابن السكيِّت
[٩] والبيان لابن مقلة
[١٠] والترجيح والموازنة لأبي الحسن بن أبي عمرو التَّوقاني
[١١] وتكملةُ الصناعةِ في شرح نقد قُدامة لعبد اللطيف بن يوسف البغدادي
[١٢] والفلك الدائر على المثل السائر لابن أبي حديد
[١٣] وكتاب الشعر والشعراء للجاحظ
[١٤] والبرهان لعبد الواحد بن خلف الأنصاري
[١٥] وعيار الشِّعر لابن طباطبا
[١٦] وشرح المفتاح لمولانا قطب الدين الشيرازي
[١٧] والمعيار لعز الدين الزنجاني
[١٨] والتبيان لابن خطيب زملكا
[١٩] والتنبيهات على مافي «التبيان» من التمويهات للشيخ أبي [المُطَرِّف] أحمد بن عبد الله المخزومي المغربي

[٢٠] والمصباح لبدر الدين بن مالك

وشرح ضوء المصباح لبدر الدين بن النخوية الحموي الذي سمّاه إسفار الصباح

[٢١]

[٢٢] وطريق الفصاحة لابن النفيس المصري

[٢٣] ومقدمة ابن الأثير الجزَريّ

[٢٤] ولُمَعُ الصناعة لمحمد بن أحمد الأردَسْتاني

[٢٥] وقَطْعُ الدَّابر من الفلك الدائر

[٢٦] والتجريد للشيخ ميثم البحراني

[٢٧] والمنتخب للشاغوري

[٢٨] والأقصى القريب في صناعة الأديب لزين الدين التنوخي المعري

[٢٩] والبديع لقاضي القضاة شهاب الدين ابن قاضي القضاة شمس الدين الخوبي

والتلخيص لقاضي القضاة جلال الدين القزويني خطيب الجامع بدمشق المحروسة

[٣٠] وهو آخر ما صنف في عصري

وأكثر هذه الكتب موجودة عندي، وتخلّف عندي غيرها مما لم أضطر إلى مطالعته لقلّة اشتهاره. والحمد لله حق حمده، وصلّى الله على سيدنا محمد وآله وصحبه وسلم، وحسبنا الله ونعم الوكيل.

تمّ وكمل والحمد لله وحده.

سابع عشر رجب الأحب الحرام الفرد المبارك. من سنة ست وستين وسبعمائة

٧٦٦ هـ.

وصلواته على خير خلقه محمد وآله.

تمت الكافية البديعية بعون الله تعالى وحسن توفيقه في سادس عشرين غرّة المحرّم الحرام من شهور سنة تسع وأربعين وثمانمائة.

chapter five

SUPERFLUOUS PROLIFERATION OR GENERATIVE INNOVATION?

The accumulation of cultural capital along lines that prompt and valorize new ideas lays down solid national and popular bases for a worldwide cultural system. Cities and city-states in the Islamic world happened to be the spaces, media, and dynamic players in this transaction. But as with any kind of accumulation, there is always the possibility of overproduction alongside inventiveness. Together with significant contributions in the *badīʿiyyah* tradition and classical verse (which nevertheless continued to lose much of its cultural primacy), however, there appeared works such as Yūsuf al-Shirbīnī's *Kitāb hazz al-quḥūf bi-sharḥ qaṣīd Abī Shādūf* (Brains Confounded by the Ode of Abū Shādūf), noted earlier, that are sufficiently satirical to call into question the validity of the rhetorical corpus, compendiums, and *badīʿiyyah* tradition, especially in uncongenial environments such as an impoverished countryside. Indeed, a large body of the so-called elite culture may fail to provide the right "cultural script" for the countryside.

Yūsuf al-Shirbīnī's work was completed in 1097/1686 and later published in printed form at the government press of Būlāq in 1274/1858; it was reprinted six times thereafter as a "commercial venture by an entrepreneur."[1] The book is not merely a humorous account of the life of peasants, their habits of speech and lifestyles, and a satirical profile of country jurists, nor is it merely about the hypocrisy of many orders of *fuqarāʾ* (mendicants). Since the work caters more to oral performance than to reading publics, we need to examine the semiotic levels of its narrative, starting with the title itself. The title is meant to parody the ongoing vogue for commentary (*sharḥ*) or explicatory compendiums that are supposed to accompany odes or poems,[2] a trend established by Ṣafī al-Dīn al-Ḥillī in particular, not only in the encomiums to the Prophet and *badīʿiyyah* tradition but also in the other *shurūḥ* (explications) of poems or epistles that were among the distinctive features of production throughout the fourteenth through the seventeenth centuries. The fact that the illustrious name of Sharaf al-Dīn Abū ʿAbdullāh Muḥammad ibn Saʿīd al-Būṣīrī (d. 696?/1297?) is repeated, parodied, and grossly overstepped in al-Shirbīnī's work is meant to draw attention to the communication gap between what is taken for granted as fashionable and the actual loss of touch with the countryside. The countryside, as represented in the highly accentuated Abū Shādūf's *qaṣīd*, either distorts what it hears or has no sense of the legacy of poetry, the Qurʾān, and hadith—apart, that is, from the things learnt from ignorant imams or from no less ignorant parents. The author, in the role of an arch-narrator who every now and then emerges under his own signature, compiles from his subject/narrator-poet's corpus detailed accounts of preachers, jurists, and imams who are castigated for their ignorance and perfidy. The term *hazz al-quḥūf* (brains confounded; also implying a drum or cap quivering out of bewilderment or incomprehension) undermines the gravity and sonority that are the intention of a series of long rhyming titles for odes in the *badīʿiyyah* tradition or in their commentaries and relevant or consequential book-length explications and debates. The rhyming in the title (*quḥūf* and *Shādūf*) is specifically intended to debunk this ongoing practice as a technique that is not confined to the title alone but rather covers a variety of topics, including prosody, derivation, morphology, conjugation, and fake documentation. On the other hand, its double narrators (and indeed its double-layered narrative—operating between, on the one hand, the high classical narrative of historical or literary significance and, on the other hand, the colloquial, slang, and variegated peasants' discursive plane) offer a dense graphic account of a dreadful way of life. It also presents the listener/reader with a deliberate juxtaposition, one that exemplifies the collapse during the medieval period of the divide between the spoken and the written, especially in historiography and poetry (noticeable in the writings of ibn Iyās, ibn Ḥijjah, and Ṣafī al-Dīn al-Ḥillī). We can also observe the way in which the text juxtaposes urban and rural practices in confrontation, while from a purely textual perspective the narrator exercises a sole monopoly on narrative or commentarial space. The narrative account offered by the text, the layered languages, and the multiple narratives serve to contrafact compendiums and especially commentaries (*shurūḥ*), at the same time bringing into the open the disparity between what has been practiced and observed or discussed and the life of another "nation," characterized by poverty and thickheadedness—traits that the narrator ascribes, not without many a paradox, to peasants.

While attributing a grossness in life, language, communication, naming, dialogue, practice, and lovemaking to peasants as one aspect of a disposition nurtured in the countryside, beyond the reach of urbanity, the self-reflexive author glosses over positive aspects of their communal life and reiterates that peasants are prone to jealousy, fighting, name-calling, insult, and aggression. He also depicts scenes where the Ottoman military and their rural representatives humiliate, beat, and murder peasants who cannot comply with their unbearable tax policies. In the following section, I will sketch the ways in which al-Shirbīnī deliberately embarks on his work as a contribution to contrafaction, one that starts with the title itself and moves on to the *sharḥ* (commentary, spoof exposition, or even sardonic exegesis), in the process passing through a constellated prosimetrum of *qaṣīd* (verse) and prose and supplying each segment with a deliberately amassed reservoir of narratives, quotes, examples from poetry, history, and theology, and an impressive lexical repertoire of insults, grossness, and lewdness.

The Transgeneric Medium: *Hazz al-quḥūf*

The publication of *Hazz al-quḥūf* is worth noting not only for its deliberate role as an example of contrafaction, but also for its own offshoots, which set it apart as a complex product that parodies and contrafacts while carving out a path of a mixed transgeneric medium. It contains not only parody but also spurious transmission, along with highly graphic detail of life in the countryside. Its mixture of genres, styles, and diction occurs historically during the period of the Ottoman rule of Egypt, but in terms of knowledge acquisition, its registers poke fun at an era of fecund production, one that is certainly abundant and yet so completely irrelevant to the peasantry that it incites the author to denigrate it. However, beneath the veneer of sarcasm there is also recognition. The author is intimately aware of this abundance of textual production, but he is also angry at its aloofness and disconnection. Sarcasm, parody, and contrafaction are all strategies of the learned that gain legitimacy through a referent, be it a single primal text or a collection of these produced over a period of time. Sarcasm, like parody, dismantles its basic text or textual method in order to establish something anew.

In other words, if the earlier period functions as signs for the world of the Mamluk period, *Hazz al-quḥūf* shatters these signs in order to locate them anew within other interstices. Ideas of the rural world and of peasant life demand the creation of another worldview, one in a "perpetual state of decomposition and composition," similar to what Foucault notices in the archaeology of eighteenth-century European knowledge.[3] Leaving only a handful of names and books untouched and untainted, al-Shirbīnī gestures derisively in a fashion that, to borrow Foucault's phrasing, results in a process whereby the "written word went into abeyance."[4] Indeed, *Hazz al-quḥūf* gestures toward a separation between things and words. As Foucault writes in defining the epistemological shift to modernity: "Discourse was still to have the task of speaking that which is, but it was no longer to be anything more than what it said."[5] Yet, in its multiple roles, *Hazz al-quḥūf* plays havoc with canonical texts, including well-known lexicons, giving them absurd titles that nevertheless convey a partial reminiscence that harks back to the primal text. The new titles, as the "deferred presence of the first name, its secondary sign, its figuration, its rhetorical panoply,"[6] stand for a threshold to modernity, one that may stealthily recognize a tradition, a canon, but that struggles toward a more thorough engagement with life in its entirety, not as lived in urban areas but primarily in the neglected rural space of the peasantry.

Al-Būṣīrī's renowned Mantle Ode is not the only text in al-Shirbīnī's mind; there are others, especially those heavily clothed with a detailed commentary in rhetoric, grammar, literary and theological references, self-reflexive interventions, and anecdotal or apocryphal paraphernalia. If we search in *Hazz al-quḥūf* for a register of names of authors, poets, preachers, historians, and imams, not to mention apocryphal citations, fake references, crutch-shifters ("as a poet says . . ."), authentic references, and religious or theological loci, we can easily tell where the author as narrator is deliberately bluffing. The decision to come up with different spellings or pronunciations for the name al-Būṣīrī, as the *adīb* (littérateur) al-Abīṣīrī or al-Abū Ṣīrī,[7] perhaps points to a deliberate strategy of evasion or to an internalization of how peasants hear and claim that illustrious name, in that the Mantle Ode was so popular that no one, even the invented figure of Abū Shādūf, could have missed it. To avoid this Mantle Ode and focus instead on al-Būṣīrī's *Hamziyyah*, the ode rhymed in *hamzah* as the last letter (*Umm al-Qurā fi madḥ khayr al-warā*; i.e., The Mother of Villages in Praise of the Best of Mankind), is another evasive strategy. The Mantle Ode was the one celebrated everywhere. Although enjoying fame, al-Būṣīrī's *Hamziyyah* cannot be compared to his Mantle Ode (*Al-Kawākib al-Durriyyah fī madḥ khayr al-bariyyah*; i.e., The Pearly Stars in Praise of the Best of All Creation). Although the *Hamziyyah* ode is also the topic of commentaries and contrafactions, the Mantle Ode generated a poetic commotion and a resurgence in rhetoric.[8] Through a systematic self-debasement found in Abū Shādūf's *qaṣīd*—a deliberate undermining of self-laudatory poems and commentaries—the author/narrator and commentator draws comparisons with similarly gross examples, such as the one by the emir of the Alexandria port-city, Murjān al-Ḥabashī, who wrote a contrafaction to al-Būṣīrī's *Hamziyyah*. Al-Shirbīnī states: "With his vile verses and supine stanzas the emir attempted to outdo the *Hamziyyah* of that glorious, scholarly, ascetic, and pious man of letters, al-Būṣīrī, may the Almighty have mercy on him and benefit us through him."[9] The narrator is even more blunt in his criticism of the emir's contrafaction to the Wine Ode of the "Divine Axis and Sempiternal Tabernacle, My Master, ʿUmar ibn al-Fāriḍ,"[10] which he describes as being "more burdensome than boulders and filthier than sewer waters, whose arrangement seemed like courses of muddy clods, and whose shape resembled a pimp's beard."[11] *Hazz al-quḥūf* contains many imitations and contrafactions that take the recent past, the middle period in particular, as their point of departure.

More telling is the method pursued in the commentary on Abū Shādūf's ode. The poem could well be the work of al-Shirbīnī, for the fictitious character Abū Shādūf is only a pretext to bring about the other side of "literate" and oral culture. It is distanced in such a manner as to enable him to claim it as a countryside production, where there is a linguistic reservoir of its own; or, as he himself puts it, "the linguistic peculiarities of the countryside . . . are undoubtedly on a par with the farting of ants."[12] Associating these peculiarities with rural life as nurturing "coarseness of expression," "crookedness of tongues," and "uncouthness of speech," the author/narrator and explicator sketches a wedge, a divide, or an inseparable abyss between the two lifestyles, the urban and the rustic.[13]

The Subject of Parody and Contrafaction

Behind this sketch of rural life, its speech, and its modes of thought and behavior, which occupies almost one third of the narrative, there lies a plan. In order to find a way through this work's thicket of descriptions and surreptitious byways and thereby engage with a cultural movement that was still alive in the seventeenth century, it is worthwhile first to explore the landmark commentaries and expositions that distinguish the literate culture of the middle period: each commentary treats of a poem or a treatise, which generates a further explicatory process that becomes its own cultural reservoir. Ibn Nubātah has to his credit many commentaries, especially his *Sarḥ al-ʿuyūn fi sharḥ risālat ibn Zaydūn* (Roaming Gently in the Explication of the Epistle of ibn Zaydūn), a work that led in particular to two of Ṣalāh al-Ṣafadī's works and commentaries: *Tamām al-mutūn fī sharḥ risālat ibn Zaydūn al-jiddiyyah* (The Conclusive Text in Explaining ibn Zaydūn's Solemn Epistle) and *Al-Ghayth al-musjam*. Al-Ḥillī's *Sharḥ al-kāfiyah al-badīʿiyyah* led to dozens of others,[14] but especially to ibn Ḥijjah's *Khizānat al-adab*. Each commentary follows a systematic method, treating the selected poem line by line in order to explain the etymological, morphological, and philological dimensions of words, phrases, structures, and rhetorical figures, and to introduce digressions about other relevant texts, which eventually provide us with a panoramic view of a cultural context. The practice of these commentaries was so popular that it was overused and perhaps rendered obsolete by the seventeenth century. Moreover, it was an urban product thoroughly entrenched in the life and practices of cities; it even urbanized the colloquial and served it back to the street in new forms—namely, the nonclassical subgenres in poetry, the ones that come under the rubric of *ʿāmmī* (colloquial).[15] Al-Shirbīnī in *Hazz al-quḥūf* dislodges the entire practice of these commentaries, not only by creating a distance between a hilarious ode and the commentator, but also by giving himself the freedom to poke fun at many practices that are normally buttressed by serious material or apocryphal detail. His work explodes the entire linguistic corpus, subverting its massive growth and proliferation into the sciences, its lexicographic treasuries (the titles of which often included the word "ocean," as noted in chapter 3), and its ever-expanding grammatical and rhetorical base. Let us take as an example the way in which he refers to word etymology, derivation, and conjugation. Whenever he goes over a word, its derivation, and morphological pattern, he pokes fun at voluminous dictionaries such as Fīrūzābādī's "Ocean." He tells the reader: "I have read in The Blue Ocean and Piebald Cannon" that such and such word derives from the following, or is of the pattern of another.[16] The work itself might have found a prototype in al-Ṣafadī's *Ikhtirāʿ al-Khurāʿ* (The Concoction of Craziness), since it contains two lines of nonsensical verse that invite another hilarious commentary. As Humphrey Davies notices, "The two works also share a *mise-en-scène* (the verses in question are brought to the attention of a gathering of littérateurs one of whose members is commissioned to write a commentary 'to be strung to fit their strange string') and certain . . . comic devices, such as false etymologies, incorrect meters, and the straight-faced assertion of the patently false."[17] These features, as he concludes, "impart a sense of kinship to the two texts."

Countryside and City: Textual Juxtaposition

Al-Ṣafadī's *Ikhtirāʿ al-Khurāʿ* appears to be the closest ancestor to al-Shirbīnī's poem, since Muḥammad ibn Maḥfūẓ al-Sanhūrī's *Muḍḥik dhawī al-dhawq wal-niẓām fī ḥall shadhara min kalām ahl al-rīf al-ʿawwām* (The Book to Make Men of Taste and Order Laugh Concerning the Deciphering of a Snippet of the Poetry of the Common People of the Countryside; written in 1058/1648–1649) draws on the same ancestor to a substantial degree.[18] No less of a source (also noticed by Humphrey Davies) is ʿAlī ibn Sūdūn al-Bashbughāwī (810–868/1407–1464) with his well-known text *Nuzhat al-nufūs wa-muḍḥik al-ʿabūs* (Bringing a Laugh to a Scowling Face),[19] especially in the latter's use of a "zany explanation" of words that otherwise do not demand intrusive etymological excavation. Although these works are of significance in that they form part of an available inventory, they are only a partial contribution to the cultural reservoir associated with the Islamic republic of letters. Al-Shirbīnī's method of accumulating the humorous and whatever partakes of "license and buffoonery," elements that comprise a substantial portion of his *Hazz al-quḥūf*, is set in sharp relief when juxtaposed with a sustained body of other material of quotes and explanations of a more serious and elevated quality. This latter body of work foregrounds two main issues. The first relates to al-Shirbīnī's desperate desire to bring to people's attention a neglected life, one that involves the linguistic reservoir of the countryside and falls outside the orbit of city notables and writers or poets, including artisans, craftsmen, traders, and professionals, whose work bears the stamp of urbanity. The other issue relates to his surreptitious strategy of drawing attention to a neglected peasantry, all under the guise of exposition and diatribe. The apparent exaltation of urban life in which he indulges cannot be taken at face value. His lavish praise of Cairo—with its women, lifestyles, and learned people, in vivid contrast to an uncouth countryside—exceeds limits and often sounds like a sardonic importation from self-congratulating learned circles.

There is a good deal of truth in what his work proclaims and defends. And yet there is also the counterargument that, through his juxtaposition of urban and rural, we come to know more about the rural linguistic repertoire not only in relation to lifestyles but also in connection with the oppression exercised by the Ottomans in rural areas. Although parodies and scathing satires build on juxtapositions and oppositions, one aim of al-Shirbīnī's work is to establish a dialectical opposition between countryside and city. The countryside is a locale where conflict and exchange interweave and where an excessively discursive assertion of the inherent coarseness of the peasantry defeats itself, especially in cases where the Ottoman authority intrudes to enforce tax collection. Al-Shirbīnī's sardonic account of Ottoman oppression cannot have been the first of its kind, since obviously there were earlier narrative and poetic productions that sought to expose the massive misuse of power and rampant corruption. But al-Shirbīnī's work nevertheless asks us to recognize and assess the unrest in the lands controlled by the Ottomans, a phenomenon that led the Mamluks to regain political power after 1711. In a gesture designed to legitimize pre-Ottoman times and also to recall relatively better days, the Mamluks harped on the expectations of people in Egypt and other regions. The most significant event was ʿAlī Bey al-Kabīr's seizure of power from the Ottomans in 1760 and the expansion of his authority yet further, resulting in the annexation of Damascus (1771), Jaffa (1773), and neighboring lands. The significance of these moves lies not only in geographical expansion and political rule, but also in the upsurge of a discourse of justice and fairness with Qurʾānic underpinnings, which undermined the Ottoman claim to Islamic rule.[20] But the political instability would soon be manipulated by an Ottoman official, Ḥasan Pasha al-Jazāʾirlī, who landed in Egypt in 1786 to impose another counter-face to Ottoman rule. He, too, claimed to have come in order to impose justice and put an end to social exploitation.

The grievances of the peasants that are mentioned by al-Shirbīnī in his work do not in any way negate the general representation of the peasantry as coarse and uncultured. The author, however, leaves many gaps to call into question the motto that runs throughout the commentary: "Man will not escape his nature / Till the milk returns to udder / Apples will never sprout from the twig / Of one whose roots are a sycamore fig!"[21] Indeed, he allows that same motto to undergo more than a mere challenge in cases where social and political elements intervene to provoke an unexpected response.[22] Although the value of education is constantly underscored and highlighted, other social factors are made to rehearse the troubles that exist within the system. The countryside and its jurists or Sufis do not fare well; for even when they align themselves with the correct application of religious rituals, these alignments are predicated on situations of physical abuse. A son can be told to beat his ignorant mother who is unable to conduct her prayers or recite a Qurʾānic verse correctly. On the other hand, even when the author digresses on the topic of coarse lovemaking and the language used for that particular purpose, there are two dimensions to his discourse: first, the appeal to antecedent or contemporaneous authority that is renowned for its celebration of open discussion of intercourse in its many manifestations, forms, and practices. The social or moral economy, as Humphrey Davies terms it, as one constructed on an opposition between *laṭāfah* (refinement, grace) and *kathāfah* (coarseness or crudeness), may hold true for most of the discursive terrain, especially when applied wholesale to an urban/rural divide; indeed, the author as narrator apologizes on behalf of a city lad, even if the same gesture or response is condemned in a peasant. Second, there are numerous digressions on pretentious people, women who proclaim virtue and practice whoredom,[23] and men who are no less implicated in double-dealing; all of these faults seem to apply more to city dwellers than to rural inhabitants. Keen on courting young boys and men, the narrator himself gives the impression of a misogynist who may not find much sympathy in the countryside.[24] The all-encompassing divide between the urban and rural domains seems to fracture on many occasions, leaving us with a work that is implicated in a double bind of exposition and concealment, the trademark in the culture of the medieval and premodern eras.

The Polymath as Knowledge Subject

The complex of Mamluk knowledge, with its overlapping of rhetoric and poetics and its break from traditional forms, emanates from a diversified effort aimed at reorientation, revision, rejuvenation, or occasionally, continuity, all within the framework of a sociopolitical order that was not necessarily authoritarian. It enlists the participation of undistinguished compilers and commentators from among so-called commoners, who are given voice and space to defend their own way of life. The scholarly spectrum is often distinguished by a combination of expertise and eclecticism. To have the same historian, poet, epistolographer, critic, and rhetorician practice all of these fields with equal commitment, including often daring conversations with peers, is no ordinary matter, especially when the collapse of genres and the dismantling of established correlations "between subject matter and mode of representation" are prominently in the foreground—even in compendiums or treasuries produced under such a homogenizing rubric.[25]

With this in mind, the presence of writing from the Mamluk era in al-Shirbīnī's work demands further notice. Among poets, he draws on ibn al-Fāriḍ, al-Būṣīrī, ibn ʿArabī, and Ṣafī al-Dīn al-Ḥillī, and overlooks many others. Among religious authorities and writers, he draws on ibn Daqīq al-ʿĪd, al-Suyūṭī, and ʿAbd al-ʿAzīz al-Dirīnī (d. 697/1297–1298). He returns to an even earlier period to quote al-Ghazālī's (d. 505/1111) dismay at the large number of ignoramuses among instructors and jurists. There are many other anonymous attributions (referred to by such phrases as "if it be said" or "a poet says"), a means of poking fun at practitioners of *fan-qala* (derived from *fa-in-qīla*, "if it be said"; or *qāla ʾākhar*, "as somebody else says").[26] Both al-Dirīnī and ibn Daqīq al-ʿĪd furnish an aura of moral certainty, thus balancing the faltering codes and systems that could no longer hold social and political sway. However, both prominent pious scholars reside in the countryside, a fact that seems to challenge al-Shirbīnī's unqualified denunciation of rural life. Both scholars were highly acclaimed for their knowledge of jurisprudence, language, and Sufism. Many anecdotes circulated about their miracles. Both were reported to be disenchanted with the pretentiousness and mediocrity of people who claimed to be *faqīhs* and the like.[27] Ibn Daqīq al-ʿĪd describes poverty as the worst evil that the state has to deal with, a point that propelled him to defend the rights of the poor and to resist oppression.[28] The verses of poetry that al-Shirbīnī attributes to the two scholars were more or less in line with what compilers of compendiums and commentaries of the middle period had already amassed. ʿUmar ibn ʿAlī ibn al-Fāriḍ (576–632/1181–1235) receives more attention than others,[29] and one can tell that the author's quotes and comments convey the ongoing popularity of ibn al-Fāriḍ's poetry, especially his well-known Wine Ode, which takes wine as a symbolic medium for ecstatic drunkenness in divine love. It can be argued that popularity is not necessarily a factor in al-Shirbīnī's selectivity, which starts with a deliberate intent to parody an ongoing and firmly established *shurūḥ* tradition. Al-Shirbīnī's work also shows a liking for Sufism, and it only disputes the function of poetasters and pretenders from among the *fuqarā*ʾ (sing. *faqīr*) or dervishes. Within this Sufi tendency, Sufis such as ibn al-Fāriḍ are accorded precedence for their intoxication in divine love, a theme that functions as leitmotif and motto across Sufi poetry.[30]

Shifting Grounds in the Acquisition of Knowledge

The ode and the rhetorical compendium serve as stimuli for the accelerated activity in the production of compendiums and commentaries. That they are invoked by al-Shirbīnī may well be an indication of his anxiety both to emulate and also to debunk the practice through a consistent application of nonsense, steeped in farcicality and unrestrained buffoonery, which fuses the middle-period hilarity of ibn Sūdūn (d. 1464) with the solemnity of al-Ḥillī.[31] By combining these two aspects of middle-period production and giving them full play in his work, al-Shirbīnī perhaps demonstrates that the premodern era is no less multifaceted and engaged with social and ideological issues. What was initially raised in the form of a series of rebellions and usurpations instigated under the rubric of justice and equality was only the tip of the iceberg. Culture itself was to go through its own, somewhat hazy, restructuration of priorities.

By the end of the eighteenth century, across the broad swath of Islamic regions, there was a sense of unease focused on the lack of consolidated engagement with the needs and aspirations of communities and scholars. Nevertheless, amid these concerns and signs of agitation, specific subgenres and Sufi utterances continued to provide comfort. At this chronological juncture, a few precautions need to be observed that challenge attempts at generalization and compartmentalization. Without falling into the tempting trap of skipping a century and drawing comparisons between the early twentieth century and eighteenth-century Europe, there is nevertheless something to be gained in a specific exploration relating to positive knowledge. This observation should not be confused with Ṭāhā Ḥusayn's recognition of a shared unease and a search for the new in both eighteenth-century Europe and the Muslim world.[32] It is focused on a symptomatic attention to natural history, research in positivist philosophy, and the classification of records, words, and documents that Michel Foucault signals as an epistemic shift in Europe.[33] Moreover, these factors cannot be understood apart from the struggle within Islamic societies for release from a single dynastic order and its ever-shifting mercantile alliances. The seemingly independent philological and lexical pursuits, as rightly noticed by Peter Gran, turn their compilers' abodes into assemblies with which merchants and other entrepreneurs were keen to connect, not only for moral support and compensation for the lack of a people-based governance, but primarily for the sake of a solid base within a society with shifting political alliances. The Shaykh or learned person, *ʿālim*, was held in esteem, and until the modern period he had a say in affairs. On the other hand, the assembly or *majlis* could turn into an educational and training site, while sustaining its role as a consortium for news and other reports.

Perhaps a survey of these assemblies in Iraq, Egypt, Syria, Yemen, Hejaz, Tunisia, and Morocco can lead us into the reasons behind this active space, which on many occasions gave birth to some of the most distinguished projects, such as al-Zabīdī's voluminous lexicon, *Tāj al-ʿarūs*. Indeed, Gran shows how the *Wafāʾiyya* salon in Cairo, for example, grew into a cultural space larger than the Sufi order itself and more involved in social life. Significantly, this salon, which was active starting from the last decades of the seventeenth century, carried further the literary and broad cultural effort that had suffered for years under a dogmatic official discourse. Hence the interest of the *majlis* in the house of the Prophet, visitations to shrines, open recognition of the Ghadīr Khumm *waṣiyyah* (the admonition and command said by the Prophet at Khumm pond),[34] and the imamate succession thereafter as usually proclaimed in Fatimid theological thought. A different line was taken by the Khalwatī-Bakrīya, as another Sufi order, whose subscription to conservative Islam kept them far removed from the masses and the rising learned segment. More relevant is the fact that the first salon continued over a long time to include illustrious names in theology, rhetoric, and poetry among its members. Al-Zabīdī, for one, not only had a significant impact on his disciples and students but also made connections with visitors to Cairo, especially from North Africa. It "became proverbial," states Peter Gran, "among them that to visit Cairo was to visit al-Zabīdī."[35] We need to keep in mind that this Moroccan presence has a long history in Egypt, with one side that branches into commerce and business and another that branches into Sufism and scholarship, before the days of ibn al-ʿArabī and later ibn Khaldūn. The Morrocan visitors were always distinguished by their local and national dress. Al-Zabīdī was on excellent terms with them and had obviously made use of their communications in his rigorous cultural pursuit. In Sufi salons as well as in individual ones such as al-Zabīdī's, promising scholars were to become among the most influential figures at the turn of the eighteenth century. Their books, treatises, and *ḥawāshī* (a series of commentaries and glosses) were a distinctive feature of the knowledge grid at the turn of the century.

Apart from these scholars' discussions in theology, grammar, and philological inquiry and their intervention in some issues that related to the interests of their society, there was also a significant turn toward *Ahl al-Bayt* (the Family or House of the Prophet) and the consequent celebration and discussion of the poetry devoted to its members, which twelfth-century jurists in particular used to ban.[36] This shift is more than rhetorical. It is epistemic in the sense that it turns upside down a dominating discourse of limitations and checks. It therefore fits squarely within the broad pursuit of knowledge. Texts, writers, and spheres of discussion confirm this movement, which was not confined to Egypt and Morocco but was also in evidence in other regions, such as Yemen, Hejaz, and Syria. Ḥasan al-ʿAṭṭār's scholarly itinerary can attest to a significant recapitulation of Islamic knowledge in its multiple domains, including ones that connect to nontheological pursuits.[37] Furthermore, apart from al-Zabīdī's lexicon *Tāj al-ʿarūs* (The Bride's Crown) and al-ʿAṭṭār's rich production, we need to consider al-Jabartī's celebration of Napoleon's scientists and of their organized research and library.[38] Such recognition comes not only because of a sense of lack, but also because of a scholarly basis in an already established local order—albeit one that is fractured and individual. In Gran's surmise, and in agreement with Maxime Rodinson, the "cultural revival took the form of a neoclassical revival of Islamic culture and . . . increasingly emphasized utilitarian resolutions of problems, which permitted critical thought to dominate over the authoritative dispensations of the earlier Ottoman period."[39] Across other Islamic lands, there are other conspicuous tendencies toward empirical explorations that attempt to balance the Sufi trend condoned and encouraged by the Ottomans, one within which panegyrics to the Prophet build on a legacy that could not be dismissed as a passing phenomenon in an effete culture.[40]

The Sacral as a Life Force: Al-Ḥillī's *Badīʿiyyah*

In literary and cultural scholarship we are often all too ready to accept the emergence of a particular institution, a book, a treatise, an article, a novel, a play, or even a maxim as a defining moment in our genealogies or histories. As noted earlier, Pascale Casanova, for example, cites particular works and institutions as major restructurations in a literary world-system. This is why patience is required in arguing the case for any defining moment, as I will do here for the astounding appearance of al-Būṣīrī's Mantle Ode, an ode that gave birth to many others over time and across the Islamic regions, especially to its subgenre, the *badīʿiyyah* ode. Although it escaped the parody and contrafaction of al-Shirbīnī, the *badīʿiyyah* ode tradition witnessed an excessive multiplication; hence its emergence and maturation deserve some attention as a candidate for a defining point in the Islamic literary world-system. In this part of my exploration into modes of construction of knowledge, I will focus on catalyzing moments, such as the advent of the *badīʿiyyah* as an ode and as a mode duly played out in a communicative sphere and practiced or received by four prominent figures in their poetry and criticism, as well as in their epistolary art. My purpose here is not to localize the argument or situate it only in terms of critical history. The works of certain writers happen to make a significant impact on a cultural scene and generate discussion, and hence bear the characteristics of ongoing contemporary conversations with peers and with others, including the ordinary public, about encyclopedic texts, along with occasional plunges into the massive corpus bequeathed to them by their forebears. Read against each other or in combination, their texts and conversations present dynamic and invigorating arguments that seriously challenge the modernist deference to a European Enlightenment–style critique of Arab-Islamic medieval productions.

Especially in literary matters of a broad cultural concern, there are many forebears who stand out in the areas of rhetoric, poetics, and systematic critical readings, but we can single out a few who complement and consolidate other lines of inquiry involving analogical reasoning, philosophy, and pure scientific discourse—topics that will be discussed elsewhere in this study. These are Ṣafī al-Dīn al-Ḥillī (d. 750/1349), ibn Nubātah al-Miṣrī (686–768/1287–1366), Ṣalāh al-Dīn ibn Aybak al-Ṣafadī (696–764/1296–1363), and Abū Bakr ibn Ḥijjah al-Ḥamawī (767–837/1366–1434). I also include their predecessor Abū Yaʿqūb al-Sakkākī (d. 626/1229), whose *Miftāḥ al-ʿulūm* opened wide horizons in critical philology, logic, and speculative thinking and involved Islamic theologians, thinkers, and grammarians in especially fruitful debates, as manifested in the quality and quantity of production. In their conversations with each other, the writings of these thinkers surprisingly convey not only a double epistemological/rhetorical shift, one that is signified by a sustained innovative stance, but also the existence of a genuine republic of letters, involving contemporaries from different geographical regions and diverse social layers. In terms of the scope of discussions and seismic and dynamic exchanges, this republic of letters equals or even goes beyond the heyday of the ʿAbbasid period. So long as the Mamluk sultan was not a "caliph" and the ruler's court was not the magnetic or gravitational center of the Islamic world, formal governance or representation of the *ummah* was open to dispute and difference, which ultimately generated multiple definitions of the moral order, especially in the ongoing conceptualization of knowledge.[41] In the following, I will first focus on al-Ḥillī and then explore the role of al-Sakkākī's *Miftāḥ al-ʿulūm.*

Al-Ḥillī was not only credited with a firsthand knowledge of popular and street verse studies and practices, but was also the author of *Al-Kāfiyah al-badīʿiyyah* and its *Al-Ishārāt al-Ilāhiyyah fi sharḥ al-kāfiyah al-badīʿiyyah fi ʿulūm al-balāghah wa maḥāsin al-badīʿ* (The Divine Guidance in Explicating the Sufficient Ode in the Sciences of Rhetoric and Innovative Adornments; better known as *Sharḥ*, i.e., Rhetorical

Compendium). The *badīʿiyyah* as term and noun derives from another basic category in rhetoric, *badīʿ* (the new, inventive, and innovative), which covers figures, devices, and adornments that evolve at certain times as an inclusive rhetoric.[42] While the term recalls an already available or newly coined register through conjugation, derivation, and conjunction, it also connotes *bidʿah* or heresy, that is, deviation from strict formal (official) or Sunni doctrine.[43] Through a reorientation in a panegyric to the Prophet that echoes but outgrows the panegyric Mantle Ode of his early contemporary, al-Būṣīrī, al-Ḥillī's *badīʿiyyah* explodes the linguistic base located in the theological correlation of *badīʿ/bidʿah* with heresy and reorients it through a poetic celebration of the Prophet. By stripping tradition of its paraphernalia and retaining it in his poetry, al-Ḥillī argues powerfully for the rhetorical endeavor, not only as a gateway to literate knowledge but also as inevitably tied to a clear-sighted recognition of the inimitability of the Qurʾān. His endeavor shifts attention to rhetors and poets as the ones who are best equipped to explain the Qurʾān and hadith.[44] Whatever may have been created by jurists under statist obligation is thereby placed under suspicion. The significance of this endeavor cannot be overestimated. While it appears initially to be derived from a deep-rooted lyrical subjectification found in Arabic, Persian, Urdu, and Turkish in particular, it actually intrudes into the scholastic monopoly of the Qurʾan, destabilizes its centrality, and aligns itself with the Prophet in a language that empties the concept of inimitability of its limited application to the Holy Text alone. Thus al-Ḥillī's *badīʿiyyah* ode, along with its compendium in rhetoric, cannot be cited merely as a contribution to a humanist tradition, unlike a handful of his love poems, nor can it be viewed as primarily scholastic.[45] It is, in fact, an entirely new medium, although its place was carved out by al-Būṣīrī's Mantle Ode. It obviously made its appearance at the right time and place, for it caught fire all over an Islamic world blighted by wars and invasions. On the other hand, al-Ḥillī's invocation of al-Mutanabbī's popular verses of *fakhr* (boasting) with respect to the vogue of his poetry signifies this stage of in-betweenness at the intersection of particular modes and schools of thought. The Mantle Ode and its immediate successor corpus were able both to invoke and to provoke very different interests and responses from multiple literary or scholastic positions.

Al-Ḥillī's reputation as another al-Mutanabbī, a master of language, a gallant and valorous fighter, may well have added to this vogue.[46] Strongly grounded in classical textual knowledge, Qurʾānic studies, and language sciences, armed with an acute sense of the power and richness of rhetoric, and perhaps further invigorated by a well-deserved tribal or even "national" poetic pride and hence a proclivity to boasting, al-Ḥillī embarked on unearthing, studying, and enhancing advanced compendia of rhetoric, as will be discussed further. On the other hand, his serious scholarly demeanor, poetic talent, and linguistic fecundity were never detrimental to his inclination to write licentious verse as well, which led him to still more explorations in the same vein, all within a cultural milieu that espoused both jest and serious literary activity.

From Court to Reading Communities

Along with "Al-Zawrāʾ," a single poem that gave birth to a generative semiotic of nationalist underpinnings,[47] al-Ḥillī was also the author of a renowned book-length ode (*Al-Kāfiyah al-badīʿiyyah*; i.e., the Sufficient Ode) and its supplementary but also separate explication or metacriticism, the *Sharḥ*. Free of any financial or political need but nonetheless showered with gifts and admiration, he was the poet/rhetor par excellence. His magisterial discourse, poetry, and presence helped to enhance and promote a rising professional class, consisting of not only scribes but also scholars, littérateurs, and critics, whom he addressed in the singular in his explicatory supplement as the "littérateur-critic and astute scholar." The so-called *badīʿiyyah* ode[48] succeeded in generating heated and wide-ranging discussions and recapitulations in rhetoric in Mamluk Egypt and throughout the Islamic world. According to the bibliographic concordance of Ḥājjī Khalīfah (Kâtip Çelebi; 1609–1657, Istanbul), his ode "was dictated in assemblies and then he explained it . . . clearly and extensively."[49] It became fashionable, invoking the emulation and participation of no less than fifty Muslim and Christian poets between the fourteenth and nineteenth centuries.[50] It led to a growing corpus of studies on eloquence; many books focused on al-Ḥillī's work, while poets embarked on contrafactions, rejoinders, and textual engagements that were to have a definite impact on the Islamic milieu.[51] Al-Ḥillī himself was not a member of a chancery,[52] but in the end his work was central to the functions of that institution, as I will discuss further. By combining poetry, poetics and rhetoric, and criticism, he helped enhance cultural growth and indirectly enabled the state and system of governance, in both the political center and the peripheries, to benefit from the efforts of the administrative class of noteworthy scribes, polymaths, and poets. Even more significant to this discussion is al-Ḥillī's mastery of poetics, the ease and flow of his language, the richness of his poetic reservoir, and the fecund imagination with which he ignited discussion and helped to catalyze his milieu.

In this context we are involved with a sphere of discussion and conversation among scribes and writers who are no less active in the establishment of a textual homeland, a nation of poetry and narration within which rhetorical institutionalization draws and carves out a "calligraphic" empire, to again borrow and expand Brinkley Messick's term.[53] Al-Ḥillī himself is known to have read hundreds of books and conversed with learned communities in different parts of the Islamic world (a topic that will be explored later under the rubric of textual ancestries).[54] Such a sphere of discussion might have seemed hard to conceive, had it not been for a long-established tradition of book production and book reading, which enlisted the collaboration of numerous participants. The copyist (*warrāq*), for example, is a laborer who happens to acquire knowledge through his profession and hence cannot resist the urge to revolt against total reification, leaving behind an imprint that takes the form of editorial intervention, omission, addition, or even a concluding short poem in praise of the text. The latter was the case with the copyist for ibn Abī al-Iṣbaʿ's book, Ḍiyāʾ al-Dīn Mūsā b. Mulḥam, who, as noted in chapter 3, concluded his work with a poetic piece of his own in praise of the book. In the copyist's concluding poem he makes the point that despite the smallness of ibn Abī al-Iṣbaʿ's book, it is so dense and rich in rhetoric as to deserve a comparison with Moses' rod, which challenged the Pharaoh's magicians: "Hadn't you seen Moses's rod, relatively small, but with an unlimited volume?"[55] In other words, until sometime in the nineteenth century, the book-production industry (manuscript preparation, dictation, copying, editing, and marketing) is central to any study of Islamic knowledge in the middle period.[56]

Keys to Sciences?

One can argue that the subtle but solid interrelatedness between the multifaceted productivity of al-Ḥillī and al-Sakkākī's epoch-opening book rests on the shared problematization of rhetoric as basic to an Islamic knowledge in its interdisciplinary concerns, which are much larger than the specific concerns of scholasticism. Even al-Sakkākī's title, *Miftāḥ al-ʿulūm* (Key to the Sciences), challenges authorities in the field since it claims to offer a unique and unrivalled method and analysis. A predecessor of al-Sakkākī by more than two centuries, the encyclopedic scholar al-Kātib al-Khwārazmī (known to live during the years 356–387/975–987) also had his *Mafātīḥ al-ʿulūm* (Keys to the Sciences). Between the two, there lies a significant turn in the trajectory of the acquisition of knowledge.[57]

Bearing in mind the seemingly harmonious rise in several fields and disciplines—across such spectrums as philosophy, theology, logic, grammar, and language—it seems reasonable to suggest that each field was able to benefit from the others while at the same time generating a literary milieu with multiple concerns and interests. As part of a developing tradition of rhetoric, literary criticism, epistolary art, and manual production, all these endeavors receive impetus as a result of the foregrounding of language in all its fecundity and richness. With Ṣafī al-Dīn al-Ḥillī's inauguration of a poetic genre of *badīʿiyyah* and its supplementary guide in rhetoric as a precedent, ibn Manẓūr's lexicon, *Lisān al-ʿArab*, brings words and constructions into a textual communal space where negotiation and exchange are a basis for societal activity and intellectual dialogue. Brought into communal use through a definite shift of allegiance away from rulers and patrons and toward the Prophet, poetry and rhetoric now acquire and retain a presence as community property and become gateways to discussion and new production. Discussed and read in assemblies and public sessions, these works are no longer the monopoly of the elite. Popularized as such, al-Ḥillī's Sufficient Ode democratizes rhetoric. In other words, a discursive space emerges as common property, having as its fulcrum the Prophet's person, message, and family. Rhetoric is disseminated through odes that are usually welcomed by the populace as panegyrics to the Prophet, and such reception thus helps in reconstructing, or enforcing the reconstruction of, political and ideological priorities. No wonder, then, that prominent scholars from among al-Ḥillī's admirers mention his Shīʿism ungrudgingly.[58]

Textual Communities and Cultural Production

In this republic of letters, interest in debate and discussion is not confined to the established circles of theologians, jurists, historians, and eminent littérateurs. As readership and reading sessions become essential elements in the circulation and vogue of works and come to be regarded as a service to Islam under certain prevalent notions of knowledge, types of literate and aural exchange developed that involved both the learned and their clientele. Within that context we can envisage an impetus and a space for innovation and competitiveness. Moreover, even in matters of correct "reading," scholars such as al-Ṣafadī, ibn Ḥajar al-ʿAsqalānī (d. 852/1448), al-Suyūṭī (d. 911/1505), and Aḥmad al-Nuwayrī, the author of *Nihāyat al-arab* (The Ultimate Goal of the Learned), took specific precautions to ensure the absence of *taṣḥīf* (misreading).[59] Such effort should not be dismissed as minor or incidental, not only because it relates to the idea of flawless calligraphic training and the need to avoid problems caused by a single shape for a number of different letters in writing and reading, but also because this is part of the process of supply and demand for skillful copyists. Scholars operating from within established circles had to engage with such requirements and to help promote their merchandise. Problems in reading and their bearing on marketability go beyond *taṣḥīf*, for at times, readers of public texts (such as anthologies and histories intended for public readings) who were already granted an *ijāzah* in *samāʿ* (certificate in audition) might skip difficult words or pages,[60] a situation that could be even more problematic in public spaces other than mosques that were selected for reading and discussion sessions. What

Ṣafī al-Dīn al-Ḥillī sets out to achieve with respect to his poetry and compendium in rhetoric and their use in assemblies and gatherings can apply with equal force to other authors.

Nevertheless, the spread of public reading practices along with the rise of the "public text," viewed as material anthologized or serially divided into folios suitable for specific time spans and reading sessions, cannot be viewed independently of a larger movement in cultural production and social mobility. It rests on a number of factors that also explain such a phenomenal vogue as the one enjoyed by the *badīʿiyyah* and its concomitant exegesis in rhetoric and cultural context. It also provides a better perspective on the rise in encyclopedic knowledge and its dynamic creators who participate in a republic of letters, where it is possible for us as readers to identify specific connections and networks that make up coteries and movements. To recapitulate and also to lay the ground for the next chapters, I summarize these dynamic factors as follows:

First, there is a growing commitment to knowledge, in its humanist and also scholastic dimensions, as an obligation sanctioned by tradition and desperately needed under circumstances that were politically unstable. There was also a counter-contention, found among some of the learned and common people, that knowledge was significant as a bulwark against rigidity and dogma and the attendant political deterioration.[61] In this context, Arabic and its sciences (i.e., grammar, rhetoric, and exegesis) maintained their place of honor. But during the late twelfth and thirteenth centuries in particular there was a more consolidated tendency aimed at providing for self-teaching, for the seeker of knowledge, the autodidact, whose needs vary but rest primarily on the knowledge of rhetoric and grammar in its inclusive terms.[62] Apart from the "foreign sciences" that theologians taught discreetly or in guided readings (i.e., self-teaching reading lists prepared by the instructor) for fear of being sacked from their secured positions,[63] there was an emphasis on a number of reading strategies. In the second half of the tenth century, al-Kātib al-Khwārazmī describes in his encyclopedic work, *Mafātīḥ al-ʿulūm* (Keys to the Sciences), his plan, one that he deems necessary for everyone, including secretaries who must have a grasp of "technical terms":[64] "I have divided the book into two treatises: the first, on the religious sciences and those Arabic sciences connected to them; and the second treatise on the foreign sciences, those of the Greeks and other peoples from among the nations."[65]

ʿAbd al-Laṭīf al-Baghdādī (1162–1231), a physician-humanist, advises students not to study works on science unaided, but he also stresses the value of learning books by heart, while not focusing on two or more at the same time.[66] Followed by al-Sakkākī's (d. 1229) *Miftāḥ* (Key), in which the same title is used for a work with this combination of subject (sciences) and method (key), al-Khwārazmī's book must have been regarded by his successors as being too general to synthesize the problematic in the makeup of knowledge, with its crossroads and pluralities. Thus al-Sakkākī's *Miftāḥ* (Key) proposes a systematic classification that from the outset takes grammar as the foundational logic and basis for reasoning, the source and token for the established episteme since the twelfth century. Grammar becomes so inclusive as to subsume within it the concerns of history, pure science, Gnosticism, epistemology, mathematics, rhetoric, and theological discussions of the Qur'ān.[67] These seeming disparate elements are tightly woven together by means of sharp and meticulously brief logical arguments, of the kind that was obviously in demand at that time. With its systematic classifications under precisely argued components, the *Miftāḥ* defines and tabulates an epistemological turn. It is no coincidence that a contemporary of al-Sakkākī, Fakhr al-Dīn al-Rāzī (d. 606/1209), revisits the books of his revered master in rhetoric, ʿAbd al-Qāhir al-Jurjānī, and reclassifies them more systematically.[68] Apart from its inclusive study of rhetoric, al-Sakkākī's *Miftāḥ* follows a sustained logical reasoning in order to account both grammatically and rhetorically for the most intricate and thorny issues in knowledge formation, including the problem of the "creation" of the Qur'an.[69] The author opens his argument by confronting the reader with this statement: "Be aware that those who knock at the door of *istidlāl* (deductive reasoning and argumentation), even though they may agree on the topic of the Qur'ān as inimitable, differ on the reason for this inimitability."[70] He proceeds to deconstruct five perspectives on this point without providing easy answers. The reader is left with questions rather than certainties. The whole structure of the book is systematically composed in order to account for reasons behind every phenomenon associated with grammar, conjugation, and rhetoric. But these reasons are all located within the principles of *ʿilm al-kalām* (analogical/theological reasoning), accompanied by a strong rationalist approach that places the opinions of "*al-mutaqaddimīn wa al-mutaʾakhkhirīn*" (precursors and successors) on a plateau of argument, where the reader is given the chance to see through these arguments while, significantly, becoming familiarized with the terms "absolutes," "eternities," "absolute cognition," "cognition," "private cognition," "necessities," and "possibilities," terms that are loaded with meanings in the manner of speculative theologians.[71] But the arguments are taken further on the basis of a different scale, one in which antithetical reasoning is called upon to reconstruct what can be evidential. Grammatical forms, especially the conditional, are brought in as part of the *istidlāl* logic (deductive method), before the recourse to analogy (*qiyās*) as conducive to induction. The method rarely leaves gray areas in knowledge formation as it relates to language.[72] The significance of this systematic thought continues a line and schema of knowledge construction initiated by ibn Wahb al-Kātib (d. after 334/946), whose focus is on clarity of expression insofar as this relates to running the state. He sets the terms and conditions for statecraft, money, and land taxation as part and parcel of a knowledge grid where even astronomy and astrology have a place as integrated parts of statecraft and Islamic polity.[73] In both the texts of ibn Wahb and al-Sakkākī's Key, there is a unique organization and systematic reasoning that could have set the path for an uninterrupted growth, had they not been challenged by a traditionalist appeal to the layman in an era of precarious politics.

Second, knowledge could be nurtured, pursued, and inculcated as a gateway to a good profession and also to better sociability. The massive production of self-teaching manuals is a case in point.[74] The literary fervor of the times expresses itself in a textual archive of lexicons, compilations, commentaries, disputations, and encyclopedias (*mawsūʿāt*) in jurisdiction, theology, history, and topography; in thorough textual excavations in, and transcription of, street or community performance, song and poetry, daily anecdotal reports, economic manuals, formularies, annals, guides, and registers for specific jobs and professions; in market inspection manuals, medical and chemical treatises, explorations into sexual practices and erotica as fashion, and more. As manifestations of taste and market demand, these works function not only as ultimate sources of knowledge, but also as self-generative mechanisms for further interest and desire, a point that will be explored further in the next chapters.

Third, social mobility increased not only the participation of women in learning processes[75] but also that of people from many walks of life, such as traders, artisans, and craftsmen.[76] Throughout the period in question, there was a fervent demand for literary culture that quite often led many to abolish elitist constraints. The counter-discourse to the bans on popular preaching on moral, theological, or scholarly grounds grew in quantity and volume. The condescending manner with which codified discourse can relate the fact that a "commoner" rose to the level of hadith collector and literary scholar tells us a good deal about a multidimensional destabilizing process that operated through the processes of knowledge formation. In this context, the record of the Damascene hadith scholar Aḥmad ibn Shiḥna (d. 730/1329) is only one among many.[77] No wonder, then, that we find scholars from the intermediate terrain between the stratified positions of commoner and elite who adopt the opposite view of Ḥanbalite jurists such as ibn Qayyim al-Jawziyyah (d. 750/1350). As an example, ʿAlī b. al-Wafā (d. 1404), a Sufi storyteller and a son of a Sufi scholar and storyteller, argues the case in one of his treatises, *Al-Bāʿith ʿalā al-khalāṣ min sūʾ al-ẓann bi-al-khawāṣṣ* (The Means of Deliverance from the Low Opinion in the Elites), providing a series of refutations that were obviously gaining ground against codified discourse.[78] The book was meant to serve as a challenge to Zayn al-Dīn al-ʿIrāqī (d. 1404), who had composed a book against storytelling: *Al-Bāʿith ʿalā al-khalāṣ min ḥawādith al-quṣṣāṣ* (The Means of Deliverance from the Innovations of the Storytellers).[79] On the other hand, there is also a growing tendency to abolish authoritative transmission and the specifics of the *samāʿ* tradition, a trend that can be noted in Ṣafī al-Dīn al-Ḥillī's own performance for large gatherings and in the fact that he was encouraged by ʿAlāʾ al-Dīn ibn al-Athīr, *kātib al-sirr* (chief secretary and keeper of secrets) for Sultan al-Nāṣir Muḥammad ibn Qalāwūn of Egypt (1285–1341), to collect his own poetry. The author and poet could act on his own with no intermediary, colleague, or disciple.

In this contentious milieu involving means, methods, and material, poetry is not absent: on the contrary, its affordability and ease make it readily available as a way of unsettling conservative attitudes in more than one direction. Such poetry varies. As I will argue in chapter 8, the Sufi *ghazal* tradition is no less subversive and undermining than the innovative ode in the hands of al-Ḥillī and his followers or contemporaries.

In summary, one can argue a case for a poetic tradition that undermines the censorship of conservative jurists, who were to ban poetry not only from children's schools but also from mosques and religious training institutions. Many collections were censored on political, ideological, or moral grounds,[80] and the authors of extant texts were unable to have their names listed in contemporaneous biographical entries.[81] The nature of this poetic effort invites further reading and analysis, not on ethnic grounds, but primarily in terms of a discursive confrontation between a conservative polemic and dissent. Popular writing was obviously enough of a challenge to provoke a firm conservative response, which in its hegemonic fervor sweeps away many other writers whose practices convey the very subject of their condemnation. In an ongoing campaign of conservative and authoritarian intimidation, official discourse manipulates circumstances, such as wars and sultans' dispositions and interests, as ways of sustaining a campaign of terror, enlisting the support of common people through an appeal to shared beliefs. Indeed, this finds its dramatic and narrative representation in Muḥammad b. Muḥammad b. ʿAlī al-Anṣārī al-Bilbaysī's (d. 746/1345) *maqāmah*, *Kitāb al-mulaḥ wa-l-ṭuraf min munādamāt arbāb al-ḥiraf* (Pleasantries and Curiosities from the Companionship of the Masters of Trade). Here, as Hirschler argues along the lines of Thomas Bauer's early reading, a "self-conscious" social group emerges consisting of craftsmen, traders, and low-salaried personnel, who confront a judge representing formal discourse and codified knowledge. Each of the forty-five traders and craftsmen has a say, in Cairene colloquial language, to rebut the judge's censure against their company and their wine drinking.[82] The confrontational site is centered especially on the application of Islamic law under conditions of stringent authority, but the site itself also connotes a self-conscious professional affiliation. It implicitly and defiantly confronts a formal discourse that was at the time still disparaging specific professions as being lowly. In ibn al-ʾUkhuwwah's manual, such professions as cuppers, weavers, watchmen, *ḥammāmīs* (public bath masseurs), scavengers, fishermen, and the like, should be accorded no weight in legal proceedings. "Their choice of a base trade is proof of the meanness of their intelligence," he argues.[83] The spectrum of trade, craft, and profession is large, and all of it falls under the purview of the wide responsibilities of the *muḥtasib* (market inspector). Ibn al-ʾUkhuwwah mentions a long list by name: flour merchants, bread bakers, sellers of roast meat, sausage-makers, sellers of liver and appetizers, butchers, vendors of cooked heads, cooked-meat sellers, pickled-meat sellers, sellers of soup, fish fryers, makers of zulabīya, dessert-makers, makers of syrups, druggists, sellers of savories, milk sellers, drapers, bazaar criers, weavers, tailors, repairers and fullers, silk weavers, dyers, cotton spinners, linen-makers, money changers, goldsmiths, shoemakers, farriers, brokers of slaves and houses, brokers of animals, masseurs (at public baths), sellers of *sidr* (lotus leaves), cuppers, phlebotomists, physicians, oculists, surgeons, preceptors, mosque attendants, muezzins, preachers, astrologers, public letter-writers, sellers of earthenware and waterpots, sellers of clay and molders, makers of sewing needles and pack-needles, makers of spindles, comb-makers, henna-makers, pressers of olive and sesame oil, sieve-makers, tanners and leather bottle–makers, makers of padded quilts, makers of fur coats, makers of reed matting, sellers of straw, timber merchants, carpenters, sawyers, builders, painters, whitewashers, lock-makers, plasterers, and lime-burners.[84] Including each professional register, the dialogue in Muḥammad al-Bilbaysī's "Pleasantries and Curiosities from the Companionship of the Masters of Trade" is another variation on both theology and linguistic availability for the common audiences. The colloquial oeuvre, juxtaposed with the judge's formal discourse, brings us to the discussion of both correct use of Arabic and the occasional lapsing in *ʿāmmiyyah*. It also confronts us with transformations in specific practices, linguistic and lexical circulation, terms of reciprocity and communication, and other divides. Although partly originating in the chancery, this activity takes place for the most part in assemblies and streets, but also and more conspicuously in compendiums, encyclopedias, and treatises that speak to each other in order to complement, dispute, defy, undermine, or simply negate and de-write. In both spectrums, the *faṣīḥ* and *ʿāmmī* (the written and the spoken), there is interchangeability and exchangeability, as can be seen in the case of al-Ḥillī discussed above. Grammarians and rhetoricians, however, were keen on bringing these spectrums together, by legitimizing the *ʿāmmī* through appropriation and reclamation in the contents of the lexicon. As custodians of language, lexicographers and rhetors pose not only as legislators for Arabic and hence Islamic polity, but also as the ultimate voices for an Islamic order in its combined scholastic, humanist, and social-economic pursuits, an entity whose dimensions are much larger and more effective than those of the Mamluk or any other state.

chapter six

DISPUTATION IN RHETORIC

> It is in the rhetorical quality that culture, society, and tradition animate the thought; a stern hostility to it is leagued with barbarism, in which bourgeois thinking ends.
>
> —Adorno, *Negative Dialectics*, 56

> The disclaiming of rhetoric is itself a figure of rhetoric.
>
> —Christine Brooke-Rose, "Whatever Happened to Narratology?," 284

It is within rhetoric that controversy, consensus, and dissent occur. Operating as the most dynamic field of knowledge and the most demanding in inventiveness and praxis, rhetoric is also the playground where persuasion, intimidation, and control are exercised. Its accessibility to manipulation can also turn it into a hegemonic order whereby a few catchwords and analogical applications are able to win over the masses in the face of a contending power, be it a person, text, or faction. This sphere also spills over into centers of learning, *majālis* (assemblies), and marketplaces, a phenomenon already evidenced in the *maqāmāt* of al-Hamadhānī and Abū Qāsim al-Ḥarīrī, and also in *ḥisbah* (market inspectors') manuals. Within this sphere, a network for learning/instruction evolves that bolsters the structure of the republic of letters. Its material, scholastic, and humanist dimensions extend across ethnic and regional divides and elevate its presence to a symbolic level of contestation and argumentation. Played out in full, this republic is the site for power conflict, where every kind of discourse can be manipulated. Fakhr al-Dīn al-Rāzī's (d. 606/1209) *Munāẓarāt* (Debates), for instance, shows us how certain theologians cover up their failure in disputation by an appeal to the ordinary feelings and beliefs of the common people. On the other hand, the sustained traditionalist conflict with rationalist philosophy and the Sufism of ibn al-ʿArabī, for example, bequeaths us with a corpus of rhetorical manipulation, aimed not only at winning over the common people but also enlisting the center of power to its side. Rhetoric can also be the sacral stratagem to undo traditionalist mechanisms, through not only diversion but also a discursive rehabilitation of rhetoric that exposes the shallowness of stark exoteric readings of texts with deep and abstruse levels of meaning. As this topic will be discussed in detail later, I will limit my argument here to specific sacral applications that assemble around them massive lexical maps, registers, and practices and that seek to respond to societal needs and a certain ethical economy that shakes up and at times unsettles the dichotomy between traditionalist and speculative theology.

Al-Ḥillī's compendium in rhetoric will be discussed further, but it is appropriate to begin by relating it to a sustained effort by his predecessors to provide training in prose writing. Apart from bringing his *badīʿiyyah* to a large body of consumers who were spread across the Islamic regions (as evidenced in Ḥājjī Khalīfah's report), his compendium is intended to serve a professional class of scribes. Although scribes had been drawing for some time on a solid library of manuals and formularies, his compendium provides something new, not only in recognizing the efforts of others in a proper scholarly fashion, but also in explaining where the author stands. His contribution is then integrated into a textual archive that is already sufficiently solid to elevate the status of writing and writers in general.

In Pursuit of *Adab*

In order to explore the rise of a strong and diversified cultural community, we need to sketch the function of writing through the "people of the pen" (*ahl al-qalam*) as the state apparatus in human form, a group that happens to include among its members some of the most renowned literary scholars, grammarians, philologists, jurists, and chancery functionaries. With the exception of a few reputed poets or established authorities in jurisprudence, it is nearly impossible to encounter rhetors, grammarians, and linguists who were not at one time in their careers chancery functionaries. The initial schools of grammar and their relevant literary activities were predicated on an anecdotal story that the first Umayyad caliph, Muʿāwiyah ibn Abī Sufyān, after noticing people reading the Qurʾān incorrectly, commissioned Abū al-Aswad al-Duʾalī to compile rules for its correct reading.[1] The story was probably calculated to promote the Umayyad political agenda through an institutionalization of the Qurʾānic text, that is, the application of certain interpretive methodologies to its writing, circulation, and exegesis in a combined effort whose goal was constructing comparisons. No wonder, then, that the arts of discourse are subsumed in scholarship devoted to Qurʾānic inimitability, an activity that involved speculative and traditionalist theologians, rationalists, philologists, and grammarians, whose focus varies accordingly. Taking the Qurʾān as the referent in lexical matters (with some reliance on pre-Islamic poetry), grammarians, for instance, had to go beyond their immediate concerns with grammatical structures and use these structures in a larger sign-system that remained in touch with poets, as being the most resourceful in lexical acquisition. They also needed a mastery of rhetoric and disputation. The linguist and grammarian ibn Jinnī (d. 392/1002), for example, was reported as saying that he had tested the poet Abū al-Ṭayyib al-Mutanabbī (d. 345/965) on the meaning of some words and was astounded to hear him exhausting every possible meaning and synonym. Al-Ḥillī not only makes improvements on pre-Islamic poets but also has a book entitled *al-Aghlāṭī* (a lexicon of incorrect language use).

The term *kitābah* (writing) evolves in this context as an inclusive effort aimed at the institutionalization of literary knowledge; it is intended to be the gateway to all textual knowledge. Cognates of *kitābah* take form in such superb epistles as that of ʿAbd al-Ḥamīd al-Kātib (d. 132/750), addressed to the secretarial class or *kuttāb* (scribes), or the epistle of ibn al-Muqaffaʿ (d. 760), *Al-Durrah al-yatīmah* (The Precious Pearl), and of Abū Riyāsh Aḥmad b. Ibrāhīm al-Shaybānī (d. 339/950), *Al-Risālah al-ʿAdhrā fī mawāzīn al-balāghah wa-adawāt al-kitābah* (The Virgin or Unblemished Epistle in Rhetorical Criteria and the Tools of Writing).[2] We can assume that, prior to this systematization of the art of writing, those cognates could not be widely different from their like in other cultures: the letter or writing itself (*littera*), which comes through a discipline (*litteratura*) espoused by the man of letters (*litteratus*), who is skilled in this kind of writing (*literate*).[3] Al-Shaybānī introduces typologies and categories into the writing profession itself, with a guide to lead scribes into domains that are associated with administration and business.[4] Writing in early ʿAbbasid culture was already advanced to the extent that the polymath al-Jāḥiẓ (776–869) authored two significant epistles of relevance: one on the drawbacks and failures of *kuttāb*, and another on the role and significant presence of the book. The first concern was echoed by one of his late contemporaries, ibn Qutaybah (d. 276/889?), but the unique discourse on the merits of the "book" that introduces al-Jāḥiẓ's *Kitāb al-Ḥayawān* speaks for an age that takes the centrality of book production as pivotal to an expanding Islamic polity.[5] Inclusive of whatever is to be associated with decency, warmth, intelligence, cordiality, good company, science, refinement, fun, wisdom, friendship, prestige, and so forth, the book constitutes not only a cultural community but also a robust citizenry. Combining *ʿilm* (science) and *adab* (ethics, as a humanist pursuit of the good life), the book as the trope for knowledge enjoys an elevated status in a discursive space established and grounded in a shared knowledge framework, which the craft of writing incessantly advocates as being an obligation in an orderly society. The *kuttāb* are the arbiters and practitioners in this Islamic state, and al-Jāḥiẓ's address to an unidentified addressee who holds a grudge against books is meant as an exercise in edification, a streamlined discourse institutionalizing the authority of the book, which is central to a state run by written obligations, laws, and expectations. Being central to a social and political order, this written tradition canonizes its texts, starting with the Qurʾān and its growing interpretive methodologies, to ensure understanding, obligation, and use.

In this rich verbal exchange with hundreds of players, one in which narrative, poetry, and criticism are widely transmitted and elicit engagements and rejoinders from writers in the Maghrib, India, pre-Reconquista Andalusia, and nearly every other Islamic region, a corpus develops not only of poetry and the epistolary art but also of discussion and semiotic interchange. Titles that reflect on each other, whether in agreement or conflict, abound, as has already been shown, but at times they glide into other semantic fields, as in the title *Qahwat al-inshāʾ* (Intoxication of the Chancery) by ibn Ḥijjah. Although this work is meant as a glorification of both the institution and refined writing, its tendency to prioritize prose, not poetry, as an accomplishment as intoxicating as any highly distilled drink cuts across a number of established behavioral, discursive, and semantic norms. The book's title draws on an acceptable blend of jest and seriousness, pleasure and solemnity. Thus the title conflates the feats and effects of the chancery in an Islamic state with wine; the competence in performance is on a level with intoxication; the dignified atmosphere of the chancery is deliberately debunked to fit into the domain of pubs and taverns. Indeed, its writers and secretaries (*kuttāb*) are transferred to another level of correspondence and equivalence, where cupbearers, tavern owners, and bartenders attend to pleasure-seekers rather than to members of an Islamic polity. The book itself, which took thirteen or fourteen years to complete, is an inclusive text that contains chancery correspondence, as well as the author's own epistles and letters, which were no less popular than the best production of the period's epistolographers. Ibn Ḥijjah explains the purpose of his work in terms of providing readers with "Cairene sweets" and "Aleppo's fruits," starting with Aleppo. These range from samples of his belletristic writings to treatises, anecdotes, and many significant chancery papers that serve as documentary records and reflections on literary and cultural life in al-Shām and Egypt.[6] In contrast, ibn Nubātah's title *Khubz al-shaʿīr* (Barley Bread) is quite different from ibn Ḥijjah's, in that it is intended to be a supreme example of the use of double entendre, since his own work is presumably raided by al-Ṣafadī without due acknowledgments. The title plays on readers' sensibilities: it is far-fetched, yet homely and intimate, as if to simultaneously encourage and discourage curiosity. It cuts across classical and popular spheres and manages to shake up a literate society that is still governed by moral contracts and codes of social ethics. The market and street are brought together within elite domains, in that the title illustrates an economy of unfair transaction that eventually raises doubts about the integrity of the learned.

In these transactional productions, copyists also have their say. They often feel free to change the title of a compendium or fit a few pages into another, simply because they need to show their role in this lucrative business, especially when the author is no longer alive. Scribes as littérateurs and littérateurs per se found themselves submerged in heated discussions, controversies, exposures, and even vilification. Worth noting is the case of the bookseller, copyist, and author Muḥammad ibn Ibrāhim ibn Yaḥya al-Waṭwaṭ (d. 718/1318), known as *al-Kutubī* (the bookseller). A wealthy *kutubī* and a knowledgeable writer, he was not in need of chancery jobs. Apart from participating fully in cultural life through a network of copyists, connections with authors, and a significant interest in natural sciences and geography, he produced *Mabāhij al-fikar wa manāhij al-ʿibar* (The Delights of Thought and Means of Edification). This book is important for the art of writing because its encyclopedic wealth in natural sciences is presented in a literary format. Written in a refined style and illustrated with examples of poetry and literary prose, the book is an excellent example of the aesthetic principles of the era. Challenging negative verdicts on the cultural climate of the period under discussion, it also sets the model for other encyclopedic works, such as that of al-Nuwayrī. The bookseller al-Waṭwaṭ (not to be confused with the poet and critic Rashīd al-Dīn) was more of a polymath than an *ʿālim* (scientist/scholar), but his career is yet another example that can lead us to a better understanding of the constitution of knowledge in this era.

There are some basic guides for understanding the substance and practice of knowledge in the medieval Islamic world. A known scholar from the middle period, ibn al-Akfānī (d. 749/1348), writes in his *Irshād al-qāṣid ilā asmā al-maqāṣid* (Guiding the Resolute to the Most Supreme Principles/Goals) that *adab* is defined as an aural and written practice signifying a stepping-stone to wider knowledge. The definition of al-Akfānī given by Makdisi fits well into his broad categorization of literary humanism:

> *Adab* is a field of knowledge by virtue of which mutual understanding is achieved; it is acquired through word-signs and writing. The word and writing are its subject-matter as part of their role in the communication of ideas. The benefit of *adab* is that it discloses intentions in the mind of one

> person and communicates them to another, whether present or absent. *Adab* is the ornament of both tongue and fingertips. By virtue of *adab* man is distinguished from the rest of animals. I have begun with the concept of *adab* because it is the first element of perfection; he who is devoid of it will not achieve perfection through any other human mode of perfection. Its objects are concentrated in ten disciplines, namely, (1) lexicography; (2) morphology; (3) rhetoric of *al-maʿānī* (semantics); (4) *al-bayān* (clarity in expression); (5) *al-badīʿ* (innovative trope; inventiveness in style); (6) metrics; (7) rhyme; (8) syntax; (9) rules of writing, (10) and the rules of reciting, because a person's thinking can be expressed in either words or writing.[7]

The term *adab* refers to both a field and a practice, meaning that there is a littérateur, *adīb*, who is distinctly different from the "scientist" or *ʿālim*, especially when both terms can be inclusive of all learned people. Al-Ṣafadī, who was referred to as "shaykh" by ibn Nubātah and ibn Ḥijjah and recognized throughout the Islamic world as being both versatile and highly learned, has another insight into the matter. He defines the *adīb* as one who can be inclusive enough to speak authoritatively about both poetry and prose, like al-Jāḥiẓ, al-Ḥasan ibn Wahb, and Muḥammad ibn ʿAbd al-Malik.[8] He relies on the authority of ibn Qutaybah (d. 276/889?), who states: "Whoever would like to be a scholar or learned person [*ʿālim*] has to be concerned with one art, but whoever plans to be a littérateur has to have a broader knowledge."[9] To understand this growing differentiation in terms, we may need to go back to Badīʿ al-Zamān al-Hamadhānī's (d. 1007) term "*al-Maqāmah al-ʿilmiyyah*," translated as "the *Maqāmah* of Knowledge," where emphasis is laid on the endless commitment to learning.[10] The two terms *adīb* and *ʿālim* often overlap, but the term *ʿālim* undergoes further deflection to refer to the theological sciences and jurisprudence. Abū al-Faraj ibn al-Jawzī (d. 597/1201), for one, uses the terms *ʿulamāʾ* (learned) and *ṭālib ʿilm* (aspiring scholar). The road to *ʿilm* (learning and knowledge) for jurists is "to be acquainted with each science, with a focus on jurisprudence."[11] Himself a prominent jurist, al-Jawzī criticized grammarians and philologists such as ibn al-Khashshāb, who displayed minimal knowledge of jurisprudence. In another context, he expounds on the concept as "the knowledge of facts, exploration of ancient tradition, familiarity with people's ethics, the knowledge of truth and its obligations." He criticizes those who "only retain words concerning what is allowed and prohibited; this is not beneficial *ʿilm*."[12] He further sets criteria by putting a distance between the learned and those who wield power, noting that only through distance and austerity can the learned offer guidance to other people.[13] He specifically warns the learned against acting as counselors to sultans, but notes that if they find themselves forced into that situation, they should act with caution. But, he adds, since "times are rotten and foul" and "rulers are corrupt, and the learned are turned into hypocrites," it is better for communities to avoid their (rulers') assemblies.[14]

Although this kind of warning had already been emphasized by Abū Ḥāmid al-Ghazālī and other scholars, the chancery nevertheless functioned throughout the middle period as a statist center, drawing many professionals into its domain and enlisting the services of numerous scholars. Chancery politics was not uniform everywhere, but there is evidence of nepotism along with advancement based on merit, a point that al-Qalqashandī discusses at length.[15] Littérateurs were drawn to the chancery, but many also chose to remain outside its corridors. The different chancery functions and its structure as a central state apparatus should not detract from its significance in the makeup of an Islamic order. Its ups and downs, its successes and failures, often reflect the composition of the republic of letters, the survival or demise of cultural capital, and the communities and networks of leading intellectuals.

Throughout the course of Islamic history and before the advent of a European modernity, the term *adab* as literature was inclusive of poetry and prose but not restricted to them. Its semantic field included refinement and good manners, in the tradition of the notion of *belles lettres*, while at the same time partaking of an all-inclusive network of knowledge with no specific boundaries. It was only with the arrival of European modernity through colonization or incorporation that *adab* became institutionalized as a term referring specifically to literary writing, a process mediated through colleges fashioned after French and British models, all the way to the Higher Teachers' Colleges in Egypt and later Baghdad. Those colleges also happened to include among their graduates the most influential literary figures associated with literary modernity.[16] Foucault comes up with an interesting surmise when he concludes that language lost its inscription in things to turn forever into discourse, surviving in that form only in literature: "It may be said in a sense that 'literature', as it was constituted and so designated on the threshold of the modern age, manifests, at a time when it was least expected, the reappearance, of the living being of language."[17] He adds: "From the nineteenth century, literature began to bring language back to light once more in its own being: though not as it had still appeared at the end of the Renaissance. For now we no longer have that primary, that absolutely initial, word upon which the infinite movement of discourse was founded and by which it was limited; henceforth, language was to grow with no point of departure, no end, and no promise. It is the traversal of this futile yet fundamental space that the text of literature traces from day to day."[18]

Although al-Ṣafadī, ibn Nubātah, and ibn Ḥijjah are littérateurs, this appellation does not imply a systematic way of thinking or application. Notwithstanding al-Ṣafadī's openness, he displays a distinctly conservative theological stand that aligns him with ibn Taymiyyah and against rationalist thought, the Muʿtazilīs, and Greek philosophy. In political terms, it leads him to draw on every dynasty in order to make a case that eventually falls within a grand and absolute dismissal of Muʿtazilīs and a counter-alliance with an opposite view.[19] But throughout his work, rhetoric and pertinent speech occupy a prominent position. Without equivocation, he allows others to report Muʿāwiyah as saying: "The learned are almost the masters."[20] Al-Ṣafadī is not unique in this preoccupation with what he regards as a problematic engagement with rationalist thought. Ibn Nubātah had already and more succinctly delved into the issue when he insightfully problematized the controversy between Muʿtazilīs and traditionalists through a gloss, in which he explains the dearth of rationalist thought beyond the quotes that we come across in the refutations by counter-rationalists and traditionalists. This rationalist thought, he intimates, is available only in the books of "*al-uṣūliyyīn*" (traditionalists),[21] meaning that this thought—and every other thought that has been censored by the official institution since al-Mutawakkil's times—was obliterated and dismissed. In comparison to al-Ṣafadī's opinion, ibn Nubātah's critique is more attuned to a balanced reading of intellectual life, a distinction that cannot be applied in the same way to al-Ṣafadī.

Being more open-minded than traditionalist, al-Ṣafadī resides in an in-between space that resists extremism. In characterizing al-Ḥillī, whom he greatly admires and emulates, al-Ṣafadī merely mentions his fervent Shīʿism (i.e., belief in the right of ʿAlī, the Prophet's cousin, to fight back against the Meccan aristocracy in its manipulation of the murder of the third caliph, ʿUthmān).[22] He uses a softer epithet in describing the lexicographer ibn Manẓūr as "prone to Shīʿism without *rafḍ* [i.e., rejection of the first caliphs]," a phrase that also occurs in al-Suyūṭī's biographical entry on ibn Manẓūr.[23] The recurrence of that phrase betrays a predominant discriminating tone against marginalized groups and communities to be found in official discourse. Indeed, this phenomenon is well worth exploration, since there is also a contending, albeit subdued, discourse that occasionally challenges and undermines the prevalent tendency to distort historical detail. More than four centuries separate Abū al-Faraj ibn al-Jawzī (d. 597/1201) from al-Shirbīnī's contemporary ibn ʿAbī al-ʿĪd al-Mālikī, for instance, but both share a common discussion site, in the sense that subtle refutation can be pursued within official discourse as a way of restoring balance to Islamic history. In one instance, ibn al-Jawzī resorts to the work of ibn Ḥanbal in order to cite him in a refutation of Abū ʿAbd al-Raḥmān al-Sulamī, a scholar and Sufi (d. 412/1021) who was so prejudiced against ʿAlī that he misconstrued historical facts and Prophetic hadiths. The question that ibn al-Jawzī raises on this occasion falls within the common Islamic obligation to accept the rightly guided caliphs: how is it possible for a Muslim to attribute misunderstanding of a hadith to ʿAlī? "The learned are in agreement that ʿAlī never goes into a fight unless right is on his side."[24] On the other hand, at a later time, al-Mālikī gathers a number of anecdotes to demonstrate not only the grace of the Prophet's family but also their magnanimity and high standards of benevolence.[25]

Excursions in literary pursuits are not exclusive to poetry and prose. Under the pretext of explicating a renowned ode, the *Lāmīyyat al-ʿajam*, by the martyr al-Tughrāʾī (1062–1121), al-Ṣafadī takes the liberty of pursuing every available referent or allusion, no matter where it takes him. Here there is an overlap between the domains of *adab* and both hagiography and historiography. Keeping in mind the elaboration on the knowledge, expertise, and humility of the subject of this explication, consider ibn Daqīq al-ʿĪd's self-elegy:[26]

You have exhausted yourself between the jobs of a humiliated laborer
Struggling for survival and the caution of the hopeful.
You have wasted your prime,
without the gain of the bawdy or the self-importance of the notable.
You have repelled fortune in this world and the next,
ending up in solitude.

This hermitic life of struggle and renunciation of pleasure leads al-Ṣafadī to elevate ibn Daqīq al-ʿĪd to the status of sanctity, accepting for the sake of his contention the premise that the history of Islam works in centennial cycles of renewal and rejuvenation. This renewal occurs whenever there is a devout person from among the learned, not al-Mahdī, whom ibn Khaldūn (d. 1406) leaves open as a possibility, but a just and compassionate man of God who will "renew for the *ummah* its religion"—such as the Umayyad caliph, ʿUmar ibn ʿAbd al-ʿAzīz, for the first hundred years, and al-Shāfiʿī a century later. Al-Dhahabī takes over this hagiographic account; he proposes Abū Ḥāmid al-Isfarāʾīnī as the devout culmination for four centuries, whereas al-Ghazālī towers over five centuries of Islamic history, followed by Shaykh ʿAbd al-Ghanī al-Maqdisī (d. 600/1204)[27] and ibn Daqīq al-ʿĪd (1228–1302) for the ensuing centuries.[28] Here, hagiography stands side by side with historical narrative, but it becomes sidetracked whenever a poet brings into the discussion his study of figures and tropes. Hagiography turns into a field of practice for theories of rhetoric. This hagiographic reconstruction cannot be overlooked in our reading of a republic of letters. Its presence and transmission among prominent traditionalists and others may have functioned as a deterrent to rational inquiry into causes and effects.

The Littérateur's Anecdotal Network

By reporting al-Dhahabī's account of temporal cycles and alluding to them at a particular point in his biography of ibn Shurayḥ (when a learned shaykh stands up in ibn Shurayḥ's assembly in AH 303 and proclaims the upcoming cycles), al-Ṣafadī is playing multiple roles: he is the biographer, reporter, transmitter, *bricoleur*, and, in Ebrahim Moosa's image of al-Ghazālī,[29] the engineer. He collects, reads, analyzes, synthesizes, and at times creates, all in order to guide us into his interpretive web. Once there, we find ourselves as readers deeply involved, the pretext being the need to find our way through a variety of pieces of information that start with the subject, that is, the poet al-Tughrāʾī, and then turn to a discussion of rhetorical figures or linguistic turns. These also come in the form of rhetorical questions, for example: "If a person like Shaykh Taqī al-Dīn ibn Daqīq al-ʿĪd can complain so much, what are we to say with respect to the playful and reckless?" In rewriting reports and anecdotes, buttressing them with information from every division of knowledge, enlivening them with personal verse, and introducing material that is both readable and worthy of discussion—whether through direct reading, recollection, retrieval from antecedent authority, audition, authorized transmission, or direct correspondence—al-Ṣafadī is not alone in his age. However, he is clearly among the most encyclopedic, conversant, and dynamically integrated of his contemporary colleagues. Reported material inserted in the form of interjections brings the recent past into the present and diverts assemblies of the learned through the use of flamboyant excursions of a less stately kind, blending all into a heteroglossia of the marketplace. We end up in constellations where human agency is both present and absent. It is there as a defining presence with a speech and role, but, as long as it also merges with other sites that conjoin or absolve each other, the conversation gradually establishes and cements shared codes that are identifiable as multivoiced constellations or compilations. Al-Ṣafadī's interjections or digressions usually demand the use of the term *rajʿ* (return) as a means of resuming the previous discussion.[30] But when al-Ṣafadī comments on al-Tughrāʾī's expressed desire to leave Baghdad, he (the former) is on solid ground, established and entrenched in literary dialogue. Opposed to this expressed desire are the words of poets whose nostalgia or sorrow upon leaving Baghdad find expression in lyrics of great poignancy.[31]

Al-Ṣafadī, like other littérateurs of this period, is quite at home with his contemporaries or recent predecessors.[32] Through audition or authorized transmission, the conversation between littérateurs and hadith scholars or jurists creates a number of constellations representing textual and social communities, which in turn serve to invigorate discussion, consolidate assemblage, and engender multiple forums and platforms. This kind of constellation takes a number of directions within the domain of *adab*. First, the practice of relying on textual and auditory fragments, epigrams, and unique or rare poetic language from other works is taken for granted; these are atemporal in the sense that a quotidian detail, allusion, image, or incident may incite the author to recall something that is either similar or starkly opposite. Thus, exquisite erotic verse may recall another category of poetry, but in terms of dexterity it may also invoke something ribald. Ibn al-Ḥajjāj is available to be quoted, not necessarily in the context of ribaldry or lewdness, but rather for the neat correspondence in his artistry, imagery, and wit to conversely refined and elevated verse, such as that of ibn Nubātah al-Saʿdī's (939–1015; not to be confused with Jamāl al-Dīn ibn Nubātah al-Miṣrī) celebration of the white blaze (*ghurrah*) on the forehead of a handsome horse. Ibn al-Ḥajjāj makes use of the phrase "as daybreak [Ṣabāḥ] slaps its forehead" from that poet in order to address his own woman, named Ṣabāḥ:

Ṣabāḥ was angry to see me holding my penis;
  hence I responded with a reprobate's retort
For God's sake, why don't you slap its face,
  to make the poet's speech come true?[33]

This example might seem incidental to the rest of the literary corpus, were it not for the fact that other compilers, poets, and writers drew on a similar reservoir of anecdotes, allusions, and invocations.[34]

Second, there is a tendency to place explicatory matter or criticism within a broader textual context of grammatical and rhetorical use. Even coarse but playful verse is studied with the principal purpose of accounting for unique or rare applications of specific figures of speech, devices of expressiveness, and images. The effort to make a case for each figure of speech or item in rhetoric necessarily leads to an excursus. Al-Ṣafadī's *Al-Ghayth* is a case in point. Working through a framework that takes its lead from the ode under study (*Al-Ghayth al-musjam*), al-Ṣafadī's excursions into a number of sciences come as a follow-up to, or a continuation of, what is deemed worthy of examination. For instance, "*iltifāt*" is a trope involving redirection as a rhetorical figure, one that marks a change from first- to second-person singular or from one verb tense to another for a specific purpose or context. Al-Ṣafadī faults Ḍiyāʾ al-Dīn ibn al-Athīr for not applying it as "the exit from one kind or condition to another, taking a path other than the first."[35] As he comments on the subject and a specific verse of his own, in which he complains about the difficulties he faces in his own life, he soon realizes that he may be burdening his companion with too many complaints, and so he switches to the use of his companion as his addressee, as a way of alleviating the gloom, delighting the companion, and coming up with invigorating and joyful verse. This is a poetic redirection, a practice that shows not only a poet's responsible reaction to a particular situation, but also a talent for improvisation, itself an indication of naturalness and both linguistic and musical fecundity.

An Open-Market Cultural Economy

The recourse to another poet's image, diction, or verse is potentially subject to the challenge that it is a weakness rather than a strength. Al-Ṣafadī's explanation of the practice goes as follows: partial use of another poet's verse for the purposes of another occasion can signify efficient craftsmanship. Such partial use cannot be plagiarism, he argues, as long as the successor-poet improves on the original.[36] Such a free and open interpretation of plagiarism may sound paradoxical in view of the accusations leveled against writers and poets; but perhaps it is better to read such openness in the context of other examples of open exchange, not only on the material level between the chancery and the street, but also in the context of titles, writers' reflections, disputes, obituary compendiums, linguistic mobility, and the continuing weakening of the distinction between low and high styles of writing, or between coarse and noble. These are all symptoms of cultural exuberance, poetic and linguistic fecundity, faith in an open-market cultural economy, and a robust understanding of unregulated exchange. The nuanced but also firmly established basis for the massive critical corpus subsumed under the rubric of plagiarism (*sariqāt*) coincided with the rise of the Islamic empire. Freed from tribal and provincial obligations over time, poets and writers in any given region became increasingly familiar with other writers spread across the Islamic world, along with writers in other cultures. In other words, the loosening of restrictions, boundaries, and binding applications enabled the establishment of a dynamic conversation that included raids on each others' literary territories and, as a result, generated serious discussions of literary limits, obligations, and responsibilities.

Speculative Theology at Work

The growth of a theoretical corpus on plagiarism, rhetoric, and lexicography, along with treasuries and manuals on different branches of knowledge, should be regarded as evidence of thriving cultural activity and a lucrative book industry. Almost every *sharḥ* (explicatory essay or compendium) turns into an exegetic transposition to the nonsacral domain. It builds its own interpretive methods and divisions that specify *lafẓ* and *maʿnā* (expression and meaning) in tandem with the specific concerns of the explicator at a certain point in the discussion. Within the framework of this cultural spectrum that traverses Islamic regions, and despite harrowing political upheavals, we come across the works of such eminent Muslim scholars as Najm al-Dīn ʿAlī al-Kātibī al-Qazwīnī (d. 675/1276) in philosophy, astronomy, and mathematics. Known as the student of Naṣīr al-Dīn al-Ṭūsī (d. 1274) and the teacher of other prominent scholars, al-Qazwīnī provides us with a rich web of literary connections and a communicative sphere that both enhanced current knowledge and stimulated further exploration and discovery. Both a polymath and a highly specialized scholar, he wrote works on logic and philosophy that elicited a number of commentaries. In particular, there are two significant ones on his book *Al-Risālah al-shamsīyah*, the first by his disciple, Saʿd al-Taftazānī, and the second by Quṭb al-Dīn al-Rāzī (Muḥammad ibn Jaʿfar, d. 766/1364). In this context it is difficult to overestimate Naṣīr al-Dīn al-Ṭūsī's compelling presence as scientist, philosopher, theologian, and statesman. His engaging commentary *Talkhīṣ al-muḥaṣṣal* (The Summa of the Harvest; i.e., a commentary on Fakhr al-Dīn al-Rāzī's *Muḥaṣṣal afkār al-mutaqaddimīn wa al-mutaʾakhkhirīn min al-ʿulamāʾ wa-al-ḥukamāʾ wa-al-mutakallimīn* [Harvest of the Thought of the Ancients and Moderns from Scholars, Philosophers, and Theologians]) needs to be noted as part of the current interrogation of the climate of ideas and field of discussion across the Islamic regions, from Herāt (part of present-day Afghanistan) to Khurāsān, Cairo, Morocco, and India. Although al-Ṭūsī's summa is meant as a contribution to the marginalia of his controversial subject matter, these very same marginalia create their own inroads into Islamic rationalist thought, the politics of the Islamic state, theology, and even Arabic rhetoric.[37] His summa turns out to be more in the nature of a new opening into a process of speculative reasoning that illustrates not only the divides between al-Rāzī and al-Ṭūsī, but also their vigorous argumentation against the traditionalist thought that was making some inroads, at least in the Arab east.[38] Although Fakhr al-Dīn al-Rāzī sustains an Ashʿarite view of ibn Sīnā, Naṣīr al-Dīn al-Ṭūsī demonstrates a rigorous familiarity with Ashʿarites and Muʿtazilites and makes use of such knowledge to engage his subject on a number of points that have been central to theological reasoning,[39] including the knowledge of God, essence, space and *ʿaraḍ* (occasion/effect; and accident), political power and community leadership (*imāmah*), and the inimitability of the Qurʾān.[40]

The Encyclopedic East

Al-Ṭūsī was more than a polymath; he was an architect, astronomer, biologist, chemist, physicist, physician, and a theologian, not to mention a guiding imam (to be emulated and followed by the Shīʿī community). He succeeded in convincing Hulagu Khan to construct the Raṣad Khāneh Observatory (1259) in Azerbaijan (south of Tabriz), to the west of Maragheh, the capital of Hulagu's Ilkhanate (Il-Khanids, 1256–1353) empire. He was also credited with the establishment within the observatory of an enormous library of four hundred thousand books, where a large number of scholars and scientists worked and were paid by the state. There are many anecdotes about the way he made use of his astrological knowledge to convince the ruthless ruler to change his mind.[41] Another exemplary figure in the science of speculative theology is ʿAḍud al-Dīn al-ʾIjī (d. 756/1355). In his *Kitāb al-mawāqif* (The Book of Stations), the personal voice towers over a vast encyclopedic compilation of theological and philosophical knowledge, turning it into the summa on that particular science. Its six divisions cover the following topics: conceptualizations of knowledge; the ontological question of being; the theory of *ʿaraḍ* as central to the discussion of *jawhar* (essence); theories of composite and simple bodies; theories of the soul, intellect, angelic intelligence, and rational theology; and a concluding section with a discussion of eschatology and prophetology. Al-ʾIjī's work clearly shows the impact of his teacher, Aḥmad ibn Ḥasan al-Jarabārdī (746/1345), and of Nāṣir al-Dīn al-Bayḍāwī's (d. 1286) compendium on *kalām*, *Maṭāliʿ al-anwār* (The Rising of Lights).

Al-ʾIjī's summa fits well into the category of library concordance in an age of compendious pursuits. Most contemporary to it are ʿAlāʾ al-Dawlah al-Simnānī's (d. 736/1336; from Simnan east of Tehran) encyclopedic work on the metaphysics of Sufism, and ʿIzz al-Dīn Muḥammad b. Maḥmūd ʿĀmūlī's (d. 735/1335) compendium, *Nafāʾis al-funūn* (The Precious Elements of Sciences), which includes both the sciences of the ancients and Islamic knowledge. Al-ʾIjī's summa was commented on by al-Sharīf al-Jurjānī (d. 1413), the author of *al-Taʿrīfāt* (The Book of Definitions), a work that has been in continual use as the major reference dictionary for philosophical and rhetorical terminology. Another encyclopedic figure and polymath with more contributions to Shīʿī philosophy and Sufism (and ibn al-ʿArabī in particular) is Sayyid Ḥaydar al-ʿĀmūlī (alive in 787/1386).

Cultural activity beyond the immediate Mamluk domains was thus active and no less encyclopedic and compendious than it was within those domains. Rather than taking the Mamluk period to task for its conspicuous concern with compendia, we should view Islamic culture during that period as geared toward the generation of knowledge, in a trend that involves numerous writers, scholars, and readers and creates its own basic compendious context. Significantly, even when a scholar such as the prolific but also specialized Sayyid Ḥaydar al-ʿĀmūlī names one of his many books *Jāmiʿ al-asrār* (The Compendium of Mysteries) and engages with the esoteric and with questions of inner thoughts, conscience, and paths of faith, belief, and truth, there always remains space for specialized pursuits, and speculative theology in particular. Opposed to these tendencies is the work of ibn Taymiyyah (d. in prison in Damascus in 728/1328). His polemics and *kalām*-oriented treatises have specific targets, such as Sufism, Shīʿism, and philosophy.

Defining a Cultural Milieu: Multiple Genealogies

The question that should be central to any inquiry into the formation of patterns of knowledge is this: How can compendious authorship be pursued and manuals and references or guides be prepared without the existence of a substantial cultural milieu that encourages collation, planning, and systematic theorization or preparation of keyword manuals and terminology guides? Even when one acknowledges ibn Khaldūn's (d. 1406) regret over the decline of philosophical inquiry, the continuous increase in such scholarship beyond the Arab center is indicative of a dynamism that the exhausted center could not sustain.

The contributions of these scholars to the study of rationalist (speculative) theology and philosophy is no minor achievement, especially if we examine them in terms of Fakhr al-Dīn al-Rāzī's (d. 606/1209) *Munāẓarāt* (Debates). In one such debate he pays specific attention to ways of coping with mediocre jurists and scholars who try to manipulate the sentiments of common people and incite them against rationalist theology. This same question is also raised by ibn Ṭufayl (d. 1185) in his famous narrative, *Ḥayy ibn Yaqẓān*. We also have ibn Taymiyyah and al-ʾIjī, two scholars representing opposite extremes, both of whom die in prison. In other words, we are dealing both with an open literary culture and with a power struggle that takes the discursive field of theology as the domain through which to conduct an invasion of an Islamic polity as a congressional community, one that stretches across many lands and regions but retains shared concerns, practices, and expectations. The issue of an open cultural economy and its converse poses an interesting question, because it confronts us, as readers and students of cultural mutation, with genealogies of power, law, and intellectual activism. No matter how receptive the street may be to less controversial activist production, it can be incited to oppose this activism, especially in the domain of *kalām* (speculative/rationalist theology). Although we find few sustained readings of the concept of *kalām* as a systematic pursuit, we do possess some single contributions, specific interventions, debates, obituaries, and biographical entries with relevant gleanings, along with additional documentation to be found in compendiums. The most obvious genealogy for institutionalized knowledge as power, exemplified by the ʿAbbasid caliph al-Muʾmūn's (r. 813–833) alignment with philosophers and speculative theologians, could not endure for long, but its scope and methodologies continued to function, albeit with much less momentum and permeation. But the relatively decentralized middle period provides sufficient space for different genealogies to develop, within which the author/scientist, now a much more conspicuous agent, was able to produce not only a summa, as in the case of al-ʾIjī's *Kitāb al-mawāqif* (Book of Stations), but also disciples and new concepts. In other words, we have at least three significant genealogies, which function on the level of mentors and disciples, encyclopedic production, and groundbreaking theorems. The notion of "license" (*ijāzah*) signifies this triple development, which was uniquely popular in the medieval period. Ibn Nubātah's license to al-Ṣafadī to report and transmit on his behalf encapsulates these multiple aspects.[42] A genealogical tree of scholarly mentorship and affiliation is thus established. The ancestor-figure always shines as a magnanimous presence, whose skill and knowledge have earned him a certain authority. Although this authority is significant by itself, it also reflects in different ways on subsequent production. Alongside tightly organized summas, compendia, and *shurūḥ* (like those of al-ʾIjī and Ṣafī al-Dīn al-Ḥillī), there is a dispersal of single works and compilations over a large canvas that accommodates multiple voices and views. In the absence of clear-cut institutionalization, the tenuous relationship between ever-changing sites of political power and knowledge constructs makes scholars always wary and careful not to get too close to such sites. The positive outcome is the enormous effort expended by individual scholars and their disciples to produce encyclopedic and other massive works in numerous fields, especially in theology: works on *kalām*; eschatology; comparative religion; logic and philosophy; natural sciences; and the *adab* traditional historiography.

In addition to individual works in any one of these fields, a writer such as al-Ṣafadī might use the occasion of explicating a poem to summarize or engage with all of the above fields as worthy of attention or as material that encourages gloss and commentary. Ibn Khaldūn was right when he accused theological explorations in the Arab lands of degenerating into mere exhausted reversions to so-called principles and roots. However, alongside those signs of exhaustion, significant contributions to scholastic theology, literary endeavor, natural sciences, and historiography continued to be made.[43] Hence, early twentieth-century criticism of the middle period fails to account for the reasons behind this dispersion and expansion.

Al-Ṣafadī's Navigations: Theology and Traditionalists

Rhetoric held sway not as a separate philological pursuit but as a dominant feature, one that cuts across a number of axial splits, from the theological and philosophical to the mathematical, medical, geographical, and literary. A seemingly passing reading on al-Ṣafadī's part of a verse by a jurist/poet such as al-Shāfiʿī (d. 204/820), al-Khalīl ibn Aḥmad (known as al-Farāhīdī; d. 175/791, or 170/786, or 160/776), or ibn Durayd (d. 321/932), for example, leads to a further exploration involving the poetry written or reported by such jurists and learned scholars as al-Shaykh Taqī al-Dīn ibn Daqīq al-ʿĪd and the hadith scholar ibn Sayyid al-Nās (d. 734/1334). In ibn Daqīq al-ʿĪd's poetry, one comes across juridical terminology and maxims such as "*taʿāruḍ al-māniʿ wa-l-muqtaḍī*" (the conflict between injunction and contingency), referring to the case of a learned person who is being described as worthy of a munificent reward, but whose impiety rules out the possibility.[44] By agreement among compilers, professional languages have a place in literature, especially when they are relating the responses, in their writings or correspondence, of professionals such as physicians, mathematicians, and musicians, among others. These responses provide a magnificent reservoir for the community as a whole, especially when they are addressed to the divine or the sovereign, since in that case they deviate from the habitual and introduce into the discourse another level of language, thus dislodging the usual linguistic and rhetorical platitudes.[45] In some cases, professional languages blend with rhetoric so neatly that they bring literature, and poetry in particular, to the street, that being the domain of use and application. Religious symbols, icons, and practices, especially in Christianity, explode their way into sites and scenes that, as al-Ṣafadī suggests, dance in music and color. In this context he is relying on the poetry of recent predecessors such as ibn Sanāʾ al-Mulk (Abū al-Qāsim Hibat Allāh; al-Qāḍī al-Saʿīd; d. 608/1211), earlier writers such as ibn al-Ḥajjāj, or immediate contemporaries such as ibn Dāniyāl, Sayf al-Dīn ibn al-Mishadd, Sirāj al-Dīn al-Warrāq, Abū al-Ḥusayn al-Jazzār, Abū Dharr al-Ḥalabī, and al-Shihāb al-Ḥijāzī.[46]

For instance, al-Ṣafadī's subtle engagement with the preoccupations of poets, critics, and philosophers regarding common concerns such as visions, intuitions, dreams, and so forth, is no passing or whimsical occurrence. Rather, it develops into a detailed discussion of imagination and fancy, one that emerges as a byproduct of the metaphorical level of poetic discourse, which may well baffle those foreign to the domain. Al-Ṣafadī describes the active "imaginative faculty" (*al-quwwah al-mukhayyilah*) as the one whose action "is not confined to awakening only, because in sleep it functions even better . . . as it utilizes the psychological insight located in the front part of the brain."[47] He adds: "Although this imaginative power can function under any circumstances, it does not imagine things by itself, because it is not a willed power. In awakening it has the capacity to function as it likes. In sleep, there is another condition that enforces actions." He explains: "This case is of one of the following four occurrences: The first involves the presence of sensory images in the imagination as they are realized by the senses. A sleeping person draws upon those that are most recent. In other words this involves the connection of sense to imagination." Furthermore, "it is the opposite of the imagination's reach into the sensory, such as dreams or as the one who sees himself in sleep eating something, only to wake up with the same taste in his mouth." The second type of occurrence "relates to the power of the intellect as it looks into a case, like travelling and meeting a friend, entertaining hope or fear. It utilizes the imagination to recall those images that will remain there during sleep in order to be acted on along with their meanings. This is termed 'the soul's monologue.' Some consider it a sort of anxiety and hesitation [*waswās*]." The third occurrence is more attuned to the reflection of external circumstance and the soul's mood (*mizāj*), and leads to fluctuations in vision. The fourth case receives more attention on al-Ṣafadī's part: it "relates to a representation realizable by the soul and passing on to the imaginative faculty, which the donor of images releases in sleep. The science of visionary expression is the one that deals with the application of that similitude to its signified. At times, this is an open encounter with no representation." He mentions examples from Greek visionaries and also from *Al-Futūḥāt al-Makkiyyah* (The Meccan Conquests) of al-Shaykh Muḥyī al-Dīn ibn al-ʿArabī.[48]

Literary Venues

Within this same category of literary venues falls the application of theological and philosophical terminology, which spills over into poetic imagery and thus is further evidence of a cultural network, a circulated system of knowledge that is widely available to participants in this literary culture. A so-called cultural script is already laid out, according to this reading. It thus becomes part of a shared code, which, while indicating a sophisticated understanding of ongoing discussions over the ages, undergoes a process of semantic deflection that transforms its meaning and direction as part of the transaction. For instance, the concept known in Arabic as *al-jawhar al-fard* (the unique atom/substance/essence; the indivisible entity) comes into usage with speculative theologians with respect to existence and nonbeing or vacuum—that being a topic regarding the movement of particles in time and space, discussed, for example, by Abū Isḥāq Ibrāhim ibn Sayyār al-Naẓẓām (d. between 220/835 and 230/845), ibn Sīnā (d. 428/1037), and other rationalists and speculative theologians, in particular the Ashʿarites.[49] But the concept was so frequently disseminated and argued among the learned community that it invaded rhetoric and poetry, too, not only as an image worthy of application and deflection, but also as a problem in physics that a poet such as Abū al-Ṭayyib al-Mutanabbī (d. 354/955) could apply to his own existence and beingness: "I am nothing but an arrow in the air / returning without an anchor."

The question posed by ibn Sīnā at this juncture runs as follows: Is there time at the intersection between the movement up and the movement down?[50] The *āna* (nowness) enters the discussion as central to the underlining principle of discreteness in theological reasoning, whereby the nondivisible entity (*al-jawhar al-fard*) is an ultimate beyond divisibility, an *ʿaraḍ* (accident) in time and space. The world consists of finite *jawhars*, which lack physical proportions unless they are occupied by the incidental or occasional.[51] Because the rational theological thought takes the God-reason-world schema as the basis for its disputation, the conceptualization of indefinite re-creation has to end up with an indefinite, *jawhar*, and a definite or ever-changing (occasional) *ʿaraḍ*. Abū al-Maʿālī ʿAbd al-Malik ibn ʿAbdullāh al-Juwaynī (d. 478/1085) argues in his work *Al-Shāmil fī ʾuṣūl al-dīn* (The Comprehensive in the Principles of Religion)[52] that there is a division on this matter among speculative theologians: Muʿtazilites maintain that the *jawhar* is a magnitudeless abstract at the endpoint of divisibility, whereas the Ashʿarites reject the idea. Speculative theologians think of *jawhar* as unrenewable, while the *ʿaraḍ* (occasional/passing) is its changing character in a dialectic of being and nonbeing. At this juncture the dividing line between Muʿtazilites and Ashʿarites is situated in their discussions of the idea of creation and creator. The nonexistence of the *ʿadam* (nonbeing/vacuum, nothingness) in Ashʿarite thought is a virtual being in a process of re-creation, which in the end disputes the concept of unchanging entities.

The significance of the discreteness principle for the present argument lies in the way that it reverts back to contexts of debate not only among polymaths, poets, and scholars, but also among the remaining Ashʿarite theologians, such as ʿAḍud al-Dīn al-ʾIjī, who continues to place more faith in *ʿaraḍ* (occasion, effect) and an emphasis not on natural causes but rather on God-caused physical effects. This kind of reasoning is bound to evade the implications of a schema of cause and effect and to deny both philosophy and astronomy their viability. Hence al-ʾIjī, for example, looks upon the celestial spheres as "imaginary" and "more tenuous than a spider's web," a point that his late contemporary al-Sharīf al-Jurjānī (d. 1413) disputes. The latter notes that "even if they do not have an external reality, yet they are things that are correctly imagined and correspond to what [exists] in actuality."[53]

The availability of these speculative theological terms in the middle period thus attests to a communicative sphere that obviously derived its components not only from salons and meetings, but also and more importantly from all of the material and communicative venues of the literary culture. Hence, al-Ṣafadī's *al-jawhar al-fard*, "the indivisible" atom or particle, leads us back to a climate of ideas that had received its impetus earlier, during the heyday of the ʿAbbasid caliphate. The rationalist and speculative tendency had taken its toll on official discourse, as duly noted and approved by al-Jāḥiẓ (d. 868). It angered his contemporary ʿAbd Allāh ibn Qutaybah (d. 276/889?), who looked at it as a surge in nonsensical terminology among speculative theologians and rationalists or logicians: to him, such terminology explains little and betrays linguistic incompetence and a lack of familiarity with, or grounding in, the "sciences of the Arabs, their languages and literatures."[54] Ibn Qutaybah elaborates on the matter as a category of analysis and as a boundary between upholders of the latter sciences, and the rationalists and theologians who come up with such phrases as *jawhar*, "which stands by itself," and *ʿaraḍ*, "which cannot."[55] This categorical divide was applied in the writer's manual in epistolary art, *Adab al-kātib*, a manual that has served ever since as a canonical text in the training of chancery secretaries. Ibn Qutaybah went so far as to criticize the major influence in this type of discourse, namely, Aristotle, whom he accuses of overblown enunciations to signify commonalities. "Had the author of *Ḥadd al-manṭiq* (Logic of Modalities; i.e., *Prior Analytics*) been among us to listen to the minute discourse in religion, jurisprudence, rituals and obligations, and grammar, he would have been struck dumb."[56]

The conflict here is larger than a matter of ethnicity. (Ibn Qutaybah's father was non-Arab, and his contenders or opponents were of a mixed ethnic origin, although prominently Arabs.) It relates to a power struggle that takes language as the battlefield. It is in defense of profession and status that Arabic—minus the conjugations and deflections of logicians and speculative theologians—was fostered and staunchly defended against what is thought of as defective, impure, and ungrammatical usage. And yet the upsurge in theoretical and speculative reasoning also alarmed Abū Saʿīd al-Sīrāfī (d. 368/979), a rigorous grammarian with a good grasp of logic, who expressed his dismay at the proliferation of philosophical and logical terminology appropriated from Greek and Latin through the linguistic medium of Syriac. This proliferation was to continue into the middle period, as al-Ṣafadī admits.[57] Indeed, terms like *qadīm* and *muḥdath* (ancient and modern; eternal and temporal or created) and *al-jawhar al-fard* would gradually be emptied of their theoretical framework and meaning in physics in order to fit, not into al-Naẓẓām's recognition of the physical property of the *ʿaraḍ* (occasional or accidental) in relation to the indivisibility of the *jawhar*, but rather into the poet ibn Sanāʾ al-Mulk's application to the uniqueness of the beloved. As he says in celebration of her lips and mouth (here, *jawhar* is a double-entendre: atom/essence, but alluding primarily to gem and pearl):

> Had al-Naẓẓām observed the *jawhar* of her mouth
> he would not have doubted that it is the unique essence.[58]

But, as al-Ṣafadī is eager to demonstrate, this type of appropriation by poetics and rhetoric of the discursive domains of other disciplines is a trend that runs through most compendious production. In the case of jurisprudence, such appropriation also allows a space to make fun of the growing rigidity in its written corpus. Playful use of jurisprudence abounds in middle-period compilations.[59] This mode usually fits well into specific subgenres, which al-Ḥillī and others treated as deviations from the classical in order to establish links with the language of the street. To prove his point with respect to the nonclassical poetic forms of *dūbayt* and *mawāliyā*, for example, al-Ṣafadī would not allow jurists to have the final say on matters of theology and logic. As if to anticipate al-Shirbīnī's devastating ridicule of the amassed body of systematized jurisdiction, he employs these nonclassical or popular poetic forms in order to offer some playful examples of the application of Islamic law. He reports, for example, the following story:

> Someone said: "I entered al-Medina, and I saw a very charming young boy whom I approached to solicit, and he agreed to come with me. When we were by ourselves, I remembered God and decided against the plan on which I was bent. He asked me to pay, but I told him that there could be no payment for nothing. The dispute turned nasty, eventually somebody showed up, and we asked him for his opinion. He began by providing us with a chain of transmitters, starting with his father and

reaching as far back as al-Shāfiʿī, who reportedly said: 'If the door is closed and the curtain is drawn, then the dowry is due. Give him his right.' I gave the boy two dirhams. I said to the man: 'May God protect us from the likes of you, you pimp! I've never encountered anyone who decides such business according to the legal opinions of al-Shāfiʿī along with such a chain of transmitters.' "[60]

Logic, Grammar, and Jurisprudence

The humorous and playful aspect of this kind of anecdotal literature leads us into the sphere of social life, but it also directs a sardonic glance at the use of jurisprudence, its elasticity, and its openness to interpretation. Moreover, this type of sarcastic gloss provides the author, al-Ṣafadī, with a pretext to delve into the reasons behind the increasingly important role of jurists. There is, first, the traditionalist school of law, which received its impetus as a result of Aḥmad ibn Ḥanbal's *miḥnah* (trial), an event that would gain increasing traction with many jurists, along with the *ʿāmmah* (common people), culminating in ibn Taymiyyah's staunch opposition not only to rationalism but also to Sufism, Shīʿism, and whatever he deemed to be a deviation from *sunna* (official Islamic tradition).[61] This traditionalist upsurge might not have occurred had it not been in dialectic opposition to the initial vogue of Muʿtazilī thought. That rationalist trend in speculative theology had gained the support of the emerging intellectual class and the court, groups that endorsed it as being conducive to the interests of the expanding Islamic empire.

We might expect a littérateur such as al-Ṣafadī to avoid forums such as these and to be concerned only with rhetoric as the ultimate practice in literary production. However, the author inserts himself into the discussion in order to assert the kind of presence that is more or less that of a navigator and negotiator. He resists traditionalist thought and its modes of reading and analysis, and he simultaneously raises suspicions concerning what smacks of inconsistency in the logic of rationalists. In this process of navigation there is a degree of undecidability, and yet there is also an eclectic perspective and an open-mindedness. The undecidability is based on selectivity and deliberate choice. As a method, it is contaminated by its subject. Becoming entangled in the issue of rationalist philosophy and translations from Greek sources, al-Ṣafadī decides to dwell on the debate between Mattā ibn Yūnus (d. 940) and Abū Saʿīd al-Sīrāfī (d. 368/979), an event that is dated to 330/932. Taking place in the assembly of the renowned minister and littérateur ibn al-Furāt, the debate helps to explain, at least in part, a selective method of translation that prioritizes the source language (Greek) as necessarily privileged in its transfer to the target language (Arabic). As postulated, this very premise may have been one of the reasons that set Shaykh Ṣalāḥ (as al-Ṣafadī was called by his contemporaries) against theological reasoning. He applies *sunna* as a negotiator among schools rather than as an upholder of any one of them. Hence he devises a comparative method that brings together a traditionalist example and a rationalist one, namely, the thought of ibn Taymiyyah and of ibn al-Muqaffaʿ, and then differentiates the one from the other. Notwithstanding the broad knowledge of the two men, he stipulates, they both lack discretion and the proper use of reason and intellect. He quotes al-Khalīl ibn Aḥmad al-Farāhīdī, who was asked about ibn al-Muqaffaʿ, as follows: "I saw a man whose knowledge is superior to his mind." Al-Ṣafadī adds: "The same verdict applies to the learned imam, Taqī al-Dīn Aḥmad ibn Taymiyyah . . . his knowledge is massive, but he is of an imperfect mind that leads him into trouble."[62] Nor is this all that leads al-Ṣafadī to draw this conclusion. In matters of analysis and deduction, he detects a failure in reasoning, which he attributes to the same combination of great knowledge with insufficient reasoning ability. In this case, al-Ṣafadī is speaking about his own experience with the imam ibn Taymiyyah and the series of questions that were posed in the imam's assembly with respect to specific verses found in the Qurʾān. It appears that ibn Taymiyyah responded in much the same fashion as other Qurʾānic scholars. Al-Ṣafadī considered these responses to be so commonplace that they failed to account for the rhetorical and grammatical intricacy that loads Qurʾānic verses with meanings that are irreducible to literal interpretation. In these encounters, al-Ṣafadī, who was avowedly an attendee at the assembly, has turned into the master, someone who forced the imam to relent and recognize the masterly knowledge of a challenger.[63]

Traditionalist Alarm at Translating the Greeks

Ibn Taymiyyah appears in al-Ṣafadī's *Al-Ghayth* as an extreme traditionalist whose presence is needed to expound on the interrelationship between the acquisition of knowledge, methodology, the skills of learning and analysis, and translation. Nothing can be more challenging than this intersection of skills and methods. It demands a discussion of the burgeoning movement of translation, its history and development, and its destabilizing impact on thought and rhetoric. In al-Ṣafadī's explicatory critique, the contentions of the rationalist Muʿtazilī school draw attention in the context of the translation movement, or simply as a cultural trend that branched out in many other influential directions which were to have a bearing on Islamic theological thought and cultural production. Although al-Ṣafadī was sufficiently well informed to be placed at the intersection between translation, rhetoric, and rationalist and speculative thought, he was not well equipped to construct a sustained logic. Both fluency and immense learning blur his vision and lead him to introduce his argument at this important intersection with a transmitted hadith, duly endorsed by Anas ibn Mālik (d. 93/714), to the effect that the Prophet on his deathbed said that his nation will be splintered into seventy-two factions, all doomed to hellfire except *al-Jamāʿah* (i.e., congregation, meaning "practitioners" in official discourse [*sunna*]). While citing this hadith, al-Ṣafadī falls into contradictions and fails to interrogate its inherent political motivations following the battles of the Camel [al-Jamal] (AD 656), Ṣiffīn (657), and al-Ḥarra (680), the last being a conflict waged by the second Umayyad caliph Yazīd against the city of the Prophet, al-Medina. In conformity with these transmissions, al-Ṣafadī loses control of his quasi-rational analysis and falls into the trap of exuberant fluency and rhetorical fecundity, concluding with a verse of his own that runs as follows:

> The passing of nights multiplies its [*sunna*] renewal
> and the passing of days endows it with the prettiness of youth.[64]

This display of exuberance demands a better explanation for his antagonism toward the Muʿtazilites, whose use of logic and reason he associates with the expanding movement of translation from Greek science.[65]

Let us therefore examine his attitude as preliminary to a discussion of the sensitive connection between, on the one hand, ibn Taymiyyah's unqualified rejection of Muʿtazilite thought, and, on the other, al-Ṣafadī's sharp critique of ibn Taymiyyah as inadequate in his reasoning and use of intellect. It is also worth noticing that al-Ṣafadī specifies the political and theological affiliation of his referent, thus casting additional doubt on his reading. He starts his own narrative of the origin of the Muʿtazilites with a quote from "Abū Bakr al-Ṣayrafī, al-Faqīh al-Shāfiʿī al-uṣūlī" (the Shāfiʿī essentialist/traditionalist jurist), who says: "The moment the Muʿtazilites reared their head, God sent Abū al-Ḥasan al-Ashʿarī to confine them down in the bottom."[66] He then describes a disputation between Abū al-Ḥasan and his father-in-law, Abū ʿAlī al-Jibāʾī, in which Abū al-Ḥasan ties up his teacher and father-in-law in logic. He asks him:

> "*A-waswasta*?" (Are you in doubt?)
>
> "No, not in doubt," his teacher replied, "but the shaykh's donkey is stuck on the [stone] bridge" (i.e., I am stuck).

Citing similar cases, al-Ṣafadī raises the case of two Muʿtazilites, Ṣāliḥ ibn ʿAbd al-Quddūs and Abū al-Hudhayl al-ʿAllāf. The former's son died, and al-ʿAllāf found him "on fire for the loss of his son." Al-ʿAllāf was surprised:

> "I have found no reason for your inordinate sorrow: for you humans are just like plants."
>
> "Abū Hudhayl," he replies, "I am sorrowful because he hasn't read the *Kitāb al-shukūk*" (The Book on Qualms/Perplexities/Uncertainties).

The conversation goes on:

> "And what is this book about?"
>
> "It's a book which I wrote down. Whoever reads it will doubt what was as if it never were, and doubt whatever was not as if it were."

Ibrāḥim al-Naẓẓām (who was young at the time and a member of the coterie of al-ʿAllāf) replies:

> "Then you need to believe that he was not dead even if he were; and that he had read the book, even if he had not."[67]

In rhetoric this is what al-Ṣafadī terms *ilzām* (obligating), when logic refutes what is logically argued. Al-Ṣafadī seems to have come across the same source that an earlier contemporary, ibn Nubātah, mentions in his *Sarḥ al-ʿuyūn*.[68] While these selections are meant to reflect negatively on the Muʿtazilites, they nevertheless convey a scenario in which discursive argumentation evolves as a natural facet common to all participants, whose acquaintance with translated material in logic and philosophy facilitated and enhanced these cultural transactions. On the other hand, these selections and comments underline another side of the republic of letters, that is, its strained dialogues and factional disputes. The lauded victory of Abū al-Ḥasan al-Ashʿarī (d. 324/935 or 936) amounts to no less than the victory of grammarians and philologists in the battle against the application of logic by people whom the first faction thinks of as linguistically incompetent, and hence unfitting for administrative rule, chancery, and other jobs that entail leadership. Al-Sīrāfī's blunt refutation of Mattā ibn Yūnus, discussed in the next chapter, amounts to excluding him and other logicians from a community of grammarians, philologists, lawmakers, and epistolographers. In M. G. Carter's neat surmise, accusations of linguistic incompetence are "ipso facto attempts to exclude a person from that elite."[69]

chapter seven

TRANSLATION, THEOLOGY, AND THE INSTITUTIONALIZATION OF LIBRARIES

Especially in areas of inquiry where logic holds sway, translations of texts were a given in the ʿAbbasid age. They were less common in the medieval period, not only because of a mounting traditionalist reaction, but also because theologians had built on the solid legacy in argumentation bequeathed by the ʿAbbasids and the Greek translations of that period. As a movement, translation would take different directions, which tended to be more pragmatic and opportunistic, as we noticed in the case of the Turkish grammar of Abū Ḥayyān of Granada. This shift signifies not only a comparable turn in power relations, whereby Turkish assumed ascendance, but also an expansion in the conceptualization of the republic of letters as the space where cultural production changes hands and traverses territories. This shift also redirects debates to focus not only on opening up the main languages of the Islamic region to each other through systematic transference, but also on questioning the legacy of the past with respect to the methods, means, and purpose of inquiry.

The association between the Muʿtazilites and Greek science, for example, is taken for granted by Islamic scholars. Al-Ṣafadī was no exception. He even narrates how the caliph al-Maʾmūn, upon striking a truce with the king of Cyprus, asked him for books by the Greeks, since "they had a treasury that no one was allowed to explore." The king's advisors were against granting the caliph's request, but one priest rejoined: "Provide it [the books] to them, for, whenever these sciences were introduced to an orderly state [*dawlah shar'iyyah*], they were bound to corrupt and cause dissension among its scholars." Al-Ṣafadī also reports the negative comments of ibn Taymiyyah, who could not abide these sciences: "I doubt that God will ever forgive al-Ma'mūn for the damage done to this nation by the spread of these sciences among its people."[1] Here, al-Ṣafadī opposes ibn Taymiyyah, based on a question of historical evidence: "Yaḥyā ibn Khālid al-Barmakī had started a translation project from Persian sources at an earlier date. But the first person to translate Greek books was Khālid ibn Yazīd ibn Mu'āwiyah because of his keen interest in chemistry."[2] But ibn Taymiyyah's absolute rejection of such sciences reaches its most unequivocal expression in one of his legal proclamations, or *fatwas*: "You'll never find anyone familiar with it [Greek logic] and adhering to its principles in argumentation who is not defective in opinion and debate, and also ineffectively equipped to function with the necessary clarity and learning."[3] His verdict has its basis in the struggle for lexicographic space, for it merely reiterates a position that was already upheld by ibn Qutaybah (d. 276/889?), who argues against philosophy and logic as the science that "has disastrous consequences for verbal expression, ties up the tongue, [and] leaves one speechless and inarticulate before disputants."[4]

Ibn Nubātah was not as sanguine as al-Ṣafadī on matters that might align him with traditionalist thought. His treatment of the Mu'tazilite thinker Abū Isḥāq al-Naẓẓām, for instance, tends to be mild, appreciative, and balanced. He is anxious to show that al-Naẓẓām was highly sophisticated and that his thinking and logic were dialectically developed. If there were any controversy on al-Naẓẓām's thought, he maintains, it was because he was very "advanced in sciences, very keen on reaching into the inner meaning of things, but other schools of law could not tolerate such depth and meticulousness."[5] He notes in particular al-Naẓẓām's views that "*jawhar* [atom, substance; essence] is constituted of configured effects" and, concerning the Qur'ān, that "it is in human power to come up with something similar, but God deters [*ṣarafa*] them [the Arabs] from doing so." According to ibn Nubātah, when al-Naẓẓām was a young boy, his father brought him to al-Khalīl ibn Aḥmad to be taught.[6] The latter quizzed the boy on a number of issues, and the answers were concise, brief, and highly sophisticated. Ibn Nubātah quotes al-Khalīl as saying: "O my son, we need to learn from you."[7] He also quotes al-Jāḥiẓ at length, as one of al-Naẓẓām's most loyal students and sufficiently familiar with his teacher to be able to comment on his thought and poetry. These anecdotes have a strong philosophical bent. What is of significance in the context of our discussion of a republic of letters is ibn Nubātah's tendency in his *Sharḥ* to give logic and philosophy their due, not only by devoting pages to al-Naẓẓām, al-Jāḥiẓ, al-Kindī, and the concepts of essence, *ʿaraḍ*, and phenomena, but also by making appropriately concise selections that help readers and listeners become acquainted with Islamic culture in its heyday. He further differs from al-Ṣafadī in his obvious predilection for prominent philosophical and theological figures and movements as relevant to his topic (i.e., in his commentary on ibn Zaydūn's epistle). For him there is no place for superfluous digressions. Hence, he avoids discussion of the ways in which Greek thought entered Islamic culture. What interests him instead are the ways in which this logic and philosophy have been assimilated into Islamic writing and thought. His focus on the first generation of Islamic logicians, theologians, and philosophers also implies that there was a smooth fusion of Greek logic with Islamic thought and reasoning. Following al-Nadīm and other ʿAbbasid sources, ibn Nubātah places this fusion within an Islamic order presided over by the caliph al-Maʾmūn, whose reported dream of Aristotle has become sufficiently proverbial to legitimize further the translation movement. In that dream, Aristotle was asked: "What is good speech?" He responded: "Whatever stands to reason." The caliph then asked: "And what more?" Aristotle responded: "What its listener appreciates." The dream continued: "And what more?" "What brings no trouble." "And what else?" Aristotle replied, "Apart from this, everything else is the braying of a donkey."[8] Ibn Nubātah's account presents the caliph as an Aristotelian whose own translation project was behind the dynamic translation movement. As we will note shortly, acquaintance with Greek thought either directly or through the intermediary of translation attests to a nonalienating translation process, one that merges nicely into the target culture without an accentuated and hence estranging violence. Conversely, al-Ṣafadī takes the mention of people, movements, and concepts as the justification for lengthy expositions, which even lead to a discussion of translation as a practice and art. Digression as such is part of a comprehensive method that is central to the encyclopedic littérateur, while also being notably different from the methods of the specialized scientist.

Within each digression, however, there is a degree of specificity that conveys the other side of the littérateur as polymath. Here, al-Jāḥiẓ has obviously already established the norm, one that numerous scholars, such as Isḥāq ibn Sulaymān ibn Wahb al-Kātib (d. after 334/946), Qudāmah ibn Jaʿfar (d. 948), and al-Tawḥīdī (d. 414/1024), were to follow. In his digression on translation, for example, al-Ṣafadī sums up his knowledge of the translational scene as follows:

> Translators have two methods in transference. One is followed by Yūḥannā ibn al-Baṭrīq (d. 815?), ibn al-Nāʿimah al-Ḥimṣī, and others. This method is concerned with every single and individual Greek word and its [meaning] signified; along with their equivalent in Arabic lexica.[9] This method is followed throughout until the text at hand is Arabized. This is a faulty method for two reasons: first, Arabic lexica may not have the same synonym or equivalence for the Greek word, and hence many Greek words remain as they are. The other reason relates to structure, syntax, and subject and predicate proportions [agreement], which do not necessarily match each other in different languages. There are also the pitfalls of misused verbal transposition. The second method of Arabization is the one followed by Ḥunayn ibn Isḥāq [808–873], al-Jawharī [al-ʿAbbās ibn Saʿīd al-Jawharī, d. 860],[10] and others. Using this method, the translator approaches the sentence in the source language to garner its own meaning before substituting it with a matching equivalent sentence in the target language, regardless of the issue of parallelism in words. This is a better method, and hence ibn Isḥāq's books required no editing except in mathematical sciences (which he had not mastered), unlike works that he Arabized in medicine, logic, natural science, and metaphysics, which require no improvement.[11]

At this juncture it is worth noting that this same quote from al-Ṣafadī finds corroboration and endorsement in the stipulations on translation included by the philosopher, mathematician, architect, and Sufi poet Bahāʾ al-Dīn al-ʿĀmilī (d. 1030/1621) in his *al-Kashkūl* (Beggar's Bowl),[12] to be reframed in full by Sulaymān Khaṭṭār al-Bustānī in his Arabization of Homer's *Iliad* in 1904. Al-Bustānī notes that "these two schools in translation to which Ṣalāḥ al-Ṣafadī refers six centuries ago are the same ones that are still used today, with no third one in between." He concludes his endorsement of the second method as follows: "It is feasible to state that our method falls within the school of Ḥunayn ibn Isḥāq (d. 873) and al-Jawharī."[13]

This celebration of Ḥunayn ibn Isḥāq as translator is corroborated by his enormous collection of translated works on medicine, mathematics, logic, and philosophy. Placed in charge of the *Bayt al-ḥikmah* (House of Wisdom) by the caliph al-Maʾmūn, he was a major figure in the systematic introduction of the knowledge of many nations, especially Greek philosophy, logic, medicine, and other sciences. He also served as the private physician to the caliph al-Mutawakkil. Ibn Isḥāq proved to be well equipped for such responsibilities. His mastery of Greek, Syriac, and Persian, along with Arabic, was recognized by his contemporaries. His method was preferred to that of a later translator, Abū Bishr Mattā ibn Yūnus (d. 940). The difference between the two is significant, being tied to the understanding of the relationship between logic and grammar. In *Kitāb al-Burhān* (The Book of Documentation), his commentary on and translation of Aristotle's *Posterior Analytics*, Mattā ibn Yūnus stipulates the need for a paradigm that takes utterances as indicative of the use and significance of things to which they refer in a language. He concludes that logic is thus more universal than grammar; Aristotelian logic in Arabic translation offers the tool for a better understanding of the cosmos, God, and humans. Mattā ibn Yūnus, however, was not as versatile in Greek as his predecessor Ḥunayn ibn Isḥāq, who was almost able to pass himself off as a native speaker of Greek and of the other languages he had mastered. There had been similar efforts at translation before ibn Isḥāq's time, as well as a familiarity with Greek, Roman, and Persian cultures; this was also the case among the pioneering logicians who introduced into Arabic grammar further conjugation and deflection, coining words and phrases that entered ninth-century discourse, as testified to by no less an authority than al-Jāḥiẓ. Speaking of the discourse established and disseminated by speculative theologians, for example, he writes: "They distinguish between nullity (*buṭlān*) and nihility (*talāshin*) and they adopt the terms 'thisness' (*hādhiyyah*), identity (*huwiyyah*), and quiddity (*māhiyyah*). In the same way, al-Khalīl ibn Aḥmad assigned names to the meters of the *qaṣīdas* . . . whereas the [Bedouin] Arabs had not known the meters by those names. Similarly, the grammarians gave names to the circumstantial accusative (*ḥāl*), the adverbial accusatives (*ẓurūf*), and such things, and often referred to them." Al-Jāḥiẓ further explains that theologians worked in every field to make them serviceable and available for current usage. This discursive proliferation was so rampant that a preacher in "the heart of the Caliph's palace said, 'God brought him out of the door of nonbeing (*laysiyyah*) and let him enter the door of being (*aysiyyah*).' These expressions are permissible in the art of *kalām* when existing words lack the requisite range of meaning. The expressions of the *Mutakallimūn* [theologians] are also befitting to poetry."[14] On another note, we find philosophers, in particular since the ninth century, who introduced new vocabulary while trying to coordinate with translators on matters of expression, correspondence, and equivalence. Abū Isḥāq al-Kindī's contributions in this respect are especially worth mentioning. Along with an emphasis on such categories as intellectual virtues (*al-faḍā'il al-'aqliyyah*) and bodily desires (*al-shahawāt al-badaniyyah*), there are also the mathematical sciences (*al-riyāḍāt*), matters of a problematic nature (*masā'il*) that relate to the issue of the brute soul (*al-nafs al-bahīmiyyah*), and so forth.[15]

These linguistic transformations were occurring as part of the general opening up of language to accommodate change. Their outcome would continue to inform the language of al-Ṣafadī in his discussions of essence and occasion and of imagination and fancy, let alone in his excursions on existence, being and nonbeing, void and substance, and also human love. He was only one among many who took seriously the shift away from Bedouin language. Does this phenomenon suggest, one might ask, that speculative theologians were able to infuse Arab culture with new coinage only because of the translation movement? Or had they already initiated a change into expressions and terminology that would bring together intellect and passion, and metaphysics and science? While certainly partly their own contribution, the emerging discourse was also indebted to Greek thought, which made its way into Islamic culture through a de-foreignization of the source language and a smooth passage into the target language of Arabic, as though it were already implicitly built-in. Through his adept concealment of a Greek foreign provenance, for instance, Ḥunayn ibn Isḥāq eased the passage of Greek thought through Arab linguistic mediums so that it was able to fit into categories that, as al-Jāḥiẓ's astute overview indicates, cover every field of knowledge. Paradoxically, the traditionalists who voiced their alarm centuries later and viewed this translation project as a deviation from essential principles and roots were unable to rid their own discourse of the alleged contamination. They could not escape either the terms or the logic that had arrived through speculative theology and linguistic navigations led by Ḥunayn ibn Isḥāq and other adepts in logic and philosophy. In brief, ibn Isḥāq's (d. 873) method constituted a smooth transplantation process, one that can be seen even in al-Ṣafadī's style centuries later at the very intersection of resistance.[16] His analysis of "'thisness' (*hādhiyyah*), identity (*huwiyyah*), and quiddity (*māhiyyah*)," along with many other speculations on concepts of being, draws heavily on that same smooth discursive incursion that is associated with the theological manipulation of language and Ḥunayn ibn Isḥāq's de-foreignization method. Opposed to this method is the one followed by Mattā ibn Yūnus (mentioned earlier), one that translated the Greek texts through the medium of Syriac and thus doubly altered the target. Its basic premise is that the Greek thought acquired through Aristotle is free from locality and "Greekness," and hence is a translatable commodity that can be passed off as universal knowledge. This premise was to incite argument and opposition, for both traditionalists and grammarians were alarmed by its foreignness; they viewed it as no less a threat than the later Frankish raids (the Crusades), which gave rise to a contending conservative view of Islamic culture led by ibn Taymiyyah. It is also no wonder that ibn Manẓūr (1233–1311)—as mentioned in earlier chapters—lamented the reluctance among certain segments of the society to speak Arabic and commented: "People compete in compilations of translations in foreign tongues and also in showing their competence in them."[17]

Ibn Manẓūr's comments can be taken as an expression of insecurity and anxiety over the fate of the Arabic language, not only because of a surge in the use of foreign languages and their translation, but also because by that time loan words may have begun to occupy a disturbing proportion of the Arabic lexicon. Earlier, during the famous debate between Mattā ibn Yūnus and Abū Saʿīd al-Sīrāfī, the latter had argued the case from a different perspective, postulating both a mastery of the target language in every detail and an equal mastery of the source and any other source-medium, such as Syriac. Abū Saʿīd al-Sīrāfī stipulated that as long as each language has its own properties, the process of transfer from a source language to another, target language entails change and confusion. The middle period, with which we are concerned here, is not impervious to this same debate—it was already available in a number of sources, especially in the section under the eighth night in Abū Ḥayyyān al-Tawḥīdī's work *al-Imtāʿ wa-l-muʾānasah* (The Book of Entertainment and Pleasant Company). Al-Tawḥīdī's account of the debate, "The Discussion between Abū Bishr Mattā and Abū Saʿīd al-Sīrāfī on the Merits of Logic and Grammar," is worth examining in detail as a basis for my further discussion of translation, language, logic, and grammar.[18] Although it appears in the text as an intervention on the part of grammarians against the onslaught of logicians and their avowed neglect of Arabic, the debate provides a highly sophisticated reading of translation as a densely wrought experience that requires not only an expert's grasp of source and target, but also a trained engagement with logic and grammar in both source and target languages, along with a grasp of a variety of other linguistic phenomena. Apart from this commonplace premise, there is also the specificity that makes a language, a grammar, and its logic no mere disposable containers or carriers. Al-Sīrāfī specifically singles out for discussion the figure of Aristotle in a genealogy of Greek predecessors, ancestors, and successors. Furthermore, there is the violence that is done to language in formation or translation processes, whereby epistemological and semiotic layers undergo mutation and transformation within specific constraints or conditions. Al-Sīrāfī's argument on this point runs as follows:

> No one language exactly corresponds with another language in all respects, or has conterminous properties in its nouns, verbs, and particles, in its mode of composition, arrangement, employment of metaphor and of exact expression, duplication and simplification, copiousness, poverty, verse, prose, rhyme, meter, tendency, and other things too numerous to

> mention. Now no one, I fancy, will object to this judgment, or question its correctness, at least no one who relies on any fragment of intelligence or morsel of justice. How, then, can you rely on any work which you know only by translation, after this account? On the contrary, you require knowing the Arabic language much more than the Greek ideas, albeit the ideas are not Greek or Indian, just as the languages are not Persian, Arabic, or Turkish. Notwithstanding, you assert that the essence of the ideas is in intelligence, study, and reflection, and then nothing remains but using correct language. Why, then, do you despise the Arabic language, when you interpret the books of Aristotle in it, albeit you are unacquainted with its real character?[19]

Al-Sīrāfī seems even more alarmed by the intervention of another medium, Syriac, since this will doubly distance meanings and syntax and lead to further confusion. He argues: "You translate from the Syriac: but what do you say of ideas that are travestied by transference from Greek to another language, Syriac; and then from that language to another, Arabic?"

As an improvised response, al-Sīrāfī's debate exemplifies the *ḥijāj* (argumentation) style that would later take a number of directions. Many middle-period scholars tend to be more explanatory and informative than their predecessors; hence their preoccupation with narrative at the expense of method, a tendency that could easily slide into digressions.

Contentious Theological Grounds

Despite the dissemination of Greek thought throughout the discursive space of the learned, the emergence of the Ḥanbalite school of law, with its traditional reorientation toward basic roots and principles, spoke to a culture that was suffering from destabilization and a challenge—not only to its rules of interpretation, transmission, and emulation of antecedent authority, but also to the Arabic language itself. This trend cannot be viewed apart from the enthusiasm for dynamic commentary and abridgement that accompanied the appearance of Abū Yaʿqūb al-Sakkākī's (d. 626/1229) *Miftāḥ al-ʿulūm* (Key to the Sciences) and the expansion of lexicography that complemented it. Along with these preoccupations, there is an increase in book-length critiques that make use of their subject to establish a communicative network with other texts and authors. Although these works often convey nuanced applications of logic and rational analysis, the increasing presence of grammar and linguistic competence as the integral base for Islamic law was to become a landmark in the Islamic republic of letters. Evidence of this type of critical and lexicographic activity is traceable in compendiums and commentaries. Thus, a particular reading of a specific poet or writer often ends up in a compendium. The other dimension, with its blend of logic and linguistic mastery, is found more frequently in the assemblies of rhetors and scholarly circles, their *mujālasāt* and *muḥāḍarāt* (their discussions and discourses there), or in mentor/disciple interactions, as in Rashīd al-Dīn al-Waṭwāṭ's relationship with Jār Allāh al-Zamakhsharī (d. 538/1144), which left its imprint on the period under discussion. Indeed, al-Waṭwāṭ's celebrated status as one who wrote simultaneously in both Arabic and Persian can be cited in support of Abū Saʿīd al-Sīrāfī's emphasis on a bilingual mastery of language and grammar. The recapitulation of translation as a movement of acculturation can thus be seen as logically integral to the overall cultural initiative.

But invasions and wars are always attended by fear, an emotion that inhibited the work of many scholars, including al-Ṣafadī, whose enormous knowledge may be regarded as a defensive strategy aimed at warding off a sense of impending loss. Although conducive to a feasible livelihood, an enormous breadth of reading could also result in a debacle of one sort or another, as with Abū Ḥāmid al-Ghazālī's (d. 1111) intellectual perplexity in the face of the thorny questions that philosophical discourse and theological speculation had left in his mind. This perplexity may help to explain why a brilliant scholar and polymath such as al-Ṣafadī found comfort in consensus. His view of translation is propelled by a taste for and commitment to consensus; he himself argues that it is due to books in philosophy and logic that "secessionists and Sunna opponents find rationalist premises . . . they include [these premises] in their explorations, broaden the limits of their disputation, and use them to construct the rules of their innovations [i.e., heresies]."[20] Ibn Taymiyyah's rejection of any negotiation with philosophy represented the extreme of a movement whose aim was to reconsider the issue of knowledge construction in Islam. No matter how we view this traditionalist and anti-rationalist school, it certainly was one factor behind the failure of a republic of letters to sustain itself—a republic that could have resumed leadership through interrogation rather than compliance. If the tenth century witnessed a significant thrust in disputation, there was also a contending movement that would gather force later on in the period within state institutions (i.e., the chancery) and the *masjid* (congressional mosque). The hierarchy of knowledge described by the physician ibn Buṭlān (d. 460/1068) as the one widely upheld until early in his own lifetime runs as follows: "the Islamic sciences, the philosophical and natural sciences, and the literary arts."[21] What he laments, in contrast, as failure and ignorance in a later period could apply not only to a rising conservative thrust but also to statist institutions and their functionaries.

The Oneiric Imagination

The proliferation of secretarial and scribal manuals after the waning of the ʿAbbasid era (750–1258) suggests an effort to establish the chancery as the governmental center, even more extensive in its power and scope than the sultan and his court. In contrast, sites of knowledge such as schools, mosques, and assemblies adopted a more or less middle path from the eleventh century onward, not only to escape the circumscribed packaging of dogma but also to be able to explore the nonempirical side of knowledge. Although al-Ghazālī stands foremost among scholars who often write within this frame of reference, oneiric imagination had already been evident from the time of ibn Sīrīn's (d. 110/728) reinterpretation of dreams as a form of *taʾwīl* (interpretation), which places the construction of dreams on a highly symbolic, nonliteralist level, as Ebrahim Moosa rightly notices.[22] No wonder, then, that Tāj al-Dīn al-Subkī (d. 769/1368) provided a documentary record of dreams that involve encounters with the Prophet or that relate to Qurʾānic narratives of true dreams or visions.[23] This middle way, which had gained momentum through al-Ghazālī's persuasive blend, was to strike firmer roots thanks to the intervention of Andalusian intellectuals and learned scholars from the Arab African west. Combining Greek logic with the fundamentals in Islamic law, scholars such as the Andalusian legal Mālikī scholar Abū Isḥāq al-Shāṭibī (d. 790/1388 in Granada) formulated a viable strategy that fuses the evidential system found in Aristotelian logic with Islamic juridical practice to account for the presence in the science of Islamic law of *maqāṣid* (literally: higher objectives, goals and destinations). In al-Shāṭibī's reading, these *maqāṣid* are equivalent to the four types of causes in Aristotelian logic. The attempts to resolve the apparent conflict between Greek philosophy and traditionalists are discernible in nearly every literary medium. Ibn Khaldūn summarizes the controversial role of Aristotelian logic as follows: "Know that this art was vehemently opposed by precursors and theologians. Their objections were excessive, and they warned against its use. They went as far as to ban learning and teaching it, but latecomers like al-Ghazālī and imam ibn al-Khaṭīb were somehow more tolerant towards it."[24] Al-Shāṭibī's initiative can be described as a middle ground because it aimed to achieve the fusion of logic and foundational or originary rules while establishing the latter on firm grounds, after divesting it of paraphernalia. This initiative perhaps can be viewed as a response to the needs of a culture following the simultaneous concurrence of multiple contentions and unresolved disputes. Although intended as a reorientation of a legalist tradition, al-Shāṭibī's work as jurist, scholar, and grammarian was, as ibn Khaldūn explains, probably as well received as al-Taftazānī's commentary on al-ʾIjī's *Risālah.*[25] These efforts to reclaim the discussion of *kalām* as both means and thought redirected theological scholarship into an open space of contestation or approval from the growing non-official forms of discourse.[26] Ibn al-ʿArabī's (d. 1240) contributions, already mentioned earlier in this volume, fit into a larger context that acquired significant impetus from al-Ghazālī's mediation between *kalām* and Sufism.

Ibn al-ʿArabī's major contribution was made at a time when both Khurāsān and Khwārizm were becoming centers of enormous intellectual activity, which was branching out in a number of directions and which enlisted a large number of Sufis and other scholars. Sufism was so much in vogue from the thirteenth through the eighteenth centuries that in al-Shirbīnī's time it was to become a domain for charlatans and pretenders. While putting forth language in its vernacular, written, formal, and also living being, and at the same time heaping sarcasm on proliferating lexical activity, al-Shirbīnī, whose *Hazz al-quḥūf* was discussed in chapter 5, is alerting us to a language that has previously functioned only as discourse. However, his antipathy to Sufis prevents him from reflecting to a sufficient degree on ibn al-Fāriḍ's reclamation of language in its rawness, its underlying life. Al-Shirbīnī's satire is directed not against ibn al-ʿArabī and al-Būṣīrī but against fake Sufis. Both shaykhs effected an epistemological shift in the contentious space of theology. They also challenged the formality of transmission and the presumed subservience to originary or foundational principles and roots. Ibn al-ʿArabī's voluminous work *Al-Futūḥāt al-Makkiyyah* (The Meccan Conquests, i.e., Illuminations) and al-Būṣīrī's *Burdah* (Mantle Ode) set a tone for al-Ḥillī's poetic effort to place oneiric signifying systems into an elaborate rhetorical register. Al-Ḥillī noticeably reduces the language concerning gods to human quotidian practice, a process duly symbolized by his extensive references to poets and essayists. Turning this tableau of inspiration to the advantage of the poet as artisan, and invoking the divine presence through an exchange with the Prophet in a dream, al-Ḥillī is nevertheless anxious to establish an empirical trace of some kind, a sign, in order to appease skeptics, and to do so not through traces on the human body or on a campsite, as is usual in pre-Islamic odes, but through rhetoric. The dream he claims to experience fits into a genealogy of visions that was not disputed throughout the middle and premodern period. Indeed, the dream and vision seem to have been part of a cultural script that accorded them sufficient credence in the constitution of a knowledge grid. The poet is here given agency in a medium of divinatory intervention. In other words, a literate and popular climate emerged that created its own middle way between traditionalists and rationalists.

Grammatica: The Domain of the Lords of the Pen

The recurrent reference to "lords of the pen," that being a distinctive appellation in Mamluk culture, echoes, but at the same time significantly differs from, the professional term by which members of the chancery were first designated by the Umayyad chief scribe ʿAbd al-Ḥamīd al-Kātib (d. 750?), namely, *ʾyā ahla ṣināʿat al-kitābah* (you the people of the writing craft; i.e., scribes). With the rise of paper manufacturing in the eighth century, the craft of writing also led to an increased interest in writing, accompanied by an intricate system of book production: dictation, transcription, copying, designing, and binding before going to booksellers.[27] At times, the *warrāq* (copyist and bookseller), probably a man of letters, played all of these roles.[28] In the absence of an exhaustive and comprehensive documentary record—which would need to be more detailed than that found in al-Nadīm's *Fihrist* and the voluminous compendiums of biographical records between the tenth and the seventeenth centuries—we may perhaps resort to writers' and readers' complaints about the impossibility of coping with this lucrative productivity. One of the many complaints came from religious scholars who held that once "knowledge was committed to writing, there developed an unending process of writing 'book after book after book.' "[29] Along with al-Jāḥiẓ, many scholars specifically refer to the availability of books in translation from Greek philosophy. In one of al-Kindī's epistles on the need for scholars in philosophy to be acquainted with the works of Aristotle, he addresses the unidentified recipient as follows: "I advise you about the books of Aristotle the Greek, in which he expounds his philosophy, according to their order."[30] In other words, by the ninth century we already come across the fact that knowledge is categorized and catalogued in such a manner as to help aspiring scholars and students to acquire it.

The spread of Islam, accompanied by wars and imperial expansion, all leading to the emergence of new cities, military garrisons, and urban exchange, brought together multiple races and cultures within the embrace of an Arab-Islamic milieu, in which Arabic served as the language of faith, communication, supremacy, administration, commerce, and personal and professional advancement. Even into the fourteenth century, the oral function of Arabic would continue—a topic that will be explained later with reference to popular poetry and street songs—but this phenomenon remained marginal when compared with the records of transmission and the practice of public readings of histories, the Prophet's sayings, epistles, or poetry.[31] It was primarily as a literate culture that Arab-Islamic production was able to sustain its overwhelming presence.

As such, it necessarily generated debates, disputations, inventiveness, dictionaries, grammarians' lexicons, rhetorical fecundity, and the noticeable fusion of poetry into prose as a contribution to the combination known as prosimetrum.[32]

Grammatica: A Comprehensive Framework for Knowledge

In this domain, the Arabic language sciences increased in both quantity and quality. Encompassing the sciences of Arabic, *grammatica* developed as the foundational knowledge, with wide-ranging emphases on grammar, lexical differentiation, levels of meaning, and, more importantly, rhetoric, all in order to demonstrate the power of the word of God and its inimitability, and from there to pose a challenge to the notion of the eloquent Arab. This is a point that al-Ḥillī and many of his contemporaries in the middle period take for granted, but with significant deviations.[33] Once we reach the era of Abū Yaʿqūb al-Sakkākī (d. 1228) and his *Miftāḥ al-ʿulūm* (Key to the Sciences), a work that provoked other eminent rhetors and renowned scholars to pen their own explanations, simplifications, or abridgements,[34] we are basically shifting scholarly attention to grammar as pivotal to the rhetorical enterprise. A careful survey of the names of scholars who concerned themselves with al-Sakkākī's *Miftāḥ* brings us to the central core of *grammatica*, as a comprehensive framework for knowledge. Following in the footsteps of ʿAbd al-Qāhir al-Jurjānī (d. 1078) and his loyal Egyptian follower, ibn Abī al-Iṣbaʿ, al-Ḥillī and his contemporaries are already adopting grammar in its broad sense as inclusive of rhetoric. Figures of speech and expressive devices become so not in terms of words, but rather as words in a specific order that endows them with changing meanings and multidimensional evocations. Language burgeons as the consequence of a grammatical shifting of words, conjunctions, propositions, and interrogative, propositional, assertive, or adverbial and adjectival modes of expression. Applied to the Qurʾān, grammar—and therefore rhetoric—allow us to engage with the sacred text's inimitability, which has kept Arabs spellbound.[35] Rhetoric, especially when studied and utilized by theologians and grammarians, appears to command the highest status in the hierarchy of knowledge. Arabic branches out into various disciplines and, over the course of centuries, serves as the vehicle for hundreds of book-length studies. Once in a while, those works will even refer to the ruler as the one who manages to corner such-and-such a scholar with a correction or a query that requires specific knowledge. Writing in the eleventh century, Abū al-Qāsim Jār Allāh al-Zamakhsharī (d. 538/1144) opens his book *al-Mufaṣṣal fī ʿilm al-lughah* (The Comprehensive in the Science of Language) with a scathing rebuttal of anti-Arab tendencies to be found in many of these studies. This posture enables him to valorize his endeavor and market it as a uniquely rich source, with cognates located within the discipline of writing. Al-Zamakhsharī is attuned to the well-established grammatical category that had been set out earlier in the writings of ibn Qutaybah (d. 276/889?), which placed its emphasis on the Qurʾān and hadith as sources of correct use and practice. This seemingly protective stance is one aspect of the response to foreign invasions, political disintegration, and wars; but it also confronts the challenge to Arabic that was posed by the growing use of other national languages, which were given a good deal of impetus by the emergence of city-states and smaller political configurations. Al-Zamakhsharī's coterie of students and disciples was well versed in both Persian and Arabic, and, as noted above, some, like al-Waṭwāṭ, had already written books and poetry in Persian. Several of the most significant works published on grammar, logic, Sufism, philosophy, and natural and applied sciences came from non-Mamluk regions, a point that is obvious, for example, from the series of commentaries on, and abridgements of, al-Sakkākī's *Miftāḥ*.

On the epistemological level, the development that places grammar within a broad spectrum of knowledge, as signified by al-Sakkākī's *Miftāḥ*, should not be confused with the criticism leveled at specific disciplines or pursuits in comparison with others that were thriving, such as law and the religious sciences. We know that with the rise of the Arab-Islamic empire and by the end of the ninth century, grammar as a single field of knowledge did not fare well, as the notable scholar Thaʿlab (d. 291/904) attests. We also know that in the tenth century some scholars boast of their learning by heart fifty thousand verses of poetry "as documentary proof" for Qurʾānic exegesis. There is also sufficient evidence to support the view of eighteenth-century scholar Muḥammad Amīn al ʿUmarī (d. 1203/1789) with respect to the auxiliary and subordinate status of the literary arts in relation to the religious sciences.[36] These examples, however, confirm the general thesis of this chapter that the middle and premodern periods (i.e., the postclassical) are distinguished by the presence of the comprehensive and encyclopedic littérateur, who can also be a noted poet or grammarian.

The Divine in Governance

The littérateurs of the Mamluk period could not have become highly versatile and knowledgeable in rhetoric had it not been for their forebears. They have left us lists of their preferred books and readings and of their authoritative ancestors. As part of their scrupulous care for rhetoric, they also entered the previously uncharted territories of colloquial language and slang in order to discover means and devices of expression that were rarely discussed by their predecessors. The fact that the illustrious poet Ṣafī al-Dīn al-Ḥillī theorizes about popular poetics and that the celebrated Egyptian poet and chancery scribe ibn Nubātah reads and collects the poetry of ibn al-Ḥajjāj, for example, with all its licentiousness, was part of a phenomenon that cannot be regarded simply as a kind of confrontation with elitism. It is rather an awareness of the needs of social classes that had been overlooked for a long time. On the other hand, this same phenomenon and the growing social awareness among writers who were also prominent chancery scribes establish a pattern that contrasts sharply with that of the Islamic state in an earlier period. Although the need for lexicons or even grammar was not binding early on, when spontaneous correctness in speech was still the standard, the expanding state enterprise, as a family *mulk* (monopoly of the temporal realm) or a clan-run enterprise, prompted the appearance of a number of divides and hierarchical structures that could not be regarded as genuinely Islamic, and in which lexicons and rules of grammar had a genuine role to play.

Scribes and secretaries in the earlier Islamic period were regarded as strong and reliable intermediaries between divine power and the ruler. This attitude is an offshoot of ʿAbd al-Ḥamīd al-Kātib's instructions for the training of an administrative corps and other functionaries in the legal and proper use of language for governance and professional purposes. Grammarians and philologists, including chancery scribes who were the ultimate experts in running the state, monopolized official space. In this context, ʿAbd al-Ḥamīd al-Kātib's epistle is significant because the bureaucratic branch of knowledge takes its clues from what must have been common knowledge among functionaries. The epistle describes the secretarial class as privileged. Through their expertise and knowledge, its members participated in running the state. They derived their power from the caliph, as the vicar of God. Language looms large as a factor in the orientation and perpetuation of this rule: "He [God] has set you as a body of secretaries in the noblest of stations as being persons of culture and manliness, of learning and deliberation. On you depends the good order of all that graces the office of the caliph and the rectitude of all that attends it. Through your counsels God prospers for His creatures the power that governs them, and their lands thrive."[37] This formulation empowers scribes and ruler; it is also one of the reasons behind a rupture in the role of members of the learned class. By subordinating them to the ruler and his rule and binding them with these constraints, this epistle, as the most internalized statement or decree of its kind, holds them back from devising a free role like the one exercised in late seventeenth- and eighteenth-century Europe.

Once this elevation to the highest status of leadership in direct association with both God and caliph has been acknowledged, there is little left other than to reinforce this role: "The sovereign cannot dispense with you, and there is none who can effectively function without you. You are to sovereigns what their ears, through which they hear, are to them, and what their eyes, through which they see, are to them, and what their tongues, wherewith they speak, are to them, and what their hands, through which they grasp, are to them."[38] The remainder of ʿAbd al-Ḥamīd's epistle deals with categories of knowledge—its scientific, literary, linguistic, and empirical levels and registers—and admonishes writers or secretaries to abide by God and behave with modesty, restraint, and compassion. In other words, he sets the tone for the double function of exercising authority and behaving appropriately, and he leaves to future secretaries, scribes, and other writers the task of working out manuals for the practice itself as a bureaucratic endeavor that needs specific registers, as, for example, in ibn Qutaybah's *Adab al-kātib* (The Education of the State Secretary; i.e., in linguistic and grammatical usage). With Abū Bakr Muḥammad b. Yaḥyā al-Ṣūlī's (d. ca. 335–336/946–948) *Adab al-kuttāb* (The Education of the Secretarial Class; i.e., in the art and tools of the profession), there is a shift in emphasis toward strategies to meet the administrative needs of the state in the context of an expanding empire. More advanced and comprehensive works were called for, as can be seen in the writings of Qudāmah ibn Jaʿfar (d. 948?) and his contemporary, Isḥāq ibn Ibrāhīm ibn Wahb al-Kātib (d. after 335/946). Qudamah's book, *Kitāb al-Kharāj wa ṣināʿat al-kitābah* (The Book of the Land-Tax and the Craft of Writing), and Isḥāq ibn Ibrāhim ibn Wahb al-Kātib's *Al-Burhān fi wujūh al-bayān* (Demonstrating the Modes of Eloquent Expression; or, The Proof on the Ways of Explication) share many things in common but differ in their interpretive methodologies. Both are significantly tied to an established understanding of writing as a profession and body of knowledge at the service of an Islamic polity and governance. Indeed, writing, with its linguistic base in its auxiliary sciences such as rhetoric, grammar, speech, discourse, and lexicography (i.e., cognates of *grammatica*), is equated with bureaucracy and governance.[39] *Grammatica* in this sense is "the central node in a larger network, the gravitational center of several other institutions and practices—schools, libraries, scriptoria commentaries, canonical texts and language" that "constructs readers, texts, and writers as irreducible constituents in a basic social practice."[40]

In his book, ibn Wahb al-Kātib elaborates on the equation within a dialectical reasoning that resonates with the early stipulation by ibn al-Muqaffaʿ that "*ʿilm* (science) is of two kinds: one for utility and another for the elevation of one's mind . . . but the science that sharpens and clears the mind has a better status among the knowledgeable and the learned."[41] He makes use of his linguistic grounding in discursive clarity as a pivot in identifying the process of running a state efficiently. He develops a number of strategies that direct nearly every linguistic practice and figure of speech or trope toward some kind of social and political use. What begins as rhetoric rooted in Arab-Islamic knowledge, especially in the Qurʾānic sciences, the Prophet's sayings, and those of his companions (and ʿAlī in particular), is soon processed through the filter of logic and speculative reasoning and applied pragmatically to administrative practice. Advice is offered to the secretarial class and their ilk on the best ways to adjust their speech and reference according to people's status. In matters of magnanimity or other types of behavior, logic is to serve as the supreme guide in knowledge construction. If a king or emir utters a solecism, others have to follow; they are not to show him his mistake lest he decide to retaliate. Common people need to be addressed in their own speech category in order not to lose their allegiance and understanding. Ibn Wahb al-Kātib makes good use of logic. His opening encomium is devoted to intellect and reason, followed by another section on *bayān* (clarity and style) and a third on *qiyās* (analogy; also analogous syntactical construction). These are followed by sections on *iʿtiqād* (belief), parts of speech and expression, rhetoric, and poetry. The author thus emerges as one whose mastery of the field is devoted to the service of both state and society. Figures of speech, tropes, proverbs, and maxims are reoriented socially as part of a linguistic spectrum that establishes the appropriateness of speech acts in practices of communication. This spectrum covers symbols, codes, concepts, tropes, and also the linguistic registers of various departments of the state, in finance, the military, and the bureaucracy. This author also focuses on writers, books, and chancery departments, covering the *wazīr*'s (vizier) role, that of the sultan, and the like. In other words, he may seem to be more in control of *bayān*—displaying a magisterial grasp of tradition and its rarely discussed intricacies (especially those relating to ʿAlī ibn Abī Ṭālib)—and yet he is no less occupied with what Qudāmah ibn Jaʿfar attends to in his *Kitāb al-kharāj*, that is, specific statist and professional linguistic registers. Insofar as methodology goes, he makes special use of dialectical reasoning, but he tends to shift the emphasis away from the ruler and court and toward the community. It is no wonder that ibn Wahb al-Kātib's writing is often confused with that of Qudāmah and that his book should be mistakenly attributed to Qudāmah as *Naqd al-nathr* (Criticism of Prose).

Inventories of Individual Readings

In terms of the Mamluk era's recognition of the library and archive as defined by the selective acquisition and use of material for research and reading purposes, the books of ibn Wahb and Qudāmah, along with a few others, enjoy a wide reputation, at least in the catalogued concordance of both ibn Abī al-Iṣbaʿ and Ṣafī al-Dīn al-Ḥillī. Both books function within an educational framework desperately needed by administrators, and within an Islamic polity that is becoming ethnically and socially heterogeneous. This trend is interesting because it illustrates not only an increased awareness of ideological and social divides but also a classification of knowledge in a central space between Arab-Islamic and ancient sciences. It does so by means of significant developments in interpretive and pragmatic methods designed to account for specific situations. The use of Qurʾānic referents is meant to substantiate and instantiate usage, but not to endow social and political power with any kind of divine endorsement.

These two books of ibn Wahb and Qudāmah were no less in vogue than celebrated poems from the past. Their conspicuous prominence in reading inventories (along with other books to be discussed below) and in relation to numerous discussions, books, and libraries in every field confronts us with further questions with respect to the constitution of the medieval literary and cultural world-system.[42] Other writers left us quotes, emendations, and a gloss here and there, but biographers and bibliophiles documented these and many others so as to become part of secretarial and administrative writing in general. Indeed, the tenth century is witness to this move, which went beyond ʿAbd al-Ḥamīd's superimposition of the divine order. Works such as al-Jahshiyārī's (d. 331/942) *Kitāb al-wuzarāʾ wa-l-kuttāb* (The Book of Wazirs and Secretaries) are rooted in the actual running of the state through an exploration of the functions of its highest administrators. This kind of target-specific record, which can clearly be observed in the epistles of Ibrāhīm b. Hilāl al-Ṣābiʾ (d. 384/994), demonstrates the fusion of the writing craft (*ṣanʿat al-kitābah*) with a more worldly state power ("The craft of writing has marked them with its honor and its occupation of the rank of rulers").[43] But this disposition is by no means absent from the realm of poetry and poetics, simply because writing and eloquence also have to draw on a growing but unified word-stock and a repertoire of specific and general lexica enlivened and given power and impetus by an enriched rhetorical practice.[44]

The celebration of the craft of writing is more than self-promotion. Here is a consistent movement aimed at the fusion of writing and statist performance. Even the philosopher Abū al-Naṣr al-Fārābī in his *ʾIḥṣāʾ al-ʿulūm* (Enumeration of Sciences) allots a prioritized epistemological space to the sciences of Arabic language, followed separately by the sciences of the ancients, that is, the Greeks, which are to be acquired by the exertion of human intelligence.[45] Both pursuits serve the state and the Islamic polity and hence require an effort. According to al-Kindī (d. 250/865), the sciences of Arabic language require this effort even when "conferred upon humans freely by the grace of revelation."[46] Second, although there is lingering support for the prioritization of poetry, prose begins to assume a more dominant role, along with the state's need for good prose writers. Chancery writing itself, as a pursuit of elegance and refinement, comes to compete strongly with its other subdisciplines, especially in such departments as finance and the military. Chancery performance brings with it prestige for the secretarial class and their entourage because their textual authority is no less than the other face of the power of the state. In the epistle of al-Ṣābiʾ (and also in ʿAbd al-Ḥamīd al-Kātib's earlier epistle) a linkage is affirmed between the writer/grammarian and ruler. The basis is established both linguistically and textually for the scribe/grammarian/writer to exert ideological and social influence through mastery of the lexical, syntactic, semantic, morphological, and phonological functions of language, duly supplemented and buttressed by poetic and intellectual fecundity.[47]

Central to the pursuit of competence and efficacy in running the state and consolidating the emotive links with the community is the use of poetry in prose through *ḥall al-manẓūm* (prosification of verse) as a means of polishing and enriching discourse. Within this amalgamation, the concept of art undergoes a radical shift. Both poetry and prose are seen as products of craftsmanship rather than of inspiration (*ilhām*) or divinely communicated message (*waḥy*). Even ibn Wahb devotes a few pages to discourse on multiple meanings of *ilhām* and *waḥy*, including that of signs, allusions, and gestures. With this emphasis on craft, already attested to in Abū Hilāl al-ʿAskarī's (d. 395/1005) *Kitāb al-ṣināʿatayn: al-kitābah wa-l-shiʿr* (The Book of the Two Crafts: Prose and Poetry), a sustained interest in the poetics of these two domains was bound to develop. With the rise of a poetics of *naẓm* (composition as construction), more emphasis is laid on distributional and integrative relations among elements and levels of language that are in keeping with the ascendance of innovativeness or inventiveness (*badīʿ*) as an encompassing rhetorical category. ʿAbd al-Wahhāb al-Khazrajī of the middle period (alive in 660/1260), author of *Miʿyār al-nuẓẓār fi ʿulūm al-ashʿār* (Observers' Criteria in the Study of the Sciences of Poetry), considers inventiveness (*badīʿ*) inclusive of eloquence and rhetoric.[48] Al-Khazrajī was not unlike others of his contemporaries in the middle period who were able to consult a library of works on the arts of discourse that had been accumulating for some time. These books, too, present a "republic of letters," handy and available, where authors, realities, and fancies meet one's mind and eye and place the reader within a broad range of materials and topics in a way that earlier would have seemed unimaginable.

Al-Ḥillī provides us with a list of books that he has read, analyzed, or otherwise covered. He significantly mentions that "most of these books are my own, and there are others that I was not compelled to peruse because they were little known."[49] ʿAbd al-Qāhir al-Jurjānī's (d. 471/1078) two prominent books, for example, occupy the sequence of 16–17 in al-Ḥillī's catalogue. Taken in the context of his gloss, his catalogue does not provide us with a full and complete register of his readings. It deliberately targets scholars and well-informed readers who were sufficiently familiar with the books on the list to participate in a discussion. As for al-Ḥillī's "little known" ones, he "was not compelled to peruse" or perhaps even to mention them. In other words, knowledge is legitimized in terms of familiarity, publicity, and circulation among scholars and other learned individuals. State, chancery, and the "little known" are outside this republic of letters, where acquaintance with the "prominent" or canonized texts and authors, such as ʿAbd al-Qāhir al-Jurjānī, holds sway.

Liberating the Islamic Canon

Scholars occupied with other issues have often tended to overlook the full titles of ʿAbd al-Qāhir al-Jurjānī's significant contributions to the theory of criticism through rhetoric. The first is his *Asrār al-balāghah fī ʿilm al-bayān* (The Mysteries of Eloquence in the Science of Clarity; i.e., semiotics), and the second is *Dalāʾil al-iʿjāz fī ʿīlm al-maʿānī* (Signs or Marks of Inimitability in the Science of Meaning; i.e., semantics). In other words, al-Jurjānī was not intent on dealing with innovation and inventiveness (*badīʿ*) separately from these two arts. In contrast to al-Shaybānī and many of his predecessors, al-Jurjānī's examples in *Dalāʾil al-iʿjāz* are taken from the Qurʾān, followed by further documentation from poetry.[50] By so doing, he is excluding the state and its functionaries from his discussions. In adopting the Qurʾān as the archetypal canonic text, he is organizing his works as interpretive methodologies for good reading and understanding. To put it differently, he is liberating the canon from the intrusion of others, including theologians. In preparing for his theory of *naẓm* (composition as construction), he is less inclined than his intellectual ancestor, ibn Wahb, to indulge in conceptualizations based on socio-ideological analysis. In *Dalāʾil al-iʿjāz* (Signs of Inimitability) he argues that words assume meanings that change in their relations to each other and to the levels of structure into which they fit.[51] He argues further: "We find the word at its highest degree of eloquence in one context and we see this very word in numerous other contexts devoid of any share of eloquence. This is because the quality which makes us describe the word in this context as being eloquent is a quality which is created where before it did not exist and which appears in the word after the construction has operated on it."[52]

Among al-Jurjānī's many disciples, the imam, theologian, and polymath Fakhr al-Dīn al-Rāzī (d. 606/1209) deserves special attention. His *Nihāyat al-ʾījāz fī dirāyat al-iʿjāz* (The Utmost Concision concerning the Knowledge of [Qurʾānic] Inimitability)[53] adopts a method of reading the target text that is meant to discredit the opposing view, held by the major Muʿtazilite figure Abū Isḥāq Ibrāhīm ibn Sayyār al-Naẓẓām (d. between 220/835 and 230/845) and his followers, such as al-Sharīf al-Murtaḍā (d. 436/1044). To his reading of al-Jurjānī he applies a specific methodology, breaking up the argument in subdivisions to accommodate a strict logic based on certain principles, a point duly noted by no less a figure than al-Ṣafadī. Al-Rāzī also draws on the works of al-Rummānī, al-Jāḥiẓ, Thaʿlab, Qāḍī ʿAbd al-Jabbār al-Hamdhānī, al-Zamakhsharī, and al-Waṭwāṭ. Invoking these authorities in support of al-Jurjānī's views, he maintains that the text of the Qurʾān includes examples of constructions that have given to specific figures of speech and forms their semantic power and their inimitable meanings and exuberance. To provide further evidence in support of al-Jurjānī's perspective, al-Rāzī must also counteract the opinions of the rationalists, especially al-Naẓẓām. The latter suggests that it is God who diverts the Arabs' attention from the practice of contrafaction. Al-Naẓẓām refers to the word *ṣarfah*, the noun for *ṣarafa* and *ṣarrafa* (disable; transform or convert, respectively) or *inṣarafah* (withhold) that occurs in the Qurʾān.[54] Of significance to the current discussion is not al-Naẓẓām, but rather al-Jurjānī and al-Rāzī, since al-Rāzī assigns the power of eloquence to constructions as laid out in al-Jurjānī's books.[55] Qurʾānic inimitability derives from unique structural combinations and constructions, involving both prose and poetry, that were almost unknown among the Arabs. Rather than focusing on Qurʾānic hermeneutics, al-Rāzī makes the construction of meaning the highest priority.

At this point I need to justify the premise that there is a palpable shift to a mode of textual analysis that moves the "inimitability" of the Qurʾān further away from theological reasoning, by focusing on the contexts of scholarly and congressional networking, discussions, and travel that together comprise the republic of letters. The principle of inimitability that permeates every discussion in either direct or oblique ways had been a characteristic feature of literary and scholarly endeavors since the ninth century and had involved a painstaking textual scrutiny. Even when popular poets make fun of prosodists and critics, as will be explored in the next chapter, their very denial of literary authority offers evidence of the continuing presence of this phenomenon. Prosodists and rhetors never disappear, and by the eleventh century they return to the scene with enhanced vigor across the Islamic lands. Their tools of analysis illustrate their continuing role as "physicians" of speech and writing. A wave of writings on rhetoric and its principles was at the center of the humanist scene during the eleventh century.

Implications of Textualization: The Qurʾān

In this context, a close reading of basic rhetorical figures that function within a textual body is essential. This was a task for which ʿAbd al-Qāhir al-Jurjānī is recognized, and one that has spawned positive scholarship and has been the topic of commentaries from his followers and disciples. By shifting the terms of discussion from external evidence to intrinsic matrices that work independently within a body, a text, or a *matn*, he managed to release Islamic cultural production from its enormous library of traditional theologians. In other words, notwithstanding the scholarly activity around the discussions of the concept of Qurʾānic inimitability that had been generated and provoked by al-Naẓẓām's daring proposal of *ṣarfah*, which had endured for over three centuries, the primacy of the Qurʾānic text is sustained in al-Jurjānī's work through a construction that has as its basis a specific number of figures, primarily metaphor, simile, resemblance, or representation,[56] and their widespread use in all kinds of Arabic lexica. While consolidating a textual milieu and substantiating through sacralization the authority of a grammatical and rhetorical culture, al-Jurjānī's shift in emphasis to the intrinsic body of the text that serves a more humanized theoretical apparatus brings inimitability (*iʿjāz*) and *majāz* (transference away from literal meaning) into an interlocking relationship, since both these terms are lexically linked to each other through verbal devices such as *jinās* (paronomasia) and through intellectual conceptualization.[57]

By implication, the Qurʾān opens up wide horizons for experimentation in this new and complex territory, encouraging writers and poets to find inspiration for their imagery and meanings not only in pre-Islamic poetry but also in the Qurʾān itself. Rhetoric now has to develop within this newfound concordance. Recourse to these rich sources of inspiration also involves a systematic reading and critiquing of antecedent poetic authority, an endeavor that entails not only either recognition or negation of this authority, but also a process of questioning or substantiating its basis as a social and political power. The seemingly apolitical or non-ideological pursuit of textual archaeology—including the consolidation of a rhetorical archive—now shifts attention to the person of the poet/archivist as an author operating in a textual community, which is the hub for a republic of letters.

Textual Archaeology as an Independent Pursuit

The shift toward the person of the poet/archivist as author, however, is only part of the narrative, as we notice in the compendiums of al-

Ṣafadī, ibn Nubātah, and ibn Ḥijjah where poets and their poetry are studied. There is also an underlying humanist shift that takes rhetoric as its field. Within this shift, we need to acknowledge differences in approach, especially in relation to the growing field of rhetoric. Al-Jurjānī, for instance, was not enthusiastic about elevating *badīʿ* into a category that would be broader than the standard classification of eloquence and rhetoric. In other words, his work is more in line with the linguistic and grammatical tendency later to be promoted by al-Sakkākī and his explicators. Through grammatical use and manipulation, we attain the results that are usually subsumed under the terms *grammatica*, *rhetorica*, and *dialectica* as being the common arts of discourse. We should recall that al-Jurjānī does not mention the category of *badīʿ*, or *al-madhhab al-kalāmī* (theological reasoning), as a rhetorical figure, but he uses theological reasoning throughout. The Qurʾānic text is employed as the basis for analysis only in a few examples, which lead to further exploration and discussion. On the other hand, when we approach the *badīʿiyyah* poetic genre later in both time and practice, the Qurʾān almost disappears as a referent. In fact, those panegyrics to the Prophet are characterized by their use of rhetorical figures, devices, and tropes that are able to derive further substantiation from the explicatory apparatus, that is, the compendium. Ibn Abī al-Iṣbaʿ's work *Taḥrīr al-taḥbīr fi ṣināʿat al-shiʿr wa-l-nathr wa-bayān iʿjāz al-Qurʾān* (Writing Elegant Compositions; Emancipating Innovation in the Craft of Poetry and Prose and the Demonstration of Qurʾānic Inimitability) is specifically concerned with the craft itself, its rhetorical power and effectiveness. In other words, it may be seen as a bridge that exemplifies the shift in focus on both rhetorical and epistemological levels toward the emancipated territory of a middle-period humanist enterprise. Along with al-Sakkākī's focus on eloquence and linguistics, the humanist endeavor adopts the panegyric ode to the Prophet as its gateway.

The valorization of intercessionist poetics—as supplicatory poetry to the Prophet accompanied and supplemented by a rhetorical inventory—retains its control over writing and discourse outside the contexts of the equation of the divine and the ruler, or the ruler/rule and the panegyrist, or the state and the prose writer. Notwithstanding the continuing role of the chancery as the statist location for this type of equation and its performance (a point that is deftly expressed and summed up in al-Qalqashandī's compendium),[58] the thriving domain of textual archaeology and discussion grows to become an astounding cultural force, an empire that manages to intimidate both court and ruler even though part of the material that is produced takes the form of panegyrics to, or biographies of, rulers. To balance these types of composition, there is also a genre of prison narrative, which is no less impressive for being written in the form of historical, geographical, and theological treatises. The production of prison narratives testifies to a cultural climate that forces the court to accept a margin of freedom in writing. Many prominent theologians, philosophers, religious leaders, and scientists suffered imprisonment or even died in prison. Both the traditionalist ibn Taymiyyah and the polymath and scientist al-Ṭūsī—to mention two extreme cases—wrote their most significant works while in prison. Shihāb al-Dīn al-ʿUmarī obtained the information that he included in his *al-Taʿrīf bi al-muṣṭlaḥ al-sharīf* regarding the Franks from a Genoese fellow prisoner. Aḥmad ibn Muḥammad ibn ʿArabshāh (d. 854/1450) was in prison when he wrote portions of his incomplete chronicle of Jaqmaq; his *al-Taʾlīf al-Ṭāhir* considers Jaqmaq as the ideal ruler, while the work itself carves its own space among other biographical but edifying sketches. For some elite Mamluk prisoners, prisons turned out to be places of learning; we have at least a record of sultan al-Nāṣir Muḥammad studying al-Bayhaqī's hadith exegesis while incarcerated.

In this republic of letters, another trajectory involves the tendency of writers to secure the patronage of notable members of the secretarial class—for example, the chancery family dynasties of ibn ʿAbd al-Ẓāhir or ibn Faḍl Allāh al-ʿUmarī. Also significant is the sense of pride felt by chancery writers and compilers, such as al-Qalqashandī, in being independently groomed and self-educated in scriptoria, in passing tests through personal merits of excellence, and in being "survivalists," without relying on nepotism and family networks. In his prose and chancery writing, al-Qalqashandī draws a vast map for reading (fourteen large volumes) that encompasses an Islamic empire over eight centuries. Writing embodies people, ideas, rule, governance, science, war, and every recognizable form in literate culture. It establishes multiple genealogies for knowledge construction, transcending tribal or clan genealogies. The written word emerges as the witness to a thriving culture, where the author may cross hierarchical boundaries and establish a new affiliation. The archive stands supreme.

Reconstructing the Literary Republican Model

Scholars of the middle period rarely ask the question of why the compendium becomes a conspicuous cultural factor during the medieval period, compared to earlier periods. Although it is commonplace now to come across both defenders and critics of these compendia, the issue that is generally overlooked is related to readership. How could there be such a massive production of compendia, if there were no audience for it? Why do some works draw more attention in their time than others? Compendia have a poetic and a political function of their own. They aspire to operate as encyclopedic exercises or knowledge inventories. Their specific or general knowledge structure addresses a literate audience that adopts self-education as a pursuit. Although the composite nature of these compendia and commentaries (*shurūḥ*) is the most distinctive aspect of their organization, it rarely stands in the way of the author's ingenuity and the work's significant contributions to knowledge. Apart from massive concordances of biographical records that add to each other and complement the missing or the missed, we find compendiums that are focused on poetics or restricted to their author's exegetic excursion, in which he includes a genealogical construction of a mentor's intellectual itinerary. Ibn Ḥijjah does as much in his *Khizānat al-adab* as a treasury of belles lettres. He records the license (*ijāzah*) that authorizes Ṣalāh al-Ṣafadī to collect and circulate ibn Nubātah's life story and work, which also includes ibn Nubātah's praise for al-Ṣafadī and his own self-narrative. Thus, ibn Nubātah's *ijāzah* runs as follows: "I hereby authorize you to transmit on my behalf what is permissible for me to narrate: aural or axiomatic and proverbial, in verse or prose, through oral transmission, copying, organization, embellishment, material old and recurrent, and forthcoming from sources both the old and frequent." In conclusion, he states again: "I hereby authorize you to transmit on my behalf, and report what I write and collect, as you deem necessary and in order, as befitting refining, copying, editing, and whatever that is included in your courteous request, for both charity and request only derive from your bounty, and may God pay you for your amiable allegiance, eloquent wording, and generosity, and adorn the arts with your munificent pen and not deprive companions and minds from your name and presence as the best of companions and friends."[59] The work concludes with many pages on ibn Nubātah's poetry, exemplifying the author's mastery of the field of rhetorical figures. In his encomium for ibn Nubātah, ibn Ḥijjah points out that this intellectual lineage involves an affiliation with a method that can be traced back to al-Qāḍī al-Fāḍil, the minister and chief secretary for Saladin, a writer whose style is very much concerned with the double entendre.[60] Indeed, he provides brief records of all those who came under *al-rāyah al-fāḍiliyyah* (the Fāḍilite banner; i.e., attributed to al-Qāḍī al-Fāḍil), and then records the names of those who wrote poetry and prose in the same vein. Thus, ibn Ḥijjah, for example, uses the proper name Muḥammad, confusing the reader by subtle allusions to the Prophet Muḥammad, while he is actually constructing a poem in reference to ibn Nubātah's son, named Muḥammad, and his companions. This particular segment of the work serves as a prelude to the listing of those companions, who were none other than his own contemporaries who were influenced by ibn Nubātah.[61] He also lists the people with whom he, ibn Ḥijjah, corresponded and those who maintained the same rhetorical style.[62]

Although these personal records devoted to poets and writers are used to present more examples on specific rhetorical use, the tendency is to accumulate such information in order to conclude with a remark demonstrating that the method has reached its acme and achieved an epitomic exuberance in the writings of ibn Nubātah.[63] Ibn Ḥijjah compares him with his predecessors, admitting that he may have been relatively late in time but nevertheless maintaining that he was advanced in his use of innovation, embellishing the method of al-Qāḍī al-Fāḍil, where he reigns unchallenged.[64] Among the books on which Ṣalāh al-Dīn al-Ṣafadī was authorized to report are ibn Nubātah's book on ibn Zaydūn, his selections from al-Qāḍī al-Fāḍil's writings, and other books by ibn Nubātah consisting of selections of panegyrics to the Prophet, prose writings, his own poetry, and the poetry of many others. Ibn Nubātah also mentions that he has been authorized to report on behalf of a number of well-known writers, whom he enumerates. In other words, we possess here a thoroughgoing literary itinerary and a crowded network that shows how close-knit this republic of letters actually was, and how significant and orderly were the methodologies involved in transmission, narration, reporting, discussion, and correspondence. In this network, we come across names and titles, recollections, and disputes, rejoinders and explanations, corrections and emendations, all of which create a dynamic intellectual space. An additional merit lies in its sustained recording of intellectual exchange.[65]

Literary Agency in a Global Sphere

What is particularly significant about both the authorization and the chain of transmission that is established in this republic of letters is the underlying fact that both author and authorized share not only a mutual admiration and intellectual respect but also a good knowledge of each other's character, style, and production. In this context, the fact that ibn Nubātah changes his mind and writes *Khubz al-shaʿīr* against al-Ṣafadī, accusing him of plagiarizing his own poetry, is obviously problematic. Al-Ṣafadī was not only prolific but also widely recognized in his own time as one of the most intelligent, perceptive, and exhaustive scholars. The accusation against him becomes even more complicated when we read it in ibn Ḥijjah's reproduction in his own treasury. The whole issue becomes even thornier when placed in the context of al-Nawājī's scathing critique of ibn Ḥijjah, since the former at one time had been so attached to ibn Ḥijjah that he was authorized to transcribe his *Qahwat al-inshāʾ* (The Intoxication of the Chancery). When considered in the context of contemporary praise and wide recognition, these controversies may seem incidental to al-Ṣafadī's overall production, and indeed to that of ibn Ḥijjah and nearly every other renowned writer of the period. Whenever a book appeared and made inroads on the cultural scene, responses would also come out, in the form of more books. Al-Nawājī's critique appeared at a time when ibn Ḥijjah was no longer the master of ceremonies, so to speak.[66] Although it is obviously to the credit of the milieu that disputes and refutations were common, ibn Ḥijjah, as noted in chapter 4, was also well known for boasting about his expertise and rhetorical achievement. He habitually belittled minor or less marketable poets and authors, such as ibn al-Kuwayz, Yaḥyā ibn al-ʿAṭṭār, and Zayn al-Dīn ibn al-Kharrāt. It is not surprising that the latter wrote a strong vituperative verse against ibn Ḥijjah.[67] With the death of the Mamluk ruler Muʾayyad al-Shaykh, who had taken great care of him and appointed him as chancery secretary, and following the departure of his well-established friend ibn al-Bārzī, ibn Ḥijjah left Cairo and settled in his hometown of Ḥamā, where he remained until his death.

Al-Ṣafadī's life was no less rife with problems and heated discussions. He was criticized by Badr al-Dīn al-Damāmīnī for his book *Al-Ghayth al-musjam fī sharḥ Lāmiyyat al-ʿAjam*. Al-Damāmīnī was opposed to the proliferation in the use of rhetorical figures,[68] a stance that was upheld by the Mamluk critic ʿAbd al-Wahhāb al-Khazrajī of the middle period (alive in 660/1260; not to be confused with the Yemenite ʿAlī b. al-Ḥasan al-Khazrajī, d. 812/1409); by Ḥāzim al-Qartājannī (d. 1285); and by Abū Ḥayyān al-Gharnāṭī (d. 1344). Apart from this specific criticism of proliferation as superfluity, personal preferences also lead writers to subscribe to a certain position, critical stance, or even a direction in rhetoric, such as ibn Nubātah's allegiance to *tawriyah* (double entendre) and al-Ṣafadī's predilection for *jinās* (paronomasia). When the latter published his book *Jinān al-jinās* (The Gardens of Paronomasia), ibn Nubātah, according to ibn Ḥijjah's report, read it as *Junān al-khannās* (a word play on *junūn*—The Frenzy of the Devil).[69] Surprisingly, Ṣafī al-Dīn al-Ḥillī is rarely the object of pejorative criticism, apart from a few minor value judgments on his verse to be found in ibn Ḥijjah's *Khizānat al-adab*. On the other hand, the best-known books devoted to the analysis of his *Kāfiyah* are all examples of great philological and rhetorical analysis: one by ʿAbd al-Ghanī al-Nābulusī (d. 1144/1731) and another by Abū Muḥammad b. Qāsim b. Zākūr (Fez; d. 1120/1708).[70] The Moroccan ibn Zākūr identifies some stylistic or grammatical points of difference and makes a few objections that have more to tell us about his own background as a philologist with a meticulous concern for linguistic rarities.[71] His book-length study of the *Kāfiyah* and its explication testifies to its popularity and vogue among scholars and readers, and perhaps listeners as well.[72] Ibn Zākūr was a latecomer among the admirers and imitators of the work. The acclaim that al-Ḥillī was accorded in terms of both criticism and emulation places him at the center of controversy and celebration in this republic of letters.

Individual Inventories in a Global Sphere

The use of the versatile and accomplished scholar and poet Ṣafī al-Dīn al-Ḥillī as a model for the *badīʿiyyah* and commentary tradition is no ordinary matter, especially in view of the fact that he was also a warrior and knight, thus recalling the earlier warrior-poet tradition. The qualities for which he was highly admired—his mastery of poetry and poetics, limpid style, consummate craftsmanship, and pride and valor as a fighter—must have led his contemporaries to associate him with his illustrious predecessor al-Mutanabbī, whom he quotes quite often but not overbearingly or to the exclusion of other canonized or minor poets and critics. His fame rests on his poetry and prose style, which were both established before the appearance of his panegyric to the Prophet. Providing a well-researched inventory of rhetoric, with models and explanations, was not part of his early plan. The ode to the Prophet, as he explains, precedes the rhetorical inventory because, after encountering some problems with his health, he had a vision in a dream in which he received "a message" from the Prophet "requiring a panegyric and promising consequent recovery . . . so I embarked on writing a poem that gathers the adornments of innovation and embellished with his glorious praise."[73] The compendium in rhetoric, his *Sharḥ*, followed soon after. A closer investigation of al-Ḥillī's overall plan and contribution, as spelled out in the introduction to *Sharḥ*, shows clearly the association of rhetoric, comprehension, and faith. As rightly noticed by Suzanne Stetkevych, the association that is established here between faith and rhetoric is so clear that it amounts to no less than an equation of the two.[74] The growth of studies in lexicography and rhetoric over seven centuries suggests that rhetoric is being elevated to the level of the sacral. Hence, excessive experimentation in the use of rhetoric led to a lamentable superfluity, or "*al-ḥashd al-badīʿī*."[75]

Yet al-Ḥillī is also admired for his self-restraint, which he justifies in identifying those domains that he decides to forsake in order to accommodate his audience's need for an easy and smooth perusal. By underscoring the rhetorical territories that he will leave uncharted, he perhaps deliberately invites his own contemporaries to embark on their own further excavations, thus ensnaring them not only in contrafaction but also in the rhetorical extravagance and paraphernalia that have engendered rich but cumbersome productions in the form of multivolume compendiums: "I crafted each verse to exemplify one adornment [from among the one hundred and forty]. It happens at times that there are two or three kinds in each verse as talent in construction allows." He adds, however: "Then I emptied it [the ode] from the types I invented, confining myself to the constructions I gathered so as to be immune to the dissension of the ignorant, the envious, or the [dogmatic] assertive man of learning."[76] In other words, he is laying the groundwork for others to multiply what he has already given up for a particular reason. In the sentence concerning immunity, the phrase "to be immune" or "to be resistant to" leads us directly into the context of a community of readers and scholars. The literate domain is not homogenous. Although basically inhabited by those who are well-informed, it also contains the "ignorant," the "envious," and assertive or dogmatic scholars. This heterogeneity can be seen as an invigorating element, since without it and its repercussions we would end up with a flat and inactive domain.

Before turning to his visionary experience, it is important to note that fusing a rhetorical schema and an ode into a single cultural product also implies an elevation of the work to a sacral status, not only through the equation already noted between faith and rhetoric, but also through the vision that requires this transaction, that is, an ode for recovery from ill health. The setup of this discursive space—one of negotiation between the Qurʾān as the basic canonical text and the vision as an intercessionist authorization—opens the gate for al-Ḥillī to connect to both antecedent and contemporary authority in the field of rhetoric. Reading and appropriating what is written and produced in rhetoric, and complementing the corpus with his own "inventions" and "innovations," he emerges as the custodian of letters, a *grammata*, who is in no need of the patronage of rulers or any other worldly power.[77] Through this sustained association that links the Qurʾān, the vision, and rhetoric or specifically innovative adornments, we are thus presented with a different outcome: the ode—now divinized, sacralized, and elevated through the vision—is the canonized text supplemented through the *Sharḥ* with an interpretive and self-reflexive apparatus. Although indebted to its immediate predecessor, namely, al-Būṣīrī's *Burdah* as the most popular panegyric to the Prophet under almost similar transactional terms,[78] the poem—with its theme of recovery of health—comes to resemble hagiographic narratives of miraculous offers and gifts, that being an already conventional practice.[79] The ode emerges and develops as a commanded transaction, for the "message" from the Prophet is that he "*yataqāḍānī al-madḥ wa yaʿidunī al-bur*ʾ" ([is] calling for a panegyric and promising recovery).[80] Notwithstanding this contract of exchange, the poem's rhetorical and lexical matrix shares very little with the panegyric topos. Whenever there is supplication or apostrophizing, it is given a universal application or stylistic elevation so as to generate an explanation for figures of speech that need to be brought into use as part of linguistic instantiation and practice. Arabic is thus transported in all its limpid fecundity to a communal stage involving conversational acts and practices. This is made clear in the explicatory prologue: "In its construction [the ode] I committed myself to what I am predisposed to create, with limpidity in style, ease of expression, and robustness in meaning; avoiding affectation and contrivance, and employing skillful openings and exits."[81] In terms of the generation of fields of readability and hence discussion, a discursive space is being created, one that spills over and connects with large segments of what current theorists call communication spheres of discussion. Both the ode and its explication could not have enjoyed such a vogue without an inherent combination of ease and rarity, of availability and restraint. This borrows its basic motifs from the *madhhab al-gharāmī* (amatory mode) tradition found in Arabic *ghazal* (love poetry) and its fusion into the poetics of the *sahl mumtaniʿ* (the unattainable ease). What starts thematically as a gesture of praise changes direction every now and then and becomes an amatory prelude, with a restrained but flowing rhythm and a dense use of figures and devices of expressiveness.

However, al-Ḥillī's contribution to the realm of readability and the consequent thriving of a textual community needs to be viewed beyond the immediate production of the ode and its explication. Its significance and centrality to a republic of letters as a self-conscious community of scholars and writers cannot be overestimated. The ode's seemingly nonmaterial engagement is humanist to the core; its subtle politics works its way through this sacral transaction to wreck traditionalist discourse and its constraining ethos. It is stridently inventive, yet its poetics takes place within a genealogy and chain that endow it with legitimacy. Al-Ḥillī recognizes antecedent or recent scholarly and poetic authority and then deliberately constructs a systematic practice related to the would-be canon and its supplementary material. There were certainly earlier genealogies and chains of authority in scholastic studies and disputations, not to mention processes of transmission and communication among the literati, and yet there are also missing links, perhaps best exemplified in al-Jurjānī's resistance to documentation as a way of avoiding any interruption of his own flowing analysis. With al-Ḥillī, this all becomes a standard practice, applied in full and with only a few drawbacks. Al-Ḥillī establishes the groundwork for two processes; first, a mastery of rhetorical figures in a formal or documentary record, including names of poets, critics, or philologists less accessible to the canon; second, his placement of street varieties of popular poetry at the center of knowledge acquisition. Both moves will be pursued and documented by others, but especially by his late contemporary ibn Ḥijjah, in his *Taqdīm*. The latter, as an offshoot of al-Ḥillī's *detour de force*, as it were, evolves as a journey through one hundred and fifty figures and tropes (ibn Ḥijjah repeats a few, to exceed al-Ḥillī's) that make his *Taqdīm* (*sharḥ*) not only a rich excursion through poetics and rhetoric but also a mine of social and cultural life in medieval Islam.

Public Acknowledgment of Readings

Basic as such to a large movement in criticism, poetics, and poetry, al-Ḥillī's *Sharḥ al-Kāfiyah* deserves to come first in any assessment of the culture of the period. Let us linger a little, therefore, and consider how al-Ḥillī perceives his textual lineage in the framework of a five-century corpus of rhetoric and criticism. He acknowledges the list of forty books already studied by Shaykh Zakī al-Dīn ʿAbd al-ʿAẓīm b. Abī al-Iṣbaʿ, which is inclusive of the most celebrated material in the concordance of criticism and rhetoric. To this reading list he adds thirty more works that were either unknown to his immediate ancestor or appeared soon after his death. (See the end of the gallery for these lists.) He concludes by producing a compendium in rhetoric that lists the contributions of his predecessors up to ibn Abī al-Iṣbaʿ, who lists ninety figures and devices categorized under "inventiveness" or "innovation" as a rhetorical base. Al-Ḥillī expands this catalogue to one hundred and forty. The significance of this concordance lies in its substantiation of a corpus of knowledge that has been accumulated by eminent scholars over centuries. Although the brilliant and knowledgeable ibn Abī al-Iṣbaʿ, the author of *Taḥrīr al-taḥbīr* (Writing Elegant Compositions), is renowned for his solid mastery of the earlier traditions of rhetoric and criticism, al-Ḥillī adds another formidable parentage to the same lineage. As a poet and eloquent speaker himself, he reads his contribution as being no less important than that of the eminent poet al-Mutanabbī. In fact, he concludes the explicatory preface to his *Sharḥ* with lines from his strong ancestor-poet that dismiss any competitors:

Leave off every other voice but mine;
Mine is the call to be uttered, the others [are but] echoes.[82]

Al-Ḥillī's dynamic role and his reinstallation of an enormous corpus in rhetoric and criticism at the very center of literary life are testified to by both bibliophiles and contrafactors or emulators. He builds on a sustained growth in rhetoric and literary criticism by offering a systematic treatment of literary and cultural phenomena as craft-oriented and open to transactions, exchange, and plagiarism. Significantly, al-Ḥillī expounds on poetry and rhetoric as a commodity; from this comes his substantiation of craftsmanship through the provision of a compendium in a competitive field of production, where authors apply their skill and expertise in full. It is to the credit of this combined project—an ode and its commentary or explication—that so many emulations and contrafactions are composed, amounting to the emergence of a new literary mode. They all attest to a theoretical maturation that at the same time runs the risk of exhaustion. On the other hand, this increasingly fashionable type of production should have fostered a dynamic movement in the cultural scene, which had already witnessed a coordinated movement in lexicography, biography, history, philosophy, grammar, and other branches of knowledge. Elevated to the sacred, al-Ḥillī's *Kāfiyah* is implicated in a double bind of textual economics: it claims the sacral through the "message" and the transaction; hence it can reach diverse social groups and sucessfully win over people through a self-perpetuating narrative, litany, and a few opening supplications in verse. It also liberates the would-be fashionable ode from the more clear-cut properties of the Mantle Ode as defined by al-Būṣīrī's popular poem.[83] As an example of its initial impact, we can refer to its immediate successor or contemporary ode, the one by ibn Jābir al-Andalusī (d. 780/1378), which is discussed by his explicator and friend Abū Jaʿfar al-Albīrī. Ibn Jābir's ode, *Al-Ḥillah al-sayrā fī madḥ khayr al-warā*, is known as "the blind man's ode" since its author was blind.[84] ʿIzz al-Dīn al-Mawṣilī (d. 789) contributes his own poem to the genre; its closeness to the themes of the Mantle Ode is clear from its title: *Al-Tawaṣṣul bi-l-Badīʿ ilā al-tawassul bi-l-shafīʿ* (Using Innovativeness in Supplicating for the Prophet's Intercession).[85]

The Encyclopedic Literary and Social Consortium

Ibn Ḥijjah's ode, as explained in his *Taqdīm*, is sufficiently liberated from many of the properties of al-Būṣīrī's Mantle Ode to claim its place within a different cultural script, one that justifies poetry in terms of its rhetorical corpus or *sharḥ*, not its panegyrics. Hence the dream motif disappears. Al-Ḥillī takes this base for granted in order to elevate the Mantle Ode to a sublimated level where its subject, the Prophet, and tropes of speech merge into a special kind of production that possesses the sonority, cadence, and sublimity needed to incite rapture. The ode turns into an exuberant experience, a source of intoxication for whirling dervishes, and also a mode of sustenance for the scholar. Using his own ode to contrafact al-Ḥillī's and to undermine and improve on the latter's

Kāfiyah, ibn Ḥijjah undergoes a kind of "anxiety of influence," as identified by Harold Bloom. Along with ibn Nubātah, al-Ḥillī manages to excite and provoke a talented generation of poets and critics, who cannot resist the lure of the master and his towering presence in the literary realm. Experiencing this "anxiety" and driven by his desire for self-aggrandizement in a competitive sphere, ibn Ḥijjah provides us with a treasury of contemporary literature and culture, a feat which at the time no one else could have achieved. What starts as an explication of his ode turns into an elaborate excursus on literature and the life of his society and culture. Each figure of speech or rhetorical trope invites explanation in relation to its use and in particular its misuse by his contemporaries. In his treasury we come face-to-face with a sample of almost everything, especially erotica and Sufi illuminations, as the next chapter will show.

We have at our disposal so many encyclopedia-like compilations that combine the personal, the public, the humanist, and the scholastic, along with authorial interventions and acquisitions of details from living persons, that it can be argued that we have a series of significant microcosmic "republics of letters" where discussion and the consolidation of knowledge take place. Side by side with Yāqūt's and ibn Khallikān's biographical dictionaries, with their testimonials, memoranda, authorizations, reports, and autobiographical details, the period under consideration offers many other variations, of which ibn Ḥijjah's *Khizānat al-adab* is among the most distinguished. It is also among the few compilations that manage to preserve its author's contemporary culture, especially the community life and street poetry.

chapter eight

PROFESSIONS IN WRITING

Street Poetry and the Politics of Difference

As part of my plan to examine literary production free from such common dichotomies as conformity and dissent, or progression and regression, I turn now to the enormous body of poetic experimentation in the premodern period—an under-theorized topic that is likely to expand our understanding of the republic of letters. The rules and means of assessment associated with this movement are to be adduced from the practice itself, which has left us with a large collection of verse that can be claimed as both an exercise in dexterity and technical resourcefulness and also a notable social and economic phenomenon. Elitist yardsticks, with their inbuilt checks and balances, have failed us in this premodern territory, and we need to examine this production from a different perspective. Notwithstanding the fact that there are other public spaces for instruction and the acquisition of knowledge, such as mosques, endowed libraries, and copyists' and booksellers' shops, the street still plays a large and different role, one that makes use of these places and institutions to create its own discussion sphere and in due time force new directions in culture. The street, understood as the language of common people, made its way into the writings and compilations of highly recognized scholars and poets, such as al-Ḥillī and ibn Ḥijjah. Rural culture might have remained outside the attention of most poets and writers, but the few extant narratives, including al-Shirbīnī's *Hazz al-quḥūf*, seem to raise questions about the literati and their canonization of urban production, and also about the partial intellectual and social history with which modernists grapple. No less central to this rural track is the reported presence of ascetic shaykhs, saints, and Sufis, of whose direction and blessing a ruler such as Tīmūr felt desperately in need, as ibn ʿArabshāh repeatedly explains in his biography of Tīmūr. These instances and many other apparent exceptions to mainstream narratives may lead us into a more consolidated reading of the changes in the poetics and politics of the era under consideration, perhaps in line with Herder's groundbreaking view of popular literature as deeply woven into the makeup of nations and thus of humanity.[1]

In terms of linguistic decentralization, the Mamluks were instrumental in promoting the use of Turkish and Persian along with, or at the expense of, Arabic. Even so, according to Ulrich Haarmann in his study of this hybridity, certain emirs and sultans, such as Sanjar al-Dawādār and Baybars al-Manṣūrī, wrote in Arabic, while the vizier Amīr Badr al-Dīn Baydarā was noted for his interest in Arabic literature.[2] The extent of written and circulated cultural production indicates that there was a lucrative market for the acquisition of knowledge across the Islamic lands, and that cultural production in Arabic is the most distinctive feature of the period under review. Although there was a concomitant level of production in the religious sciences, other pursuits in science and literature were landmarks of knowledge. Scholars usually consider the rise in hybrid, popular-based literature as a reaction to the devastating invasions represented by both the Mongol invasions and the Crusades, which included the specific targeting of libraries and centers of knowledge.[3] This is worth keeping in mind as a surmise, but, apart from an anticipated resistance to means and outcomes of erosion and cultural effacement, there must have been other factors as well that made the street a dynamic cultural location, especially in the Mamluk period and the last stages of the Ottoman occupation (in particular, during the eighteenth century).

The enormous production characteristic of this period in fact shows a great diversity within a seeming homogeneity. There is also a noticeable liberation from traditional conventions and patterns and the emergence of multiple practices that provoke a number of contending responses. Between the valorization of Arabic as a topic of knowledge acquisition and the ultimate challenge caused by non-Arab occupation of the regions involved, a number of thematic and technical variations can be identified. The Mamluks and their Ottoman conquerors were not inclined to develop or maintain close connections to the societies under their control. The Mamluks, for instance, monopolized such sectors as the military and administration. In their state system, only the offices of Islamic law, the chancery, and endowment departments were exempted from their monopoly. Later historians and critics portray this attitude as propelled by "a sense of superiority to the natives of the conquered country, a conservation of aristocracy as a condition for rule regardless of the roots and origins of its individuals."[4] Although such an attitudinal gap certainly existed, the Mamluks are nevertheless credited for their valor in the wars against the Crusaders and Mongols; and despite insistent criticism of their internal rivalries and sense of superiority to everyone else, the Mamluks still receive loud plaudits from contemporary scholars who grant them the quality of efficient statesmanship. Thus, Bakrī al-Shaykh Amīn writes: "The Mamluks succeeded in general in cleaning great Syria [*Bilād al-Shām*] and Egypt from the remains of European invasion, and they deterred for good the devastating Mongol armies led by Hulagu, and then by Tīmūr (1336–1405). Had it not been for the Mamluks, these armies could have changed the direction of history and culture in this land."[5] He adds: "Hence, this state saved Egypt from the perils that Syria and Iraq passed through, enabling the land to enjoy a sustained culture and continuous political systems that were never achieved in any other Islamic country outside the Arabian Peninsula."[6] The same author deals with literary production in terms of political, economic, and social circumstances, including the terrible plagues, taxation, and the devastation of cities.[7]

There is sufficient extant material to support this kind of argument. It is also important, however, to regard crafts and professions as self-informing cultural processes. Such a proposal in no way negates the implications raised by structural changes within the social and political order that marginalize literariness, while opening up literature as an inclusive pursuit that forms the basis for knowledge. Poetry gradually gives way to prose so as to become a communicative medium that every now and then manages to display a unique and highly talented practice. Bearing in mind the gradual loss of the previously renowned centers of literary learning, as well as of salons or literary assemblies, and the shift of poetic focus away from the Mamluk court, which has no real sense of or care for poetry, and toward the street and its public venues, the new and different role of the craftsman or professional as both actor and practitioner gains validity. The lengthy lists of poets that we come across in compendiums include copyists, oculists, bakers, butchers, judges, jurists, and merchants.[8] This new situation implies the emergence of specific characteristics of poetic production with regard to physical space, versification, and material quality. By comparison with the earlier poetic tradition, for instance, the tendency to use an image in a conceit-like constellation now gives way to a catalogue-like listing, a procession of visual images or perceptual attributes.

Verbal Escapades

In al-Nābighah's (d. 604) poetry,[9] for example, the warlike prowess or valor that wreaks havoc on an enemy may invoke a preliminary metaphor that is consolidated through an image of endless throngs of raptors and birds of prey in the trail of a fighting army. "Whenever they [the Ghasanid army] conduct a raid / throngs of birds fly over, each summoned by another." In Mamluk times, it would seem, the poet has neither the time, need, nor talent for such a vision.[10] Both the street and the milieu demand a catalogue listing of an adjectival phrase or metaphor culled from an already accumulated stock that has been verified and sustained by a rich lexical base. Poetry possesses a number of innovative functions and technical codicils to buttress what has already been mentioned as part of a shift to externals. A noticeable example is its role as a historiographical register and index. This historicization of an event or an occasion takes the form of the Arabic alphabet.[11] Instead of a numerical history, that is, the use of the Hindu-Arabic numeral system for a historical referent or record, there was a noticeable shift to a lettered historicization, whereby letters follow the Semitic order.[12] An early example is by ibn al-Shibīb (Abū ʿAbd Allāh Saʿd al-Dīn al-Ḥusayn; d. 580/1185) in a eulogy to the ʿAbbasid caliph al-Mustanjid bi-Allāh (d. 554/1159), whom the poet identifies as thirty-second in the ʿAbbasid dynasty. But instead of the number he uses the word "lubb," which, according to this *abjadī* (A, B, C, . . .) system, equals the same number. The art requires the mention of history to enable the reader to interpret specific word configurations and images of letters. In his *Sulāfat al-ʿaṣr fī maḥāsin al-shuʿarāʾ bi-kull Miṣr* (Precedence of the Age/Pressings of the Wine-Grapes, on the Excellence of Poets from Every Place),[13] ibn Maʿṣūm (d. 1130/1707) cites poems by a number of poets, such as Shihāb al-Dīn Aḥmad ibn Muḥammad Bakāthīr al-Makkī.[14]

More pervasive is the use of riddles and puzzles under the category of mystifications (*muʿammiyāt*), as a cerebral exercise. Its root goes back to traditional codification (sing. *laḥn*, pl. *malāḥin*) when an address cannot be deciphered by an outsider. The practice was widespread among poets and jurists in the period under consideration since it builds on ibn Durayd's (d. 321/933) book *al-Malāḥin* (Ambiguities of Speech).[15] There he explains that the book is intended to offer an escape from duress in certain situations that require a binding oath or commitment. Its vogue in this period cannot be evaluated outside its political and economic context. Especially under the Ottomans, the resort to this process of mystification as a verbal escapade points to the existence of a coercive governmental system. While these verbal exercises can be accompanied by nonverbal codifications, they do not function outside the domain of court, law, and chancery. They differ therefore from other pictorial forms, such as *al-tashjīr* (taking the form of a tree), implying the branching out into the semantic field of a single word into many other derivative meanings. Jalāl al-Dīn al-Suyūṭī (d. 911/1505) dwells on this form in his *al-Muzhir fī ʿulūm al-lughah* (The Luminous Work Concerning the Sciences of Language and Its Subfields), where he supports his explanation of the definition by reference to the work of Abū al-Ṭayyib al-Lughawī (the philologist; d. 351/962).[16] In both shape and meaning, this form is akin to a genealogical tree. In poetry, for example, there is a verse that resembles a trunk or a stem; its branches spread out to the side, where its derivative words with the same rhyming system are included. Thus, the branches should also be in the same meter and rhyme as the stem (for an example, see fig. 6 in the gallery).

Craftsmen's Poetry

The vogue for this pictorial poetic practice in both the Mamluk and premodern periods should be viewed in the context of the role and presence of the street and the prominence of craftsmen as poets. The phenomenon cannot be understood separately from the illuminated manuscript tradition of books of prayers, such as *Dalāʾil al-khayrāt wa-shawāriq al-anwār fī dhikr al-ṣalāh ʿalā al-Nabī al-Mukhtār* (Guide to Blessings and Shining Lights Regarding Prayers on the Chosen Prophet), by Abū ʿAbd Allāh Muḥammad ibn Sulaymān al-Jazūlī (d. 1465). Illuminated and copied as a book of prayer, this work has also continued to serve as an amulet and part of the Sufi ritual. Both the manuscript tradition and pictorial poetry in crafts and architecture distinguish the period throughout the Islamic lands, including Andalusia. This kind of art also appears in carpentry, embroidery, art design, illumination, and carving. Other practitioners emerge from traditions of the occult and magic, whereby vows, amulets, parchments, and supplications appear in a pictorial layout. Connected to this physical arrangement is the geometrical form that makes use of such shapes as the square, circle, triangle, and so forth, to create a verbal/pictorial design where the verse begins and ends at the same point (for an example, see fig. 7 in the gallery). What concerns us here is not the poetic preciousness of the practice, but rather its relevance to the notion that this kind of approach to art is linked to an earlier era, an example of which can be seen as an architectural phenomenon in the Alhambra (al-Ḥamrāʾ) caliphal residence and palace in Granada (Andalusia). No less relevant is the feature known as *taṭrīz* (embroidery), whereby the letters at the beginning of each verse combine with those that follow to form a certain person's name. Ibn Maʿṣūm's *Sulāfat al-ʿaṣr* contains the names of poets who specialize in these domains. Others may develop a poetics of library catalogues, with the aim of addressing a specific issue or a notable through the mention of well-known titles of books. In such cases the poem evolves as an index of the most popular books among readers. One such poem is by Sharaf al-Dīn Yaḥyā b. ʿAbd al-Malik al-ʿIṣāmī.[17] In addition, there are many other inventive verbal explorations that illustrate a knack for experimentation and innovation, which cannot be simply disregarded as being signs of fatigue and a lack of robust poetics.[18]

Poetry in Islamic Knowledge

Unless we understand the place of poetry in Arab and Islamic culture, we may fail to account for its role in the makeup of Islamic knowledge. On many occasions, the poet functions not only within the limits of verse but also (and significantly so) in the accrued public sphere of a legitimacy that is acquired through poetry. In more than one instance, we encounter the same poet fulfilling multiple roles: the worldly, the Sufi, the saintly, and the devout. Within these roles, the poet explores mediums and modules and releases words from their stock significations. Poetry may have been practiced by nearly every littérateur during earlier periods (albeit recognized as the distinctive career of a few practitioners), but this was even more true during the Mamluk and premodern periods. Discourse took over at the expense of literariness. While not necessarily devaluing the role of poetry and its circulation, the rise of discourse indicates a transformation in tabulated knowledge.

Poetry in Arabic and other Asian languages was practiced by many people as a single part of a larger pursuit or career, which was their means of survival. Knowledge as a quest centers on a profession that one practiced while courting other commitments and interests. Oculists, carpenters, tailors, copyists, butchers, and other craftsmen were expected to compose poetry as an inclusive pursuit that would not interfere with their professional life and its requirements in terms of expertise and marketing. It is no surprise, therefore, that we come across a poet like Aḥmad al-Barbīr al-Dimyāṭī (d. 1160/1747), who was born in Egypt, settled in Beirut, and died in Damascus; he goes so far as to assign the term "poet" only to people who are well acquainted with every branch of knowledge: "Nobody deserves to be accounted a poet, someone deserving honor and esteem, unless he has become acquainted with some knowledge of everything. The poet speaks of every art, and no one can fulfill this function without passing through the taverns of science and taking a sip from every barrel."[19] His very phrasing and wording leads us back to common life, where heterogeneity plays havoc with the barometers of refinement and nobility. Taverns, barrels, and indiscriminating sips address disparate audiences and confront us with the register of a changing milieu.

This attribute of multiple and layered cultural grounding fully applies to the warrior, businessman, merchant, poet, rhetorician, and epistolographer Ṣāfī al-Dīn al-Ḥillī, discussed in the previous chapters. His poetic eulogy to the Prophet is pivotal to any reading of Islamic liturgical practices, especially in *dhikr* ceremonies and festivities. Meant as a tribute to the Prophet, and generating dozens of other poems in the process, his ode confronts us not only with the religious problematic (i.e., the Qurʾān-based criticism of poets) but also with a poetics/politics of accountability. Is poetry representative, imaginative, factual, or fictitious? What are the limits of credibility, legitimacy, and hence poetic faith? Can poetry claim a spiritual role? *Dhikr* (involving invocations of divine attributes in recitations in Sufi gatherings) belies the question, but to what extent can poetry function, especially when faced with the rigidity and dogmatic applications of some traditionalists? How thin, for instance, is the demarcating line between erotica and devout verse?[20]

The Esoteric and the Discursive

Heavily influenced by the preoccupation with rhetoric, poetic language plays havoc with traditionalist discourse and unsettles its practitioners. In their commentaries on the great Sufi master Muḥyī al-Dīn ibn al-ʿArabī, traditionalists habitually heap mundane accusations on the esoteric and hidden aspects of his seemingly erotic verse, which is addressed to the young female devout, al-Niẓām, or ʿAynn al-Shams (The Eye of the Sun). Especially in the erotic lyrics of the Sufi master ibn al-ʿArabī, *ghazal* elevates the feminine to divine beatitude, as proposed in the self-annotated version. However, the subtle and powerful longing expressed in such lyrics also undermines conservative theology and dogmatic applications. No wonder ibn al-ʿArabī becomes the target of conservative scholastic criticism. His *Tarjumān al-ashwāq* (The Interpreter of Desires) and *Fuṣūṣ al-ḥikam* (translated into English as *Bezels of Wisdom*) received the brunt of this onslaught because of their clarity and freedom from obscurantism, an aspect that made them accessible to traditionalists and hence to their attack. Alongside this practice, which would permeate the Islamic humanist tradition, there was also a sustained lyrical poetics that partakes of an *interior infinite*, to borrow a phrase from Mikhail Bakhtin.[21] It is both subtle and soothing, as can be seen in the lyrics of al-Shābb al-Ẓarīf (Muḥammad b Sulaymān ʿAfīf al-Dīn al-Tilimsānī, d. 688–1289), Bahāʾ al-Dīn Zuhayr (d. 656/1258), Muḥammad b. Yūsuf al-Tallaʿfarī (d. 675/1277), Jamāl al-Dīn Yaḥyā ibn Maṭrūḥ (d. 649/1251), Muḥammad ibn ʿUbayd Allāh al-Taʿāwīdhī (d. 553/1158), Abū al-Qāsim Hibat Allāh ibn Sanāʾ al-Mulk (d. 1212), and others. More in line with the politics of the medieval Islamic milieu are other poetic variants and variables, including the rise of the elegy in relation to the decline and fall of urban centers and civilizations. The many applications of this *nasīb* (amatory) poetics between Sufi and human love can be traced in numerous poetry collections across Islamic lands. On the other hand, the attacks on the Sufi poetics that soar toward unification in the divine beatitude is traced by al-Ṣafadī in the poetry of such harsh critics of Sufi poets as the grand jurist Quṭb al-Dīn al-Qasṭallānī (d. 686/1287), himself a Sufi, whose own poetry is replete with ideas and images that bear a close resemblance to the poetry of ibn al-Fāriḍ, al-Shushtarī, and ʿAfīf al-Dīn al-Tilimsānī—all of whom he harshly condemns for what he refers to as their monism. Al-Ṣafadī concludes: "Only God penetrates the secret thoughts of men and only He knows their secret intentions!"[22] In this broad spectrum, where positions and practices multiply, it is tenable to assume that, despite efforts to discipline culture and instruction by conservative jurists and market inspectors, poetry was able to sustain a degree of freedom through an unchartered poetic navigation. And obviously, the public was receptive to a variety of poetic practices.

Registers undergo semantic navigation and a blurring of boundaries. In ibn al-ʿArabī's poetry, the persona melts into the divine, raising God's seven attributes to eight: "eight bear the throne of His Person— / Me and My Attributes. Nay, I AM the Throne, so seek!"[23] On occasions, there is an even greater fusion into the Divine: "And though as selves we may be twin, / to outside eyes we must appear as one."[24] But in the uneven Sufi trajectory, the search for the Divine may end up in blaming the denying lover, in this case, God, who proves unattainable at times. More noticeable is the use made by writers in the premodern period of ibn al-ʿArabī's poetry. Even among writers who were less prone to devout verse, there was a tendency to quote him and buttress their works with some of his verses and sayings. Thus, al-Shirbīnī, whose quotes suggest that he is positively inclined to the Sufi master, quotes further: "All those who seek Your favor have been granted rain; / Your lightning has excepted only me."[25] The Sufi register can also accommodate a love scene, expressing love for both boys and women, a trend that is diligently followed by al-Shirbīnī's narrator. Perhaps there is no better trajectory to bridge this gap between devotion to the divine and occupation with everyday life and its concerns than al-Shirbīnī's combination on the same page of al-Būṣīrī, the author of the renowned Mantle Ode as panegyric to the Prophet, and ibn Sūdūn (d. 868/1464). The latter, "may God have mercy on his soul, said in the poetic form of the *mawāliyā*":

> The man of great taste stands puzzled and at a loss,
> While the billy goat advances and puts on airs.
> Lord, let me be a billy goat, son of a dumb billy goat
> If you intend no relief for my cares![26]

Ibn Sūdūn combines the will to "nonsensicality and farcicality, license and buffoonery" with a touch of "profligacy, frivolity, and effrontery" as being the only means to survive in "this age of ours."[27] Although these latter attributes are applicable to al-Shirbīnī's style, he, as readers may have noted, is not averse to relying on Sufi or recognized authorities, especially in his complaints about life and contemporary times, or in serious rhetorical applications. The latter is noticeable in his references to al-Ḥillī's *Badīʿiyyah*, which he cites in order to exemplify the "distribution" of one letter among words across a verse, or "impossible rhetorical exaggeration."[28] But even here, he cannot restrain himself from digressions, for instance, under the rubric of farting. The specific reference to al-Ḥillī and his *Badīʿiyyah* may not fall outside the framework of the intertextual preoccupations of al-Shirbīnī's work; but there must be some further explanation for such a specific reference to this particular ode, the one for which the poet composes his explicatory corpus, *Al-ʾIshārāt al-Ilāhiyyah fī sharḥ al-kāfiyah al-badīʿiyyah* (The Divine Guidance in Explicating the Sufficient Ode in the Sciences of Rhetoric and Innovative Adornments; better known as *Sharḥ*; i.e., Rhetorical Compendium).

As noted earlier in this volume, al-Ḥillī's *Al-badīʿiyyah al-kāfiyah* (The Sufficient Ode) sets the stage for contrafactions, elucidations, and commentaries that culminated in the work of his late contemporary and emulator, ibn Ḥijjah al-Ḥamawī. The latter's contribution exceeds the normative role of the ode. His ode and compendium begin as a contrafaction, but they develop into an enormous body of texts, a constellation, which interacts with and relates to its components by virtue of the dexterity of both the master narrator and the commentator who masterminds the performance and takes the cultural milieu in its entirety as his stage. Notwithstanding the status of ibn Ḥijjah's ode and its compendium as recapitulations of al-Ḥillī's earlier work, along with rhetorical apparatus, each figure in ibn Ḥijjah's ode is an occasion for an excursion into a vast textual space, where contemporaries are able to make themselves heard. While always exonerating himself, ibn Ḥijjah buttresses every model with examples from oppositional camps or dichotomous spaces, but he always utilizes the mastery of a good-humored polymath who adopts literature as an enterprise for cultural rejuvenation. These excursions bring into the seemingly smooth cultural climate a number of undermining practices; parody, travesty, and contrafaction emerge as new unsettling modes of writing, especially when they target the architects of taste, such as the prolific and encyclopedic al-Ṣafadī. Thus, ibn Ḥijjah begins by citing models of "felicitous" and "elusive" openings, quoting his own opening as superior to those of his immediate predecessors and at least as good as the prose preludes of such master prose writers as the magistrate Muḥyī al-Dīn ibn ʿAbd al-Ẓāhir, or Kamāl al-Dīn ibn ʿAbd al-Razzāq al-ʾIṣfahānī. He also quotes ibn Nubātah's opening to the anthology of the latter's poems—claimed to have been stolen by al-Ṣafadī—entitled "Barley Bread," reproducing it verbatim in order to show that al-Ṣafadī had made frequent (and untoward) raids on the poetry of ibn Nubātah.[29] Since an urbane humor characterizes the dialogue, the entire argument sounds free from any personal venom or grudge. Ibn Nubātah's reported comments on these instances of plagiarism may convey bitterness, and yet they are always wrapped in a garment of forgiveness. On the other hand, ibn Ḥijjah as reporter is willing to praise al-Ṣafadī for his great (and elusive) openings. He cites, with much accompanying fanfare, al-Ṣafadī's exordium to his widely reputed compendium of criticism, *Sharḥ lāmiyyat al-ʿAjam*.[30] As if he were a performer in the street or a *maqāmah* protagonist, the author gives the impression of being emancipated from constraints and ready to roam the stage, free and unrestrained. Even so, he is still prepared to illustrate the opposite tendency whenever his contemporary seems overly fascinated by the use of paronomasia—along with its thirty-four modes and subdivisions. This kind of minute and detailed rhetorical exploration cannot be dismissed as merely another symptom of verbosity and and a loss of intellectual focus. Rather, it marks a culminating point in a rhetorical tradition that turns it into a kind of pseudo-scientific pursuit. As long as there is speech, one might say, there will always be a purpose in pointing to its efficacy or failure.

Poetic Production in a "Democratic" Space

Within a fluid culture industry such as the one discussed here, there will inevitably be an abundance of competition, conflicts of interest, whimsical sentiments, and a tendency to plagiarize, all in the context of either eulogy or lampoon. Such characteristics cannot be seen as mere extravagances. As observed earlier, in chapter 4, ibn al-Wardī makes use of ideational liberty or license on the grounds set out by al-Jāḥiẓ (d. 255/869), who exempts similar meanings from the accusation that they are the traces of raids, that is, plagiarism: "Meanings are to be found on the highways and byways and are easily realized by the foreigner as well as the Arab, the town dweller as well as the Bedouin."[31]

It is worth noting that ibn al-Wardī was on close terms with most of his contemporaries, was "a colleague and sometimes a rival of ibn Nubātah," and was almost a mentor for al-Ṣafadī. All three composed treatises or recensions that focus on debates between the sword and pen.[32] These debates are not merely random exercises; they are discussions of stylistic dexterity or the extensive use of verse prosification (*ḥall al-manẓūm*) as a sustained method for enriching prose, not only by association with a robust poetic tradition but also through *istiʿārah* or *taḍmīn* (borrowing or incorporation) from the Qurʾān, a point that will receive more attention in due course.[33] In addition, such treatises should be regarded as engagements in ongoing debates between professions and administrative structures that are vying with each other for influence. Written by acknowledged writers who have a substantial constituency of readers (as evidenced by their lucrative cultural production and their penchant for disputation), these works also indirectly emphasize the significance of their authors' careers as central to an Islamic polity. Detailed annotation, commentaries, and an extensive use of contemporary poetry and other writings, especially in ibn Ḥijjah's *Sharḥ* (*Khizānat al-adab*) and al-Ṣafadī's *Al-Ghayth*, are intended not only as proofs of erudition and of a familiarity with culture both past and present, but also as a substantial conversation with a readership that is an indication of one's "democratic" space. Indeed, these works (and there are hundreds like them) provide an extraordinary index of not only a lucrative culture industry—with its writers, copyists, book markets, assemblies, readings, and disputes—but also a *scriptoria* economy that derives its self-conscious sense of emancipation from the boundless cultural capital. Such a phenomenon demands the kind of study that transcends the parameters and limits usually set in Western scholarship on the so-called "Orient," including the importation of such "principles" into surveys of modern Arabic culture and textual and philological studies. Indeed, the kind of surplus that emerges as an inevitable outcome in an uneven, premodern market economy should not be confused with superfluity as a pejorative reference. The participants involved in this cultural context are none other than the professional authors, critics, epistolographers, scribes, and poets who are the primary producers and owners of the means of production. In this case, the means of production are not the industrial machine and its components, but rather elements of intellectual property—talent, eloquence, words, and mastery of a field of knowledge—elements that are usually gathered together under the two terms *ʿulūm* and *rusūm*, as mentioned in chapter 2 and explained elsewhere in my discussion of al-Qalqashandī's *maqāmah*.[34]

On many occasions, however, we come across writers who lament their failure to secure a good standard of living through a literary skill. In Abū Hilāl al-ʿAskarī's time it was not easy to survive as a writer. Apparently al-ʿAskarī was a cloth-merchant by profession, and he complains of the double commitment of being a merchant while also writing poetry and criticism—an activity that obviously could not cover expenses or satisfy any sense of importance that he may have craved. In one of his more pensive moods, he writes (in verse): "Anyone seeing my condition among others / would curse paper, ink and pen."[35]

In this context, it is worth keeping in mind that Badīʿ al-Zamān al-Hamadhānī (969–1007) set the stage for the unique status of the vagrant intellectual, a salesman whose cultural capital is nothing but good health and eloquence. Although in a few of his *Maqāmāt* he heaps praise on an emir who was quite generous toward an author, the protagonist in his work breaks up the "differentiated" form of patronage, to use Lefevere's term, into other variables. The economic component, for example, turns into a changing transaction between an author and his audiences across Islamic lands. The author will obtain support wherever he is capable of marketing his eloquence or his ruses. Nobody forces on him any ideological commitment; and on many occasions he even baffles his audience, as in the "Maqāmah of Asylum."[36] Emerging from these situations with a certain amount of gain and an untarnished ideological stance, he eludes categorization, even under the differentiated form of patronage. The inherent instability within this type of vagrancy dodges systematization and brings into literature a changing dynamic. Taking the locations of his different assemblies as an ultimate substitute for patronage and its privileged sites, al-Hamadhānī lays out for his readers in profusion his sources of eloquence and wit, disputing and hence shaking up every other site of power, including the most sacred and hallowed. In one of these assemblies, the *Maqāmah* of Nishapur (in which he invokes his habitual linguistic and assonant fecundity),[37] he makes use of a particular location, Mecca, to strike a parallel genitive and partial paronomasia between *muḥtāj* (needy) and *ḥajj* (pilgrimage)—Mecca of the needy, not Mecca of pilgrimage. Although his talent was exceptional, al-Hamadhānī was also heir to the Arab poetic *Ṣuʿlūk* (brigand) tradition, in which poetry is a record, an itinerary of rebellion punctuated by intimations of love and longing. Al-Hamadhānī shifts the scene to urban centers, where a new transaction takes place, an enforced exchange whereby the vagrant, an eloquent and knowledgeable protagonist, markets his cultural products by means of ruses. This practice is far removed from al-Jāḥiẓ's subtle satire and restrained humor. It coincides, however, with the rise of popular tales, such as Abū al-Muṭahhar al-Azdī's *Ḥikāyat Abī al-Qāsim* (The

Tale of Abū al-Qāsim), a tenth-century narrative that takes us straight to stories of parasites and that Abū al-Qāsim narrates with gusto as it unfolds in a mixed linguistic register.[38] Heaping insults and rants on the company he gate-crashes, while at the same time cajoling them to accept him, the protagonist brings street language into a privileged space, opening up the liminal space for new knowledge constructions of popular culture. No wonder, then, that ibn Ḥajjāj's poetry, composed around the same time (late tenth century), takes as its locale an off-center quarter in Baghdad culture, *al-Zaṭṭ*, where people have their own etymologic pairing and freedom with language. Many of Abū al-Qāsim's anecdotes about his friends among merchants and garbagemen find their way into "The Tale of the Barber and the Young Merchant of Baghdad" in *A Thousand and One Nights*.[39] When juxtaposed as such, societies and their languages open themselves to become linguistic heterogeneities that bid farewell to chancery prose and its belletristic tradition.

On the other hand, it was common among critics and epistolographers of the time to share ibn Ḥijjah's suggestion that the double entendre (*tawriyah*) should be put to frequent use by poets whose profession requires it, especially if these professions relate to the marketplace. He mentions Abū al-Ḥusayn al-Jazzār (the butcher), al-Sarrāj al-Warrāq (d. 695/1295) (scribe-copyist, saddlemaker), Shams al-Dīn al-Muzayyin (the barber), Yaḥyā al-Khabbāz (the baker), and so on.[40] Ibn Ḥijjah notes that someone said to al-Sarrāj al-Warrāq: "Had it not been for your patronymic and profession, half of your poetry would be lost," a point that is mentioned in al-Ṣafadī's *Al-Ghayth.* The source is ʿImād al-Dīn Ismāʿīl ibn al-Qaysarānī, who in turn quotes his own father as the person who told this to al-Sarrāj al-Warrāq.[41] Combining in this patronymic derivation and profession (copyist, saddlemaker) a variety of professions and meanings, the poet was known for short poems that take their start from professional attributes to make a point of one sort or another. Certainly, the analogy to industrial capital cannot and should not be sustained. The point here is that, being independent of the hegemonic order of the court and free from subordination, writers can function as professionals with a knowledge capital of their own. That capital emanates from their exertions in cultural production, marketing, and the extraction value in order to be able to cover not only the labor expenses of copyists, binders, and others, but also the writer's own expenses, which would include cultivating the desired public image implied by a prestigious social role. Only when those who are untalented or unqualified try to flood the market with imitative literature do we find the kind of superfluity that has been habitually decried. Rosenthal refers to Abū al-Barakāt Hibat Allāh al-Baghdādī's (d. 1164 or 1165) complaints against the overproduction of books in the twelfth century, in his *al-Mu'tabar fī al-ḥikmah*, and concludes that "even for secular scholars, the great increase in books (*al-kutub wa-l-taṣānīf*) made it possible for ignoramuses to infiltrate the ranks of qualified intellectuals, and actually diminish the quality of books."[42] The phenomenal proliferation of book writing and compilation is a prominent feature of the other side of book production in socially and politically malleable and peripatetic communities.

Such overproduction takes many directions. Notwithstanding the complaints directed at the less learned or scholarly material, the indexical archive of biographical dictionaries, bibliographic guides, lexicons, and manuals confronts us with dynamic processes of knowledge formation that cannot be linked to a specific function of the state. The destruction of Baghdad libraries, schools, and markets was without doubt an unparalleled cultural catastrophe in the Arab east, and the fear of a similar event elsewhere may well have been on the minds of book collectors, perhaps leading them to increase their acquisitions. More significant than that, however, is the rise of a generative-textual referentiality, a process whereby each polymath's book evolves as documentary record of rarities, choices, anecdotes, figures of rhetoric, entertaining narratives, insights, commentaries, and the like. Each book becomes a library of its own, a textual space sustaining its author's thesis (*khuṭbah*), which usually stands out as a prologue to a book. Each encyclopedic or treasury-like production tends to vie with another of the same type, not necessarily to duplicate it, but rather to demonstrate the author's competitive mastery of a field manifested in his erudite coverage and analysis of new examples, details, extensive criticism, and analytic strategies for dealing with writings both ancient and contemporary. Moreover, the same writer, poet, or scribe is not merely a recipient of street language but also a master of its theorization and application through circulation as an indispensable aspect of knowledge. Along with other common and distinctive features, one can argue that there is a substantial epistemological turn here, which can explain the inability of what Adorno calls the "antipodes" or "patriarchs of modernity" to come to grips with disruptive explorations that absorb antecedent knowledge,[43] its *ʿulūm* and *rusūm*, while exploring new paths and legitimizing other earlier models that have never been accommodated as central to knowledge.

The common features of this endeavor—analyzed further below—can be summed up as follows. First, the author, being a versatile littérateur, is no longer tied to earlier prescriptions of knowledge as generally applied in ʿAbd al-Ḥamīd al-Kātib's *Risālah* (epistle), for example, a feature that continues to inform strategies and basic knowledge formation in epistolary art. Each littérateur must also contribute new findings, adding thereby to the accumulation of knowledge. Second, as though experiencing Harold Bloom's anxiety of influence in relation to the ancients (including most of the poets of the Umayyad and ʿAbbasid periods), this same littérateur continues to remind readers that he or she is unprecedented in specific cases of inventiveness. Third, the professionalism and collegiality that ʿAbd al-Ḥamīd al-Kātib demands in his epistle fail to mitigate the kind of blunt (and at times scathing) criticism aimed at what is regarded as faulty analysis. Hence, we come across fervent exchanges among poets, critics, and epistolographers, who fault each other or accuse each other of theft. Fourth, although the Qurʾān and its studies remain pivotal, the shift to panegyrics to the Prophet deprives rulers of any possible claim to representation as the vicars of God on earth. These panegyrics engender a rich rhetorical treasury that shifts emphasis from the divine to the human, each trope or figure being one of substantiation, not abstraction. Fifth, while poetry witnesses an upsurge in both volume and power, the supplemental commentaries devoted to it tend to buttress the shift to prose as a basic mode of communication. Poetry itself is subject to greater experimentation in form and themes, tendencies that show diversity and prolixity in the practice of layout as a spatial management on the page. In such a context the humorous but sustained use of platitudes must have been one way to please street and assembly audiences. Sixth, the rise of prosimetrum—works mixing verse and prose—plays the dual role of enriching language through revitalization and navigation between poetry, the Qurʾān, and prose. Finally, elitist prose may still be dominant, in keeping with a valorization of a classical mode of expression, and yet most of the prominent poets, authors, and scribes have their own licentious verse and common and popular poetry and songs, and make many inroads into "*ʿāmmiyah*" (colloquial) rarities and pleasantries; the point is that they are also addressing and reaching out to the common public. In other words, the shift to the common public signifies epistemologically a shift in Islamic polity structures. Authors are subservient neither to ibn al-Nadīm's measures of elegance versus "insipidity" nor to the demands and protocols of the royal court and its entourage. All of this helps explain why traditionalists since the time of al-Shayzarī and ibn Taymiyyah have occasionally made vindictive comments about the proliferation of deviationist practices.

Artisans as Poets

The participation of professionals and traders in poetic composition testifies to this shift in literate culture, especially since the names used by many of these poets bear their professional or working titles, as agnomina, eponyms, nicknames, or surnames. It is no coincidence that a large number of traders and artisans of the middle period are listed in belletristic compendiums or constellations. No matter how restrictive book production might have been, the fact that traders are a noticeable presence throughout the period in question testifies to a number of material and cultural realities. First, there was a considerable degree of malleability that allowed traders and craftsmen to invade the literary scene and to retain a noticeable status there. Second, the quality of this productivity in terms of performance was very high, as can be seen in ibn Dāniyāl's shadow plays and poetry, as well as the poetry, prose writing, and anecdotes of others. Different explanations for this phenomenon can also be suggested: these traders have a conspicuous social role and thus cannot be ignored. Their anecdotes and poetry gain wide circulation in tandem with their social role and status. As both productive social groups and individuals, their sayings and professional languages introduce a new element that is seductive and intriguing for the rest of the social spectrum. Even when their works verge on playful obscenity, there is still a lucrative market and a public demand for them, which copyists accommodate through commercial transactions. The entire endeavor, moreover, should be seen in the context of a dynamic milieu that is untrammeled by subservience to a center of authority. Self-liberated poets and critics can argue their case as they see fit, indulging in experimentation and at the same time invoking enough intellectual acumen to theorize it. Although popular forms of poetry outside the framework of the classical *qaṣīdah* tradition were already in evidence, their growth and variety impelled the poet as critic to develop a schema that would authorize the marginal works and place them in scriptoria alongside the literary canon. Within this new climate of ideas, where practitioners were now dispersed among miscellaneous public spaces, the entire undertaking gradually became a genuine presence in the intellectual milieu. By implication, the new critical endeavor to systematize and categorize the languages of the street was intended not only to concede validity to these languages and their social groups, but also to revise the classical canon in order to accommodate the street within its terms of reference. The system of prosody that al-Khalīl ibn Aḥmad had originally recorded as based on Bedouin criteria and that scholars had legislated as the basic prosody for poetry underwent an appropriation by no less a master of classical prosody and popular verse than Ṣafī al-Dīn al-Ḥillī. Thus, the republic of letters was forced to expand its parameters so as to host the street, and it did so in the relative absence of the court, whose role as a literary and cultural center had diminished since the decline of the caliphate.

Street Poetry

Al-Ḥillī's most significant contribution, from the present perspective, is thus not his wine poetry and homoeroticism but rather his pioneering collection and analysis of popular verse (on a par with his founding *badīʿiyah*, *dīwān*, and groundbreaking compendium in rhetoric). The title that he chose for the work on popular verse, namely, *Al-ʿĀṭil al-ḥālī wa-al-murakhkhaṣ al-ghālī fī al-azjāl wa-al-mawālī* (The Unadorned Bejeweled and the Cheapened Rendered Costly),[44] is another play on paronomasia and antithesis. By way of explanation, the title means that the collection is free from grammatical and eloquent correctness as practiced in classical Arabic, but is nonetheless bejeweled with what it misses in terms of high moral ethics; among the reprobate and the dissipated it is cheap, but for those who are grave and morally upright it is costly. Although al-Ḥillī justifies these poetic forms and modes as being well known, whether in part or whole, in the east and west of the broader region, his own taste is for what Baghdadis used to sing at night on the city streets in the ʿAbbasid period during the month of Ramadan. Four of these poems exhibit a sustained level of solecism, although one of them (*al-mawāliyā*) can be read either as being in pure and correct Arabic or as written at a lower level of the language. I note here parenthetically that al-Ḥillī's contemporary, ibn Ḥijjah, quotes examples of *tawriyah* (double entendre) in his *Taqdīm* taken from his contemporary Shams al-Dīn al-Wāsiṭī, composed in the metrical form of *dūbayt*, and also from the poet al-Qāḍī ʿAlāʾ al-Dīn b. al-Juwaynī (the Ṣāḥib al-Dīwān, or chief chancery secretary in Baghdad), whose poems composed in both *dūbayt* and *mawāliyā* contain a mixture of colloquial and classical registers. They are set within the specific metric for each mode.[45] The *zajal*, *kān-wa-kān*, and *qūmā* are partially colloquial, solecistic (*malḥūn*), and hence different from other forms such as *qarīḍ*, *muwashshaḥ*, and *dūbayt*, which are in *faṣīḥ* (pure and classical) Arabic.[46] Al-Ḥillī's study, along with its examples, is unique because for the first time it offers a full engagement with popular lore that is penned by a prolific poet with a strong mastery of classical poetics and a significant contribution to rhetoric. Since these poetic forms originate for a reason and in response to specific situations, their audiences are to be located in their sites of origination, with all their political and social complications. But other studies were also made, such as those of another of al-Ḥillī's contemporaries, ʿAbd al-Wahhāb al-Banwānī, entitled *Rafʿ al-shakk wa-l-bayn fī taḥrīr al-fannayn, al-zajal wa-l-mawāliyā* (Dispelling Doubt, Falsehood, and Discord in the Explication of the Two Arts: *Zajal* and *Mawāliyā*); ibn Iyās's *Al-Durr al-maknūn fī sabʿ funūn* (The Hidden Pearls Concerning the Seven Categories [of Poetry]); and al-Ṣafadī's *Alḥān al-sawājiʿ min al-mabādiʾ wa-l-marājiʿ* (The Harmonious Cadence in Principles and Orientations). These initiatives raise serious questions about the appropriate response to the complexity of the period under consideration. With works such as these, the poet/critic and rhetor is confronting us with the realities of a society in its totality. Considered as a linguistic phenomenon, it involves both a past and present and challenges one-sided readings of its complexity.

Both al-Ṣafadī and ibn Ḥijjah assiduously gathered these popular poems as rarities, spices for what might have otherwise lapsed into a kind of uniformity and sameness. However, these two authors are not the only sources, for, as Kāmil Muṣṭafā al-Shaybī (al-Shaibi) has shown, there are dozens of compendiums, historical accounts, and compilations that contain poetry by professionals, craftsmen, artisans, Sufis, women poets, and others.[47] Al-Shaybī mentions a number of poets whose short poems were known during the middle period all over the Arab east. An anonymous poet, for example, wrote a poem of ninety-four verses admonishing professionals, craftsmen, and traders, one after another, to refrain from cheating their customers.[48] Presumably familiar with the marketplace and its transactions and economies, the poet details the specifics of each trade. Moreover, in this particular mode of composition the poet is required to mention his or her name within one of the concluding verses. The required presence of this signature calls for some explanation. One might argue that, since many poets are writing or reciting in the same vein, there is a possibility of overlap, where one poet is mixed up with another, with the risk of being plagiarized and misquoted. On the other hand, the need for this signature may also be linked to a semiotic bent, an assertion of specific identification demanded in a market for lucrative popular poetry in which the laws of supply and demand function not only in material terms but also in moral ones, including social relations, love affairs, and other prospects. Kāmil Muṣṭafā al-Shaybī speculates that this imprint or signature, known under the term *al-istishhād* (nouns: *shāhidah*, *shāhid*, and so on; sign/witness), was first used in a long poem by Aḥmad ibn al-Jawzī, the grandson of the renowned shaykh and polymath Jamāl al-Dīn ibn al-Jawzī, who himself composed in the *kān-wa-kān* form.[49] An example of this kind of usage can be seen in the following concluding couplet from a long poem in the *mawāliyā* form by al-Qayyim al-Ghubārī ("measurer of verse and prosody" in the first verse is punning on his name and that of formal prosodists):

This is al-Ghubārī, a measurer of verse and prosody,
  and, as said, his measurements are certified, sanctioned, and balanced,
He knows the rhymes and the correct meters:
  Vicissitudes of fortune precipitate sorrows subsequent to joy.[50]

The conclusion of the *mawāliyā* always reminds audiences of the brevity of life and the need for atonement.[51] Another poet who numbers among vendors, traders, or craftsmen is Badr al-Dīn al-Zaytūnī (d. 924/1518), who composed works in the forms of the seven categories[52] and also for *khayāl al-ẓill* (puppet shadow theatre). One of his lyrics is a love poem written in *kān-wa-kān*, in which he addresses a woman in whom he is interested:

You whose love takes me hostage
  my heart yearns for you
adulation overwhelms me
  and I am passing through tormenting longing
the heart cannot bear so much
  but love and longing mercilessly surge.[53]

Still another poet, Ibrāhīm ibn Muʿḍad ibn Shaddād (known as al-Jaʿbarī; d. 687/1288), deploys for his poetry of longing the *kān-wa-kān* form. On the other hand, Burhān al-Dīn ibn Zuqāʿah's (d. 816/1413) professions as cook and tailor find full expression in his poetry. Along with other craftsmen, he introduces into Arabic a malleable space, containing internal disjunctions where relational sets and layered socioeconomic conditions open up to the use of dialects, jargon, and generic group languages that justify and also question Bakhtin's arguments in his "Discourse in the Novel."[54] Expanding the dialogic principle in poetry and turning the form into a diaglossic space, the poem is no less functional than the novel in capturing and dynamizing the cultural and social mode of writing and recitation. Bringing these voices into poetry through reference to their crafts, these poets generate a heteroglossic space of dispersion, dialogization, and conversation. By invoking these speech types they aspire to militate against centripetal linguistic dynamics, in the process destabilizing and supplanting the ever-present stronghold of ideological systems in the battle for linguistic space. Like the other poets, ibn Zuqāʿah does not restrict his verse to an exterior index of social and human practices but instead uses the occasion to conclude on a pious note that usually conflicts with the stern, restrictive, and unitary discourse so typical of the emerging conservative tenor in theological debate. In this capacity, for example, he says:

> You who would like to see a tailor
>   shorten the cloth of disobedience
> and ask the God of the throne
>   for a garb of blessings.[55]

Another poem only reaches its conclusion after a long and detailed description of the speaker's own circumstances, set within a register of cookery, meals, ragout preparation, and pan-fried dishes, along with abundant comparisons between the condition of the speaker and varieties of fruits and vegetables. In the end, the poem emerges as an index of cookery as practiced at the level of common social life.[56]

There are also poems in the more traditional *qaṣīdah* form that speak of this common social life, as in the elegy composed by the Egyptian judge Sirāj al-Dīn al-Qusī (d. 533/1138) on the occasion of the passing of two friends, a weaver and a sailor, in which he invokes the tools and instruments associated with their occupations. But this involves a change in the very conceptualization of the world. Its wholeness, as macrocosmically intertwined with a person's life and career, is now redrawn. Concreteness and representability take over.

The significance of these poems in terms of conceptualization lies in the transposition of the devices of expressiveness, the figures and evocations of mythical or religious registers, onto another level of more down-to-earth vocabulary that confronts us as readers with life as it is. It is not the sky, time, or cosmic phenomena that are drawn upon in order to express calamity and loss, but rather the personified tools that are used to bewail the loss while longing for the missing management of the meticulous user. This shift, no matter how ironic it may sound, signifies a changing understanding of poetry and poetics, which for many centuries had been the preserve of the privileged and highly educated class.[57] At the level of profession and material production, the case becomes yet more problematic. In a preindustrial age, there is as yet no alienation precipitated by the separation of the craftsman or professional from the tool or machine in its preindustrial status. Hence there exists no surplus value to further emphasize the gap and enforce further exploitation or accumulation of capital. The tool and its immediate owner still cherish a reciprocal devotion, which is picked up and celebrated in verse that recreates the relationship in a multidimensional graphic, expressive, and verbal *mise-en-scène* involving multiple voicing and performative enactments. Tools are made to perform their role in reciprocity with the owner's affection and devotion to a profession.

Other examples of this trend abound in an age that witnessed the vogue of popular forms of poetry. Among the names that received some attention in compendiums or separate monographs are Abū Dharr al-Ḥalabī (d. 884/1479), ibn Tāj al-Dīn Mūsā (d. 844/1440), and Zayn al-Dīn ibn al-ʿAjmī (d. 795/1392). However, there is more to be gleaned on the semiotic level than the mere existence of registers for professions and crafts that invade the poetry of these figures and attest to what twentieth-century narratologists, such as Bakhtin, refer to as multiple voicing and heteroglossia. Apart from a significant destabilization of an official or codified discourse, there is also a noticeable shift in names, nicknames, and attributes. Although not all these attributives, nicknames, and denominations indicate a personal intervention, they usually involve some kind of family, communal, or institutional mediation. The most conspicuous among these appellations, especially in the middle period and throughout the Islamic territories, is the genitive compound construction whereby the word *dīn* (religion) becomes part of the first name, as in "Tāj al-Dīn" and "Nūr al-Dīn" (the crown of religion and the light of religion, respectively). An honorific as it is, its proliferation requires an explanation. This attributive and possessive use was so widespread and in such an unprecedented manner that it raises questions concerning the shift from an earlier vogue of single proper names, nicknames, professional affiliations, and/or compound attributives such as "Jār Allāh" and other variations on honorifics. The reader may perhaps ask whether this shift in signification betrays an overt fear for the survival of religion as an institution and a practice following long periods of invasions and plagues, in an era that was also known for visits to shrines and the reliance on, and resorts to, parchments, amulets, rituals, and ceremonials. Especially in non-Arab regions, and in Asia in particular, names and honorifics make up a distinctive marker in Islamic geographies.

On the semantic level, this popular tradition is as diversified in its origins and propensities as is appropriate for common publics. An exception to popular modes of poetry that relates to the taste of privileged classes is the *dūbayt*. This poetic genre, for example, derives from a Persian origin and hence is practiced by classes and professional strata that rarely associate with common life. Its practitioners may include, according to al-Shaybī, kings, sultans, physicians, ministers, philosophers, and also recognized poets across ethnic divides and boundaries.[58] As the tales of *A Thousand and One Nights* illustrate, the *kān-wa-kān* genre, in contrast, tended to be in vogue among all classes, as a popular means of expressing musings, emotions, passions, expectations, and also the usual themes of poetry subsumed under the subcategories of elegy, panegyric, erotic longing, debauchery, and simple life stories. Its recitation or inscription rarely omits reference to its poet, especially since the verse addresses people who need no sublime touches in order to invoke an image different from what they actually are. To make use of Ranciére's comment on the breakup of Aristotelian divisions among genres, this practice of nonclassical modes of poetry is "first and foremost rooted in the aesthetic logic of a mode of visibility that, on the one hand, revokes the representative tradition's scales of grandeur and, on the other hand, revokes the oratorical model of speech in favor of the interpretation of signs on the body of people, things, and civilizations."[59]

Although the *kān-wa-kān* originated in Baghdad and gained momentum among the populations of the marshes in Iraq,[60] it proved sufficiently flexible to find a place in both Egyptian and Syrian colloquial language as well. As evidence for this flexibility, we can point to the availability and mobility of the *kān-wa-kān* as a register for numerous professions and crafts, the kind of listing that befits a *ḥisbah* (market inspector's) manual.[61] However, the genre supersedes these manuals in its intimate listing of the specifics of each craft, detailing its tools and practice in a rhythm that mnemonically establishes a place for itself in a collective memory.

Sufis in the Public Domain

Didactic and edifying poetry written in the *kān-wa-kān* mode constitutes a large portion of what has survived. In the Sufi trend in particular there are many women poets, and we can tell that the privacy of their sphere made it impossible for their other poetry to be circulated as widely as that of their male counterparts. The Sufi portion of this female output, however, made its way easily into the street and hence to compendiums, to achieve a crowning point with the verse of Fāṭimah al-Jamāliyyah (sixteenth century). She was in charge of social and religious celebrations in Cairo at that period. Well known as a woman Sufi, Fāṭimah clearly had many followers, and her *kān-wa-kān* poems were popular enough to be cited. Apart from writing poetry for these celebrations, she composed poetry on Sufism as a practice, with its rituals of restraint and austerity.[62] Her poetry also extends to other social issues, including a child's learning of the Qur'ān, education, a girl's success in a craft, and the like. In this mode the didactic and edifying verse should not be seen as rigid performance, since the form of the *kān-wa-kān* in particular is light and smooth enough to reach people: its instructive touch can be seen as a mere intervention into what is otherwise a recited or textual body of virtually realistic scenes and occasions. Even when coming from a well-known and popular Sufi shaykh such as ʿUbayd al-Ḥarfūsh (d. 801/1399),[63] it avoids the constrained model of instructive verse. His *kān-wa-kān*, which adopts the figure of al-Ḥallāj (executed 922) as persona, reconstructs a widely circulated version of al-Ḥallāj's Sufism, but is situated in a retrospective *kān-wa-kān* that uses Sufi wine as the intoxicating medium of divine adoration and love:

You, who supplied me with unadulterated cups of love
 and told me don't sing and disclose the secrets
But had He supplied a mountain one single drop from what has
 been given to me

the mountain would have sung and shouted and turned among
mountains into dust.[64]

Mnemonic and short, this kind of poetry is usually met with approval. Both Shams al-Dīn al-Kūfī (d. 685/1277) and Aḥmad ibn al-Jawzī (d. after 678/1279) wrote edifying verse in the same form.[65] Similar poets include Ṣafī al-Dīn al-Ḥillī and ibn Nuqṭah (d. 597/1201) in Iraq.[66] In Egypt they include Abū ʿAbd Allah Khalaf ibn Muḥammad al-Miṣrī, known as al-Qayyim al-Ghubārī (d. 791/1389); Ibrāhīm ibn ʿAlī, better known as Ibrāhīm al-Miʿmār, also as Ghulām al-Nūrī (al-Nūrī's Lad; d. 749/1348); and Abū al-Najā Muḥammad ibn Muḥammad al-ʿŪfī (831–924/1428–1518). In Syria we find Abū al-Ḥasan al-Ḥarīrī (d. 645/1247) and Zayn al-Dīn Abū Ḥafṣ ibn al-Wardī (d. 749/1348). Ibrāhīm al-Miʿmār was highly acclaimed in his time as an illiterate (i.e., unable to read) who was nevertheless richly endowed with a dense rhetorical register. Combining the use of figures of speech with new meanings and suggestive comparisons, he earned for himself a distinguished poetic career. Moreover, he never aspired to easy gain or undeserved merit. When he was told that Tīmūr Lang, who occupied the lands of the Arab east and settled in al-Shām, always begged God to forgive his sins, Ibrāhīm improvised the following lines: "It is our blight to have an emir who oppresses people and asks for forgiveness / he is like a butcher who slaughters in the name of God."[67] Al-Miʿmar died as a result of the plague that devastated the fourteenth-century Mediterranean world and Europe.

While it is true that this poetry provides space for traders and professionals and enters the street and the life of people, it also introduces to literate culture a novel blend of orality and scriptoria, being recited and performed in both public and private spaces, especially the marketplace. The ways in which genres and subgenres are received and become prevalent relate to the nature of societies, for the *al-muwashshaḥ* genre became popular in Andalusia and al-Maghrib and was later mingled (and often confused) with the *zajal* in the Arab east, whereas the nonclassical subgenres, usually associated with popular verse, such as the *dūbayt*, *kān-wa-kān*, *qūmā*, and *mawāliyā*, were popular in both Egypt and the entire Arab east. The *kān-wa-kān* that was initiated in Iraq, among the Baghdadis in particular, received a different name in Egypt and was widely practiced under the name *zaklash* (pl. *zakālish*).[68] An early contemporary to this emerging phenomenon of popular verse, Zayn al-Dīn al-Tanūkhī (d. 692/1293), explains the nature of the vogue as follows: "It is not a matter of ease or difficulty that decides scarcity in prose among people or abundance of poetry among others; it is a matter of taste. Hence the Moroccans make greater use of the *muwashshaḥ*, the Persians of the *dūbayt*, the Iraqis of *kān-wa-kān*."[69] Al-Shaybī qualifies the judgment, citing the evidence of the Moroccan Taqī al-Dīn ʿAlī b. ʿAbd al-ʿAzīz ibn Jābir (d. 684/1285), who settled in Baghdad and gathered verses in the *kān-wa-kān* mode.

Homoerotics?

If the *kān-wa-kān* mode lends itself easily to edification, that tendency is even more evident in poetry involving erotic pleasantries. This takes a number of directions, where the *ghazal* tradition provides a substratum for love expressions addressed to specific individuals, boys or girls. Al-Ḥillī addresses one poem to a boy who is incessantly demanding payments: "I have a lover who acts as a brick builder [demanding money, not bricks] and I am the supplier of gold [not brick or clay] / whenever he turns around and sees me, he'll reiterate: give me."[70] In another piece, the addressee is named ʿAlī:

> I haven't tasted a sip ever more bitter than the taste of passion:
> May God help my heart against the one I love.
> People learn from me prowess and perseverance: yet I cannot
> show the same towards a cruel estranged one
> The one I love is like a peach: with color, taste, and scent:
> how numerous his attributes: but how little his constancy.[71]

Al-Qayyim Khalaf al-Ghubārī (d. 791/1389) composes another example of this trend, addressing a lover named Ṣalāh. The poem is rich with examples of paronomasia and paradox as he plays on the etymology and derivation of the proper name Ṣalāh, meaning "reform" or "goodness," also providing the poet with further etymological and rhyming excursions in order to include the word *rāḥ*, implying both a departure and wine:

I woke up to have my unadulterated drink: to be followed by joy
and rapture, sadness departs: intoxicated so much: I spent all the
money I had.
Do you know who corrupts my correctness in love?
My lover Ṣalāh: Unequalled in charm, his beauty is proverbial.[72]

The Egyptian oculist ibn Dāniyāl offers us a neat combination in performing arts, involving the literary style of the *maqāmah* genre and a celebration of homosexual passion, especially in his shadow play *Al-Mutayyam* (The Love Stricken). The site of fighting beasts becomes the pretext for the pursuit of passion for the adored youth. While the author clearly commands advanced skills of literary expression and allusion, the presence of slang is an indication of the blended culture in Mamluk Cairo, one that subsumes the street and its idiolects as substantial realities in a mobile social life.[73] His work fits well into the countermovement in cultural production that supplies urbanized groups and guilds with colloquial or usable material, in the form of songs, poetry, and narrative. Poetry is also receptive to colloquialism to cater to the most subtle erotic insinuations. No wonder jurists and writers of manuals on market inspection banned poetry on moral and political grounds.[74]

Ibn Ḥajjāj's Poetics

It is possible to shun Abū ʿAbdullāh ibn al-Ḥusayn ibn al-Ḥajjāj's (d. 391/1001) pornographic and licentious poetry and to equate it with Shīʿī poetry on some scale of what is considered dangerous poetry. However, it is important to note that much openly erotic verse by ibn al-Ḥajjāj borrows its terminology not directly from the street but rather, and primarily, from street images and euphemisms.

Ibn Nubātah, as the best-known Egyptian poet of the middle period, collected ibn al-Ḥajjāj's poetry into a single large volume, while the noted contemporary of ibn al-Ḥajjāj, al-Sharīf al-Raḍī (d. 391/1000), produced a small collection at an earlier date. The historical record tells us many stories about the poet, who was able to secure the respect and admiration of the Būyid rulers (r. 932–1062). We know that he was twice a market inspector and was imprisoned several times. It is also on record that in his later years he made a living from his poetry, leading a respectable life that was at variance with his verse. He certainly precedes Ṣafī al-Dīn al-Ḥillī in collecting colloquial speech, images, songs, and expressions of the undesirable elements in the district of *al-zaṭṭ* (gypsies) in Baghdad. More important, the bookseller who owned his volume of poetry never allowed it to be copied; he is reported to have said that he was investing in it, just as he would in a charming slave girl; it was entertaining and also lucrative because it attracted customers to come to his shop, leave him some of their provisions, and offer him money for reading from it. In other words, we are left with a text by ibn al-Ḥajjāj that also supplies entertainment during the Mamluk period. It garners the commitment and devotion of no less a poet and scholar than ibn Nubātah and circulates far enough to arouse the indignation of market inspectors and jurists. Ibn Nubātah exempts ibn al-Ḥajjāj from being like any other poet: "The verses of the exceptional littérateur Abū ʿAbdullāh ibn al-Ḥajjāj constitute a unique nation of its own, resurrected apart from all others, a wonderful progeny that matures through playfulness and revelry; nobody's imagination has ever come up with its like."[75] Al-Ṣafadī, the fourth figure in the grand company of al-Ḥillī, ibn Ḥijjah, and ibn Nubātah within this republic of letters, described ibn al-Ḥajjāj as smart, handsome, popular, feared, and well respected.[76] The renowned chancery secretary and author ibn Faḍl Allāh al-ʿUmarī (d. 749/1349) devotes a few pages to ibn al-Ḥajjāj in his *Masālik al-Abṣār fī mamālik al-amṣār* (Pathways of Vision, on the Realms of Regions).[77] The third in this company, ibn Ḥijjah, also shares a fascination with ibn al-Ḥajjāj. He retains from ibn al-Ḥajjāj's verses parts that have been shunned and banned by jurists and market inspectors. Thus, in order to exemplify "fluency" (*insijām*) as a figure of speech and expressive device for unstrained wording and freedom from convulsions, "like a descending cascade of water," he cites from ibn al-Ḥajjāj the most wanton of his references to sexual impotence.[78] Using this as a prelude to contemporaneous verse, he quotes from ibn Nubātah to exemplify "innovative embedding," where the image of dry wasted dates stands for ibn Ḥajjāj's signification of impotency.[79] As if it were not enough to quote from these sources, he goes on to cite other poets, including the scholar and poet Badr al-Dīn ibn Muḥmmmad ibn al-Damāmīnī (d. 827/1424), who again makes use of ibn Ḥajjāj's image as part of jovial discourse among the learned.[80] Ibn Ḥajar al-ʿAsqalānī, the hadith scholar and polymath, is reported to have sent ibn Ḥijjah selected handwritten passages that were meant to be exemplifications of a number of rhetorical figures.[81] He quotes one in the same frivolous vein that has been shunned by jurists. This time the quotation comes from no less than a grand imam, ibn Ḥajar himself, whose homoeroticism is no more than a pornographic piece that must have been part of a playful game among these astute scholars.[82] Ibn Ḥijjah cannot conclude this section without a quote from his own poetry, which is more of a mixture of ribaldry and explicit sexual reference.[83] All these citations are subsumed within his representation of the variations on the double entendre (concealment) as a rhetorical figure.

Homoerotic Compilations

The middle period adopted a blend of hedonistic, playful, and also Sufi expressions. Indeed, the three elements fuse in one way or another in the career of poets such as al-Shābb al-Ẓarīf (i.e., the Young Dandy) ʿAfīf al-Dīn al-Tilimsānī, who composes mystical, wine, and love poetry and indulges in his own displays of dandyism. In the renowned Persian anthology *Nozhat al-Majāles* (The Joy of Assemblies) by the Persian poet Jamāl-al-Dīn Khalīl Sharvānī, compiled in the middle of the seventh/thirteenth century, we find 4,125 selected quatrains that mainly focus on homoeroticism and pedophilia.[84] There are other accounts and compilations, but worthy of special note, and more in the form and style of Badīʿ al-Zamān al-Hamadhānī's *Maqāmāt*, is Ḥamīd al-Dīn Abū Bakr's *Maqāmāt-e-Ḥamīdī*, also composed in Persian. This twelfth-century chief justice of Balkh offers in his collection one *maqāmah* that has as its two contenders a Sodomite (*laṭiy*) and a fornicator (*zāny*). Rather than taking sides, the narrator—much in the manner of al-Jāḥiẓ in his epistles—lets each character defend his case, concluding that both provide good justifications that are worth considering. More in the spirit of administrative manuals and the "mirror for princes" genre, the prince of Ṭabarestān, Onṣor-al-Maʿāli Kay-Kāvus, uses his *Qābūs-nāma* to recommend a similar process of mediation, for a bisexual attitude is taken to be the most viable middle ground. Considered in terms of an open pleasurable space, these works portray a series of relationships that take wine, boon-companionship, and delicacy as components and properties for a humanist entertaining *majlis*.[85]

Jurists and judges such as the Tunisian Sharaf al-Dīn Abū al-ʿAbbās Aḥmad ibn Yūsuf al-Tīfāshī (d. 651/1253) come up with an elaborate interpretation of the ways in which life can turn into a more enjoyable and experience the moment we become aware of its wide prospects. Al-Tīfāshī, for example, discusses whatever partakes of sensual experience, setting the terms for pleasures like music, song, dance, wine drinking, and other forms of entertainment including the shadow theatre. His *Mutʿat al-asmāʿ* (The Joy of Music and Song) and *Surūr al-nafs bi-madārik al-ḥawāss al-khams* (The Delight of the Soul in the Attainments of the Five Senses),[86] as well as other books of his, provide contemporary scholarship with material for the study of homoeroticism.[87] Al-Tīfāshī also composed *Nuzhat al-albāb fī mā lā yūjad fī kitāb* (Delight of the Hearts at What Is Never Found in Books), a work that serves to fill in the missing link in a lost tradition of passion and love as known and perhaps practiced.

Among these books, especially those that celebrate the qualities of young boys, was al-Nawājī's *Marātiʿ al-Ghizlān* (The Prairie [or, Meadow] of Gazelles).The homoerotic lyrics found throughout the book make it one of the major sources on the subject, but it obviously builds on compiled material that was in circulation at that time, including al-Tīfāshī's works and Jamāl-al-Dīn Khalīl Sharvānī's anthology *Nozhat al-Majāles* (The Joy of Assemblies), mentioned above. This type of ongoing conversation among books is, after all, one of the most distinctive aspects of the republic of letters, which transcends geographical, ethnic, religious, or even linguistic divides. A writer more focused on a masculinist concern with virility is Muḥammad al-Nafzāwī, who was a counselor to the Tunisian Ḥafṣīd ruler, Abū Fāris, early in the fifteenth century, and whose famous work, *al-Rawḍ al-ʿĀtir fī nuzhat al-khāṭir*

(The Perfumed Garden),[88] was to become popular in erotic and aphrodisiac literature only much later, through an 1876 French translation published in Algiers. In order to fit the book into an acceptable cultural milieu in the face of possible dogmatic opposition, the author's excursions in endless sexual practices, including sodomy, are bracketed in piety. Even more focused on virility is *Rujūʿ al-shaykh ilā ṣibāh fi al-quwwa ʿalā ʿal-bāh* (Rejuvenation in Old Age; or The Return to Youth through Virility), which was written by no less a figure than the Ottoman shaykh al-Islam Kemalpaşazâde, the leading historian and scholar during the reign of the Ottoman sultan Selim I (r. 1512–1520). Throughout the period under consideration, the concern with heteroerotic and homoerotic politics and their manifestations in poetry and daily communication set the path for a rich and diversified culture throughout the Ottoman, Safavid, and Qajar periods.

Delicacy and Wine Rituals

The dandyism vogue as an expression of excessive delicacy may have been less widespread in the middle period than during the heyday of the ʿAbbasid Caliphs, but it was obviously common among writers, artists, artisans, and members of the elite Mamluk corps. Apart from the *qāḍī* (magistrate), alchemist, and poet ibn Daqīq al-ʿĪd, there were others; the fact that they are identified by name suggests that the trend was not all that widespread. Amir Janīk al-Ashrafī was such a one.[89] But there was certainly a tendency all over the Islamic region to celebrate entertainment, pleasure, and wine. A notable scholar, Muḥammad ibn Ḥasan Shams al-Dīn al-Nawājī (d. 859/1455), produced a well-known anthology on wine. Its title, *Ḥalbat al-Kumayt* (The Racecourse of the Bay), plays on color to signify dark reddish wine, like the color of a dark bay horse. The wine and cup, when circulated around a wine-drinking *majlis*, are metaphorically compared to racehorses. Indeed, as if this anthology with its celebration of pleasurable pursuits were not enough, he coupled it with another entitled *Kitāb al-ṣabūḥ* (The Book of Dawn Wine Drinking).

Books on rhetoric and literary compilations and compendiums abound with references to wine-sessions (*majālis*) and homoerotic verse.

But these are not the staple focus of compendiums; they tend to demonstrate a wide knowledge of almost everything. Ever since the appearance of Ṣafī al-Dīn al-Ḥillī's *Sharḥ*, other scholars and poets tended to emulate his example by providing a large canvas for rhetorical figures and applications; they are also anxious to demonstrate to their actual or implied audience a level of skill and knowledge that will equal or even surpass that of the master. Al-Ḥillī was careful not to undertake an excursus of expositions; his purpose, rather, is to explain the art of rhetoric as practiced in his own ode. Both al-Ṣafadī and ibn Ḥijjah take off from that point in order to provide the reader (or even listener) with digressions on grammar, social life, poetics, history, and even theology and philosophy. If homoeroticism occupies a certain amount of space, it does so only as a social entertainment and also as an occasion, like others in different domains and interests, for mapping out new kinds of writing or anecdotes that are characteristic of the middle period. Thus, al-Ṣafadī, for example, cites a number of verses in which poets explain why sneaking into the lover's private domain, where there is quietude and the latter slips into a seeming slumber, is an intoxicated condition that justifies a slow and measured intercourse. Relying on the authority of Abū Yaʿlī Muḥammad ibn Muḥammad ibn al-Habāriyyah (d. 509/1115), he explains why others reject this approach, arguing for an interactive mode, which is part of the practice of the elite. The reference goes on to explain that "people like us, beggars, have no luck or even possibility of mingling with such people." Al-Ṣafadī continues: "an interactive relationship [*mufāʿalah*] is to be between two persons who are of matching desire, approximately the same intentions, or on familiar grounds with each other."[90] This statement is a prelude to further explications, humorous anecdotes, and also serious discourse on the matter. Throughout the process, he quotes ibn al-Habāriyyah's contemporaries, such as Abū al-Faḍl Muḥammad b. Muḥammad b. Aysūn al-Munajjim al-Mawṣilī and al-Qāḍī Abū al-Ḥusayn al-Asnandānī al-Mahlamī, along with some antecedent authorities, before moving on to cite some of his own contemporaries, for example, Jamāl al-Dīn b. al-Ḥājib.[91] But no matter how selective he needs to be to provide a concise compendium in the form of *sharḥ*, he cannot resist a humorous, albeit obscene, anecdote related by ibn al-Habāriyyah that runs as follows:

> Once we were in Iṣfahān, at the vizier's abode accompanied by a great number of notables . . . when all was quiet and a silence enveloped us, we heard loud screams, shrieking voices, requests and yells, so we stood up to investigate. What confronted us was the shaykh and littérateur, Abū Jaʿfar al-Qaṣṣāṣ, fucking the blind poet, Abū ʿAlī al-Ḥasan b. Jaʿfar al-Bandnījī, while the latter kept screaming in agony. He was yelling: "I'm a blind shaykh, what is it that impels you to fuck me?" The other man took no notice until he was done. Then he stood up and said: "I've always hoped to fuck Abū al-ʿAlāʾ al-Maʿarrī for his unbelief, apostasy, atheism, but that could not have happened. So when I saw you to be a noble blind shaykh, I did this for his sake." He then proceeded to recite in poetry.[92]

This anecdote may be part of an entertaining bawdy conversation, but it is here cited by al-Ṣafadī alongside his discourse on logic.[93] In the above instance, it is deprived of any joyful connotations; the incident would verge on a case of rape, were it not deliberately placed in the category of a two-faced, playful act of vindication. As the anecdote is narrated, the blind shaykh is in agony, but not the revengeful one, who, in his drunkenness, was determined to target any blind littérateur who reminded him of the renowned poet, critic, and skeptic Abū al-ʿAlāʾ al-Maʿarrī (d. 449/1058).

The anecdotal mention of the *majlis* in Iṣfahān may invoke further considerations that relate to the formation of the republic of letters. This narrative reverses the trope of an interactive and reciprocal relationship, which talks of an equal human exchange in terms of desire and intercourse. As is usual in digressions devoted to rhetoric, paradoxical situations and unsettling anecdotes creep in to soften and entertain an otherwise disciplined discourse. The reverse anecdote implicates grave rhetoric in sites of abuse and also laughter. It also destabilizes and perturbs any claims to centrism in politics, human life, and genres. Any attempt at establishing a hierarchy of genres will inevitably undergo deflection, detraction, and infraction. Apart from the emergence of multiple Islamic centers and the concomitant fall, destruction, or obfuscation of other centers as a result of a series of wars and invasions, the overall outcome is one of fluid mobility among cultures and peoples, a mobility that engenders new modes and hybrid and heterogeneous modules. To illustrate such trends, let us now draw on a few selective cases in Turkish, Persian, and Indic poetics.

Exploring Islamic Poetics

The growth of an otherwise nascent Turkic poetry in the middle and premodern period is usually associated with a few poets who happened to be well versed in Arabic and Persian poetry and poetics.[94] Fuzûlî (d. 1556), for one, was famed for his skill in Arabic, Persian, and Ottoman Turkish. Apart from his many poetic achievements, his fame usually rests on his *mesnevî* as verse romance in the narrative tradition, exemplified at its best in *Leylî vü Mecnun*. Although Şeyh Gâlib (d. 1799) is also known for writing in the same narrative mode (as in *Hüsn ü Aşk* [Beauty and Love]), the fact that he belonged to the Mevlevî Sufi order and his thorough involvement in the rituals of that order give his poetry an ornate and complex style, usually known as *sebk-i hindî*, or "Indian style." Other poets who traverse and bridge the middle and premodern period are different from these two; they fit better into the space between popular street poetry and the courtly tradition of the pre-Islamic Arabic *qaṣīdah* (ode). Nedîm's (d. 1730) poetry, for instance, reveals a classical bent for solid and formal structure that is combined with a populist taste reminiscent of al-Ḥillī's oeuvre. Side by side with rhetorically laden verse is the street poetics, which conveys an impression of the poet in his most leisurely and communicative modes. Preceding him in the same classical practice is Nef'î (d. 1635), the accomplished emulator of the Arabic *qaṣīdah* tradition.[95] Like pre-Islamic and Islamic poets who compose their odes within that tradition, his poetic works lead him into panegyric and vituperative genres that may be no less rewarding (and at the same time dangerous) than the effects enjoyed or suffered by ancient Arab poets. It is not surprising that Nef'î lost his life as a result of his poetry. Both these poets provide an example very different from that of Mahmud Abdülbâkî Bâkî (d. 1600) and others whose poetic excursions are mainly celebratory, adopting the methods of al-Ḥillī and ancient Arab and later 'Abbasid-era traditions to establish a rhetoric of striding triumphalism during the reign of Süleyman the Magnificent.[96]

Although our information on poetic innovations and mixed genres in Indic and other Asian languages is less than what is available for Arabic, Persian, and Ottoman Turkish, it still provides significant insights that can bring us closer to the wide world of the Islamic republic of letters. Genres, transgenres, and practices involve an interaction, *mufāʿalah*, a process that al-Ṣafadī applies to literary, cultural, and human practices. In the court of the Persianized Shah Jahan Mughal (r. 1628–1657) in India, for example, we have, according to Allison Busch's reading,[97] two poets, Sundar and Kavindra, who use Brajbhasha to mediate a discursive and oral communication space. Within this space, language can maintain its functional efficacy through the inclusion of tropes and themes, while still manipulating its other attributes (such as pairing), in order to extend its reach into a broader interactive space, which might otherwise prove difficult. Busch cites examples from these two court poets for the Mughal Shah Jahan.[98] The pairing of opposites is a pervasive trope in the Arabic tradition that is subsumed in rhetoric under the terms *muzāwajah* (doubling) and *ṭibāq* (antithesis) whenever the same wording or sound and function is involved. It can thus be viewed as a viable navigational tool among diverse cultural sites.[99]

Sufi *Šāheds* and Homoerotics

Persian middle and premodern poetry offers extensive examples of two poetic territories: Sufism and *ghazal*. These territories often overlap whenever the "beloved" is portrayed as a transfiguration of divine beatitude. Nevertheless, a number of indexical and thematic terms and levels of categorization specify variables among a large body of invariables. On the level of naming, an indefinite "beloved" who has no specific proper name or identification, but is called "Young Turk," "soldier," or "*sāqī*" (cupbearer), can easily be interpreted within a Sufi register. Such is the case, for example, in the poetry of the author of *Sawāneḥ*, Aḥmad Ğazāli (d. ca. 1123), and in that of ʿAyn-al-Qużāt Hamadānī (1098–1131),[100] Farīd ud-Dīn ʿAṭṭār (d. 1221), Awḥad-al-Din of Kermān (635/1237), Fak̲r-al-Din ʿErāqi (d. 1289), Jalāl al-Dīn Muḥammad Rūmī (d. 1273), and Qāsem-al-Anwār (d. 1433). The concept of *Šāheds* (*shāhid*: witness and sign) is the most delicate of the intersections involving homoerotics and Sufism, since a long observance and focus on the beloved mean, for the Sufi, *ḥulūl* (incarnation) of the divine in a human form that demands of the Sufi lover surrender and even self-annihilation. Indeed, the infatuation felt by the most prominent ruler of the Ghaznavid Empire (977–1185), Maḥmūd of Ğazna (d. 1030), for the slave boy Ayās, the future army commander, was taken as evidentially God-ordained and meant as an exemplary *Šāhed*.

The case is different when we approach homoeroticism as a widely encountered and celebrated theme in the *nasībs* and *tašbibs* (erotic and adoration verse) of the *ghazal* tradition.[101] Strongly and deeply rooted in the pre-Islamic ode, these erotic preludes and their urbanite variables in short pieces and lyrics from the seventh through the tenth centuries laid the groundwork for the emergence of an exquisite elaboration, which is encountered in Persian poetry thereafter. As documented in Abū al-Faraj al-ʾIṣfahānī's (d. 967) voluminous *Kitāb al-aghānī* (Book of Songs), *ghazal* grew in tandem with urban life, but it has its roots deep in an early pre-Islamic tradition. The Book of Songs attests to the powerful role played by the milieu—urban life, court patronage, and discussion and correspondence among poets and people of literary taste—in developing and even deciding the contours of lyricism. The Book of Songs was dedicated to the prince of Aleppo, Sayf al-Dawlah al-Ḥamadānī, who was a knight, poet, scholar, and strong patron of writers and poets. Indeed, no matter how strong and refined the *ghazal* tradition was to become soon after this work appeared, it harks back to a vigorous heritage of music and song. One of the most significant landmarks in the humanist tradition, the Book of Songs cannot be omitted from any discussion of a republic of letters, not only because of its amalgam of thousands of songs and musical pieces, but also, significantly, because of its emphasis on human communication among poets, courtiers, singers, musicians, and others.[102] In this large collection, too, we find side by side both homoeroticism and common *ghazal*. The Book of Songs is often placed in the context of the court of the ʿAbbasid caliph al-Amīn and his *ghulāmiyyah* entourage (of women dressed as beardless youths), thus anticipating al-Nawājī's (d. 1455) much later *Marātiʿ al-ghizlān* (The Prairie of Gazelles).[103] Through citations of documents and surveys, it discusses whatever can be subsumed under the categories of sociability, song, and music. But al-Nawājī complements what was already a set practice in the heyday of Persian homoerotic poetry. His collection of erotic verse, *Marātiʿ al-ghizlān*, is unique, not only in the amount of verse by his contemporaries but also in its register of the objects of desire. Verse is addressed to particular young people, named ʿIsā, Jamāl, Shaʿbān, and so on. In specific lyrics by ibn al-Kharrāṭ, al-Qīrāṭī, Badr al-Dīn b. Ḥabīb, ibn al-Warrāq, ibn Nubātah, ibn Ḥajalah, al-Ṣafadī, and others, we encounter verses addressed, variously, to a Turk, a black boy, and a fair-skinned other. These verses carry further what was already a common practice among Persian poets. In one lyric, we read:

I have chosen from among the sons of the Turks
A young male gazelle.
In my burning desire to possess him
I consumed my life to no purpose.
I asked him one day:
"What will put out the fire
That you have lit in me,
O, most fearsome of men?"
He answered: "My lips."[104]

The celebration of the Turk as the subject of love began to take shape during the reign of the Samanid dynasty (r. 819–1005) and continued under the Ghaznavids and Kwārazmshāhs. Purchased as slaves, held as captives in wars, or simply brought from Central Asia and Anatolia, pubescent and adolescent youths by their very presence helped in the formation of an aesthetic imaginary whereby the beloved took their physical form. Observed and communicated with while in uniform as a soldier, the youth in reality or fiction infatuates the love-stricken speaker, the lyrical subject who joins Farrūkhī (d. 1038) in shouting:

Put down your weapons, boy! Bring me kisses
All this trouble and strife serves no purpose at all!

Or, in another lyric:

> O Turk, remove and throw aside this battle raiment
> Take up the lyre and put down your shield and sword.[105]

There is a similar use of infantry registers in Manučehri (d. 1041), as shield and battle are transformed to fit into the battle for the youth's heart:

> Do you see that when that Turk takes the lyre in hand
> Self-restraint flees a hundred parasangs from the hearts of saints!

Or in Hāfez (d. 1389) more than three centuries later:

> If that Turk of Shiraz should gain my heart
> I bestow upon him Samarkand and Bukhara for his black beauty spot [*khāl*].[106]

Hāfez's homoerotic theme rests on an aggrandized lyrical subject who, in this empire of gifts for compliance, is no less than a ruler in full control and possession of both domains and human fates. On another occasion, the persona adopts the role of a pious person whose piety cannot resist the charm of a young cupbearer. As the personification of the beloved, this image is no newcomer to erotic poetry. In wine poetry, including the Sufi verse of ibn al-Fāriḍ, the *sāqī* is the focus of physical attention and love celebration:

> Pardon me if the thread of my rosary came undone
> My hand was in the arm of the silver-calved *sāqī*.
> (Hāfez, *Divān*, no. 202)[107]

Another paradigm for this homoerotic poetry borrows from a *ghazal* tradition, with its Sufi niche of supplicatory poetics, as is the case in the ʿErāqī School, best exemplified as a movement in the poetry of Masʿūd Saʿd and Farīd al-Dīn al-ʿAṭṭār (d. 1221). The beloved may appear as a dancer, poet, soldier, goldsmith, polo player, drummer, baker, or even a blind youth. The beloved has the upper hand throughout; he is the epitome of charm and physical attraction, who is sought after by everyone, as befits a paragon of beauty and loveliness. In this uneven transaction the lover is the supplicator—submissive, lamenting, and indeed at times lamentable. The transaction was so stereotyped that in *Nozhat al āšeqīn* (The Lovers' Entertainment),[108] Zangi narrates the story of a certain Sufi who fell in love with a young prince and was so overwhelmed when the latter, for fun, began to bestow on him attention and love, that he died on the spot. Hāfez, after all, speaks of this transaction with the "thief of hearts" in these terms:

> If the wine-serving *môḡ-bača* [magian boy] would shine in this way
> I will make a broom of my eyelashes to sweep the entrance of the tavern.
> (*Divān*, no. 9)[109]

Since the pages, tavern waiters, and cupbearers of such poetry usually hail from non-Muslim communities (Zoroastrian or Christian), al-ʿAṭṭar speaks of them as follows:

> A Christian child suddenly attacked my heart and my soul
> The love of his tresses scandalized me throughout the world.
> (al-ʿAṭṭār, *Divān*, p. 158)[110]

In his *Ḡazaliat* Saʿdī (d. 1290) speaks of youth as the subject of love:

> A beau with a candle in hand is an affliction
> (A beau) heavy-headed with love's slumber and intoxicated with wine.[111]

Since the physical attributes of the youth stand out as the most prominent aspect, many poets speak in terms similar to Farrūkhī's "silver-bodied, ruby-lipped children," thus placing this poetry within the realms of pederasty. It is hardly surprsing that Suzāni (d. 1173) advises the youth to keep to this youthfulness:

> Be mindful, o boy, that you would not grow a beard
> So that a beard would not plunge you in sorrow and grief, o boy!
> (Suzāni, *Divān*, p. 396)[112]

According to the Persian poet Jamāl-al-Dīn Khalīl Sharvānī, the compiler of *Nozhat al-Majāles* (Joy of the Assemblies), quatrains that deal with these kinds of relationship have their own registers of retorts, insults, pleas, farewells, and returns. In these registers there are also specific catalogues of dress, drink, embrace, love, encounters, and other details pertaining to homoerotics. Women are therefore placed under a separate section.[113]

The Carnivalesque Street

The rich corpus of anecdotal literature that exists in this area also contains humor and laughter, itself a practice and outcome that should not be disregarded, in particular when the square, street, and ebullient *majlis* are the focus of discussion. Within the catalogue of the sensory that al-Tīfāshī identifies, the shadow theatre holds a special place. It provides a more or less carnivalesque scene that engages a number of senses while at the same time stimulating a critical insight, one that turns the hierarchal social or political structure upside down. Laughter is indicative of the role played by these spaces, dislodging the hierarchical limits of the "vertical world" and purging it of the "contagion of 'antiphysis' that had infected it."[114] In shadow theatre, and especially in ibn Dāniyāl's shadow plays, indirection takes multiple routes toward sardonic laughter. Through such methods, time retains its visibility and draws attention to concrete situations. In shadow plays, as in market and street gatherings, narratives or poetry assume a concrete life of their own through the interaction between storytellers and poets and their audiences. It thus comes as no surprise that we have on record expressions of market inspectors' fears concerning these gatherings, as I have argued in *The Islamic Context of the Thousand and One Nights*.[115] The street is the stage on which the body and its physiological expressions in terms of eating and drinking practices are given free rein, which takes them far beyond normative conservative restraints.[116] This helps explain why the street and the poor or suburban quarters are ready and willing to submit themselves to their actual users, such as the *ḥarāfīsh* "riff-raff" in medieval Cairo. Tightly organized through communion and contingency, the Cairene riff-raff took over the street as their stage, where, by sheer expediency, the real is turned into a carnival. It is thereby claimed as their residence, and their sultan is their ruler. The nation is already divided between a Mamluk elite and its entourage and the poor with their own rituals of action and laughter.[117] It is on the street that the humanist tradition manifests itself in full.

Playful excursus in homoeroticism also subsumes within its limits both passionate love and passing affairs. The latter builds on a tradition, however, even when the experience is new and has all the hallmarks of a genuine relationship. Perhaps in response to the partner's expectations, as well as the expectations of the public, this reliance appears in forms and images that infuse the new poetry with a historical memory, one that claims a mnemonic lineage while undergoing serious examination and undermining. The vogue for *al-madhhab al-gharāmī* (the amatory mode) courts both sexual and innocent relationships, but, whenever the latter theme prevails, images and syntax are sanitized; the dominant creed precludes license and buffoonery. Thus we may encounter two separate love poems by the same poet, each with its own register and form: one that sublimates and another that degenerates. Al-Ḥillī, for example, tried his hand at both types, leaving behind some exquisite verse that survives side by side with hilarious experiments in ribaldry. Hence, the single image of a cupbearer that draws on the ʿAbbasid poet Abū Nuwās (d. 810) and diligently surveys the attractions of the youthful body as they are seen and longed for by the voyeur, can be transformed into a sublime poetic of love and longing, but it may also deliberately plummet into graphic physical detail that is warped in a moment of ecstatic drunkenness. It can also plunge further into buffoonery and grotesque street shows, which blatantly affront authority through the ironic and paradoxical reclamation of the Banū Sāsān,[118] that being the name adopted by self-identified underworld groups of ruffians and beggars.[119] Al-Ḥillī's *Sāsānid Qaṣīdah* builds on Badīʿ al-Zamān al-Hamadhānī's *Sāsānid Maqāmah* (no. xix), which depicts the complex historical, political, and economic connotations associated with organized beggary. The *maqāmah*, along with Abū Dulaf's *qaṣīdah*, sets the stage for the controversial social scene in Mamluk Cairo. The wide use of the term and its implications are attested to by ibn Dāniyāl's recourse to the same issue in his shadow play *ʿAjīb wa-Gharīb*, where the parade that al-Hamadhānī's

Sāsānid Maqāmah describes makes a comeback with updated details on social vice during the Mamluk era.

The development of the Banū Sāsān theme offers an ironic example of the wheel of fortune, or the paradigm of rise and fall. At these intersections, when time and place coalesce to be claimed by the fringes and margins of society, a reversal of the carnivalesque movement takes place to purge the street of a "transcendent worldview" and "clean away symbolic and hierarchical interpretations still clinging to this vertical world."[120] Whenever this happens, a culture of the body emerges in tandem with an expanded street culture.[121] The graphic and detailed account of these groups and the available historical material on the *ḥarāfīsh* in the streets of Cairo present us not only with a colossal body of idiolects and practices, but also with corporeal sites that present the street and its corners as the natural habitat for the homeless. Within this space, the needs and habits of the human body are expressed and exhibited. Group solidarity is evident there as well, as if to counter the punishments of public shaming, in which the human body is ridiculed. It is also within the context of these fringes that the street is inundated in times of need, war, and social trouble, as documented by late ʿAbbasid and Mamluk historians and scribes.[122] Within such a social framework, polarized discourses involving courtly regulations, rigid conservatism, and analogical reasoning or Sufi language are all emptied of binaries and projected at random across idiolects of ribaldry, jest, and laughter. Indeed, Abū al-Ḥasan al-ʿUkbarī, the beggars' poet in the tenth-century Islamic world, and Abū Dulaf introduced the slang and latest antics of the Banū Sāsān underworld into the celebrated assembly of the famous littérateur, the vizier al-Ṣāḥib ibn ʿAbbād.[123] It is thus no surprise that the renowned bawdy poet ibn Ḥajjāj concludes his ongoing discussion of the public and private in moral conduct, sex, and sanitized language as follows: "Is there ever a house without a privy, / And could any intelligent person stay in such a house?"[124]

Unease at Sufi Love Language

Idiolects involve acts and speech acts and hence are central to a culture emphasizing the human body. But the seemingly physiological appropriation of the corporal can nevertheless take an elusive itinerary, one that conveys the concrete indices of a culture of the body, so that a referent will bear and also communicate flesh at the very moment when it is neatly borne on a plane of tender passion. Such, for example, is Sufi love poetry. Although the poetry of the Sufi shaykh ibn al-Fāriḍ (d. 1235) was interpreted during the thirteenth century within the confines of dominant philological concerns and grammatical pursuits and is unable to divest itself entirely of the fashionable contemporary concern with rhetorical figures, ibn al-Fāriḍ nevertheless composed exquisite verses of love and devotion.[125] Thus he says in a poem rhyming on the consonant "F", which is not an easy task for devotional poetry:

> My heart tells me you are to annihilate me
> my soul is the ransom, whether you know or not.[126]

In another Sufi verse that can easily be read in the context of human love, he states:

> I have warned you,
> knowing passion and my enemy;
> so choose for yourself
> what is sweet.
>
> But if you want to live well,
> then die love's martyr,
> and if not, well,
> love has its worthy ones.
>
> Not to die in love
> is not to live by love; before you harvest honey,
> you must surely face the bees.[127]

Making use of a pre-Islamic poetic tradition that uses the journey topos as an itinerary for the poet's loss and his resolve to come to terms with a seemingly adversarial situation, ibn al-Fāriḍ imports its concrete indices and telos into his poetry in order to reconstruct a spiritual encounter that sounds no less representational and real for being Sufi. In fact, the pre-Islamic *qaṣidah* (ode), with its tripartite structural pattern that starts at the ruined encampment (*aṭlāl*), the deserted campsite that evokes longing and passionate desire, lies at the very core of the expressed and deeply felt love for divine beatitude. However, for the Sufi devotee, the deserted campsite is only another name for a temporal state, merely betokening a pre-eternal covenant. In Michael Sells's eloquent reading of Islamic Sufi poetics, the ruins dig deep into the "origin of poetic consciousness." Both the "pre-eternal covenant (in which the human and divine were together and to which the human strives to return)" and the pre-eternal wine intensify the feeling of loss and the difficult Sufi struggle to retain that union.[128] The speaking "I," the persona that permeates the ode, traverses time and space, the temporal and the eternal, as central to the Sufi journey for union with the divine. In ibn al-Fāriḍ's "The Poem of the Sufi Way," the subject persona harps on this union, a feature for which outsiders offer different and also controversial interpretations:

> She and I are in essence one;
> he who slandered me against her
> and the one who turned away from her,
> only appeared as attributes.[129]

Indeed, as part of the spiral journey into consciousness and Sufi intoxicating adoration, there is bound to be fusion. Union negates duality:

> In the sobriety after effacement,
> I was none other than her,
> my essence adorned my essence
> when she removed her veil.[130]

In moving toward this pre-eternal state, the Sufi heart has to pour out the agonies of this striving for union:

> So my heart, melt
> in burning flowing love;
> O my love pains, help me
> to dissolve and fade away.[131]

The wine that is a staple of the ʿAbbasid poetic tradition and Persian lyricism now returns in Sufi poetry, not as the path or modus operandi to intoxication, but instead as the intoxicating union itself, *ittiḥād*. Sufi wine poetry adopts its motifs from the wine tradition, behind which lies enormous compilations of wine varieties, their antique distillation and preservation, source, quality, and effect, a tradition to which the Tunisian blind poet, al-Ḥaṣrī al-Qayrawānī (d. 488/1095), devotes his *al-Mukhtaṣar fī al-anbidhah wa-l-khumūr* (The Abridged Dictionary of Wines and Liquors). Making use of this repository, ibn al-Fāriḍ lets the subject persona say:

> But they said: "You've drunk sin!"
> No, indeed, I drank only
> that whose abstention
> is sin to me.[132]

In Dāwūd al-Qayṣarī's (d. 747/1346) commentary on ibn al-Fāriḍ's ode, the "drinker loses his sense of self as all of the properties of his human nature disappear along with the natural traits regarding the designations of actions, characteristics, and essence."[133] In the third and fourth stages in love, it is God's will to assume "His servant's senses and will, thereby plunging him into ecstasy and rapture, annihilating the lover's being and essence into His own, where the lover abides forever."[134] Dāwūd al-Qayṣarī explains how the poet reaches that self-annihilation after passing through the arduous journey required in order to conquer weaknesses and temptation: "In the presence of unification, the entity is the receptacle for divine self-manifestations contiguous with perfection. Whereas in the [higher] presence of divine knowledge, the servant's entity is annihilated in the entity of Him Who possesses beauty and majesty."[135] Ibn al-Fāriḍ's two odes, "The Wine Ode" and "The Poem of the Sufi Way," were no less popular than the poetry of ibn al-ʿArabī, receiving commentaries from scholars across the Islamic lands, including Saʿd al-Dīn al-Farghānī (d. 699/1300), the Sufi poet ʿAfīf al-Dīn al-Tilimsānī (d. 690/1291), ʿIzz al-Dīn al-Kāshānī (d. 735/1344), al-Qayṣarī, and ʿAbd al-Ghanī al-Nābulusī (d. 1143/1731).

Ibn al-Fāriḍ's Sufi poetry of love and wine cannot be understood outside of a Sufi tradition.[136] Before him were the Baghdad Sufis, as eloquently studied by the late Iraqi thinker and writer ʿAzīz al-Sayyid Jāsim (executed in 1991).[137] In the Persian tradition were Sanāʾī (d. 1131) and Farīd al-Dīn al-ʿAṭṭār (d. 1221). Saʿdī al-Shīrāzī (d. 1291), who followed ibn al-Fāriḍ, gained fame for what some scholars describe as Sufi love-verse clothed in the garb of human infatuation with the youthful body, a poetry written and communicated in an acceptable stylized poetics that made his poetry even more accessible in other regions. Jalāl al-Dīn al-Rūmī (d. 1273), a near contemporary of Saʿdī, went still further in his soul-searching quest for union with the beloved. No less allusive and more esoteric and controversial than these poets is ibn al-ʿArabī. The preface to his collection of poems, *Tarjumān al-ashwāq* (The Interpreter of Desires), may be for scholars the most confusing part of his corpus, since it is there that he plainly explains how he met the daughter of a certain Meccan shaykh, Makīn al-Dīn Abū Shujāʿ Zāhir al-ʾIṣfahānī, named al-Niẓām. He states that he was impressed by, and indeed infatuated with, the girl. Her knowledge, grace, beauty, and accomplishment were the occasion for his celebration, and he concludes that in his poetry, "whoever I mention in name is hers, and every abode I recall is hers." He warns against hurried presumptions that "honorable souls" will shun. He also emphasizes the Sufi path of indirection and spiritual intimations that should distract us from purely surface meanings. Ibn al-ʿArabī provides an interpretation for each verse, suggesting a seemingly far-fetched significance that conforms to a Sufi register. If the reader of ibn al-ʿArabī's poetry is unaware of the interpretation appended to the text and his disclaimer, he or she will certainly approach this poetry as erotic verse of the highest order. But even if it is interpreted only in esoteric terms, this work, *Tarjumān al-ashwāq*, was no less controversial. We have on record the first obituary for ibn al-ʿArabī, penned by the Ḥanbali hadith scholar ibn Nuqṭah (d. 629/1231), which unequivocally states its writer's "dislike for his verses." This seemingly passing note was soon to be seized upon by opponents such as Muḥammad ibn Aḥmad al-Dhahabī (1274–1348), who loads ibn Nuqṭah's note with his own proposed explication: "It seems to me that he [ibn Nuqṭah] referred to the unity [of God and man] (*ittiḥād*), the wine [themes], [Christian] churches, and [ancient] maxims, which abound in [ibn al-ʿArabī's] poetry."[138] In other words, al-Dhahabī proposes his own condemnation of ibn al-ʿArabī's use of the terms *ḥulūl* (usually translated as fusion, incarnation), *ittiḥād* (unification, unity, monism), and *waḥdat al-wujūd* (unity of being; confused with pantheism), as he understands them. These terms drew the most attention and controversy. Al-Dhahabī was a prominent conservative scholar, and his criticisms would soon reappear in the writings of later scholars, such as ibn Ḥajar al-ʿAsqalānī (d. 852/1449), who was prone to give names to what might not have been in ibn Nuqṭah's mind. He quotes the following verses of ibn al-ʿArabī from *Tarjumān al-ashwāq* as the focus of his disapproval:

My heart has become capable of every form;
It is a pasture for gazelles and a convent
For Christian monks,
A temple for idols and the pilgrim's
Kaʿba and the tables of the Torah and the manuscripts
of the Qurʾān.[139]

Other scholars untrammeled by animosity and the tendency to refutation focused more closely on the actual detail of the poems, referring to ibn al-ʿArabī's "unique mastery of [mystical] gnosis (*maʿrifah*) . . . , path of the People of Truth, ascetic discipline, spiritual exertion, and [writing in] the language of the Sufis," as ibn al-Dubaythī (d. 639/1241) puts it in his *Dhayl taʾrīkh Baghdād* (Epilogue to the History of Baghdad).[140] His disciple, ibn al-Najjār (d. 643/1245), appends a piece of poetry that ibn al-ʿArabī improvised in his presence, and which he includes in his *Al-Mustafād min dhayl taʾrīkh Baghdād* (Useful Extract from the Epilogue to the History of Baghdad). The poem runs:

Oh you, who wavers bewilderingly between
true knowledge and passion!
These two opposites merge
for him, who has attained
the highest degree of realization.[141]

Crucial to the notion of a republic of letters is the role that language plays in this debate over ibn al-ʿArabī's poetry. The apparent clarity to be found in his poetry and in the *Fuṣūṣ al-ḥikam* (*Bezels of Wisdom*) was responsible for the adversarial stance adopted by conservative theologians and traditionalists. Ṣalāḥ al-Dīn's (Saladin's) biographer, Abū Shāmah (d. 665/1268), a prominent epistolographer in his own right, wrote admiringly of ibn al-ʿArabī's verse as follows: "He composed fine poetry and long works in prose on the path of the Sufis."[142] Ibn al-ʿArabī's discourse, apart from his *Bezels of Wisdom*, is often marked by digressions and obfuscation; it is sufficiently abstruse and esoteric to confuse his contenders. There is very little with which they can dispute except matters of interpretation, where their own misunderstanding of anything that falls outside their own formal and codified discourse is clearly evident. Foremost among this tissue of misunderstandings is ibn Taymiyyah's change of heart upon reading *The Bezels*. He writes: "At first I was among those who held a good opinion of Ibn al-ʿArabī and praised him highly for the useful advice he provides in his books. This useful advice is found in the pages of the 'Revelation,' the 'Essence,' the 'Tightly Knit and Tied,' the 'Precious Pearl,' the 'Positions of the Stars,' and similar writings. At that time, we were unaware of his real goal, because we had not yet studied the *Fuṣūṣ* and similar works."[143] Al-Dhahabī was to follow the same line as that of the better-known Shaykh ibn Taymiyyah, addressing thereby jurists and common people alike. In Alexander Knysh's words, al-Dhahabī is known for his "advocacy of the community-oriented, fideistic theology that was shared by most of Ibn Taymiyyah's disciples."[144] Regarding some of ibn al-ʿArabī's poetic pieces and his *Fuṣūṣ* in particular as *kufr* (atheism), al-Dhahabī and many others shunned this kind of esoteric knowledge, the "obscure gnosis," which he associates with ibn al-ʿArabī.[145] But we can detect some uncertainty in his refutation, which avoids an unequivocal condemnation. He qualifies his critique as follows:

> Ibn al-ʿArabī was characterized by such qualities as eloquence, acumen, good memory, mastery of Sufism, and proficiency in esoteric knowledge (*ʿirfān*). If it had not been for ecstatic utterances in his speech, he would certainly have been [approved] by scholarly consensus. His slips of the tongue may have occurred in a state of ecstatic intoxication and mystical rapture. Therefore, we wish him a favorable [outcome in the Hereafter].[146]

Ibn al-ʿArabī's language cuts across a broad spectrum of doctrinal disputation and has been the focus of a good deal of attention, though there has been little effort to interpret its poetics as emerging naturally from a rich tradition of Arabic poetry and rhetoric. As his language soars through select, malleable spaces that recall the dense poetics of his forebear, Muḥammad al-Niffarī (d. 965),[147] it also negotiates with traditional lore without falling into the trap of imitation. Genuine and heartfelt, it emerges sufficently fresh to dislodge more codified discourse. Hence the alarm among traditionalists. As a direct result, ibn al-ʿArabī is the subject of both refutation and apology. It is well known, for example, that the Ottoman scholar-statesman Kemalpaşazâde (d. 940/1534) issued a ban on defamations of ibn al-ʿArabī; and that al-Shaykh Makkī (Muḥammad ibn Muẓaffar) composed an apology in the name of Sultan Selim, a work that was later followed by a no less influential one from the Sufi shaykh and scholar ʿAbd al-Wahhāb al-Shaʿrānī (d. 973/1565). The details of this history are not unique, to be sure, because ibn al-Fāriḍ suffered a similar posthumous fate. Taqī al-Dīn ʿAbd al-Raḥmān ibn Bint al-Aʿazz, Sultan Sayf al-Dīn Qalāʾūn's vizier, for example, leveled a slander, albeit less vituperative and widespread, against ibn al-Fāriḍ as "inclined toward the heresy of incarnation [*ḥulūl*]."[148] Later in his life, however, this same vizier was reported to "ask for God's forgiveness for what [he] . . . said against his [ibn al-Fāriḍ's] good reputation."[149] In the case of both these Sufi poets, less prominent jurists and a number of popular religious authorities tended to pamper commoners who might, as the renowned al-Dhahabī, for example, believes, be led astray by the utterances and statements of these poets. Thus, language is the site for contestation, and Sufi poetics becomes the focus for discussion and controversy.

The divide takes a sharp turn, however, when it comes to the treatment of Sufism itself. Although ibn Taymiyyah is regarded as a staunch opponent of Sufism, his letters and legal statements include many qualifications that differentiate between the grand Sufis and their abstruse phrasing, on the one hand, and those who dwell only on the surface meaning, on the other. Ibn al-ʿArabī's reservations with respect to misreadings of his use of the terms *ḥulūl*, *ittiḥād*, and *waḥdat al-wujūd* need to be borne in mind. In his *The Meccan Revelations* he states that "God forbids incarnation in or with beings and occasions," and "nobody claims unification unless he is a blasphemer."[150] To the same effect, ibn Taymiyyah asserts that agnostics (*ahl al-maʿrifah*)[151] cannot "believe in God's incarnation in them or in other creatures, or in His unification. And if something is reported on behalf of the great shaykhs, it is distortion, made up by liars from among licentious monists who are misled by Satan."[152] He even goes out of his way to interpret the famous verse of al-Ḥallāj, the one that caused him to be summoned before the jurists who then demanded of the caliph that he be killed. The verse begins: "It is I whom I adore . . . ," and ibn Taymiyyah explains: "The poet means moral unification, as the union of one lover with another, adoring the same, and hating the same, with the same utterance and action, in similarity and resemblance, not a unification in detail, as each is absorbed into the other, to be so self-annihilated as to be blind to one's self, as someone says: 'I, so absented by you from myself / to believe you are I.' This resemblance is a proper unification."[153]

Esoteric Poetics

Sufism relies on an esoteric poetics, but it makes use not only of early Islamic odes to the Prophet but also, and primarily, of a tradition whereby the amatory prelude of the *qaṣīdah* paves the way for sites of longing, adoration, and devotion. The image of the deserted encampment, the topoi for the departing lover/beloved, the sites that punctuate these poetic openings and that have ever since become topographic indices of a vanished era, all these are adopted and transformed in praise poems to the Prophet and also in Sufi poetry. What is new here is the density of feeling associated with the use of these topoi, a trend that explores new territories in its expressiveness through indirection, facilitated through the medium of wine poetry with its rich repertoire in the Arabic and Persian traditions. Self-annihilation makes use of sense and perception in order to read an alterity into sites and sounds, "like a transparent glass that assumes the color of its contents," as al-Ghazālī stipulates.[154] These sources of inspiration are, needless to say, part of a poetic tradition of long standing. They are now invoked in an esoteric register of allusion, symbol, code, and gesture that has already been enriched by

Arab poets.The matter is discussed at some length by al-Ghazālī. In his reading, the referent and the topoi assume meaning in view of the beholder's own passion. If this passion is toward God, everything else reminds the beholder of God. He argues:

> So he over whose heart the love of God has control is reminded by the blackness of the hair on the temples of a like thing, the darkness of unbelief, and by the brightness of the cheek, of the light of Faith, and by the mention of union, of the meeting God Most High, and by the mention of parting, of the separation from God Most High in the company of the rejected, and by the mention of the censurer who disturbs the gladness of the union, of the obstacles of the world and its defects that disturb the endurance of intercourse with God Most High.[155]

Referents, topoi, and beholders change relationships and effects. They also help establish a milieu that enables poets to interact, intertextualize material, and appropriate as much as they wish in a poetic endeavor that was already perused by both classical and premodern Arab scholars and critics as part of the library of works on plagiarism.

The Sufis also borrow from this repertoire, but only in the sense that they redirect registers and sites toward their own cryptic and highly symbolic and allusive usage. It thus comes as no surprise that not all of the later critics, philologists, and scholars were able to comprehend their poetic repository and symbolic layers of language. Thus, al-Būrīnī (d. 1024/1615), for example, failed to provide a nuanced study of ibn al-Fāriḍ's poetry. His explication is concerned primarily with surface meanings rather than the deep layers of allusion, a point that has been noticed by some modern Arab scholars.[156] By way of contrast, ʿAbd al-Ghanī al-Nābulusī (d. 1143/1730) devotes his study to the Sufi intertext in ibn al-Fāriḍ's poetry, and his achievement only proves the need for the critic and scholar to be sufficiently familiar with a poet or tradition before embarking on analysis and explication.[157] Both manuscripts found their way into edited editions in France in 1853 as part of a sustained interest among Orientalists with literary, and especially Sufi, traditions.

Sufi poetry certainly gives language a new life; it releases it from verbosity, rigidity, and stock imagery. Its resort to common sites, images, and allusions is at the root of this innovation: it borrows in order to "detonate" the obvious and strip the verbal of its overuse. It provides the republic of letters with new terms of allusion and hence gestures and intimations that are badly needed in order to expunge the ineffective dimensions of common discourse. Admired by his contemporaries and later scholars, ibn al-Fāriḍ is a pivotal figure in our quest for the other side in the republic of letters, the one that adheres to the "literary" while espousing the spiritual path of Sufi agnostics.

This poetics dovetails with other religious traditions, but its esoteric hold on word and syntax is less tied to rhetoric. Its soaring tone takes a different path, one that has its point of departure in the Qurʾān or poetic tradition, and yet the interiority of the journey remains personal. Both the Sufi love poem and *badīʿiyyah* share common aspects, but they traverse distinct territories and conclude their experience differently. Both manage to dislodge formal and codified discourse through rephrasing, allegory, ambivalence, rearticulation, paradox, slippage, antinomianism, obfuscation, parody, *laḥn* (verbal gesturing and allusion), and many other stylistic applications that play a major role in the ultimate shake-up of habitual terms of writing, dispute, and syllogistic reasoning.

Between Sufi Verse and *Badīʿiyyāt*

At this juncture between Sufi verse and *badīʿiyyāt*, the ideologically entrenched world of transcendence and hierarchical categorizations undergoes a process of transformation. Along these "sacral" paths and trajectories, the linguistic and rhetorical fecundity endows the poet's endeavors with a new, robust quality, while simultaneously involving the traditionalist community in reactions that involved counteracting and deciphering the esoteric and densely rhetorical creations that confronted them. At this intersection a line of demarcation must be drawn between writing on religious subjects, on the one hand, and, on the other, the Sufi and *badīʿiyyah* pursuits and their manifestations in poetry or prose. Scholars have taken it for granted that the medieval and premodern age is distinguished by an enormous production in the religious sciences, which is only partly true. Even so, the reasons given for the substantial religious production are worth examining in more detail. As one common argument has it, a way of confronting challenges posed under the banner of religion is through a counter-religious movement. The three Crusades (489/1096–588/1192) are claimed as such challenges, and the Mongols' attacks can be included as well (starting in 616/1219 until 1260 east of Iran; later, to control Khwārizm, 1371; Mongolia, 1374; Khurāsān, 1380; Mazandaran, 1384; India, 1398; and Anatolia, 1401).[158] The Mamluks ruled as Muslims, and the Ottomans (from 1516 up to 1922) did the same. More relevant is the tendency to interpret the onslaught as basically cultural: behind the targeting of libraries in Marv, Herāt, Khwārizm, Baghdad, Damascus, Aleppo, and so on, is an effort to erase memory and knowledge. For the large body of jurists, the target was not books on philosophy and science, but rather works of Islamic law, exegesis, and source material. Other explanations oscillate between eschatological readings and socioeconomic justifications. Wars and plagues took their heavy toll on people, and a sense of ending enveloped people's minds and souls in a fatalist submission.[159] Where poetry is concerned, the *badīʿiyyah* tradition responds to these needs, but it also shifts attention to the Prophet; it can thus be seen as yet another vehicle for the Sufi focus on the Prophet as the pillar of light. Although the early origins of this idea lead us back to Abū Manṣūr al-Ḥallāj's (d. 911) *Ṭāʾ wa-sīn* and Shihāb al-Dīn Aḥmad al-Suhrawardī's (d. 587/1191) *Haykal al-nūr* (Pillar of Light; translated into English as *The Shape of Light*),[160] al-Būṣīrī's (d. 1294) seminal *Burdah* ode establishes a new tone for this line of discussion.[161] He states:

> Every miracle brought up by the noble messengers of God
> emanates from his illumination
> for he is effusing, divinely emanating sun and they are its planets
> that convey to people in darkness its light.[162]

The twentieth-century Egyptian scholar Zakī Mubārak draws on this notion as a Sufi catalyst for the Prophet's presence. He argues that it is at the center of their "Muḥammadan [esoteric] Reality," the base for the "Dome of Existence," for this Truth is the link between God and people. As he points out, ibn al-ʿArabī argues:

> Know that when God creates the universe, there are categories, and under each there are the elect, and from among the elect there are the faithful, and from among them are the selected few who are the friends of God, i.e., saints, and from among them the very remnant who are the prophets, and from among them the prophets of specific messages, and from among this condensed elect are all the messengers: He chose one of them, who is not one of them, the one in charge of all creations, the pillar for the dome of existence, at the supreme peak by designation and assignment; whose knowledge is antecedent to all humans: this is Muḥammad . . . irresistible and unchallenged, the master, and the rest are commoners.[163]

This underlying Sufi understanding is as pivotal to al-Būṣīrī's poem as it is to the *badīʿiyyah* tradition thereafter. It follows a pre-Islamic structure, making use of the erotic prelude only in the sense that the Prophet is the one intended and addressed in the opening lines. Al-Būṣīrī draws on the Sufi shaykh and poet ibn al-Fāriḍ (d. 1235), already discussed, not only in the use of rhyme but also in names and terms of Sufi adoration. In correspondence with the Sufi shaykh, he makes selective use of perceptual and visual images and expressions to compose his immensely popular Mantle Ode. If there are drawbacks, they relate to the milieu, which, as one scholar argues, is notorious for its application of grammatical and philological knowledge in poetry and narrative.[164] It is to the credit of this ode of al-Būṣīrī, however, that a chain of similar poems has flourished ever since.[165] While we may now regard such production as superfluous, it obviously did not sound so to its premodern audiences; nor does it sound so nowadays to the large audiences who regularly participate in occasions when it is publicly recited, or who watch or listen to presentations on satellite TV shows and social media venues. The *Burdah*, its reception, and its use over time provide us with parameters for taste and faith all over the Islamic world, thus helping us to understand the lines of disconnect and disparity that separate the modern elite from the common public.

Sacral Itineraries

Not all odes in this vein reveal a strong Sufi streak. The ones that follow, and that show more variations and a sustained application of both known and new rhetorical figures, take their cue from Ṣāfī al-Dīn al-Ḥillī's *al-Kāfiyah al-badīʿiyyah* (literally, The Sufficient Ode). Even if there is some disagreement on who comes first, the blind poet ibn Jābir al-Andalusī (d. 780/1378), or his explicator, Abū Jaʿfar al-Albīrī, or al-Ḥillī, the latter is usually credited with the initial use of the term *badīʿiyyah*, leading soon after to a series of others, as discussed in chapter 5. Nearly every prominent poet tried his or her hand at the art, including al-Suyūṭī and the Sufi woman poet ʿĀʾishah al-Bāʿūniyyah.[166] Of special significance for this reading of the medieval and premodern Islamic republic of letters is the tendency to establish a tradition, a chain of authoritative poetic and rhetorical referents, which draw on each other in terms of borrowing, interpolation, addition, and appropriation. The process develops into rich constellations not only on the level of philological inquiry and lexical supplementation, but also on socioeconomic and cultural levels. They provide a comprehensive index of taste, and as a result we acquire more information about cultural pursuits, needs, beliefs, inhibitions, and fears. Their other variations relate to the so-called supplicatory poetry, also addressed to the Prophet in the form of entreaties and petitions to him to intervene on their behalf. In such supplications, a sense of difficulty, duress, and calamity looms.[167] Although there is a long list of poets who authored such supplications, there is also a conservative counter-movement mounted by ibn Taymiyyah and his followers, who shunned the practice and regarded it as blasphemous because it appealed for help to an entity other than God. But, as Bakrī Shaykh Amīn candidly admits, the Qurʾān states: "Reach God by whatever means."[168] Without these supplications and intercessions, there will be no such poetry, no sainthood, and no shrines.

A genre of poetry that is less esoteric and hence less shocking or disruptive than Sufi language is the elegy. Elegaic poems on the death or loss of individuals abound, but the ones that address the destruction of cities, centers of knowledge and learning, and sites of past glory and exuberance bring memory alive, not as mere nostalgic recollections but as verbal reconstructions of being. Although they replicate, and are thus themselves replicas, they also offer in the intensely felt dirge a kind of resuscitation, but one weighted with the symbolism of reckoning, warning, and promise. The symbolic reconstruction inflicts death on the past, which is given a post-maturation in this symbolic act. The latter is predicated on a verbal atemporal canvas. The hiatus that is thus created is situated amid verbal constructs and memories of centers of production and the proliferation of knowledge (such as the chancery, the compendious culture, and other constellations). Poets in this tradition regularly draw on two significant verses, one by al-Sharīf al-Raḍī (d. 406/1016) and another by Diʿbil al-Khuzāʿī (d. 246/860). Both extend the *aṭlāl* (amatory) prelude of the pre-Islamic ode. Instead of the deserted campsite, there is the deserted abode of either the beloved or the Prophet's family. Al-Khuzāʿī's verse runs as follows: "The abodes of Qurʾānic verse are empty of recitation, and the site of divine inspiration lost its features."[169] Al-Sharīf al-Raḍī's verse reverses the topoi of the ancient ode, turning the physical trace upside down and introducing a new itinerary of feeling. The deserted campsite is now gone, and hence the occasion for poetic deflection from eyesight to insight: "And my eye looked around; but as the effaced *ṭulūl* [ruins] belie the look, the heart takes over."[170] Both these poets inspired others, who elegize lost centers and their symbolic value for the Islamic polity. The fall of Jerusalem to the Franks, for example, was the occasion for a number of elegies, especially those by the poet Abū Yūsuf Shihāb al-Dīn Yaʿqūb ibn al-Mujāwir (d. 601/1204). Born in Persia and a resident of Damascus, ibn al-Mujāwir was a vizier, poet, and eloquent littérateur. Recalling Diʿbil al-Khuzāʿī's T-rhymed (ending on the letter "T") poem, he writes:

> The entire domain should weep over Jerusalem and proclaim
> its sorrow and grief;
> Mecca should do likewise, for it is Jerusalem's sister; and should
> protest to ʿArafāt itself the treatment meted out.[171]

The rest of the poem uses the occasion to incite resistance. After the Mongol invasion, the loss of Baghdad occasioned a deep sense of misery. Thus Shams al-Dīn Maḥmūd al-Kūfī was shocked to see only ruins and sites of destruction and devastation. Unable to recognize a trace of the glorious city, he echoes al-Mutanabbī and asks in agonized tones: "What goes wrong with the abodes? Its people are no longer mine; or its neighbors my neighbors."[172] Another poet, Taqī al-Dīn Ismāʿīl b. Abū al-Yusr al-Tūkhī, advises people not to visit the devastated site:

> You visitors to Baghdad refrain from going
> there is no host, nor protection there
> the crown of the caliphate and the site
> that honored the place is in ruins.[173]

From Andalusia to Herāt and Khwārizm, the sense of destruction, devastation, and loss touched a sensitive chord in poetic sensibilities, invoking a corpus of elegies that serves not only as a historical index of wars and their attending calamities on the personal, communal, and cultural levels, but also as journeys into the unconscious of nations torn between the need for a secure center and repugnance toward violence. Especially for those writers whose moments of jubilation soar high when they are placed among their peers and accommodated in libraries, a peaceful abode is what they all yearn for. In such an environment, it is no surprise that the chancery in an established state becomes the recipient of so many encomiums.

CONCLUSION

Al-Khātimah

The argument presented here for a medieval Islamic republic of letters implies an umbrella term that subsumes within its frame of reference multiple coexisting and/or successive communities of literary world-systems that existed across Asia and Africa. Literary and broad cultural networks took as their main venues the *ḥajj*, other travels, assemblies, projects requiring teamwork, and numerous compendiums and successive commentaries, all constituting an interactive dialogue over a relatively long temporal stretch that witnessed the generation of modes and patterns in logical reasoning and literary forms and practices, along with diversified styles in commentary and documentation. Taking the Arabic language as the pervasive medium and space for this proliferation in knowledge, my argument gathers these outcomes under a number of categories that constitute a tabulated and organized knowledge system.

This approach may prompt a counterargument, one that takes the Western model or models as its example. In the West, writers and philosophers had a say in the makeup of the Enlightenment and, to a certain extent, in the rise of empires and colonial systems. Many became architects of and theorists for territorial and cultural domination. They also brought with them the institutionalization of literature as a specific pursuit aimed at the canonization of certain names and texts, which would serve in the long run as landmarks in literary nationalism and the discreet legitimization of imperial power and acumen. Colonized societies witnessed this valorization through colleges of higher education in arts and sciences, institutions where people learned more of Shakespeare than of their own cultures. Moreover, Western intellectuals were able to have an impact on public opinion, since they were living in a largely free society that had the upper hand in running world affairs. That offered them an advantage that Afro-Asian intellectuals could only partially achieve, usually with difficulty and under duress.

Such considerations as these should not stop us from raising other questions with respect to prototypical formations that predate the European Enlightenment model, questions relating to the Islamic constellation of knowledge as a movement with its own identifiable features and regenerative processes that could have nourished the present and led it safely out of wars, disasters, and colonial incursions. A question that may recur relates to the seeming failure of that constellation of knowledge to survive in a sustainable manner, involving growth and order. One can also offer examples (and there are many) of scientists and intellectuals in this republic of letters who served as effective mediators with emperors and ruthless rulers; Al-Ṭūsī and ibn Khaldūn were not the only ones. Every national literature across Asia and Africa offers a rich legacy of such figures; and in the particular case of Arabic literature, Arab, Berber, and African-Asian intellectuals bequeathed a massive cultural output that is daunting in its very diversity and imposing presence and in the challenge that it offers to modern individual researchers and scholars.

Even so, we must conclude that such constellations as these falter and fail to furnish sustainable world-systems in the Islamic regions, ones that would have been capable of averting the doom that we usually associate with the encroachment of colonialism. Nevertheless, they need to be studied within the framework of inherent or applied constitutive elements, elements such as dynastic succession and caliphal monopoly that stifled the possibilities for collective resistance to specific patterns of governance. Due to the complexity of a culture of such dimensions and range, we cannot expect easy answers. At each intersection, we come across multiple problems and possible resolutions.

Social and urban mobility caused by wars and invasions, for instance, paradoxically generated vivacious networks among migrant scholars and writers. But by the same token, these wars made the sustainable growth of solid mercantile and professional communities an impossibility, a fact that was dwelt on by contemporaneous historians and scholars, especially in relation to Tīmūr's enforced capture and deportation of craftsmen to be part of his new order in Samarqand. As a result of such deportations, for example, the textile industry that was the landmark of the economy in al-Shām (Syria) was ravaged, according to ibn ʿArabshāh. Apart from wars and their destructive consequences, there must be other reasons that halt sustainability and divert attention away from the enhancement of scientific discovery or the continuity of rationalist thought within its Islamic framework. As an example that may seem inconsequential, I draw once more on ʿAbd al-Ḥamīd al-Kātib's epistle as a foundational text. It permanently set the tone of, and argument for, the chancery as an institution with a large number of scribes, functionaries, and writers whose role was to be the ears, eyes, and tongues of the ruler and hence to share authority as his counselors. The text emanates from the principle "might is right," which was assiduously implemented in a rising empire. In other words, scribes, as the distinguished elite, complemented and enhanced state politics as specifically defined by rulers and dynasties. Co-opted as professionals and functionaries, their role outside their chancery jobs was laid down as one of complacency and conciliation, devoid of individuality or dissent. This institutionalization, which occurred early in the composition of the chancery as "people of the pen," cannot be understood apart from a systematic codification of prose, with its centrality to the discourse of power that struck very deep roots in the Umayyad image of the state. By forcing the language of power onto every other interpretation of Islam, this codification was bound to impose an official discourse of checks that empties the faith of its poetry and turns it into indices against difference, which is often treated as deviation and heresy. In other words, an overruling conformist discourse can be identified as one of the reasons behind the lack of a durably consolidated cultural capital. The mounting stress on consensus as an intimidating means of stifling and repressing deviations and difference became an essential part of official discourse, with its systematization of doctrinal checks.[1] As many manuals and commentaries also demonstrate, especially in the middle period, the roles of grammarians and jurists overlapped. Their combined profession ensured not only inclusion in the leading community but also a good job, as ibn al-ʾUkhuwwah noticed.

The reverse took place in Tīmūr's court, in the context of Tīmūr's search for a more accommodating theological perspective. Unfortunately, this effort was coupled with and thus incapacitated by wars of destruction. According to ibn Khaldūn's hypothesis, the traditionalists won the battle against speculative theology and philosophy. In tandem with the consolidation and expansion of state power, the belletristic tradition received a further impetus that enabled it to compete very strongly with nearly every other literary medium and domain. Prose rather than poetry grew and developed: it was a lucrative field of production, essential to a hegemonic discourse centered in the chancery and its early prototypes, and increasingly in demand in accordance with statist needs, social mobility, and trans-ethnic inclusion and assimilation. In other words, during the middle period and insofar as the formation of a state or empire is concerned, there was no noticeable deviation from the institutionalization of the chancery as a professional and functionary space based on the ethos of exchange: benefits in exchange for allegiance. As the location that incorporated some of the most dynamic elements in epistolary art and prose writing, the medieval chancery showed minimal or even no concern with internal issues, a fact that could be cited among the negative elements in the constitution of knowledge.

These probable drawbacks and detrimental forces could all be put forward to justify the durability/intermittence paradigm mapped out in ibn Khaldūn's theory of history and rule. His theory of rise and fall, based on tribal solidarity and gradual disintegration, can be applied here on the condition that we take into consideration a variety of factors that have forestalled a sustained growth in knowledge construction. The lack of emphasis on consolidated economies, dynastic preoccupation with the accumulation of riches at the expense of the Muslim nation, rivalries, and the ultimate destruction of cities and industries all helped to disintegrate the social and political fabric of Islamic communities and states. In no way, however, can these factors negate the complexity, diversity, and magnitude of medieval cultural production, which has daunted modernists and their counterparts in the West and caused them to fall back on a series of negations and denials of merit. The various domains of the republic of letters across the Islamic world were to express themselves in their vernacular literatures, although not necessarily as part of a humanist secularization, unlike the struggles in the West against the dominance of Latin and the Church. The Sufi strand, for one, notwithstanding its grounding in a thorough Qurʾānic hermeneutic, manifested a number of accentuations, enunciations, and Sufi Orders that turned Sufism into a poetic enterprise and practice in a God-loving universe. In terms of a humanist paradigm, with its focus on reason, Sufism might seem an aberration and a case of waywardness. But its significance for the republic of letters extends even beyond its deconstruction of the prosaic and the mundane; for its striking freedom and newness in vision and illumination also necessarily downplay structures of authority and power. Furthermore, even when there was an avowed application of Islamic law in one region or another, there were always local variables stemming from national, social, and also traditional values and interests.

Hence, there was more than one literary world-system in the Islamic world, and more variables are in play than those assumed by Pascale Casanova in her Parisian model of a metropolitan center that plays both centripetal and centrifugal roles. But, to formulate a conclusion to this study of the medieval Islamic republic of letters, one can argue for the binary of heterogeneity and uniformity not only along metropolitan and peripheral lines but also, and more pointedly, through sociopolitical, economic, and literary trends. Although for a long time historiography has tended to account more readily for the grand event or happening and paid less attention to social, communal, and local life, the middle period witnessed the appearance of many compilations and books that deal with urban and rural space, annals, and anecdotes that might otherwise have been beyond the reach of belletristic prose. Difference and dissent are played out in full in many of these compilations. Hence, the medieval or postclassical period provides particular instances that constitute a distinctive feature of the milieu and its social and ethnic mobility. As if in a countermovement to the factors that brought about disastrous migrations, exodus, and destruction, the cultural scene also gained some of its diversity and difference from the chancery. Social and demographic mobility brought to the literary scene sustained modes of parody and contrafaction, thus offering support to the burgeoning number of subgenres, while at the same time consolidating and diverting others.

At times, however, a subgenre such as the *badīʿiyyah*—initially a traditional tripartite *qaṣīdah* with a personal claim on the poet's part that it is a gift to the Prophet in exchange for his intercession and the poet's recovery from illness—outgrows and outpaces its foundational base, the *qaṣīdah*. One can even propose that it opens up a wide horizon for variability from the long-established *qaṣīdah* form, which is often associated with rule and power. Al-Būṣīrī, a poet of Amazigh (Berber) descent who settled in Cairo, was one of the many who flocked to the city from every region of the Islamic world. Along with Alexandria, Cairo, as discussed earlier, proved particularly accommodating to scholars and poets from North Africa and the Maghreb. Although al-Būṣīrī's poem generates an oneiric imagination among fellow poets and invokes emulation and contrafaction, its value for rhetoric stems from its power to engender the subgenre that al-Ḥillī significantly terms *badīʿiyyah*, with its systematic valorization of tropes and figures of speech as a body of knowledge that is subsequently subsumed under rhetoric. The significance of both the original poem and its innovative successor for a literary value system stems not only from its being recited all over the Islamic world, but also from its popular use as an amulet and its subsequent growth into a sacral and talismanic edifice; it became a "mantle" for not only individuals and communities but also for an Islamic nationhood. This fact, along with the proliferation of Sufism and other forms of popular knowledge, cannot be discounted in any assessment of Islamic culture. Sufi, street, and popular poetry and poetics manifest their variables as humanist endeavors and ways of expression in a God-loving universe.

According to a modernist paradigm, with its basic equation between secularism and humanism, these Islamic practices find no place within a humanist system. Their wide acceptance and practice have been depreciated by Arab and Afro-Asian modernists as regressive and hence not conducive to progress and modernity. Indeed, they have not even been regarded as falling within the terms of Herder's celebration of folk and popular-national traditions as necessarily enriching a republic of letters. In Islamic culture, and especially in the period under consideration, the phenomenal growth of Sufism, folk narrative and poetry, and popular belief and practice complemented and perhaps enriched the belletristic tradition, as we understand from the notable grammarian ibn al-Khashshāb. An ironic twist that also requires interrogation relates to the *Thousand and One Nights* (Arabian Nights), as another confederational site of folk, popular, and urban tales narrated and collected over time by storytellers, copyists, detractors, editors, and translators and publishers. While achieving its fame in Europe after its first appearance in translation in 1704, this collection, the product of the same middle period, could not find a place in an Arab belletristic tradition. That very tradition presents to us the other face of the literary world-system, namely, its consecration of power and maintenance of discipline through formulas, manuals, and codified schema. Lexicography and compendiums, along with historiography, also fall within this trend, since they necessarily aimed at fitting all knowledge within some orderly schema. However, that aim does not preclude diversity and difference. In Islamic culture, the struggle among traditionalists, speculative theologians, and rationalists concerning historiographical or dehistoricized argumentation takes as its starting point canonical texts, and especially the Qurʾān. It is this specific battle, debated over centuries, that has led to an enormous production in hermeneutics, rhetoric, and other fields of knowledge. Hence, the long-established Western equation between secularism and humanism needs to be challenged whenever it is applied outside the specific domain of a European Renaissance. Only through a better engagement with this past, with rigorous interrogation of its successes and failures, can modernists build up a sustainable view of the present and thus be at peace with themselves. Diversity and dissent constitute a marked feature of Islamic culture, one that valorizes and invigorates a republic of letters with its many conspicuous or discrete worlds in what amounts to no less than a seismic *Islamica*.

APPENDIX

Tīmūr's Debate with Damascene Theologians outside the Gates of Damascus (803/1401)

Tīmūr with ibn Khaldūn and the Damascene theologians and *faqīhs* (experts in Islamic law), excerpted from Ahmad ibn Arabshah, *Tamerlane, or Timur the Great Amir*, trans. J. H. Sanders (London: Luzac and Co., 1936), 143–51 (vol. 2, ch. 6).

CHAPTER VI

HOW THE LEADERS WENT FORTH, AFTER THE SULTAN HAD DEPARTED, AND SOUGHT SECURITY FROM TIMUR

Therefore when their opinion had deceived them and they knew that fatal evil was descending upon them, the great men of the city assembled and the leaders that were present, namely the chief judge Muhiuddin Mahmud son of Al-Az Hanifi and his son the chief judge Shahabuddin and the chief judge Taqiuddin Ibrahim Son of Muflah Hanbali and the chief judge Shamsuddin Mahomed Hanbali of Nablus and Qazi[1] Nasiruddin Mahomed son of Abiltib, who had charge of secret affairs, and Qazi Shahabuddin Ahmed son of Vazir

1. Or Cadi, i.e., judge.

Al Shahid, on whom at that time the dignity of vazir[2] conferred authority above the rest, and Qazi Shahabuddin Habani the Shafeite and Qazi Shahabuddin Ibrahim son of Qusha Hanifi, deputy judge—Allah have mercy upon them!—but the Shafeite Qazi that is Alauddin son of Abul Baqa fled with the Sultan; and the Malikite chief judge Burhanuddin Shazali died a martyr as I have related. These leaders therefore went out and sought security from him, after they had taken counsel and consented among themselves, and their speech had been joined on the thread of agreement.

But when the Sultan had committed to the winds the sails of the full ship of his armies, there fell into the sea of Timur's army the chief judge Valiuddin son of Khaldun, who was among the principal leaders, and one of those who had arrived with the Sultan, and who, when the Sultan was driven to flight, took no heed and so fell into the net. He was living in the college Al Adalia and those leaders approached him, concerning the direction of this crisis and by united judgment set him over this business, for they could not take him as an associate; for he was by sect, as well as in respect of eloquence and poetry a Maliki, and in knowledge of tradition and history an Asmai.[3]

Therefore he set out with them, clad in a turban light and elegantly shaped and a robe long, like himself, with a narrow border, like the beginning of a dark night, and they wished him to go before them, approving whatever he might say or do for them or against them; and when they went into Timur's presence, they stood before him and remained standing, trembling and afraid, until he mercifully bade them sit and be of good courage. Then with geniality and smiling pleasantly upon them, he marked their condition and with the probe of his mind tried their words and deeds. And when he saw that the dress of Ibn Khaldun was different from theirs he said:

"This man is not one of them" and the course was opened for speech and his tongue was loosened. And what he said, I will soon tell.

2. I.e., vizier. The form "vasir" or "wazir" is more correct.

3. The famous Ibn Khaldun, author of *Universal History* and other works, was born in Tunis in A.D. 1322, and lived successively at Fez, Granada, Tiemcen, Tunis and Egypt. He died in 1406.

Then they folded up the carpet of speech and unfolded the rug of feasting and presently they brought heaps of boiled meat and set before each what was suitable and some abstained therefrom through zeal for restraint, some in that turn of affairs were through fear distracted from eating, but some ate with outstretched hand and were not slow in appetite and drew not back, but urged and roused the others to eat, reciting that verse: "Eat like one, who, if he lives, will be praised by his people, but if he dies, will come to Allah with full belly."

And among those who ate freely was the chief judge Valiuddin.

Meanwhile Timur glanced at them and with dull eye secretly observed them. But Ibn Khaldun also glanced towards Timur and when Timur looked at him, looked down; then, when his glance turned from him, again lightly regarded him. Then he said in a loud voice: "O Lord and Amir! Praise to Allah Almighty! truly I have had the honour of admission to the kings of mankind and I have restored life to their memory by my chronicles. Of the kings of the Arabs I have seen that one and that; to this Sultan and this I have been admitted; I have visited East and West and everywhere talked with Amirs and governors, but thanks be to Allah! that my life has been extended and by Allah! that I have lived long enough to see this man, who is truly a king and knows rightly how to rule the Sultanate. But if the food of kings suffice to avert destruction, truly the food of our Lord Amir suffices for this, nay, suffices to gain glory and honour."

By this speech, Timur was more pleased, so that he almost leapt for joy and began a conversation with him, in which he relied on him above all and asked him concerning the kings of the West, their exploits, the days of their power, and memorable deeds. Then he expounded to him concerning it, things which charmed him and drew him almost beyond himself into admiration.

And Timur was very skilled in the history of kings and peoples and expert in the annals of East and West, of which I will give below excellent examples.

Now while they were sitting one day in the presence of that keen observer, lo! they brought prisoner Sadaruddin Manavi, whom pursuers caught in Mislon, while he was following the Sultan in his flight, and put him in chains and brought him to Timur. He was clad in a turban like a tower and gauntlets like saddle-bags and passing those who already sat, without apology took a higher place, wherefore Timur blazed with anger and the assembly was filled with flame, his lungs swelled, and he boiled with wrath, and he roared and snorted and anger flooded his body and overflowed and he ordered certain of his attendants to set an example of punishment on Qazi Sadaruddin and they dragged him over the ground like a dog, tore his clothes and heaped curses and abuse upon him and smote him excessively with their feet and fists. Then he ordered them to bind him with tighter bonds, sharpen his pain and vex him from time to time with constant torments and doubled afflictions. Therefore he was cast out, like a wicked man on the day of judgment driven away with back turned, who has no defender from Allah.

Then Timur returning to the contriving of his wonted evil and cunning, clothed each of those leaders with a robe of honour and set them in honour and dignity at his court. Then he sent them away cheered, having gained calm and joy, but in his heart evils and heavier matters were turning, which presently broke forth.

I have written:

"Like a victim which he who offers it adorns and honours, but soon gives it to eat to death as guest."

And he promised them and their followers security on condition that they should hand over for him the Sultan's goods and all his and his Amirs' utensils, means, riches, beasts of burden, cattle, slaves and domestics: and they performed these commands of his, bearing out to him all those things, whether hidden or open.

But the fort was equipped for sustaining a siege and its governor was called Azdar, who fortified it and rightly equipped it with every munition, expecting vigorous aid from the Sultan or some divine obstacle, whereby he might be freed from trouble.

But Timur in the beginning neglected it and did not consider it or attend thereto; but when the goods had been brought and transferred to his treasury, he imposed on the city a tribute of security, for the exaction of which he wished to employ those leaders over whom he set his own masters of accounts and scribes and agents and the managers of his treasury. But the chief control of that business he entrusted to Allahdad, one of his ministers of state, whom he especially trusted, uterine brother of Seifuddin, who was mentioned at the beginning of the book, and added to them any and every unjust oppressor and men reared in the bosom of inhumanity and who had sucked the paps of oppression.

Then by the voice of a herald he proclaimed peace and security and that they should not vex one another. But when certain Jagatais after hearing this edict and its publication put forth their hands to plunder, Timur so soon as he learnt it, ordered them to be fixed to the cross in a public place. Therefore they crucified them in the silk market, where the vegetable market begins. This act of his was most pleasant to the people, who had good hopes of his goodness and justice and opened the small gate of the city; and they began to inquire exactly about the state of the city to the very kernel and distributed this tribute between the wards, the ministers of oppression and insolence shouting to each other from near and far "Now for vengeance!" and they made the court of gold[4] a place of robbery and they began to drive the people into that trap, among whom one attacked another and he hunted the hares of that land with native hounds. And now autumn, like the army of Egypt, had retired and winter with its biting cold, like Timur's army, had descended on the world.

Then he made his way to the palace of Qasrablaq and thence to the house of Amir Butakhas, ordering that that palace should be laid waste and burnt. And entering the city with a great host through the Little Gate he performed the public prayers in the mosque of the sons of Omayya[5] and ordered the Hanifites to go before the Shafeites,[6] and there the chief Qazi Muhiuddin Mahmud, son of Alaz, the Hanifite, already mentioned, held discourse. Then affairs and evils befell, the tale of which would be tedious.

And between Abdul Jabar son of Abdul Jabar Rahman of Khwarizm the Mutazalite[7] and the doctors of Syria, especially the chief Qazi Taqiuddin Ibrahim son of Muflah the Hanbalite, there arose disputes, controversies, and arguments, in all which as though the interpreter of Timur he spoke with

4. This it seems had been the residence of the governor.

5. Or the Omayyads.

6. The Sunni Moslems are divided into four sects: Hanifite, Shafeite, Malikitis and Hanbalites. They differ in ritual and law.

7. The Mutazalites believe that man has free will, that the Koran was created and not eternal and they deny bodily resurrection. They are opposed to the orthodox Sunnis.

them in his name: especially about the battles of Ali and Muavia and what was done between them in that time in the past; and also about the affairs of Yazid and other things and the killing of Husein, the blessed martyr, and that it was injustice and sin, which cannot be denied; and that the man who thinks it lawful falls into unbelief; and that without doubt that unlawful deed was committed by aid of the people of Syria; that they if they approve it, must be held unbelievers; if they disapprove, then rebels, evil and wicked; and that those Syrians who live now are of the same sect as those of the past. To which they gave various answers, of which he rejected some and accepted others; until Nasiruddin son of Abiltib, who was secretary of secret matters, replied well and aptly, if he sought advantage: "May Allah Almighty prolong the life of our lord and Amir! as for me, I carry back my family to Umar and Othman and my first ancestor was one of the leaders of that time and was present at those battles and plunged into those combats and was a man of the right cause and a champion of truth, but among his wonderful deeds, whereby he showed himself zealous for the right, is this, that when he had found the head of our lord Husein, he removed it from the neglect and shame in which it lay, then cleansed and washed it, reverenced and kissed it, filled it with spices, treated it with reverence and buried it in a tomb, and so earned the highest rank of favour with Allah Almighty and hence O cloud pouring forth rain![8] received the name of Abiltib.[9] But, however that may be, those peoples have now passed and all those clouds of trouble have been dispersed. What had to be swallowed, is now finished and what had to be tasted, whether bitter or sweet. As for discords, Allah has given us ease, since he has freed us from them; and as for shedding of blood, Allah has made our swords clean from it. And now we profess the faith of those, who rely on tradition and accepted doctrine."

And when he heard this speech, Timur said:

"Ah, by Allah! this is wonderful! Is this the reason, why you are called sons of Abiltib?"

He replied: "Certainly; and my witnesses of this are both distant and near; for I am Mahomed, son of Umar, son of Mahomed, son of Abilkasim, son of Abdulmunaam, son of Mahomed, son of Abiltib Umari Othmani."

8. A respectful address to Timur.

9. I.e., father of sweet odours.

Then he said: "Pardon me, O noble seed! If I had not plain excuse, I would carry you on my neck and shoulders; nevertheless you shall enjoy honour and benevolence, with which I will treat you and your friends."

Then he dealt quietly with them and followed them with honour and reverence; further he put to them a cunning question, that contained harm and danger, saying:

"Which is more excellent, the rank of knowledge or the rank of birth?" And they grasped and perceived the aim of it, but for fear held themselves back from giving an answer since they all knew that they were being led into danger. But Qazi Shamsuddin of Nablus, the Hanbalite, hastily replied, saying: "The rank of knowledge is more excellent than the rank of birth and its dignity is higher with the Creator as with men; and a learned man of low birth excels an ignorant of noble birth and a man base-born, but excellent, is better in the office of Imam than a noble Said, and the proof of this is clear, for the companions of the Prophet agreed in preferring Abu Bakr to Ali, knowing that Abu Bakr was more learned than they and firmer and prior in profession of the Faith. And this proof is confirmed by the saying of the Prophet: 'My people will not agree concerning error.' "

Then he began to strip off his garment, listening to Timur, whether he would reply, and he loosened its knots, and said to his soul: "Thou art only a loan; and the cup of death must be drunk, which is the same, whether it happens soon or late. And death with martyrdom is most excellent worship of Allah and the good state of him who is convinced that he is going to Allah is a word of truth before an unjust Sultan."

And Timur asked, "What is this madman doing?"

Then he said "O illustrious lord! Your armies are scattered, like the tribes of Israel, and there are men in them who fashion new religions and are drawn into diverse sects, and are sundered and divided by religion; and there is no doubt that the meetings held in your presence are made public and the excellent inquiries there held loosen and bind men's breasts. Therefore when this speech is established against me and someone hears it, who is not a Sunni, especially one who defends the succession of Ali and being a heretic calls Abu Bakr a schismatic, I am sure that death is prepared for me and that there is no defender to save me, but that he will slay me publicly and that my blood will be shed on that day. And since this is so, I prepare myself for this felicity and I will seal with martyrdom the sentences of my judgeship."

And Timur said, "By Allah! How ready and bold this man is in speech and how shameless!" Then looking at the assembly he said: "Let not this man be admitted henceforth."

Now Abdul Jabar was the doctor[10] of Timur and his Imam and one of those who in his presence plunged in the blood of Muslims. He was excellent in learning, a perfect lawyer, a careful inquirer, precise and a subtle debater. His father, Alnuman, was at Samarkand the head of the most learned men of all time, so that he was called the second Alnuman[11] and was among those who deny vision in the future life; therefore Allah blinded his eyes like his mind in this life. Most of his learned contemporaries in Transoxiana counted him as their head and consulted him in questions which they raised. And the difference between the Sunnis and Mutazalis is not concerning the *branches*, but they differ about the roots of religion in many questions, in which the latter hold the path of error.

Now there was employed to seize wealth from the people of Syria every wicked and cruel man and violent unbeliever and those who were in the greatest poverty, such as Sadaqa, son of Alharibi, and Ibn Almuhadit and Abdul Malik, son of Altukriti, who was surnamed Sumaqa, and other like men of the posterity of evil and their sons—and that, in the presence of the great men of the city and its leaders before mentioned and the chief citizens, who were not permitted to resist or even to withdraw for a moment or devise delays and in the·presence of his secretaries, accountants, treasurers and clerks, among whom were Khwaja Masaud Samnani and Maulana Umar and Tajuddin Salmani, who were all in the court of gold, a famous place. And Allahdad was staying inside the Little Gate in the house of Ibn Mashkur. And everyone, who had in his heart hatred against anyone, or hidden malice or feud or envy or annoyance, handed over his own brothers to those wicked and harsh men, evil, violent, and fierce.

10. Man of learning.
11. Founder of the Hanifites.

"They do not ask their brother, when he summons them
In misfortunes, to prove what he says."

Nay, on the slightest proof and least indication they built on the ground of the existence of that wretched man high towers out of the mountains of torture and raised over the gardens of his being out of the sky of punishments clouds of vengeance, which sounded over him bursting with thunder and sent forth upon him thunders of ruin and destruction.

Then he began during this time the siege of the fort, for which he provided all the equipment he could and ordered a building to be raised in the opposite direction commanding it, whereby they might ascend and overthrow the fort; and they gathered materials and timber, which they packed together and poured thereon stones and earth, which they levelled; and this was on the Syrian and Arabian sides.

Then they climbed upon the building and stormed the fort hand to hand with lance and sword. And he entrusted the siege to the chief among his principal Amirs, by name Jahanshah, who took in hand the business entrusted to him and bringing up ballistas shattered its lower part and as it were suspended it.

In the fort among the warriors was a company lacking in numbers, and excellent among them were Shahabuddin Zardakash of Damascus and Shahabuddin Ahmad Zardakash of Haleb, who inflicted great loss on his army and whenever it approached their position, wrought destruction and slaughter, and dealt havoc among the army with fire and thunder and lightning more than could be counted or measured.

But when a violent flood from the swelling seas of that army had surrounded the fort and the cloud of its javelin-throwers was raining down javelins and the thunderstorms of its armed men raining down a direct onset, punishment came upon the fort from above and below and from right and left and the hands of the fighters were wearied with constant combat and strife.

Therefore they sought security and surrendered to him without delay.

And all the terrible things and prodigious destinies befell at the beginning of the second month of Rabia and in the months of Jumadi and Rajab; nevertheless he did not accomplish his purpose concerning the fort until after a siege of forty-three days. Meanwhile he gave himself to seeking excellent men and masters of arts and crafts and men that had skill. And the silk-workers wove for him an all-silk tunic embroidered with gold without any seam, of wonderful workmanship. And he had built in the cemetery of the Little Gate two adjoining shrines over the grave of the wives of the Prophet, on whom be the Mercy of Allah! and ordered slaves of Zinj[12] to be collected, of whom he sought to possess more and preferred them to others.

12. Zanzibar.

NOTES

Preliminary Discourse

1. The term "medieval," as in the title of this work, is used throughout as an inclusive cultural template covering the premodern and hence what is also termed the "postclassical" or the "middle period." In practice, I use the adjectives "postclassical," "medieval," "middle," and "medieval and premodern" or "middle and premodern" interchangeably. The inclusive "medieval" therefore goes beyond the usual historicization of culture in terms of particular events, such as the fall of Baghdad to the Buyids (932–1062) and Seljuqs (1040–1194) and its ultimate fall to the Mongols in 1258. Rather, my usage engages with cultural dynamics that make up a broad landscape of specific cultural attributes.

2. The French scholar Pierre Bayle (d. 1706) coined the phrase "Republic of Letters" (*République des Lettres*) at the end of the seventeenth century, using the term to indicate a community or network of intellectuals, like a "republic," who were able to create and sustain an intellectual and informational exchange through correspondence, the circulation of epistles, poems, books, and journals, assemblies (like the Arab *majlis*), and so forth. See Dena Goodman, *The Republic of Letters: A Cultural History of the French Enlightenment* (Ithaca and London: Cornell University Press, 1994), 2, 15. The term was later applied to Diderot's *Encyclopedia* (1751), which enlisted the participation of prominent figures such as Jean le Rond d'Alembert (d. 1783) and Voltaire (d. 1778).

3. For a helpful overview of the position of grammar early in the history of Islamic civilization, see George Makdisi, *The Rise of Colleges: Institutions of Learning in Islam and the West* (Edinburgh: Edinburgh University Press, 1981), 123–40.

4. The term "traditionalist" is used alternately with *salafī*, as the adjective from *salafiyyah*. In current usage, both are synonymous with "fundamentalist" and "fundamentalism." Although originally used in reference to ancestors, often the companions and early followers of the Prophet, its later use refers to a school of thought that resists theological and rationalist reasoning.

5. See Muḥammad Murtaḍā al-Zabīdī, *Tāj al-ʿarūs min jawāhir al-qāmūs* (The Bride's Crown Inlaid with the Jewels of the Qāmūs), ed. Nawāf al-Jarrāḥ (Beirut: Dār Ṣādir, 2011), 2:481–83.

6. Technically, the term *badīʿiyyah*, as explained by ʿAlī Abū Zayd, refers to "odes that appeared in the 8th/14th century and continued until the 14th/20th century; aiming to praise the prophet; while accumulating maximum figures of innovation and inventiveness with each verse having one of these. Following al-Būṣīrīa's *Burdah* each ode adopts the same *baṣīt* meter and the letter M rhyming scheme." ʿAlī Abū Zayd, *Al-Badīʿyyāt fī al-adab al-ʿArabī* (Beirut: ʿĀlam al-Kutub, 1983), 7.

7. For more on the copyists' profession, with special reference to al-Ḥasan ibn al-Haytham (Alhazen; d. 430/1038) as a copyist, see Bakrī Shaykh Amīn, *Muṭālaʿāt fī al-shiʿr al-Mamlūkī wa-al-ʿUthmānī* (Readings in Mamluk and Ottoman Poetry) (Beirut: Dār al-ʿIlm lil-Malāyīn, 2007), 75.

8. Throughout this volume, whenever two years or two centuries are provided, separated by a slash, the first refers to the Hijra calendar (AH) and the second to the Julian and Gregorian calendars (AD). A single date refers to AD, unless AH is explicitly specified.

9. Abū al-Ḥusayn Isḥāq b. Ibrāhīm b. Sulaymān b. Wahb al-Kātib, *Al-Burhān fi wujūh al-bayān* (Demonstrating the Modes of Eloquent Expression), and Abū Yaʿqūb al-Sakkākī, *Miftāḥ al-ʿulūm* (Key to the Sciences).

10. For these modernists, including Salāmah Mūsā, Ṭāhā Ḥusayn, and Aḥmad Ḥasan al-Zayyāt, see Salāmah Mūsā, *Al-Tathqīf al-dhātī* (Self-Teaching; Autodidactus) (Cairo: Maṭbaʿat Dār al-Taqaddum, n.d.), 80; in Muḥammad ʿĀbid al-Jābirī, *Al-Khiṭāb al-ʿArabī al-muʿāṣir* (Contemporary Arabic Discourse) (Beirut: Dār al-Ṭalīʿah, 1982; repr. 1986), 36; also Salāmah Mūsā, *Mā hiya al-Nahḍah* (What Is the Renaissance?) (Cairo: Dār al-Jīl, n.d.), 130. Ṭāhā Ḥusayn's article appeared in *al-Jadīd* (1930); reprinted in *Akhbār al-adab* 186 (2 February 1997), 30. Cited by Roger Allen, "The Post-Classical Period: Parameters and Preliminaries," in *Arabic Literature in the Post-Classical Period*, ed. Roger Allen and D. S. Richards, The Cambridge History of Arabic Literature (Cambridge and New York: Cambridge University Press, 2006), 14, 15. From among Arabs who echoed the concept of a much needed rejuvenation through Europe, see Aḥmad Ḥasan al-Zayyāt, "Fī al-Adab al-ʿArabī," *Al-Jadīd* 1, no. 2 (6 February 1928): 19–20. Ṭāhā Ḥusayn has already drawn on the need in his

preface to al-Zayyāt's translation of Goethe's *Werther*. See Muhsin al-Musawi, *Islam on the Street* (Lanham, MD: Rowman and Littlefield, 2009), 8. See also Shaden M. Tageldin, "Proxidistant Reading: Toward a Critical Pedagogy of the Nahḍah in U.S. Comparative Literary Studies," *Journal of Arabic Literature* 43, no. 2/3 (Fall 2012): 240. For a detailed study, see Muhsin al-Musawi, "The Republic of Letters: Arab Modernity?" *Cambridge Journal of Postcolonial Literary Inquiry* 10 (2014): 1–16. More on this point is found in my forthcoming monograph, *The "Canon of Politics": Arab Modernists' Struggle with the Past.*

11. Pascale Casanova, *The World Republic of Letters*, trans. M.B. DeBevoise (Cambridge, MA, and London: Harvard University Press, 2004), 54.

12. Ignatii Lulianovich Krachkovskii, *Tārīkh al-adab al-jughrāfī al-ʿArabī* (Istoriia arabskoi geograficheskoi literatury) (Beirut: Dār al-Gharb al-Lubnānī, 1987), 435.

13. Quoted in Carl F. Petry, *The Civilian Elite of Cairo in the Later Middle Ages* (Princeton: Princeton University Press, 1981), xxi.

14. Shihāb al-Dīn Abū al-ʿAbbās Aḥmad b. ʿAlī b. Aḥmad ʿAbdullāh al-Qalqashandī, *Ṣubḥ al-aʿshā fī ṣināʿat al-inshā* (The Dawn of the Benighted in the Craft of Fine Writing), ed. Muḥammad Ḥusayn Shams al-Dīn (Beirut: Dār al-Kutub al-ʿIlmiyyah, 1988), 1:31.

15. Casanova, *The World Republic of Letters*, 46–47.

16. Casanova uses here Benedict Anderson's phrase from his *Imagined Communities: Reflections on the Origin and Spread of Nationalism* (London: Verso, 1983), 66. Cited in *The World Republic of Letters*, 47.

17. Ibn Baṭṭūṭah's travel accounts cover lands, customs, habits of thought, practices, hearsay, and eyewitness news. See his account of Shaykh Jamāl al-Dīn ibn Muṭahhar's (d. 1325) presumed role in converting the Tartar king of Iraq, Muḥammad Kudābandah Öljaitu (r. 1304–1316), to Shīʿism: *Tuḥfat al-nuẓẓār fī gharāʾib al-amṣār wa- ʿajāʾib al-asfār* (The Observer's Delight in Surprises of Cities and Wonders in Journeys), in *The Travels of ibn Baṭṭūṭa, A.D. 1325–1354*, trans. and ed. H.A.R. Gibb, C. Defrémery, and B.R. Sanguinetti, vol. 2, Works issued by the Hakluyt Society, 2nd series, no. 117 (Cambridge: Hakluyt Society, Cambridge University Press, 1962; repr., Millwood, NY: Kraus, 1986), 302–4; also 313–14, 410, 416–17. Ibn Baṭṭūṭah's accounts of Sufis are abundant; see, for instance, his sojourn in Jidda, 360–61; the judges of Mārdīn, 302–5, 352–55. More interesting, as I argue in a forthcoming contribution, is his readiness to accept rebelliousness against power; see 404–5, 417–21. See also Tim Mackintosh-Smith, *Travels with a Tangerine: A Journey in the Footnotes of Ibn Battuta* (New York: Welcome Rain Publishers, 2002).

18. Jawaharlal Nehru, *Glimpses of World History* (Oxford: Oxford University Press, 1989), 752.

19. André Lefevere, *Translation, Rewriting, and the Manipulation of Literary Fame* (London and New York: Routledge, 1992), 89.

20. For dating the Mamluk period, see ʿAbduh ʿAbd al-ʿAzīz Qalqīlah, *Al-Naqd al-adabī fī al-ʿaṣr al-Mamlūkī* (Literary Criticism in the Mamluk Period) (Cairo: Maktabat al-Anjilū al-Miṣriyyah, 1972; based on his 1969 dissertation), 11 and fn. 1. He argues the case for these historical limits in terms of rule: Al-Muʿizz Aybak al-Turkumānī ruled Egypt in 1250, and Tūmān was defeated by the Ottomans in 1517. See also ʿUmar Mūsā Bāshā, *Tārīkh al-adab al-ʿArabī: al-ʿaṣr al-Mamlūkī* (The History of Arabic Literature: The Mamluk Age) (Damascus: Dār al-Fikr, 1989), 29–39. The new Wālī of Egypt in 1805 was Muḥammad ʿAlī Pāshā (4 March 1769–2 August 1849). He eliminated the Mamluk leaders in 1811. Inviting them to the Cairo Citadel in honor of his son, Ṭusūn, he had them trapped and murdered.

21. For a brief listing of these libraries and collections from 594/1197 well into the nineteenth century, see Amīn, *Muṭālaʿāt fī al-shiʿr al-Mamlūkī wa- l-ʿUthmānī*, 68–70.

22. For a survey, see Jane Clark, "Ibn al-ʿArabī," in *Essays in Arabic Literary Biography, 925–1350*, ed. Terri De Young and Mary St. Germain (Wiesbaden: Harrassowitz, 2011), 94–115.

23. Ibn Khaldūn was another example of the growing republic of letters: he was Tunisian by birth, a Moroccan and Andalusian notable and scholar, and a resident of Cairo and Damascus in a similar capacity.

24. Saʿd al-Dīn al-Taftazānī received his education in Herāt, Ghijduvān, Feryumed, Gulistān, Khwārizm, Samarqand, and Sarakhs, where he spent most of his life.

25. Writing to Yaʿqūb Ṣarrūf in 1920, Mayy Ziyādah referred to the correspondence between Voltaire (d. 1778) and Jean le Rond d'Alembert (d. 1783) with respect to their *Encyclopedia* project that brought many European intellectuals on board, and that was seen as evidence of a "republic of letters." B. Khaldi, *Egypt Awakening in the Early Twentieth Century* (New York: Palgrave, 2012), 11.

26. The remainder of the Abbasid rule was passed under Turkish dominance, 847–946; Buyid rule, 964–1055; and Seljuk domination, 1055–1258.

27. Cited in Joe Cleary's review, "The World Literary System: Atlas and Epitaph; *The World Republic of Letters* by Pascale Casanova," *Field Day Review* 2 (2006): 199.

28. Ibid.

29. Many books come under titles dealing with both publics; Abū al-Qāsim Muḥammad al-Ḥarīrī's (1054–1122) *Durrat al-ghawwāṣṣ fi awhām al-Khawāṣṣ* (The Diver's Pearl in the Delusions of the Elite) is one.

30. Examples will be mentioned later in this volume.

31. On this point, see my *Scheherazade in England: A Study of Nineteenth-Century English Criticism of the Arabian Nights* (Washington, DC: Three Continents, 1981).

32. Thomas Austenfeld sums up the point as follows: to "attain recognition, she argues, writers must be granted a space in this imaginary republic, and in order to be recognized as innovative—her key criterion of excellence—writers must be legitimized by being 'consecrated' in Paris, the tolerant world-center of literature since the late 16th century, either through translation into French or by recognition of 'the authorities.' Her bold claim, in other words, is to declare Paris 'the Greenwich meridian' of literary recognition." Austenfeld, "Review of Pascale Casanova's *World Republic of Letters*," *South Atlantic Review* 71, no. 1 (Winter 2006): 142.

33. Ibrāhīm ibn Muḥammad ibn Aydamr ibn Duqmāq, *Al-Jawhar al-thamīn fī siyar al-mulūk wa al-salāṭīn* (The Precious Stone in the Conduct Accounts of Kings and Sultans) (Ṣaydā: Al-Maktabah al-ʿAṣriyyah, 1999), 223.

34. See Peter Gran's study of capitalist economy in mid-eighteenth century Egypt, *Islamic Roots of Capitalism: Egypt, 1760–1840* (Syracuse, NY: Syracuse University Press, 1998; repr. of 1979 ed.), xv.

35. Cleary, "World Literary System," 199.

36. On Edward Said's explorations of the dangers for Third World readers of the internalization of the Western imperialist philological machinery "for the establishment of identitarian truth-claims around the world," see Aamir R. Mufti, "Orientalism and the Institution of World Literatures," *Critical Inquiry* 36, no. 3 (Spring 2010): 462.

37. On the rhetorical disclaimers of modernity, see Christine Brooke-Rose, "Whatever Happened to Narratology?" *Poetics Today* 11, no. 2, Narratology Revisited I (Summer 1990): 283–93.

38. For surveys of Jamāl al-Dīn ibn Nubātah, Ṣalāḥ al-Ṣafadī, and Abū Bakr. b. ʿAlī ibn ʿAbdullāh ibn Ḥijjah al-Ḥamawī, see Thomas Bauer, "Ibn Nubatah," Everett K. Rowson, "Khalīl b. Aybak al-Ṣafadī," and Devin Stewart, "Ibn Ḥijjah al-Ḥamawī," in *Essays in Arabic Literary Biography, 1350–1850*, ed. Joseph E. Lowry and Devin J. Stewart (Wiesbaden: Harrassowitz, 2009), 184–202, 341–57, and 137–47, respectively.

39. The terms *sukhf* and *mujūn* were used interchangeably under specific conditions in urban life when refinement and high taste shunned vulgarity. But the terms differ: *sukhf* means frivolity and shallow-mindedness, whereas *mujūn* denotes obscenity. See J. E. Montgomery, "Sukhf," *Encyclopedia of Islam* (CD-ROM ed. v. 1.0, 1999), and G. J. van Gelder, *The Bad and the Ugly: Attitudes towards Invective Poetry (hijāʾ) in Classical Arabic Literature* (Leiden: Brill, 1988), 16.

40. For an overview of Ghulām ʿAlī Āzād Bilgrāmī, see Shawkat M. Toorawa, "Āzād Bilgrāmī," in *Essays in Arabic Literary Biography, 1350–1850*, 91–97.

41. Ahmad ibn Arabshah, *Tamerlane, or Timur the Great Amir*, trans. J. H. Sanders (London: Luzac and Co., 1936), 150–51. See Appendix A in the present volume.

42. *Kalām* means speculative and dialectic theology and is usually associated with a strong element in Islamic thought that has put down deep roots since Abū al-Ḥasan al-Ashʿarī (d. 324/935). It is also called " scholastic" theology, as a science of its own formation and growth. It was at one time heavily involved in disputes with the Muʿtazila (literally, "seceders") who withdrew from al-Ḥasan al-Baṣrī's (d. 110/728) assembly after a heated debate on the determination of the gradations of sin and sinners in Islam, and who allowed for a middle or "intermediate" ground. For more, see Ian Richard Netton, *A Popular Dictionary of Islam* (London: Curzon Press, 1992), 185–86.

43. Ibid., 143–49.

44. Ibid., 151.

45. In Foucauldian terms, the tabulated (i.e., amenable to statistical analysis) space of knowledge appears in its most visible form in the "theories of language, classification, and money." See Michel Foucault, *The Order of Things: An Archaeology of the Human Sciences* (New York: Vintage Books–Random House, 1994), 75.

46. The Moroccan traveler ibn Baṭṭūṭah devotes numerous pages not only to the compassionate presence of Sufis and their succor to travelers, but also to the high regard in which they were held across Ottoman and East Asian territories. See especially *The Travels of ibn Baṭṭūṭa*, 2:401, 418–21.

47. These institutions were not restricted to Sufis, and, as Makdisi shows, they were widely used for formal teaching of religious sciences. See *The Rise of Colleges*, 20–24.

Chapter One. Seismic *Islamica*

1. See Walter Joseph Fischel, *Ibn Khaldūn and Tamerlane: Their Historic Meeting in Damascus, 1401 A.D. (803 A.H.); A Study Based on Arabic Manuscripts of Ibn Khaldūn's "Autobiography"* (Berkeley and Los Angeles: University of California Press, 1952).

2. Ibid., 62–65. Also ibn Arabshah, *Tamerlane, or Timur the Great Amir*, 143–44.

3. For a summary of the views of early modern European historians and scholars on the eminence of ibn Khaldūn as a knowledge architect, see Howard Miller, "Tamburlaine: The Migration and Translation of Marlowe's Arabic Sources," in *Travel and Translation in the Early Modern Period*, ed. Carmine Di Biase (Amsterdam and New York: Rodopi, 2006), 255–66.

4. Addressing Tīmūr, ibn Khaldūn explains why he had long desired to meet the emperor. He mentions first: "Sovereignty exists only because of a group loyalty . . . , and the greater the number in the group, the greater is the extent of sovereignty." He adds: "Scholars, first and last, have agreed that most of the peoples of the human race are of two groups, the Arabs and the Turks" (Fischel, *Ibn Khaldūn and Tamerlane*, 36).

5. Also covered in a modern biographical fictional work by the Moroccan Ben Salem Himmich, *Al-ʿAllāmah*; in English, *The Polymath*, trans. Roger Allen (Cairo and New York: American University in Cairo Press, 2004).

6. ʿAbd al-Raḥmān ibn Khaldūn's book is entitled *Kitāb al-ʿibar wa dīwān al-mubtadaʾ wa al-khabar fī ayyām al-ʿArab, wa al-ʿAjam wa al-Barbar wa man ʿāṣarahum min dhawī al-sulṭān al-akbar* (Book of Lessons, Record of Beginnings and Events in the History of the Arabs, Non-Arabs, and Berbers and Their Powerful Contemporaries), published in Cairo by the governmental Būlāq Press, 1867–1868. The use of the term *ʿajam* is in line with the Qurʾānic use, meaning non-Arabs. The term was used among Indian writers throughout the period in question in reference to themselves and to those specifically from Persia. On the other hand, we find a poet like Qays ibn al-Mulawwaḥ (first/seventh century) using the term as antonymous to the pure and correct: *aʿjam/faṣīḥ* (faulty and unclear/flawless and clear). See Régis Blachère, *Historie de la Littérature Arabe* (1952); an annotated Arabic translation is used here: Régis Blachère, *Tārīkh al-adab al-ʿArabī* (Damascus: Dār al-Fikr, 1998), 783. In an article devoted to the conceptualization of *Shuʿūbīyah*, Roy P. Mottahedeh highlighted the use as one between *ʿAjam* (meaning non-Arabs) and Arabs. See his "The Shuʿūbīyah and the Social History of Early Islamic Iran," *International Journal of Middle East Studies* 7 (1976): 161–82. The divide based on genealogical and ancestral terms rather than residential and identitarian ones was not unique to western Asia, for in Abū Bakr Muḥammad ibn al-Walīd al-Ṭurṭūshī's (d. 520/1127) *Sirāj al-mulūk* (The Kings' Lamp), the distinction is made between Berbers and Arabs, and it was cited among the reasons for a disintegrating Andalusia. As long as there is manipulation of power and the use of racial justification for material gain, there is bound to be misuse, which theoretically runs counter to the Islamic egalitarian principle.

7. Fischel, *Ibn Khaldūn and Tamerlane*, 71.

8. For an early critique of this dominant paradigm, see Gran, *Islamic Roots of Capitalism*, 25.

9. Respectively, see Fischel, *Ibn Khaldūn and Tamerlane*, 70–71, fn. 54; also 68, fn. 41; ibn Arabshah, *Tamerlane, or Timur the Great Amir*, 143–44.

10. Gran, *Islamic Roots of Capitalism*, 64, 68, 84.

11. Also known as the "prodigy of the age," he was born in Hamadhān and died at Herāt. For an overview, see Jaakko Hàmeen-Anttila, "Badīʿ al-Zamān ibn al-Ḥusayn al-Hamadhānī," in *Essays in Arabic Literary Biography, 925–1350*, 38–51.

12. Ibn Arabshah, *Tamerlane, or Timur the Great Amir*, 16.

13. In defense of the author of the biographical work, the translator J.H. Sanders writes: "The author, who wrote as a good Moslem, is sometimes charged with bias against the 'great amir,' but I find no injustice in the account, except in the first few pages where he vaguely depreciates Timur's origin" (ibid., 16).

14. See the appendix to this volume.

15. Taking issue with George Makdisi, Dabashi explains his rationale for redirecting discussion, not westward, between Islam and Europe, but eastward to Khurāsān, Shiraz, Herāt, Marv, Khwārizm, Balkh, Bukhārā, and finally Samarqand. Hamid Dabashi, *The World of Persian Literary Humanism* (Cambridge, MA: Harvard University Press, 2012), 2, 15, 16, 18, 36, 52, 79–80; see George Makdisi, *The Rise of Colleges*, and *The Rise of Humanism in Classical Islam and the Christian West with Special Reference to Scholasticism* (Edinburgh: Edinburgh University Press, 1990).

16. See Ross Dunn, *The Adventures of Ibn Battuta: A Muslim Traveler of the 14th Century* (Berkeley: University of California Press, 1989).

17. On the level of popular religion, Tīmūr made a point of destroying palaces while ordering his emirs to build marble domes over the tombs of the wives of the Prophet, in the cemetery of the Little Gate in Damascus. These orders were carried out in twenty-five days. Fischel, on the authority of ibn ʿArabshāh and other historians, *Ibn Khaldūn and Tamerlane*, 92; also ibn Arabshah, *Tamerlane, or Timur the Great Amir*, 151.

18. "Franks" and "Frankish" are the terms used by Arabs during the European invasions of the Levant and Jerusalem (tenth to thirteenth centuries); the phrase replaced the use of color in describing Europeans and Byzantines, as *Rūm*. For more, see Nizar F. Hermes, *The [European] Other in Medieval Arabic Literature and Culture: Ninth–Twelfth Century AD* (New York: Palgrave Macmillan, 2012).

19. G.J. Toomer, *Eastern Wisdom and Learning: The Study of Arabic in Seventeenth-Century England* (Oxford: Clarendon Press, 1996), 21; Muhsin al-Musawi, *Anglo-Orient* (Tunis: Centre de Publication Universitaire, 2000), 62–63.

20. I am indebted to Alexander D. Knysh's synthesis of the source material on this detail; see his *Ibn ʿArabi in the Later Islamic Tradition: The Making of a Polemical Image of Medieval Islam* (Albany: State University of New York Press, 1999), 142–44.

21. Ibid., 144.

22. Ibid., 145.

23. Khaled El-Rouayheb, "Opening the Gate of Verification: The Forgotten Arab-Islamic Florescence of the 17th Century," *International Journal of Middle East Studies* 38, no. 2 (May 2006): 263–81.

24. The official translator was ʿAbd al-Jabbār ibn al-Nuʿmān al-Khwārazmī (d. 1403). Fischel, *Ibn Khaldūn and Tamerlane*, 1–5.

25. Cited by Shams al-Dīn Aḥmad ibn Muḥammad Abī Bakr ibn Khallikān, *Wafayāt al-Aʿyān*, ed. Iḥsān ʿAbbās, ʿIzz al-Dīn ʿUmar Aḥmad Mūsā, and Wadād Qādī, 8 vols. (Beirut: Dār al-Thaqāfah 1994), 5:184.

26. The long title means: Guiding the Resourceful to Knowing the Littérateur.

27. Knysh, *Ibn ʿArabi in the Later Islamic Tradition*, 8, 10, 192.

28. S. Sperl and C. Shackle, eds., *Qasida Poetry in Islamic Asia and Africa: Classical Traditions and Modern Meanings*, 2 vols. (Leiden: Brill, 1996).

29. Franklin Lewis, "Sincerely Flattering Panegyrics: The Shrinking Ghaznavid Qasida," in *The Necklace of the Pleiades*, ed. F. D. Lewis and S. Sharma (Leiden: Leiden University, 2010), 224.

30. Ibid.

31. See Julie Scott Meisami, *Medieval Persian Court Poetry* (Princeton: Princeton University Press, 1987), 56, 59, on the Persian *qaṣīdah*. See also Jerome W. Clinton, *The Dīwān of Manūchihrī Dāmghānī: A Critical Study*, Studies in Middle Eastern Literatures 1 (Minneapolis: Bibliotheca Islamica, 1972).

32. Meisami, *Medieval Persian Court Poetry*, 40–41, 58–59, 87. See also J. T. P. De Bruijn, *Of Piety and Poetry: The Interaction of Religion and Literature in the Life and Works of Ḥakīm Sanāʾī of Ghazna*, Publication of the de Goeje Fund 25 (Leiden: Brill, 1983), 148.

33. A fuller discussion is found in A. A. Seyed-Gohrab, " 'My Heart is the Ball, Your Lock the Polo-Stick': The Development of Polo Metaphors in Classical Persian Poetry," in *The Necklace of the Pleiades*, ed. Lewis and Sharma, 183–205. See also Victor Danner, "Arabic Literature in Iran," in *Cambridge History of Iran*, vol. 4, *From the Arab Invasion to the Seljuqs*, ed. R. N. Frye (Cambridge: Cambridge University Press, 1975), 566–94.

34. His "nights" were conducted in the *majlis* of the famous Buyid minister ibn Saʿdan in Rayy (Tehran). These were brought together under the title

al-Imtāʿ wa-l-Muʾānasa (Enjoyment and Conviviality). Al-Tawḥīdī died in Shiraz in 414/1023.

35. For the role of Abū Sulaymān al-Sijistānī, author of *Ṣiwān al-ḥikmah* (Vessel of Wisdom), in the establishment of a foundational epistemological base, see Joel L. Kraemer, *Philosophy in the Renaissance of Islam: Abū Sulaymān Al-Sijistānī and His Circle* (Leiden: Brill, 1986); also the entry on al-Sijistānī in *Routledge Encyclopedia of Philosophy*, ed. Edward Craig, vol. 8 (London: Routledge, 1998). Abū Sulaymān al-Sijistānī should not be confused with Abū Yaʿqūb al-Sijistānī, the author of *Kitāb al-yanābīʿ*. To avoid confusion, see Paul Ernest Walker, ed. and trans., *The Wellsprings of Wisdom: A Study of Abū Yaʿqūb al-Sijistānī's Kitāb al-Yanābīʿ; including a complete English translation with commentary and notes on the Arabic text* (Salt Lake City: University of Utah Press, 1994).

36. Dabashi, *The World of Persian Literary Humanism*, 30.

37. See Cleary, "World Literary System," 201.

38. The Indian poet's full name is Mawlānā al-Sayyid Ghulām ʿAlī Āzād Bilgrāmī ibn Nūḥ, author of many books and volumes of poetry, including, in Arabic, *Subḥat al-marjān fī āthār Hindustān*; *Ghazalān al-Hind*; and *Shifāʾ al-ʿalīl*. In *Subḥat al-marjān fī āthār Hindustān*, he included his "Al-Qaṣīdah al-badīʿiyyah," where he uses Indian figures of speech. See Ghulām ʿAlī Āzād Bilgrāmī, *Subḥat al-marjān fī āthār Hindūstān*, 2 vols., ed. Muḥammad Faḍl al-Raḥmān al-Nadwū al-Siwānī (ʿAlīgarh: Jāmiʿat ʿAlīgarh al-Islāmiyya, 1976–1980), 1:34–35. I am indebted to Vivek Gupta for drawing my attention to the author's discussion of that lyric. It is worth reiterating, moreover, that Āzād was also the author of a *badīʿiyyah*, a panegyric to the Prophet with an elaborate application of rhetoric, that won him the high praise of the king of Yemen, who named him Ḥassān al-Hind after the renowned Ḥassān ibn Thābit.

39. Julie Scott Meisami, "A Life in Poetry: Hafiz's First Ghazal," in *The Necklace of the Pleiades*, ed. Lewis and Sharma, 165–67. It is possible for the verse to be confused with that of another caliph, the Umayyad al-Walīd ibn Yazīd ibn ʿAbd al-Malik, a renowned reveler (d. 126/744). See Régis Blachère, *Histoire de la littérature arabe* (1952), as translated in *Tārīkh al-adab al-ʿArabī*, 768–71.

40. The term was regularly employed in classical Arab theory to denote plagiarism.

41. A standard study is the following: Asʿad Khairallah, *Love, Madness, and Poetry: An Interpretation of the Magnun Legend* (Beirut: Orient-Institut der Deutschen Morgenlandischen Gesellschaft, 1980).

42. In answer to the grammarian and philologist Abū Saʿīd al-Sīrāfī, who was faulting al-Mutanabbī, al-Maghribī retorts: "Who authorized Abū Saʿīd on

this matter? Poets alone, not tutors (i.e., grammarians) may pass judgment on poetry!" Makdisi, *The Rise of Humanism*, 140.

43. For example, Shaykh Zakariya Khanqah in Lenasia, South Africa, had its unique recitation session in October 1995.

44. See Suzanne P. Stetkevych, *The Mantle Odes: Arabic Praise Poetry to the Prophet Muḥammad* (Bloomington: Indiana University Press, 2010), 269 n. 2. See also Rajāʾ al-Sayyid al-Jawharī, ed., *Kitāb Ṭirāz al-Ḥullah wa- Shifāʾ al-Ghullah lil-Imām Abī Jaʿfar Shihāb al-Dīn . . . al-Andalusī, Sharḥ al-Ḥullah al-Siyarāʾ* (Alexandria: Muʾassasat al-Thaqāfah al-Jāmiʿiyyah, 1410/1990), 11–66.

45. For praise poems to the Prophet, see Sperl and Shackle, *Qasida Poetry in Islamic Asia and Africa*, vol. 2: in Urdu, 268; in Panjabi, 298; in Sindhi, 302, 306; in Hausa, 372.

46. Abū Zayd, *Al-Badīʿiyyāt fī al-adab al-ʿArabī*, 136–37, 160–63.

47. Dabashi, *The World of Persian Literary Humanism*, 38–40, 54.

48. *Al-Kawākib ad-durrīya fī madḥ Khayr al-Barīyah* (Celestial Lights in Praise of the Best of Creation). Other translations have it as "Pearly Stars in . . . ." For a comprehensive study, see S. Stetkevych, *The Mantle Odes*, ch. 2.

49. Fischel, *Ibn Khaldūn and Tamerlane*, 41–42.

50. For the *Maqāmah*, see Peter Gran, trans., "The Maqāmāt al-ʿAṭṭār," in Gran, *Islamic Roots of Capitalism*, appendix I, 189–91. See also his "Ḥasan al-ʿAṭṭār," in *Essays in Arabic Literary Biography, 1350–1850*, 56–68. Using Baudrillard's concept of refraction, whereby translatability takes place as identity with and superiority to the colonized, Shaden Tageldin cogently argues that the French Orientalist in Shaykh Ḥasan al-ʿAttār's (1766–1835) *Maqāmah* uses Arab and Muslim canonical works to impact, seduce, and indeed captivate the native who speaks of himself in the *Maqāmah* as powerless: "the intoxication of literature sent me reeling toward him," adding, "My attraction to him intensified as, when I said to him, 'Indeed, I am a guest who has dropped by to visit your neighbor' . . . , he instantly sang to me" from al-Buṣīrī's nasīb prelude in the Mantle Ode: "Was it the memory of those you loved at Dhū Salam / That made you weep so hard your tears were mixed with blood?" Shaden M. Tageldin, *Disarming Words: Empire and the Seductions of Translation in Egypt* (Berkeley: University of California Press, 2011), 79. Needless to say, Peter Gran's version contains no such details. In his version: "Then they sought from me a clarification of some of the verses of the Burda" (*Islamic Roots of Capitalism*, 190). In Europe and America, Gran was the first to draw attention to Shaykh Ḥasan al-ʿAṭṭār's *Maqāmah*; see esp. appendix I, 189–91. For the full text, see Shaykh Ḥasan al-ʿAṭṭār, *Al-Maqāmāt al-Suyūṭiyah: li-Jalāl al-Dīn Sayyidī ʿAbd al-Raḥmān al-Suyūṭī. Mudhayyalah bi-Maqāmah li-Ḥasan al-ʿAṭṭār* (Cairo: Sāliḥ al-Yāfī, 1859). See

Elliott Colla, "'Non, non! Si, si!': Commemorating the French Occupation of Egypt (1798–1801)," *MLN* 118, no. 4 (September 2003): 1043–69.

51. I have used Suzanne P. Stetkevych's translation in *The Mantle Odes*. Another significant translation is by Sperl, in Sperl and Shackle, *Qasida Poetry in Islamic Asia and Africa*, 2:388–411. An earlier version is by W. A. Clouston, *Arabian Poetry* (1881; repr., London: Darf Publishers, 1986), 319–44; for Kaʿb ibn Zuhayr's Mantle ode, 305–18.

52. Tageldin, *Disarming Words*, 80–81.

53. Raymond Williams, *Marxism and Literature* (Oxford: Oxford University Press, 1977), 132. He argues further: "It is that we are concerned with meanings and values as they are actively lived and felt, and the relations between these and formal or systematic beliefs are in practice variable." He adds: "We are talking about characteristic elements of impulse, restraint, and tone; specifically affective elements of consciousness and relationships: not feeling against thought, but thought as felt and feeling as thought: practical consciousness of a present kind, in a living and inter-relating continuity" (132).

54. Faiz Allāh Bhār, *Tuḥfat al-muslimīn: A Moslem Present; An Anthology of Arabic Poems about the Prophet and the Faith of Islam* (Bombay: Education Society, 1893).

55. Yūsuf ibn Ismāʿīl Nabhānī (d. 1932), *Al-Majmūʿah al-Nabhāniyyah fī al-madāʾiḥ al-nabawiyyah*, 4 vols. (Beirut: Al-Maṭbaʿah al-Adabiyyah, 1902; repr., Beirut: Dār al-Maʿrifah, 1974).

56. Especially in Ṣafī al-Dīn al-Ḥillī's *Al-ʿĀṭil al-ḥālī wa-al-murakhkhaṣ al-ghālī fī al-azjāl wa-al-mawālī* (The Unadorned Bejeweled and the Cheapened Rendered Costly Concerning Zajals and Mawwals). There will be more on this point later in the book. For an overview, see Terri DeYoung's entry, "Ṣafī al-Dīn al-Ḥillī," in *Essays in Arabic Literary Biography, 925–1350*, 75–88.

57. For application to Persian space, see Dabashi's citation from Jiri Becka, in *The World of Persian Literary Humanism*, 219; and Jiri Becka, "Tajik Literature from the 16th Century to the Present," in *History of Iranian Literature*, ed. Jan Rypka (Dordrecht: D. Reidel, 1968), 483–545.

58. Bilgrāmī writes in the prologue for *Subḥat al-marjān fī āthār Hindūstān*: "I have conveyed to littérateurs and accomplished scholars what I intended to introduce in terms of inventiveness in figures and embellishments, then I followed what authors of these *badīʿiyyāt* have set, to bring about an Ode that surpassess spring flowers and fishes out of the deep sea the best of pearls, to renew innovation and inventiveness in this age." His ode exemplifies each figure in a verse, adding to what is already known figures that he imported from Indian rhetoric. See Abū Zayd, *Al-Badīʿiyyāt fī al-adab al-ʿArabī*, 141–43; also 293, 296, and so on, where the author records Bilgrāmī's contributions to rhetoric.

59. These terms apply to theological categorizations: although all refer to the leadership of the Islamic community, *wilāyah* (as the designated leadership by jurists) is theorized and explained by Āyatullāh al-Khumaynī (d. 1989). On the other hand, although *imām* is used in reference to a person leading the prayer, its specific use among Shīʿites gives it a political and religious sanctity, since the *imāms* are none other than the descendants of the Prophet through his daughter Fāṭimah.

60. An example is the longing for an unseen city in a lyric of Saʿdī al-Shīrāzī. See Dabashi's significant note and translation of the poem and *ghazal* itinerary, *The World of Persian Literary Humanism*, 150.

61. ʿAbd al-Raḥmān al-Jabartī, *ʿAjāʾib al-āthār fī al-tarājim wa al-akhbār* (The Most Wondrous Traces in Biographies and Reports) (Cairo: Lajnat al-Bayān al-ʿArabī, 1959–1967). English edition: *ʿAbd al-Raḥmān al-Jabartī's History of Egypt*, ed. Thomas Philipp and Moshe Perlmann, 4 vols. (Stuttgart: Franz Steiner Verlag, 1994).

62. Yūsuf al-Shirbīnī, *Kitāb hazz al-quḥūf bi-sharḥ qaṣīd Abī Shādūf* (Brains Confounded by the Ode of Abū Shādūf), ed. and trans. Humphrey Davies (Leuven: Peeters, 2005).

63. Dabashi, *The World of Persian Literary Humanism*, 82.

64. Cleary's paraphrase of Casanova, "World Literary System," 201.

65. Franz Rosenthal, *The Classical Heritage in Islam* (London: Routledge, 1992), 47–48.

66. Ibid., 48.

67. Ibid., 47.

68. Abū ʿUthmān ibn Baḥr al-Jāḥiẓ (d. 255/869) tactfully alludes to this officialdom as the discourse of "*nābitat ʿaṣrinā*," a reference to the pro-Umayyad forces that were to influence official discourse ever since. Abū ʿUthmān ibn Baḥr al-Jāḥiẓ, "Risālah fī Banī Umayyah," in Aḥmad Zakī Ṣafwat, *Jamharat Rasāʾil al-ʿArab*, 2nd ed. (Cairo: Muṣṭafā al-Bābī al-Ḥalabī, 1971), 4:56–68, esp. 4:58–60.

69. Cited in Kamran Scot Aghaie, *The Martyrs of Karbala: Shīʿi Symbols and Rituals in Modern Iran* (Seattle: University of Washington Press, 2004), 10–11.

70. Hamid Dabashi, *Shiʿsm: A Religion of Protest* (Cambridge, MA: The Belknap Press of Harvard University Press, 2011), 15–16, 83–95, 217–25.

71. Lūṭ ibn Yaḥyā b. Saʿīd b. Mikhnaf (d. AH 157), *Kitāb Maqtal al-Ḥusayn*. His father was a companion of Imam ʿAli. His reports are trustworthy and used by Muḥammad b. ʿAmr Wāqidī (d. AH 207), ibn Qutaybah (d. AH 276), Ṭabarī (d. AH 310), Masʿūdī (d. AH 345), al-Mufīd (d. AH 413), Shahrastanī (d. AH 548), Khaṭīb al-Khwarazmī (d. AH 568), ibn al-Athīr (d. AH 630), Sibṭ ibn al-Jawzī (d. AH 654), and others.

72. In 1871 Matthew Arnold published "A Persian Passion Play," in his *Essays in Criticism* (London: Macmillan, 1871). He used French sources, especially Joseph Arthur Comte de Gobineau (d. 1882), who was once stationed in Iran. The latter is known for his racial demography and racist theory of the Aryan master race in his book *An Essay on the Inequality of the Human Races* (1853–1855).

73. See n. 68 above.

74. Specifically, this use of "Imamate" refers to the Shīʿite interpretation of the designated right to lead accorded to distinguished descendants of the Prophet through his daughter: the Imamate is an authorized institution.

75. Boaz Shoshan, "On Popular Literature in Medieval Cairo," *Poetics Today* 14, no. 2, Cultural Processes in Muslim and Arab Societies: Medieval and Early Modern Periods (Summer 1993): 349–65; Dwight F. Reynolds, "Musical Dimensions of an Arabic Oral Epic Tradition," *Asian Music*, 26, no. 1, Musical Narrative Traditions of Asia (Autumn 1994–Winter 1995): 53–94; Peter Heath, "A Critical Review of Modern Scholarship on 'Sīrat 'Antar ibn Shaddad' and the Popular Sīra," *Journal of Arabic Literature* 15 (1984): 19–44; David Woodward, "Reality, Symbolism, Time, and Space in Medieval World Maps," *Annals of the Association of American Geographers* 75, no. 4 (December 1985): 510–21; and Harold Scheub, "A Review of African Oral Traditions and Literature," *African Studies Review* 28, no. 2/3 (June–September 1985): 1–72.

76. Fredric Jameson argues for the "persistence of buried master-narratives" as an "unconscious activity," which usually takes specific forms such as popular epics. See Fredric Jameson, "Foreword," in Jean-François Leotard, *The Postmodern Condition: A Report on Knowledge* (Minneapolis: University of Minnesota Press, 1984), xii; also Jameson, *The Political Unconscious* (Ithaca, NY: Cornell University Press, 1981), 20, where he maintains, "It is in detecting the traces of that uninterrupted narrative, in restoring to the surface of the text the repressed and buried reality of this fundamental history, that the doctrine of a political unconscious finds its function and its necessity."

77. See more in Casanova, *World Republic of Letters*, 75–79.

78. See Heath, "A Critical Review of Modern Scholarship on 'Sīrat ʿAntar ibn Shaddad' and the Popular Sīra"; Basiliyus Bawardi, "First Steps in Writing Arabic Narrative Fiction: The Case of 'Ḥadīqat al-Akhbār,'" *Die Welt des Islams*, n.s., 48, no. 2 (2008): 170–95; Muhsin al-Musawi, "Abbasid Popular Narrative: The Formation of Readership and Cultural Production," *Journal of Arabic Literature* 38, no. 3, In Honor of Jaroslav Stetkevych, Who First Made "The Mute Immortals Speak," Part I (2007): 261–92; Dwight Reynolds, "Popular Prose in the Post-Classical Period," in *Arabic Literature in the Post-Classical Period*, ed. Roger Allen and D. S. Richards, The Cambridge History of Arabic

Literature (Cambridge: Cambridge University Press, 2006), 258–59; and, in the same volume, Dwight Reynolds's "The Thousand and One Nights: A History of the Text and Its Reception," 270–91, and "Sirat Bani Hilal," 307–19.

79. After the fall of Baghdad in 1258, Mamluk Cairo became the center toward which every Muslim scholar and intellectual gravitated, either by going there in person or by engaging from afar with its scholars. The migration of scholars to Cairo was uneven; the vicissitudes of fortune, catastrophic events, travel on the pilgrimage to Mecca, a desire to discuss matters with Cairo scholars, and the choice to seek one's fortune in better lands can all be cited as reasons behind this migration. The Muslim empire in the heyday of the Abbasids gave way to a number of independent or semi-autonomous entities, ranging from the fighting factional states in Andalusia to the Fatimids and Ayyubids in Egypt, and the Tahirids (r. 821–873), Ghaznavids (r. 977–1185), and the Buyids (r. 934–1055) further to the east.

80. Gran, *Islamic Roots of Capitalism*, 62–65. The complete title is *Tāj al-ʿarūs min jawāhir al-Qāmūs* (The Bride's Crown Inlaid with the Jewels of the *Qāmūs*). It was written and compiled as commentary and expansion on the *Qāmūs* (Dictionary) of Fīrūzabādī. For an overview, see Monique Bernards, "Muḥammad Murtaḍā al-Zabīdī," in *Essays in Arabic Literary Biography, 1350–1850*, 419–28.

81. Lefevere, *Translation, Rewriting, and the Manipulation of Literary Fame*, 1–10. See also Paul E. Losensky's pertinent application to al-ʿAṭṭār, "The Creative Compiler: The Art of Rewriting in al-ʿAṭṭār's *Tazkirat al-awlīyā*ʾ," in *The Necklace of the Pleiades*, ed. Lewis and Sharma, 107–19.

82. Dabashi, *The World of Persian Literary Humanism*, 214–19.

83. Anna Contadini, *A World of Beasts: A Thirteenth-Century Illustrated Arabic Book on Animals (the Kitāb Naʿt al-Ḥayawān) in the Ibn Bakhtīshūʿ Tradition* (Leiden: Brill, 2012), 64–65 and n. 34.

84. Ibid.

85. Ibid., 4, plate 3.

86. Ibid., 155, plate 22.

87. Ibid., plate 17.

88. For more on painting, see Dabashi, *The World of Persian Literary Humanism*, 215–17.

89. Oleg Grabar, *The Formation of Islamic Art* (New Haven: Yale University Press, 1987); and Richard Ettinghausen, "The Flowering of Seljuq Art," *Metropolitan Museum Journal* 3 (1970): 113–31.

90. *Yatīmat al-dahr*, IV, 168; cited and translated by W. J. Prendergast, in Badīʿ al-Zamān al-Hamadhānī, *The Maqāmāt of Badīʿ al-Zamān al-Hamadhānī*, trans. with introduction and notes by W. J. Prendergast (London: Luzac & Co.,

1915), 7. Online at http://www.sacred-texts.com/isl/mhm/mhm48.htm. Repr., London: Curzon, 1973.

91. Dabashi maintains that Arab humanism "remained canonical in its commitment to the imperially imposed language of the Arab conquerors and their tribal racism." *The World of Persian Literary Humanism*, 79–80.

92. Cited from ibn Khallikān, De Slane's translation, in al-Hamadhānī, *The Maqāmāt of Badīʿ al-Zamān al-Hamadhānī*, trans. Prendergast (1915), 2. http://www.sacred-texts.com/isl/mhm/mhm48.htm.

93. On the historicity of knowledge and the reconstitution of "the general system of thought," see Foucault, *The Order of Things*, 75, 76.

94. Dabashi, *The World of Persian Literary Humanism*, 52, 87.

95. Ross Dunn, "The Adventures of Ibn Battuta: A Muslim Traveler of the 14th Century," Keynote Address, March 2, 2005, Ibn Battuta Event, UCLA International Institute, University of California, Los Angeles. At www1.international.ucla.edu/article.asp?parentid=21336.

96. For a study of local histories of Iran with a specific focus on al-Bayhaqī, see Parvaneh Pourshariati, "Local Historiography in Early Medieval Iran and the Tārīkh-i Bayhaq," *Iranian Studies* 33, no. 1/2 (Winter–Spring 2000): 144; Q.S. Kalimullah Husaini, "Life and Works of Zahir Uʾ D-Din Al-Bayhaqi, the Author of Tarikh-i-Bayhaq," *Islamic Culture* 28 (1954): 297–318.

97. ʿAlī ibn Abī Ṭālib, *Peak of Eloquence*, trans. Askari Jafri, ed. Muhammad Wasi (India: Alwaʿẓ International, 2010). See also Tahera Qutbuddin, trans., *Dustūr maʿālim al-ḥikam* (Treasury of Virtues); *The Miʾat kalimah* (100 Proverbs) (New York: New York University Press, 2013).

Chapter Two. A Massive Conversation Site

1. Richard Schwab, introduction to Jean le Rond d'Alembert, *Preliminary Discourse to the Encyclopedia of Diderot*, trans. Richard N. Schwab with the collaboration of Walter E. Rex (Chicago: University of Chicago Press, 1995), ix–lii.

2. Ibid., xii.

3. Ikhwān al-Ṣafāʾ, *Rasāʾil Ikhwān al-Ṣafāʾ wa Khullān al-Wafāʾ* (Epistles of the Pure Brethren and the Sincere Friends), 4 vols. (Beirut: Dār Ṣādir, n.d.), with a preface by Buṭrus al-Bustānī. The name for the group could have been self-chosen, possibly evoked by ibn al-Muqaffaʿ's use of the term in his tale "Al-Ḥamāmah al-muṭawwaqah" (The Dove with a Ring) in *Kalīlah wa-Dimnah*.

4. Ikhwān al-Ṣafāʾ, *Rasāʾil*, preface by Buṭrus al-Bustānī, 1:5–20.

5. On the authority of his master Abū Sulaymān al-Manṭiqī (912–985) and the Muʿtazilī theologian ʿAbd al-Jabbār al-Hamadānī (936–1025), Abū Ḥayyān al-Tawḥīdī (b. between 922–932, d. 1023) identified the names: the *qāḍī* Abū al-Ḥasan ʿAlī b. Hārūn al-Zanjānī and his three friends, Abū Sulaymān Muḥammad b. Maʿshar al-Bustī, better known as al-Maqdisī, Abū Aḥmad al-Nahrajūrī, and al-ʿAwfī. All of these men came from Basra and were linked to the chancellery secretary Zayd b. Rifāʿa. See Buṭrus al-Bustānī's preface, vol. 1; also S.M. Stern, "The Authorship of the Epistles of the Ikhwan-as-Safa," *Islamic Culture* 20 (1946): 367–72, and "New Information about the Authors of the 'Epistles of the Sincere Brethren,'" *Islamic Studies* 3 (1964): 405–28; and Y. Marquet, "Ikhwān al-Safāʾ," in *Encyclopedia of Islam* (Leiden: Brill, 1968), 3:1071–76; repr., *Encyclopedia of Islam*, CD-ROM Edition, v. 1.0 (Leiden: Brill, 1999).

6. Ikhwān al-Ṣafāʾ, *Al-Risālah al-jāmiʿah* (The Comprehensive Epistle) or *Jāmiʿat al-jāmiʿah* (Super Comprehensive Epistle), ed. Muṣṭafā Ghālib (Beirut: Dār Ṣādir, 1974).

7. Foucault, *The Order of Things*, 73.

8. Ismāʿīlīs, or "seveners," are named after the seventh Shīʿite Imam Ismāʿīl b. Jaʿfar al-Ṣādiq (103–138/721–755).

9. See, for example, Fakhr al-Dīn al-Rāzī's response in the third debate with a so-called al-Nūr al-Ṣābūnī from Bukhārā, who called on attendees to join his cry that "God is the benevolent creator," trying, according to al-Rāzī, to arouse "rowdiness"; al-Rāzī told him, "you departed from the canon of research and reasoning [*naẓar*], and embarked on arousing the mobs and the illiterate, but this is the city of the learned, the clever, and the reasonable." See Fakhr al-Dīn al-Rāzī, *Al-Munāẓarāt*, ed. ʿĀrif Tāmir (Beirut: Muʾassasat ʿIzz al-Dīn, 1992), no. 3, p. 119.

10. The Brethren admonish their reader as follows: "Know, brother, that analogy between the author of these epistles and the seekers of knowledge and devotees to wisdom [philosophy], and those who chose salvation and safety is like a generous person with a green and fresh orchard." They add: "So those who get hold of these epistles should not let them go into the hands of those who do not deserve them or who are not well-disposed to them, but should not repress their circulation nor withhold them from reaching those who deserve them" (Ikhwān al-Ṣafāʾ, *Rasāʾil*, 1:43–45).

11. See Schwab's introduction to d'Alembert, *Preliminary Discourse*, ix–x, and his reference to Frederick the Great's Letter of 1780 to d'Alembert.

12. Foucault, *The Order of Things*, 75.

13. See Toomer, *Eastern Wisdom and Learning*; George Saliba, *Islamic Science and the Making of the European Renaissance* (Cambridge, MA: MIT

Press, 2007); Charles Burnett, *Arabic into Latin in the Middle Ages: The Translations and Their Intellectual and Social Context* (Farnham, Surrey: Ashgate Variorum, 2009); Montgomery Watt, *The Influence of Islam on Medieval Europe* (Edinburgh: Edinburgh University Press, 1972); and Peter M. Holt, "The Treatment of Arab History by Prideaux, Ockley and Sale," 290–302, in *Historians of the Middle East* (London: Oxford University Press, 1962).

14. Foucault, *The Order of Things*, 74.

15. See Makdisi, *The Rise of Humanism*, 264; M.F. Jamil, "Islamic Wirāqah, 'stationery,' during the Early Middle Ages," PhD diss., University of Michigan, 1985; Shawkat Toorawa, *Ibn Abī Ṭāhir Ṭayfūr and Arabic Writerly Culture: A Ninth-Century Bookman from Baghdad* (London: RoutledgeCurzon, 2005), 56–57; Muhsin al-Musawi, *The Islamic Context of the Thousand and One Nights* (New York: Columbia University Press, 2009), 151–52.

16. Foucault, *The Order of Things*, 31. On the move to *tadwīn* (from orality to textualization), see Abū al-Ḥusayn Isḥāq b. Ibrāhīm b. Sulaymān b. Wahb al-Kātib, *Al-Burhān fi wujūh al-bayān* (Demonstrating the Modes of Eloquent Expression), ed. Ḥanafī M. Sharaf (Jīzā: Maktabat al-Shabāb, 1969), 71–72. The doctoral dissertation made use of an earlier Baghdadi edition, ed. Aḥmad Maṭlūb and Khadījah al-Ḥadīthī (Baghdad: Baghdad University Publication, 1967).

17. Foucault, *The Order of Things*, 32.

18. Ibid., 33.

19. Ikhwān al-Ṣafā', *Rasā'il*, 4:235.

20. Julie Scott Meisami's words in reference to Conger's surmise. See Meisami, *Medieval Persian Court Poetry*, 32. See also George Perrigo Conger, *Theories of Macrocosms and Microcosms in the History of Philosophy* (New York: Columbia University Press, 1922), 49–51.

21. Conger, *Theories of Macrocosms and Microcosms*, 51.

22. See ibn Wahb al-Kātib's quotes from the Qur'ān where *'āyāt* recurs, *Al-Burhān*, ed. Sharaf, 56–57.

23. On the place of reason in the Qur'an, see ibid., 51–56.

24. Foucault, *The Order of Things*, 42. He explains: "Ever since the Stoics, the system of signs in the Western world had been a ternary one, for it was recognized as containing the significant, the signified, and the 'conjuncture.' "

25. Ibn Wahb al-Kātib, *Al-Burhān*, ed. Sharaf, 71–72.

26. See al-Jāḥiẓ, "Risālah fī Banī Umayyah," 56–68.

27. Quoted from R. Walzer by M.G. Carter, "Language Control as People Control in Medieval Islam: The Aim of the Grammarians in Their Cultural Context," *Al-Abḥath* 31 (1983): 66. For more, see Richard Walzer, "New Light on the Arabic Translations of Aristotle," *Oriens* 6 (1953): 91–142.

28. Foucault defines this hermeneutics in relation to the European Renaissance as "the totality of the learning and skills that enable one to make the signs speak and to discover their meaning" (*The Order of Things*, 29).

29. Writing in the preface to his lexicon, ibn Manẓūr laments the fact that there is a common reluctance among certain segments of society to speak Arabic. He explains the decreasing interest in Arabic on the basis of a lucrative market for translations, a trend that might well have been cited conversely as evidence of a thriving culture industry: "People compete in compilations of translations in foreign tongues and also in showing their competence in them. Hence I have compiled this work in an age whose people aren't proud of their native language." Muḥammad b. al-Mukarram ibn Manẓūr, *Lisān al-ʿArab* (Beirut: Dār Iḥyāʾ al-Turāth, 2010), Introduction, 18, 79.

30. Robert Irwin, "Mamluk Literature," *Mamluk Studies Review* 7, no. 1 (2003): 3.

31. An excerpt is available in translation from his commentary on Alfīyyah. See Sidney Glazer, "A Noteworthy Passage from an Arab Grammatical Text," *Journal of the American Oriental Society* 62 (1942): 106–8.

32. See Cleary's synopsis, "World Literary System," 201.

33. András Bodrogligeti, "A Collection of Poems from the 14th Century," *Acta Orientalia Academiae Scientiarum Hungaricae* 16 (1963): 245–311; *A Fourteenth Century Turkic Translation of Saʿdi's Gulistan* (Bloomington: Indiana University, 1970); "A Grammar of Mamluke-Kipchak," in *Studia Turcica*, ed. L. Ligeti (Budapest: Akadémisi Kiadó, 1971), 89–102; and "Notes on the Turkish Literature in the Mamluke Court," *Acta Orientalia Academiae Scientiarum Hungaricae* 14 (1962): 273–82. For more, see Irwin, "Mamluk Literature," 4.

34. Irwin, "Mamluk Literature."

35. Muḥammad ibn ʿAbd al-Raḥmān al-Sakhāwī, *Al-Iʿlān bi-al-tawbīkh liman dhamma al-tārīkh*, trans. Franz Rosenthal, in *A History of Muslim Historiography*, 2nd ed. (Leiden: Brill, 1968). It is worth noting how specific terms, phrases, and epithets circulate and function as leitmotifs in a semiotic landscape of linguistic and semantic exchange. *Al-Tibr al-masbūk* was also referenced as "The Forged Sword." For instance, Abū Ḥamid al-Ghazālī used the first two words, *Al-Tibr al-masbūk fī naṣīḥat al-mulūk* (usually referenced as: The Forged Sword in Counseling Kings or The Counsel of Kings; and also, Ingots of Gold for the Advice of Kings) (Cairo: Maṭbaʿat al-ʾĀdāb wa-l-Muʾayyid, 1899). In this concordance is Aḥmad ibn ʿAlī Maqrīzī's (d. 1442) *Kitāb al-sulūk li maʿrifat duwal al-mulūk* (usually referenced as Book of Entrance to the Knowledge of the Dynasties of the Kings), which served as a prototype for Shams al-Dīn al-Sakhāwī's (902/1497) *Kitāb al-Sulūk*. Another book by al-Sakhāwī is

al-Dhahab al-masbūk fī dhikr man ḥajja min al-khulafā' wa-l-mulūk (The Cast Gold in the Concordance of Those Who Performed the Pilgrimage from among Caliphs and Kings); the first two words appear also in Ismā'īl ibn 'Alī Abū al-Fidā's (d. 1331) *Al-Tibr al-masbūk fī tawārikh akābir al-mulūk* (The Cast Gold in the Histories of the Greatest Kings).

36. Geoffrey Tantum, "Muslim Warfare: A Study of a Medieval Muslim Treatise on the Art of War," in *Islamic Arms and Armour*, ed. Robert Elgood (London: Scolar Press, 1979), 194–96.

37. Walter G. Andrews, "Speaking of Power: The 'Ottoman kaside,'" and Walter G. Andrews and Mehmed Kalpakli, "Across Chasms of Change: The kaside in Late Ottoman and Republican Times," both in *Qasida Poetry in Islamic Asia and Africa*, ed. Sperl and Shackle, 1:281–300 and 1:301–26, respectively.

38. Lefevere, *Translation, Rewriting, and the Manipulation of Literary Fame*.

39. Ibid., 17.

40. *The Travels of ibn Baṭṭūṭa*, 2:422.

41. Ibid.

42. Ikhwān al-Ṣafā', *Rasā'il*, 1:43–45.

43. For some brief discussions, see George Makdisi, "Ṭabaqāt Biography: Law and Orthodoxy in Classical Islam," *Islamic Studies* 32 (1993): 371–96; and Wael B. Hallaq, "Was al-Shāfi'ī the Master Architect of Islamic Jurisprudence?" *International Journal of Middle East Studies* 25 (1993): 587–605.

44. Ulrich Haarmann, "Arabic in Speech, Turkish in Lineage: Mamluks and Their Sons in the Intellectual Life of Fourteenth-Century Egypt and Syria," *Journal of Semitic Studies* 33 (1988): 81–114.

45. Reuben Levy, trans., *A Mirror for the Princes: The Qabus Nama of ibn Iskandar* (New York: Dutton, 1951).

46. Irwin, "Mamluk Literature," 15.

47. Ibn Arabshah, *Tamerlane, or Timur the Great Amir*, 28.

48. Fischel, *Ibn Khaldūn and Tamerlane*, 89 n. 120.

49. Ibid.

50. Ibid., 37.

51. Ibid.

52. Ibn Arabshah, *Tamerlane, or Timur the Great Amir*, 32.

53. Cities such as Jurjān, Iṣfahān, Seistān, and Herāt were laid waste. See ibid., esp. 23, 33, 45.

54. *The Travels of ibn Baṭṭūṭa*, 2:367–68.

55. See 'Ārif Tāmir's reference to schools of thought in the introduction to *Risālat jāmi'at al-jāmi'ah li Ikhwān al-Ṣafā'* (Beirut: Dār al-Nashr al-Jāmi'ī,

1959); also in his introduction to al-Rāzī, *Al-Munāẓarāt* (The Debates), ed. Tāmir, 75 fn. 1.

56. An example is Aḥmad b. ʿAlī ibn Ḥajar al-ʿAsqalānī, *Al-Durar al-Kāmina fī Aʿyān al-miʾah al-thāmina* (The Hidden Pearls of the Eighth-Century Notables), 4 vols. (Beirut: Dār al-Jīl, 1989).

57. Muḥammad ibn Shākir ibn Aḥmad al-Kutubī, *Fawāt al-wafayāt, wa-huwa dhayl ʿalā kitāb Wafayāt al-aʿyān li-ibn Khallikān*, ed. Muhḥammad Muḥyī al-Dīn ʿAbd al-Ḥamīd (Cairo: Maktabat al-Nahḍah al-Miṣrīyah, 1951); al-Ṣafadī, *Kitāb al-Wāfī bi-al-Wafayāt*, ed. Hilmūt Rītir and Iḥsān ʿAbbās . . . [et al.] (Beirut: Al-Maʿhad al-Almānī lil-Abḥāth al-Sharqīyah fī Bayrūt, 2008–2010).

58. Shihāb al-Dīn Aḥmad ibn ʿAbd al-Wahhāb al-Nuwayrī was also an administrator and historian in the reign of the Bahri Mamluk sultan al-Nāṣir Muḥammad ibn Qalāwūn (r. 693–694/1293–1294, 698–708/1299–1309, 709–741/1310–1341). He compiled his treasure trove during the period 714–731/1314–1330. M. Chapoutot-Remadi, "Al-Nuwayrī," *The Encyclopedia of Islam*, 2nd ed. (Brill), 8:158. See also Elias Muhanna, "Encyclopaedism in the Mamluk Period: The Composition of Shihāb al-Dīn al-Nuwayrī's (d. 1333) *Nihāyat al-Arab fī Funūn al-Adab*," PhD diss., Harvard University, 2012. Muhanna suggests translating the title as "The Ultimate Ambition in the Arts of Erudition."

A different approach is by al-Ghuzūlī. In ʿAlāʾ al-Dīn al-Ghuzūlī's (d. 815/1412) *Maṭāliʿ al-budūr fī manāzil al-surūr* (Shining Full Moons in the Abodes of Delight), he offers "delights" in the form of a house with many rooms and parts; each site accommodates something special, while adjoining sections and structural properties satisfy worldly delights by invoking selections from literature at large. For more information on the writer, see Michael Cooperson, "ʿAlāʾ al-Dīn al-Ghuzūlī," in *Essays in Arabic Literary Biography, 1350–1850*, 107–17.

59. Martin Irvine uses "macrogenres" as an inclusive term for the lexicon, the gloss and commentary, the compilation, the library, and the encyclopedia. I find it in correspondence with terms that were used in that period and continued in use among later scholars under the rubric of *mawsūʿāt* or compendiums and encyclopedias. Martin Irvine, *The Making of Textual Culture: 'Grammatica' and Literary Theory, 330–1100* (Cambridge: Cambridge University Press, 1994), 426.

60. It is of some significance that Ṣafī al-Dīn al-Ḥillī (d. 750/1349), the pioneer in the *badīʿiyyah* as a specifically thematic, ideational exercise in expressiveness, uses "*mukhtaraʿāt*" and other terms to indicate unprecedented newness or inventiveness. See al-Ḥillī, *Sharḥ al-kāfiyah al-badīʿiyyah fi ʿulūm al-balāghah wa- maḥāsin al-badīʿ* (The Explication of the Sufficient *Badīʿiyyah* Ode in Rhetorical Sciences and Adornments in Innovativeness), ed. Nasīb Nashāwī (Beirut: Dār Ṣādir, 1982; repr. 1992), 6. Abū Bakr ibn Ḥijjah al-Ḥamawī (767–837/

1366–1434) also used the term. See Abū Bakr ibn ʿAlī Taqī al-Dīn ibn Ḥijjah al-Ḥamawī, *Khizānat al-adab wa-ghāyat al-arab* (The Ultimate Treasure Trove of Literature), ed. Kawkab Diyāb (Beirut: Dār Ṣādir, 2001).

61. See Konrad Hirschler's record and analysis of specific "public" texts that were read for a group by their authors, or by those whom they authorized or by other participants. Hirschler, *The Written Word in the Medieval Arabic Lands* (Edinburgh: Edinburgh University Press, 2012), 26–27.

62. See ʿĀrif Tāmir's edition of al-Rāzī's *Al-Munāẓarāt*, where he mentions some cases that go back mostly to the tenth century. I discuss this topic further in the last chapter.

63. See Joseph Sadan, "Kings and Craftsmen—A Pattern of Contrast," *Studia Islamica* 56 (1982): 5–49; and 62 (1985): 89–120.

64. For comparable frameworks, see Foucault, *The Order of Things*, 42–44.

65. The Ashʿarite school of theology is named after the founder, Abū al-Ḥasan al-Ashʿarī (d. 324/936).

66. This is an inclusive term that covers *ʿulūm al-awāʾil* or the Greeks, usually attended to in many epistles. Al-Qalqashandī's *ʿulūm* covers the Qurʾān, its sciences, statecraft principles, heritage of the Arabs, orations and epistles, dynasties and chivalry, rhetoric, grammar, and chancery skills. *Rusūm* covers calligraphy, knowledge of chancellery correspondence, geography and cultures of other nations, etc. See Muhsin al-Musawi, "Vindicating a Profession or a Personal Career? Al-Qalqashandī's *Maqāmah* in Context," *Mamluk Studies Review* 7, no. 1 (2003): 111–35, esp. 128–29. For the quotations from Adorno, see Theodor W. Adorno, *Negative Dialectics* (New York: Continuum–The Seabury Press, 1979), 53.

67. Abū Manṣūr al-Thaʿālibī used the term *muʿāraḍah* for the title of one of his books; see *Al-Kināyah wa-l-taʿrīḍ* (Concomitance and Metonomy). For more on the term, see Pierre Cachia, *The Arch Rhetorician or the Schemer's Skimmer: A Handbook of Late Arabic Badīʿ Drawn from ʿAbd al-Ghanī al-Nabulsī's Nafaḥāt al-azhār ʿalā nasamāt al-ashʿār* (Wiesbaden: Harrassowitz, 1998), 64, 66–67, 72–73. This term should not be confused with *muʿāraḍah* as contrafaction.

68. See ibn Wahb al-Kātib, *Al-Burhān*, ed. Sharaf, 98–99. He explains how through its use "the other takes the obvious meaning." The term *taqiyyah* derives from *waqā* ("to shield oneself"). Translated as "precautionary dissimulation," it justifies evasion or concealment to escape danger.

69. Al-Shirbīnī, *Kitāb hazz al-quḥūf*, ed. Davies.

70. During the same period, the ninth century (seventeenth century of the Christian era), ibn Abī al-ʿĪd al-Mālikī compiled his *Ḥilyat al-kuramāʾ wa-bahjat al-nudamāʾ* (The Adornment of the Honorable and the Delight of Boon-Companions) (Beirut: Books-Publisher, 2010), where he opens the first few pages with a comparison between the knowledgeable and those who are preten-

tious and sham among jurists, warning that to have a long beard and a seemingly pious demeanor should not be confused with actual depth and knowledge. See 14–17. See also, in preparation for this rising phenomenon, Abū al-Faraj ʿAbd al-Raḥmān ibn al-Jawzī, *Ṣayd al-khāṭir* (Random Thoughts) (Beirut: Dār al-Kitāb al-ʿArabī, 2010). Al-Jawzī, despite his conservatism, draws attention to a rising body of sham jurists. He was also vehemently opposed to Sufis. See 77, 88, 122, 175–76, 188, 214, 249, 288.

71. *The Travels of ibn Baṭṭūṭa*, 2:300.

72. Ibid., 2:286.

73. In Saʿd al-Dīn al-Taftazānī's *Al-Muṭawwal: Sharḥ Talkhīṣ al-Miftāḥ* (The Elaborate or Expanded: The Explication of the Resumé of the Key) (Beirut: Dār Iḥyāʾ al-Turāth al-ʿArabī, 2004), 98–99, 100–102.

74. Makdisi, *The Rise of Humanism*, 219.

75. Ibid., 222–23.

76. See ibn Wahb al-Kātib, *Al-Burhān*, ed. Sharaf, 253.

77. Al-Qalqashandī, *Ṣubḥ al-aʿshā*, 1:84, 173–76.

78. Quoted in Makdisi, *The Rise of Humanism*, 127.

79. The complete title is *Tāj al-lughah wa-Ṣiḥāḥ al-ʿArabiyyah* (The Crown of Language and the Correct Arabic). A shorter title is *al-Ṣiḥāḥ fī al-lughah* (The Correct Language).

80. The commentaries are so numerous that ʿAbdullāh Muḥammad al-Ḥabashī published a bibliography of them; see his *Jāmiʿ al-shurūḥ wa al-ḥawāshī* (A Compendium of Commentaries and Marginalia), 3 vols. (Abu Dhabi: Al-Mujammaʿ al-Thaqāfī, 2006).

Chapter Three. The Lexicographic Turn in Cultural Capital

1. See Cleary, "World Literary System," 202.

2. Abū al-Naṣr Ismāʿīl ibn Ḥammād al-Jawharī's lexicon appears under variable titles according to circulated editions soon after its appearance. Typical is *Muʿjam al-Ṣiḥāḥ fī al-lughah* (The Lexicon of Correct Arabic), which is originally *Tāj al-lugha wa ṣiḥāḥ al-ʿArabiya* (The Crown of Language and Correct Arabic), better known by its short title, *al-Ṣiḥāḥ fī al-lugha* (The Correct or Purist Language). On lexicons, see John A. Haywood, *Arabic Lexicography: Its History, and Its Place in the General History of Lexicography*, 2nd ed. (Leiden: Brill, 1965), ch. 6. See also M. G. Carter, "Arabic Lexicography," in *Religion, Learning and Science in the ʿAbbasid Period*, ed. M. J. L. Young, J. D. Latham, and R. B. Serjeant, The Cambridge History of Arabic Literature (Cambridge: Cambridge University Press, 1990), 106–17.

3. According to the catalog description (Indiana University Lilly Library, DR 403 .M82215 vol. 1), *Vankulu Lügati* has "the most extensive front matter of all the seventeen books in the Müteferrika series. It opens with a foreword by Müteferrika and contains a copy of the original imperial edict (*ferman*) issued by Sultan Ahmed III (r. 1703–1730), followed by religious decrees (*fetvas*) issued by leading religious figures in the administration giving religious clearance to Müteferrika to establish a press. The religious decrees are followed by a copy of the pamphlet entitled 'The Usefulness of Printing' (*Vesiletü'ʾt-tibaʿa*), which Müteferrika wrote and presented to Grand Vizier Damad Ibrahim Paşa. In this pamphlet, Müteferrika lists ten reasons why an imperial printing house should be established."

4. William J. Watson, "Ibrahim Muteferrika and Turkish Incunabula," *Journal of the American Oriental Society* 88, no. 3 (1968): 435–41. See also Alastair Hamilton, Maurits H. van den Boogert, and Bart Westerweel, *The Republic of Letters and the Levant* (Leiden: Brill, 2005), 266–67.

5. For more, see Stefan Reichmuth, "Murtaḍā az-Zabīdī (d. 1791) in Biographical and Autobiographical Accounts: Glimpses of Islamic Scholarship in the Eighteenth Century," *Die Welt des Islams* 39, no. 1 (1999): 64–102.

6. Joseph E. Lowry, "Ibn Maʿṣūm," in *Essays in Arabic Literary Biography, 1350–1850*, 175.

7. In the period under discussion, these are: Muḥammad b. Aḥmad Abū al-Manāqib al-Zanjānī's (d. 656/1258) *Tahdhīb al-ṣiḥāḥ* (i.e., al-Jawharī's); Zayn al-Dīn Muḥammad al-Rāzī's (d. 666?/1268) *Mukhtār al-ṣiḥāḥ*; Muḥammad b. ʿAlī al-Anṣārī al-Shaṭibī's (d. 684/1285) *Ḥawāshī ʿalā mukhtār al-ṣiḥāḥ*; Muḥammad b. Mukarram b. Manẓūr's (d. 711/1311) *Lisān al-ʿArab*; Muḥammad b. Yūsuf al-Andalusī Abū Ḥayyān's (d. 745/1344) *Tuḥfat al-arab fī gharīb al-Quran*; Aḥmad b. Muḥammad al-Maqrī al-Fayyūmī's (d. 770/1368) *Al-Miṣbāḥ al-munīr*; Majd al-Dīn Muḥammad al-Fīrūzabādī's (d. 817/1415) *Al-Qāmūs al-muḥīṭ*; Jalāl al-Dīn al-Suyūṭī's (d. 911/1505) *al-Muzhir*; Shihāb al-Dīn Aḥmad al-Khafājī's (d. 1069/1659) *Sharḥ durrat al-ghawwāṣ*; Murtaḍā al-Zabīdī's (d. 1205/1790) *Tāj al-ʿarūs*. Many others preceded them, but deserving special mention are ibn Sīda's (d. 458/1066) *Al-Muḥkam wa al-muḥīṭ al-aʿẓam* and al-Ṣaghānī's (d. 650/1252) *al-ʿUbāb*, *Majmaʿ al-baḥrain*, *al-Takmila*, *al-Dhayl*, *al-Shawārd*, and *al-Aḍdād*.

8. For an overview of this significant base, which requires more work, see Carter, "Arabic Lexicography"; Haywood, *Arabic Lexicography*; and Ulrich Haarmann, *Quellenstudien zur frühen Mamlukenzeit* (Freiburg im Breisgau: K. Schwarz, 1970).

9. Aḥmad Fāris Affendī al-Shidyāq [editor of *al-Jawāʾib*], *Al-Jāsūs ʿalā al-qāmūs* (Spying on al-Fīrūzabādī's Lexicon) (Istanbul: Maṭbaʿat al-Jawāʾib, AH 1299).

10. Ibid. See also ibn Manẓūr, *Lisān al-ʿArab*, 8 vols. (Beirut: Dār Iḥyāʾ al-Turāth, 2010), introduction, 1:79.

11. See the note by the editors, ibn Manẓūr, *Lisān al-ʿArab*, 1:9.

12. Al-Shidyāq, *Al-Jāsūs ʿalā al-qāmūs*, 80–97.

13. Ibid., 105.

14. Needless to say, the list is long, and there are many lexicons that take over from preceding efforts or carry on a more specialized and focused research. Ibn Manẓūr recognized that each lexicon has its merits, since each complier had his own sources and channels of transmission and documentation. Hence, he credits each with some value and subtly acknowledges limits. *Lisān al-ʿArab*, 1:16–17.

15. Al-Shidyāq, *Al-Jāsūs ʿalā al-qāmūs*, 81.

16. They include *Tahdhīb al-lugha* by Abū Manṣūr al-Azharī (d. 370/981?); *al-Muḥkam* by ibn Sīdah al-Andalusī (d. 458/1066); *al-Ṣiḥāḥ* by Abū al-Naṣr Ismāʿīl b. Ḥammād al-Jawharī (d. 398/1008); *Ḥāshiyat al-Ṣiḥāḥ* by Muḥammad ibn Barrī (d. 582/1187); *al-Nihāyah* by Abū al-Saʿādāt ibn al-Athīr al-Jazrī (d. 630/1232); along with *Jamharat al-lughah* by ibn Duraid (d. 321/934), which is not listed. See editors' note, ibn Manẓūr, *Lisān al-ʿArab*, 1:13.

17. Ibn Manẓūr, *Lisān al-ʿArab*, 1:18.

18. Majd al-Dīn Muḥammad b. Yaʿqūb al-Fīrūzābādī, *Muʿjam al-Qāmūs al-Muḥīṭ*, ed. Khalīl Maʾmūn Shīḥā (Beirut: Dār al-Maʿrifah, 2009), 22.

19. On these poems mourning his wife, see Gran, *Islamic Roots of Capitalism*, 62, 222 n. 20.

20. Ibid., 62.

21. Ibid., 63.

22. Ibid., 61. There is a further note in the concluding chapter on al-Ḥarīrī as a controversial subject for medievalists.

23. Abū Yaʿqūb Yūsuf al-Sakkākī, *Miftāḥ al-ʿulūm* (Key to the Sciences), ed. Naʿīm Zarzūr (Beirut: Dār al-Kutub al-ʿIlmiyyah, 1983).

24. Gran, *Islamic Roots of Capitalism*, 69.

25. Al-Shirbīnī, *Kitāb hazz al-quḥūf*, ed. Davies.

26. Gran, *Islamic Roots of Capitalism*, 66–67.

27. Ibid.

28. Yazīd ibn Muʿāwiyah (d. 683), the second Umayyad caliph, purportedly tapped the severed head of al-Ḥusayn, the Prophet's grandson, while reciting a poem by ibn al-Zibaʿrī that celebrated victory over the Prophet at the Battle of ʾUḥud in 625. For a long time that poem served as the Umayyads' mode of recall of their sense of vengeance against the family of the Prophet. Al-Jāḥiẓ, "Risālah fī Banī Umayyah," 62.

29. Al-Fīrūzābādī, *Muʿjam al-Qāmūs al-Muḥīṭ*, 24.

30. Ṭāhā Ḥusayn's article with this critique first appeared, as noted earlier, in *al-Jadīd* (1930); reprinted in *Akhbār al-adab* 186 (2 February 1997): 30; cited by Allen, "The Post-Classical Period: Parameters and Preliminaries," 14, 15. For more on modernists with a similar view, see Muḥammad ʿĀbid al-Jābirī, *Al-Khiṭāb al-ʿArabī al-muʿāṣir* (Contemporary Arabic Discourse) (Beirut: Dār al-Ṭalīʿah, 1989), 36.

31. For a comparative perspective, see Herbert Weisinger, "The Middle Ages and the Late Eighteenth Century Historians," *Philological Quarterly* 28 (January 1948): 63–79.

32. Brinkley Messick, *The Calligraphic State: Textual Domination and History in a Muslim Society* (Berkeley: University of California Press, 1993), 1.

33. Foucault, *The Order of Things*, 40.

34. Ibid.

35. Ibid., 41.

36. Ibid.

37. Ibid.

38. Ibid., 42.

39. Ibn Sina, *Remarks and Admonitions*, Part One: Logic, trans. S. Inati (Toronto: Pontifical Institute of Medieval Studies, 1984).

40. As cited in ibn Ḥijjah, *Khizānat al-adab*, 1:46; Qalqīlah, *Al-Naqd al-adabī fi al-ʿaṣr al-Mamlūkī*, 170; and also in Jamāl al-Dīn ibn Nubātah, *Talṭīf al-mizāj min shiʿr ibn al-Hajjāj* (Refining the Mood with the Poetry of ibn al-Ḥajjāj), ed. Najm ʿAbdullāh Muṣṭafā (Suese: Dār al-Marʿārif, 2001), 49.

41. In Cairo, the historian al-Maqrīzī mentions the Fusṭāṭ book market and the booksellers' and copyists' markets (*Sūq al-kutubīyīn*/*Sūq al-warrāqīn*). These markets grow or decline in accordance with topographical and demographic changes. We should remember that *Khizānat al-kutub* (the Ayyubid library collection housed at the citadel, which kept only a selected list from the famous earlier Fatimid collection) was lost in a raging fire in 1292. On the other hand, whatever survived found its way into collections supported by wealthy patrons, such as ibn Khaldūn's friend the wealthy emir Jamāl al-Dīn Maḥmūd ibn ʿAlī al-Ustādār, who "purchased [books] from the royal citadel" for his Jamālī *madrasah*. Recorded, too, is the gift by Baybars II of five hundred volumes to the restored mosque of al-Hākim. No less significant with regard to these libraries and collections was their linguistic diversity, with works in Turkish, Arabic, and Persian. The chronicler and historian ibn Dawādārī notes, for example, that there was a fascinating "Turkish book" in the impressive Arabic collection of emir Badr al-Dīn Baysarī al-Shamsī (d. 1298). Among known private collections and libraries were those of the Sāmānid Nūḥ b. Naṣr (d. 954), al-Ṣāḥib ibn ʿAbbād

(d. 995), and Muʾayyid al-Dīn al-ʿAlqamī, the minister for the last ʿAbbasid caliph, al-Mustaʿṣim (d. 1258). The bibliophile Yāqūt al-Ḥamawī made use of the library in Marv to compile his compendiums and dictionaries. Indeed, Cairo, Aleppo, and Damascus were known for their libraries, as described by Muslim and Western travelers. The Jerusalem fourteenth-century notable Burhān ad-Dīn Ibrahim an-Nāṣirī had a magnificent collection, as described in Ulrich Haarmann, "The Library of a Fourteenth Century Jerusalem Scholar," *Der Islam* 61 (1984): 327–33. See, respectively, Irwin, "Mamluk Literature," 1; Petry, *Civilian Elite of Cairo*; Mohamed Makki Sibai, *Mosque Libraries: An Historical Study* (London: Mansell, 1987); Donald Little, "Religion under the Mamluks," *Muslim World* 73 (1983): 170; and Ulrich Haarmann, "Turkish Legends in the Popular Historiography of Medieval Egypt," in *Proceedings of the Sixth Congress of Arabic and Islamic Studies*, ed. Frithiof Rundgren (Leiden: Brill, 1975), 99, 102. For more, see B. Amīn, *Muṭālaʿāt fī al-shiʿr al-Mamlūkī wa al-ʿUthmānī*, 66–76.

42. Ibn Duqmāq, *al-Jawhar al-thamīn fī siyar al-mulūk wa al-salāṭīn* (The Precious Stone in the Conduct Accounts of Kings and Sultans), 223.

43. Between 1261 and 1517, the ʿAbbāsid token caliphs were al-Mustanṣir II, al-Ḥakīm I, al-Mustakfī I, al-Wāthiq I, al-Ḥakīm II, al-Muʿtaḍid, al-Mutawakkil I, al-Mustaʿṣim, al-Wāthiq II, al-Mustaʿīn, al-Muʿtaḍid II, al-Mustakfī II, al-Qāʿim, al-Mustanjid, al-Mutawakkil II, al-Mustamsik, and al-Mutawakkil III.

44. Al-Maqrīzī, *Al-Sulūk li-maʿrifat duwal al-mulūk*, vols. 1 and 2 (Cairo: Muḥammad Muṣṭafā Ziyādah, 1941), 454.

45. See especially Fawzī Muḥammad Amīn, *Adab al-ʿaṣr al-awwal al-mamlūkī: malāmiḥ al-mujtamaʿ al-Miṣrī* (Suese: Dār al-Maʿrifah al-Jāmiʿyyah, 2009), 12–17. For an extensive reading of ibn Dāniyāl's oeuvre, see Li Guo, *The Performing Arts in Medieval Islam: Shadow Play and Popular Poetry in Ibn Dāniyāl's Mamluk Cairo* (Leiden: Brill, 2012).

46. Muhsin al-Musawi, "Pre-modern Belletrist Prose," in *Arabic Literature in the Post-Classical Period*, ed. Allen and Richards, 101–33; Jonathan P. Berkey, *Popular Preaching and Religious Authority in the Medieval Islamic Near East* (Seattle and London: University of Washington Press, 2001). See also Petry, *Civilian Elite of Cairo*, 17–18; C.E. Bosworth, *Medieval Arabic Culture and Administration* (London: Variorum Reprints, 1982); J.H. Escovitz, "Vocational Patterns of the Scribes of the Mamluk Chancery," *Arabica* 23 (1976): 42–62. In relation to the role of chancery scribes, see al-Musawi, "Vindicating a Profession or a Personal Career?"

47. Maḥmūd Ruzq Salīm's quote from al-Maqrīzī's *Ighāthat al-ʾummah*, in Salīm, *Ṣafī al-Dīn al-Ḥillī* (Cairo: Dār al-Maʿārif, 1980), 16. See also Hirschler, *The Written Word in the Medieval Arabic Lands*, 25.

48. Makdisi, *The Rise of Humanism*, 51; also Hirschler, *The Written Word in the Medieval Arabic Lands*, 46, 48–49.

49. See, in particular, Yāqūt al-Ḥamawī's (d. 626/1229) itinerary, in Makdisi, *The Rise of Humanism*, 49; also Hirschler's use of Bauer, *The Written Word in the Medieval Arabic Lands*, 190–91. Ibn Baṭṭūṭah mentions in ʿAdan its "pious qāḍī Sālim b. ʿAbdallāh al-Hindī; [whose] . . . father . . . had been a slave, employed as a porter, but the son devoted himself to learning and became a master and leader [in the religious sciences]." *Tuḥfat al-nuẓẓār fī gharāʾib al-amṣār wa- ʿajāʾib al-asfār* (The Observer's Delight in Surprises of Cities and Wonders in Journeys), in *The Travels of ibn Baṭṭūṭa*, 2:373.

50. E.g., Makdisi, *The Rise of Humanism*, 49.

51. See more in Berkey, *Popular Preaching and Religious Authority*; Hirschler, *The Written Word in the Medieval Arabic Lands*, 26–27, 40–41, 45–47, and esp. 186–93; and Thomas Bauer, "Literarische Anthologien der Mamlükenzeit," in *Die Mamlüken: Studien zu ihrer Geschichte und Kultur*, ed. S. Conermann and A. Pistor-Hatam (Hamburg: EB-Verlag, 2003), 71–122.

52. Makdisi's *The Rise of Humanism* is of particular significance to any reconstruction of textual communities in the postclassical era.

53. J. Brugman, *An Introduction to the History of Modern Arabic Literature in Egypt* (Leiden: Brill, 1984); and al-Musawi, *Islam on the Street*.

54. Much is written on this "charm" or "seduction." See Abdelfattah Kilito, *Thou Shalt Not Speak My Language*, trans. Wael Hassan (Syracuse: Syracuse University, 2008), e.g., p. 9; originally published in Arabic, *Lan tatakallam lughatī* (Beirut: Dār al-Talīʿah, 2002). For exemplary discussions of moving "beyond Eurocentrism" as a means to organize world and Middle Eastern history, see Peter Gran's *Islamic Roots of Capitalism* and *Rise of the Rich: A New View of Modern World History* (Syracuse: Syracuse University Press, 2008); and Samir Amin's *Eurocentrism* (New York: Monthly Review, 2010 [1989]) and *The Arab Nation* (New York: Zed Press, 1978).

55. Especially on paratexts as thresholds, fringes, or zones between texts and off-texts, see Gerard Genette, *Paratexts: Thresholds for Interpretation*, trans. Jane E. Lewin (Cambridge: Cambridge University Press, 1997), 1–15.

56. Al-Ḥillī, *Sharḥ al-kāfiyah al-badīʿiyyah fi ʿulūm al-balāghah wa-maḥāsin al-badīʿ* (The Explication of the Sufficient *Badīʿiyyah* Ode in Rhetorical Sciences and Adornments in Innovativeness), ed. Nashāwī, 101.

57. Contadini, *A World of Beasts*, 64–65, fn. 34.

58. Ibn Abī al-Iṣbaʿ, *Taḥrīr al-taḥbīr* (although it means "writing" elegant compositions in Gelder's translation, the implication, as rationalized by his editor, is "emancipating innovation"), ed. Ḥifnī Muḥammad Sharaf (Cairo: Al-Majlis al-Aʿlā lil-Shuʾūn al-Islāmiyyah, 1995), 622.

59. In André Lefevere's reading, patronage is either differentiated or undifferentiated. It is differentiated when the economic factor is not tied to the ideological; but undifferentiated patronage brings the factors of economics, ideology, and status together as "dispensed by one and the same person" or institution. See Lefevere, *Translation, Rewriting, and the Manipulation of Literary Fame*, 17.

60. Cachia, *The Arch Rhetorician*, 7.

61. See al-Ḥillī, *Sharḥ al-kāfiyah al-badīʿiyyah fi ʿulūm al-balāghah wa-maḥāsin al-badīʿ* (The Explication of the Sufficient *Badīʿiyyah* Ode in Rhetorical Sciences and Adornments in Innovativeness), especially the introduction.

62. Peter Adamson, *The Arabic Plotinus: A Philosophical Study of the Theology of Aristotle* (London: Gerald Duckworth, 2002), 1.

63. Ibid., 18.

64. For a translation of the prologue in the order it appears in the original, see ibid., 27–30.

65. Ibn Arabshah, *Tamerlane, or Timur the Great Amir*.

66. ʿAbd Allāh ibn al-Ḥusayn Yazdī, *Al-Ḥāshiyah ʿalā Tahdhīb al-manṭiq lil-Taftazānī* (Qum: Muʾassasat al-Nashr al-Islāmī, 1984).

67. Muḥammad ibn ʿAbd al-Rahmān Jālāl al-Dīn al-Qazwīnī, *Talkhīṣ al-Miftāḥ* (The Resumé of the Key) (Beirut: Dār al-Jīl, n.d.), 1:8–14.

68. Ibid., 1:97, 98, 99.

69. Quotations from al-Taftazānī's *Al-Muṭawwal*: *Sharḥ Talkhīṣ al-Miftāḥ*, 13. The sequence of the quote is reordered to make "lack" a reason for the editor's scholarly effort, which is seemingly meant to be so in the original.

70. For a concordance of these abridgements and explications, see Muḥammad ʿAbd al-Munʿim Khafājah, ed., *Al-ʾĪḍāḥ fī ʿūlūm al-balāghah* (Beirut: Dār al-Jīl, n.d.), 1:8–14.

71. Al-Sharīf al-Jurjānī's *Ḥāshiyah* (commentary) comes as marginal notes or footnotes to the *Muṭawwal*. The editor and publisher included these, along with al-Qazwīnī, in their version of al-Taftazānī's *Al-Muṭawwal: Sharḥ Talkhīṣ al-Miftāḥ*, wa maʿahu ḥāshiyat al-ʿallāmah al-Sayyid al-Sharīf al-Jurjānī, ed. Aḥmad ʿAzzū (Beirut: Dār Iḥyāʾ al-Turāth, 2004), 97, 98, 99.

72. Jurjī Zaydān, *Tārīkh Ādāb al-lughah al-ʿArabiyyah* . . . (The History of Arabic Language . . .), 4 vols. (Cairo: Maṭbaʿat al-Hilāl, 1931), 4:6, 11.

73. In Wolfhart P. Heinrichs's translation of this title, it reads as "Frequented Places for Clarification: Commentary on the Poetic Prooftexts of the 'Epitome' "; i.e., al-Khaṭīb al-Qazwīnī's *Talkhīṣ al-Miftāḥ* (Epitome [or Resumé] of the Key). See his entry, "ʿAbd al-Raḥīm al-ʿAbbāsī," in *Essays in Arabic Literary Biography, 1350–1850*, 12–20.

74. ʿAbd al-Raḥīm ibn ʿAbd al-Raḥmān al-ʿAbbāsī, *Kitāb Sharḥ shawāhid al-Talkhīṣ al-musammā Maʿāhid al-tanṣīṣ* (Designating Familiar Texts: A

Commentary on the Evidentiary Verses in *al-Talkhīṣ*) (Miṣr: Al-Maṭbaʿah al-Bahiyyah, 1899).

75. Ibn Sanāʾ al-Mulk's full name: Abū al-Qāsim hibat Allāh b. Abī al-Faḍl Jaʿfar b. al-Muʿtamid, known as al-Qāḍī al-Saʿīd. He worked under the direction of al-Qāḍī al-Fāḍil. See "Dār al-Ṭirāz," *Encyclopaedia of Islam*, 2nd ed., ed. P. Bearman, Th. Bianquis, C. E. Bosworth, E. van Donzel, and W. P. Heinrichs (Brill Online, 2014), referenced 19 July 2014.

76. In *Sūrat al-Nūr*, 24:35: "Allāh is the Light of the heavens and the earth. The parable of His Light is as a niche and within it a lamp: the lamp is in a glass, the glass as it were a brilliant [pearly] star, lit from a blessed tree. . . ."

77. See al-Musawi, "Vindicating a Profession or a Personal Career?"

78. Rashīd al-Dīn al-Waṭwāṭ served as chief secretary (Ṣāḥib dīwān al-inshāʾ) in Khwārizm to ʿAzīz Khwārazm Shāh (d. 1156) and his successor Ēl-Arsalān (d. 568/1172). See Rashīd al-Dīn al-Waṭwāṭ, *Ḥadāʾiq al-siḥr fī daqāʾiq al-shiʿr* (The Groves of Enchantment in the Secrets of Poetry), ed. Ibrāhim Amīn al-Shawārbī (Cairo: Lajnat al-Taʾlīf wa-l-Tarjamah wa-l-Nashr, 1945).

79. Ibid., 30–36.

80. Ibid.

81. See the last four pages of the gallery of this volume: An Inventory of al-Ḥillī's Reading List and Library in Rhetoric, appended to his *Sharḥ*.

82. On the technical impact of the *badīʿiyyah*, Suzanne P. Stetkevych argues: "Ṣafī al-Dīn al-Ḥillī . . . is usually credited with creating the first such poem. Later practitioners, beginning with ʿIzz al-Dīn al-Mawṣilī (d. 789/1387), added the further proviso that each verse contain a *tawriyah* (pun) on the rhetorical term for the device exhibited therein." *The Mantle Odes*, 154.

83. See El-Rouayheb, "Opening the Gate of Verification," 268.

84. Ibid. Although meaning 'verification,' the term *taḥqīq* is equivalent to commentary and annotation, an authenticating method that was pursued in the thirteenth century onwards. As for the term *aʿājim*, it began to undergo deflection to mean partly 'Persians' only after the rise of the sectarian divide. In Islamic times, and well before the fifteenth century, it meant 'non-Arabs.' Jār Allāh al-Zamakhsharī (d. 1144), himself of Persian origin and born in Khwārizm, used the term *ʿajami khalq Allāh* (the non-Arabs among God's creatures). See the preface to his *Al-Mufaṣṣal fī ʿIlm al-lughah* (Beirut: Dār Iḥyāʾ al-ʿUlūm, 1990), 11–12. On the other hand, ibn Khaldūn used *ʿajam* to mean other nations in his *Kitāb Al-ʿIbar wa dīwān al-mubtadaʾ wa-al-khabar fī ayyām al-ʿArab wa al-ʿAjam wa al-Barbar wa man ʿaṣarahum min dhawī al-sulṭān al-akbar.* As noted also by Nabil Matar, *In the Lands of the Christians: Arabic Travel Writing in the Seventeenth Century* (New York and London: Routledge, 2003): "Although the very concept

of 'Europe' did not exist either among the Christian Arabs or Muslims, there was a curiosity about the Rūm (the Qurʾanic name for the Byzantines), the infraj (Franks) and the ʿajam (Spaniards)" (xviii). Muḥammad ʿAbd al-Wahhāb al-Ghassānī al-Andalusī uses the term to refer to non-Arabic speaking people. See his *Riḥlat al-Wazīr fī iftikāk al-asīr, 1690–1691* (The Travels of the Vizier to Release the Hostage, 1690–1691), ed. Nūrī al-Jarrāḥ (Abū Dhabī: Dār al-Suwaydī lil-Nashr wa-l-Tawzīʿ, 2002).

85. For more on the seventeenth century, see El-Rouayheb, "Opening the Gate of Verification," 265; his interpretation of "*kutub al aʿājim*" should be ignored.

86. For references to this usage, see Qalqīlah, *Al-Naqd al-adabī fi al-ʿaṣr al-Mamlūkī*, 43. Ibn Ḥijjah included this in his *Sharḥ* (mistakenly called *Khizānat al-adab*) as "Risālat al-sayf wa al-qalam." See ibn Ḥijjah, *Khizānat al-adab*, ed. Diyāb, 1:360.

87. Jean Baudrillard writes in *Simulacra and Simulation*, trans. Sheila Faria Glaser (Ann Arbor: University of Michigan Press, 1994), 1:

> If once we were able to view the Borges fable in which the cartographers of the empire draw up a map so detailed that it ends up covering the territory exactly (the decline of the Empire witnesses the fraying of this map, little by little, and its fall into ruins, though some shreds are still discernible in the deserts—the metaphysical beauty of this ruined abstraction testifying to some pride equal to the empire and rotting like a carcass, returning to the substance of the soil, a bit as the double ends by being confused with the real through aging)—as the most beautiful allegory of simulation, this fable has now come full circle for us, and possesses nothing but the discrete charm of second order simulacra.

88. Brooke-Rose, "Whatever Happened to Narratology?," 284.

89. Suzanne P. Stetkevych, *Abū Tammām and the Poetics of the ʿAbbāsid Age* (Leiden: Brill, 1991), 16–17. In her translation, al-Jāḥiẓ says:

> For the Mutakallimūn [speculative theologians] selected expressions for their concepts, deriving terminology for things for which the Arab language had no word. In doing so they have set the precedent in this for all who came after them, and the model for all who followed. Thus they say accident (*ʿaraḍ*) and essence (*jawhar*); to be (*aysa*) and not to be (*laysa*). They distinguish between nullity (*buṭlān*) and nihility (*talāshin*), and they use the terms "thisness" (*hādhiyyah*), identity (*huwiyyah*), and quiddity

> (*māhiyyah*). In the same way al-Khalīl ibn Aḥmad attached names to the metres of the *qaṣīdahs* . . . whereas the [Bedouin] Arabs had not known the metres by those names. Similarly the grammarians named and referred to the circumstantial accusatives (*ḥāl*), the adverbial accusatives (*ẓurūf*) and such things. . . . Likewise the mathematicians draw upon names which they have designated as signs in order to understand one another. . . . Someone preaching in the heart of the Caliph's palace said, "God brought him out of the door of nonbeing (*laysiyyah*) and made him enter the door of being (*aysiyyah*)." . . . These expressions are permissible in the art of Kalām when existing words lack the required range of meaning. The expressions of the Mutakallimūn are also befitting to poetry.

But see also ʿĀrif Tāmir on the use of these terms by al-Karmānī and al-Fārābī, in al-Rāzī, *Al-Munāẓarāt* (The Debates), ed. Tāmir, 28–29.

Chapter Four. The Context of an Islamic Literate Society

1. Reported by Imam ʿAlī, cited by the calligrapher, in Sayyid Ibrāhīm, "Al-Khaṭṭ al-ʿArabī fī al-ʿaṣr al-ḥadīth," *Al-Hilāl* (1939; special issue): 150.

2. For more, see S. Stetkevych, *The Mantle Odes*, 269 n. 3.

3. Muslim ibn Ḥajjāj (d. 875), *Ṣaḥīḥ Muslim* (Beirut: Dār al-Kitāb al-ʿArabī, 2004), hadith no. 5919.

4. Abū Bakr. b. ʿAlī b. ʿAbdullāh ibn Ḥijjah al-Ḥamawī deliberately names his book-length poem—a contrafaction specifically to Ṣafī al-Dīn al-Ḥillī's panegyric to the Prophet—"Taqdīm Abī Bakr," meaning it as *tawriyah*, a pun or word play (double entendre). His title means that his ode surpasses preceding texts and authors, perhaps as his namesake the Caliph Abū Bakr precedes other companions, including ʿUmar, whom al-Ḥillī holds in high esteem. The ode also has its own extensive compendium and an abridged exegesis, which he names *Thubūt al-Ḥijjah ʿalā al-Mawṣilī wa al-Ḥillī* (The Damning Proof against al-Mawṣilī and al-Ḥillī). It seems, according to Qalqīlah's reading, that a later copyist recalled ʿAbd al-Qādir ibn ʿUmar al-Baghdādī's (d. 1093/1682) *Khizānat al-adab wa lubb lubāb lisān al-ʿArab* (The Treasury of Literature and the Essence of the Arab Language) and saw that ibn Ḥijjah's explication goes beyond a mere apparatus in rhetoric in support of his long poem, because he brought into the voluminous work contemporary and past writings, including contemporary poetry that is inaccessible elsewhere. Needless to say, ibn Ḥijjah explains that he names his poem "Taqdīm Abī Bakr" in terms of comparison with those of al-Ḥillī and

al-Mawṣilī. See ibn Ḥijjah, *Khizānat al-adab* (The Ultimate Treasure Trove of Literature), ed. Diyāb, 1:349–50. Maḥmūd al-Rabdāwī takes the Būlāq version as the one that witnessed the slippage, *Ibn Ḥijjah Shāʿiran wa nāqidan* (Damascus: Dār Qutaybah, 1982), 193–94; and see Kawkab Diyāb's use of this documentation, in *Khizānat al-adab*, 1:64–65. For more on ʿAbd al-Qādir ibn ʿUmar al-Baghdādī's *Khizānat al-adab wa lubb lubāb lisān al-ʿArab*, where he explains al-Raḍī al-Astrābādhī's commentary on the *Kāfiyah of ibn al-Ḥājib* (d. 646), see Bāshā, *Tārīkh*, 92–94. See also Suzanne P. Stetkevych, "From Jahiliyya to Badīʿiyyah: Orality, Literacy, and the Transformations of Rhetoric in Arabic Poetry," *Oral Tradition* 25 (2010): 211–30.

5. The commitment to popular songs and street poetry is part of the recognition of poets as the legislators for language. See again Makdisi, *The Rise of Humanism*, 140.

6. Al-Hamadhānī, *The Maqāmāt of Badīʿ al-Zamān al-Hamadhānī*, trans. Prendergast (1915), online at http://www.sacred-texts.com/isl/mhm/mhm48.htm, 58. In the Arabic edition, *Maqāmāt*, ed. Shaykh Muḥammad ʿAbduh (Beirut: Dār al-Mashriq, 2002), 65.

7. See Makdisi, *The Rise of Colleges*, 140.

8. See also on this point Everett Rowson, "An Alexandrian Age in Fourteenth-Century Damascus: Twin Commentaries on Two Celebrated Arabic Epistles," *Mamluk Studies Review* 7, no. 1 (2003): 106.

9. See how al-Ṣafadī specifically uses the term to indicate that he heard it and was allowed to transmit, in the quotes he had from Ṣafī al-Dīn al-Ḥillī: Khalīl ibn Aybak al-Ṣafadī, *Kitāb al-Ghayth al-musjam fī sharḥ Lāmiyyat al-ʿajam*, 2 vols. (Al-Dār al-Bayḍāʾ: Dār al-Rashād, 1990), 1:123; and also from ibn Nubātah; and from Shihāb al-Dīn Maḥmūd, 1:123–24.

10. The quote cited in Makdisi with respect to the *samāʿ* of a text by the poet al-Khalīʿ (d. 250/864), copied by Yāqūt al-Mawṣilī al-Kātib (d. 618/1221 or 1222) from the grammarian ibn al-Khashshāb's (568/1172) copy, states that the rest of the book "was read without authoritative transmission or a license (*wajadatan*) because it was not collated with al-Ḍabbī's text by authoritative transmission." Makdisi, *The Rise of Humanism*, 101–2. On the origin of the concept and its early applications, see Makdisi, *The Rise of Colleges*, 140–41.

11. For ibn Nubātah's authorization and al-Ṣafadī's request, see ibn Ḥijjah's *Khizānat al-adab*, 3:324–34.

12. Shams al-Dīn Muḥammad ibn Ḥasan al-Nawājī (1386–1455), *Kitāb al-Ḥujjah fī sariqāt ibn Ḥijjah* (The Damning Evidence of ibn-Ḥijjah's Plagiarisms), manuscript, undated. MS Arab 285, Houghton Library, Harvard University, http://nrs.harvard.edu/urn-3:FHCL.HOUGH:2600641.

13. Ibn Zaydūn's epistle is in the voice of the princess Wallādah bint al-Mustakfī and is written in a sarcastic and scathingly satirical tone addressed to Aḥmad ibn ʿAbdūs, who vied for her love aginst ibn Zaydūn. Ibn Nubātah's study and explication is titled *Sarḥ al-ʿuyūn fī sharḥ risālat ibn Zaydūn*, ed. Muḥammad Abū al-Faḍl Ibrāhīm (Beirut/Ṣaydā: Al-Maktabah al-ʿAṣriyyah, 1998). Al-Ṣafadī included his discussion in *Kitāb al-Ghayth al-musjam fī sharḥ Lāmiyyat al-ʿAjam*.

14. "Shifters," as devices to express shifting deixis, as traces of authorial intervention, and as indices of subjective presence, are used by Otto Jesperson, named and discussed by Roman Jacobson, and exercised and practiced by Roland Barthes. See Lubomīr Doležel, *Possible Worlds of Fiction and History: The Postmodern Stage* (Baltimore: Johns Hopkins University Press, 2010), 17. On their use in Arabic, see Muhsin al-Musawi, *Arabic Poetry: Trajectories of Modernity and Tradition* (London: Routledge, 2006), and the reference to ʿAbd Allāh ibn Muslim ibn Qutaybah, *Kitāb al-shiʿr wa- al-shuʿarāʾ*, ed. M.J. de Goeje (Leiden: Brill, 1904), 14–15; Reynolds A. Nicholson, *A Literary History of the Arabs* (Cambridge: Cambridge University Press, 1956), 77–78. See also Makdisi, *The Rise of Humanism*, 98–99.

15. See ibn Nubātah's authorized transmission to Ṣalāh al-Ṣafadī, in ibn Ḥijjah's *Khizānat al-adab*, 3:324–34.

16. This view had no success, and it failed early on. It argues that "desinential inflections" are ordained by God. See Makdisi, *The Rise of Humanism*, 124.

17. See Messick, *The Calligraphic State*.

18. Apart from ibn Ḥijjah's *Taqdīm*, which is intended to supersede, contrafact, and undermine al-Ḥillī's, we have Shams al-Dīn al-Nawājī, *Al-Ḥujjah fi sariqāt ibn Ḥijjah* (exposing the latter's presumed plagiarisms), and his *Al-Durr al-nafīs fī mā zāda ʿalā jinān al-jinās li-l-Ṣafadī wa ajnās al-tajnīs li-l-Ḥillī* (an excursus in paronomasia expounding on two of its prominent users); Badr al-Dīn al-Damāmīnī, *Nuzūl al-Ghayth al-ladhī insajam ʿalā sharḥ lāmiyyat al-ʿajam* (which critiques al-Ṣafadī's book *Al-Ghayth*); Ṣalāh al-Dīn al-Ṣafadī, *Niṣrat al-thāʾir ʿalā al-mathal al-sāʾir* (against ibn al-Athīr's book under that title); ibn Ḥijjah's *Kashf al-lithām ʿan wajh al-tawriyah wa-al-istikhdām* (against al-Ṣafadī's book *Faḍḍ al-Khitām . . .*), and so forth.

19. Shams al-Dīn al-Sakhāwī, *Al-Ḍawʾ al-lāmiʿ li-ahl al-qarn al-tāsiʿ* (Cairo: Maktabat Al-Qudsī, 1953), 11:53.

20. The Arabic term "istikhdām" is the "use of a word that bears two radically different meanings, each of which is intended in turn." See Cachia, *The Arch Rhetorician*, 72–73, n. 107.

21. Ṣafī al-Dīn al-Ḥillī, *Al-Kāfiyah al-badīʿiyyah fī al-madāʾiḥ al-nabawiyyah* (literally, The Sufficient Ode of Rhetoric in Encomiums to the Prophet).

22. For more on this side, see ibn Ḥijjah al-Ḥamawī, *Bulūgh al-amal fī fann al-zajal* (The Achievement of the Desirable in the Art of Zajal), ed. Riḍā Muḥsin al-Qurayshī (Damascus: Wizārat al-Thaqāfah wa-al-Irshād al-Qawmī [Ministry of Culture], 1974), 26, 29–33.

23. For a survey of these, covering nearly all of the most prominent critics of the period under consideration, see Qalqīlah, *Al-Naqd al-adabī fi al-ʿaṣr al-Mamlūkī*, 370–89.

24. Al-Jāḥiẓ mentions this in *Al-Ḥayawān*, ed. ʿAbd al-Salām Hārūn (Cairo: Maktabat wa-Maṭbaʿat Muṣṭafā al-Bābī al-Ḥalabī, 1938), 3:131; Kamal Abu Deeb, *Al-Jurjani's Theory of Poetic Imagery* (Warminster: Aris and Phillips, 1979), 60. Abū Hilāl al-ʿAskarī repeats the same in his *Kitāb al-Sināʿatayn: al-kitābah wa- al-shiʿr* (The Book of the Two Arts: Prose and Poetry), ed. Mufīd Qamīḥah (Beirut: Dār al-Kutub al-ʿIlmiyyah, 1981; repr. 1989), 72. See also George J. Kanazi, *Studies in the Kitāb aṣ-Ṣināʿatayn of Abū Hilal al-Askari* (Leiden: Brill, 1989), 93. He specifies that distinction resides "in the excellence and limpidity of the *lafẓ*, its beauty and splendor, purity and refinement, and degree of smoothness and polish, with proper construction and articulation, and freedom from distortion in structure and composition."

25. Al-Qāḍī ʿAlī ibn ʿAbd al-ʿAzīz al-Jurjānī, *Al-Waṣāṭah bayna al-Mutanabbī wa-khuṣūmihī* (The Mediation between al-Mutanabbī and His Opponents), ed. Muḥammad Abū al-Faḍl Ibrāhīm (Cairo: Maṭbaʿat ʿIsā al-Bābī al-Ḥalabī, 1966). For extensive discussions of this controversy and the numerous contributions and rejoinders, see Qalqīlah, *Al-Naqd al-adabī fi al-ʿaṣr al-Mamlūkī*, 370–416; Iḥsān ʿAbbās, *Tārīkh al-naqd al-adabī ʿinda al-ʿArab: naqd al-shiʿr min al-qarn al-thānī ḥattā al-qarn al-thāmin al-hijrī* (1993; 4th print., Amman: Dār al-Shurūq, 2006), 131, 197, 250–56, 268, 288, 375, 463, 563, 671–73. See also S. Stetkevych, *Abū Tammām and the Poetics of the ʿAbbasid Age*.

26. Qalqīlah, *Al-Naqd al-adabī fi al-ʿaṣr al-Mamlūkī*, 563.

27. Al-Ṣafadī, *Kitāb al-Ghayth*, 1:190–91. The reference, taken by al-Tughrāʾī, is to the unique verse of al-Sharīf al-Raḍī in the elegiac nostalgic mode of *nasīb* (And my eye looked back, for since the ruins faded, the heart is the one to reminisce).

28. Qalqīlah, *Al-Naqd al-adabī fi al-ʿaṣr al-Mamlūkī*, 379; referring to Yaḥyā ibn Ḥamzah al-ʿAlawī, *Al-Ṭirāz*.

29. Zayn al-Din ʿUmar ibn al-Muzaffar ibn al-Wardī, *Diwān ibn al-Wardī* (Cairo: Dār al-Āfāq al-ʿArabiyyah, 2006), 264. Also in ibn Ḥijjah's *Khizānat al-adab*, 1:49. He is also the author and compiler of *Kharīdat al-ʿajāʾib wa farīdat al-gharāʾib* (The Pearl of Wonders and the Uniqueness of Things Strange) (Cairo: Maktabat al-Thaqāfah al-Dīniyyah, 2008).

30. Cited in ibn Ḥijjah's *Khizānat al-adab*, 1:46. Also Qalqīlah, *Al-Naqd al-adabī fi al-ʿaṣr al-Mamlūkī*, 170; and ibn Nubātah, *Talṭif al-mizāj min shiʿr ibn al-Ḥajjāj* (Refining the Mood with the Poetry of ibn al-Ḥajjāj), ed. Muṣṭafā, 49. See also Sinan Antoon, *The Poetics of the Obscene: Ibn al-Hajjaj and Sukhf* (New York: Palgrave Macmillan, 2014).

31. See Yūsuf ibn Ismāʿīl al-Nabhānī, *Al-Hamziyyah al-alfiyyah al-musammāt Tibat al-gharrāʾ fī madḥ Sayyid al-anbiyāʾ* (Beirut: Al-Maṭbaʿah al-Adabiyyah, 1896), and *Al-Majmūʿah al-Nabhāniyyah fī al-madāʾiḥ al-nabawiyyah* (1902; repr. 1974).

32. Yāqūt al-Ḥamawī (d. 626/1229), for example, was fortunate in that his master, a businessman from Baghdad, allowed him to attend sessions in Arabic grammar, the art of prose writing, philology, and other areas that helped him later in his work as a copyist and as author of a voluminous biographical dictionary, *Muʿjam al-udabāʾ: Irshād al-arīb ilā maʿrifat al-adīb* (The Dictionary of the Learned . . .). On the other hand, the jurist Aḥmad ibn al-ʾUkhuwwah (d. 548/1153) worked as an authorized reader of public texts in public sessions. See Hirschler, *The Written Word in the Medieval Arabic Lands*, 41. For more on the application of textual archaeology, see Irvine, *The Making of Textual Culture*, 425.

33. For some tentative applications of this construction, see Paul L. Heck's study *The Construction of Knowledge in Islamic Civilization: Qudamā b. Jaʿfar and His Kitāb al-Kharāj wa-ṣināʿat al-kitāba* (Leiden: Brill, 2002), in which, under the guidance of his advisor Wadad al-Qadi, he comes up with some pertinent suggestions, mainly involving three divides: of language and administration, geography, and jurisprudence. Under the first divide are the following subcategories: the grammatical, the bureaucratic, and the linguistic. Qudāma ibn Jaʿfar (d. 337/948) was a jurist, administrator, epistolographer, critic, and littérateur. See also Carter, "Language Control as People Control in Medieval Islam"; and O. Bakar, *The Classification of Knowledge in Islam* (Cambridge: Cambridge University Press, 1998).

34. As keenly noticed by Makdisi in *The Rise of Humanism*, there is always a concordance in official discourse that continues to function. The caliph al-Qādir (r. 381–422/991–1031) enforced a traditionalist creed, known after him as Qādirī, that was directed against "anthropomorphists, the Karramiya, the Shīʿa (especially the extremist Rafida [who reject the choice of the first caliphs] and Ismaʿiliya), the Ashʿariya, and the Muʿtazila," leading to the banning of *kalām* theology from the curriculum of colleges of law, and so on. But this kind of view would continue even centuries later in historical surveys and accounts, such as that of al-Dhahabī (d. 748/1347), who shared the same creed and preserved the discriminatory attitude. It finds its way in other accounts within a genealogy of inclusion/exclusion. See Makdisi, *The Rise of Humanism*, 8–9. For a

brief discussion of Ashʿariyyah as a dominating school of law under the Seljuqs, see al-Razi, *Al-Munāẓarāt*, ed. Tāmir, 7, fn. 1; and 51, fn. 1, on Muʿtazila.

35. Ḍiyāʾ al-Dīn Muḥammad ibn Muḥammad al-Qurashī al-Shāfiʿī ibn al-ʾUkhuwwa, *The Maʿālim al-Qurba fī Ṭalab al-Ḥisba*, ed. Reuben Levy, Gibb Memorial series, n.s. 12 (London: Luzac, printed by Cambridge University Press, 1938), 57.

36. Ibid.

37. Isḥāq Ibrāhīm Mūsā al-Lakhmī al-Shāṭibī, *Al-Muwāfaqāt fi ʾuṣūl al-sharīʿah* (Beirut: Dār al-Fikr al-ʿArabī), 1:21. The Andalusian al-Shāṭibī (d. 790/1388), mentioned by the second mendicant in the *Thousand and One Nights*, had many renowned mentors, including Abū ʿAbd Allah al-Sharīf al-Tilimsānī (d. 771/1369). He left behind numerous works in theology and jurisprudence that have an abiding impact on Islamic law. See also Abū Ḥāmid al-Ghazālī, an excerpt from *Iḥyāʾ ʿulūm al-dīn* (The Revival of Religious Sciences) on *ḥisbah*, included in al-Shayzarī's *The Book of the Islamic Market Inspector*, trans. Ronald Paul Buckley (Oxford: Oxford University Press, 2000), 183.

38. Al-Musawi, *The Islamic Context of the Thousand and One Nights*, 120. In his *The Mediaeval Islamic Underworld: The Banū Sāsān in Arabic Society and Literature* (Leiden: Brill, 1976), Clifford E. Bosworth writes: "The *qāṣṣ* was thus not infrequently an influential figure in popular eyes, for whereas the dialectical subtleties of the scholastic theologians and the legal niceties of the traditionalists and lawyers were quite above the heads of the masses, the edifying tales of the story-tellers made some sort of religious knowledge available to the illiterate majority" (1:26–27).

39. Ibn al-Jawzī, *Ṣayd al-khāṭir*, 77, 88, 122, 175, 176, 188, 214, 248, 249.

40. An early anthology of ibn Ḥajjāj's (d. 391/1001) poetry, with its subtleties in ribald and obscene excursions and clever allusions, was by Hibat Allāh Badīʿ al-Zamān al-Asṭurlābī (d. 534/1139 or 1140). See al-Asṭurlābī, *Durrat al-tāj min shiʿr ibn al-Ḥajjāj* (The Crown Pearl of ibn al-Ḥajjāj's Poetry), ed. ʿAlī Jawād al-Ṭāhir (Baghdad and Berlin: Manshūrāt al-Jamal, 2009). A standard anthology is ibn Nubātah's *Talṭīf al-mizāj min shiʿr ibn al-Ḥajjāj* (Refining the Mood with the Poetry of ibn al-Ḥajjāj), ed. Muṣṭafā. For a survey, see Mary St. Germain, "Abū ʿAbd Allāh ibn al-Ḥajjāj," in *Essays in Arabic Literary Biography, 925–1350*, 122–29; also Antoon, *The Poetics of the Obscene*. For more, see Boaz Shoshan, "High Culture and Popular Culture in Medieval Islam," *Studia Islamica* 73 (1991): 84 fn. 57.

41. Abū Saʿīd al-Sīrāfī (d. 368/979) says to Mattā ibn Yūnus in a famous debate (330/932): "You are wrong. Logic, grammar, sound, correct expression, correct inflexion, statement, narration, predication, interrogation, request, desire, exhortation, invocation, appellation, and petition, all belong to the same

region by virtue of similarity and resemblance." Also: "Grammar, then, is Logic, only abstracted from the Arabic language, and Logic is Grammar, only rendered intelligible by language." D. S. Margoliouth, "The Discussion between Abu Bishr Matta and Abu Saʿid al-Sirafi on the Merits of Logic and Grammar," *Journal of the Royal Asiatic Society of Great Britain and Ireland* (January 1905): 116, 117; see also Muhsin Mahdi, "Language and Logic in Classical Islam," in *Logic in Classical Islamic Culture*, ed. G. E. von Grunebaum (Wiesbaden: Harrassowitz, 1970), 50–83.

42. Saʿd al-Dīn Masʿūd b. ʿUmar al-Taftazānī, *Sharḥ al-talkhīṣ* (Beirut: Dār al-Kutub, n.d.), 1:15.

43. Jamāl al-Dīn al-Isnāwī, *Al-Kawkab al-durrī fī mā yatakharraj ʿala al-ʾuṣūl al-naḥwiyyah min al-furūʿ al-fiqhiyya* (The Pearly Star in the Extraction of Juridical Secondary Rulings on the Bases of Grammatical Principles) (Amman: Dār ʿAmmār, 1985), 233–34.

44. For more on this point, see Ḥasan Khamīs al-Malkh, *Naẓariyyat al-aṣl wa-al-farʾ fī al-naḥw al-ʿArabī* (The Theory of Origin and Branch in Arabic Grammar) (Amman: Dār al-Shurūq, 2001), 102–8.

45. For an insight into an aesthetic movement toward *badīʿ* as a dynamic, not static, poetic, see Jaroslav Stetkevych, *The Zephyrs of Najd: The Poetics of Nostalgia in the Classical Arabic Nasīb* (Chicago: University of Chicago Press, 1993), 6–15 and 180–201.

46. See note 18 above.

47. See ibn Ḥijjah, *Khizānat al-adab*, 3:331. Ibn Nubātah mentions Muḥyī al-Dīn Abū Muḥammad ʿAbd Allāh b. Shaykh Rashīd ʿAbd al-Ẓāhir; he also mentions Bahāʾ al-Dīn b. al-Naḥḥās and Shams al-Dīn Ibn. al-Mattīnī, along with many hadith scholars.

48. For a short account of the poet, see W. P. Heinrichs, "Ṣāfī al-Dīn ʿAbd al-ʿAzīz b. Sarāyā," in *Encyclopedia of Islam*, CD-ROM Edition, v. 1.0 (Leiden: Brill, 1999).

49. For a brief introductory survey of an early period discussion of the prioritization of prose, see al-Ḥasan Bū Tibyā, *Mufāḍalah bayna al-naẓm wa-al-nathr wa-ashkāl al-tadākhul baynahumā fī al-ʿaṣr al-ʿAbbāsī* (Marrākish: Imprimerie al-Waṭaniyya, 2002).

50. Al-Nābulusī's manual of rhetoric is summarized and systematized by Pierre Cachia under the title *The Arch Rhetorician*.

51. Ibid., item 107, p. 69.

52. Ibid., item 106, p. 72.

53. Foucault, *The Order of Things*, 33.

54. Ibid., 34.

55. Ibid., 35.

56. Ibid., 35–36.

57. In Geert Jan van Gelder's "A Good Cause: Fantastic Aetiology (*Ḥusn al-taʿlīl*) in Arabic Poetics," in *Takhyīl: The Imaginary in Classical Arabic Poetics: Pt. 2, Studies*, ed. Geert Jan van Gelder and Marlé Hammond (London: Gibb Memorial Trust, 2008), 223.

58. Ibid.

59. Ibid.

60. These include (with their dates of death): al-Fārābī (339/950), Abū Hilāl al-ʿAskarī (395/1005), al-Zamakhsharī (538/1144), Averroes (Abū al-Walīd ibn Rushd, 595/1198), al-Jurjānī, Abū Barakāt al-Baghdādī (560/1164), al-Waṭwaṭ (573/1182), Fakhr al-Dīn al-Rāzī (606/1209), al-Sakkākī (626/1229), Ḥāzim al-Qarṭājannī (684/1285), ʿAbd al-Wahhāb ibn Ibrāhīm al-Zanjānī (660/1262), Zayn al-Dīn al-Rāzī (666/1276), Abū al-Baqāʾ al-Rundī (684/1285), al-Khaṭīb al-Qazwīnī (739/1338), al-Taftazānī, Bahāʾ al-Dīn al-ʿĀmilī (1621), ibn Ḥijjah (837/1434), Yaḥyā ibn Ḥamzah al-ʿAlawī (749/1348), ʿAbd al-Raḥīm al-ʿAbbāsī (963/1556), ibn Maʿṣūm (1104/1692), and, most prominently, ibn Abī al-Iṣbaʿ (656/1256) and Ṣafī al-Dīn al-Ḥillī.

61. See, for example, by Ijī: *Risālat adab al-baḥth wa-al-munāẓarah* (The Epistle on the Art of Research and Debate); *Al-Mawāqif fī ʿilm al-kalām* (The Stations in the Science of Speculative Theology); *Al-Fawāʾid al-ghiyāthiyah fī al-ʿulūm al-balāghiyyah* (The Bountiful Sources in the Sciences of Rhetoric); *Jāmiʿ al-bayān fī tafsīr al-Qurʾān* (The Compendium of Tropical Language in Qurʾānic Hermeneutics); and his commentary on ibn al-Ḥājib's *al-Muntahā*, known as *al-Ḥāshiyah al-ʿAḍudiyyah* (Aḍud's Marginalia).

62. Foucault, *The Order of Things*, 63.

63. It is worth noting that the official discourse, with its worldly underpinnings, was so overwhelming that even Abū Yaʿqūb al-Sakkākī could only allude to the issue when arguing the case for Qurʾānic inimitability: "they were so confounded that they refrained from opposition by words and resorted to fighting with swords . . . all out of aggressiveness, envy, and stubbornness." *Miftāḥ* (The Key), 1.

64. Foucault, *The Order of Things*, 50.

65. Ibid.

66. See Knysh, *Ibn ʿArabi in the Later Islamic Tradition*.

67. This is traceable in particular in Shams al-Dīn al-Dhahabī's *Taʾrīkh al-Islam*, which is representative of ibn Taymiyyah's disciples. To them, one's reliance should be absolutely on faith and literal meaning in matters of religion; everything else, such as scientific reasoning or philosophy and ecstatic meditations, is shunned. See Knysh, *Ibn ʿArabi in the Later Islamic Tradition*, 115, 123.

68. Cleary's wording, "World Literary System," 200.

69. Ibn Arabshah, *Tamerlane, or Timur the Great Amir*, 176.

70. Ibid., 147–49.

71. Frederick the Great, Letter of 1780 to d'Alembert, in *Oeuvres* (Berlin, 1854), 25:166, as cited by Schwab in his introduction to d'Alembert, *Preliminary Discourse to the Encyclopedia of Diderot*, ix–x.

72. Ibn Ḥijjah, *Khizānat al-adab*, 3:524.

73. See Jacques Rancière, *The Politics of Aesthetics*, trans. Gabriel Rockhill (New York: Continuum, 2004), 32.

74. In Rancière's phrasing, it "evokes the representative tradition's scales of grandeur and, on the other hand, revokes the oratorical model of speech in favor of the interpretation of signs on the body of people, things and civilizations." Ibid.

75. Ibn Ḥijjah, *Khizānat al-adab*, 3:516.

76. Ibid., 3:525.

Chapter Five. Superfluous Proliferation or Generative Innovation?

1. See Al-Shirbīnī, *Kitāb hazz al-quḥūf*, ed. Davies, 1:xvii–xviii. Cited hereafter as *Hazz al-quḥūf.*

2. See also Humphrey Davies' note where he rightly observes that the *shurūḥ* commentators' preoccupations most prominently parodied by al-Shirbīnī are meter; etymology, conventions of verbal paradigm- and morphological pattern-identification, and the use of lexical authorities in support of the latter; probative verse quotations; and the rhetorical debate as heuristic tool (*mas'ala, fangala*, etc.). Ibid., 2:lxviii–lxix.

3. Foucault, *The Order of Things*, 67.

4. Ibid., 43.

5. Ibid.

6. Ibid.

7. See *Hazz al-quḥūf*, 1:6, 154, and elsewhere. In the second instance al-Shirbīnī refers to al-Būṣīrī as the "pious, ascetic littérateur, and the glorious learned . . . may God benefit us from him."

8. See Suzanne P. Stetkevych, "From Text to Talisman: Al-Buṣīrī's Qaṣīdat al-Burdah (Mantle Ode) and the Poetics of Supplication," *Journal of Arabic Literature* 37, no. 2 (2006): 145–89; modified as chapter 2 in her *The Mantle Odes*, 70–148; see esp. 81–82.

9. *Hazz al-quḥūf*, 2:165–66.

10. Ibid., 2:168.

11. Ibid.

12. Davies' translation, *Hazz al-quḥūf*, 1:xxviii.

13. Ibid.

14. For a listing of odes and applications in rhetoric, see Abū Zayd, *Al-Badīʿiyyāt fī al-adab al-ʿArabī*, 71–180.

15. For more on these seven categories, see Roger Allen, *The Arabic Literary Heritage* (Cambridge: Cambridge University Press, 1998), 133–38.

16. This functions almost as a refrain or leitmotif for each section on etymology morphology, or paradigm (*maṣdar*). See examples in *Hazz al-quḥūf*, 2:64, 96, 106, 112, 130, 135, 142, 160, 161, 163, 246, 265, 268, 274, 439, and 457.

17. *Hazz al-quḥūf*, 2:xxvii–xxviii.

18. See Davies, in ibid., 2:xxxi.

19. See Arnoud Vrolijk, *Bringing a Laugh to a Scowling Face: A Study and Critical Edition of "Nuzhat al-nufūs wa-muḍḥik al-ʿabūs" by ʿAlī ibn Sūdūn al-Bashbughāwī* (Leiden: Brill, 1998).

20. For more information, see ʿAbd al-Wahhāb Bakr, *Al-Dawlah al-ʿUthmāniyyah wa Miṣr fī al-niṣf al-thānī min al-qarn al-thāmin ʿashar* (Cairo: Dār al-Maʿārif, 1982). See also Gran, *Islamic Roots of Capitalism*, xix, 11.

21. *Hazz al-quḥūf*, 2:28.

22. Ibid.

23. Ibid., 2:197.

24. Ibid. His claim to have written an epistle entitled "Riyāḍ al-uns mimmā jarā bayna al-ayr wa-al-kuss" (roughly: Meadows of Entertainment with Respect to What Took Place between the Penis and the Kunt) may be mere buffoonery in the same misogynist direction.

25. I quote Jacques Rancière for his application to the nineteenth-century French scene; see *The Politics of Aesthetics*, 32.

26. *Hazz al-quḥūf*, 2:124, 125.

27. Ibid., 2:93.

28. Ibid., 2:280–83.

29. Ibid., 2:168, 169, 260, 300, 342, 403, 405, 432.

30. For an explanation of how *nasīb*-turned-*ghazal* functions in turn as "metaphor for another metaphor," see Jaroslav Stetkevych's analysis, *The Zephyrs of Najd*, 80–102.

31. For an entry on ibn Sūdūn, see Arnoud Vrolijk, "Ibn Sūdūn," in *Essays in Arabic Literary Biography, 1350–1850*, 223–28.

32. See Ṭāhā Ḥusayn's preface to Aḥmad Ḥasan al-Zayyāt's translation of *The Sorrows of Young Werther*: *ʾĀlām Veirtar* (Cairo: Lajnat al-Taʾlīf wa Tarjamah wa al-Nashr, 1920).

33. Foucault, *The Order of Things*, 131.

34. In reference to the pond or pool called Khumm, an oasis between Mecca and Medina where the Prophet mentioned his cousin by name as the one to whom Muslims are obliged to show allegiance. Many Sunni sources approved of this hadith as authentic. Specifically, the Prophet raised ʿAlī's hands and made it known that whoever held him, the Prophet, as his master, should hold ʿAlī in the same way.

35. Gran, *Islamic Roots of Capitalism*, 64.

36. See, for example, ʿAbd al-Raḥmān Naṣr al-Dīn al-Shayzarī's (d. 1193) *ḥisbah* manual, in which he was unequivocally against any such mention: in Al-Shayzarī, *The Book of the Islamic Market Inspector*, trans. Buckley. See also al-Musawi, *The Islamic Context of the Thousand and One Nights*, 184–85.

37. See Gran's listing, *Islamic Roots of Capitalism*, 196–208.

38. Sheikh ʿAbd al-Raḥmān al-Jabartī (1753–1825) in *Tārīkh Muddat al-Faransīs bi Miṣr* (Al-Jabartī's *Chronicle of the First Seven Months of the French Occupation of Egypt*), trans. S. Moreh (Leiden: Brill, 1975).

39. Gran, *Islamic Roots of Capitalism*, 181.

40. For more on the Ottoman official stand, see Knysh, *Ibn ʿArabi in the Later Islamic Tradition*, 4.

41. For more, see Heck, *The Construction of Knowledge in Islamic Civilization*.

42. It is customary to speak of rhetoric as summed up in Muḥammad ibn ʿAbd al-Raḥmān al-Qazwīnī's (d. 1338) *Talkhīs al-Miftaḥ*: *ʿilm al-maʿānī* (the science of meanings); *ʿilm al-bayān* (the science of clarity and stylistics, covering tropes); *ʿilm al-badīʿ* (the science of innovation and newness, adornments and figures of speech and figures of expressiveness; i.e., *badīʿ lafẓī* and *badīʿ maʿnawī*). See more in Herbjørn Jenssen, *The Subtleties and Secrets of the Arabic Language*: *Preliminary Investigations into al-Qazwini's Talkhis al-Miftah* (Bergen: Centre for Middle Eastern and Islamic Studies, 1998). For a survey that covers rhetoric but needs more orientation in Arabic criticism, see Philip Halldén, "What Is Arab Rhetoric?" *International Journal of Middle East Studies* 37, no. 1 (February 2005): 19–38.

43. See Makdisi on the defection of Ashʿarī (d. 324/935) to the Ḥanbalite camp, for Aḥmad ibn Ḥanbal "overcame the innovations of innovators, the deviation of deviators." *The Rise of Humanism*, 6.

44. See Makdisi's quotes on who is deemed good enough to read rhetoric and poetry and hence to interpret the Qurʾān. *The Rise of Humanism*, 70, 106–7, 151–52.

45. For a reading that differs from Makdisi's polarized scholasticism and humanism, see Dabashi, *The World of Persian Literary Humanism*, 12–13.

46. For the best documentary record of how his contemporaries thought highly of him, as unprecedented in poetry, see the entry on al-Ḥillī by his contemporary Ṣalāh al-Dīn ibn Aybak al-Ṣafadī, from *Aʿyān al-ʿAṣr* [The Notables of the Age]: *Ṣafī al-Dīn al-Ḥillī*, ed. ʿAdnān Darwīsh (Damascus: Ministry of Culture, 1995), 51. Ibn Qādī Shuhbah quotes many of his contemporaries, adding that he "heard from the imams of *adab* that there are verses in his poetry that are more powerful and better than al-Mutanabbī's. He has unprecedented meanings, and inimitable epistles which nobody can claim crafting their equal. All the learned, notables, and poets admit that he was the poet of the age, an imam in Arabic sciences, language, and epistolary art" (14–15). Al-Ḥillī's ode is basically a contrafaction to al-Būṣīrī's Mantle Ode. See S. Stetkevych, "From Text to Talisman." But al-Ḥillī made it an exercise in language games that excited generations and led to the growth of an amazing field of readability and at times recitation. From Yemen and Morocco to Turkey and India, there are *badīʿiyyāt.* See Abū Zayd, *Al-Badīʿiyyāt fī al-adab al-ʿArabī*, 141–423.

47. See Muhsin al-Musawi, *Reading Iraq* (London: I. B. Tauris, 2006), 63, 164 fn. 108. The verse reads as follows: "White are our deeds (we are good and generous); black are our battles (they make our foes grieve); our fields are green (we are affluent not needy); and our swords are red (we are cavaliers and knights who defeat their enemies)." The poem that opens with a plea for a female addressee to "ask the sharp-edged stout lances of our great feats / and get the attestations of swords if we fail their expectations" refers to the Zawrāʾ battle (Al-Zawrā' is also one of the sobriquets for Baghdad), after his tribe, which made up the population of the city, Ḥilla, rose "like one man" and fought a battle against their enemies, who had killed his uncle in his own mosque. He was among the frontline fighters, and they achieved a glorious victory.

48. Al-Ḥillī mentions that he composed 145 lines with 140 rhetorical devices, but with variants on some, the number reached 151. See al-Ḥillī, *Sharḥ al-kāfiyah al-badīʿiyyah*, 54–55. For more on the definition, see Cachia, *The Arch Rhetorician.*

49. Quoted by Nashāwī in al-Ḥillī, *Sharḥ al-kāfiyah al-badīʿiyyah*, ed. Nashāwī, 3, from Ḥājjī Khalīfah (Kâtip Çelebi), For more, see the latter's *Kashf al-ẓunūn ʿan asāmī al-kutub wa-al-funūn* (The Removal of Doubt from the Names of Books and the Sciences), ed. Gustav Flügel (London: R. Bentley for the Oriental Translation Fund of Great Britain and Ireland, 1835–1858; Beirut: Dār al-Kutub al-ʿIlmiyyah, 2008).

50. See Ibn Ḥijjah, *Khizānat al-adab*, ed. Diyāb, 1:190–208; and Abū Zayd, *Al-Badīʿyyāt fī al-adab al-ʿArabī*, 351–58.

51. For a concordance, see Abū Zayd, *Al Badīʿiyyāt fī al-adab al-ʿArabī*, 351–58.

52. His request to the rulers of Mārdin to be given the job of a chancery scribe was made under duress when he was forced into exile from his hometown.

53. Messick, *The Calligraphic State.*

54. For more on al-Ḥillī's preparation for writing down his book on rhetoric, see his *Sharḥ al-kāfiyah al-badīʿiyyah*, ed. Nashāwī, 51–56.

55. See Ibn Abī al-Iṣbaʿ, *Taḥrīr al-taḥbīr*, ed. Sharaf, 622 (although it means "writing" elegant compositions in Gelder's translation, the implication as rationalized by his editor is "emancipating innovation"). See also van Gelder, "A Good Cause," 230. Cachia translated the term as "fanciful cause," *The Arch Rhetorician*, 96.

56. For an excellent coverage of the book industry, see Makdisi, *The Rise of Humanism*, 49–51, 62–63, 76–78, 244–66.

57. Al-Khwārazmī's full name: Abū ʿAbd Allāh Muḥammad ibn Aḥmad ibn Yūsuf al-Kātib al-Khwārazmī.

58. Majd al-Dīn Fīrūzabādī says: "I met the littérateur and poet Ṣafī al-Dīn in 747 A.H. in Baghdad, who was old then, gifted in poetry and prose and expertise in the sciences of Arabic language and poetry. He was Shīʿī to the core. Whoever would have seen him would never think that he was the same person who was able to produce that poetry which was like pearls still in shells." Quoted in Salīm, *Ṣafī al-Dīn al-Ḥillī*, 79. Salīm also quotes Ṣalāḥ al-Dīn al-Ṣafadī, who holds the poet in high esteem and also mentions him as "kāna Shīʿiyyan" (he was a Shīʿī). One can tell that an exclusive official discourse infiltrated the biographical and literary corpus. Less oriented in this official discourse, Abū Muḥammad al-Ḥasan ibn Ḥabīb al-Ḥalabī (Badr al-Dīn) wrote as follows: "He was the poet of the East, ranked above many predecessors, and demonstrated the limits of the poets of the seven odes [the pre-Islamic Muʿallaqāt]. He excelled in the literary arts and collected the scattered Arab sayings. He was famous everywhere, and his poetry and prose were on everybody's tongue; very well mannered, with an appealing presentation, brilliant conversation, and of great lineage and fame, intelligence and valor." Quoted in Salīm, ibid., 79.

59. See Hirschler, *The Written Word in the Medieval Arabic Lands*, 92–93.

60. Ibid., 41.

61. See Berkey, *Popular Preaching and Religious Authority*, 56–63; also Hirschler, *The Written Word in the Medieval Arabic Lands*, 41–43.

62. Apart from al-Qāḍī al-Fāḍil (ʿAbd al-Raḥīm al-Baysānī) and his popular epistolographic style in his formulary of letters, there are Abū Yaʿqūb al-Sakkākī's *Miftāḥ al-ʿulūm* (Key to the Sciences); Ḍiyāʾ al-Dīn ibn al-Athīr's (d. 637/1239) *Al-Mathal al-sāʾir fī adab al-kātib wa-al-shāʿir* (The Popular Model for the Discipline of Writer and Poet); Shihāb al-Dīn ibn Faḍl Allah al-ʿUmarī's (d. 749/1349) *Al-Taʿrīf bi al-muṣṭalaḥ al-sharīf* (Getting Acquainted with the

Terminology of the Noble Arts); and al-Qalqashandī's (d. 821/1418) *Ṣubḥ al-a'shā fī ṣinā'at al-inshā* (Daylight of the Benighted in the Art of Literary Composition), and so on. See Makdisi, *The Rise of Humanism*, 224. Makdisi also provides a translation of ibn al-Athīr's epistle on the grounding of aspiring scribes, 355–65.

63. See more on the case of the Ḥanbalite scholar Saif al-Dīn al-Amīdī (d. 631/1233), who was sacked from his chair of law, and the requests he received to teach philosophy; in Makdisi, *The Rise of Humanism*, 42–43, 225.

64. See more in C.E. Bosworth, "A Pioneer Arabic Encyclopedia of the Sciences: Al-Khawārizmī's Keys of the Sciences," *Isis* 54, no. 1 (March 1963): 97–111.

65. Quoted in Makdisi, *The Rise of Humanism*, 219–20.

66. Ibid., 223.

67. Early on, since the tenth century, grammar grows into a field of knowledge that is greater than its specific application with respect to the standard use of Arabic. Makdisi writes: "Grammar, a term used to encompass the literary arts including poetry, was an indispensable aid to understanding the language of the Koran and hadith, though subordinate to them and to the law as a subject of the curriculum." *The Rise of Colleges*, 76.

68. Al-Rāzī's book is addressed to the Seljuk vizier Abū al-Ma'ālī Suhail ibn 'Abd al-'Azīz al-Mustawfī. See editor's note in Fakhr al-Dīn al-Rāzī, *Nihāyat al-'ījāz fī dirāyat al-i'jāz* (The Utmost Concision concerning the Knowledge of Inimitability), ed. Nasrullah Hacimuftuoglu (Beirut: Dār Ṣādir, 2004), 24.

69. Al-Sakkākī, *Miftāḥ al-'ulūm* (Key to the Sciences), ed. Zarzūr, 512–13.

70. Ibid.

71. Ibid., 512–23.

72. On the issue of *qiyās* as deductive method, see J. van Ess, "The Logical Structure of Islamic Theology," in *Logic in Classical Islamic Culture*, ed. G.E. von Grunebaum (Wiesbaden: Otto Harrassowitz, 1970), 21–50. It is good to know that *Miftāḥ al-'ulūm* devotes a chapter to poetry and women's sharp wit and wisdom.

73. See, in Sharaf's edition, how ibn Wahb explains the procedures, mechanics, and laws that govern taxation, army organization, scribes in finance and calculus, the state of the police, jurisdiction, writing as inclusive of clarity and mystification as needed, and so forth. Ibn Wahb al-Kātib, *Al-Burhān*, ed. Sharaf, 254–362.

74. For a brief list of these manuals, see Makdisi, *The Rise of Humanism*, 224.

75. Hirschler, *The Written Word in the Medieval Arabic Lands*, 44–46, 50, 110, 139.

76. See ibid., 43–45, 192.

77. Ibid., 66.

78. See Berkey, *Popular Preaching and Religious Authority*, 71, fn. 5–6, and 117; 73, fn. 15, and 118; 75, fn. 24, and 118; Hirschler, *The Written Word in the Medieval Arabic Lands*, 184–85; and Michael Chamberlain, *Knowledge and Social Practice in Medieval Damascus, 1190–1350* (Cambridge: Cambridge University Press, 1994).

79. See Reynolds, "Popular Prose in the Post-Classical Period," 258–59.

80. See Hirschler, *The Written Word in the Medieval Arabic Lands*, 88–89.

81. Ibid., 190–91. See Thomas Bauer, "Ibrahim al-Miʿmar: Ein dichtender Handwerker aus Ägyptens Mamlukenzeit," *ZDMG–Zeitschrift der Deutschen Morgenländischen Gesellschaft* 152 (2002): 63–93.

82. Hirschler, *The Written Word in the Medieval Arabic Lands*, 192.

83. Ibn al-ʾUkhuwwa, *The Maʿālim al-Qurba fī Ṭalab al-Ḥisba*, 86.

84. Ibid., 1–3.

Chapter Six. Disputation in Rhetoric

1. The counternarrative speaks of the Prophet's cousin ʿAlī as the one who taught Abū al-Aswad. See Makdisi, *The Rise of Humanism*, 124, for more on this, as perpetuated in al-Anbārī's chain of authorities.

2. Al-Shaybānī is also known for a commentary on *Al-Ḥamāsah of Abū Tammām*. See Makdisi, *The Rise of Humanism*, 77.

3. Irvine, *The Making of Textual Culture*, 4.

4. Formularies and manuals for scribes and other writers are numerous: Ibn Sahl al-Balkhī (d. 934) writes *Faḍl ṣināʿat al-kitābah* (The Merit of the Craft of Writing); Aḥmad ibn Muḥammad ibn Yūsuf al-ʾIṣfahānī composes, along with *Ṭabaqāt al-khuṭabāʾ* (Classes of Orators), another manual entitled *Kitāb adab al-kuttāb* (Book of Scribal Practice); Aḥmad ibn al-Faḍl al-Ahwāzī contributes *Manāqib al-kuttāb* (Qualities of Secretaries); and Aḥmad ibn Muḥammad al-Naḥḥās al-Miṣrī (d. 337/949) authors *Adab al-kuttāb* (Secretarial Practice). There are also treatises of broader scope, such as Abū Hilāl al-ʿAskarī's (d. ca. 400/1009) *Kitāb al-Ṣinaʿatayn: al-kitāba wa-l-shiʿr* (The Book on the Two Crafts: Prose and Poetry); ʿAlī ibn Khalaf's (d. 455/1063) *Mawādd al-bayān* (Principles of Clarity); and *Kitāb qawānīn al-dawāwīn* (Book of Rules for Diwans) by the Ayyubid minister, al-Asʿad ibn Mammātī (d. 606/1209). By the late thirteenth century, the status of the chancery was so firmly established that ʾUthmān ibn Ibrāhīm al-Nābulusī (d. 685/1286) was able to make the chancery a career, beginning as mamluk to Sultan Najm al-Dīn Ayyūb but soon "honored" with the position of chief secretary in charge of all *dīwāns*.

Al-Akfānī's (d. 749/1348) list of ten disciplines of *adab* reflects Ḍiyā᾽ al-Dīn ibn al-Athīr's (d. 636/1239) list in his scribal training manual, *Al-Mathal al-sā᾽ir fī adab al- kātib wa al-shā῾ir* (The Popular Model for the Practice of Secretaries and Poets), of a number of prerequisites for the aspirant to proficiency in the secretarial art, namely, grammar, syntax, morphology, lexicography, proverbs, and the history of the Arabs and their battles. The tradition of manual composition reached a culminating point in the writings of ῾Abd al-Malik ibn Muḥammad al-Tha῾ālibī (d. 429/1038) in his *Nathr al-naẓm wa-ḥall al-῾iqd* (Prosification of Poetry and the Untying of the Knot), and in Ḍiyā᾽ al-Dīn ibn al-Athīr's *Washy al-marqūm fī ḥall al-manẓūm* (The Embroidered Tapestry in Prosification). Ibn ῾Abd Kān (d. 270/883), head of the first chancery of Aḥmad ibn Ṭūlūn in Egypt, was a pioneer in that his style shows a distinct concentration on syntactical balance via short, terse sentences. Ibn Munjib al-Ṣayrafī (d. 542 or 550/1148 or 1155), chief chancery clerk for the Fatimid caliph al-Ḥāfiẓ, also merits recognition, not only for his *Qānūn dīwān al-rasā᾽il* (The Canon for Chancery) but also for his own mastery of prosification. Ibn Khalaf, whose writings also belong to the Fatimid period, lays emphasis in wording a letter on its value-laden language; as he explains, codes should emerge from the addresser's personal ideology so as to convey its message and impart its full meaning.

5. Toorawa, *Ibn Abī Ṭāhir Ṭayfūr and Arabic Writerly Culture*, 83–84, 60–70, referring to books and paper, respectively.

6. Taqī al-Dīn Abū Bakr ibn ῾Alī Abdullāh ibn Ḥijjah al-Ḥamawī, *Kitāb Qahwat al-inshā᾽*, ed. Rudolf Veselý (Berlin: K. Schwarz; Beirut: Matba᾽at Dirgham, 2005), introduction, 11, 17.

7. Quoted with some editorial changes from Makdisi, *The Rise of Humanism*, 93. Although *adab* was used inclusively to refer to fine writing, refined behavior, command of a literary and cultural repertoire, a multidisciplinary knowledge of language and grammar, and a good literary memory, *ẓarf* is only part of it; hence the *ẓarīf* as refined sociable company can be an *adīb*, but not every *ẓarīf* is so. Wolfhart Heinrichs notices that by the fourth century/tenth century, there are three significations, referring to moral and correct standards; use and practice of literary knowledge; and command of disciplines that fall under this rubric. See W. Heinrichs, "The Classification of the Sciences and the Consolidation of Philology in Classical Islam," in *Centres of Learning: Learning and Location in Pre-Modern Europe and the Near East*, ed. J.W. Drijvers and A.A. MacDonald (Leiden: Brill, 1995), 119–20; also S.A. Bonebakker, "*Adab* and the Concept of Belles-Lettres," in *῾Abbāsid Belles-Lettres*, ed. Julia Ashtiany et al., The Cambridge History of Arabic Literature (Cambridge: Cambridge University Press, 1990), 16–30; and Bo Holmberg, "*Adab* and Arabic Literature," in *Literary*

History: Towards a Global Perspective (Berlin and New York: W. de Gruyter, 2006), 1:180–205.

8. Al-Ṣafadī, *Kitāb al-Ghayth*, 1:12–13. Hereafter cited as *Al-Ghayth.*

9. Ibid., 1:11.

10. According to the narrator:

> It [knowledge] is neither inherited from paternal uncles, nor borrowed from the generous. Therefore I adopted, as a means of attainment thereto, the making of clods a bed, the taking of a stone for a pillow, repelling weariness, braving danger, prolonging vigils, making a companion of travel, much reading and meditation. And I found it to be a thing suitable only for planting, and it is not planted save in the mind. A quarry that is ensnared but rarely and is not caught, save in the breast. A bird that is deluded only by the snaring of the word, and nought catches it but the net of memory. Therefore I laid it upon my soul and confined it within my eye. I spent my means, but stored my mind. I wrote elegantly by virtue of much reading, and passed on from reading to investigation and from investigation to composition, and I relied therein on divine guidance.

Al-Hamadhānī, *The Maqāmāt of Badīʿal-Zamān al-Hamadhānī*, trans. Prendergast (1915), 153. http://www.sacred-texts.com/isl/mhm/mhm48.htm.

11. Ibn al-Jawzī, *Ṣayd al-khāṭir*, 212–13.

12. Ibid., 214.

13. Ibid., 260.

14. Ibid., 268.

15. See al-Musawi, "Vindicating a Profession or a Personal Career?"

16. See Brugman, *An Introduction to the History of Modern Arabic Literature in Egypt*, 98–99; and al-Musawi, *Islam on the Street*, 226.

17. Foucault, *The Order of Things*, 43.

18. Ibid., 44.

19. *Al-Ghayth*, 1:79, 80–81, 83, 75, and 103.

20. Ibid., 1:104.

21. Jamāl al-Dīn ibn Nubātah, *Sarḥ al-ʿuyūn fi sharḥ risālat ibn Zaydūn* (Roaming Gently in the Explication of the Epistle of ibn Zaydūn), ed. Muḥammad Abū al-Faḍl Ibrāhīm (Beirut/Ṣaydā: Al-Maktabah al-ʿAṣriyyah, 1986), 226–31.

22. The specific application of the term to a rejection of the rightly guided caliphs has nothing to do with Shīʿism, for ʿAlī recognized the problem but refused to make an issue of it.

23. See the biography of ibn Manẓūr, written by Amīn Muḥammad ʿAbd al-Wahhāb and Muḥammad al-Ṣādiq al-ʿUbaidī, in *Lisān al-ʿArab*, 1:9–10. Both al-Ṣafadī and al-Suyūṭī are quoted, along with others.

24. Ibn al-Jawzī, *Ṣayd al-khātir*, 257–58.

25. Al-Mālikī, *Ḥilyat al-kuramāʾ wa-bahjat al-nudamāʾ*, 55–56.

26. Ibn Daqīq's full name is Shaykh Taqī al-Dīn Abū al-Fatḥ Muḥammad al-Qushayrī. The lyric was reported as an authorized audition by the hadith scholar Abū al-Fatḥ ibn Sayyid al-Nās. Al-Ṣafadī got it directly from the latter; *Al-Ghayth*, 1:105.

27. The full name of Shaykh ʿAbd al-Ghanī al-Maqdisī is Taqī al-Dīn Abū Muḥammad b. ʿAbd al-Wāḥid b. ʿAlī (ca. 541–600/1146–1204).

28. *Al-Ghayth*, 1:105–6. In his short essay entitled *Tuḥfat al-Mujtahidīn bi Asmāʾ Mujaddidīn* (The Gem of the Striving Scholars: The Names of the Renewers of Religion), al-Suyūṭī listed the Renewers as follows: first century: ʿUmar ibn ʿAbd al-ʿAzīz; second century: al-Shāfiʿī; third century: Ibn Surayj and al-Ashʿarī; fourth century: al-Bāqillānī, Sahl al-Suʿlūkī, and Abū Hāmid al-Isfarāyīnī; fifth century: al-Ghazālī; sixth century: al-Fakhr al-Rāzī and Abū al-Qāsim al-Rāfiʿī; seventh century: Ibn Daqīq al-ʿĪd; eighth century: al-Bulqīnī and al-ʿIrāqī; ninth century: Taqī al-Dīn Abū Muḥammad b. ʿAḍud al-Dīn al-ʾIjī and ʿAbd al-Wāḥid b. ʿAlī, etc.

29. Ebrahim Moosa, *Ghazālī and the Poetics of Imagination* (Chapel Hill: University of North Carolina Press, 2005), 30, 35–38.

30. *Al-Ghayth*, 1:105.

31. Ibid., 1:115–18.

32. Ibid., 1:197–201.

33. In ibid., 1:211. Al-Ṣafadī refers to this borrowing in his discussion of figures of speech, images, and so on.

34. See ibn Ḥijjah, *Khizānat al-adab*, 3:498, for an example of getting material incorporated.

35. *Al-Ghayth*, 1:206–7.

36. Ibid., 1:258–59.

37. Fakhr al-Dīn al-Rāzī, *Muḥaṣṣal afkār al-mutaqaddimīn wa al-mutaʾakhkhirīn min al-ʿulamāʾ wa-al-ḥukamāʾ wa-al-mutakallimīn* (Harvest of the Thought of the Ancients and Moderns from Scholars, Philosophers, and Theologians), ed. Ṭāhā A. [Abd al-Raʾūf] Saʿd (Cairo: Maktabat al-Kulliyāt al-Azhariyyah, 1978); and, incorporated in the same volume, Naṣīr al-Dīn al-Ṭūsī, *Talkhīṣ al-muḥaṣṣal* (The Summa of the Harvest), ed. Ṭāhā A. Saʿd (Cairo: Maktabat al-Kulliyāt al-Azhariyyah, 1978).

38. See, for example, al-Ṭūsī on the philosophers' and theologians' views on the difference between "knowledge of God" by reasoning or by obligation, *Talkhīṣ al-muḥaṣṣal*, 47–49.

39. The two schools in speculative theology, Muʿtazalites and Ashʿarites, have many things in common, and their differences are only a few, but these

differences are philosophically dividing. The early Muʿtazilites include Wāṣil ibn ʿAṭṭāʾ (d. 131/748), ʿAmr ibn ʿUbayd (d. 145/762), Abū al-Huthayl al-ʿAllāf (d. 227/841), Ibrāhīm ibn Sayyār al-Naẓẓām (d. between 220/835 and 230/845), and al-Jāḥiẓ (d. 255/868). Although much of their thought has been lost, extant material is preserved in their opponents' rejoinders and also by some of the later Muʿtazilite thinkers, such as Abū al-Ḥusayn al-Khayyāt (d. 300/912), Abū al-Qāsim al-Balkhī (d. 319/931), Abū ʿAlī al-Jibāʾī (d. 303/915), and his son Abū Hāshim (d. 321/933). Following them were Abū Rashīd al-Naisābūrī (d. 415/1024) and al-Qāḍī ʿAbd al-Jabbār al-Hamadānī (d. 415/1024) and his student Aḥmad ibn Mattawayh (d. 450/1060). The Ashʿarite school is named after Abū al-Ḥasan al-Ashʿarī (d. 324/935), who broke away from the Muʿtazilites. Prominent among them were Abū Bakr al-Bāqillānī (d. 403/1012), Abū al-Maʿālī al-Juwainī (d. 478/1085), and al-Ghazālī (d. 505/1111).

40. See al-Rāzī's *Muḥaṣṣal* and al-Ṭūsī's commentary: *Talkhīṣ al-muḥaṣṣal*, 58–59, 97–98, 112–13, 132–33, 138–39, 208–9, 240–42 (al-Ṭūsī's commentary incorporates al-Rāzī's *Muḥaṣṣal*).

41. Editor's (Ṭāhā A. Saʿd) introduction, Al-Ṭūsī, *Talkhīṣ al-muḥaṣṣal*, 11–12.

42. We know that al-Ṭūsī, for example, who perhaps resembled ibn Sīnā in keeping a record of his early grounding, studied philosophy with Farīd al-Dīn Ḍamad in Nishapur and mathematics with Muḥammad Ḥasīb; he attended the debates and lectures of Qutb al-Dīn al-Miṣrī; and he met the Sufi master Farīd al-Dīn al-ʿAṭṭār (killed by the Mongol invaders). He traveled to Mosul, where he studied astronomy with Kamāl al-Dīn Yūnus; and he met and studied with many other scholars and scientists. See editor's introduction to al-Ṭūsī's *Talkhīs al-Muhaṣṣal.*

43. "Already the teachers of dogma, sensing their inability to add anything original to the mass of dialectic in defense of orthodoxy, had begun to make commentaries on statements of faith and articles of belief." See Earl Edgar Elder, trans. with introd. and notes, *A Commentary on the Creed of Islam: Saʿd al-Dīn al-Taftazānī on the Creed of Najm al-Dīn al-Nasafī* (New York: Columbia University Press, 1950), xvi.

44. See *Al-Ghayth*, 1:204.

45. See, for example, the selections that al-Ṣafadī makes in his *Al-Ghayth*, 1:204–7.

46. Ibid., 1:207–11.

47. Ibid., 1:245.

48. See ibid., 1:245–47.

49. For a concise reading of the difference between Ashʿarites and Muʿtazilites on this matter, see al-Rāzī's *Muḥaṣṣal* and al-Ṭūsī's response, *Talkhīṣ al-*

muḥaṣṣal. Both provide significant insights that also define the departure in Ashʿarite theology from the Muʿtazilites; see *Talkhīṣ al-muḥaṣṣal*, 47, 58–59, 112–13, 132–33, 138–39.

50. For a brief survey and study of *kalām* and its application to physical theory, see Alnoor Dhanani, *Physical Theory of Kalam* (Leiden: Brill, 1994), 6–7. See also his "Kalām, Atoms and Epicurean Minimal Parts," in *Tradition, Transmission, Transformation*, ed. Jamil F. Ragep and Sally P. Ragep (Leiden: Brill, 1996), 157–71. In the consideration of things and their properties, the question is what is accidental and what is indivisible. Three positions developed among speculative theologians: Abū ʿAmr Ḥafṣ al-Fard (d. 195/810), Ḍirār ibn ʿAmr (d. 200/815), and al-Ḥusayn al-Najjār (d. 230/845) postulated that accidents *(aʿrāḍ)* define the world. Hishām ibn al-Ḥakam (d. 179/795), Abū Bakr ʿAbd al-Raḥmān b. Kaysān al-Aṣamm (d. 201/817), Ibrāhīm ibn Sayyār al-Naẓẓām (d. between 220/835 and 230/845), and his followers believed that the created world consisted of bodies. Other theologians thought that the created world is constituted of combined corporeal atoms and incorporeal accidents, which inhere in atoms. Based on Alnoor Dhanani's reading, Muzaffar Iqbal concludes: "This atomistic doctrine was a totally independent development in the Islamic intellectual thought, without any links to the Greek Atomism for there is no mention of any Greek texts having been translated at this early stage." Muzaffar Iqbal, *Islam and Science* (Aldershot, Hampshire: Ashgate Publishing, 2002), 32–33.

51. In Kamāl al-Dīn Maytham ibn ʿAlī al-Baḥrānī (d. 679/1280), *Qawāʿid al-marām fī ʿilm al-kalām* (The Orderly Principles in the Science of Theological Reasoning) (Qum: Mihr Press, 1977), 41, the revisionist reading of predecessors surveys and adds to or emends this account. Hence, the created, or *muḥdath*, is either existing in space and time, or coexisting with it, or coexisting with neither. In the last case it is indivisible and cannot accept division. This is the *jawhar al-fard*.

52. Abū al-Maʿālī ʿAbd al-Malik ibn ʿAbdullāh al-Juwaynī, *Al-Shāmil fī ʾuṣūl al-dīn* (The Comprehensive in the Principles of Religion) (Alexandria: Al-Maʿarif, 1969), 159.

53. For a general view of education and science, see Toby Huff, *The Rise of Early Modern Science: Islam, China, and the West* (Cambridge: Cambridge University Press, 2003), 149–200. On al-Sharīf al-Jurjānī, see Jamil F. Ragep, "Freeing Astronomy from Philosophy: An Aspect of Islamic Influence on Science," *Osiris*, 2nd ser., 16, Science in Theistic Contexts: Cognitive Dimensions (2001): 55–57. Al-ʾIjī (or, al-Ījī) and al-Jurjānī are quoted by Ragep, 55 and 57, respectively.

54. ʿAbd Allāh ibn Muslim ibn Qutaybah, *Adab al-kātib* (Beirut: Al-Maktabah al-ʿAṣriyyah, 2002), 14–15.

55. Ibid., 15.

56. Ibid., 16.

57. The increasing use of the terms in literary debates, outside speculative theology, is noticeable, as in the MS *Al-Jawhar al-fard fi mufakharat al-narjis wa-al-ward* (The Unique Gem on the Rivalry of the Narcissus and the Rose), ed. Ibtisām Marhūn al-Ṣaffār, a series of poems probably by Abū al-Ḥasan ʿAlī ibn al-Musharraf Mārdīnī (fl. 1442); identification of author made from comparison of openings with those in Berlin MS Pet. 654, fols. 79b–83a, and Berlin MS Mf. 1178, fols. 85b–87a, where the author is given as al-Maridini (see Berlin entry nos. 8439 and 6111). Ibtisām Marhūn al-Ṣaffār mentions that document (but obviously did not publish it).

58. *Al-Ghayth*, 1:249–51.

59. Ibid., 1:392–93.

60. Ibid.

61. Ibn Khaldūn (d. 808/1406), writing about the scholastic theology of his time, bemoaned its decline from its exalted position of the past. "It had once been useful in repulsing heretics and innovators in their attacks on the faith, but they had passed from the scene of action. During this period of impending decline philosophy took the brunt of the attack in place of the Muʿtazilite doctrines. However, the writers rehashed the arguments of the past and were not at all timid about beating the dead horse of Muʿtazilitism." Cited by Elder, *A Commentary on the Creed of Islam*, xvi.

62. *Al-Ghayth*, 2:436–37.

63. Ibid., 2:24–25.

64. Ibid., 2:51–55.

65. Al-Ṣafadī provides a summary of the Muʿtazilite philosophy, and the burgeoning of the school following Wāṣil ibn ʿAṭā's departure from al-Ḥasan al-Baṣrī's assembly and the consequent rift between its proponents and Abū al-Ḥasan al-Ashʿarī. See ibid., 2:51–55. He also lists the names of the prominent figures and notables in the school, 2:55.

66. Ibid., 1:80. Perhaps al-Ṣafadī had in mind al-Ashʿarī's *Al-Ibānah fī uṣūl al-diyānah*; see ʿAlī ibn Ismāʿīl al-Ashʿarī, *Al-Ibānah fī uṣūl al-diyānah* (The Elucidation of Islam's Foundation); a translation, with introduction and notes by Walter C. Klein (New Haven: American Oriental Society, 1940; repr., New York: Kraus, 1967).

67. *Al-Ghayth*, 1:81–82.

68. Ibn Nubātah, *Sarḥ*, 328.

69. Carter, "Language Control as People Control in Medieval Islam," 72.

Chapter Seven. Translation, Theology, and the Institutionalization of Libraries

1. *Al-Ghayth*, 1:79.

2. Ibid.

3. Taqī al-Dīn ibn Taymiyyah, *Majmūʿ Fatāwā ibn Taymiyyah* (Ribat: Maktabat al-Maʿārif, n.d.), 9:6.

4. M.G. Carter's citation, in "Language Control as People Control in Medieval Islam," 72; ibn Qutaybah, *Adab al-kātib*, ed. M.M. ʿAbd al-Ḥamīd (Cairo: Al-Maktabah al-Tijāriyyah al-Kubrā, 1963), 4.

5. Ibn Nubātah, *Sarḥ*, 326.

6. Al-Khalīl ibn Aḥmad was a renowned Arab philologist who is credited with authoring and compiling the first lexicon, *al-ʿAyn*, and also the first codification and formulation of Arabic prosody.

7. Ibn Nubātah, *Sarḥ*, 326–27.

8. See ibid., 213. Rosenthal's source gives a larger context; see his *The Classical Heritage in Islam*, 48–49.

9. Both translators followed translations from Greek into Syriac and from Syriac into Arabic. See D.M. Dunlop, "The Translation of al-Bitriq and Yahya (Yuhanna) b. al-Batriq," *Journal of the Royal Asiatic Society* (1959): 140–50. For more on translations from Greek, see Dimitri Gutas, *Greek Thought, Arabic Culture: The Graeco-Arabic Translation Movement in Baghdad and Early ʿAbbāsid Society (2nd–4th/8th–10th Centuries)* (London and New York: Frances and Taylor, 1998).

10. Al-ʿAbbās ibn Saʿīd al-Jawharī was a conspicuous presence during the caliph al-Maʾmūn's reign (813–833) and was one of the court astronomers and astrologers.

11. *Al-Ghayth*, 1:79. It is noticeable that the author moves freely between translation, transference, and Arabization, unlike al-Jāḥiẓ, who is meticulous in his terminology. Rosenthal uses "translation" as the defining term for all styles; see *The Classical Heritage in Islam*, 17.

12. For more, see Devin J. Stewart, "Bahāʾ al-Dīn al-ʿĀmilī," in *Essays in Arabic Literary Biography, 1350–1850*, 27–48.

13. Sulayman Khaṭṭār al-Bustānī, *Ilyādhat Hūmīrūs: muʿrrabah naẓman wa-ʿalayhā sharḥ tarīkhī adabī* (Miṣr: Al-Hilāl, 1904; repr., Suese: Dār a-Maʿārif, n.d.), 2 vols., 1:75–76.

14. See S. Stetkevych, *Abū Tammām and the Poetics of the ʿAbbāsid Age*, 16–17; quotations with slight changes. A direct quotation is also given above, n. 89, ch. 3.

15. See Adamson, *The Arabic Plotinus*, 36–37, 46–47.

16. On the problems and anxieties attending smooth, almost native, translation, see Lawrence Venuti, *The Scandals of Translation: Towards an Ethics of Difference* (London: Routledge, 1998), 184.

17. Ibn Manẓūr, *Lisān al-ʿArab*, 1:18.

18. D. S. Margoliouth's translation is used: Margoliouth, "The Discussion between Abu Bishr Matta and Abu Saʿid al-Sirafi on the Merits of Logic and Grammar."

19. Ibid., 118.

20. Ibid., 80.

21. Makdisi, *The Rise of Colleges*, 75.

22. Moosa, *Ghazālī and the Poetics of Imagination*, 76–77.

23. Tāj al-Dīn al-Subkī, *Ṭabaqāt al-shāfiʿyyah al-kubrā*, 10 vols. (Cairo: Dār Iḥyāʾ al-Kutub al-ʿArabiyyah; ʿĪsā Bābī al-Ḥalabī, 1976), 7:227.

24. ʿAbd al-Raḥmān ibn Khaldūn, *Al-Muqaddima* (Beirut: Dār al-Kutub al-ʿIlmiyyah, 1993), 403. In Rosenthal's translation, there are passages in which ibn Khaldūn condemns the confusion between logic and philosophy and speaks of this as pernicious. See Franz Rosenthal, *The Muqaddimah: An Introduction to History* (Princeton: Princeton University Press, 2005), 353, 390, esp. 405.

25. Ibn Khaldūn states, "I found in Egypt numerous works on the intellectual sciences composed by the well-known person Saʿd al-Dīn al-Taftazānī, a native of Herāt, one of the villages of Khurāsān. Some of them are on *kalām* and the foundations of *fiqh* and rhetoric, which show that he had a profound knowledge of these sciences. Their contents demonstrate that he was well versed in the philosophical sciences and far advanced in the rest of the sciences which deal with Reason." Elder, *A Commentary on the Creed of Islam*, xxi.

26. Since this study is not concerned with monographic contributions, but rather with encyclopedic and compendious ones that demonstrate a field of discussion, I leave out the former. There are, however, monographs on *kalām* that tell us more about the undying activity. See, for example, al-Baḥrānī's (d. 679/1280) *Qawāʿid al-marām fī ʿilm al-kalām* (The Orderly Principles in the Science of Theological Reasoning).

27. For a concise description of book manufacturing, copying, and dictation, see Makdisi, *The Rise of Humanism*, 262–71.

28. See more on this point in George N. Atiyeh, ed., *The Book in the Islamic World* (Albany: State University of New York Press, 1995), xiv. Primary notes are in al-Khaṭīb al-Baghdādī, *Taqyīd al-ʿilm*, ed. Youssef Eche (Yusuf al-ʿIshsh) (Damascus: Al-Maʿhad al-Faransī, 1949; repr. 1975). For more, see Franz Rosenthal, " 'Of Making Many Books There Is No End': The Classical Muslim View," in *The Book in the Islamic World*, ed. Atiyeh, 33–56; Toorawa, *Ibn Abī Ṭāhir Ṭayfūr and Arabic Writerly Culture*, 13–15, 26–27, 32–33.

29. See Rosenthal, "'Of Making Many Books There Is No End,'" 36, citing ibn Qayyim al-Jawziyyah, *al-Ṭuruq al-ḥukmiyyah*. See also Abd al-Hamid K.M.H. al-Shaiji, "Critical Study and Edition of Al-Turuq al-Hukmiyya fi-i-Siyasa al-Sharʿiyya of Imam Shams al-Din b. Muhammad b. Abu Bakr Ibn Qayyim al-Jawziyya," PhD diss., University of Wales, Lampeter, 2001.

30. Adamson's translation, *The Arabic Plotinus*, 36.

31. On occasions, the poet in his capacity as the "scribe of the scroll" or epistolographer, for instance, can either read in public or, when not present himself, request that his writing be read. When Abū Bakr ibn Ḥijjah al-Ḥamawī was in the company of the Sultan Shaykh al-Maḥmūdī (al-Malik al-Muʾayyad) in his journey to Byzantium, he wrote an epistle describing the journey, requesting the king to have it sent to Cairo and to be read in public in the Muʾayyadī Mosque and al-Azhar by no less than the Chief Justice ibn Ḥajar al-ʿAsqalānī (d. AH 816). See Kawkab Diyāb's reference to ibn Taghrī Bīrdī, in ibn Ḥijjah, *Khizānat al-adab*, ed. Diyāb, 1:32.

32. This is very close in practice to Badīʿ al-Zamān al-Hamadhānī's use of poetry in prose in his epistles to al-Khwārazmī, which al-Qalqashandī singles out as examples of *fann al-imtizāj*. See al-Qalqashandī, *Ṣubḥ al-aʿshā*, 1:280. See also Vahid Behmardi, "Rhetorical Values in Buyid Persia According to Badiʿ al-Zaman al-Hamadhani," in *The Weaving of Words: Approaches to Classical Arabic Prose*, ed. Lale Behzadi and Vahid Behmardi (Beirut: Orient-Institut-Verlag, 2009), 155. For an early study of this style, see Wolfhart Heinrichs, "Prosimetrical Genres in Classical Arabic Literature," in *Prosimetrum: Cross-Cultural Perspectives on Narrative in Prose and Verse*, ed. Joseph Harris and Karl Reichl (Cambridge: D.S. Brewer, 1997), 249–76.

33. The term *grammatica* is equivalent to *adab* and *studia adabiya*, inclusive of: 1. philology (grammar, lexicography, along with *naḥw* and *lughah*, i.e., grammar and language); 2. *shiʿr*, inclusive of the sciences of metrics and rhyme; 3. rhetoric: inclusive of all that pertains to eloquence and can apply to oratory, speech, writing and letter writing or the epistolary art; 4. history: including ancient genealogies, tribal times, historiographical archive, chronicles, and classification of groups and societies; 5. moral philosophy, embracing rules, regulations, governance, description of specific posts and occupations, guiding ethics, and so forth. See Makdisi, *The Rise of Humanism*, 121. If we understand by rhetoric also its inclusion of *al-madhhab al-kalāmī* (analogical or speculative reasoning), as emanating from al-Jāḥiẓ's Muʿtazilite background and permeating the *badīʿ* tradition thereafter, then *jadal* becomes part and parcel of *adab*, too. In this sense, *adab* comprises the otherwise triple arts of discourse in Latin: grammatica, rhetorica, and dialectica. See Irvine, *The Making of Textual Culture*, 7.

34. These include works by Muḥammad ibn ʿAbd al-Raḥmān Jalāl al-Dīn al-Qazwīnī (d. 724/1338) in his *Talkhīṣ* (Resumé), and Saʿd al-Dīn Masʿūd al-Taftazānī (d. 791/1389) in his *Mukhtaṣar* (Condensation).

35. See ʿAbd al-Qāhir al-Jurjānī, *Dalāʾil al-iʿjāz*, ed. Yāsīn al-Ayyūbī (Beirut/Ṣaydā: Al-Maktabah al-ʿAṣriyyah, 2002), 304.

36. See Makdisi, *The Rise of Colleges*, 76–77.

37. D. Latham's translation, in "The Beginnings of Arabic Prose Literature: The Epistolary Genre," in *Arabic Literature to the End of the Umayyad Period*, ed. A. F. L. Beeston et al. (Cambridge: Cambridge University Press, 1983), 167.

38. Ibid.

39. See Heck, *The Construction of Knowledge in Islamic Civilization*, 12; and Irvine, *The Making of Textual Culture*, 7–8.

40. Irvine, *The Making of Textual Culture*, 5.

41. Ibn al-Muqaffaʿ, "Al-Durrah al-yatīmah" (The Solitary Gem), in *Rasāʾil al-bulaghāʾ* (Epistles of the Rhetoricians), ed. Muḥammad Kurd ʿAlī (Cairo: Dār al-Kutub al-ʿArabīyah al-Kubrā, 1913).

42. For more on libraries as state institutions in early Islamic history, see Makdisi, *The Rise of Colleges*, 24–27.

43. In al-Ṣābīʾ's letter, after enumerating the responsibilities of the "writers of prose," he concludes: "The craft of writing has marked them with its honor and its occupation of the rank of rulers, for theirs is a towering importance in accordance with the lofty stature which they attain." See Heck, *The Construction of Knowledge in Islamic Civilization*, 18 (fn. 36), 19.

44. Ibid. For more on specific registers, see C. E. Bosworth, "Abū ʿAbdallāh al-Khawārazmī on the Technical Terms of the Secretary's Art," *Journal of the Economic and Social History of the Orient* 12 (1969): 113–64; C. E. Bosworth, "The Terminology of the History of the Arabs in the Jahiliyya according to al-Khwārazmī's 'Keys of the Sciences,'" in *Studies in Judaism and Islam*, ed. S. Morag et al. (Jerusalem: Magnes Press, Hebrew University, 1981), 27–43; Heinrichs, "The Classification of the Sciences"; also Carter, "Language Control as People Control in Medieval Islam"; and Bakar, *The Classification of Knowledge in Islam*.

45. Heinrichs, "The Classification of the Sciences."

46. See Heck, *The Construction of Knowledge in Islamic Civilization*, 20, fn. 40 (Heck's phrasing).

47. See ibn Wahb al-Kātib, *Al-Burhān fī wujūh al-bayān* (Demonstrating the Modes of Eloquent Expression), ed. Aḥmad Maṭlūb and Khadījah al-Ḥadīthī (Baghdad: Baghdad University Publication, 1967), 191–245; on speech, including solecism and incorrect usage, 246–64.

48. See Qalqīlah, *Al-Naqd al-adabī fi al-ʿaṣr al-Mamlūkī*, 56.

49. Al-Ḥillī, *Sharḥ al-kāfiyah al-badīʿiyyah*, 356.

50. See, for example, his discussion of poetry: al-Jurjānī, *Dalāʾil al-iʿjāz*, 166, 169, etc.

51. Al-Jurjānī argues: "Individual words, which are conventional elements of language, have not been created in order that what they represent may itself be discovered or known, but in order that they may be joined one with another, thus expressing, by their inter-relations, valuable information. This is an honorable science and a great foundation principle. What proves (the validity) of this principle is that if we alleged that individual words . . . were invented so that the identity of what they symbolize may be known, it would lead to an undoubted absurdity." Kamal Abū Deeb's translation, in Abu Deeb, *Al-Jurjani's Theory of Poetic Imagery*, 37.

52. Ibid., 42.

53. The book is addressed to the Seljuk *wāzīr* Abū al-Maʿālī Suhail ibn ʿAbd al-ʿAzīz al-Mustawfī. See editor's note, in al-Rāzī, *Nihāyat al-ʾījāz fī dirāyat al-iʿjāz*, 24.

54. *Ṣarrafa*: manage, or direct (*Laqad ṣarrafnā li-l-nāsī fī hādhā ʾl-Qurʾāni min kulli mathal* [Qurʾān, 17:89]; we provided and directed in this Qurʾān a medley of examples), or from *inṣarafa*: (*Thumma inṣarafū ṣarafa Allāhu qulūbahum* [Qurʾān, 9:127]; they withheld, God diverted their hearts).

55. Fakhr al-Dīn al-Rāzī also alludes to that point in *Muḥaṣṣal*, inviting al-Ṭūsī's response thereafter: see al-Ṭūsī, *Talkhīṣ al-muḥaṣṣal*, 208.

56. See Abu Deeb's quotes and comments, *Al-Jurjani's Theory of Poetic Imagery*, 67, 155, 167, 313. Al-Jurjānī argues in *Asrār al-balāghah*: "It has been shown that *istiʿārah* is based on transferring a word, which is conventionally set to designate a particular referent, to apply it to another referent, on the condition previously made. This criterion does not apply to *tamthīl*, which has been defined as a relation of similarity revealed [between an object and] a unified group of other objects" (155).

57. On the use of *majāz* in exegesis, see J. Wansbrough, "Majāz al-Qurʾān: Periphrastic Exegesis," *Bulletin of the School of Oriental and African Studies* 33 (1970): 247–66.

58. Al-Qalqashandī, *Ṣubḥ al-aʿshā*, 1:38; 11:148–49.

59. Ibn Ḥijjah, *Khizānat al-adab*, 3:333–34.

60. See ibid., 3:365–66. The double entendre for ibn Ḥijjah is a shared meaning between two terms: one of them is approximate and "its verbal signification is conspicuous, and the other is remote and the verbal referent is concealed. The speaker intends the remote but implies it in the approximate, hence deluding the listener that what is meant is the approximate; but it is not so. This

is why this figure is called delusion or elusion." He goes on to define four types of the double entendre. See ibid., 3:533–34.

61. They are: Ṣalāh al-Dīn al-Ṣafadī, Zayn al-Dīn ibn al-Wardī, Burhān al-Dīn al-Qīrāṭī, Shams al-Dīn b. al-Sāyigh, Badr al-Dīn b. al-Sāḥib, Shihāb al-Dīn b. Abī Ḥijlah, Ibrāhīm al-Muʿmār, Badr al-Dīn Ḥasan al-Zagharī al-Ghizzī, Yaḥyā al-Khabbāz al-Ḥamawī, and Shihāb al-Dīn al-Ḥalabī.

62. Ibn Ḥijjah, *Khizānat al-adab*, 3:66–68.

63. Ibid., 3:521.

64. Ibid., 3:335.

65. See ibid., 3:324–34.

66. See al-Sakhāwī, *Al-Ḍawʾ al-lāmiʿ*, 11:144. For Shams al-Dīn al-Nawājī, see his *Al-Ḥujjah fī sariqāt ibn Ḥijjah*.

67. Ibn al-ʿAṭṭār's compilation is entitled *Ḥawāʾij al-ʿAṭṭār fī ʿiqr al-ḥimār* (Al-ʿAṭṭār's Goods in the Donkey's Stable); ibn al-Kharrāṭ's verse is in *Ṣawṭ al-ʿAdhāb ʿalā sharr al-dawāb* (The Whip of Torture on the Worst of Brutes), mentioned by Kawkab Diyāb: see Diyāb's introduction, in ibn Ḥijjah, *Khizānat al-adab*, 1:52, where references are made to primary and secondary sources.

68. See Qalqīlah, *Al-Naqd al-adabī fi al-ʿaṣr al-Mamlūkī*, 151.

69. See ibn Ḥijjah, *Khizānat al-adab*, 1:382.

70. See Muḥammad ibn Qāsim ibn Zākūr al-Fāsī, *Al-Ṣanīʿ al-Badīʿ fi sharḥ al-ḥilyat dhāt al-badīʿ* (The Inventive Craftsmanship in Explicating the Innovative Adornment), ed. Bushrā al-Badāwī (Rabat: Muhammad V University, diss. 53; 2001), 46.

71. See ibid., 52–54.

72. Ibid.

73. See al-Ḥillī, *Sharḥ al-kāfiyah al-badīʿiyyah*, 54.

74. See S. Stetkeyvch, "From Jahiliyya to Badīʿiyyah."

75. See Qalqīlah, *Al-Naqd al-adabī fi al-ʿaṣr al-Mamlūkī*, 151, 428–36.

76. Al-Ḥillī, *Sharḥ al-kāfiyah al-badīʿiyyah*, 55.

77. See Irvine's reading of medieval Europe, *The Making of Textual Culture*, 14.

78. S. Stetkevych, "From Text to Talisman"; also in *The Mantle Odes*, 70–150.

79. Irvine, for example, recounts Bede's story in his *Historia ecclesiastica*, in which the illiterate Caedmon "had night-duty, and has a vision in his sleep. In his dream Caedmon is instructed to sing the *principium creaturarum*, the first event in the master narrative of sacred history, the poem which he remembers . . . and recites the next day for the rest of the community." *The Making of Textual Culture*, 433.

80. Al-Ḥillī, *Sharḥ al-kāfiyah al-badīʿiyyah*, 54.

81. Ibid., 55.

82. Suzanne P. Stetkevych, *The Poetics of Islamic Legitimacy* (Bloomington: Indiana University Press, 2002), 191; and see her "From Jahiliyya to Badīʿiyyah."

83. S. Stetkevych, *The Poetics of Islamic Legitimacy*, 191.

84. For a good survey of these odes, see ʿAlī Abū Zayd, *Al-Badīʿyyāt fī al-adab al-ʿArabī*, 351–58.

85. Ibid.

Chapter Eight. Professions in Writing

1. Casanova, *The World Republic of Letters*, 104–5, 224–25.

2. Haarmann, "Arabic in Speech, Turkish in Lineage." In this sense, the fact that a few Mamluk sultans—including al-Ẓāhir Rukn al-Dīn Baybars al-Bundukdārī (d. 658/1260), Manṣūr Sayf al-Dīn Qalāwūn (d. 678/1279), Naṣīr al-Dīn Muḥammad ibn Qalāwūn (d. 693/1293), Ashraf ʿAlāʾ al-Dīn Qujuq (d. 742/1341), al-Ẓāhir Sayf al-Dīn Barqūq (d. 784/1382), Ashraf Sayf al-Dīn Qāytbāy (d. 873/1468), and Ashraf Qanṣūwah al-Ghūrī (d. 906/1500)—paid great attention to knowledge and notable scholars should not serve as our only yardstick.

3. See, for instance, B. Amīn, *Muṭālaʿāt fī al-shiʿr al-Mamlūkī wa-al-ʿUthmānī*, 59.

4. Ibid., 44.

5. Ibid., 40–41.

6. Ibid.

7. Ibid., 43.

8. Along with ibn Ḥijjah's *Khizānat al-adab*, we have also *Silk al-durrar* by Muḥammad al-Murādī, *Khulāṣat al-athar* by al-Muḥibbī, and so on.

9. The reference is to the pre-Islamic poet al-Nābighah al-Dhubiyānī, whose real name was Ziyād ibn Muʿāwiyah (535–604).

10. B. Amīn draws on the comparison without going into the implication, in *Muṭālaʿāt fī al-shiʿr al-Mamlūkī wa-al-ʿUthmānī*, 95. I am indebted to him for his documentary survey of Mamluk and Ottoman poetry.

11. The art goes back to Abū Maʿshar al-Falakī (Latinized: Albumasar, Albusar; d. 886). In his books on astrology, he develops a numerologist system whereby each letter corresponds to a number.

12. Jalāl al-Dīn al-Suyūṭī (d. 911/1505) dwells on this in his *Al-Muzhir fī ʿulūm al-lughah* (The Luminous Work Concerning the Sciences of Language and Its Subfields), 2 vols. in one (Beirut: Al-Maktabah al-ʿAṣriyyah, 2004), 2:257–65.

13. On ibn Maʿṣūm, see Lowry's entry on him in *Essays in Arabic Literary Biography, 1350–1850*, 175–84.

14. Ibid., 172–74. ʿAlī ibn Aḥmad ibn Maʿṣūm's (d. 1130/1707) work *Sulāfat al-ʿaṣr fi maḥāsin ahl al-ʿaṣr* also occurs under other titles (*Fī maḥāsin ʿayān miṣr* and *Fī maḥāsin al-shuʿarāʾ bi-kull miṣr*). The title *Sulāfat al-ʿaṣr* means precedence in time; its opposite, *dhuʾābat*, means dregs or the dying end of a candle or torch; it may also refer to the essence of pressed wine-grapes.

15. The author's full name is Abū Bakr Muḥammad ibn al-Ḥasan al-Azdī ibn Durayd: *Kitāb al-Malāḥin*, ed. ʿAbd al-Ilāh Nabhān (Damascus: Wizārat al-Thaqāfah, 1992).

16. The author's full name is ʿAbd al-Wāḥid b. ʿAlī al-ʿAskarī al-Ḥalabī, Abū al-Ṭayyib al-Lughawī.

17. Cited in B. Amīn from ibn Maʿṣūm, *Muṭālaʿāt fī al-shiʿr al-Mamlūkī wa-al-ʿUthmānī*, 222–23.

18. For more on these types of poem, see B. Amīn, *Muṭālaʿāt fī al-shiʿr al-Mamlūkī wa-al-ʿUthmānī*, 186–208, 218–24.

19. Quoted in ibid., 82.

20. For a general reading of the controversy over religion and poetry, see Vicente Cantarino, *Arabic Poetry in the Golden Age* (Leiden: Brill, 1975), 9–19.

21. Cited from Mikhail Bakhtin's *Rabelais and His World*, trans. Helene Iswolsky (Bloomington: Indiana University Press, 1984), 44; also cited with specific applications in Muhsin al-Musawi, *Anglo-Orient* (Tunis: Centre de Publication Universitaire, 2000), 27.

22. Cited from Khalīl b. Aybak al-Ṣafadī, *Kitāb al-Wāfī bi-al-wafayāt*, ed. Hellmut Ritter, 24 vols. (Istanbul: Maṭbaʿat al-Dawlah, 1931), 2:135; also in Knysh, *Ibn ʿArabi in the Later Islamic Tradition*, 45.

23. *Hazz al-quḥūf*, 2:182.

24. Ibid., 2:425.

25. Ibid., 2:292.

26. Ibid., 2:6.

27. Ibid.

28. Ibid., 2:278–79; 2:321.

29. Ibn Ḥijjah, *Khizānat al-adab*, 1:352–58.

30. Ibid., 1:365.

31. For al-Jāḥiẓ's premise on meanings, see his *Al-ḥayawān*, 3:131–32. See also Muhsin al-Musawi, "Arabic Rhetoric," in *Oxford Encyclopedia of Rhetoric*, ed. Thomas O. Sloane (Oxford and New York: Oxford University Press, 2001), 30.

32. A discussion of these three treatises that evidentially build on ibn Nubātah's is by Geert Jan van Gelder, "Conceit of Pen and Sword," *Journal of Semitic Studies* 32, no. 2 (1987): 329–60; and Adrian Gully, "The Sword and the Pen in the Pre-Modern Arabic Heritage: A Literary Representation of an Important Historical Relationship," in *Ideas, Images, and Methods of Portrayal:*

Insights into Classical Arabic Literature and Islam, ed. Sebastian Günther (Leiden: Brill, 2005), 403–30.

33. For a survey of sources, see Geert Jan van Gelder, "Forbidden Firebrands: Frivolous 'Iqtibās' (Quotation from the Qur'ān) according to Medieval Arabic Critics," *Quaderni di Studi Arabi* 20/21 (2002–2003): 3–16.

34. Although al-Qalqashandī cites a long list of requirements, he puts less emphasis on *ʿulūm al-awāʾil*, or the Greeks, compared to other epistles. See al-Musawi, "Vindicating a Profession or a Personal Career?" 128–29.

35. Cited in Kanazi, *Studies in the Kitāb aṣ-Ṣināʿatayn of Abū Hilal al-Askari*, 10.

36. *The Maqāmāt of Badīʿ al-Zamān al-Hamādhānī*, trans. Prendergast (1915). http://www.sacred-texts.com/isl/mhm/mhm48.htm. See nos. xxiv, xxxiii.

37. Al-Hamadhānī, *Maqāmāt*, ed. Shaykh Muḥammad ʿAbduh, 199–201.

38. See Muhsin al-Musawi, "Abbasid Popular Narrative: the Formation of Readership and Cultural Production," *Journal of Arabic Literature* 38, no. 3, In Honor of Jaroslav Stetkevych, Who First Made "The Mute Immortals Speak," Part I (2007): 261–92; *Mujtamʿ Alf Laylah wa-Laylah* (Tunis: Dār al-Nashr al-Jāmiʿī, 2000); and *The Islamic Context of the Thousand and One Nights*, 189–208.

39. Al-Musawi, *The Islamic Context of the Thousand and One Nights*, 15, 202, 216, 244–45.

40. See ibn Ḥijjah, *Khizānat al-adab*, ed. Diyāb, 1:60–61.

41. See *Al-Ghayth*, 2:435.

42. Rosenthal, "'Of Making Many Books There Is No End,'" 36. Al-Baghdādī flourished in the first half of the twelfth century and had as a prominent disciple Fakhr al-Dīn al-Rāzī. According to Shlomo Pines, his voluminous book *al-Muʿtabar* should be translated as "the book of what has been established by personal reflection." The full title is *Kitāb al-Muʿtabar*, ed. and trans. Shlomo Pines, 3 vols. (Hyderabad: Osmania Publication Bureau, 1938–1939). See Shlomo Pines, *Studies in Abū ʾl-Barakāt al-Baghdādī: Physics and Metaphysics*, The Collected Works of Shlomo Pines, vol. 1 (Jerusalem: Magnes Press; Leiden: Brill, 1979).

43. Adorno, *Negative Dialectic*, 53.

44. Règis Blachère, "*Al-ʿAṭil al-ḥālī wa-l-muraḫḫaṣ al-ġālī* by al-Ḥillī Ṣafiyy al-dīn; W. Hoenerbach," *Arabica*, T. 5, Fasc. 3 (September 1958): 296–97; R. B. Serjeant, "*Die vulgärarabische Poetik al-Kitāb al-ʿĀtil al-ḥālī wal-muraḫḫaṣ al-ġālī des Ṣafīyaddīn Ḥillī* by Wilhelm Hoenerbach; Ṣafīyaddīn Ḥillī," *Bulletin of the School of Oriental and African Studies* 21, no. 1/3 (1958): 405–7.

45. See ibn Ḥijjah, *Khizānat al-adab*, 3:530–32.

46. Ṣafī al-Dīn al-Ḥillī, *Al-ʿĀṭil al-ḥālī wa-al-murakhkhaṣ al-ghālī fī al-azjāl wa-al-mawālī* (The Unadorned Bejeweled and the Cheapened Rendered Costly), ed. Ḥusayn Naṣṣār (Cairo: Al-Hayʾah al-Miṣriyyah al-ʿĀmmah lil-Kitāb [GEBO], 1981), 2–4.

47. See Kāmil Muṣṭafā al-Shaybī (self-spelled al-Shaibi), ed. and compiled, *Dīwān al-kān -wa-kān fī al-shiʿr al-shaʿbī al-ʿArabī al-qadīm* (Dīwān al-kān -wa-kān in Ancient Arabic Popular Poetry) (Baghdad: General Cultural Foundation, 1987). His book was published under my supervision when I was in charge of culture in Iraq (1983–1990).

48. Ibid., 45.

49. The full name of the latter is Jamāl al-Dīn Abū al-Faraj ʿAbd al-Raḥmān b. ʿAlī Muḥammad al-Bakrī (511–597/1117–1201). Ibid., 15, 40–41.

50. Ibid., 41. The poem is included in ʿAbd al-Wahhāb al-Banwānī's (d. 860/1456) *Rafʿ al-shakk wa-l-bayn fī taḥrīr al-fannayn, al-zajal wa-l-mawāliyā* (Dispelling Doubt, Falsehood, and Discord in the Explication of the Two Arts: *Zajal and Mawāliyā*). More on poets in this tradition is found in ibn Iyās's *Al-Durr al-maknūn fī sabʿ funūn* (The Hidden Pearls of the Seven Arts/Categories); and al-Ṣafadī's *Alḥān al-sawājiʿ min al-mabādiʾ wa-l-marājiʿ* (The Harmonious Cadence in Principles and Orientations).

51. For more on the poet, see Margaret Larkin, "The Dust of the Master: A Mamlūk-Era 'Zajal' by Khalaf al-Gubārī," *Quaderni di Studi Arabi*, n.s., 2 (2007): 11–29.

52. The seven arts (categories) are explained in ibn Iyās's *Al-Durr al-maknūn fī sabʿ funūn* (The Hidden Pearls of the Seven Arts).

53. Al-Shaybī, *Dīwān al-kān -wa-kān fī al-shiʿr al-shaʿbī al-ʿArabī al-qadīm*, 44. Hereafter, *Dīwān.*

54. Bakhtin, "Discourse in the Novel," in *The Dialogic Imagination: Four Essays*, ed. Michael Holquist, trans. Caryl Emerson and Michael Holquist (Austin: University of Texas Press, 1981), 263.

55. Al-Shaybī, *Dīwān*, 44.

56. Ibid., 197–211.

57. See the text of the poem in ibid., 212.

58. Ibid., 34.

59. Rancière, *The Politics of Aesthetics*, 34.

60. According to ibn Saʿīd al-Maghribī, the *kān-wa-kān* is the one called *mawāliyā* in the *baṭāʾiḥ* of Iraq (the marshes) because they, the people of these marshes, used it. He heard it himself sung by sailors. Al-Shaybī corrects the confusion and explains the slight difference between the two (*Dīwān*, 32). Reference is made to ibn Saʿīd, *Al-Muqtaṭaf min azāhīr al-ṭuraf.*

61. Al-Shaybī, *Dīwān*, 45–46.

62. Ibid., 259–92.

63. His full name is Abū ʿAlī ʿAbd Allah ibn Saʿd b. ʿAbdullāh al-Kāfī al-Miṣrī (al-Ḥurayfīsh al-Makkī).

64. See al-Shaybī, *Dīwān*, 181–82.

65. Ibid., 38.

66. Ibn Nuqṭah was an Iraqi wandering poet (*muzaklash*) who was described as "wandering in Baghdad's markets" during the day reciting *kān-wa-kān* and *mawāliyā*, and also at night during Ramadan. Poetry was natural to him, and he was ribald and brazen, known for singing, and illiterate. He took as a craft the making of women's slippers. See al-Shaybī's list of references to Mamluk historiography and biographical dictionaries, ibid., 78–79.

67. Ibid., 123.

68. The name *zaklash* is taken from the wandering poet, i.e., *muzaklash*, ibn Nuqṭah, whose full Baghdadi name is Abū Manṣūr Muḥammad ibn Abī Bakr ibn Shujāʿ (d. 597/1201). See more in al-Shaybī, ibid., 11; and see also ʿAlī ibn-Ẓāfir al-Azdī (d. 613/1226), *Badāʾiʿ al badāʾih*, ed. Muḥammad Abū al-Faḍl Ibrāhīm (Cairo: Maktabat al-Anjlū, 1971), 249.

69. Cited in al-Shaybī, *Dīwān*, 34, from ibn Jābir, *Al-Aqṣā al-qarīb fī ʿilm al-bayān* (Cairo: Al-Saʿādah Press, 1909), 40.

70. Al-Shaybī, *Dīwān*, 138–40.

71. Ibid., 157–58.

72. Ibid., 163–65.

73. See Muḥammad ibn Dāniyāl, *Three Shadow Plays*, ed. Paul Kahle, Derek Hopwood, and Mustafa Badawi (Cambridge: Cambridge University Press, 1992); also, Everett Rowson, "Two Homoerotic Narratives from Mamlūk Literature: al-Ṣafadī's *Lawʿat al-shākī* and ibn Dāniyāl's *al-Mutayyam*," in *Homoeroticism in Classical Arabic Literature*, ed. J. W. Wright, Jr., and Everett K. Rowson (New York: Columbia University Press, 1997), 172–84.

74. See al-Musawi, *The Islamic Context of the Thousand and One Nights*, 84; and Hirschler, *The Written Word in the Medieval Arabic Lands*, 89.

75. See ibn Nubātah, *Talṭīf al-mizāj min shiʿr ibn al-Ḥajjāj* (Refining the Mood with the Poetry of ibn al-Ḥajjāj), ed. Muṣṭafā, 49.

76. Al-Ṣafadī, *Kitāb al-Wāfī bi-al-wafayyāt*, 6:331–34. Al-Ṣafadī used al-Thaʿālibī and ibn Khullikān, *Wafayāt al-aʿyān* (Obituaries of the Notables), 2:171; Yāqūt, *Irshād al-arīb*, 6:206.

77. Aḥmad ibn Yaḥyā ibn Faḍl Allāh al-ʿUmarī (1301–1349), *Masālik al-abṣār fī mamālik al-amṣār*, 27 vols. in 15 (Beirut: Dār al-Kutub al-ʿIlmiyyah, 2010), 15:262–63.

78. Ibn Ḥijjah, *Khizānat al-adab*, 3:91.

79. Ibid., 3:360.

80. Ibid., 3:498.

81. Ibid., 3:499.

82. Ibid., 3:506.

83. Ibid., 3:520.

84. Siavash Lornejad and Ali Doostzadeh, *On the Modern Politicization of the Persian Poet Nezami Ganjavi*, ed. Garnik S. Asatrian, Yerevan Series for Oriental Studies 1 (Yerevan: Caucasian Centre for Iranian Studies, 2012), 157.

85. For a reading of the *majlis* as a poetic space in the ʿAbbasid period, see Samer Ali, *Arabic Literary Salons in the Islamic Middle Ages* (Notre Dame: University of Notre Dame Press, 2010).

86. The title of the complete text that contains *Surūr al-nafs bi-madārik al-ḥawāss al-khams* is *Faṣl al-khitāb fī madārik al-ḥawās al-khams* (The Final Say in the Reach of the Five Senses); abridged by ibn Manẓūr as *Surūr al-nafs.*

87. Daniel Newman, trans., *Sensual Delights of the Heart: Arab Erotica by Ahmed al-Tifashi* (London: Saqi Books, 2013).

88. *The Perfumed Garden*, by Shaykh Nefwazi [*sic*], trans. Sir Richard Francis Burton (Benares, 1886).

89. See Mohammed Ferid Ghazi, "Un group sociale: 'Les Raffinés' (*ẓurafāʾ*)," *Studia Islamica* 1 (1959): 59. Cited in Irwin, "Mamluk Literature," 9.

90. *Al-Ghayth*, 2:323.

91. Ibid., 2:327.

92. Ibid., 2:324.

93. Ibid., 2:375–76.

94. For general surveys, see *Encyclopedia of the Ottoman Empire*, ed. Gábor Ágoston and Bruce Alan Masters (New York: Facts on File, 2009), 338; Elias John Wilkinson Gibb, *A History of Ottoman Poetry, 1319–1901*, ed. E. G. Browne (London: Lowe-Brydone, 1958); Kemak Cicek, ed., *The Great Ottoman Turkish Civilization*, vol. 4 (Ankara: Yeni Türkiye, 2000); Walter G. Andrews, *An Introduction to Ottoman Poetry* (Minneapolis: Bibliotheca Islamica, 1976), and *Poetry's Voice, Society's Song: Ottoman Lyric Song* (Seattle: University of Washington Press, 1985).

95. Although his name was Ömer, he was nicknamed Nefʿî by his friend Gelibolulu Ali, meaning "Utilitarian." After writing vituperative verse against Vizier Bayram Paşa, he was brutally strangled and thrown into the sea. Although known for his satires, he was among the pillars of the *Dīwān* tradition that comprises the *qaṣīdah*, the lyric in the ghazal tradition, and the romance verse-narrative.

96. Walter Feldman, "The Celestial Sphere, the Wheel of Fortune, and Fate in the Gazels of Naili and Baki," *International Journal of Middle East Studies* 28, no. 2 (May 1996): 193–215.

97. Allison Busch, "Hidden in Plain View: Brajbhasha Poets at the Mughal Court," *Modern Asian Studies* 44, no. 2 (2010): 267–309.

98. Allison Busch, *Braj beyond Braj: Classical Hindi in the Mughal World*, IIC Occasional Publication 12 (New Delhi: Indian International Centre, 2009[?]), 1–32, esp. 10–11.

99. See Cachia, *The Arch Rhetorician*, 51–52.

100. Also spelled Ain-al Quzat Hamedānī or ʿAyn-al Qudat Hamadhānī.

101. Ehsan Yarshater, "The Theme of Wine-Drinking and the Concept of the Beloved in Early Persian Poetry," *Studia Islamica* 13 (1960): 43–53, and "Love-Related Conventions in Saʿdi's *gāzals*," in *Studies in Honour of Clifford Edmund Bosworth*, vol. 2, ed. Carole Hillenbrand (Leiden: Brill, 2000), 420–38.

102. Hilary Kilpatrick, *Making the Great Book of Songs: Compilation and the Author's Craft in Abū l-Faraj al-Iṣbahānī's Kitāb al-aghānī* (London and New York: RoutledgeCurzon, 2003).

103. See *The World History of Male Love*, "Gay Poetry," *The Meadow of the Gazelles*, 2002, at http://www.gay-art-history.org/gay-history/gay-literature/gay-poetry/muhammad-al-nawaji-mudhakkarat/muhammad-al-nawaji-mudhakkarat.html. For the Arabic manuscript, see http://arks.princeton.edu/ark:/88435/ms35t868t.

104. www.gay-art-history.org/gay-history/gay-literature/gay-poetry.

105. I am indebted in this section to the *Columbia Encyclopedia*, 6th ed., 2012, http://www.encyclopedia.com.

106. "Homosexuality," section iii, "Persian Literature," in *Encyclopedia Iranica*, http://www.iranicaonline.org/articles/homosexuality-iii. Originally December 15, 2004. Last updated: March 23, 2012. This article is available in print: *Encyclopedia Iranica*, vol. 12, fasc. 4, pp. 445–48, and fasc. 5, pp. 449–54.

107. Ibid. "Rešta-ye tasbiḥ agar begsast maʿḏuram bedār / Dastam andar sāʿed-e sāqi-ye simin sāq bud." Also, http://afghanistanonlineforums.com/cgi-bin/yabb2/YaBB.pl?num=1218478844/181.

108. Zangi's *Nozhat al-ʿāšeqin* (note the [š] has the [sh] sound). Ibid. See *Encyclopaedia Iranica*, "Homosexuality," section iii, "In Person Literature," at www.iranicaonline.org/articles/homosexuality-iii.

109. *Encyclopaedia Iranica*, "Homosexuality," section iii, "In Person Literature," at www.iranicaonline.org/articles/homosexuality-iii.

110. Ibid.

111. Ibid.

112. Ibid.

113. For the text of the Persian anthology *Nozhat al-Majāles*, see http://www.archive.org/details/NozhatAl-majales.

114. See Mikhail Bakhtin, "Forms of Time and Chronotope in the Novel," in *The Dialogic Imagination: Four Essays*, ed. Holquist, 168.

115. Al-Musawi, *The Islamic Context of the Thousand and One Nights*, 84, 185.

116. Bakhtin, "Forms of Time and Chronotope in the Novel," 168.

117. William M. Brinner, "The Significance of the Ḥarāfīsh and Their 'Sultan,'" *Journal of the Economic and Social History of the Orient* 6, no. 2 (July 1963): 190–215.

118. Tracing the terms *sāsī* and *sāsānī* as they turn into derisive usage, Abū al-Ḥasan ʿAlī al-Bayhaqī (ibn Funduq; d. 565/1169) only corroborates their application since the mid-tenth century. Rather than referring to the pomp of the vanquished Sasanid Empire, these epithets are applied to beggars and others on the fringes of society. See Parvaneh Pourshariati, "Local Historiography in Early Medieval Iran and the *Tārīkh-i Bayhaq*," *Iranian Studies* 33, no. 1/2 (Winter–Spring 2000): 154.

119. Dāwūd al-ʿAṭṭār al-Isrāʾīlī, in *Minhāj al-Dukkān*, copied by Mūsā ibn al-Shāmī (Cairo, 739/1338), mentions this fact in a medical manuscript, reprinted in multiple editions.

120. Bakhtin, "Forms of Time and Chronotope in the Novel," 168.

121. See especially Salīm's quotes in his *Ṣafī al-Dīn al-Ḥillī*, 52.

122. Hilāl al-Ṣābī, *Rusūm dār al-khilāfah* (Regulations at the Caliph's Palace). The book was dedicated to Caliph al-Qāʾim (r. 1031–1075). Ed. M. ʿAwwād (Baghdad, 1964); trans. Elie A. Salem (Beirut: American University in Beirut Press, 1977).

123. Bosworth, *Mediaeval Islamic Underworld*, 1:63, 67–68, 74–75. For a very informative study of unfolding cultural divides, see Shoshan, "High Culture and Popular Culture in Medieval Islam."

124. Bosworth, *Mediaeval Islamic Underworld*, 1:64.

125. See Th. Emil Homerin, trans. and introd., *ʿUmar ibn al-Fāriḍ: Sufi Verse, Saintly Life* (New York: Paulist Press, 2001).

126. Ibn al-Fāriḍ, *Dīwān ibn al-Fāriḍ* (Beirut: Dār Ṣādir, 1958; 2nd printing, 2002), 151–53.

127. Homerin, *ʿUmar ibn al-Fāriḍ: Sufi Verse, Saintly Life*, 37.

128. See Michael A. Sells, "Preface," in ibid., xvi.

129. Homerin, *ʿUmar ibn al-Fāriḍ: Sufi Verse, Saintly Life*, 189.

130. Ibid., 210.

131. Ibid., 171.

132. Ibid., 50.

133. Ibid., 55; Homerin cites from Dāwūd al-Qayṣarī (d. 747/1346), *Sharḥ al-Qaṣīdh al-Khamrīyah* (Commentary on the Wine Ode), Cairo, Dār al-Kutub al-Miṣrīyah-MS 56.

134. Homerin's comment, *ʿUmar ibn al-Fāriḍ: Sufi Verse, Saintly Life*, 53.

135. Cited and translated, ibid., 56.

136. See Dabashi, *The World of Persian Literary Humanism*, 3.

137. ʿAzīz al-Sayyid Jāsim, *Mutaṣawwifat Baghdād* (Beirut: Al-Markaz al-Thaqāfī al-ʿArabī, 1990).

138. Cited from Muḥammad ibn Aḥmad al-Dhahabī's *Tārīkh al-Islām wa-tabaqāt al-mashāhīr wa-al-aʿlām*, table 64, p. 353; in Knysh, *Ibn ʿArabi in the Later Islamic Tradition*, 26. I am indebted to Knysh for his synthesis of the debate on ibn al-ʿArabī's controversial poetics.

139. Quoted in Knysh, *Ibn ʿArabi in the Later Islamic Tradition*, 287; from ibn al-ʿArabī, *Tarjumān al-ashwāq, A Collection* of *Mystical Odes*, ed. and trans. R.A. Nicholson (London: Royal Asiatic Society, 1911), 66–67; and Michael Sells, "Ibn ʿArabī's Garden among the Flames: A Reevaluation," *History of Religions* 23, no. 4 (May 1984): 287–31.

140. Knysh, *Ibn ʿArabi in the Later Islamic Tradition*, 27. For Muḥammad ibn Saʿīd ibn al-Dubaythī, see his *Al-Mukhtaṣar al-muḥtāj ilayh min tārīkh Abī ʿAbd Allāh Muḥammmad Saʿīd ibn Muḥammad ibn al-Dubaythī*, ed. Muṣṭafā Jawād, 2 vols. (Baghdad: Al-Majmaʿ al-ʿIlmī al-ʿIrāqī, 1951). For ibn al-Najjār al-Baghdādī, see his *Al-Mustafād min dhayl taʾrīkh Baghdād*, ed. Bashshār ʿAwwād Maʿrūf (Beirut: Muʾassasat al-Risālah, 1986).

141. Knysh, *Ibn ʿArabi in the Later Islamic Tradition*, 29; and ibn al-Najjār al-Baghdādī, *Al-Mustafād*, 27.

142. ʿAbd al-Raḥmān b. Ismāʿīl Abū Shāmah, *Tarājim rijāl al-qarnayan al-sādis wa- al-sābiʿ* (Biographies of the Men of the Sixth and Seventh Centuries) (Cairo: s.n., 1947), 170.

143. Cited from MRM [*Majmūʿat al-rasāʾil w-al-masāʾil*, ed. Muḥammad Rashīd Riḍā, 5 vols. (Cairo: Lajnat al-Turāth al-ʿArabī, 1976)], 4:179, in Knysh, *Ibn ʿArabi in the Later Islamic Tradition*, 96.

144. Knysh, *Ibn ʿArabi in the Later Islamic Tradition*, 115.

145. Ibid.

146. Cited in Knysh, *Ibn ʿArabi in the Later Islamic Tradition*, 117; from al-Dhahabī's *Taʾrīkh*, table 64, pp. 358–59.

147. Muḥammad Ibn ʿAbd al-Jabbār al-Niffarī, *The Mawāqif and Mukhāṭabāt of Muḥammad Ibn ʿAbd ʾl-Jabbār al-Niffarī*, with other fragments, edited for the first time, with translation, commentary, and indices, by Arthur John Arberry, printed by the Cambridge University Press for the Trustees of the "E. J. W. Gibb Memorial" (London: Luzac & Co., 1935).

148. Cited and translated by Homerin, *ʿUmar ibn al-Fāriḍ: Sufi Verse, Saintly Life*, 314.

149. Ibid., 317.

150. Cited by B. Amīn, *Muṭālaʿāt fī al-shiʿr al-Mamlūkī wa-al-ʿUthmānī*, 238, from ibn al-ʿArabī's *Al-Futūḥāt al-Makkiyyah* (Meccan Revelations), 1:80. The first sentence was modified.

151. Ibn Taymiyyah uses the term without the usual Sufi connotation, i.e., *ʿārif* = Sufi gnostic.

152. B. Amīn, *Muṭālaʿāt fī al-shiʿr al-Mamlūkī wa-al-ʿUthmānī*, 238, from ibn Taymiyyah, *Majmūʿ fatāwī* (Collected Legal Opinions) (Cairo: Kurdistān Press, AH 1326), 11:74; and from ʿAbd al-Qādir ʿIsā, *Ḥaqāʾiq ʿan al-taṣawwuf* (The Facts of Sufism) (Aleppo: Maktabat al-ʿIrfān, 5th printing, 1993), 550.

153. Cited in B. Amīn, *Muṭālaʿāt fī al-shiʿr al-Mamlūkī wa-al-ʿUthmānī*, 238–39, from ibn Taymiyyah, *Majmūʿat al-rasāʾil* (Complete Letters), 5 vols. (Cairo: Muḥammad Rashīd Riḍā-Maṭbaʿat al-Manār, 1922–1930), 1:52.

154. Abū Ḥāmid al-Ghazālī, *Iḥyāʾ ʿulūm al-dīn* (The Revival of Islamic Sciences) (Cairo: Al-Azhar Press, 1302/1884), 2:229.

155. Duncan Black Macdonald, ed. and trans.,"Emotional Religion in Islam as Affected by Music and Singing. Being a Translation of a Book of the Iḥyā ʿUlūm ad-Dīn of al-Ghazzālī with Analysis, Annotation, and Appendices," *Journal of the Royal Asiatic Society* 33, no. 2 (April 1901): 238.

156. See B. Amīn, *Muṭālaʿāt fī al-shiʿr al-Mamlūkī wa-al-ʿUthmānī*, 244, for one example.

157. Ibid.

158. See Dabashi, *The World of Persian Literary Humanism*, 167.

159. See B. Amīn, *Muṭālaʿāt fī al-shiʿr al-Mamlūkī wa-al-ʿUthmānī*, 230–31.

160. Shihāb al-Dīn Aḥmad al-Suhrawardī, *The Shape of Light*, trans. Shaykh Tosun Bayrak al-Jerrahi al-Halveti (Louisville, KY: Fons Vitae, 1998).

161. Apart from modern translations in English, especially Clouston's (1881), there were a number of other early translations: in English by Faizullabhai (Bombay, 1893), in French by R. Basset (Paris, 1894), and in German by C.A. Ralfs (Vienna, 1860).

162. Lines 52–53, my translation. For a full and slightly different translation, see S. Stetkevych, *The Mantle Odes*, 98. For another translation, see http://www.sunnah.org/aqida/light_of_the_prophet_sall.htm.

163. Cited in B. Amīn, *Muṭālaʿāt fī al-shiʿr al-Mamlūkī wa-al-ʿUthmānī*, 262–63, from Zakī Mubārak, who in turn quotes *The Meccan Revelations*.

164. B. Amīn, *Muṭālaʿāt fī al-shiʿr al-Mamlūkī wa-al-ʿUthmānī*, 266.

165. See S. Stetkevych, *The Mantle Odes*, 70–150; and ʿAlī Abū Zayd, *Al-Badīʿyyāt fī al-adab al-ʿArabī*, 71–180.

166. For a list, see also, along with earlier sources, Zakī Mubārak, *Al-Madā'iḥ al-nabawiyyah* (Encomiums to the Prophet) (Cairo: Dār al-Kātib al-'Arabī, 1967), 204. On 'Ā'ishah al-Bā'ūniyyah, see the entry on her by Th. Emil Homerin, *Essays in Arabic Literary Biography, 1350–1850*, 21–27.

167. Well known among these forms of supplicatory poetry are the poems by Majd al-Dīn al-Watrī al-Baghdādī (d. 980/1572), 'Abd al-Raḥīm b. Aḥmad al-Bur'ī al-Yamānī (d. 803/1400), Yaḥyā ibn Yūsuf al-Ṣarṣarī (killed by the Mongol invaders, 656/1258), Maḥmūd ibn Salmān b. Fahd al-Ḥalabī (d. 725/1325), 'Umar ibn al-Wardī (d. 749/1349), Muḥammad ibn Muḥammad ibn Ma'tūq (d. 707/1307), and many others.

168. See B. Amīn, *Muṭāla'āt fī al-shi'r al-Mamlūkī wa-al-'Uthmānī*, 274. The *'āyah* says: *wa ibtaghū ilayhī al-wasīlah*.

169. Di'bil al-Khuzā'ī's verse reads as follows in Arabic:

مَدَارِسُ آيَاتٍ خَلَتْ مِن تلاوةٍ ومنزلُ وحيٍ مقفرُ العرصاتِ

From *Dīwān Di'bil ibn 'Alī al-Khuzā'ī*, ed. 'Abd al-Ṣāḥib ibn 'Imrān Dujaylī (Beirut: Dār al-Kitāb al-Lubnānī, 1972). Online at http://www.adab.com.

170. Al-Sharīf al-Raḍī's verse runs as follows:

وتلفتت عيني فمذ خفيت   عنها الطلول تلفت القلب

Online at http://www.adab.com.

171. See Allen, *The Arabic Literary Heritage*, 161.

172. These selections of elegies, except the last two, al-Khuzā'ī and al-Raḍī, are cited from B. Amīn, *Muṭāla'āt fī al-shi'r al-Mamlūkī wa-al-'Uthmānī*, 99–114.

173. Ibid.

Conclusion

1. For an early exercise of consensus against *khilāf* (dissent and difference), see Makdisi, *The Rise of Colleges*, 106–7.

BIBLIOGRAPHY

ʿAbbās, Iḥsān. *Tārīkh al-naqd al-adabī ʿinda al-ʿArab: naqd al-shiʿr min al-qarn al-thānī ḥattā al-qarn al-thāmin al-hijrī*. 1993; 4th printing, Amman: Dār al-Shurūq, 2006.

Al-ʿAbbāsī, ʿAbd al-Raḥīm ibn ʿAbd al-Raḥmān. *Kitāb Sharḥ shawāhid al-Talkhīṣ al-musammā Maʿāhid al-tanṣīṣ* (Designating Familiar Texts: A Commentary of the Evidentiary Verses in *al-Talkhīṣ*). Miṣr: Al-Maṭbaʿah al-Bahiyyah, 1899.

Abu Deeb, Kamal. *Al-Jurjani's Theory of Poetic Imagery*. Warminster: Aris and Phillips, 1979.

Abū al-Fidā, Ismāʿīl ibn ʿAlī. *Al-Tibr al-masbūk fī tawārikh akābir al-Mulūk* (The Cast Gold in the Histories of the Greatest Kings). Cairo: Maktabat al-Thaqāfah al-Dīniyyah, 1995.

Abū Shāmah, ʿAbd al-Raḥmān b. Ismāʿīl. *Tarājim rijāl al-qarnayn al-sādis wa-al-sābiʿ* (Biographies of the Men of the Sixth and Seventh Centuries). Cairo: s.n., 1947.

Abū Zayd, ʿAlī. *Al-Badīʿiyyāt fī al-adab al-ʿArabī*. Beirut: ʿĀlam al-Kutub, 1983.

Adamson, Peter. *The Arabic Plotinus: A Philosophical Study of the Theology of Aristotle*. London: Gerald Duckworth, 2002.

Adorno, Theodor W. *Negative Dialectics*. New York: Continuum–The Seabury Press, 1979.

Aghaie, Kamran Scot. The *Martyrs of Karbala: Shiʿi Symbols and Rituals in Modern Iran*. Seattle: University of Washington Press, 2004.

Ali, Samer. *Arabic Literary Salons in the Islamic Middle Ages*. Notre Dame: University of Notre Dame Press, 2010.

Allāh Bhār, Faiz. *Tuḥfat al-muslimīn: A Moslem Present; An Anthology of Arabic Poems about the Prophet and the Faith of Islam*. Bombay: Education Society, 1893.

Allen, Roger. *The Arabic Literary Heritage*. Cambridge: Cambridge University Press, 1998.

———. "The Post-Classical Period: Parameters and Preliminaries." In *Arabic Literature in the Post-Classical Period*, ed. Roger Allen and D. S. Richards. The Cambridge History of Arabic Literature. Cambridge and New York: Cambridge University Press, 2006.

Amīn, Bakrī Shaykh. *Muṭālaʿāt fī al-shiʿr al-Mamlūkī wa-al-ʿUthmānī*. Beirut: Dār al-ʿIlm lil-Malāyīn, 2007.

Amīn, Fawzī Muḥammad. *Adab al-ʿaṣr al-awwal al-mamlūkī: malāmiḥ al-mujtamaʿ al-Miṣrī*. Suese: Dār al-Maʿrifah al-Jāmiʿiyyah, 2009.

Amin, Samir. *The Arab Nation*. New York: Zed Press, 1978.

———. *Eurocentrism*. New York: Monthly Review, 2010.

Anderson, Benedict. *Imagined Communities: Reflections on the Origin and Spread of Nationalism*. London: Verso, 1983.

Andrews, Walter G. *An Introduction to Ottoman Poetry*. Minneapolis: Bibliotheca Islamica, 1976.

———. *Poetry's Voice, Society's Song: Ottoman Lyric Song*. Seattle: University of Washington Press, 1985.

———. "Speaking of Power: The 'Ottoman kaside.'" In *Qasida Poetry in Islamic Asia and Africa*, ed. S. Sperl and C. Shackle, 2 vols., 1:281–300. Leiden: Brill, 1996.

Andrews, Walter G., and Mehmed Kalpakli. "Across Chasms of Change: The kaside in Late Ottoman and Republican Times." In *Qasida Poetry in Islamic Asia and Africa*, ed. S. Sperl and C. Shackle, 2 vols., 1:301–26. Leiden: Brill, 1996.

Antonius, George Habib. *The Arab Awakening: The Story of the Arab National Movement*. London: H. Hamilton, 1938.

Antoon, Sinan. *The Poetics of the Obscene: Ibn al-Hajjaj and Sukhf*. New York: Palgrave Macmillan, 2014.

Arnold, Matthew. "The Literary Influence of the Academies" and "Heinrich Heine." In *Essays in Criticism, 1st Series*. 1865; London and New York: Macmillan, 1902.

———. "A Persian Passion Play." In *Essays in Criticism*. London: Macmillan, 1871.

Al-Ashʿarī, ʿAlī ibn Ismāʿīl. *Al-ibānah ʿan uṣūl al-diyānah* (The Elucidation of Islam's Foundation); a translation, with introduction and notes by Walter C. Klein. New Haven: American Oriental Society, 1940; repr., New York: Kraus, 1967.

Al-ʿAskarī, Abū Hilāl. *Kitāb al-Sināʿatayn: al-kitāba wa- al-shiʿr* (The Book of the Two Arts: Prose and Poetry). Ed. Muḥammad Abū al-Faḍl Ibrāhim. Cairo: ʿIsā al-Bābī al-Ḥalabī, 1952.

———. *Kitāb al-Sināʿatayn: al-kitābah wa- al-shiʿr* (The Book of the Two Arts: Prose and Poetry). Ed. Mufīd Qamīḥah. Beirut: Dār al-Kutub al-ʿIlmiyyah, 1981; repr. 1989.

Al-ʿAsqalānī, Aḥmad b. ʿAlī ibn Ḥajar. *Al-Durar al-Kāmina fī Aʿyān al-miʾah al-thāmina* (The Hidden Pearls of the Eighth-Century Notables). 4 vols. Beirut: Dār al-Jīl, 1989.

Al-Asṭurlābī, Hibat Allāh Badīʿ al-Zamān. *Durrat al-tāj min shiʿr ibn al-Ḥajjāj* (The Crown Pearl of ibn al-Ḥajjāj's Poetry). Ed. ʿAlī Jawād al-Ṭāhir. Baghdad and Berlin: Manshūrāt al-Jamal, 2009.

Atiyeh, George N., ed. *The Book in the Islamic World*. Albany: State University of New York Press, 1995.

ʿAṭṭār, Farīd al-Dīn. *The Conference of the Birds*. Trans. Dick Davis and Afkham Darbandi. Harmondsworth, Middlesex: Penguin, 1984.

Al-ʿAṭṭār, al-Israʾīlī Dāwūd ibn Abī al-Naṣr. *Minhāj al-Dukkān*. Copied by Mūsā bin Shāmī. 2 vols. 739/1338; 1870; Cairo: Maktabat al-Jumhūriyyah al-Miṣriyyah, 1970; Beirut: Dār al-Manāhil, 1992; Frankfurt: Maʿhad Tāʾrīkh al-ʿUlūm al-ʿArabiyyah wa- al-Islāmiyyah fī Jāmiʿat Frankfūrt, 1997.

Al-ʿAṭṭār, Shaykh Ḥasan. *Al-Maqāmāt al-Suyūṭiyah: li-Jalāl al-Dīn Sayyidī ʿAbd al-Raḥmān al-Suyūṭī. Mudhayyalah bi-Maqāmah li-Ḥasan al-ʿAṭṭār* ["Maqāmah fī Dukhūl al-Faransīs"]. Cairo: Sāliḥ al-Yāfī, 1859.

Austenfeld, Thomas. "Review of Pascale Casanova's *World Republic of Letters*." *South Atlantic Review* 71, no. 1 (Winter 2006): 141–44.

Al-Azdī, ʿAlī ibn-Ẓāfir. *Badāʾiʿ al badāʾih*. Ed. Muḥammad Abū al-Faḍl Ibrāhīm. Cairo: Maktabat al-Anjlū, 1971.

Al-Baghdādī, ʿAbd al-Qādir ibn ʿUmar. *Khizānat al-adab wa lubb lubāb lisān al-ʿArab* (The Treasury of Literature and the Essence of the Arab Language). Beirut: Dār Ṣādir, 1968.

———. *Kitāb al-Muʿtabar* (The Book of What Has Been Established by Personal Reflection). Ed. and trans. Shlomo Pines. 3 vols. Hyderabad: Osmania Publication Bureau, 1938–1939.

Al-Baḥrānī, Kamāl al-Dīn Maytham ibn ʿAlī. *Qawāʿid al-marām fī ʿilm al-kalām* (The Orderly Principles in the Science of Theological Reasoning). Qum: Mihr Press, 1977.

Bakar, O. *The Classification of Knowledge in Islam*. Cambridge: Cambridge University Press, 1998.

Bakhtin, Mikhail. "Discourse in the Novel." In *The Dialogic Imagination: Four Essays*, ed. Michael Holquist, trans. Caryl Emerson and Michael Holquist. Austin: University of Texas Press, 1981.

———. "Forms of Time and Chronotope in the Novel." In *The Dialogic Imagination: Four Essays*, ed. Michael Holquist, trans. Caryl Emerson. Austin: University of Texas Press, 1981.

———. *Rabelais and His World*. Trans. Helene Iswolsky. Bloomington: Indiana University Press, 1984.

Bakr, ʿAbd al-Wahhāb. *Al-Dawlah al-ʿUthmāniyyah wa Miṣr fī al-niṣf al-thānī min al-qarn al-thāmin ʿashar*. Cairo: Dār al-Maʿārif, 1982.

Bāshā, ʿUmar Mūsā. *Tārīkh al-adab al-ʿArabī: al-ʿaṣr al-Mamlūkī* (The History of Arabic Literature: The Mamluk Age). Damascus: Dār al-Fikr, 1989.

Basnett, Susan. *Comparative Literature: A Critical Introduction*. London: Blackwell, 1993.

Baudrillard, Jean. *Simulacra and Simulation*. Trans. Sheila Faria Glaser. Ann Arbor: University of Michigan Press, 1994.

Bauer, Thomas. "Communication and Emotion: The Case of Ibn Nubātah's Kindertotenlieder." *Mamluk Studies Review* 7, no. 1 (2003): 48–95.

———. "Ibn Nubatah." In *Essays in Arabic Literary Biography, 1350–1850*, ed. Joseph E. Lowry and Devin J. Stewart, 184–202. Wiesbaden: Harrassowitz, 2009.

———. "Ibrāhim al-Miʿmār: Ein dichtender Handwerker aus Ägptens Mamlukenzeit." *ZDMG–Zeitschrift der Deutschen Morgenländischen Gesellschaft* 152 (2002): 63–93.

———. "In Search of 'Post-Classical Literature': A Review Article." *Mamluk Studies Review* 11, no. 2 (2007): 137–67.

———. "Literarische Anthologien der Mamlükenzeit." In *Die Mamlüken: Studien zu ihrer Geschichte und Kultur*, ed. S. Conermann and A. Pistor-Hatam, 71–122. Hamburg: EB-Verlag, 2003.

———. "Mamluk Literature: Misunderstandings and New Approaches." *Mamluk Studies Review* 9, no. 2 (2005): 105–32.

———. "Al-Nawājī." In *Arabic Literary Biography, 1350–1850*, ed. Joseph E. Lowry and Devin J. Stewart, 321–31. Wiesbaden: Harrassowitz, 2009.

Bawardi, Basiliyus. "First Steps in Writing Arabic Narrative Fiction: The Case of 'Ḥadīqat al-Akhbār.'" *Die Welt des Islams*, n.s., 48, no. 2 (2008): 170–95.

Becka, Jiri. "Tajik Literature from the 16th Century to the Present." In *History of Iranian Literature*, ed. Jan Rypka, 483–545. Dordrecht: D. Reidel, 1968.

Behmardi, Vahid. "Rhetorical Values in Buyid Persia According to Badiʿ al-Zaman al-Hamadhani." In *The Weaving of Words: Approaches to Classical Arabic Prose*, ed. Lale Behzadi and Vahid Behmardi, 151–64. Beirut: Orient-Institut-Verlag, 2009.

Berkey, Jonathan P. "Culture and Society during the Late Middle Ages." In *Cambridge History of Egypt*, ed. Martin W. Daly and Carl F. Petry, 1:375–411. Cambridge: Cambridge University Press, 1998.

———. *Popular Preaching and Religious Authority in the Medieval Islamic Near East*. Seattle and London: University of Washington Press, 2001.

———. "Tradition, Innovation, and the Social Construction of Knowledge in the Medieval Islamic Near East." *Past and Present* 146 (February 1995): 38–65.

Bernards, Monique. "Muḥammad Murtaḍā al-Zabīdī." In *Essays in Arabic Literary Biography, 1350–1850*, ed. Joseph E. Lowry and Devin J. Stewart, 419–28. Wiesbaden: Harrassowitz, 2009.

Al-Bilbaysī. *Al-Mulaḥ wa-al-ṭuraf min munādamāt arbāb al-ḥiraf*. Ed. A. al-Fāʿūrī and M. Khraysāt. Irbid: Muʾassasat Ḥamādah, 2009.

Bilgrāmī, Ghulām ʿAlī Āzād. *Subḥat al-marjān fī āthār Hindūstān*. 2 vols. Ed. Muḥammad Faḍl al-Raḥmān al-Nadwū al-Siwānī. ʿAlīgarh: Jāmiʿat ʿAlīgarh al-Islāmiyya, 1976–1980.

Al-Bishrī, ʿAbd al-ʿAzīz. "Muhimu al-adīb fī al-Sharq an yakūna adīban Sharqiyyan" (How Disturbing for a Littérateur in the East to Be an Oriental Littérateur [this title can mislead one to read it as the 'mission of . . . to be . . .']). *Al-Hilāl* (1939): 117–19.

Blachère, Régis. "*Al-ʿAṭil al-ḥālī wa-l-muraḫḫaṣ al-ġālī* by al-Ḥillī Ṣafiyy al-dīn; W. Hoenerbach." *Arabica*, T. 5, Fasc. 3 (September 1958): 296–97.

———. *Historie de la Littérature Arabe* (1952). Arabic translation: *Tārīkh al-adab al-ʿArabī*. Damascus: Dār al-Fikr, 1998.

Bodrogligeti, András. "A Collection of Poems from the 14th Century." *Acta Orientalia Academiae Scientiarum Hungaricae* 16 (1963): 245–311.

———. *A Fourteenth Century Turkic Translation of Saʿdi's Gulistān*. Bloomington: Indiana University, 1970.

———. "A Grammar of Mamluke-Kipchak." In *Studia Turcica*, ed. L. Ligeti, 89–102. Budapest: Akadémisi Kiadó, 1971.

———. "Notes on the Turkish Literature in the Mamluke Court." *Acta Orientalia Academiae Scientiarum Hungaricae* 14 (1962): 273–82.

Bonebakker, S. A. "*Adab* and the Concept of Belles-Lettres." In *ʿAbbasid Belles-Lettres*, ed. Julia Ashtiany et al., 16–30. The Cambridge History of Arabic Literature. Cambridge: Cambridge University Press, 1990.

Bosworth, C. E. "Abū ʿAbdallāh al-Khawārazmī on the Technical Terms of the Secretary's Art." *Journal of the Economic and Social History of the Orient* 12 (1969): 113–64.

———. "A *Maqāmah* on Secretaryship: Al-Qalqashandī's Al-Kawākib al-Durriyah fī al-Manāqib al-Badriyya." *Bulletin of the School of Oriental and African Studies* 27 (1964): 291–98. Repr. in Bosworth, *Medieval Arabic Culture and Administration*, 292–98.

———. *The Mediaeval Islamic Underworld: The Banū Sāsān in Arabic Society and Literature*. Leiden: Brill, 1976.

———. *Medieval Arabic Culture and Administration*. London: Variorum Reprints, 1982.

———. "A Pioneer Arabic Encyclopedia of the Sciences: Al-Khawārizmī's Keys of the Sciences." *Isis* 54, no. 1 (March 1963): 97–111.

———. "The Terminology of the History of the Arabs in the Jahiliyya according to al-Khwārazmī's 'Keys of the Sciences.'" In *Studies in Judaism and Islam*, ed. S. Morag et al., 27–43. Jerusalem: Magnes Press, Hebrew University, 1981.

Brinner, William M. "The Significance of the Ḥarāfīsh and Their 'Sultan.'" *Journal of the Economic and Social History of the Orient* 6, no. 2 (July 1963): 190–215.

Brooke-Rose, Christine. "Whatever Happened to Narratology?" *Poetics Today* 11, no. 2, Narratology Revisited I (Summer 1990): 283–93.

Brugman, J. *An Introduction to the History of Modern Arabic Literature in Egypt*. Leiden: Brill, 1984.

Bulliet, R. "The Age-Structure of Medival Islamic Education." *Studia Islamica* 57 (1983): 105–17.

Burnett, Charles. *Arabic into Latin in the Middle Ages: The Translations and Their Intellectual and Social Context*. Farnham, Surrey: Ashgate Variorum, 2009.

Busch, Allison. *Braj beyond Braj: Classical Hindi in the Mughal World*. IIC Occasional Publication 12. New Delhi: India International Centre, 2009[?].

———. "Hidden in Plain View: Brajbhasha Poets at the Mughal Court." *Modern Asian Studies* 44, no. 2 (2010): 267–309.

Al-Bustānī, Buṭrus. *Muḥīṭ al-muḥīṭ*. Beirut: [s.n.], 1867.

———. Preface to *Rasāʾil Ikhwān al-Ṣafāʾ wa Khullān al-Wafāʾ* (Epistles of the Pure Brethren and the Sincere Friends). 4 vols. Beirut: Dār Ṣādir, n.d.

Al-Bustānī, Sulaymān Khaṭṭār. *Ilyādhat Hūmīrūs: muʿarrabah naẓman wa-ʿalayhā sharḥ tārīkhī adabī* (The *Iliad* Arabized in verse, with a historical and literary explanation). Miṣr: Al-Hilāl, 1904; repr., Suese: Dār a-Maʿārif, n.d.

Cachia, Pierre. *The Arch Rhetorician or the Schemer's Skimmer: A Handbook of Late Arabic Badīʿ Drawn from ʿAbd al-Ghanī an-Nabulsī's Nafaḥāt al-azhār ʿalā nasamāt al-ashʿār*. Wiesbaden: Harrassowitz, 1998.

Calinescu, Matei. *Five Faces of Modernity*. Durham, NC: Duke University Press, 1987.

Cantarino, Vicente. *Arabic Poetry in the Golden Age*. Leiden: Brill, 1975.

Carter, M. G. "Arabic Lexicography." In *Religion, Learning and Science in the ʿAbbāsid Period*, ed. M. J. L. Young, J. D. Latham, and R. B. Serjeant, 106–17. The Cambridge History of Arabic Literature. Cambridge: Cambridge University Press, 1990.

———. "Language Control as People Control in Medieval Islam: The Aim of the Grammarians in Their Cultural Context." *Al-Abḥath* 31 (1983): 65–84.

Casanova, Pascale. *The World Republic of Letters*. Trans. M. B. DeBevoise. Cambridge, MA, and London: Harvard University Press, 2004.

Chamberlain, Michael. *Knowledge and Social Practice in Medieval Damascus, 1190–1350*. Cambridge: Cambridge University Press, 1994.

Chapoutot-Remadi, M. "Al-Nuwayrī." In *Encyclopedia of Islam*, 2nd ed. (Brill Online, 2014), 8:158.

Chipman, Leigh. *The World of Pharmacy and Pharmacists in Mamluk Cairo*. Leiden: Brill, 2010.

Cicek, Kemak, ed. *The Great Ottoman Turkish Civilization*. Vol. 4. Ankara: Yeni Türkiye, 2000.

Clark, Jane. "Ibn al-ʿArabī." In *Essays in Arabic Literary Biography, 925–1350*, ed. Terri De Young and Mary St. Germain, 94–115. Wiesbaden: Harrassowitz, 2011.

Cleary, Joe. "The World Literary System: Atlas and Epitaph; *The World Republic of Letters* by Pascale Casanova." *Field Day Review* 2 (2006): 196–219.

Clifford, W. W. "*Ubi Sumus?* Social Theory and Mamluk Studies." *Mamluk Studies Review* 1 (1997): 45–61.

Clinton, Jerome W. *The Dīwān of Manūchihrī Dāmghānī: A Critical Study*. Studies in Middle Eastern Literatures 1. Minneapolis: Bibliotheca Islamica, 1972.

Clouston, W. A. *Arabian Poetry* [1881]. London: Darf Publishers, 1986.

Colla, Elliott. "'Non, non! Si, si!' Commemorating the French Occupation of Egypt (1798–1801)." *MLN* 118, no. 4 (September 2003): 1043–69.

Conger, George Perrigo. *Theories of Macrocosms and Microcosms in the History of Philosophy*. New York: Columbia University Press, 1922.

Conrad, L. "Seven and Tasbīʿ: On the Implications of Numerical Symbolism for the Study of Medieval Islamic History." *Journal of the Economic and Social History of the Orient* 31 (1988): 42–73.

Contadini, Anna. *A World of Beasts: A Thirteenth-Century Illustrated Arabic Book on Animals (the Kitāb Naʿt al-Ḥayawān) in the Ibn Bakhtīshūʿ Tradition*. Leiden: Brill, 2012.

———, ed. *Arab Painting: Text and Image in Illustrated Arabic Manuscripts*. Leiden: Brill, 2007.

Cooperson, Michael. "ʿAlāʾ al-Dīn al-Ghuzūlī." *In Essays in Arabic Literary Biography, 1350–1850*, ed. Joseph E. Lowry and Devin J. Stewart, 107–17. Wiesbaden: Harrassowitz, 2009.

Culler, Jonathan. "On the Negativity of Modern Poetry: Friedrich, Baudelaire, and the Critical Tradition." In *Languages of the Unsayable: The Play of Negativity in Literature and Literary Theory*, ed. Sanford Budick and Wolfgang Iser, 189–208. New York: Columbia University Press, 1989.

Czapkiewicz, Andrzej. *The Views of the Medieval Arab Philologists on Language and Its Origins in the Light of As-Suyūṭī's "Al-Muzhir."* Kraków: Nakładem Uniwersytetu Jagiellońskiego, 1988.

Dabashi, Hamid. *Shiʿsm: A Religion of Protest*. Cambridge, MA: The Belknap Press of Harvard University Press, 2011.

———. *The World of Persian Literary Humanism*. Cambridge, MA: Harvard University Press, 2012.

Al-Damāmīnī, Badr al-Dīn Muḥammad ibn Abī Bakr. *Nuzūl al-Ghayth al-ladhī insajam ʿalā sharḥ lāmiyyat al-ʿajam* [which critiques al-Ṣafadī's book, *al-Ghayth*]. Baghdad: Diwān al-Waqf al-Sunnī, Markaz al-Buḥūth wa-al-Dirāsāt al-Islāmiyah, 2010.

Danner, Victor. "Arabic Literature in Iran." In *Cambridge History of Iran*, vol. 4, *From the Arab Invasion to the Seljuqs*, ed. R.N. Frye, 566–94. Cambridge: Cambridge University Press, 1975.

Davis, Natalie. *Trickster Travels: A Sixteenth-Century Muslim Between Two Worlds*. New York: Hill and Wang, 2006.

De Bruijn, J.T.P. *Of Piety and Poetry: The Interaction of Religion and Literature in the Life and Works of Ḥakīm Sanāʾī of Ghazna*. Publication of the de Goeje Fund 25. Leiden: Brill, 1983.

De Gobineau, Joseph Arthur Comte. *An Essay on the Inequality of the Human Races* [1853–1855]. New York: H. Fertig, 1915; 1967.

DeYoung, Terri. "Ṣafī al-Dīn al-Ḥillī." In *Essays in Arabic Literary Biography, 925–1350*, ed. Terri DeYoung and Mary St. Germain, 75–88. Wiesbaden: Harrassowitz, 2011.

Dhanani, Alnoor. "Kalām, Atoms and Epicurean Minimal Parts." In *Tradition, Transmission, Transformation*, ed. Jamil F. Ragep and Sally P. Ragep, 157–71. Leiden: Brill, 1996.

———. *Physical Theory of Kalam*. Leiden: Brill, 1994.

Dodge, B. *Muslim Education in Medieval Times*. Washington, DC: Middle East Institute, 1962.

Doležel, Lubomīr. *Possible Worlds of Fiction and History: The Postmodern Stage*. Baltimore: Johns Hopkins University Press, 2010.

Dunlop, D. M. "The Translation of al-Bitriq and Yahya (Yuhanna) b. al-Batriq." *Journal of the Royal Asiatic Society* (1959): 140–50.

Dunn, Ross. *The Adventures of Ibn Battuta: A Muslim Traveler of the 14th Century*. Berkeley: University of California Press, 1989.

———. "The Adventures of Ibn Battuta: A Muslim Traveler of the 14th Century." Keynote Address, March 2, 2005, Ibn Battuta Event, UCLA International Institute, University of California, Los Angeles. www1.international.ucla.edu/article.asp?parentid=21336.

Elayyan, R. M. "The History of the Arabic-Islamic Libraries: 7th to 14th Centuries." *International Library Review* 22 (1990): 119–35.

Elder, Earl Edgar, trans. with introd. and notes. *A Commentary on the Creed of Islam: Sa'd al-Dīn al-Taftazānī on the Creed of Najm al-Dīn al-Nasafī*. New York: Columbia University Press, 1950.

Elsharky, Marwa. "Knowledge in Motion: The Cultural Politics to Modern Science Translations in Arabic." *Isis* 99, no. 4 (December 2008): 701–30.

Escovitz, J. H. "Vocational Patterns of the Scribes of the Mamluk Chancery." *Arabica* 23 (1976): 42–62.

Ettinghausen, Richard. "The Flowering of Seljuq Art." *Metropolitan Museum Journal* 3 (1970): 113–31.

Feldman, Walter. "The Celestial Sphere, the Wheel of Fortune, and Fate in the Gazels of Naili and Baki." *International Journal of Middle East Studies* 28, no. 2 (May 1996): 193–215.

Fernandes, L. *The Evolution of a Sufi Institution in Mamluk Egypt: The Khanqah*. Berlin: K. Schwarz, 1988.

———. "Mamluk Politics and Education: The Evidence of Two Fourteenth Century Waqfiyyas." *Annales Islamologiques* 23 (1987): 87–98.

Al-Fīrūzābādī, Majd al-Dīn Muḥammad b. Ya'qūb. *Mu'jam al-Qāmūs al-Muḥīṭ*. Ed. Khalīl Ma'mūn Shīḥā. 4th printing. Beirut: Dār al-Ma'rifah, 2009.

Fischel, Walter Joseph. *Ibn Khaldūn and Tamerlane: Their Historic Meeting in Damascus, 1401 A.D. (803 A.H.); A Study Based on Arabic Manuscripts of Ibn Khaldūn's "Autobiography."* Berkeley and Los Angeles: University of California Press, 1952.

Foucault, Michel. *The Order of Things: An Archaeology of the Human Sciences*. New York: Vintage Books–Random House, 1994.

Genette, Gerard. *Paratexts: Thresholds for Interpretation*. Trans. Jane E. Lewin. Cambridge: Cambridge University Press, 1997.

Germain, Mary St. "Abū ʿAbd Allāh ibn al-Ḥajjāj." In *Essays in Arabic Literary Biography, 925–1350*, ed. Terri DeYoung and Mary St. Germain, 122–29. Wiesbaden: Harrassowitz, 2011.

Ghālib, Muṣṭafā, ed. *Al-Risālah al-Jāmiʿah*. Beirut: Dār Ṣādir, 1974.

Al-Ghassānī al-Andalusī, Muḥammad ʿAbd al-Wahhāb. *Riḥlat al-Wazīr fī iftikāk al-asīr, 1690–1691* (The Travels of the Vizier to Release the Hostage, 1690–1691). Ed. Nūrī al-Jarrāḥ. Abū Dhabī: Dār al-Suwaydī lil-Nashr wa-al-Tawzīʿ, 2002.

Al-Ghazālī, Abū Ḥāmid. *Iḥyāʾ ʿulūm al-dīn* (The Revival of Islamic Sciences). Cairo: Al-Azhar Press, 1302/1884.

———. *Al-Tibr al-masbūk fī naṣīḥat al-mulūk* (usually referenced as The Forged Sword in Counseling Kings or The Counsel of Kings; or, Ingots of Gold for the Advice of Kings). Cairo: Maṭbaʿat al-ʾĀdāb wa-al-Muʾayyad, 1899.

Ghazi, Mohammed Ferid. "Un group sociale: 'Les Raffinés' (ẓūrafāʾ)." *Studia Islamica* 1 (Paris, 1959): 38–71.

Gibb, Elias John Wilkinson. *A History of Ottoman Poetry, 1319–1901*. Ed. E. G. Browne. London: Lowe-Brydone, 1958.

Glazer, Sidney. "A Noteworthy Passage from an Arab Grammatical Text." *Journal of the American Oriental Society* 62 (1942): 106–8.

Goodman, Dena. *The Republic of Letters: A Cultural History of the French Enlightenment*. Ithaca, NY, and London: Cornell University Press, 1994.

Grabar, Oleg. *The Formation of Islamic Art*. New Haven: Yale University Press, 1987.

Gran, Peter. "Ḥasan al-ʿAṭṭār." In *Essays in Arabic Literary Biography, 1350–1850*, ed. Joseph E. Lowry and Devin J. Stewart, 56–68. Wiesbaden: Harrassowitz, 2009.

———. *Islamic Roots of Capitalism: Egypt, 1760–1840*. Syracuse: Syracuse University Press, 1998.

———. *Rise of the Rich: A New View of Modern World History*. Syracuse: Syracuse University Press, 2008.

Gruendler, Beatrice, and Louise Marlow. Introduction to *Writers and Rulers: Perspectives on Their Relationship from Abbasid to Safavid Times*, ed. Beatrice Gruendler and Louise Marlow, v–xi. Wiesbaden: Reichert, 2004.

Gully, Adrian. "Arabic Linguistic Issues and Controversies of the Late Nineteenth and Early Twentieth Centuries." *Journal of Semitic Studies* 42, no. 1 (Spring 1997): 75–120.

———. "The Sword and the Pen in the Pre-Modern Arabic Heritage: A Literary Representation of an Important Historical Relationship." In *Ideas, Images, and Methods of Portrayal: Insights into Classical Arabic Literature and Islam*, ed. Sebastian Günther, 403–30. Leiden: Brill, 2005.

Guo, Li. *The Performing Arts in Medieval Islam: Shadow Play and Popular Poetry in Ibn Dāniyāl's Mamluk Cairo*. Leiden: Brill, 2012.

Gutas, Dimitri. *Greek Thought, Arabic Culture: The Graeco-Arabic Translation Movement in Baghdad and Early ʿAbbāsid Society (2nd–4th/8th–10th Centuries)*. London and New York: Frances and Taylor, 1998.

Haarmann, Ulrich. "Arabic in Speech, Turkish in Lineage: Mamluks and Their Sons in the Intellectual Life of Fourteenth-Century Egypt and Syria." *Journal of Semitic Studies* 33 (1988): 81–114.

———. "The Library of a Fourteenth Century Jerusalem Scholar." *Der Islam* 61 (1984): 327–33.

———. *Quellenstudien zur frühen Mamlukenzeit*. Freiburg im Breisgau: K. Schwarz, 1970.

———. "Turkish Legends in the Popular Historiography of Medieval Egypt." In *Proceedings of the Sixth Congress of Arabic and Islamic Studies*, ed. Frithiof Rundgren. Leiden: Brill, 1975.

Al-Ḥabashī, ʿAbdullāh Muḥammad. *Jāmiʿ al-shurūḥ wa al-ḥawāshī* (A Compendium of Commentaries and Marginalia). 3 vols. Abu Dhabi: Al-Mujammaʿ al-Thaqāfī, 2006.

Ḥājjī Khalīfah (Kâtip Çelebi). *Kashf al-ẓunūn ʿan asāmī al-kutub wa-al-funūn* (The Removal of Doubt from the Names of Books and the Sciences). Ed. Gustav Flügel. London: R. Bentley for the Oriental Translation Fund of Great Britain and Ireland, 1835–1858; Beirut: Dār al-Kutub al-ʿIlmiyyah, 2008.

Al-Ḥakīm, Tawfīq. "Tabiʿātunā naḥwa al-shabāb" (Our Responsibilities towards Youth). In *Yaqẓat al-fikr*. Cairo: Maktabat al-Anglū-Miṣriyyah, 1947.

———. *Yaqẓat al-fikr* (Awakening of the Mind). Cairo: Maktabat al-ʾĀdāb, 1986.

Hallaq, Wael B. "Was al-Shāfiʿī the Master Architect of Islamic Jurisprudence?" *International Journal of Middle East Studies* 25 (1993): 587–605.

Halldén, Philip. "What Is Arab Rhetoric?" *International Journal of Middle East Studies* 37, no. 1 (February 2005): 19–38.

Al-Hamadhānī, Badīʿ al-Zamān. *Maqāmāt*. Ed. Shaykh Muḥammad ʿAbduh. Beirut: Dār al-Mashriq, 2002.

———. *The Maqāmāt of Badīʿ al-Zamān al-Hamadhānī*. Trans. with introduction and notes by W. J. Prendergast. London: Luzac & Co., 1915. Online at http://www.sacred-texts.com/isl/mhm/mhm48.htm. Repr. with new foreword, London: Curzon, 1973.

Hämeen-Anttila, Jaakko. "Badīʿ al-Zamān ibn al-Ḥusayn al-Hamadhānī." In *Essays in Arabic Literary Biography, 925–1350*, ed. Terri DeYoung and Mary St. Germain, 38–51. Wiesbaden: Harrassowitz, 2011.

Hamilton, Alastair, Maurits H. van den Boogert, and Bart Westerweel. *The Republic of Letters and the Levant*. Leiden: Brill, 2005.

Hanna, Nelly. "Culture in Ottoman Egypt." In *Cambridge History of Egypt*, vol. 2, *Modern Egypt from 1517 to the End of the Twentieth Century*, ed. M. W. Daly, 87–112. Cambridge: Cambridge University Press, 1998.

Al-Ḥarīrī, Abū al-Qāsim Muḥammad. *Durrat al-ghawwāṣ fi awhām al-Khawāṣṣ* (The Diver's Pearl in the Delusions of the Elite). Baghdad: Maktabat al-Muthannā, [1871] 1964.

Haywood, John A. *Arabic Lexicography: Its History, and Its Place in the General History of Lexicography*. 2nd ed. Leiden: Brill, 1965.

Heath, Peter. "A Critical Review of Modern Scholarship on 'Sīrat ʿAntar ibn Shaddad' and the Popular Sīra." *Journal of Arabic Literature* 15 (1984): 19–44.

Heck, Paul L. *The Construction of Knowledge in Islamic Civilization: Qudamā b. Jaʿfar and His Kitāb al-Kharāj wa-ṣināʿat al-kitāba*. Leiden: Brill, 2002.

Heinrichs, Wolfhart P. "ʿAbd al-Raḥīm al-ʿAbbāsī." In *Essays in Arabic Literary Biography, 1350–1850*, ed. Joseph E. Lowry and Devin J. Stewart, 12–20. Wiesbaden: Harrassowitz, 2009.

———. "The Classification of the Sciences and the Consolidation of Philology in Classical Islam." In *Centres of Learning: Learning and Location in Pre-Modern Europe and the Near East*, ed. M. Drijvers and A. A. MacDonald, 119–39. Leiden: Brill, 1995.

———. "Prosimetrical Genres in Classical Arabic Literature." In *Prosimetrum: Cross-Cultural Perspectives on Narrative in Prose and Verse*, ed. Joseph Harris and Karl Reichl, 249–76. Cambridge: D. S. Brewer, 1997.

———. "Ṣāfī al-Dīn ʿAbd al-ʿAzīz b. Sarāyā." In *Encyclopedia of Islam*, CD-ROM Edition, v. 1.0. Leiden: Brill, 1999.

Hermes, Nizar F. *The [European] Other in Medieval Arabic Literature and Culture: Ninth–Twelfth Century AD*. New York: Palgrave Macmillan, 2012.

Al-Ḥillī, Ṣafī al-Dīn. *Al-ʿĀṭil al-ḥāli wa-al-murghghaṣ al-ghālī fī al-azjāl wa-al-mawālī* (The Unadorned Bejeweled and the Cheapened Rendered Costly). Ed. Ḥusayn Naṣṣār. Cairo: Al-Hayʾah al-Miṣriyyah al-ʿĀmmah lil-Kitāb [GEBO], 1981.

———. *Al-Kāfiyah al-badīʿiyyah fī al-madāʾiḥ al-nabawiyyah* (literally, the Sufficient Ode of Rhetoric in Encomiums to the Prophet), with *Sharḥ al-kāfiyah al-badīʿiyyah fi ʿulūm al-balāghah wa- maḥāsin al-badīʿ* (The Explication of the Sufficient *Badīʿiyyah* Ode in Rhetorical Sciences and Adornments in Innovativeness). Beirut: Dār Ṣādir, 1992.

———. *Sharḥ al-kāfiyah al-badīʿiyyah fi ʿulūm al-balāghah wa- maḥāsin al-badīʿ* (The Explication of the Sufficient *Badīʿiyyah* Ode in Rhetorical Sciences and Adornments in Innovativeness). Ed. Nasīb Nashāwī. Beirut: Dār Ṣādir, 1982.

Himmich, Ben Salem. *Al-ʿAllāmah*. English edition: *The Polymath*. Trans. Roger Allen. Cairo and New York: American University in Cairo Press, 2004.

Hirschler, Konrad. *The Written Word in the Medieval Arabic Lands*. Edinburgh: Edinburgh University Press, 2012.

Holmberg, Bo. "*Adab* and Arabic Literature." In *Literary History: Towards a Global Perspective*, 1:180–205. Berlin, New York: W. de Gruyter, 2006.

Holt, Peter M. "Literary Offerings: A Genre of Courtly Literature." In *The Mamluks in Egyptian Politics and Society*, ed. Thomas Philipp and Ulrich Haarmann, 3–16. Cambridge: Cambridge University Press, 1998.

———. "The Treatment of Arab History by Prideaux, Ockley and Sale." In *Historians of the Middle East*, ed. Bernard Lewis and Peter M. Holt, 290–302. London: Oxford University Press, 1962.

Homerin, Th. Emil. "ʿĀʾishah al-Bāʿūniyyah," *Essays in Arabic Literary Biography, 1350–1850*, ed. Joseph E. Lowry and Devin J. Stewart, 21–27. Wiesbaden: Harrassowitz, 2009.

———, trans. and introd. *ʿUmar ibn al-Fāriḍ: Sufi Verse, Saintly Life*. New York: Paulist Press, 2001.

Hourani, Albert. *Arabic Thought in the Liberal Age*. London: Oxford University Press, 1962.

Huff, Toby. *The Rise of Early Modern Science: Islam, China, and the West*. Cambridge: Cambridge University Press, 2003.

Ḥusayn, Ṭāhā. Preface to Goethe, *Ālām Veirter* (*The Sorrows of Young Werther*), trans. Aḥmad Ḥasan al-Zayyāt. Cairo: Lajnat al-Taʾlīf wa Tarjamah wa al-Nashr, 1920.

Ibn Abī al-Ḥadīd, Hibat Allāh. *Al-Falak al-dāʾir ʿalā al-Mathal al-sāʾir*. Ed. Aḥmad al-Ḥūfī and Badawī Ṭabānah. Cairo, n.d.

Ibn Abī al-Iṣbaʿ. *Taḥrīr al-taḥbīr*. Ed. Ḥifnī Muḥammad Sharaf. Cairo: Al-Majlis al-Aʿlā lil-Shuʾūn al-Islāmiyyah, 1995.

Ibn Abī Ṭālib, ʿAlī. *Peak of Eloquence*. Trans. Askari Jafri. Ed. Muhammad Wasi. India: Alwaʿẓ International, 2010.

Ibn al-ʿArabī, Muḥyī al-Dīn. *Tarjumān al-ashwāq, A Collection of Mystical Odes*. Ed. and trans. R.A. Nicholson. London: Royal Asiatic Society, 1911.

Ibn Arabshah, Ahmad. *Tamerlane, or Timur the Great Amir*. Trans. J.H. Sanders. London: Luzac and Co., 1936.

Ibn Baṭṭūṭa [Baṭṭūṭah], Muḥammad ibn ʿAbdallah. *The Travels of ibn Baṭṭūṭa, A.D. 1325–1354*. Trans. and ed. H.A.R. Gibb, C. Defrémery, and B.R. Sanguinetti. Vol. 2, Works issued by the Hakluyt Society, 2nd ser., no. 117.

Cambridge: Hakluyt Society, Cambridge University Press, 1962; repr., Millwood, NY: Kraus, 1986.

———. *Tuḥfat al-nuẓẓār fī gharā'ib al-amṣār wa- ʿajā'ib al-asfār* (The Observer's Delight in Surprises of Cities and Wonders in Journey). Cairo: Maṭbaʿat at-Taqaddum, 1904.

Ibn Dāniyāl, Muḥammad. *Three Shadow Plays*. Ed. Paul Kahle, Derek Hopwood, and Mustafa Badawi. Cambridge: Cambridge University Press, 1992.

Ibn al-Dubaythī, Muḥammad ibn Saʿīd. *Al-Mukhtaṣar al-muḥtāj ilayh min tārīkh Abī ʿAbd Allāh Muḥammmad Saʿīd ibn Muḥammad ibn al-Dubaythī.* Ed. Muṣṭafā Jawād. 2 vols. Baghdad: Al-Majmaʿ al-ʿIlmī al-ʿIrāqī, 1951.

Ibn Duqmāq, Ibrāhīm ibn Muḥammad ibn Aydamr. *Al-Jawhar al-thamīn fī siyar al-mulūk wa al-salāṭīn* (The Precious Stone in the Conduct Accounts of Kings and Sultans). Ṣaydā: Al-Maktabah al-ʿAṣriyyah, 1999.

Ibn Durayd, Abū Bakr Muḥammad ibn al-Ḥasan al-Azdī. *Kitāb al-Malāḥin* (Ambiguities of Speech). Ed. ʿAbd al-Ilāh Nabhān. Damascus: Wizārat al-Thaqāfah, 1992.

Ibn al-Fāriḍ. *Dīwān ibn al-Fāriḍ*. Beirut: Dār Ṣādir, 1958; 2nd printing, 2002.

Ibn Ḥajjāj, Muslim. *Ṣaḥīḥ Muslim*. Beirut: Dār al-Kitāb al-ʿArabī, 2004.

Ibn Ḥijjah al-Ḥamawī, Taqī al-Dīn Abū Bakr ibn ʿAlī ʿAbdullāh. *Bulūgh al-amal fi fann al-zajal*. Ed. Riḍā Muḥsin al-Qurayshī. Damascus: Wizārat al-Thaqāfah wa-al-Irshād al-Qawmī (Ministry of Culture), 1974.

———. *Kashf al-lithām ʿan wajh al-tawriyah wa-al-istikhdām.* Beirut: Al-Maṭbaʿah al-Unsiyah, 1894–1895.

———. *Kashf al-lithām ʿan wajh al-tawriyah wa-al-istikhdām* (against al-Ṣafadī's book, *Faḍḍ al-Khitām . . .*). Beirut: Dār al-Kutub al-ʿIlmiyyah, 2011.

———. *Khizānat al-adab wa-ghāyat al-arab* (The Ultimate Treasure Trove of Literature). Ed. Kawkab Diyāb. Beirut: Dār Ṣādir, 2001.

———. *Kitāb Qahwat al-inshā'*. Ed. Rudolf Veselý. Berlin: K. Schwarz; Beirut: Matba'at Dirgham, 2005.

Ibn Hishām al-Anṣārī. *Mughnī al-Labīb* (Sufficient Knowledge of the Sensible One). Ed. Dr. Emil Yaqub. 3 vols. Beirut: Dār al-Kutub al-ʿIlmiyyah, n.d.

Ibn Ilyās al-Ḥanafī. *Al-Durr al-maknūn fī sabʿ funūn* (The Hidden Pearls of the Seven Arts/Categories). www.Islamicareastudies. Date: 17C AD. Number: ADD. 9570/2. AC 750/2. Fiche 32114–15.

Ibn Jābir. *Al-Aqṣā al-qarīb fī ʿilm al-bayān*. Cairo: Al-Saʿādah Press, 1909.

Ibn al-Jawzī, Abū al-Faraj ʿAbd al-Raḥmān. *Ṣayd al-khāṭir* (Random Thoughts). Beirut: Dār al-Kitāb al-ʿArabī, 2010.

Ibn Khaldūn, ʿAbd al-Raḥmān. *Kitāb al-ʿibar wa dīwān al-mubtada' wa al-khabar fī ayyām al-ʿArab, wa al-ʿAjam wa al-Barbar wa man ʿāṣarahum min dhawī al-sulṭān al-akbar* (Book of Lessons, Record of Beginnings and

Events in the History of the Arabs, Non-Arabs, and Berbers and Their Powerful Contemporaries). Cairo: Būlāq Press, 1867–1868.

———. *Al-Muqaddima*. Beirut: Dār al-Kutub al-ʿIlmiyyah, 1993.

———. *Al-Taʿrīf bi-ibn Khaldūn wa-Riḥlatihī gharban wa-sharqan*. Cairo: Lajnat al-Taʾlīf wa-al-Tarjamah wa-al-Nashr, 1951.

Ibn Khallikān, Shams al-Dīn Aḥmad ibn Muḥammad Abū Bakr. *Wafayāt al-Aʿyān*. Ed. Iḥsān ʿAbbās, ʿIzz al-Dīn ʿUmar Aḥmad Mūsā, and Wadād Qāḍī. 8 vols. Beirut: Dār al-Thaqāfah, 1994.

Ibn Manẓūr, Abū al-Mukarram. *Lisān al-ʿArab*. 8 vols. Beirut: Dār Iḥyāʾ al-Turāth, 2010.

Ibn Maʿṣūm, ʿAlī ibn Aḥmad. *Sulāfat al-ʿaṣr fi maḥāsin ahl al-ʿaṣr* [it occurs also under other titles]: *fī maḥāsinʿayān miṣr* and *fī maḥāsin al-shuʿarāʾ bi-kull miṣr*. Cairo: Aḥmad Nājī al-Jamālī wa-Muḥammad Amīn al-Khānjī, 1906; Beirut/Ṣaydā: Al-Maktaba al-ʿAṣriyya li-al-Ṭibāʿa wa-al-Nashr, 1986; Dimashq: Dār Kinān lil-Ṭibāʿah wa al-Nashr wa-al-Tawzīʿ, 2009.

Ibn al-Muqaffaʿ. "Al-Durrah al-yatīmah" (The Solitary Gem). In *Rasāʾil al-bulaghāʾ* (Epistles of the Rhetoricians), ed. Muḥammad Kurd ʿAlī. Cairo: Dār al-Kutub al-ʿArabīyah al-Kubrā, 1913.

Ibn al-Najjār al-Baghdādī. *Al-Mustafād min dhayl taʾrīkh Baghdād* (Useful Extract from the Epilogue to the History of Baghdad). Ed. Bashshār ʿAwwād Maʿrūf. Beirut: Muʾassasat al-Risālah, 1986.

Ibn Nubātah, Jamāl al-Dīn. *Sarḥ al-ʿuyūn fī sharḥ risālat ibn Zaydūn* (Roaming Gently in the Explication of the Epistle of ibn Zaydūn). Ed. Muḥammad Abū al-Faḍl Ibrāhīm. Beirut/Ṣaydā: Al-Maktabah al-ʿAṣriyyah, 1986; repr. 1998.

———. *Talṭīf al-mizāj min shiʿr ibn al-Hajjāj* (Refining the Mood with the Poetry of ibn al-Ḥajjāj). Ed. Najm ʿAbdullāh Muṣṭafā. Suese: Dār al-Maʿārif, 2001.

Ibn Qutaybah, ʿAbd Allāh ibn Muslim. *Adab al-kātib*. Ed. M. M. ʿAbd al-Ḥamīd. Cairo: Al-Maktabah al-Tijāriyyah al-Kubrā, 1963.

———. *Adab al-kātib*. Beirut: Al-Maktabah al-ʿAṣriyyah, 2002.

———. *Kitāb al-shiʿr wa- al-shuʿarāʾ*. Ed. M. J. de Goeje. Leiden: Brill, 1904.

Ibn Sina, *Remarks and Admonitions*, Part One: Logic. Trans. S. Inati. Toronto: Pontifical Institute of Medieval Studies, 1984.

Ibn Taymiyyah, Taqī al-Dīn. *Kitāb minhāj al-sunna al-nabawīyah fi naqḍ kalām al-Shīʿa wa-al-Qadarīyah*. Būlāq: Al-Maṭbaʿah al-Kubrā al-Amīrīyah, AH 1321(1903–1904).

———. *Majmūʿ al-fatāwā li-Shaykh al-Islām Aḥmad b. Taymiyyah*. Ed. M. ʿAṭāʾ. Beirut: Dār al-Kutub al-ʿIlmiyyah, 2000.

———. *Majmūʿ Fatāwā ibn Taymiyyah*. Ribat: Maktabat al-Maʿārif, n.d.

Ibn al-ʾUkhuwwa, Ḍiyāʾ al-Dīn Muḥammad ibn Muḥammad al-Qurashī al-Shāfiʿī. *The Maʿālim al-Qurba fī Ṭalab al-Ḥisba*. Ed. Reuben Levy. Gibb Memorial Series, n.s., 12. London: Luzac, printed by Cambridge University Press, 1938.

Ibn Wahb al-Kātib, Abū al-Ḥusayn Isḥāq b. Ibrāhīm b. Sulaymān. *Al-Burhān fī wujūh al-bayān* (Demonstrating the Modes of Eloquent Expression). Ed. Aḥmad Maṭlūb and Khadījah al-Ḥadīthī. Baghdad: Baghdad University Publication, 1967.

———. *Al-Burhān fi wujūh al-bayān* (Demonstrating the Modes of Eloquent Expression). Ed. Ḥafnī M. Sharaf. Jīzā: Maktabat al-Shabāb, 1969.

Ibn al-Wardī, Zayn al-Din ʿUmar ibn al-Muzaffar. *Diwān ibn al-Wardī*. Cairo: Dār al-Āfāq al-ʿArabiyyah, 2006.

———. *Kharīdat al-ʿajāʾib wa farīdat al-gharāʾib* (The Pearl of Wonders and the Uniqueness of Things Strange). Cairo: Maktabat al-Thaqāfah al-Dīniyyah, 2008.

Ibn Zākūr al-Fāsī, Muḥammad b. Qāsim. *Al-Ṣanīʿ al-Badīʿ fi sharḥ al-ḥilyati dhāt al-badīʿ* (The Inventive Craftmanship in Explicating the Innovative Adornment). Ed. Bushrā al-Badāwī. Rabat: Muhammad V University, diss. 53; 2001.

Ibrāhim, Sayyid. "Al-Khaṭṭ al-ʿArabī fī al-ʿaṣr al-ḥadīth." *Al-Hilāl* (1939, special issue): 150.

Ijī, ʿAḍud al-Dīn ʿAbd al-Raḥmān ibn Aḥmad. *Al-Fawāʾid al-ghiyāthiyah fī al-ʿulūm al-balāghiyyah* (The Bountiful Sources in the Sciences of Rhetoric). Cairo: Dār al-Kitāb al-Miṣrī; Beirut: Dār al-Kitāb al-Lubnānī, 1990.

———. *Al-Ḥāshiyah*. Cairo: Maktabat al-Kulliyāt al-Azhariyyah, 1973–1974.

———. *Jāmiʿ al-bayān fī tafsīr al-Qurʾān* (The Compendium of Tropical Language in Qurʾānic Hermeneutics). Beirut: Dār al-Kutub al-ʿIlmiyyah, 2004; Kuwait: Gharas, 2007.

———. *Kitāb al-Mawāqif fī ʿilm al-kalām* (The Stations in the Science of Speculative Theology). Beirut: Dār al-Jīl, 1997.

———. *Risālat adab al-baḥth wa-al-munāẓarah* (The Epistle on the Art of Research and Debate). Al-Riyāḍ: Dār Umayyah lil-Nashr wa-al-Tawzīʿ, 1991.

———. *Sharḥ Mukhtaṣar al-Muntahā al-ʾuṣūlī li- ibn al-Ḥājib*, known as *al-Ḥāshiyah al-ʿAḍudiyyah* (Aḍud's Marginalia). Beirut: Dār al-Kutub al-ʿIlmiyyah, 2004.

Ikhwān al-Ṣafāʾ. *Rasāʾil Ikhwān al-Ṣafāʾ wa Khullān al-Wafāʾ* (Epistles of the Pure Brethren and the Sincere Friends). 4 vols. Beirut: Dār Ṣādir, n.d.

———. *Al-Risālah al-jāmiʿah* (The Comprehensive Epistle) or *Jāmiʿat al-jāmiʿah* (Super Comprehensive Epistle). Ed. Muṣṭa Ghālib. Beirut: Dār Ṣādir, 1974.

Iqbal, Muzaffar. *Islam and Science*. Aldershot, Hampshire: Ashgate Publishing, 2002.

Irvine, Martin. *The Making of Textual Culture: 'Grammatica' and Literary Theory, 350–1100*. Cambridge: Cambridge University Press, 1994.

Irwin, Robert. "Mamluk Literature." *Mamluk Studies Review* 7, no. 1 (2003): 1–30.

Al-Isnāwī, Jamāl al-Dīn. *Al-Kawkab al-durrī fī mā yatakharraj 'ala al-'uṣūl al-naḥwiyyah min al-furū' al-fiqhiyya* (The Pearly Star in the Extraction of Juridical Secondary Rulings on the Bases of Grammatical Principles). Amman: Dār 'Ammār, 1985.

Al-Jabartī, 'Abd al-Raḥmān. *'Ajā'ib al-āthār fī al-tarājim wa al-akhbār* (The Most Wondrous Traces in Biographies and Reports). Cairo: Lajnat al-Bayān al-'Arabī, 1959–1967. English edition: *'Abd al-Raḥmān al-Jabartī's History of Egypt*. Ed. Thomas Philipp and Moshe Perlmann. 4 vols. Stuttgart: Franz Steiner Verlag, 1994.

———. *Tārīkh Muddat al-Faransīs bi Miṣr* (Al-Jabartī's *Chronicle of the First Seven Months of the French Occupation of Egypt*). Trans. S. Moreh. Leiden: Brill, 1975.

Al-Jābirī, Muḥammad 'Ābid. *Al-Khiṭāb al-'Arabī al-mu'āṣir* (Contemporary Arabic Discourse). Beirut: Dār al-Ṭalī'ah, 1982; repr. 1986.

Al-Jāḥiẓ, Abū 'Uthmān. *Al-Ḥayawān*. Ed. 'Abd al-Salām Hārūn. Cairo: Maktabat wa-Maṭba'at Muṣṭafā al-Bābī al-Ḥalabī, 1938.

———. *Kitāb al-ḥayawān*. Ed. Muḥammad 'Abd al-Salām Hārūn. Beirut: Dār al-Jīl, 1996.

———. "Risālah fī Banī Umayyah." In Aḥmad Zakī Ṣafwat, *Jamharat Rasā'il al-'Arab*, 2nd ed., 4:56–68. Cairo: Muṣṭafā al-Bābī al-Ḥalabī, 1971.

Jameson, Fredric. "Foreword." In Jean-François Leotard, *The Postmodern Condition: A Report on Knowledge*, vii–xxi. Minneapolis: University of Minnesota Press, 1984.

———. *The Political Unconscious*. Ithaca, NY: Cornell University Press, 1981.

Jamil, M. F. "Islamic Wirāqah, 'stationery,' during the Early Middle Ages." PhD diss., University of Michigan, 1985.

Jāsim, 'Azīz al-Sayyid. *Mutaṣawwifat Baghdād*. Beirut: Al-Markaz al-Thaqāfī al-'Arabī, 1990.

Al-Jawharī, Rajā' al-Sayyid, ed. *Kitāb Ṭirāz al-Ḥullah wa- Shifā' al-Ghullah lil-Imām Abī Ja'far Shihāb al-Dīn . . . al-Andalusī, Sharḥ al-Ḥullah al-Siyarā'*. Alexandria: Mu'assasat al-Thaqāfah al-Jāmi'iyyah, 1410/1990.

Jenssen, Herbjørn. *The Subtleties and Secrets of the Arabic Language: Preliminary Investigations into al-Qazwini's Talkhis al-Miftah*. Bergen: Centre for Middle Eastern and Islamic Studies, 1998.

Al-Jurjānī, ʿAbd al-Qāhir. *Dalāʾil al-iʿjāz*. Ed. Yāsīn al-Ayyūbī. Beirut/Ṣaydā: Al-Maktabah al-ʿAṣriyyah, 2002.

Al-Jurjānī, al-Qāḍī ʿAlī ibn ʿAbd al-ʿAzīz. *Al-Waṣāṭah bayna al-Mutanabbī wa-khuṣūmihī* (The Mediation between al-Mutanabbī and His Opponents). Ed. Muḥammad Abū al-Faḍl Ibrāhīm. Cairo: Maṭbaʿat ʿIsā al-Bābī al-Ḥalabī, 1966.

Al-Juwaynī, Abū al-Maʿālī ʿAbd al-Malik ibn ʿAbdullāh. *Al-Shāmil fī ʾuṣūl al-dīn* (The Comprehensive in the Principles of Religion). Alexandria: Al-Maʿārif, 1969.

Jwaideh, Wadie. *The Introductory Chapters of Yāqūt's Muʿjam al-Buldān*. Leiden: Brill, 1959.

Kalimullah Husaini, Q. S. "Life and Works of Zahir UʾD-Din Al-Bayhaqi, the Author of Tarikh-i-Bayhaq." *Islamic Culture* 28 (1954): 297–318.

Kanazi, George J. *Studies in the Kitāb aṣ-Ṣināʿatayn of Abū Hilal al-Askari*. Leiden: Brill, 1989.

Al-Kātib, ʿAbd al-Ḥamīd. "Risālah ilā al-kuttāb." In *Rasāʾil al-bulaghāʾ* (Epistles of the Rhetoricians), ed. Muḥammad Kurd ʿAlī. Cairo: Dār al-Kutub al-ʿArabīyah al-Kubrā, 1913.

Khafājah, Muḥammad ʿAbd al-Munʿim, ed. *Al-ʾĪḍāḥ fī ʿulūm al-balāghah*. Beirut: Dār al-Jīl, n.d.

Khairallah, Asʿad. *Love, Madness, and Poetry: An Interpretation of the Magnun Legend*. Beirut: Orient-Institut der Deutschen Morgenlandischen Gesellschaft, 1980.

Khaldi, B. *Egypt Awakening in the Early Twentieth Century*. New York: Palgrave, 2012.

Al-Khaṭīb, ʿAdnān. *Al-Muʿjam al-ʿArabī.* 1966; amended edition, 1994; Beirut: Maktabat Lubnān, 1994.

Al-Khaṭīb al-Baghdādī. *Taqyīd al-ʿilm*. Ed. Youssef Eche (Yusuf al-ʿIshsh). Damascus: Al-Maʿhad al-Faransī, 1949; repr. 1975.

Khouri, Mounah A. *Poetry and the Making of Modern Egypt*. Leiden: Brill, 1971.

Kilito, Abdelfattah. *Lan tatakallam lughatī.* Beirut: Dār al-Ṭalīʿah, 2002. English edition: *Thou Shalt Not Speak My Language*. Trans. Wail Hassan. Syracuse: Syracuse University Press, 2008.

Kilpatrick, Hilary. *Making the Great Book of Songs: Compilation and the Author's Craft in Abū l-Faraj al-Iṣbahānī's Kitāb al-aghānī.* London and New York: RoutledgeCurzon, 2003.

Knysh, Alexander D. *Ibn ʿArabi in the Later Islamic Tradition: The Making of a Polemical Image of Medieval Islam*. Albany: State University of New York Press, 1999.

Krachkovskii, Ignatii Lulianovich. *Tārīkh al-adab al-jughrāfī al-ʿArabī* (Istoriia arabskoi geograficheskoi literatury). Beirut: Dār al-Gharb al-Lubnānī, 1987.

Kurd ʿAlī, Muḥammad. "Ḥālatunā al-ʿilmiyyah wa al-ijtimāʿiyyah." *Al-Muqtabas* 2, no. 12 (1907): 617–23.

———. "Malakat al-ʿArabiyyah." *Al-Muqtabas* 1, no. 8 (1906): 430–35.

———. *Rasāʾil al-bulaghāʾ* (A Collection of Literary Epistles by ʿAbd Allāh ibn Al-Muqaffaʿ and ʿAbd Al-Hamīd ibn Yaḥya al-Kātib). Cairo: Al-Ẓāhir, 1908.

Al-Kutubī, Muḥammad ibn Shākir ibn Aḥmad. *Fawāt al-Wafayāt.* Ed. Iḥsān ʿAbbās and Wadād Qāḍī. 5 vols. Beirut: Dār Ṣādir, 1973.

———. *Fawāt al-wafayāt, wa-huwa dhayl ʿalā kitāb wafayāt al-aʿyān li-ibn Khallikān*. Ed. Muḥammad Muḥyī al-Dīn ʿAbd al-Ḥamīd. Cairo: Maktabat al-Nahḍah al-Miṣrīyah, 1951.

Larkin, Margaret. "The Dust of the Master: A Mamlūk-Era 'Zajal' by Khalaf al-Gubārī." *Quaderni di Studi Arabi*, n.s., 2 (2007): 11–29.

Latham, D. "The Beginnings of Arabic Prose Literature: The Epistolary Genre." In *Arabic Literature to the End of the Umayyad Period*, ed. A. F. L. Beeston et al., 164–79. Cambridge: Cambridge University Press, 1983.

Lefevere, André. *Translation, Rewriting, and the Manipulation of Literary Fame.* London and New York: Routledge, 1992.

Levy, Reuben, trans. *A Mirror for the Princes: The Qabus Nama of ibn Iskandar.* New York: Dutton, 1951.

Lewis, Franklin. "Sincerely Flattering Panegyrics: The Shrinking Ghaznavid Qasida." In *The Necklace of the Pleiades*, ed. F. D. Lewis and S. Sharma, 209–49. Leiden: Leiden University, 2010.

Little, Donald P. "Historiography of the Ayyūbid and Mamlūk Epochs." In *Cambridge History of Egypt*, ed. Carl F. Petry, 1:412–44. Cambridge: Cambridge University Press, 1998.

———. "Religion under the Mamluks." *Muslim World* 73 (1983): 165–81.

Lornejad, Siavash, and Ali Doostzadeh. *On the Modern Politicization of the Persian Poet Nezami Ganjavi*. Yerevan Series for Oriental Studies 1, ed. Garnik S. Asatrian. Yerevan: Caucasian Centre for Iranian Studies, 2012.

Losensky, Paul E. "The Creative Compiler: The Art of Rewriting in al-ʿAṭṭār's *Tazkirat al-awlīyāʾ*." In *The Necklace of the Pleiades*, ed. F. D. Lewis and S. Sharma, 107–19. Leiden: Leiden University, 2010.

Lowry, Joseph E. "Ibn Maʿṣūm." In *Essays in Arabic Literary Biography, 1350–1850*, ed. Joseph E. Lowry and Devin J. Stewart, 175–84. Wiesbaden: Harrassowitz, 2009.

Macdonald, Duncan Black, ed. and trans. "Emotional Religion in Islam as Affected by Music and Singing. Being a Translation of a Book of the Iḥyā

ʿUlūm ad-Dīn of al-Ghazzālī with Analysis, Annotation, and Appendices." *Journal of the Royal Asiatic Society* 33, no. 2 (April 1901): 195–252.

Mackintosh-Smith, Tim. *Travels with a Tangerine: A Journey in the Footnotes of Ibn Battuta.* New York: Welcome Rain Publishers, 2002.

Mahdi, Muhsin. "Language and Logic in Classical Islam." In *Logic in Classical Islamic Culture*, ed. G. E. von Grunebaum, 50–83. Wiesbaden: Harrassowitz, 1970.

Makdisi, George. *The Rise of Colleges: Institutions of Learning in Islam and the West.* Edinburgh: Edinburgh University Press, 1981.

———. *The Rise of Humanism in Classical Islam and the Christian West with Special Reference to Scholasticism.* Edinburgh: Edinburgh University Press, 1990.

———. "Ṭabaqāt Biography: Law and Orthodoxy in Classical Islam." *Islamic Studies* 32 (1993): 371–96.

Al-Mālikī, ibn Abī al-ʿĪd. *Ḥilyat al-kuramāʾ wa-bahjat al-nudamāʾ* (The Adornment of the Honorable and the Delight of Boon-Companions). Beirut: Books-Publisher, 2010.

Al-Malkh, Ḥasan Khamīs. *Naẓariyyat al-aṣl wa-al-farʾ fī al-naḥw al-ʿArabī* (The Theory of Origin and Branch in Arabic Grammar). Amman: Dār al-Shurūq, 2001.

Maqdisi, Usama. *Artillery of Heaven: American Missionaries and the Failed Conversion of the Middle East.* Ithaca, NY: Cornell University Press, 2007.

Al-Maqrīzī, Taqī al-Dīn Aḥmad ibn ʾAlī. *Kitāb al-sulūk li maʿrifat duwal al mulūk* (usually referenced as Book of Entrance to the Knowledge of the Dynasties of the Kings). 4 vols. Cairo: Lajnat al-Taʾlif wa al-Tarjama wa al-Nashr, 1956–1973.

———. *Al-Sulūk li-maʿrifat duwal al-mulūk.* Vols. 1 and 2. Cairo: Muḥammad Muṣṭafā Ziyādah, 1941.

Margoliouth, D. S. "The Discussion between Abu Bishr Matta and Abu Saʿid al-Sirafi on the Merits of Logic and Grammar." *Journal of the Royal Asiatic Society of Great Britain and Ireland* (January 1905): 79–129.

Marlow, Louise. "The Way of Viziers and the Lamp of Commanders." In *Writers and Rulers: Perspectives from Abbasid to Safavid Times*, ed. Beatrice Gruendler and Louise Marlow, 169–93. Wiesbaden: Reichert, 2004.

Marquet, Y. "Ikhwān al-Safāʾ." In *Encyclopedia of Islam*, 3:1071–76. Leiden: Brill, 1968. Repr., *Encyclopedia of Islam*, CD-ROM Edition, v. 1.0. Leiden: Brill, 1999.

Al-Marṣafī, Shaykh Ḥusayn. *Risālat al-kalam al-thamān.* Ed. Aḥmad Zakarīyā Shalaq. Cairo: Al-Hayʾah al-Miṣrīyah al-ʿĀmmah lil-Kitāb [GEBO], 1984.

Matar, Nabil. *In the Lands of the Christians: Arabic Travel Writing in the Seventeenth Century*. New York and London: Routledge, 2003.

Maẓhar, Ismāʿīl. *Al-Nahḍa Dictionary*. 2 vols. Cairo: Renaissance Bookshop, n.d.

McCarthy, Richard J. *The Theology of Al-Ashʿarī: The Arabic Texts of al-Ashʿarī's Kitāb al-Lumaʿ and Risālat Istihsān al-khawd fī ʿilm al-kalām, with briefly annotated translations and appendices containing material pertinent to the study of al-Ashʿarī*. Beirut: Imprimerie Catholique, 1953.

Meisami, Julie Scott. "A Life in Poetry: Hafiz's First Ghazal." In *The Necklace of the Pleiades*, ed. F.D. Lewis and S. Sharma, 163–81. Leiden: Leiden University, 2010.

———. *Medieval Persian Court Poetry*. Princeton: Princeton University Press, 1987.

Messick, Brinkley. *The Calligraphic State: Textual Domination and History in a Muslim Society*. Berkeley: University of California Press, 1993.

Miller, Howard. "Tamburlaine: The Migration and Translation of Marlowe's Arabic Sources." In *Travel and Translation in the Early Modern Period*, ed. Carmine Di Biase, 255–66. Amsterdam and New York: Rodopi, 2006.

Miura, Toru. "The Ṣāliḥiyya Quarter in the Suburbs of Damascus: Its Formation, Structure, and Transformation in the Ayyūbid and Mamlūk Periods." *Bulletin d'études orientales* 47 (1995): 154–75.

———. "The Salihiyya Quarter of Damascus at the Beginning of Ottoman Rule: The Ambiguous Relations between Religious Institutions and *Waqf* Properties." In *Syria and Bilad al-Sham under Ottoman Rule: Essays in Honour of Abdul-Karim Rafeq*, ed. Peter Sluglett and Stefan Weber, 269–91. Leiden: Brill, 2010.

Montgomery, J.E. "Sukhf." In *Encyclopedia of Islam*, CD-ROM Edition, v. 1.0. Leiden: Brill, 1999.

Moosa, Ebrahim. *Ghazali and the Poetics of Imagination*. Chapel Hill: University of North Carolina Press, 2005.

Mottahedeh, Roy P. "The Shuʿūbīyah and the Social History of Early Islamic Iran." *International Journal of Middle East Studies* 7 (1976): 161–82.

Mubārak, Zakī. *Al-Madāʾiḥ al-nabawiyyah* (Encomiums to the Prophet). Cairo: Dār al-Kātib al-ʿArabī, 1967.

———. "Mustaqbal al-adab al-ʿArabī" (The Future of Arabic Literature). *Al-Hilāl* (1939, special issue): 129–31.

Al-Mudawwar, Amīn Nakhlah. *Ḥaḍārat al-Islām fī Dār al-Salām* (Islamic Civilization in the Abode of Peace [i.e., Baghdad]). Cairo: Al-Amīriyyah Press, Būlāq, 1937.

Mufti, Aamir R. "Orientalism and the Institution of World Literatures." *Critical Inquiry* 36, no. 3 (Spring 2010): 458–93.

Muhanna, Elias. "Encyclopaedism in the Mamluk Period: The Composition of Shihāb al-Dīn al-Nuwayrī's (d. 1333) *Nihāyat al-Arab fī Funūn al-Adab*." PhD diss., Harvard University, 2012.

Al-Muqaddasī. *The Best Divisions for Knowledge of the Regions: A Translation of Ahasan al-Taqasim fi Maʿrifat al-Aqalim*. Trans. B. Collins. Reading: Garnet, 1994.

Mūsā, Salāmah. *Mā hiya al-Nahḍah* (What Is the Renaissance?). Cairo: Dār al-Jīl, n.d.

———. *Al-Tathqīf al-dhātī* (Self-Teaching; Autodidactus). Cairo: Maṭbaʿat Dār al-Taqaddum, n.d.

Al-Musawi, Muhsin. "Abbasid Popular Narrative: The Formation of Readership and Cultural Production." *Journal of Arabic Literature* 38, no. 3, In Honor of Jaroslav Stetkevych, Who First Made "The Mute Immortals Speak," Part I (2007): 261–92.

———. *Anglo-Orient*. Tunis: Centre de Publication Universitaire, 2000.

———. *Arabic Poetry: Trajectories of Modernity and Tradition*. London: Routledge, 2006.

———. "Arabic Rhetoric." In *Oxford Encyclopedia of Rhetoric*, ed. Thomas O. Sloane, 29–33. Oxford and New York: Oxford University Press, 2001.

———. *The Islamic Context of the Thousand and One Nights*. New York: Columbia University Press, 2009.

———. *Islam on the Street*. Lanham, MD: Rowman and Littlefield, 2009.

———. *Mujtamʿ Alf Laylah wa-Laylah*. Tunis: Dār al-Nashr al-Jāmiʿī, 2000.

———. "Pre-modern Belletrist Prose." In *Arabic Literature in the Post-Classical Period*, ed. Roger Allen and D. S. Richards, 101–33. The Cambridge History of Arabic Literature. Cambridge: Cambridge University Press, 2006.

———. *Reading Iraq*. London: I. B. Tauris, 2006.

———. "The Republic of Letters: Arab Modernity?" *Cambridge Journal of Postcolonial Literary Inquiry* 10 (2014): 1–16.

———. *Scheherazade in England: A Study of Nineteenth-Century English Criticism of the Arabian Nights*. Washington, DC: Three Continents, 1981.

———. "Vindicating a Profession or a Personal Career? Al-Qalqashandī's *Maqāmah* in Context." *Mamluk Studies Review* 7, no. 1 (2003): 111–35.

Al-Nabhānī, Yūsuf ibn Ismāʿīl. *Al-Hamziyyah al-alfiyyah al-musammāt Tībat al-gharrāʾ fī madḥ Sayyid al-anbiyāʾ*. Beirut: Al-Maṭbaʿah al-Adabiyyah, 1896.

———. *Al-Majmūʿah al-Nabhāniyyah fī al-madāʾiḥ al-nabawiyyah*. 4 vols. Beirut: Al-Maṭbaʿah al-Adabiyyah, 1902; repr., Beirut: Dār al-Maʿrifah, 1974.

Nābulusī, ʿAbd al-Ghanī. *Nafaḥāt al-azhār ʿalā nasamāt al-asḥār fī madḥ al-Nabī al-mukhtār bi-fann al-badīʿ*. Dimashq: Ḥabīb Afandī, 1882.

Al-Nabulusī, ʿUthmān. *Lumaʿ al-Qawānīn*. Ed. C. Becker and C. Cahen. Port Said, n.d.

Al-Nafzāwī, Muḥammad. *The Perfumed Garden*, by Shaykh Nefwazi [*sic*]. Trans. Sir Richard Francis Burton. Benares, 1886.

Al-Nawājī, Shams al-Dīn Muḥammad ibn Ḥasan. *Al-Durr al-nafīs fī mā zāda ʿalā jinān al-jinās lil-Ṣafadī wa ajnās al-tajnīs lil-Ḥillī* (The Precious Jewels in the Addenda to al-Ṣafadī's *jinān al-jinās* [Gardens of Paronomasia] and al-Ḥillī's *ajnās al-tajnīs* [Modes of Paronomasia] . . .). Cairo: Maktabat al-Azhar, 1987.

———. *Kitāb ḥalbat al-kumayt fī al-adab wa-al-nawādir al-mutaʿalliqah bi-al-khamriyāt*. Būlāq: Al-Maṭbaʿah al-Mayriyah al-ʿĀmirah, 1859; Beirut: Dār al-Warrāq, 2008.

———. *Kitāb al-Ḥujjah fī sariqāt ibn Ḥijjah* (The Damning Evidence of ibn-Ḥijjah's Plagiarisms). Manuscript, undated, MS Arab 285. Houghton Library, Harvard University. http://nrs.harvard.edu/urn-3:FHCL.HOUGH:2600641.

———. *Kitāb Marātiʿ al-ghizlān fī waṣf al-ghilmān al-ḥisān*. Princeton University MS. http://arks.princeton.edu/ark:/88435/ms35t868t.

———. *ʿUqūd al-laʾāl fī al-muwashshaḥāt wa-al-azjāl*. Baghdad: Dār al-Rashīd li al-Nashr, 1982.

Nehru, Jawaharlal. *Glimpses of World History*. Oxford: Oxford University Press, 1989.

Netton, Ian Richard. *A Popular Dictionary of Islam*. London: Curzon Press, 1992.

Newman, Daniel, trans. *Sensual Delights of the Heart: Arab Erotica by Ahmed al-Tifashi*. London: Saqi Books, 2013.

Nicholson, Reynolds A. *A Literary History of the Arabs*. Cambridge: Cambridge University Press, 1956.

Al-Niffarī, Muḥammad ibn ʿAbd al-Jabbār. *The Mawāqif and Mukhāṭabāt of Muḥammad Ibn ʿAbd ʾl-Jabbār al-Niffarī*, with other fragments, edited for the first time, with translation, commentary, and indices, by Arthur John Arberry. Printed by the Cambridge University Press for the Trustees of the "E. J. W. Gibb Memorial." London: Luzac & Co., 1935.

Al-Nuʿaymī. *Al-Dāris fī taʾrīkh al-madāris*. Ed. J. al-Ḥasanī. Damascus: Al-Majmaʿ al-ʿIlmī al-ʿArabī, 1948–1951.

Al-Nuwayrī, Shihāb al-Dīn Aḥmad b. ʿAbd al-Wahhāb. *Nihāyat al-arab fī funūn al-adab* (The Ultimate Goal of the Learned in the Humanities). Beirut: Dār al-Kutub al-ʿIlmiyyah, 2004–2005.

Petry, Carl F. *The Civilian Elite of Cairo in the Later Middle Ages*. Princeton: Princeton University Press, 1981.

Pines, Shlomo. *Studies in Abū ʾl-Barakāt al-Baghdādī: Physics and Metaphysics*. The Collected Works of Shlomo Pines, vol. 1. Jerusalem: Magnes Press; Leiden: Brill, 1979.

Piterberg, Gabriel. "Tropes of Stagnation and Awakening in Nationalist Historical Consciousness: The Egyptian Case." In *Rethinking Nationalism in the Arab Middle East*, ed. Israel Gershoni and James Jankowski, 42–61. New York: Columbia University Press, 1997.

Pourshariati, Parvaneh. "Local Historiography in Early Medieval Iran and the Tārīkh-i Bayhaq." *Iranian Studies* 33, no. 1/2 (Winter–Spring 2000): 133–64.

Al-Qalqashandī, Shihāb al-Dīn Abū al-ʿAbbās Aḥmad b. ʿAlī b. Aḥmad ʿAbdullāh. *Ṣubḥ al-aʿshā fī ṣināʿat al-inshā* (The Dawn of the Benighted in the Craft of Fine Writing). Ed. Muḥammad Ḥusayn Shams al-Dīn. Beirut: Dār al-Kutub al-ʿIlmiyyah, 1988.

Qalqīlah, ʿAbduh ʿAbd al-ʿAzīz. *Al-Naqd al-adabī fi al-ʿaṣr al-Mamlūkī* (Literary Criticism in the Mamluk Period). Cairo: Maktabat al-Anjilū al-Miṣriyyah, 1972.

Al-Qayṣarī, Dāwūd. *Sharḥ al-Qaṣīdah al-Khamrīyah* (Commentary on the Wine Ode). Cairo, Dār al-Kutub al-Miṣrīyah-MS 56.

Al-Qazwīnī, Muḥammad ibn ʿAbd al-Raḥmān Jālāl al-Dīn. *Talkhīṣ al-Miftāḥ* (The Resumé of the Key). Beirut: Dār al-Jīl, n.d.

Al-Qazwīnī, Najm al-Dīn al-Kātibī. *Al-l-Risālah al-Shamsīyah*. Sharḥ (explicated by) Muḥammad ibn Muḥammad Quṭb al-Taḥtānī. [Cairo]: Al-Maṭbaʿah al-Azharīyah, 1311 [1894].

Qutbuddin, Tahera, trans. *Dustūr maʿālim al-ḥikam* (Treasury of Virtues); *The Miʾat kalimah* (100 Proverbs). New York: New York University Press, 2013.

Al-Rabdāwī, Maḥmūd. *Ibn Ḥijjah Shāʿiran wa nāqidan*. Damascus: Dār Qutaybah, 1982.

Ragep, Jamil F. "Freeing Astronomy from Philosophy: An Aspect of Islamic Influence on Science." *Osiris*, 2nd ser., 16, Science in Theistic Contexts: Cognitive Dimensions (2001): 49–71.

Rancière, Jacques. *The Politics of Aesthetics*. Trans. Gabriel Rockhill. New York: Continuum, 2004.

Al-Rāzī, Fakhr al-Dīn. *Muḥaṣṣal afkār al-mutaqaddimīn wa-al-mutaʾakhkhirīn min al-ʿulamāʾ wa-al-ḥukamāʾ wa-al-mutakallimīn* (Harvest of the Thought of the Ancients and Moderns from Scholars, Philosophers, and Theologians). Ed. Ṭāhā A. Saʿd. Cairo: Maktabat al-Kulliyāt al-Azhariyyah, 1978.

———. *Al-Munāẓarāt*. Ed. ʿĀrif Tāmir. Beirut: Muʾassasat ʿIzz al-Dīn, 1992.

———. *Nihāyat al-ʾījāz fī dirāyat al-iʿjāz* (The Utmost Concision concerning the Knowledge of Inimitability). Ed. Nasrullah Hacimuftuoglu. Beirut: Dār Ṣādir, 2004.

Reichmuth, Stefan. "Murtaḍā az-Zabīdī (d. 1791) in Biographical and Autobiographical Accounts: Glimpses of Islamic Scholarship in the Eighteenth Century." *Die Welt des Islams* 39, no. 1 (1999): 64–102.

Reynolds, Dwight F. "Musical Dimensions of an Arabic Oral Epic Tradition." *Asian Music* 26, no. 1, Musical Narrative Traditions of Asia (Autumn 1994–Winter 1995): 53–94.

———. "Popular Prose in the Post-Classical Period." In *Arabic Literature in the Post-Classical Period*, ed. Roger Allen and D. S. Richards, 258–59. The Cambridge History of Arabic Literature. Cambridge: Cambridge University Press, 2006.

———. "Sirat Bani Hilal." In *Arabic Literature in the Post-Classical Period*, ed. Allen and Richards, 307–19.

———. "The Thousand and One Nights: A History of the Text and Its Reception." In *Arabic Literature in the Post-Classical Period*, ed. Allen and Richards, 270–91.

Riḍā, Muḥammad Rashīd. *Majmūʿat al-rasāʾil wa al-masāʾil*. Ed. Muḥammad Rashīd. 5 vols. Cairo: Lajnat al-Turāth al-ʿArabī, 1976.

Roper, Geoffrey. "Texts from Nineteenth-Century Egypt: The Role of E. W. Lane." In *Travelers in Egypt*, ed. Paul and Janet Starkey, 244–54. London: I. B. Tauris, 2001.

Rosenthal, Franz. *The Classical Heritage in Islam*. London: Routledge, 1992.

———. *The Muqaddimah: An Introduction to History*. Princeton: Princeton University Press, 2005.

———. "'Of Making Many Books There Is No End': The Classical Muslim View." In *The Book in the Islamic World*, ed. George N. Atiyeh, 33–56. New York: State University of New York Press, 1995.

El-Rouayheb, Khaled. "Opening the Gate of Verification: The Forgotten Arab-Islamic Florescence of the 17th Century." *The International Journal of Middle East Studies* 38, no. 2 (May 2006): 263–81.

Rowson, Everett. "An Alexandrian Age in Fourteenth-Century Damascus: Twin Commentaries on Two Celebrated Arabic Epistles." *Mamluk Studies Review* 7, no. 1 (2003): 97–110.

———. "Khalīl b. Aybak al-Ṣafadī." In *Essays in Arabic Literary Biography, 1350–1850*, ed. Joseph E. Lowry and Devin J. Stewart, 341–57. Wiesbaden: Harrassowitz, 2009.

———. "Two Homoerotic Narratives from Mamlūk Literature: al-Ṣafadi's *Lawʿat al-Shākī* and ibn Dāniyāl's *al-Mutayyam*." In *Homoeroticism in*

Classical Arabic Literature, ed. J. W. Wright, Jr., and Everett K. Rowson, 158–91. New York: Columbia University Press, 1997.

Ruʿaynī, Aḥmad ibn Yūsuf. *Kitāb Ṭirāz Al-Ḥullah wa-shifāʾ Al-ghullah: Sharḥ Al-Ḥullah Al-siyyarā fī madḥ Khayr Al-Warā: Badīʿīyah Naẓamahā Al-Imām Shams Al-Dīn Abū ʿAbd Allāh Muḥammad Ibn Jābir Al-Andalusī, T 780 H.* Alexandria: Muʾassasat al-Thaqāfah al-Jāmiʿīyah, 1990.

Al-Ṣābī, Hilāl. *Rusūm dār al-khilāfah* (Regulations at the Caliph's Palace). Ed. M. ʿAwwād (Baghdad, 1964). Trans. Elie A. Salem. Beirut: American University in Beirut Press, 1977.

Sadan, Joseph. "Kings and Craftsmen—A Pattern of Contrast." *Studia Islamica* 56 (1982): 5–49; and 62 (1985): 89–120.

Al-Ṣafadī, Ṣalāh al-Dīn Khalīl ibn Aybak. *Alḥān al-sawājiʿ min al-mabādiʾ wa-la-marājiʿ* (The Harmonious Cadence in Principles and Orientations). Cairo: Al-Hayʾah al-Miṣrīyah al-ʿĀmmah lil-Kitāb, 2005–2007.

———. *Aʿyān al-ʿaṣr* (The Notables of the Age): *Ṣafī al-Dīn al-Ḥillī*. Ed. ʿAdnān Darwīsh. Damascus: Ministry of Culture, 1995.

———. *Kitāb al-Ghayth al-musjam fī sharḥ Lāmiyyat al-ʿAjam* (The Book of the Smoothly Flowing/Life-Giving Rain in Explicating al-Ṭughrāʾī's ʿAjam Ode Rhyming in L . . .). 2 vols. Al-Dār al-Bayḍāʾ: Dār al-Rashād, 1990.

———. *Kitāb al-Wāfī bi-al-wafayāt*. Ed. Hellmut Ritter, 24 vols. Istanbul: Maṭbaʿat al-Dawlah, 1931.

———. *Kitāb al-Wāfī bi-al-wafayāt*. Ed. Hilmūt Rītir wa Iḥsān ʿAbbās . . . [et al.]. Beirut: Al-Maʿhad al-Almānī lil-Abḥāth al-Sharqīyah fī Bayrūt, 2008–2010.

———. *Niṣrat al-thāʾir ʿalā al-mathal al-sāʾir*. Damascus: s.n., 1972.

Al-Sakhāwī, Shams al-Dīn Muḥammad ibn ʿAbd al-Raḥmān. *Al-Ḍawʾ al-lāmiʿ li-ahl al-qarn al-tāsiʿ*. Cairo: Maktabat Al-Qudsī, 1953.

———. *Al-Dhahab al-masbūk fī dhikr man ḥajja min al-khulafāʾ wa-al-mulūk* (The Molded Gold in the Concordance of Those Who Performed the Pilgrimage from among Caliphs and Kings). Cairo: Al-Maṭbaʿah al-Āmīrīyah, 1896.

———. *Al-Iʿlān bi-al-tawbīkh li-man dhamma al-tārīkh*. Trans. Franz Rosenthal. In Franz Rosenthal, *A History of Muslim Historiography*. 2nd ed. Leiden: Brill, 1968.

Al-Sakkākī, Abū Yaʿqūb Yūsuf. *Miftāḥ al-ʿulūm* (Key to the Sciences). Ed. Naʿīm Zarzūr. Beirut: Dār al-Kutub al-ʿIlmiyyah, 1983.

Saliba, George. *Islamic Science and the Making of the European Renaissance*. Cambridge, MA: MIT Press, 2007.

Salīm, Maḥmūd Ruzq. *Ṣafī al-Dīn al-Ḥillī*. Cairo: Dār al-Maʿārif, 1980.

Sawaie, Mohammed. "Rifaʿa Rafiʿ al-Ṭahtawi and His Contribution to the Lexical Development of Modern Literary Arabic." *International Journal of Middle East Studies* 32, no. 3 (August 2000): 395–410.

Scheub, Harold. "A Review of African Oral Traditions and Literature." *African Studies Review* 28, no. 2/3 (June–September 1985): 1–72.

Schwab, Richard. Introduction to Jean le Rond d'Alembert, *Preliminary Discourse to the Encyclopedia of Diderot*, trans. Richard N. Schwab with the collaboration of Walter E. Rex, ix–lii. Chicago: University of Chicago Press, 1995.

Sedra, Paul. *From Mission to Modernity*. London: I. B. Taurus, 2011.

Sells, Michael A. "Ibn ʿArabī's Garden among the Flames: A Reevaluation." *History of Religions* 23, no. 4 (May 1984): 287–31.

———. "Preface." In Th. Emil Homerin, *ʿUmar ibn al-Fāriḍ: Sufi Verse, Saintly Life*. New York: Paulist Press, 2000.

Serjeant, R. B. "*Die vulgärarabische Poetik al-Kitāb al-ʿĀtil al-ḥālī wal-muraḫḫaṣ al-ġālī des Ṣafīyaddīn Ḥillī* by Wilhelm Hoenerbach; Ṣafīyaddīn Ḥillī." *Bulletin of the School of Oriental and African Studies* 21, no. 1/3 (1958): 405–7.

Seyed-Gohrab, A. A. " 'My Heart Is the Ball, Your Lock the Polo-Stick': The Development of Polo Metaphors in Classical Persian Poetry." In *The Necklace of the Pleiades*, ed. F. D. Lewis and S. Sharma, 183–205. Leiden: Leiden University, 2010.

Al-Shādhilī, Abū al-Mawāhib. *Illumination in Islamic Mysticism*; a translation, with an introduction and notes, based upon a critical edition of Abū al-Mawāhib al-Shādhilī's treatise entitled *Qawānīn ḥikam al-ishraq*, by Edward Jabra Jurji. Princeton: Princeton University Press; London: Oxford University Press, 1938.

Al-Shaiji, Abd Al-Hamid K. M. H. "Critical Study and Edition of *Al-Turuq al-Hukmiyya fi-i-Siyasa al-Sharʿiyya* of Imam Shams al-Din b. Muhammad b. Abu Bakr Ibn Qayyim al-Jawziyya." PhD diss., University of Wales, Lampeter, 2001.

Sharlet, Jocelyn. *Patronage and Poetry in the Islamic World: Social Mobility and Status in the Medieval Middle East and Central Asia*. London: I. B. Tauris, 2011.

Al-Shāṭibī, Isḥāq Ibrāhīm Mūsā al-Lakhmī. *Al-Muwāfaqāt fi ʾuṣūl al-sharīʿah*. Beirut: Dār al-Maʿrifah, 1975.

Al-Shawkānī, Muḥammad. *Ṭalab al-ʿilm wa-ṭabaqāt al-mutaʿallimīn: Adab al-ṭālib wa muntahā al-ʾArab* (loosely: The Search for Knowledge and Classes of Learners: The Most Desired Manners in the Acquisition of Islamic Knowledge). Ṣanʿāʾ: Dār al-Arqam, 1981.

Al-Shaybī, Kāmil Muṣṭafā, ed. and compiled. *Dīwān al-kān -wa-kān fī al-shiʿr al-shaʿbī al-ʿArabī al-qadīm* (Dīwān al-kān-wa-kān in Ancient Arabic Popular Poetry). Baghdad: General Cultural Foundation, 1987.

Al-Shayzarī, ʿAbd al-Raḥmān. *The Book of the Islamic Market Inspector*; including Abū Ḥāmid al-Ghazālī's *ḥisbah* manual, an excerpt from *Iḥyāʾ ʿulūm al-dīn* (The Revival of Religious Sciences). Trans. Ronald Paul Buckley. Oxford: Oxford University Press, 2000.

Al-Shidyāq, Aḥmad Fāris Affendī. *Al-Jāsūs ʿalā al-Qāmūs* (Spying on al-Fīrūzabādī's Lexicon). Istanbul: Maṭbaʿat al-Jawāʾib, AH 1299.

Al-Shirbīnī, Yūsuf. *Kitāb hazz al-quḥūf bi-sharḥ qaṣīd Abī Shādūf* (Brains Confounded by the Ode of Abū Shādūf). Ed. and trans. Humphrey Davies. Leuven: Peeters, 2005.

Shoshan, Boaz. "High Culture and Popular Culture in Medieval Islam." *Studia Islamica* 73 (1991): 67–107.

———. "On Popular Literature in Medieval Cairo." *Poetics Today* 14, no. 2, Cultural Processes in Muslim and Arab Societies: Medieval and Early Modern Periods (Summer 1993): 349–65.

Sibai, Mohamed Makki. *Mosque Libraries: An Historical Study*. London: Mansell, 1987.

Sibṭ ibn al-Jawzī, Yūsuf ibn Qizughlī. *Mirʾāt al-Zamān*. Mecca, 1987.

Sperl, S., and C. Shackle, eds. *Qasida Poetry in Islamic Asia and Africa: Classical Traditions and Modern Meanings*. 2 vols. Leiden: Brill, 1996.

Steenbergen, Jo Van. "Qalāwūnid Discourse, Elite Communication and the Mamluk Cultural Matrix: Interpreting a 14th-Century Panegyric." *Journal of Arabic Literature* 43 (2012): 1–28.

Stern, S. M. "The Authorship of the Epistles of the Ikhwan-as-Safa." *Islamic Culture* 20 (1946): 367–72.

———. "New Information about the Authors of the 'Epistles of the Sincere Brethren.'" *Islamic Studies* 3 (1964): 405–28.

Stetkevych, Jaroslav. *The Zephyrs of Najd: The Poetics of Nostalgia in the Classical Arabic Nasīb*. Chicago: University of Chicago Press, 1993.

Stetkevych, Suzanne P. *Abū Tammām and the Poetics of the ʿAbbāsid Age*. Leiden: Brill, 1991.

———. "From Jahiliyya to Badīʿiyyah: Orality, Literacy, and the Transformations of Rhetoric in Arabic Poetry." *Oral Tradition* 25 (2010): 211–30.

———. "From Text to Talisman: Al-Buṣīrī's Qaṣīdat al-Burdah (Mantle Ode) and the Poetics of Supplication." *Journal of Arabic Literature* 37, no. 2 (2006): 145–89.

———. *The Mantle Odes: Arabic Praise Poetry to the Prophet Muḥammad*. Bloomington: Indiana University Press, 2012.

———. *The Mute Immortals Speak: Pre-Islamic Poetry and the Poetics of Ritual*. Ithaca, NY: Cornell University Press, 1993.

———. *The Poetics of Islamic Legitimacy*. Bloomington: Indiana University Press, 2002.

Stewart, Devin J. "Bahāʾ al-Dīn al-ʿĀmilī." In *Essays in Arabic Literary Biography, 1350–1850*, ed. Joseph E. Lowry and Devin J. Stewart, 27–48. Wiesbaden: Harrassowitz, 2009.

———. "Ibn Ḥijjah al-Ḥamawī." In *Essays in Arabic Literary Biography, 1350–1850*, ed. Lowry and Stewart, 137–47.

Al-Subkī, Tāj al-Dīn. *Ṭabaqāt al-shāfiʿyyah al-kubrā*. 10 vols. Cairo: Dār Iḥyāʾ al-Kutub al-ʿArabiyyah, ʿĪsā Bābī al-Ḥalabī, 1976.

Al-Suhrawardi, Shihab al-Din Yahya. *The Shape of Light*. Trans. Shaykh Tosun Bayrak al-Jerrahi al-Halveti. Louisville, KY: Fons Vitae, 1998.

Al-Sulamī. *Fatāwā*. Ed. M. al-Kurdī. Beirut: Muʾassasat al-Risālah, 1996.

Al-Suyūṭī, Jalāl al-Dīn. *Itmām al-dirāyah* (Completion of Knowledge). Cairo: Al-Adabiyyah Press, n.d.

———. *Al-Muzhir fī ʿulūm al-lughah* (The Luminous Work Concerning the Sciences of Language and Its Subfields). Būlāq, Cairo: Maṭbaʿah al-Miṣrīyah, 1865.

———. *Al-Muzhir fī ʿulūm al-lughah* (The Luminous Work Concerning the Sciences of Language and Its Subfields). 2 vols. in 1. Beirut: Al-Maktabah al-ʿAṣriyyah, 2004.

———. *Al-Muzhir fī ʿulūm al-lugha*. Ed. Jād al-Mawlā et al. Cairo: n.p., n.d.

———. *Tuḥfat al-Mujtahidīn bi Asmāʾ Mujaddidīn* (The Gem of the Striving Scholars: The Names of the Renewers of Religion). Landberg MSS 754, Beinecke Library, Yale University.

Al-Ṭabarī, ʿAlī ibn Sahl Rabbān. *The Book of Religion and Empire: A Semi-Official Defense and Exposition of Islam*; written at the court and with the assistance of the Caliph Mutawakkil (A.D. 847–861) by Ali Tabari. Translated, with a critical apparatus from an apparently unique manuscript in the John Rylands Library, by Alphonse Mingana. Manchester: Manchester University Press, 1922.

Al-Taftazānī, Saʿd al-Dīn. *Al-Muṭawwal: Sharḥ Talkhīṣ al-Miftāḥ* (The Elaborate or Expanded: The Explication of the Resumé of the Key). Beirut: Dār Iḥyāʾ al-Turāth al-ʿArabī, 2004.

———. *Sharḥ al-talkhīṣ*. Beirut: Dār al-Kutub, n.d.

Al-Taftazānī, Saʿd al-Dīn, and al-Sharīf al-Jurjānī. *Al-Ḥāshiyah of al-Taftazānī and al-Sharīf al-Jurjānī* [on al-Ijī's commentary, supplemented by Shaykh Ḥusayn al-Harawī's]. Cairo: Maktabat al-Kulliyāt al-Azhariyyah, 1974.

Tageldin, Shaden M. *Disarming Words: Empire and the Seductions of Translation in Egypt*. Berkeley: University of California Press, 2011.

———. "Proxidistant Reading: Toward a Critical Pedagogy of the *Nahḍah* in U.S. Comparative Literary Studies." *Journal of Arabic Literature* 43, no. 2/3 (Fall 2012): 227–68.

Tāmir, ʿĀrif. Introduction to *Risālat jāmiʿat al-jāmiʿah li Ikhwān al-Ṣafāʾ*. Beirut: Dār al-Nashr al-Jāmiʿī, 1959.

Tantum, Geoffrey. "Muslim Warfare: A Study of a Medieval Muslim Treatise on the Art of War." In *Islamic Arms and Armour*, ed. Robert Elgood, 194–96. London: Scolar Press, 1979.

Tibyā, al-Ḥasan Bū. *Mufāḍalah bayna al-naẓm wa-al-nathr wa-ashkāl al-tadākhul baynahumā fī al-ʿaṣr al-ʿAbbāsī*. Marrākish: Imprimerie al-Waṭaniyya, 2002.

Toomer, G. J. *Eastern Wisdom and Learning: The Study of Arabic in Seventeenth-Century England*. Oxford: Clarendon Press, 1996.

Toorawa, Shawkat M. *Ibn Abī Ṭāhir Ṭayfūr and Arabic Writerly Culture: A Ninth-Century Bookman from Baghdad*. London: RoutledgeCurzon, 2005.

———. "Āzād Bilgrāmī." In *Essays in Arabic Literary Biography, 1350–1850*, ed. Joseph E. Lowry and Devin J. Stewart, 91–97. Wiesbaden: Harrassowitz, 2009.

Al-Ṭurṭūshī, Abū Bakr Muḥammad ibn al-Walīd. *Sirāj al-mulūk* (The Kings' Lamp). Cairo: Al-Dār al-Miṣriyah al-Lubnaniyah, 1994.

Al-Ṭūsī, Naṣīr al-Dīn. *Talkhīṣ al-muḥaṣṣal* (The Summa of the Harvest). Ed. Ṭāhā A. Saʿd. Cairo: Maktabat al-Kulliyāt al-Azhariyyah, 1978.

Al-ʿUmarī, Aḥmad ibn Yaḥyā ibn Faḍl Allāh. *Masālik al-abṣār fī mamālik al-amṣār*. 27 vols. in 15. Beirut: Dār al-Kutub al-ʿIlmiyyah, 2010.

Van Ess, J. "The Logical Structure of Islamic Theology." In *Logic in Classical Islamic Culture*, ed. G. E. von Grunebaum, 21–50. Wiesbaden: Harrassowitz, 1970.

Van Gelder, Geert Jan. *The Bad and the Ugly: Attitudes towards Invective Poetry (hijāʾ) in Classical Arabic Literature*. Leiden: Brill, 1988.

———. "Conceit of Pen and Sword." *Journal of Semitic Studies* 32, no. 2 (1987): 329–60.

———. "Forbidden Firebrands: Frivolous 'Iqtibās' (Quotation from the Qurʾān) according to Medieval Arabic Criticism." *Quaderni di Studi Arabi* 20/21 (2002–2003): 3–16.

———. "A Good Cause: Fantastic Aetiology (*Ḥusn al-taʿlīl*) in Arabic Poetics." In *Takhyīl: The Imaginary in Classical Arabic Poetics: Pt. 2, Studies*, ed. Geert Jan van Gelder and Marlé Hammond. London: Gibb Memorial Trust, 2008, 221–37.

———. "Poetry for Easy Listening." *MSR* 7, no. 1 (2003): 31–48.

Venuti, Lawrence. *The Scandals of Translation: Towards an Ethics of Difference*. London: Routledge, 1998.

Vrolijk, Arnoud. *Bringing a Laugh to a Scowling Face: A Study and Critical Edition of "Nuzhat al-nufūs wa-muḍhik al-ʿabūs" by ʿAlī ibn Sūdūn al-Bashbughāwī*. Leiden: Brill, 1998.

———. "Ibn Sūdūn." In *Essays in Arabic Literary Biography, 1350–1850*, ed. Joseph E. Lowry and Devin J. Stewart, 223–28. Wiesbaden: Harrassowitz, 2009.

Walker, Paul Ernest, ed. and trans. *The Wellsprings of Wisdom: A Study of Abū Yaʿqūb al-Sijistānī's Kitāb al-Yanābīʿ; including a complete English translation with commentary and notes on the Arabic text*. Salt Lake City: University of Utah Press, 1994.

Walzer, Richard. "New Light on the Arabic Translations of Aristotle." *Oriens* 6 (1953): 91–142.

Wansbrough, J. "Majāz al-Qurʾān: Periphrastic Exegesis." *Bulletin of the School of Oriental and African Studies* 33 (1970): 247–66.

Watson, William J. "Ibrahim Muteferrika and Turkish Incunabula." *Journal of the American Oriental Society* 88, no. 3 (1968): 435–41.

Watt, Montgomery. *The Influence of Islam on Medieval Europe*. Edinburgh: Edinburgh University Press, 1972.

Al-Waṭwāṭ, Rashīd al-Dīn. *Ḥadāʾiq al-siḥr fī daqāʾiq al-shiʿr* (The Groves of Enchantment in the Secrets of Poetry). Ed. Muḥammad Fahmī. Cairo: Maktabat al-ʾĀdāb, 1939.

———. *Ḥadāʾiq al-siḥr fī daqāʾiq al-shiʿr* (The Groves of Enchantment in the Secrets of Poetry). Ed. Ibrāhim Amīn al-Shawārbī. Cairo: Lajnat al-Taʾlīf wa-al-Tarjamah wa-al-Tarjamah wa al-Nashr, 1945. For another edition: Cairo: Maktabat al-Thaqāfah, 2004.

Weisinger, Herbert. "The Middle Ages and the Late Eighteenth Century Historians." *Philological Quarterly* 28 (January 1948): 63–79.

Wichtenstader, Ilse. *Classical Arabic Literature*. New York: Schocken Books, 1976.

Williams, Raymond. *Marxism and Literature*. Oxford: Oxford University Press, 1977.

Woodward, David. "Reality, Symbolism, Time, and Space in Medieval World Maps." *Annals of the Association of American Geographers* 75, no. 4 (December 1985): 510–21.

Yākūt, ibn ʿAbd Allāh. *The Irshād Al-Arīb Ilā Maʿrifat Al-Adīb; Or, Dictionary of Learned Men, of Yāqūt*. Trans. D. S. Margoliouth. Leiden: Brill; London: Luzac, 1907–1927.

Yarshater, Ehsan. “Love-Related Conventions in Saʿdi’s *gāzals*.” In *Studies in Honor of Clifford Edmund Bosworth*, vol. 2, ed. Carole Hillenbrand, 420–38. Leiden: Brill, 2000.

———. “The Theme of Wine-Drinking and the Concept of the Beloved in Early Persian Poetry.” *Studia Islamica* 13 (1960): 43–53.

Yazdī, ʿAbd Allāh ibn al-Ḥusayn. *Al-Ḥāshiyah ʿalā Tahdhīb al-manṭiq lil-Taftazānī*. Qum: Muʾassasat al-Nashr al-Islāmī, 1984.

Al-Yāzijī, Ibrāhīm. *Abḥāth lughawiyyah: al-lughah ʿunwān al-ummah wa mirʾāt aḥwālihā* (Linguistic Research: Language Is the Identity of a Nation and the Mirror of Its State). Ed. Yūsuf Qazmā Khūrī. Beirut: Dār al-Ḥamrāʾ, 1993.

Yücesoy, Hayrettin. “Translation as Self-Consciousness: Ancient Sciences, Antediluvian Wisdom, and the ʿAbbāsid Translation Movement.” *Journal of World History* 20, no. 4 (2009): 523–57.

Al-Zabīdī, Muḥammad Murtaḍā. *Tāj al-ʿarūs min jawāhir al-qāmūs*. Ed. Nawāf al-Jarrāḥ. Beirut: Dār Ṣādir, 2011.

Al-Zamakhsharī, Jār Allāh. *Al-Mufaṣṣal fi ʿIlm al-lughah*. Beirut: Dār Iḥyāʾ al-ʿUlūm, 1990.

Zaydān, Jurjī. *Tārīkh Ādāb al-lughah al-ʿArabiyyah*: [yashtamil ʿala tārikh al-lugha al-ʿArabiya wa-ʿulūmihā wa-ma ḥawathu min al-ʿulūm wa-al-ādāb ʿalā ikhtilāf mawādihā . . . min dukhūl al-salādjiqa Baghdad sanat 447 h.ʾilā dukhūl al-faransāwiyyīn Miṣr sanat 1213 h. (1798 m.)] (The History of Arabic Language, Its Sciences, and What It Comprises of Variegated Sciences and Arts since the Seljuk’s Occupation of Baghdad . . . until the Entry of Egypt by the French. . . . Consisting of the Fruitful Production of Talents and Minds of the Abbasid, the Mongol and the Ottoman Periods). 4 vols. Cairo: Maṭbaʿat al-Hilāl, 1931.

Al-Zayyāt, Aḥmad Ḥasan. “Fī al-Adab al-ʿArabī.” *Al-Jadīd* 1, no. 2 (6 February 1928): 19–20.

———. *Tārīkh al-adab al-ʿArabī*. Cairo: Lajnat al-Taʾlīf wa-al-Tarjamah wa-al-Nashr, 1928.

INDEX

aʿājim (non-Arabs): *ʿajam* as term, 329n.6, 352n.84; contributors to, 116; method of, 116–17; in relation to seventeenth-century geopolitics, 116–17; replacing *qudamāʾ* as a phrase, 116; verification or *taḥqīq* (commentary, annotation), 116; al-Zamakhsharī on, 115–16

ʿAbbāsī, ʿAbd al-Raḥīm ibn ʿAbd al-Raḥmān, al-: loaded title *Sharḥ shawāhid*, 112; peritexts, paratexts, and referents, 112; and textual analysis, 112

ʿAbbasid Age: as damaging to Islamic polity, 205–6; ibn Nubātah on al-Maʾmūn's dream, 207; ibn Taymiyyah's verdict against al-Maʾmūn, 206; reiterating traditionalists, 206; al-Ṣafadī on Greek logic, 205–6; translations, 205. *See also* ʿAbbasid caliphate

ʿAbbasid caliphate: Hārūn al-Rashīd testing philologists on correct use, 86; heyday of, 100; in ibn Dāniyāl's shadow plays, 101; as legitimating token, 101; literate culture, 101; and al-Maʾmūn's dream of Aristotle, 206–7; al-Maqrīzī on symbolic presence of, 101; as symbolic and ceremonial in Mamluk state, 101

adab: al-Akfānī on, 180–81; as *belles lettres*, 182–83; illustrious names in, 177–78; as knowledge, 181, 193; origins of grammar, 177; overlap with *ʿilm*, 181–82; and people of the pen, 176–77; politics of people of the pen, 177; in al-Ṣafadī, 181; al-Ṣafadī and recent predecessors and poets, 195; and traditional historiography, 193; translations and issues of translation, 207–8, 210–11. *See also adīb*; knowledge; republic of letters

adīb: overlap with *ʿālim*, 181; in relation to *adab*, 369n.7; al-Ṣafadī's use as inclusive, like al-Jāḥiẓ, 181; al-Shirbīnī's use in reference to al-Būṣīrī, 151; Yāqūt's dictionary, 358n.32

270–71; Muḥammad b. Yūsuf al-Talla'farī, 253; in relation to *badī'iyyāt*, 298–99; release of language, 297–98; Shābb al-Ẓarīf (Muḥammad b Sulaymān 'Afīf al-Dīn al-Tilimsānī), 253; attacked by Quṭb al-Dīn al-Qasṭallānī, 253; Sufi experience in poetry, anticipating postmodern, 142–43; Sufi poetics, 295–97; 'Ubayd Allāh al-Ta'āwīdhī, 253

Sufi *Šāheds*: and homoerotics, 281–82

Sufism: challenge to dominant thought, 78–79; and eighteenth-century revival in interest in Battle of Badr (13 March 624), 96; and ibn al-'Arabī, 33; involving a liberated sensibility in loving God's universe, 78–79; semiology, 142–43; sham practitioners in al-Shirbīnī's *Sharḥ*, 158–59; stripping language of denotation, 142–43; Sufi networks, 46; Sufi scholars in Cairo, 10; symptomatology, 19

Suyūṭī, Jalāl al-Dīn, al-: "Arab" method of analysis, 15, 116; *Itmām al-dirāyah* published bracketing nineteenth-century version of al-Taftazānī's *sharḥ*, 109; *al-Muzhir*, 249; reference to Abū al-Ṭayyib al-Lughawī, 249; al-Shidyāq on, 92; on *tashjīr* poetry, 249

Ṭabarī, Abū Ja'far Muḥammad ibn Jarīr, al-: historian, 49; historicization of a rupture in Islamic history, 49; record of Abū Mikhnaf, 49; rejected by Tīmūr, 77–78; use by ibn Khaldūn, 76–78

Taftazānī, Sa'd al-Dīn Mas'ūd, al-: abridgement and expanded edition on rhetoric, 108–9; commentaries on his The Refinement of Logic, 107; conversation with scholars, 84–85; gathering material in Khwārizm, 84; and ibn al-'Arabī, 33; among illustrious architects of knowledge, 14; as knowledge seeker, 10; *Muṭawwal* as comprehensive, 109; *Muṭawwal*, preface to, 103; *Muṭawwal*, significance of, 84; between Mu'tazilites and Ash'arites in reasoning, 117; praise of Khwārizm as city of knowledge, 84; preempting antagonistic response, 103; reasons for working in Khwārizm, 108–9; reputation in Cairo, 45–46; scholarly debate with al-Sharīf al-Jurjānī in Tīmūr's *majlis*, 31; al-Sharīf al-Jurjānī's commentary on, 109

Tawḥīdī, Abū Ḥayyān, al-: in Abū Sulaymān al-Manṭiqī al-Sijistānī's circle, 35; account of debate between al-Sīrāfī and ibn Yūnus, 212–13; frustration at the vagaries of times, 56; humanist intellectual, 35; multicultural background, 35; patronage by Buyid vizier, 35

tawriyah (double entendre): breakdown of representation, 139–41; in dissemblance and dissimulation, 137–39; examples, 138–41; in relation to Foucault's reading of Western episteme, 139–40; roots in al-Qaḍī al-Fāḍil, 137–38;

MUHSIN J. AL-MUSAWI

is professor of Arabic and comparative studies at Columbia University.